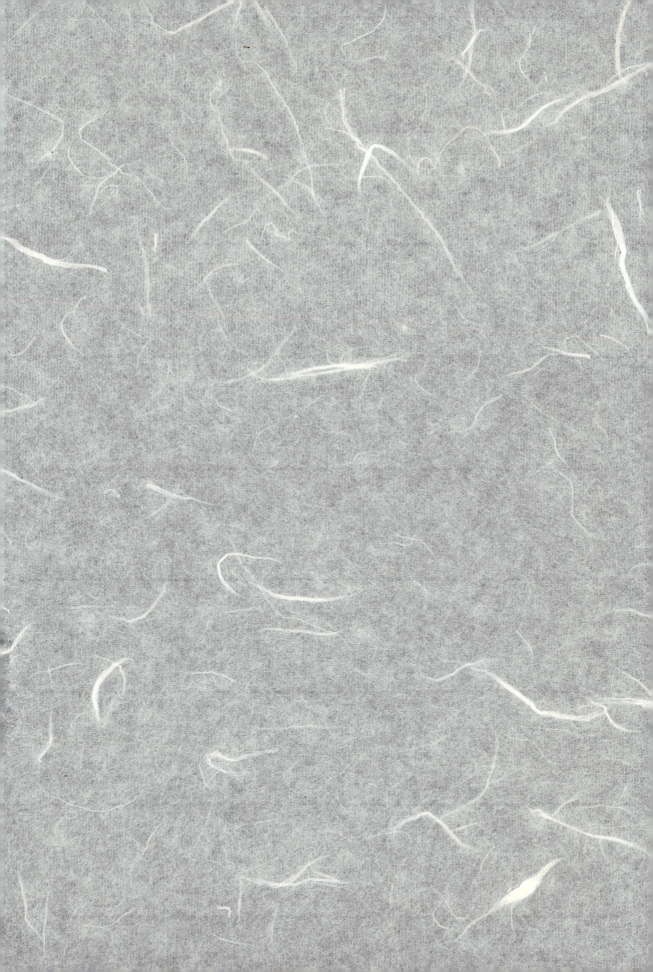

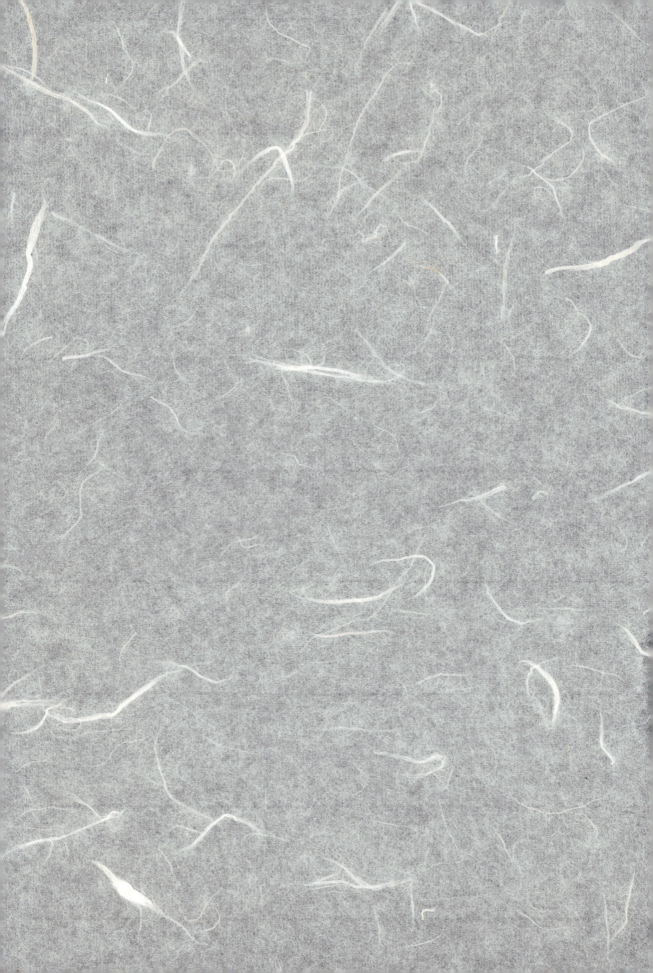

A. V. DICEY

INTRODUCTION TO THE STUDY OF THE LAW OF THE CONSTITUTION

A. V. Dicey

LibertyClassics

INDIANAPOLIS

Liberty*Classics* is a publishing imprint of Liberty Fund, Inc., a foundation established to encourage study of the ideal of a society of free and responsible individuals.

The cuneiform inscription that serves as the design motif for our endpapers is the earliest known written appearance of the word "freedom" (*ama-gi*), or liberty. It is taken from a clay document written about 2300 B.C. in the Sumerian city-state of Lagash.

Frontispiece courtesy of Professor Richard A. Cosgrove, University of Arizona.

This Liberty*Classics* edition is a reprint of the eighth edition published by Macmillan in 1915. The first edition was issued by the same publisher in 1885.

Library of Congress Cataloging in Publication Data

Dicey, Albert Venn, 1835–1922.
  Introduction to the study of the law of the
constitution.

  Reprint. Originally published: 8th ed. London:
Macmillan, 1915.
  Includes bibliographical references and index.
  1. Great Britain—Constitutional law. I. Title.
KD3989.D53 1982   342.41   81–82778
ISBN 0–86597–002–5   344.102   AACR2
ISBN 0–86597–003–3 (pbk.)

10 9 8 7 6 5 4 3 2 1

CONTENTS

PUBLISHER'S NOTE

A. V. Dicey's *Introduction to the Study of the Law of the Constitution* was first published in 1885 in London by Macmillan and Co. New editions were issued by the same publisher in 1886, 1889, 1893, 1897, 1902, and 1908. In each of these editions, Dicey attempted to reflect such constitutional changes as he believed had occurred since the previous edition.

When he prepared an eighth edition in 1914 (the eighth edition was published in 1915, but Dicey dated his preface in 1914), Dicey left the text as it had been in the seventh edition of 1908 but added a long introduction in which he discussed both actual changes in the British Constitution and various changes that were then under discussion.

In 1939, a ninth edition was prepared under the editorship of E. C. S. Wade. In this edition, a long introduction by Wade was substituted for Dicey's introduction to the eighth edition, and Dicey's appendix was omitted in favor of one by Wade. This edition was reprinted several times.

This Liberty*Classics* edition is based on the eighth edition, published in 1915, since this was the last edition that Dicey himself prepared.

FOREWORD

Very few jurists ever put forward doctrines of constitutional law which become not merely classic but which remain alive as standards. A year after the publication of Albert Venn Dicey's *Law of the Constitution* in 1885, Gladstone already was reading it aloud in Parliament, citing it as an authority. Half a century later these doctrines were still regarded so essential and fundamental that a special inquiry was necessary to determine whether more recent constitutional changes did not infringe on them. The Donoughmore Committee, whose *Report of the Committee on Ministers' Powers* appeared in 1932, endorsed those principles as a guide to further practice. Now, nearly a century later, Britain in large measure is still on the Dicey standard and so, too, is the United States. The doctrines, and even the names by which they are designated, remain part of the equipment of the student of public law. Dicey's analysis of legislative power and constitutional conventions must still be considered by anyone who desires to deal with the foundations of Anglo-American constitutional law simply because Dicey analyzed those foundations and enunciated principles, with a power and clarity never before or since attained that make those foundations intelligible.

I

Albert Venn Dicey was born 4 February 1835 at Claybrook Hall in Leicestershire, England, and he died in London 7 April 1922. He was the third son of Thomas Edward Dicey, a leading journalist of his time, by his wife Anne Mary, younger daughter of James Stephen, master in chancery. The Venn family name was given to him in honor of John Venn, the leader of the Clapham Evangelicals, whose daugher Jane married Sir James Stephen, Mrs. Dicey's brother and the elder Dicey's closest friend. The well-known Victorian scholars and publicists Sir Leslie Stephen and Sir James FitzJames Stephen were Albert Dicey's cousins. The Venns were linked by marriage to the Wedgwoods and the Darwins. Through the marriage of his parents Albert Dicey was born into what Lord Annan has called the Victorian intellectual aristocracy.

Even though Albert Dicey's parents had wed in 1814, just before the final defeat of Napoleon at Waterloo, there were no children born of the marriage until 1831. His parents, for reasons never publicly disclosed by them or their children, took the step, somewhat unusual for a middle class family, of educating their children at home; but Dicey in an "Autobiographical Fragment" surmised

> that among Whigs and especially among Whigs who, as was the case with my parents, combined a firm belief in the political principles of the Whig party with an equally firm belief in the best and most tolerant Evangelicism in matters of religion, there had grown up a suspicion that the public school system of England was marked by some very strong defects which the salutary influence of education at home might easily correct.

The results of this tuition at home were in every way fortunate.

His father had graduated from Trinity College, Cambridge as a senior wrangler in mathematics in 1811, whereupon he assumed full editorial control of the *Northampton Mercury*, one of the oldest newspapers in the country and the basis of the family's publishing business. His mother was gifted in languages. Besides training him in English composition, she taught him Greek and Latin as well as French and German, which was unusual even at that time and in that circle of austere devotion to intellectual things. Dicey recounts a story about his mother that bears retelling: it reveals something of his mother's intellectual power and influence as well as conveying an insight into Dicey's extreme modesty.

My mother had been reading with me [in 1848] the First Book of the *Iliad*. She dined on that evening at a house of good friends, among whom, naturally enough, an expression from that book, which we had noticed in the morning, was cited in Greek. My mother told me, when she came home, her amusement at hearing the words quoted, over which we had puzzled ourselves. But she added at once, "of course I did not let anyone perceive that I understood what the words meant."

An obstetrical error at the time of Dicey's premature birth left him with a muscular weakness that he bore all his life. The severity of the disorder is hard to judge, but at times it was so marked that he could not write at all; most of his life he could not write without taking frequent pauses. The affliction was severe enough to make him something of a physical oddity and to raise the question whether he would be strong enough to leave home before the age of seventeen, when he was sent to King's College School in London.

In 1854, after two years at King's College School, Dicey matriculated at Balliol College, Oxford, where he became a pupil of Benjamin Jowett. Under Jowett's personal supervision, which was kind but stringent, Dicey flourished and received a first class in classical moderations in 1856 and in *literae humaniores* in 1858. His own intellectual fervor and the reforming spirit of Jowett led Dicey, encouraged by this academic distinction, to join with other Balliol men, under the leadership of John Nichol, to form a literary society—the Old Mortality Society. This society, which has attracted considerable scholarly interest because of the later fame of many of its members, was a forum in which serious undergraduates could sharpen their intellects on questions that might lie outside their normal course of study by presenting papers which were followed by rigorous discussion. Membership and activity in the Old Mortality Society was especially important for Dicey because it gave him self-confidence in public speaking, at which, by all accounts, he became a master. In 1859 he was elected president of the Oxford Union. Although the presentations and discussions of the Old Mortality were academic, theoretical, and speculative, removed from the conditions of the real world, it bears mention that from time to time, particularly at the prodding of T.H. Green, the society did take up contemporary questions, political, social, and religious. According to Lord Bryce the discussions in this "quite remarkable" body were conducted openly and freely, devoid of dogmatism, because everyone "assumed individualism as obviously and absolutely right."

Dicey went down from Oxford in 1861 to read law in London. He left with an excellent degree, a fellowship at Trinity College, which he relinquished upon his marriage in 1872, a circle of friends, who remained close until death, and his first book, *The Privy Council,* winner of the Arnold Prize Essay in 1860, ready for publication. He returned to Oxford in 1883, when he began his intellectually productive period. The intervening years were spent in legal practice, having been called to the bar in 1863 as a member of the Inner Temple. His accomplishments led in 1876 to his appointment as junior counsel to the Commissioners of the Inland Revenue. Although he did handle some important briefs, the political career for which he hoped did not materialize. It also became clear before long that because of his physical weakness he could not realistically expect elevation to the bench. During this time Dicey married, began his scholarly writing, and travelled, with some frequency outside of England.

It was from these travels that he gained the knowledge to lay the foundation for the pioneering character of the *Law of the Constitution* in the field of comparative constitutional law. Dicey's extraordinarily accurate knowledge of continental constitutions was initiated in the course of his travels to Belgium, France, Switzerland, and Germany; the regimes of these countries excited him as examples of constitutional governments different from but similar to Britain. Indeed, Dicey's genius as a constitutional lawyer came from his ability to draw sharp distinctions between very similar but fundamentally different constitutional arrangements. Much of his understanding for these subtle but profound differences came from first-hand observations.

In 1870 he made a voyage to America with Bryce who used the opportunity to gather much of the material for *The American Commonwealth,* which he published in 1888. These travellers seemed bent on learning everything possible about the United States, and through their Oxford friends and family contacts met an impressive number of prominent Americans. Dicey made a full record of these experiences in his diary.

Above all, the travellers wanted to understand the American constitution; Dicey's diary abounds in jottings regarding the legal profession, the administration of justice, politics, and constitutional arrangements in the United States. Dicey attended the Democratic Convention at Rochester in 1870 and was able to see at close range the machine politics of which he was not an unqualified admirer. He wrote: "America is in theory the purest of Democracies, yet there are perhaps very few countries where there is less scope for independent political action, at least by individuals." Systematic party discipline, he thought, "violates the essential principles of Democracy, for it very much limits the control over their Government exercised by the people, and it sacrifices the public service to purely individual interests. The evil is very apparent in England and will become more so." Many of the observations about American politics and institutions in his diary showed his strong capacity for comparative analysis. In the opinion of his friend and former pupil, Robert Rait, the American tour very decidedly marked Dicey's later work in comparative and constitutional law. It gave him a basis for comparison, and it influenced his subsequent attitude to American constitutional problems. On at least two occasions Dicey wrote to Bryce that the *Law of the Constitution* would not have been written but for this journey.

Dicey admired the United States greatly. It proved popular government possible; it drew on a tradition of voluntary action, and it seemed to confirm his liberal principles. The United States and France were the examples he drew most frequently on to contrast by illustration with the principles of the British constitution. America expanded his imagination about the structure and formation of comparable but different legal institutions.

The academic study of modern society through the study of politics and history was one of the achievements of the movement to reform university education. Dicey admired this reform when he was still an undergraduate; when he became Vinerian professor in 1882 he brought the spirit of those reformers to bear on the field of his responsibilities.

The Vinerian Professorship had been established in Oxford in 1758 on a bequest of Charles Viner. Its first incumbent was Sir William Blackstone, author of the *Commentaries on the Laws of England*. While law, principally canon law, had most certainly been studied for a long time at Oxford—the Regius Professorship had been established by Henry VIII—the Vinerian Professorship was the first academic post created specifically for the study of English law. After the auspicious beginning in Blackstone's lectures, the subsequent Vinerian professors were uniformly undistinguished. They paid little attention to teaching; some had written unremarkable commentaries; most seemed uninterested in the post.

Not only did Dicey's considerable practice at the bar and his position as counsel to the Commissioners of the Inland Revenue help his election to the Vinerian Professorship, but also his writings, *The Privy Council* (1861), his *Treatise on the Rules for the Selection of the Parties to an Action* (1870), and *The Law of Domicil as a Branch of the Law of England* (1879) had given him a considerable reputation as a legal writer. In 1896, he published his *Digest of the Law of England with Reference to the Conflict of Laws,* which was an expansion of *The Law of Domicil* and is the most celebrated of his strictly legal works. *The Conflict of Laws,* which has been periodically brought up to date, remains today a standard work. In the words of his Vinerian successor, William Geldart, this work "not only reduced to order one of the most intricate and technical branches of law . . . but exerted a potent influence on its development."

Dicey held the Vinerian Professorship for twenty-seven years. His term of service is often referred to as the second founding. By the time of his resignation in 1909 Dicey had transformed the Vinerian chair into one of the most important posts in the world for the teaching of law. In a tribute, Sir William Holdsworth, the ninth Vinerian Professor and the author of *The History of English Law* in sixteen volumes, wrote:

> Dicey will hold in the history of the legal literature of the nineteenth century a place not unlike that which Blackstone holds in the history of the legal literature of the eighteenth century. Both have written books which have been accepted by their contemporaries as books of authority; and . . . Dicey's

work has contributed largely to the fulfilment of Blackstone's prophecy of the effects of a scientific study of English law at a university both upon the law, and upon the teaching of law. . . . In his works on the *Law of the Constitution* and *Law and Opinion in England* he has done for English public law and for the legal history of the nineteenth century all, and in some respects more than all, that Blackstone did for the public law and the legal history of the eighteenth century.

The first of the books to which Holdsworth referred, the *Introduction to the Study of the Law of the Constitution,* was originally published in 1885, two years after Dicey moved back to Oxford. It was a revision of his first Oxford lectures and based on many years of study and reflection. In it, he conceived of the legal and political elements of constitutional law in a way that, after the better part of a century, as Holdsworth said, still remains our starting point.

II

The contemporary American reader of the *Law of the Constitution* initially must understand three points. First, Great Britain, unlike the United States, does not possess a written document specifying the constitution of political power. In a narrow sense knowledge of constitutional law in the United States may be had through familiarity with the text of the Constitution and through the current state of interpretation of the written Constitution as revealed through Supreme Court decisions. This approach to knowledge of English constitutional law, due to the absence of a single written document, is impossible.

The second point proceeds from this observation. That is, how does one know, actually and conceptually, the English constitution and English constitutional law? In the *Law of the Constitution* Dicey answers these questions by stipulating three descriptive principles of law around which he organizes the book: the legislative sovereignty of Parliament; the rule of law; and the dependence in the last resort of the conventions of the constitution on the law of the constitution. He states these principles with such force and clarity that they remain today the starting point for any contemporary discussion of constitutional rules and of limitations of governmental powers. While Dicey is writing of Great Britain directly, because of their extraordinary similarity, he says much that is true of constitutional principles of the United States as well. In short, Dicey develops a conceptual structure that defines the political and legal constitution of democratic government as we know it.

Finally, the book should be read with reference to conditions when he wrote. Dicey published the *Law of the Constitution* in 1885. As he carefully explains, the text of the book was essentially fixed with the seventh edition, which appeared in 1908. That edition contained revisions up to 1908 in accord with Dicey's understanding of the changes that had taken place in the English constitution. The eighth edition, which is reprinted here, appeared in 1915 when Dicey was eighty years old. This reprints the text of 1908, but it contains an introduction of nearly one hundred pages in which Dicey recorded his thoughts on constitutional changes since 1908. The organization of this introduction, however, follows the organization of the book and may not be readily understood if the propositions and the arguments of the main text are not *first* read and absorbed. A further suggestion for the present-day reader before embarking on the introduction, but after reading the main body of the work, would be to read the Parliament Act of 1911, listed as Note XIII. Dicey seeks to show the actual, the true state and condition of English constitutional law, within the boundaries of his definition, in the period between 1885 and 1908. Were he writing in the 1980s, the book would be very different. This is the principal value of his 1915 introduction, for it shows Dicey's understanding not only of actual changes in the law but of how those changes embody changes in fundamental constitutional principles.

Some of Dicey's detractors have called this introduction the work of a tired, cranky old man, disappointed by life. There is, however, much to be learned from the introduction. For instance, in 1915 Dicey appears cool to women's suffrage, which was then one of the pressing issues of the day. But it must be understood that his chilliness represented a change. In the 1860s he was a great champion of the women's movement, and he supported John Stuart Mill's call for women's suffrage. In the well-known *Essays on Reform* in 1867, Dicey contributed a piece entitled "The Balance of Classes" in which he spoke against the arguments of the Conservatives and defended individual choice. Following his trip to the United States in 1870, he wrote:

> One of the reasons why there is less clamour for Women's Rights [in the United States] is the existence of a far smaller number of women's wrongs than with us, *e.g.,* they have in many states the right to hold property when married, as their own, and have got the full legal protection for their earnings. . . . It is impossible not to conclude that the average education of women is, compared with that of men, higher than in Europe—hence a freer opening of careers. . . . In the United States women are as a matter of fact obtaining political privileges . . . generally reserved for men.

Dicey was demonstrably a vigorous proponent of women's suffrage. In any case, the political issue of women's suffrage is moot. But it is not beside the point to read a distinguished constitutional lawyer's reflections on the effects of social and political movements on constitutional principles and on individual rights under the constitution. Dicey says that "constitutional law, as the term is used in England, appears to include all rules which directly or indirectly affect the distribution or the exercise of the sovereign power of the state." These "rules" fall into two broad categories. The first category of rules are laws, strictly understood. These laws are written and unwritten, statutory and customary, which are usually called the Common Law. These laws are known and recognized to be laws, because—this is the important determining factor—they are enforced by the courts. The other broad category of rules are what Dicey calls "conventions of the constitution." The rules of this second category are not in strictness laws, they are not enforced or enforceable by the courts; but they are the usual and customary practice of politicians and civil servants, and represent what Dicey calls "political" or "constitutional morality." The law of the constitution, then, is of two pieces: the relatively unambiguous laws, derived from judicial decisions and Parliamentary enactments, precisely expressed and recognized by the courts and the relatively ambiguous, largely implicit, conventions, which are part of political practice and morality and enter into public opinion. Dicey aims to examine the relationship between statutory law and public morality, and thereby to elucidate the relations between continuity and change in law and politics. The sovereign power of the state consists of a "legal sovereign" and of a "political sovereign."

In the *Law of the Constitution* Dicey shows how, from a strictly legal point of view, public morality must yield to law. In a later work *Lectures on Law and Public Opinion in England during the Nineteenth Century,* which was published in 1905, Dicey shows how, from other than a strictly legal point of view, public morality acts as a final sanction on law. No other modern writer has shown so penetratingly, as Dicey does in these two books, the relationships between law and the *mores maiorum*—the prevailing beliefs—in democratic regimes.

Dicey also tells us something of the importance of political morality. By deprecating the growing estrangement between law and morality through the constant addition to the statute books and the criminal law of acts which the government considers anti-social but the governed do not consider immoral Dicey offers us his most important lesson: the persistence of this state of affairs can only mean "a decline of reverence for the rule of law."

This phrase, "the rule of law," Dicey formulated into a principle of the British constitution. He did not create this phrase, but he brought it into currency, and he was responsible for elaborating the principle. By the rule of law he means: 1) the absence of arbitrary or discretionary power on the part of government; 2) every man is subject to the ordinary law of the land administered by ordinary and usual tribunals; 3) the general principles of law, the common law rules of the constitution, in contradistinction to the civil law countries of Europe, are the consequences of rights of the subject, not their source. To illuminate this difference Dicey contrasts the rule of law with the French idea of *droit administratif,* which he translates as administrative law.

Dicey makes the point that in Great Britain in 1885 there was no distinction between private and public law. One set of laws regulated and one system of courts adjudicated public and private interests alike. In subsequent decades this point ceased to be valid.

In Great Britain the officers of government were subject to the ordinary law of the land enforced by ordinary courts just as the private citizen was. In France, under the provisions of *droit administratif,* the government and its officials had special rights against private citizens and were to a great extent free from the jurisdiction of the ordinary courts. However nearly the French and English systems approach one another in actual practice, the principles governing them are different. The English system seeks to afford remedies for illegal administrative action, whereas the French hopes by setting up standards of conduct and by deterrent action to insure that the remedies will not be needed. Dicey saw that the rights of the citizen were potentially endangered by discretionary executive authority, because he equated discretion with arbitrariness, which meant that it was not subject to the rule of law. He claimed "discretionary authority on the part of the government must mean insecurity for legal freedom on the part of its subjects. . . . In this sense the rule of law is contrasted with every system of government based on the exercise by persons in authority of wide, arbitrary, or discretionary powers of constraint." Letourneur, one of the most prominent modern French writers on *droit administratif,* has made a similar point: *"Droit administratif* is by nature a law of inequalities, in which the private person, who represents purely private interests, cannot be put on the same footing as the administration charged with the task of conducting public services in the general interest." Because, he continues, "administrative action requires a unity of decision and of responsibility, it rests on a principle of authority." Dicey's central insight in this discussion is that divided jurisdiction formed the key element of *droit administratif* by permitting government interference in the private affairs of citizens. In this way *droit administratif* is inconsistent with the liberties afforded by the common law.

In America the tradition of exempting administrative authorities from the same liability as private persons has been very strong, and, in some ways, is more suitable for illustrating Dicey's point than the French *droit administratif.* The federal government, the state governments, municipal corporations of all kinds, and even some private trusts and charities inherited from eighteenth century English law the Crown's exemption from liability. Only recently have courts been willing to hold for some kind of liability for the non-governmental activities of municipal corporations. Moreover, in the United States legislatures and courts have traditionally been unwilling to make a public officer liable for acts, though clearly unlawful, if they were done through mistake or for probable cause. In such cases, both the official and the institution for which he worked were not to be held liable. Finally, until relatively recently, individual exemption from liability was not balanced by the assumption of liability by the administrative authority.

The rule of law means basically four things: equality of all citizens before the law; uniformity of courts; the unacceptability of *raison d'état* as an excuse for an unlawful act; and observance of the old maxim, *nullum crimen sine lege*. Dicey did not say he was opposed to special tribunals to handle technical matters, such as, for example, patents. But he most definitely denied the propriety of conferring quasi-judicial and wide executive authority on administrative agencies. He would be astonished and overwhelmed by the amount of discretionary authority—which in Dicey's view must be arbitrary and thus, to some degree, outside of the ordinary law of the land—with which we have in recent years invested regulatory agencies and tribunals of administrative law judges. He would certainly be opposed to the power exercised by judges, inspectors, and other officers of government in certain not especially technical areas of the law, such as labor relations, occupational safety, public education, and, in fact, hundreds of others. He would warn us of the inherent dangers in over-reliance on the "expert."

Dicey thought that there could be practical and moral checks, internal and external, which could restrain the legislative branch from the abuse of its powers. While it is true that the rights of the subject, which collectively make up the rule of law, are in theory precarious, being subject to legislative whim, they are in practice firm. He saw no such guarantees in bureaucratic agencies and administrative tribunals, which, in practice, have wide discretionary powers, especially those in which the officials are appointed on political grounds.

Dicey is absolutely right in thinking that discretionary authority is the selective and arbitrary use of power—for better or for worse—which may be used to foster political allegiance and to promote political clients. For these reasons, Dicey's discussion of the rule of law and its relation to executive discretion and judicial control is extraordinarily pertinent for understanding much of what has been happening in the United States in the past half century.

ROGER MICHENER
Committee on Social Thought
The University of Chicago

PREFACE TO THE FIRST EDITION

This book is (as its title imports) an introduction to the study of the law of the constitution; it does not pretend to be even a summary, much less a complete account of constitutional law. It deals only with two or three guiding principles which pervade the modern constitution of England. My object in publishing the work is to provide students with a manual which may impress these leading principles on their minds, and thus may enable them to study with benefit in Blackstone's *Commentaries* and other treatises of the like nature those legal topics which, taken together, make up the constitutional law of England. In furtherance of this design I have not only emphasised the doctrines (such, for example, as the sovereignty of Parliament) which are the foundation of the existing constitution, but have also constantly illustrated English constitutionalism by comparisons between it and the constitutionalism on the one hand of the United States, and on the other of the French Republic. Whether I have in any measure attained my object must be left to the judgment of my readers. It may perhaps be allowable to remind them that a book consisting of actually delivered lectures must, even though revised for publication, exhibit the characteristics inseparable from oral exposition, and that a treatise on the principles of the law of the constitution differs in its scope and purpose, as well from a constitutional history of England as from works like Bagehot's incomparable

English Constitution, which analyse the practical working of our complicated system of modern Parliamentary government.

If, however, I insist on the fact that my book has a special aim of its own, nothing is further from my intention than to underrate the debt which I owe to the labours of the lawyers and historians who have composed works on the English constitution. Not a page of my lectures could have been written without constant reference to writers such as Blackstone, Hallam, Hearn, Gardiner, or Freeman, whose books are in the hands of every student. To three of these authors in particular I am so deeply indebted that it is a duty no less than a pleasure to make special acknowledgment of the extent of my obligations. Professor Hearn's *Government of England* has taught me more than any other single work of the way in which the labours of lawyers established in early times the elementary principles which form the basis of the constitution. Mr. Gardiner's *History of England* has suggested to me the conclusion on which, confirmed as I found it to be by all the information I could collect about French administrative law, stress is frequently laid in the course of the following pages, that the views of the prerogative maintained by Crown lawyers under the Tudors and the Stuarts bear a marked resemblance to the legal and administrative ideas which at the present day under the Third Republic still support the *droit administratif* of France. To my friend and colleague Mr. Freeman I owe a debt of a somewhat different nature. His *Growth of the English Constitution* has been to me a model (far easier to admire than to imitate) of the mode in which dry and even abstruse topics may be made the subject of effective and popular exposition. The clear statement which that work contains of the difference between our so-called "written law" and "our conventional constitution," originally led me to seek for an answer to the inquiry, what may be the true source whence constitutional understandings, which are not laws, derive their binding power, whilst the equally vigorous statements contained in the same book of the aspect in which the growth of the constitution presents itself to an historian forced upon my attention the essential difference between the historical and the legal way of regarding our institutions, and compelled me to consider whether the habit of looking too exclusively at the steps by which the constitution has been developed does not prevent students from paying sufficient attention to the law of the constitution as it now actually exists. The possible weakness at any rate of the historical method as applied to the growth of institutions, is that it may induce men to think so much of the way in which an institution has come to be what it is, that they cease to consider with sufficient care what it is that an institution has become.

A. V. DICEY

All Souls College,
Oxford, 1885

PREFACE TO THE EIGHTH EDITION

The body of this work is the eighth edition, or rather a reprint of the seventh edition, of the *Law of the Constitution* first published in 1885. It is, however, accompanied by a new Introduction. This Introduction is written with two objects. The first object is to trace and comment upon the way in which the main principles of our constitution as expounded by me may have been affected either by changes of law or by changes of the working of the constitution which have occurred during the last thirty years (1884–1914). The second object of this Introduction is to state and analyse the main constitutional ideas which may fairly be called new, either because they have come into existence during the last thirty years, or because (what is much more frequently the case) they have in England during that period begun to exert a new and noticeable influence.

It has been my good fortune to receive in the composition of this Introduction, as in the writing of every book which I have published, untold aid from suggestions made to me by a large number both of English and of foreign friends. To all these helpers I return my most sincere thanks. It is at once a duty and a pleasure to mention my special obligation to two friends, who can both be numbered as high authorities among writers, who have investigated the constitution of England from different points of view. To the friendship of the late Sir William Anson I owe a debt the amount of which it is impossible to exaggerate. He was better acquainted, as his books show, with the details and the working of the whole constitution of England than any contemporary authority. Since I first endeavoured to lay down the few general principles which in my judgment lie at the basis of our constitution, I have, whilst engaged in that attempt, always enjoyed his sympathy and encouragement, and, especially in the later editions of my work, I have received from him corrections and suggestions given by one who had explored not only the principles but also all the minute rules of our constitutional law and practice. To my friend Professor A. Berriedale Keith I am under obligations of a somewhat different kind. He has become already, by the publication of his *Responsible Government in the Dominions,* an acknowledged authority on all matters connected with the relation between England and her Colonies. I have enjoyed the great advantage of his having read over the parts of my Introduction which refer to our Colonial Empire. His knowledge of and experience in Colonial affairs has certainly saved me from many errors into which I might otherwise have fallen.

It is fair to all the friends who have aided me that I should state explicitly that for any opinions expressed in this Introduction no one is responsible except myself. The care with which many persons have given me sound information was the more valued by me because I have known that with some of the inferences drawn by me from the facts on which I commented my informants probably did not agree.

A. V. Dicey
Oxford, 1914

ANALYSIS OF INTRODUCTION

INTRODUCTION

AIM

The *Law of the Constitution* was first published in 1885. The book was based on lectures delivered by me as Vinerian Professor of English Law. The lectures were given and the book written with the sole object of explaining and illustrating three leading characteristics in the existing constitution of England; they are now generally designated as the Sovereignty of Parliament, the Rule of Law, and the Conventions of the Constitution. The book, therefore, dealt with the main features of our constitution as it stood in 1884–85, that is thirty years ago. The work has already gone through seven editions; each successive edition, including the seventh, has been brought up to date, as the expression goes, by amending it so as to embody any change in or affecting the constitution which may have occurred since the last preceding edition. On publishing the eighth and final edition of this treatise I have thought it expedient to pursue a different course. The constant amendment of a book republished in successive editions during thirty years is apt to take from it any such literary merits as it may originally have possessed. Recurring alterations destroy the original tone and spirit of any treatise which has the least claim to belong to the literature of England. The present edition, therefore, of the *Law of the Constitution* is in substance a reprint of the seventh edition; it is however accompanied by this new Introduction whereof the aim is to compare our constitution as it stood and worked in 1884 with the constitution as it now stands in 1914. It is thus possible to take a general view of the development of the constitution during a period filled with many changes both of law and of opinion.[1] My readers are thus enabled to see how far either legislation or constitutional conventions have during the last thirty years extended or (it may be) limited the application of the principles which in 1884 lay at the foundation of our whole constitutional system. This Introduction therefore is in the main a work of historical retrospection. It is impossible, however (nor perhaps would it be desirable were it possible), to prevent a writer's survey of the past from exhibiting or betraying his anticipations of the future.

The topics here dealt with may be thus summed up:— The Sovereignty of Parliament,[2] the Rule of Law,[3] the Law and the Conventions of the Constitution,[4] New Constitutional Ideas,[5] General Conclusions.[6]

SOVEREIGNTY OF PARLIAMENT[7]

The sovereignty of Parliament is, from a legal point of view, the dominant characteristic of our political institutions. And my readers will remember that Parliament consists of the King, the House of Lords, and the House of Commons acting together. The principle, therefore, of parliamentary sovereignty means neither more nor less than this, namely that "Parliament" has "the right to make or unmake any law whatever; and further, that no person or body is recognised by the law of England as having a right to override or set aside the legislation of Parliament,"[8] and further that this right or

---

1 Compare the Introduction to the second edition of *Law and Public Opinion in England during the Nineteenth Century*.

2 See Part I. Chaps. I.–III., *post.*

3 See Part II. Chaps. IV.–XIII., *post.*

4 See Part III. Chaps. XIV., XV., *post.*

5 See p. lxxvi, *post.*

6 A student who wishes to understand the statements in the Introduction should read with care that part of the book on which they are a comment; thus the portions of the Introduction referring to the Sovereignty of Parliament ought to be read in connection with Part I. Chapters I.–III., *post.*

7 See Chaps. I.–III., *post.*

8 See Chap. I. p. 3, *post.* Parliament may itself by Act of Parliament either expressly or impliedly give to some subordinate legislature or other body the power to modify or add to

power of Parliament extends to every part of the King's dominions.[9] These doctrines appear in the first edition of this work, published in 1885; they have been repeated in each successive edition published up to the present day. Their truth has never been denied. We must now, however, consider whether they are an accurate description of parliamentary sovereignty as it now exists in 1914. And here it should be remarked that parliamentary sovereignty may possibly at least have been modified in two different directions, which ought to be distinguished. It is possible, in the first place, that the constitution or nature of the sovereign power may have undergone a change. If, for example, the King and the Houses of Parliament had passed a law abolishing the House of Lords and leaving supreme legislative power in the hands of the King and of the House of Commons, any one would feel that the sovereign to which parliamentary sovereignty had been transferred was an essentially different sovereign from the King and the two Houses which in 1884 possessed supreme power. It is possible, in the second place, that since 1884 the Imperial Parliament may, if not in theory yet in fact, have ceased as a rule to exercise supreme legislative power in certain countries subject to the authority of the King. Let us consider carefully each of these two possibilities.

POSSIBLE CHANGE IN CONSTITUTION OR CHARACTER OF THE PARLIAMENTARY SOVEREIGN (EFFECT OF THE PARLIAMENT ACT, 1911)

The matter under consideration is in substance whether the Parliament Act,[10] has transferred legislative authority from the King[11] and

---

a given Act of Parliament. Thus under the Commonwealth Act, 63 & 64 Vict. c. 12, the Imperial Parliament has given to the Parliament of the Australian Commonwealth power to modify many provisions of the Commonwealth Act, and the Imperial Parliament, under the National Insurance Act, 1911, has given power to the Insurance Commissioners and to the Board of Trade to modify some provisions of the Insurance Act.

9 See pp. 47–61, *post.*

10 See especially the Parliament Act, 1911, ss. 1–3, and Appendix, Note XIII., the Parliament Act.

11 The Parliament Act in no way diminishes the prerogatives of the King as they existed immediately before the passing of that Act, and it is enacted (Parliament Act. s. 6) that "nothing in this Act shall diminish or qualify the existing rights and privileges of the House of Commons."

the two Houses of Parliament to the King and the House of Commons?

The best mode of giving an answer to this question is first to state broadly what were the legislative powers of the House of Lords immediately before the passing of the Parliament Act, 18th August 1911, and next to state the main direct and indubitable effects of that Act on the legislative power of the House of Lords and of the House of Commons respectively.

THE STATE OF THINGS IMMEDIATELY BEFORE THE PASSING OF THE PARLIAMENT ACT

No Act of Parliament of any kind could be passed without the consent thereto both of the House of Lords and of the House of Commons. No doubt the House of Lords did very rarely either alter or reject any Money Bill, and though the Lords have always claimed the right to alter or reject such a Bill, they have only on very special occasions exercised this power. No doubt again their lordships have, at any rate since 1832, acknowledged that they ought to pass any Bill deliberately desired by the nation, and also have admitted the existence of a more or less strong presumption that the House of Commons in general represents the will of the nation, and that the Lords ought, therefore, in general to consent to a Bill passed by the House of Commons, even though their lordships did not approve of the measure. But this presumption may, they have always maintained, be rebutted if any strong ground can be shown for holding that the electors did not really wish such a Bill to become an Act of Parliament. Hence Bill after Bill has been passed by their lordships of which the House of Lords did not in reality approve. It was however absolutely indubitable up to the passing of the Parliament Act that no Act could be passed by Parliament without obtaining the consent of the House of Lords. Nor could any one dispute the legal right or power of the House, by refusing such assent, to veto the passing of any Act of which the House might disapprove. Two considerations, however, must be taken into account. This veto, in the first place, has, at any rate since 1832, been as a rule used by the Lords as a merely suspensive veto. The passing of the Great Reform Act itself was delayed by their lordships for somewhat less than two years, and it may well be doubted whether they have, since 1832, ever by their legislative veto, delayed legislation really desired by the electors for as much as two years. It must again be remembered that the Lords, of recent years at least, have at times rejected Bills supported by the majority of the House of Commons which, as has been proved by the event, had not received the support of the electors. Hence it cannot be denied that the action of the House of Lords has sometimes protected the authority of the nation.

THE DIRECT EFFECTS OF THE PARLIAMENT ACT[12]

Such effects can be summed up in popular and intelligible language, rather than with technical precision, as follows:

1. In respect of any Money Bill the Act takes away all legislative power from the House of Lords. The House may discuss such a Bill for a calendar month, but cannot otherwise prevent, beyond a month, the Bill becoming an Act of Parliament.[13]

2. In respect of any public Bill (which is not a Money Bill),[14] the Act takes away from the House of Lords any *final* veto, but leaves or gives to the House a *suspensive* veto.[15]

This suspensive veto is secured to the House of Lords because under the Parliament Act, s. 2, no such Bill can be passed without the consent of the House which has not fulfilled the following four conditions:

i. That the Bill shall, before it is presented to the King for his assent, be passed by the House of Commons and be rejected by the House of Lords in each of *three successive* sessions.[16]

ii. That the Bill shall be sent up to the House of Lords at least one calendar month before the end of each of these sessions.[17]

---

12 See as to "indirect effects," p. lxix, *post.*

13 See Parliament Act, ss. 1 and 3.

14 Except a Bill for extending the maximum duration of Parliament beyond five years. See Parliament Act, s. 2, sub-s. 1.

15 See s. 2.

16 See s. 2 (1).

17 *Ibid.*

iii. That in respect of such Bill at least two years shall have elapsed between the date of the second reading of the Bill in the House of Commons during the first of those sessions and the date on which it passes the House of Commons in the third of such sessions.[18]

iv. That the Bill presented to the King for his assent shall be in every material respect identical with the Bill sent up to the House of Lords in the first of the three successive sessions except in so far as it may have been amended by or with the consent of the House of Lords.

The history of the Government of Ireland Act, 1914, popularly, and throughout this Introduction generally, called the Home Rule Bill or Act, affords good illustrations of the peculiar procedure instituted by the Parliament Act. The Home Rule Bill was introduced into the House of Commons during the first of the three successive sessions on April 11, 1912; it passed its second reading in the House of Commons during that session on May 9, 1912; it was rejected by the House of Lords either actually or constructively[19] in each of the three successive sessions. It could not then possibly have been presented to the King for his assent till June 9, 1914; it was not so presented to the King till September 18, 1914. On that day, just before the actual prorogation of Parliament in the third session, it received the royal assent without the consent of the House of Lords; it thereby became the Government of Ireland Act, 1914. The Act as assented to by the King was in substance identical with the Bill sent up to the House of Lords in the first of the three sessions on January 16, 1913. But here we come across the difficulty of amending a Bill under the Parliament Act after it had once been sent up in the third session to the House of Lords. By June

---

18 S. 2 (1) Proviso. Under this enactment the House of Lords may insist upon a delay of at least two years and one calendar month, and a powerful opposition in the House of Commons may lengthen this delay.

19 Constructive rejection arises under the Parliament Act, s. 2, sub-s. 3, which runs as follows: "A Bill shall be deemed to be rejected by the House of Lords if it is not passed by the House of Lords either without amendment or with such amendments only as may be agreed to by both Houses." The Home Rule Bill was actually rejected by the vote of the House of Lords in its first and second session. It was constructively rejected in the third session by the House of Lords simply by the House not passing the Bill during such session.

1914 it was felt to be desirable to amend the Home Rule Bill in respect of the position of Ulster. On June 23 the Government brought into the House of Lords a Bill which should amend the Home Rule Act which was still a Bill, and it is difficult to find a precedent for thus passing an Act for amending a Bill not yet on the statute-book. The attempt to carry out the Government's proposal came to nothing. On September 18, 1914, the Home Rule Bill became the Home Rule Act (or technically the Government of Ireland Act, 1914) unamended, but on the very day on which the Home Rule Act was finally passed it was in effect amended by a Suspensory Act under which the Government of Ireland Act, 1914, cannot come into force until at any rate twelve months from September 18, and possibly will not come into force until the present war has ended. The Suspensory Act evades or avoids the effect of the Parliament Act, but such escape from the effect of a recently passed statute suggests the necessity for some amendment in the procedure created by the Parliament Act.

3. The House of Commons can without the consent of the House of Lords present to the King for his assent any Bill whatever which has complied with the provisions of the Parliament Act, section 2, or rather which is certified by the Speaker of the House of Commons in the way provided by the Act to have complied with the conditions of the Parliament Act, section 2.

The simple truth is that the Parliament Act has given to the House of Commons, or, in plain language, to the majority thereof, the power of passing any Bill whatever, provided always that the conditions of the Parliament Act, section 2, are complied with. But these provisions do leave to the House of Lords a suspensive veto which may prevent a Bill from becoming an Act of Parliament for a period of certainly more, and possibly a good deal more, than two years.[20]

---

20 The Parliament Act leaves the existing rights and privileges of the House of Commons untouched (*ibid.* sect. 6). No reference whatever is therein made to the so-called "veto" of the King. Its existence is undoubted, but the veto has not been exercised for at least two centuries. The well-known words of Burke, however, should always be borne in mind: "The king's negative to bills," he says, "is one of the most indisputed of the royal prerogatives; and it extends to all cases whatsoever. I am far from certain, that if several laws which I know had fallen under the stroke of that sceptre, the public would have had a very heavy loss. But it is not the *propriety* of the exercise which is in question. The exercise itself is

In these circumstances it is arguable that the Parliament Act has transformed the sovereignty of Parliament into the sovereignty of the King and the House of Commons. But the better opinion on the whole is that sovereignty still resides in the King and the two Houses of Parliament. The grounds for this opinion are, firstly, that the King and the two Houses acting together can most certainly enact or repeal any law whatever without in any way contravening the Parliament Act; and, secondly, that the House of Lords, while it cannot prevent the House of Commons from, in effect, passing under the Parliament Act any change of the constitution, provided always that the requirements of the Parliament Act are complied with, nevertheless can, as long as that Act remains in force, prohibit the passing of any Act the effectiveness of which depends upon its being passed without delay.

Hence, on the whole, the correct legal statement of the actual condition of things is that sovereignty still resides in Parliament, *i.e.* in the King and the two Houses acting together, but that the Parliament Act has greatly increased the share of sovereignty possessed by the House of Commons and has greatly diminished the share thereof belonging to the House of Lords.

PRACTICAL CHANGE IN THE AREA OF PARLIAMENTARY SOVEREIGNTY (RELATION OF THE IMPERIAL PARLIAMENT TO THE DOMINIONS[21])

The term "Dominions" means and includes the Dominion of Canada, Newfoundland, and Commonwealth of Australia, New

---

wisely forborne. Its repose may be the preservation of its existence; and its existence may be the means of saving the constitution itself, on an occasion worthy of bringing it forth."— Burke, *Letter to the Sheriffs of Bristol,* vol. iii., ed. 1808, pp. 180, 181; ed. 1872, vol. ii. p. 28. Experience has confirmed the soundness of Burke's doctrine. The existence of this "negative" has greatly facilitated the development of the present happy relation between England and her self-governing colonies. It has enabled English and colonial statesmanship to create that combination of Imperial unity with something coming near to colonial independence which may ultimately turn out to be the salvation of the British Empire.

21 For this use of the term Dominions see British Nationality & Status of Aliens Act, 1914, 4 & 5 Geo. V. c. 17, 1st Schedule. Compare especially as to British colonies with representative and responsible government pp. 47 to 61, *post.*

The Dominions for the most part consist either of a country which was a self-governing colony, or of countries which were self-governing colonies in 1884. But this statement does

Zealand, and the Union of South Africa. Each of the Dominions is a self-governing colony, *i.e.* a colony possessed both of a colonial Parliament, or representative legislature, and a responsible government, or in other words, of a government responsible to such legislature.

Our subject raises two questions:

First Question

What is the difference between the relation of the Imperial Parliament to a self-governing colony, such, *e.g.*, as New Zealand, in 1884, and the relation of the same Parliament to the Dominion, *e.g.* of New Zealand, in 1914?

Before attempting a direct answer to this inquiry it is well to point out that in two respects of considerable importance the relation of the Imperial Parliament[22] to the self-governing colonies, whether called Dominions or not, has in no respect changed since 1884.

In the first place, the Imperial Parliament still claims in 1914, as it claimed in 1884, the possession of absolute sovereignty throughout every part of the British Empire; and this claim, which certainly extends to every Dominion, would be admitted as sound legal doctrine by any court throughout the Empire which purported to act under

---

not apply with perfect accuracy to every one of the Dominions. Western Australia, for instance, which is now one of the states of the Commonwealth of Australia, did not obtain responsible government till 1890, and Natal, now a state of the Union of South Africa, did not obtain such government till 1893. The Union of South Africa itself consists to a great extent of states which in 1884, though subject to the suzerainty of the King, were (under the government of the Boers) all but independent countries.

Throughout this Introduction, unless the contrary is expressly stated, or appears from the context, no reference is made to the position either of (i.) the Crown colonies, or (ii.) the three colonies, viz. the Bahamas, Barbadoes, and Bermuda, which possess representative but not responsible government, or (iii.) British India. This Introduction, in short, in so far as it deals with the relation of the Imperial Parliament to the colonies, refers exclusively, or all but exclusively, to the relation between the Imperial Parliament and the five Dominions.

22 This term means what an English writer on our constitution would generally call simply "Parliament," that is the Parliament of the United Kingdom. The term "Imperial Parliament" is, however, a convenient one when we have to deal, as in this Introduction, with the relation between the Parliament of the United Kingdom and the Dominions, every one of which has representative legislatures of their own which are always popularly, and sometimes in Acts of Parliament, termed Parliaments. The term "Imperial Parliament" is used in colonial statutes, *e.g.*, in the Interpretation Act of the Commonwealth of Australia, No. 2 of 1901.

the authority of the King. The constitution indeed of a Dominion in general originates in and depends upon an Act, or Acts, of the Imperial Parliament; and these constitutional statutes are assuredly liable to be changed by the Imperial Parliament.

Parliament, in the second place, had long before 1884 practically admitted the truth of the doctrine in vain pressed upon his contemporaries by Burke,[23] when insisting upon the folly of the attempt made by the Parliament of England to exert as much absolute power in Massachusetts as in Middlesex, that a real limit to the exercise of sovereignty is imposed not by the laws of man but by the nature of things, and that it was vain for a parliamentary or any other sovereign to try to exert equal power throughout the whole of an immense Empire. The completeness of this admission is shown by one noteworthy fact: the Imperial Parliament in 1884, and long before 1884, had ceased to impose of its own authority and for the benefit of England any tax upon any British colony.[24] The omnipotence, in

---

23 "Who are you," to quote his words, "that should fret and rage, and bite the chains of nature? Nothing worse happens to you, than does to all nations who have extensive empire; and it happens in all the forms into which empire can be thrown. In large bodies, the circulation of power must be less vigorous at the extremities. Nature has said it. The Turk cannot govern Egypt, and Arabia, and Curdistan, as he governs Thrace; nor has he the same dominion in the Crimea and in Algiers which he has at Brusa and Smyrna. Despotism itself is obliged to truck and huckster. The Sultan gets such obedience as he can. He governs with a loose rein, that he may govern at all; and the whole of the force and vigour of his authority in the centre is derived from a prudent relaxation in all his borders. Spain, in her provinces, is, perhaps, not so well obeyed as you are in yours. She complies too; she submits; she watches times. This is the immutable condition, the eternal law, of extensive and detached empire."—Burke, *Conciliation with America*, vol. iii. (ed. 1808), pp. 56, 57.

24 This renunciation by the Imperial Parliament of the right to impose taxes upon a colony, whether a self-governing colony or not, has passed through two stages. Since 1783 taxation imposed by an Imperial Act has always been, even in the case of a Crown colony, imposed for the benefit of the colony, and the proceeds thereof have been paid to the colony. But until the repeal of the Navigation Laws in 1849 Parliament, in support of our whole navigation system, retained the practice of imposing duties on goods imported into the colonies, though the proceeds thereof were paid to the colonies so taxed. Since 1849 no Imperial Act has been passed for the taxation of any colony, and no colony is compelled by the Imperial Parliament to contribute anything in the way of taxation towards the cost of the government of the United Kingdom or towards the defence of the British Empire.

The Imperial Parliament does still impose customs duties upon the Isle of Man. See 3 & 4 Geo. V. c. 18.

short, of Parliament, though theoretically admitted, has been applied in its full effect only to the United Kingdom.

A student may ask what is the good of insisting upon the absolute sovereignty of Parliament in relation to the Dominions when it is admitted that Parliament never gives, outside the United Kingdom, and probably never will give, full effect to this asserted and more or less fictitious omnipotence. The answer to this suggestion is that students who do not bear in mind the claim of Parliament to absolute sovereignty throughout the whole of the British Empire, will never understand the extent to which this sovereign power is on some occasions actually exerted outside the limits of the United Kingdom, nor, though this statement sounds paradoxical, will they understand the limits which, with the full assent, no less of English than of colonial statesmen, are in fact, as regards at any rate the Dominions, imposed upon the actual exercise of the theoretically limitless authority of Parliament. It will be found further that even to the Dominions themselves there is at times some advantage in the admitted authority of the Imperial Parliament to legislate for the whole Empire. In the eyes, at any rate, of thinkers who share the moral convictions prevalent in most civilised states, it must seem a gain that the Imperial Parliament should have been able in 1834 to prohibit the existence of slavery in any country subject to the British Crown, and should be able to-day to forbid throughout the whole Empire the revival of the Slave Trade, or of judicial torture.

Let us now turn to the points wherein the relation of the Imperial Parliament to the self-governing colonies in 1884 differed from the existing relation of the Imperial Parliament to the Dominions in 1914.

The relation of the Imperial Parliament in 1884 to a self-governing colony, *e.g.* New Zealand.

The Imperial Parliament, under the guidance of English statesmen, certainly admitted in practice thirty years ago that a self-governing colony, such as New Zealand, ought to be allowed in local matters to legislate for itself. Parliament did, however, occasionally legislate for New Zealand or any other self-governing colony. Thus the existing English Bankruptcy Act, 1883, as a matter of fact transferred, as it still transfers, to the trustee in bankruptcy the bankrupt's property, and even his immovable property situate in any part of the British Empire,[25] and a discharge under the English Bankruptcy Act, 1883, was, and still is, a discharge as regards the debts of the bankrupt contracted in any part of the British Empire,[26] *e.g.* in New Zealand or in the Commonwealth of Australia. So again the veto of the Crown was, in one form or another[27] in 1884, and even later, used occasionally to prevent colonial legislation which, though approved of by the people of the colony and by the legislature thereof, might be opposed to the moral feeling or convictions of Englishmen. Thus colonial Bills for legalising the marriages between a man and his deceased wife's sister, or between a woman and her deceased husband's brother, were sometimes vetoed by the Crown, or in effect on the advice of ministers supported by the Imperial Parliament. No doubt as time went on the unwillingness of English statesmen to interfere, by means of the royal veto or otherwise, with colonial legislation which affected only the internal government of a self-governing colony, increased. But such interference was not unknown. There was further, in 1884, an appeal in every colony from the judgments of the Supreme Court thereof to the English Privy Council. And a British Government would in 1884 have felt itself at liberty to interfere with the executive action of a colonial Cabinet when such action was inconsistent with English ideas of justice. It was also in 1884 a clear principle of English administration that English colonists should neither directly nor indirectly take part in negotiating treaties with foreign powers. Nor had either England or the self-governing colonies, thirty years ago, realised the general advantage of those conferences now becoming a regular part of English public life, at which English ministers and colonial ministers could confer upon questions of colonial policy, and could thus practically acknowledge the interest of the colonies in everything which concerned the welfare of the whole Empire. Neither certainly did English statesmen in 1884 contemplate the pos-

---

25 See Dicey, *Conflict of Laws* (2nd ed.), pp. 329–333.

26 *Ibid.*, p. 441, and *Ellis* v. *McHenry* (1871), L. R. 6, C. P. 228, 234–236; but contrast *New Zealand Loan, etc, Co.* v. *Morrison* [1898], A. C. 349, cited *Conflict of Laws*, p. 342.

27 See pp. 56–61, *post.*

sibility of a colony standing neutral during a war between England and a foreign power.

The relation of the Imperial Parliament in 1914 to a Dominion.[28]

This relation may now, it is submitted, be roughly summed up in the following rules:

Rule 1

In regard to any matter which directly affects Imperial interests the Imperial Parliament will (though with constantly increasing caution) pass laws which apply to a Dominion and otherwise exercise sovereign power in such a Dominion.

But this rule applies almost exclusively to matters which directly and indubitably affect Imperial interests.[29]

Rule 2

Parliament does not concede to any Dominion or to the legislature thereof the right—

a. to repeal [except by virtue of an Act of the Imperial Parliament] any Act of the Imperial Parliament applying to a Dominion;

b. to make of its own authority a treaty with any foreign power;

c. to stand neutral in the event of a war between the King and any foreign power, or, in general, to receive any benefit from a foreign power which is not offered by such power to the whole of the British Empire.[30]

It must be noted that under these two rules the Imperial Parliament does retain, and sometimes exerts the right to legislate in regard to matters which may greatly concern the prosperity of a Dominion, and also does in some respects seriously curtail both the legislative power of a Dominion Parliament and the executive power of a Dominion Cabinet. As long, in short, as the present state of things continues, the Imperial Parliament, to the extent I have laid down, still treats any Dominion as on matters of Imperial concern subordinate to the sovereignty of the Imperial Parliament.

---

28 See as to meaning of Dominion, pp. xlii–xliii, note 21, *ante.*

29 See Keith, *Responsible Government in the Dominions,* p. 1316.

30 *Ibid.* pp. 1119–1122.

Rule 3

The Imperial Parliament now admits and acts upon the admission, that any one of the Dominions has acquired a moral right to as much independence, at any rate in regard to matters occurring within the territory of such Dominion, as can from the nature of things be conceded to any country which still forms part of the British Empire.

Take the following illustration of the extent of such internal independence:

Parliament does not (except at the wish of a Dominion) legislate with respect to matters which merely concern the internal interests of such Dominion, *e.g.* New Zealand.[31]

The legislature of any Dominion has within the territorial limits of such Dominion power to legislate in regard to any matter which solely concerns the internal interest of such Dominion.

The power of the Crown, *i.e.* of the British ministry, to veto or disallow in any way[32] any Bill passed by the legislature of a Dominion, *e.g.* New Zealand, is now most sparingly exercised, and will hardly be used unless the Bill directly interferes with Imperial interests or is as regards the colonial legislature *ultra vires.* Thus the Crown, or in other words a British ministry, will now not veto or disallow any Bill passed by the legislature of a Dominion on the ground that such Bill is indirectly opposed to the interests of the United Kingdom, or contradicts legal principles generally upheld in England, *e.g.* the principle of free trade.

The British Government will not interfere with the executive action of the Government (*e.g.* of New Zealand) in the giving or the withholding of pardon for crime, in regard to transactions taking place wholly within the territory of New Zealand.[33]

Any Dominion has now a full and admitted right to raise military or naval forces for its own defence. And the policy of England is in the main to withdraw the English Army from the Dominions and to encourage any Dominion to provide for its own defence and to raise

---

31 See Keith, *Responsible Government in the Dominions,* pp. 1316–1328.

32 See pp. 56–57, *post.*

33 See Keith, *Responsible Government in the Dominions,* p. 1583.

for itself a Navy, and thereby contribute to the defensive power of the British Empire.

The Imperial Government is now ready at the wish of a Dominion to exclude from its constitution, either partially or wholly, the right of appeal from the decision of the Supreme Court of such Dominion to the Privy Council.[34]

The Imperial Government also is now ready at the wish of a Dominion to grant to such Dominion the power to amend by law the constitution thereof though created under an Act of the Imperial Parliament.[35]

Rule 4

The habit has now grown up that conferences should be held from time to time in England, at which shall be present the Premier of England and the Premier of each Dominion, for consultation and discussion on all matters concerning the interest and the policy of the Empire, and that such conferences should be from time to time held may now, it is submitted, be considered a moral right of each Dominion.

These conferences, which were quite unthought of thirty years ago, and which did not receive their present form until the year 1907, mark in a very striking manner a gradual and therefore the more important change in the relations between England and the self-governing colonies.

The answer then to the question before us[36] as to the difference between the relation of England (or in strictness of the Imperial Parliament) to the self-governing colonies[37] in 1884 and her relation to the Dominions in 1914 can thus be summed up: At the former period England conceded to the self-governing colonies as much of independence as was necessary to give to such colonies the real management in their internal or local affairs. But English statesmen at that

---

34 See Commonwealth of Australia Constitution, s. 74; South Africa Act, 1909, s. 106.

35 See especially South Africa Act, 1909, s. 106.

36 See first question, p. xliii, *ante.*

37 The difference between the expression "self-governing colonies" and "Dominions" is worth noticing. The first is appropriate to 1884, the second is appropriate to 1914.

date did intend to retain for the Imperial Parliament, and the Imperial Government as representing such Parliament, a real and effective control over the action of the ministry and the legislature of each self-governing colony in so far as that control was not palpably incon- sistent with independence as regards the management of strictly local affairs. In 1914 the colonial policy of England is to grant to every Dominion absolute, unfettered, complete local autonomy,[38] in so far as such perfect self-government by a Dominion does not clearly inter- fere with loyalty of the Dominion to the Empire. The two relations of England to the self-governing colonies—now called Dominions— are, it may be objected, simply one and the same relation described in somewhat different language. The objection is plausible, but not sound. My effort has been to describe two different ways of looking at one and the same relation, and the results of this difference of view are of practical consequence. In 1884 it was admitted, as it is to-day, that the self-governing colonies must have rights of self-government. But in 1884 the exercise of self-government on the part of any colony was regarded as subordinate to real control by the English Parliament and Crown of colonial legislation which might be opposed to English interests or to English ideals of political prudence. In 1914 the self- government, *e.g.,* of New Zealand means absolute, unfettered, com- plete autonomy, without consulting English ideas of expediency or even of moral duty. The one limit to this complete independence in regard to local government is that it is confined to really local matters and does not trench upon loyalty to the Empire. The independence of the Dominion, in short, means nowadays as much of independence as is compatible with each Dominion remaining part of the Empire.

Second Question

What are the changes of opinion which have led up to the altered relation between England and the Dominions?[39]

In the early Victorian era [and even in the mid-Victorian era] there were two rough-and-ready solutions for what was regarded, with some impa-

---

38 See Minutes of Proceedings of Imperial Conference, 1911 [Cd. 5745], p. 22.

39 See *Law and Opinion*, pp. 450–457.

tience, by the British statesmen of that day as the "Colonial problem." The one was centralisation—the government, that is, except in relatively trivial matters, of all the outlying parts of the Empire from an office in Downing Street. The other was disintegration—the acquiescence in, perhaps the encouragement of, a process of successive "hivings off" by which, without the hazards or embitterments of coercion, each community, as it grew to political manhood, would follow the example of the American Colonies, and start an independent and sovereign existence of its own. After 70 years' experience of Imperial evolution, it may be said with confidence that neither of these theories commands the faintest support to-day, either at home or in any part of our self-governing Empire. We were saved from their adoption—some people would say by the favour of Providence—or (to adopt a more flattering hypothesis) by the political instinct of our race. And just in proportion as centralisation was seen to be increasingly absurd, so has disintegration been felt to be increasingly impossible. Whether in the United Kingdom, or in any one of the great communities which you represent, we each of us are, and we each of us intend to remain, master in our own household. This is, here at home and throughout the Dominions, the life-blood of our polity. It is the *articulus stantis aut cadentis Imperii.*[40]

These words are a true statement of patent facts, but it will on examination be found that the change during recent years in English opinion, and also in colonial opinion, with regard to the relation between England and the Dominions presents rather more comlexity than at first sight may be apparent[41] to a casual reader of Mr. Asquith's address. Up to the last quarter of the nineteenth century, and even as late as 1884, many Englishmen, including a considerable number of our older statemen, held that the solution of the colonial problem was to be found wholly in the willingness of England to permit and even to promote the separation from the Empire of any self-governing colony which desired independence, provided that this separation should take place without engendering any bad feeling between England and her so-called dependencies. No doubt there existed, at any rate till the middle of the nineteenth century, a limited body of experienced officials who held that our colonial system, as long as it was maintained, implied the active control by

---

40 Minutes of Proceedings of the Imperial Conference, 1911 [Cd. 5745]. Opening address of the President (Mr. Asquith), p. 22. Compare "Message of King to Governments and Peoples of the Self-governing Dominions," *Times*, Sept. 10, 1914.

41 Compare Dicey, *Law and Opinion*, pp. 450–457.

England of colonial affairs. But such men in many cases doubted whether the maintenance of the Colonial Empire was of real benefit to England, and thought that on the whole, with respect at any rate to any self-governing colony, the course of prudence was to leave things alone until it should have become manifest to every one that the hour for friendly separation had struck. The self-governing colonies, on the other hand, up at any rate till 1884, just because they were more and more left alone and free to manage their own affairs, though they occasionally resented the interference of the English Government with colonial legislation, were on the whole contented with things as they stood. They certainly did not display any marked desire to secede from the Empire. Still less, however, did they show any active wish to take part in controlling the policy of the Empire, or to share the cost of Imperial defence. Honest belief in the principle of *laissez faire* produced its natural and, as far as it went, beneficial result. It removed causes of discontent; it prevented the rise of ill-will between England and her self-governing colonies. But it did not of itself produce any kind of Imperial patriotism. The change which a student has to note is an alteration of feeling, which did not become very obvious till near the close of the nineteenth century. This was the growth (to use a current expression) of Imperialism. But this term, like all popular phrases, is from its very vagueness certain to mislead those who use it, unless its meaning be defined with some care. In regard to the British Empire it ought to be used as a term neither of praise nor of blame, but as the name for an idea which, in so far as it is true, is of considerable importance. This idea is that the British Empire is an institution well worth maintaining, and this not on mere grounds of sentiment but for definite and assignable reasons. Upon England and upon every country subject to the King of England the British Empire confers at least two benefits: It secures permanent peace among the inhabitants of the largest of existing states; it again secures, or ought to secure, to the whole of this vast community absolute protection against foreign attack. The resources of the Empire are, it is felt, practically inexhaustible; the creation of a fleet supported by revenues and also by armies drawn from every country subject to the King of England should, provided England herself stands properly armed, render invasion of the British Empire by any of the great military powers of Europe an impossibility. But then the hugeness of the Empire and the strength of the Empire, if it remains united, are enough to show that the different countries which are parts of the Imperial system would, if they each stood alone, be easily assailable by any state or combination of states which had the command of large military and naval armaments. Neither England, in short, nor any of her self-governing Dominions can fail to see that the dissolution of the Empire might take from both the mother country and the most powerful of the Dominions the means necessary for maintaining liberty and independence. Loyalty to the Empire, typified by loyalty to the King, is in short a sentiment developed by the whole course of recent history. It is a feeling or conviction which places the relation of England and the Dominions in a new light. It amply accounts for the extraordinary difference between the colonial policy accepted both by England and by the self-governing colonies in 1850, and even (to a great extent) in 1884, and the colonial policy acceptable both to England and to her all but independent Dominions in 1914. English statesmen on the one hand now proffer to, and almost force upon, each Dominion every liberty compatible with the maintenance of the Empire; but then English statesmen no longer regard with philosophic calm the dawn of the day when any one of the Dominions may desire to secede from the Empire. The Dominions, on the other hand, have no longer any reason to fear and do not desire any interference with colonial affairs either by the legislation of the Imperial Parliament or by the administrative action of officials at Downing Street who are the servants of the Imperial Parliament. But then statesmen of the Dominions show a willingness to share the cost of the defence of the Empire, and at the same time express at each of the great Conferences, with more and more plainness, the desire that the Dominions should take a more active part in the determination of Imperial policy. It is not my object, at any rate at this part of this Introduction, to consider how far it may be possible to give satisfaction to the desires of rational Imperialists, and still less ought any man of sense to express any confident opinion as to how far the sentiment of Imperialism may in the course of time increase in force

LAW OF THE CONSTITUTION

or suffer diminution. My immediate aim is to show that this new Imperialism is the natural result of historical circumstances. It is well, however, to bear in mind several considerations which Englishmen of to-day are apt to overlook. The friendly Imperialism which finds expression in the Imperial Conferences is itself the admirable fruit of the old policy of *laissez faire*. The system of leaving the self-governing colonies alone first appeased discontent, and next allowed the growth of friendliness which has made it possible for the English inhabitants, and even in some cases the foreign inhabitants, of the Dominions to recognise the benefits which the Empire confers upon the Dominions, and for Englishmen at home to see that the Dominions may contribute to the safety of England and to the prosperity of the whole Empire.[42] But we must at the same time recognise that the policy of friendly indifference to secession from the Empire, which nominally, at any rate, was favoured by many English statesmen during the nineteenth century, has come to an end. The war in South Africa was in reality a war waged not only by England but also by the Dominions to prevent secession; the concession further to the South African Union of the full rights of a Dominion is no more inconsistent with resistance to secession than was the restoration to the Southern States of the American Commonwealth of their full right to existence as States of the United States. It must, lastly, be noted, that while the inhabitants of England and of the Dominions express at each Conference their honest pleasure in Imperial unity, the growth of Imperialism already causes to many patriotic men one disappointment. Events suggest that it may turn out difficult, or even impossible, to establish throughout the Empire that equal citizenship of all British subjects which exists in the United Kingdom and which Englishmen in the middle of the nineteenth century hoped to see established throughout the length and breadth of the Empire.[43]

---

42 As they now [1914] are contributing.

43 The kind of equality among British subjects which Englishmen, whether wisely or not, hoped to establish throughout the whole Empire is best seen by considering the sort of equality which actually exists and has for many years existed in England. Speaking broadly, every British subject has in England at the present day the same political rights as every natural-born Englishman, *e.g.* an Englishman born in England and the son of English

THE RULE OF LAW[44]

The rule of law, as described in this treatise, remains to this day a distinctive characteristic of the English constitution. In England no man can be made to suffer punishment or to pay damages for any conduct not definitely forbidden by law; every man's legal rights or liabilities are almost invariably determined by the ordinary Courts of the realm, and each man's individual rights are far less the result of our constitution than the basis on which that consitution is founded.

The principles laid down in this treatise with regard to the rule of law and to the nature of *droit administratif* need little change. My object in this Introduction is first to note a singular decline among modern Englishmen in their respect or reverence for the rule of law, and secondly, to call attention to certain changes in the *droit administratif* of France.[45]

DECLINE IN REVERENCE FOR RULE OF LAW

The ancient veneration for the rule of law has in England suffered during the last thirty years a marked decline. The truth of this assertion is proved by actual legislation, by the existence among some classes of a certain distrust both of the law and of the judges, and by a marked tendency towards the use of lawless methods for the attainment of social or political ends.

---

parents settled in England. Thus a British subject, whatever be the place of his birth, or the race to which he belongs, or I may now add the religion which he professes, has, with the rarest possible exceptions, the same right to settle or to trade in England which is possessed by a natural-born Englishman. He has further exactly the same political rights. He can, if he satisfies the requirements of the English electoral law, vote for a member of Parliament; he can, if he commends himself to an English constituency, take his seat as a member of Parliament. There is no law which forbids any British subject, wherever he be born, or to whatever race he belongs, to become a member of the English Cabinet or a Prime Minister. Of course it will be said that it is extremely improbable that the offices I have mentioned will, in fact, be filled by men who are not in reality Englishmen by race. This remark to a certain extent is true, though it is not wholly true. But the possession of theoretically equal political rights does certainly give in England, or rather to be strictly accurate in the United Kingdom, to every British subject an equality which some British subjects do not possess in some of the Dominions.

44 See Part II., and especially Chap. IV., *post.*

45 See Chap. XII. *post.*

Legislation

Recent Acts have given judicial or quasi-judicial authority to officials[46] who stand more or less in connection with, and therefore may be influenced by, the government of the day, and hence have in some cases excluded, and in others indirectly diminished, the authority of the law Courts. This tendency to diminish the sphere of the rule of law is shown, for instance, in the judicial powers conferred upon the Education Commissioners by the Education Act, 1902,[47] on various officials by the National Insurance Acts, 1911 and 1913,[48] and on the Commissioners of Inland Revenue and other officials by the Finance Act, 1910.[49] It is also shown by the Parliament Act, 1911, s. 3, which enacts that "any certificate of the Speaker of the House of Commons given under this Act shall be conclusive for all purposes and shall not be questioned in any Court of law." This enactment, if strictly construed, would protect any Speaker who, either from partisanship or to promote some personal interest of his own, signed a certificate which was notoriously false from being liable to punishment by any Court of law whatever.[50] No doubt the House of Commons has been historically jealous of any judicial interference with persons acting under the authority of the House, and has on more than one occasion claimed in a sense to be above the law of the land. All that can be said is that such claims have rarely been of advantage or credit to the House, and that the present time is hardly the proper season for the curtailment by the House of legitimate judicial power. It must, however, in fairness be noted that the invasion of the rule of law by imposing judicial functions upon officials is due, in part, to the whole current of legislative opinion in favour of extending the sphere of the State's authority. The inevitable result of thus immensely increasing

---

46 See generally on this point Muir, *Peers and Bureaucrats*, especially pp. 1–94.

47 See sect. 7, and *R. v. Board of Education (Swansea Case)* [1910], 2 K. B. 167; *Board of Education v. Rice* [1911], A. C. 179.

48 See National Insurance Act, 1911, ss. 66, 67, 88 (1), and generally *Law and Opinion* (2nd ed.), pp. 41–43.

49 See especially sect. 2, sub-s. 3, ss. 33 and 96.

50 Would this enactment protect the Speaker against an impeachment for giving a certificate which he knew to be false?

the duties of the Government is that State officials must more and more undertake to manage a mass of public business, *e.g.,* to give one example only, the public education of the majority of the citizens. But Courts are from the nature of things unsuited for the transaction of business. The primary duty of a judge is to act in accordance with the strict rules of law. He must shun, above all things, any injustice to individuals. The well-worn and often absurdly misapplied adage that "it is better that ten criminals should escape conviction than that one innocent man should without cause be found guilty of crime" does after all remind us that the first duty of a judge is not to punish crime but to punish it without doing injustice. A man of business, whether employed by a private firm or working in a public office, must make it his main object to see that the business in which he is concerned is efficiently carried out. He could not do this if tied down by the rules which rightly check the action of a judge. The official must act on evidence which, though strong, may not be at all conclusive. The official must often act with severity towards subordinates whose stupidity, and not their voluntary wrong-doing, gives cause for dismissal. A judge, on the other hand, is far more concerned with seeing that the law is strictly carried out than in showing consideration to individuals. "That hard cases make bad law" is proverbial; the transaction of business, in short, is a very different thing from the giving of judgments: The more multifarious therefore become the affairs handed over to the management of civil servants the greater will be always the temptation, and often the necessity, extending to the discretionary powers given to officials, and thus preventing law Courts from intervening in matters not suited for legal decision.

Distrust of Judges and of Courts

If the House of Commons deliberately excludes the intervention of any law Court in matters which the House may deem (with very dubious truth) to concern the House alone, we can scarcely wonder that artisans should have no love for judicial decisions. In plain truth, while every man of at all respectable instincts desires what he considers justice for himself and for the class to which he belongs, almost all men desire something more than, and different from, justice for themselves and against their neighbours. This is inevitably the case with persons such as the members of trade unions, who are trying, with a good deal of success, to enforce trade rules which often arouse the censure of the public, and sometimes come into absolute conflict with the law of the land. The blackleg may be, and one may suspect often is, a mean fellow who, to put money into his own pocket, breaks rules which his fellow-workers hold to be just and beneficial to the trade generally. He, for example, has no objection, if properly paid for it, to work with men who are not members of any union. The blackleg, however, all but invariably keeps within the law of the land, and proposes to do nothing which violates any principle established by common law or any enactment to be found in the Statute Book. The trade unionists whom he offends know perfectly well that the blackleg is in the eye of the law no wrong-doer; they therefore feel that the Courts are his protectors, and that, somehow or other, trade unions must be protected against the intervention of judges. Hence the invention of that self-contradictory idea of "peaceful picketing," which is no more capable of real existence than would be "peaceful war" or "unoppressive oppression"; hence, too, that triumph of legalised wrong-doing sanctioned by the fourth section of the Trade Disputes Act,[51] 1906. It is however by no means to be supposed that artisans are the only class accustomed to decry a judge or the legislature when the one gives a judgment or the other passes a law opposed to the moral convictions of a particular part of the community.

Lawlessness

Till a time well within the memory of persons now living, it would have been very difficult to find any body of men or women who did not admit that, broadly speaking, a breach of the law of the land was also an act of immorality. No doubt at all times there have existed, as at the present day, a large number of habitual law-breakers, but though a cheat, a pickpocket, or a burglar does constantly break the law, there is no reason to surmise that cheats, pickpockets, or burglars maintain the doctrine that law-breaking is itself a praiseworthy

---

51 See *Law and Opinion*, pp. xliv–xlvi, and compare the Trade Union Act, 1913, *ibid.* p. xlviii.

or a moral act. Within the last thirty years, however, there has grown up in England, and indeed in many other civilised countries, a new doctrine as to lawlessness. This novel phenomenon, which perplexes moralists and statesmen, is that large classes of otherwise respectable persons now hold the belief and act on the conviction that it is not only allowable, but even highly praiseworthy, to break the law of the land if the law-breaker is pursuing some end which to him or to her seems to be just and desirable. This view is not confined to any one class. Many of the English clergy (a class of men well entitled to respect) have themselves shown no great hesitation in thwarting and breaking laws which they held to be opposed to the law of the Church. Passive resisters do not scruple to resist taxes imposed for some object which they condemn. Conscientious objectors are doing a good deal to render ineffective the vaccination laws. The militant suffragettes glorify lawlessness; the nobleness of their aim justifies in their eyes the hopeless and perverse illegality of the means by which they hope to obtain votes for women.

Whence arises this zeal for lawlessness? The following reflections afford an answer, though only a partial answer, to this perplexing inquiry:

In England democratic government has already given votes, if not precisely supreme power, to citizens who, partly because of the fairness and the regularity with which the law has been enforced for generations in Great Britain, hardly perceive the risk and ruin involved in a departure from the rule of law. Democratic sentiment, further, if not democratic principle, demands that law should on the whole correspond with public opinion; but when a large body of citizens not only are opposed to some law but question the moral right of the state to impose or maintain a given law, our honest democrat feels deeply perplexed how to act. He does not know in effect how to deal with lawlessness which is based upon a fundamental difference of public opinion.[52] For such difference makes it impossible that on a given topic the law should be in reality in accordance with public opinion. Thus many Englishmen have long felt a moral

---

52 See especially Lowell, *Public Opinion and Popular Government,* chap. iii.

difficulty in resisting the claim of a nationality to become an independent nation, even though the concession of such a demand may threaten the ruin of a powerful state and be opposed to the wishes of the majority of the citizens thereof. So the undoubted fact that a large number of Englishwomen desire parliamentary votes seems, in the eyes of many excellent persons, to give to Englishwomen a natural right to vote for members of Parliament. In each instance, and in many other cases which will occur to any intelligent reader, English democrats entertain a considerable difficulty in opposing claims with which they might possibly on grounds of expediency or of common sense have no particular sympathy. The perplexity of such men arises from the idea that, at any rate under a democratic government, any law is unjust which is opposed to the real or deliberate conviction of a large number of citizens. But such a conviction is almost certain to beget, on the part of persons suffering under what they deem to be an unjust law, the belief, delusive though it often is, that any kind of injustice may under a democratic government be rightly opposed by the use of force. The time has come when the fact ought to be generally admitted that the amount of government, that is of coercion, of individuals or classes by the state, which is necessary to the welfare or even to the existence of a civilised community, cannot permanently co-exist with the effective belief that deference to public opinion is in all cases the sole or the necessary basis of a democracy. The justification of lawlessness is also, in England at any rate, suggested if not caused by the misdevelopment of party government. The rule of a party cannot be permanently identified with the authority of the nation or with the dictates of patriotism. This fact has in recent days become so patent that eminent thinkers are to be found who certainly use language which implies that the authority or the sovereignty of the nation, or even the conception of the national will, is a sort of political or metaphysical fiction which wise men will do well to discard. Happily, crises arise from time to time in the history of any great state when, because national existence or national independence is at stake, the mass of a whole people feel that the authority of the nation is the one patent and the one certain political fact. To these causes of lawlessness honesty compels the addition of one cause which loyal citizens are most anxious not to bring into prominence. No sensible man can refuse to admit that crises occasionally, though very rarely, arise when armed rebellion against unjust and oppressive laws may be morally justifiable. This admission must certainly be made by any reasoner who sympathises with the principles inherited by modern Liberals from the Whigs of 1688. But this concession is often misconstrued; it is taken sometimes to mean that no man ought to be blamed or punished for rebellion if only he believes that he suffers from injustice and is not pursuing any private interest of his own.

COMPARISON BETWEEN THE PRESENT OFFICIAL LAW OF ENGLAND AND THE PRESENT DROIT ADMINISTRATIF OF FRANCE[53]

The last thirty years, and especially the fourteen years which have elapsed since the beginning of the twentieth century, show a very noticeable though comparatively slight approximation towards one another of what may be called the official law of England and the *droit administratif* of France. The extension given in the England of to-day to the duties and to the authority of state officials, or the growth, of our bureaucracy,[54] to use the expression of an able writer, has, as one would naturally expect, produced in the law governing our bureaucrats some features which faintly recall some of the characteristics which mark the *droit administratif* of France. Our civil servants, indeed, are as yet not in any serious degree put beyond the control of the law Courts, but in certain instances, and notably with regard to many questions arising under the National Insurance Act, 1911, something very like judicial powers have been given to officials closely connected with the Government.[55] And it may not be an exaggeration to say that in some directions the law of England is being "officialised," if the expression may be allowed, by statutes passed under the influence of socialistic ideas. It is even more certain that the *droit administratif* of France is year by year becoming more and more judicialised. The *Conseil d'État*, or, as we might term it, the Council, is

---

53 See Chap. XII., especially pp. 242–267, *post; Law and Opinion,* pp. xxxii–liii.

54 Muir, *Peers and Bureaucrats.*

55 See *Law and Opinion,* pp. xxxix–xliii.

(as all readers of my seventh edition of this work will know) the great administrative Court of France, and the whole relation between the judicial Courts and the Council still depends, as it has depended now for many years, upon the constitution of the Conflict Court,[56] which contains members drawn in equal numbers from the Council of State and from the Court of Cassation. It would be idle to suppose that the decisions of the Council itself when dealing with questions of administrative law do not now very nearly approach to, if indeed they are not in strictness, judicial decisions. The Council, at any rate when acting in a judicial character, cannot now be presided over by the Minister of Justice who is a member of the Cabinet.[57] Still it would be a grave mistake if the recognition of the growth of official law in England and the gradual judicialisation of the Council as an administrative tribunal led any Englishman to suppose that there exists in England as yet any true administrative tribunals or any real administrative law. No doubt the utmost care has been taken in France[58] to give high authority to the Council as an administrative tribunal and also to the Conflict Court. Still the members of the Council do not hold their position by anything like as certain a tenure as do the judges of the High Court in England, or as do the judges (if we may use English expressions) of the French common law Courts. A member of the Council is very rarely dismissed, but he still is dismissible. It must be noted further that the Minister of Justice is still the legal President of the Conflict Court, though he does not generally preside over it. When, however, the members of the Conflict Court are equally divided as to the decision of any case, the Minister of Justice does preside and give his casting vote. It is indeed said that such a case, which must almost necessarily be a difficult and probably an important one, is in truth again heard before the Minister of Justice and in effect is decided by him. A foreigner without practical acquaintance with the French legal system would be rash indeed were he to

---

56 As to the constitution of this Court see p. 239 and Appendix, Note XI. pp. 416–417, *post.*

57 See Poincaré, *How France is Governed, Trans. B. Miall.* (T. Fisher Unwin, 1913), p. 272.

58 Administrative law has in some other continental countries, *e.g.* in Germany, been far less judicialised than in France.

form or express an assured opinion as to the extent to which the decisions of the Council or the Conflict Court are practically independent of the wishes and the opinions of the Ministry of the day. Hesitation by a foreign critic is the more becoming, because it is certain, that Frenchmen equally competent to form an opinion would differ in their answer to the inquiry, whether the Council and the Conflict Court ought to be still more completely judicialised. The constitution of the Council of State and of the Conflict Court may suggest to a foreign critic that while neither of these bodies may be greatly influenced by the Ministry of the day, they are more likely to represent official or governmental opinion than are any of our English tribunals. It must further always be remembered that under the French Republic, as under every French government, a kind of authority attaches to the Government and to the whole body of officials in the service of the state (*fonctionnaires*) such as is hardly possessed by the servants of the Crown in England,[59] and especially that proceedings for the enforcement of the criminal law are in France wholly under the control of the Government. The high repute of the Council and, as it seems to a foreigner, the popularity of administrative law, is apparently shown by the success with which the Council has of recent years extended the doctrine that the state ought to compensate persons who suffer damage not only from the errors or faults, *e.g.* negligence, of officials, but also for cases in which the law is so carried out that it inflicts special damage upon individuals, that is damage beyond what is borne by their neighbours.[60] The authority again of the Council is seen in the wide extension it has given to the principle that any act done by an official which is not justified by law will, on its illegality being proved, be declared a nullity by the Council. It ought to be noted that this extension of the liability of the state must, it would seem, in practice be a new protection for officials; for if the state admits its own liability to pay compensation for damage suf-

---

59 Note, for instance, the absence of any law like the Habeas Corpus Act and the wide and arbitrary powers still left to the police under the head of the *régime de police*; Duguit, *Traité de Droit Constitutionnel*, ii. pp. 24–26, 33–45, and also the protection still extended in some instances to officials acting under the orders of their superior.

60 See pp. 262–264, *post*.

fered by individuals through the conduct of the state's servants, this admission must induce persons who have suffered wrong to forego any remedy which they may have possessed against, say, a postman or a policeman, personally, and enforce their claim not against the immediate wrong-doer but against the state itself.

One singular fact closely connected with the influence in France of *droit administratif* deserves the notice of Englishmen. In the treatises on the constitutional law of France produced by writers entitled to high respect will be found the advocacy of a new form of decentralisation termed *décentralisation par service*,[61] which seems to mean the giving to different departments of civil servants a certain kind of independence, *e.g.* leaving the administration of the Post Office to the body of public servants responsible for the management of the postal system. This body would, subject of course to supervision by the state, manage the office in accordance with their own knowledge and judgment; would, as far as I understand the proposal, be allowed to share in the gains affected by good management; and would, out of the revenue of the Post Office, make good the compensation due to persons who suffered by the negligence or misconduct of the officials. On the other hand, the officials would, because they were servants of the state who had undertaken certain duties to the state, be forbidden either to organise a strike or in any way to interrupt the working of the Post Office. It is a little difficult to see why this proposal should be called "decentralisation," for that term has hitherto borne a very different meaning. To an Englishman the course of proceeding proposed is extremely perplexing; it however is from one or two points of view instructive. This so-called decentralisation looks as if it were a revival under a new shape of the traditional French belief in the merit of administration. This reappearance of an ancient creed possibly shows that French thinkers who have lost all enthusiasm for parliamentary government look for great benefits to France from opening there a new sphere for administrative capacity. It certainly shows that Frenchmen of intelligence are turning their thoughts towards a question which perplexes the thinkers or legis-

---

61 Duguit, *Traité de Droit Constitutionnel*, 1. pp. 460–467.

lators of other countries. How far is it possible for officials, *e.g.* railway servants and others who undertake duties on the due performance of which the prosperity of a country depends, to be allowed to cease working whenever by so doing they see the possibility of obtaining a rise in the wages paid them? My readers may think that this examination into the recent development of French *droit administratif* digresses too far from the subject which we have in hand. This criticism is, it is submitted, unsound, for the present condition of *droit administratif* in France suggests more than one reflection which is strictly germane to our subject. It shows that the slightly increasing likeness between the official law of England and the *droit administratif* of France must not conceal the fact that *droit administratif* still contains ideas foreign to English convictions with regard to the rule of law, and especially with regard to the supremacy of the ordinary law Courts. It shows also the possible appearance in France of new ideas, such as the conception of the so-called *décentralisation par service* which are hardly reconcilable with the rule of law as understood in England. It shows further that the circumstances of the day have already forced upon France, as they are forcing upon England, a question to which Englishmen have not yet found a satisfactory reply, namely, how far civil servants or others who have undertaken to perform services on the due fulfilment of which the prosperity of the whole country depends, can be allowed to use the position which they occupy for the purpose of obtaining by a strike or by active political agitation concessions from and at the expense of the state. Nor when once this sort of question is raised is it possible absolutely to reject the idea that England might gain something by way of example from the experience of France. Is it certain that the increasing power of civil servants, or, to use Mr. Muir's expression, of "bureaucrats," may not be properly met by the extension of official law?[62] France has with undoubted wisdom more or less judicialised her highest administrative tribunal, and made it to a great extent independent of the Government of the day. It is at least conceivable that modern England would be benefited by the extension of official law. Nor is it quite certain that the

---

62 Consider the Official Secrets Acts.

ordinary law Courts are in all cases the best body for adjudicating upon the offences or the errors of civil servants. It may require consideration whether some body of men who combined official experience with legal knowledge and who were entirely independent of the Government of the day, might not enforce official law with more effectiveness than any Division of the High Court.

CONVENTIONS OF THE CONSTITUTION[63]

Three different points deserve consideration. They may be summed up under the following questions and the answers thereto:

FIRST QUESTION

Have there been during the last thirty years notable changes in the conventions of the constitution?

ANSWER

Important alterations have most certainly taken place; these may, for the most part, be brought under two different heads which for the sake of clearness should be distinguished from each other, namely, first, new rules or customs which still continue to be mere constitutional understandings or conventions, and, secondly, understandings or conventions which have since 1884 either been converted into laws or are closely connected with changes of law.[64] These may appropriately be termed "enacted conventions."

MERE CONVENTIONS

These have arisen, without any change in the law of the land, because they meet the wants of a new time. Examples of such acknowledged understandings are not hard to discover. In 1868 a Conservative Ministry in office suffered an undoubted defeat at a general election. Mr. Disraeli at once resigned office without waiting for even the meeting of Parliament. The same course was pursued by Mr.

---

63 See Chaps. XIV. and XV. *post.*

64 See especially the indirect effects of the Parliament Act, p. li, *post.*

Gladstone, then Prime Minister, in 1874, and again, in his turn, by Disraeli (then Lord Beaconsfield) in 1880, and by Gladstone in 1886. These resignations, following as they each did on the result of a general election, distinctly reversed the leading precedent set by Peel in 1834. The Conservative Ministry of which he was the head, though admittedly defeated in the general election, did not resign until they suffered actual defeat in the newly-elected House of Commons. It may be added, that on the particular occasion the Conservatives gained both influence and prestige by the ability with which Peel, though in a minority, resisted in Parliament the attempt to compel his resignation from office; for during this parliamentary battle he was able to bring home to the electors the knowledge that the Conservative minority, though defeated at the election, had gained thereby a great accession of strength. Peel also was able to show that while he and his followers were prepared to resist any further changes in the constitution, they fully accepted the Reform Act of 1832, and, while utterly rejecting a policy of reaction, were ready to give the country the benefits of enlightened administration. The new convention, which all but compels a Ministry defeated at a general election to resign office, is, on the face of it, an acknowledgment that the electorate constitutes politically the true sovereign power.[65] It also tends to convert a general election into a decision that a particular party shall hold office for the duration of the newly-elected Parliament and, in some instances, into the election of a particular statesman as Prime Minister for that period.[66] This new convention is the sign of many minor political or constitutional changes, such, for example, as the introduction of the habit, quite unknown not only to statesmen as far removed from us as Pitt, but to Peel, to Lord John Russell, or to Lord Palmerston, of constantly addressing, not only when out of office but also when in office, speeches to some body of electors and hence to the whole country.

---

65 See as to the possible distinction between "legal" and "political" sovereignty, pp. 27–29, *post*.

66 It is certain that at the general election of 1880 the Liberal electors who gained a victory meant that Lord Beaconsfield should resign office and that Mr. Gladstone should be appointed Prime Minister.

Another change in political habits or conventions unconnected with any legal innovation or alteration has received little attention because of its gradual growth and of its vagueness, but yet deserves notice on account of its inherent importance. It is now the established habit of any reigning king or queen to share and give expression to the moral feelings of British subjects. This expression of the desire on the part of English royalty to be in sympathy with the humane, the generous, and the patriotic feelings of the British people is a matter of recent growth. It may fairly be attributed to Queen Victoria as an original and a noble contribution towards national and Imperial statesmanship. This royal expression of sympathetic feeling, though not unknown to, was rarely practised by George III. or the sons who succeeded him on the throne.[67] It belongs to, but has survived, the Victorian age. It has indeed received since the death of Victoria a wider extension than was possible during a great part of her long reign. On such a matter vagueness of statement is the best mode of enforcing a political fact of immense weight but incapable of precise definition. At the moment when the United Kingdom is conducting its first great Imperial war it is on many grounds of importance to remember that the King is the typical and the only recognised representative of the whole Empire.[68]

Another example of new political conventions is found in the rules of procedure adopted by the House of Commons since 1881 with a view to checking obstruction, and generally of lessening the means possessed by a minority for delaying debates in the House of Commons. These rules increase the possibility of carrying through the House in a comparatively short time Bills opposed by a considerable number of members. That the various devices popularly known as the Closure, the Guillotine, and the Kangaroo have enabled one Government after another, when supported by a disciplined majority, to accomplish an amount of legislation which, but for these de-

---

67 As the King's speech when addressing the House of Parliament became more and more, and was known to have become, the utterance rather of ministerial than of royal opinion, the necessity inevitably arose of the monarch's finding some means for expressing his personal sympathy with the joy, and, above all, with the sorrow, of his people.

68 See p. cviii, note 107, *post.*

vices could not have been passed through the House of Commons, is indisputable. Whether the price paid for this result, in the way of curtailment and discussion, has been too high, is a question which we are not called upon to consider. All that need here be said is that such rules of procedure are not in strictness laws but in reality are customs or agreements assented to by the House of Commons.[69]

ENACTED CONVENTIONS

By this term is meant a political understanding or convention which has by Act of Parliament received the force of law[70] or may arise from a change of law. The best examples of such enacted conventions[71] are to be found in some of the more or less indirect effects[72] of the Parliament Act, 1911.

1. The Parliament Act in regard to the relation in legislative matters between the House of Lords and the House of Commons goes some way towards establishing in England a written or, more accurately speaking, an enacted constitution, instead of an unwritten or, more accurately speaking, an unenacted constitution.[73]

2. The Act greatly restrains, if it does not absolutely abolish, the use of the royal prerogative to create peers for the purpose of "swamping the House of Lords" in order to force through the House a Bill rejected by the majority of the peers. Such exercise of the prerogative has never but once, namely under Queen Anne in 1712, actually taken place. The certainty, however, that William IV. would use his prerogative to overcome the resistance of the House of Lords

---

69 As to the essential difference between the laws and the conventions of the constitution, see pp. cxl–cxlvi, *post*.

70 See Provisional Collection of Taxes Act, 1913.

71 A critic may indeed say, and with truth, that a convention converted by statute into a law is in strictness not a convention at all but a part of the law of the constitution. This I will not deny; but such an enacted convention may indirectly so affect the working of conventional understandings or arrangements that its indirect effects are conveniently considered when dealing with the conventions of the constitution.

72 For the direct effects of the Act see p. xxxix, *ante*.

73 See as to this distinction, p. cxliii, *post*, and note especially Parliament Act, s. I, sub-ss. 2, 3, which give a statutable definition of a Money Bill, and also contain a special provision as to the mode of determining whether a Bill is a Money Bill.

in 1832, carried the great Reform Act. The certainty that George V. would use the same prerogative carried the Parliament Act, 1911. In each case the argument which told with the King in favour of an unlimited creation of peers was that the constitution supplied no other means than this exceptional use or abuse of the royal prerogative for compelling the Lords to obey the will of the country. The Parliament Act deprives this argument of its force. Any king who should in future be urged by Ministers to swamp the House of Lords will be able to answer: "If the people really desire the passing of a Bill rejected by the House of Lords, you can certainly in about two years turn it into an Act of Parliament without the consent of the Lords."[74] The Parliament Act cuts away then the sole ground which in 1832 or in 1911 could justify or even suggest the swamping of the House of Lords.

3. Under the Parliament Act it may probably become the custom that each Parliament shall endure for its full legal duration, *i.e.* for nearly the whole of five years. For a student of the Act must bear in mind two or three known facts. A House of Commons the majority whereof perceive that their popularity is on the wane will for that very reason be opposed to a dissolution; for until it occurs such majority can carry any legislation it desires, and a dissolution may destroy this power. The payment to all unofficial M.P.s of a salary of £400 a year may induce many M.P.s who belong to a Parliamentary minority to acquiesce easily enough in the duration of a Parliament which secures to each of them a comfortable income. Between the Revolution of 1688 and the year 1784 few, if any, dissolutions took place from any other cause than either the death of a king, which does not now dissolve a Parliament, or the lapse of time under the Septennial Act, and during that period the Whigs, and notably Burke, denied the constitutional right of the King to dissolve Parliament at his pleasure; the dissolution of 1784 was denounced as a "penal dissolution." The Parliament of the French Republic sits for four years, but it can be dissolved at any time by the President with

---

74 See the Parliament Act, s. 7, "Five years shall be substituted for seven years as the time fixed for the maximum duration of Parliament under the Septennial Act, 1715."

the consent of the Senate. This power has been employed but once during the last thirty-seven years, and this single use of the presidential prerogative gives a precedent which no French statesman is tempted to follow. It is highly probable, therefore, that the direct appeal from the House of Commons to the electorate by a sudden dissolution may henceforward become in England almost obsolete. Yet this power of a Premier conscious of his own popularity, to destroy the House of Commons which put him in office, and to appeal from the House to the nation, has been treated by Bagehot as one of the features in which the constitution of England excels the constitution of the United States.

4. The Parliament Act enables a majority of the House of Commons to resist or overrule the will of the electors or, in other words, of the nation. That this may be the actual effect of the Act does not admit of dispute. That the Home Rule Bill was strenuously opposed by a large number of the electorate is certain. That this Bill was hated by a powerful minority of Irishmen is also certain. That the rejection of a Home Rule Bill has twice within thirty years met with the approval of the electors is an admitted historical fact. But that the widespread demand for an appeal to the people has received no attention from the majority of the House of Commons is also certain. No impartial observer can therefore deny the possibility that a fundamental change in our constitution may be carried out against the will of the nation.

5. The Act may deeply affect the position and the character of the Speaker of the House of Commons. It has hitherto been the special glory of the House of Commons that the Speaker who presides over the debates of the House, though elected by a party, has for at least a century and more tried, and generally tried with success, to be the representative and guide of the whole House and not to be either the leader or the servant of a party. The most eminent of Speakers have always been men who aimed at maintaining something like a judicial and therefore impartial character. In this effort they have obtained a success unattained, it is believed, in any other country except England. The recognition of this moral triumph is seen in the constitutional practice, almost, one may now say, the constitutional rule, that

a member once placed in the Speaker's chair shall continue to be re-elected at the commencement of each successive Parliament irrespective of the political character of each successive House of Commons. Thus Speakers elected by a Liberal majority have continued to occupy their office though the House of Commons be elected in which a Conservative majority predominates, whilst, on the other hand, a Speaker elected by a Conservative House of Commons has held the Speakership with public approval when the House of Commons exhibits a Liberal majority and is guided by a Cabinet of Liberals. The Parliament Act greatly increases the authority of the Speaker with respect to Bills to be passed under that Act. No Bill can be so passed unless he shall have time after time certified in writing under his hand, and signed by him that the provisions of the Parliament Act have been strictly followed. This is a matter referred to his own knowledge and conscience. There may clearly arise cases in which a fair difference of opinion may exist on the question whether the Speaker can honestly give the required certificate. Is it not certain that a party which has a majority in the House of Commons will henceforth desire to have a Speaker who may share the opinions of such party? This does not mean that a body of English gentlemen will wish to be presided over by a rogue; what it does mean is that they will come to desire a Speaker who is not a judge but is an honest partisan. The Parliament Act is a menace to the judicial character of the Speaker. In the Congress of the United States the Speaker of the House of Representatives is a man of character and of vigour, but he is an avowed partisan and may almost be called the parliamentary leader of the party which is supported by a majority in the House of Representatives.

SECOND QUESTION

What is the general tendency of these new conventions?

ANSWER

It assuredly is to increase the power of any party which possesses a parliamentary majority, *i.e.*, a majority, however got together, of the House of Commons, and, finally, to place the control of legislation, and indeed the whole government of the country, in the hands of the Cabinet which is in England at once the only instrument through which a dominant party can exercise its power, and the only body in the state which can lead and control the parliamentary majority of which the Cabinet is the organ. That the rigidity and the strength of the party system, or (to use an American expression) of the Machine, has continued with every successive generation to increase in England, is the conviction of the men who have most thoroughly analysed English political institutions as they now exist and work.[75]

Almost everything tends in one and the same direction. The leaders in Parliament each now control their own party mechanism. At any given moment the actual Cabinet consists of the men who lead the party which holds office. The leading members of the Opposition lead the party which wishes to obtain office. Party warfare in England is, in short, conducted by leading parliamentarians who constitute the actual Cabinet or the expected Cabinet. The electors, indeed, are nominally supreme; they can at a general election transfer the government of the country from one party to another. It may be maintained with much plausibility that under the quinquennial Parliament created by the Parliament Act the British electorate will each five years do little else than elect the party or the Premier by whom the country shall be governed for five years. In Parliament a Cabinet which can command a steadfast, even though not a very large majority, finds little check upon its powers. A greater number of M.P.s than fifty years ago deliver speeches in the House of Commons. But in spite of or perhaps because of this facile eloquence, the authority of individual M.P.s who neither sit in the Cabinet nor lead the Opposition, has suffered diminution. During the Palmerstonian era, at any rate, a few of such men each possessed an authority inside and outside the House which is hardly claimed by any member now-a-days who neither has nor is expected to obtain a seat in any Cabinet.

---

75 See Lowell, *Government of England*, part ii. chaps. xxiv–xxxvii.; Low, *The Governance of England*, chaps. i. to vii. Ramsay Muir, in his essay on Bureaucracy (see *Peers and Bureaucrats*, pp. 1–94), would apparently agree with Mr. Lowell and Mr. Low, though he maintains that power tends at present under the English constitution to fall from the hands of the parliamentary Cabinet into the hands of the permanent civil servants.

Any observer whose political recollections stretch back to the time of the Crimean War, that is sixty years ago, will remember occasions on which the words of Roebuck, of Roundell Palmer, of Cobden, and above all, at certain crises of Bright, might be, and indeed were, of a weight which no Government, or for that matter no Opposition, could treat as a trifle. Legislation again is now the business, one might almost say the exclusive business, of the Cabinet. Few if any, as far as an outsider can judge, are the occasions on which a private member not supported by the Ministry of the day, can carry any Bill through Parliament. Any M.P. may address the House, but the Prime Minister can greatly curtail the opportunity for discussing legislation when he deems discussion inopportune. The spectacle of the House of Commons which neither claims nor practices real freedom of discussion, and has no assured means of obtaining from a Ministry in power answers to questions which vitally concern the interest of the nation, is not precisely from a constitutional point of view, edifying or reassuring. But the plain truth is that the power which has fallen into the hands of the Cabinet may be all but necessary for the conduct of popular government in England under our existing constitution. There exists cause for uneasiness. It is at least arguable that important changes in the conventions, if not in the law, of the constitution may be urgently needed; but the reason for alarm is not that the English executive is too strong, for weak government generally means bad administration, but that our English executive is, as a general rule, becoming more and more the representative of a party rather than the guide of the country. No fair-minded man will, especially at this moment, dispute that the passion for national independence may transform a government of partisans into a government bent on securing the honour and the safety of the nation. But this fact, though it is of immense moment, ought not to conceal from us the inherent tendency of the party system to confer upon partisanship authority which ought to be the exclusive property of the nation.[76]

---

76 Several recent occurrences show the occasional appearance of ideas or practices which may mitigate rather than increase the rigidity of the party system. *In re Sir Stuart Samuel* [1913], A. C. 514, shows that under the Judicial Committee Act, 1833, s. 4, a question of law on which depends the right of a Member of Parliament to sit in Parliament may be referred

THIRD QUESTION

Does the experience of the last thirty years confirm the doctrine laid down in this treatise that the sanction which enforces obedience to the conventions of the constitution is to be found in the close connection between these conventions and the rule of law?[77]

ANSWER

The doctrine I have maintained may be thus at once illustrated and explained. The reason why every Parliament keeps in force the Mutiny Act or why a year never elapses without a Parliament being summoned to Westminster, is simply that any neglect of these conventional rules would entail upon every person in office the risk, we might say the necessity, of breaking the law of the land. If the law governing the army which is in effect an annual Act, were not passed annually, the discipline of the army would without constant breaches of law become impossible. If a year were to elapse without a Parliament being summoned to Westminster a good number of taxes would cease to be paid, and it would be impossible legally to deal with such parts of the revenue as were paid into the Imperial exchequer. Now it so happens that recent experience fully shows the inconvenience and danger of either violating a constitutional convention or of breaking the law because custom had authorised a course of action which rested on no legal basis. The House of Lords, in order to

---

to the Privy Council and be adequately and impartially dealt with by a body of eminent lawyers. The thought suggests itself that other questions affecting the conduct and the character of M.P.s which cannot be impartially investigated by any Committee of the House of Commons might be referred to the same high tribunal. The public statement, again, of Lord Kitchener that he took office in no way as a partisan, but simply as a general whose duty it was to provide for the carrying on of a war in which the welfare and honour of the nation is concerned set a precedent which might be followed in other spheres than that of military affairs. Is it of itself incredible that a Foreign Secretary of genius might without any loss of character retain office for years both in Liberal and in Conservative Cabinets? Is there any thing absurd in supposing that a Lord Chancellor respected for his legal eminence and for his judgment might serve the country as the highest of our judges and give his legal knowledge to Cabinets constituted of men with whose politics he did not agree? The English people would gain rather than lose by a check being placed on the constantly increasing power of the party system.

77 See pp. 296–302, *post.*

compel a dissolution of Parliament in 1909, rejected the Budget. Their Lordships acted within what was then their legal right, yet they caused thereby great inconvenience, which, however, was remedied by the election of a new Parliament. For years the income tax had been collected in virtue not of an Act but of a resolution of the House of Commons passed long before the income tax for the coming year came into existence. An ingenious person wishing to place difficulties in the way of the Government's proceedings claimed repayment of the sum already deducted by the Bank of England from such part of his income as was paid to him through the Bank. The bold plaintiff at once recovered the amount of a tax levied without legal authority. No better demonstration of the power of the rule of law could be found than is given by the triumph of Mr. Gibson Bowles.[78]

DEVELOPMENT DURING THE LAST THIRTY YEARS OF NEW CONSTITUTIONAL IDEAS

These ideas are (1) Woman Suffrage, (2) Proportional Representation, (3) Federalism, (4) The Referendum.

TWO GENERAL OBSERVATIONS

The brief criticism of each of these new ideas which alone in this Introduction it is possible to give, will be facilitated by attending to two general observations which apply more or less to each of the four proposed reforms or innovations.

First Observation

Political inventiveness has in general fallen far short of the originality displayed in other fields than politics by the citizens of progressive or civilised States. The immense importance attached by modern thinkers to representative government is partly accounted for by its being almost the sole constitutional discovery or invention unknown to the citizens of Athens or of Rome.[79] It is well also to note that

---

78 *Bowles* v. *Bank of England* [1913], I Ch. 57.

79 It is hardly an exaggeration to say that there exist very few other modern political conceptions (except the idea of representative government) which were not criticised by

neither representative government nor Roman Imperialism, nor indeed most of the important constitutional changes which the world has witnessed, can be strictly described as an invention or a discovery. When they did not result from imitation they have generally grown rather than been made; each was the production of men who were not aiming at giving effect to any novel political ideal, but were trying to meet in practice the difficulties and wants of their time. In no part of English history is the tardy development of new constitutional ideas more noteworthy or more paradoxical than during the whole Victorian era (1837 to 1902). It was an age full of intellectual activity and achievement; it was an age rich in works of imagination and of science; it was an age which extended in every direction the field of historical knowledge; but it was an age which added little to the world's scanty store of political or constitutional ideas. The same remark in one sense applies to the years which have passed since the opening of the twentieth century. What I have ventured to term new constitutional ideas are for the most part not original; their novelty consists in the new interest which during the last fourteen years they have come to command.

Second Observation

These new ideas take very little, one might almost say no account, of one of the ends which good legislation ought, if possible, to attain. But this observation requires explanatory comment.

Under every form of popular government, and certainly under the more or less democratic constitution now existing in England, legislation must always aim at the attainment of at least two different ends, which, though both of importance, are entirely distinct from one another. One of these ends is the passing or the maintaining of good or wise laws, that is laws which, if carried out, would really promote the happiness or welfare of a given country, and therefore which are desirable in themselves and are in conformity with the nature of

---

the genius of Aristotle. Note however that the immense administrative system known as the Roman Empire lay beyond, or at any rate outside, the conceptions of any Greek philosopher.

things. That such legislation is a thing to be desired, no sane man can dispute. If, for example, the freedom of trade facilitates the acquisition of good and cheap food by the people of England, and does not produce any grave counterbalancing evil, no man of ordinary sense would deny that the repeal of the corn laws was an act of wise legislation. If vaccination banishes small-pox from the country and does not produce any tremendous counterbalancing evil, the public opinion even of Leicester would hold that a law enforcing vaccination is a wise law. The second of these two different ends is to ensure that no law should be passed or maintained in a given country, *e.g.* in England, which is condemned by the public opinion of the English people. That this where possible is desirable will be admitted by every thoughtful man. A law utterly opposed to the wishes and feelings entertained by the inhabitants of a country, a rule which every one dislikes and no one will obey, is a nullity, or in truth no law at all; and, even in cases where, owing to the power of the monarch who enacts a law opposed to the wishes of his subjects, such a law can to a certain extent be enforced, the evils of the enforcement may far overbalance the good effects of legislation in itself wise. This thought fully justifies an English Government in tolerating throughout India institutions, such as caste, supported by Indian opinion though condemned by the public opinion and probably by the wise opinion of England. The same line of thought explained, palliated, and may even have justified the hesitation of English statesmen to prohibit suttee. Most persons, then, will acknowledge that sound legislation should be in conformity with the nature of things, or, to express the matter shortly, be "wise," and also be in conformity with the demands of public opinion, or, in other words, be "popular," or at any rate not unpopular. But there are few Englishmen who sufficiently realise that both of these two ends cannot always be attained, and that it very rarely happens that they are each equally attainable. Yet the history of English legislation abounds with illustrations of the difficulty on which it is necessary here to insist. Thus the Reform Act, 1832,[80] is in the judgment of most English historians and thinkers a

---

80 See J. R. M. Butler, *The Passing of the Great Reform Bill* (Longmans, Green & Co., 1914). This is an excellent piece of historical narrative and inquiry.

wise law; it also was at the time of its enactment a popular law. The Whigs probably underrated the amount and the strength of the opposition to the Act raised by Tories, but that the passing of the Reform Act was hailed with general favour is one of the best attested facts of modern history. The Act of Union passed in 1707 was proved by its results to be one of the wisest Acts ever placed on the statute-book. It conferred great benefits upon the inhabitants both of England and of Scotland. It created Great Britain and gave to the united country the power to resist in one age the threatened predominance of Louis XIV., and in another age to withstand and overthrow the tremendous power of Napoleon. The complete success of the Act is sufficiently proved by the absence in 1832 of any demand by either Whigs, Tories, or Radicals for its repeal. But the Act of Union, when passed, was unpopular in Scotland, and did not command any decided popularity among the electors of England. The New Poor Law of 1834 saved the country districts from ruin; its passing was the wisest and the most patriotic achievement of the Whigs, but the Act itself was unpopular and hated by the country labourers on whom it conferred the most real benefit. Within two years from the passing of the Reform Act it robbed reformers of a popularity which they had hoped might be lasting. Indeed the wisdom of legislation has little to do with its popularity. Now all the ideas which are most dear to constitutional reformers or innovators in 1914 lead to schemes of more or less merit for giving full expression in the matter of legislation to public opinion, *i.e.* for ensuring that any law passed by Parliament shall be popular, or at lowest not unpopular. But these schemes make in general little provision for increasing the chance that legislation shall also be wise, or in other words that it shall increase the real welfare of the country. The singular superstition embodied in the maxim *vox populi vox Dei* has experienced in this miscalled scientific age an unexpected revival. This renewed faith in the pre-eminent wisdom of the people has probably acquired new force from its congeniality with democratic sentiment. May we not conjecture that the new life given to a popular error is in part and indirectly due to the decline in the influence of utilitarianism? Faith in the voice of the people is closely connected with the doctrine of "natural rights." This dogma of natural rights was in England contemned and confuted by

Bentham and his disciples.[81] The declining influence of the utilitarian school appears therefore to give new strength to this doctrine. People forget that the dogma of natural rights was confuted not only by Benthamites but by powerful thinkers of the eighteenth and of the nineteenth century who had no sympathy with utilitarianism.

CRITICISM OF EACH OF THE FOUR NEW CONSTITUTIONAL IDEAS[82]

Woman Suffrage

The claim for women of the right to vote for members of Parliament, or, as now urged, to be placed in a position of absolute political equality with men, is no new demand. It was made in England before the end of the eighteenth century,[83] but no systematic, or at any rate noticeable, movement to obtain for Englishwomen the right to vote for members of Parliament can be carried back much earlier than 1866–67, when it was supported in the House of Commons by J. S. Mill.

Let my readers consider for a moment first the *causes* which have added strength to a movement which is 1866 attracted comparatively little public attention, and next the *main lines of argument* or of feeling which really tell on the one hand with the advocates and on the other with the opponents of the claim to votes for women.[84]

The Causes

These may be thus summarised. Since the beginning of the nineteenth century the number in the United Kingdom of self-supporting

---

81 See *Law and Opinion,* pp. 309, 171, 172.

82 It would be impossible, and it is not my aim in this Introduction, to state or even summarise all the arguments for or against each of these ideas; my sole object is to bring into light the leading thoughts or feelings which underlie the advocacy of, or the opposition to, each of these new ideas. See p. lxxiv–lxxv, *ante.*

83 See the *Vindication of the Rights of Women,* by Mary Wollstonecraft, published 1792. Little was heard about such rights during the great French Revolution. There is no reason to suppose that Madame Roland ever claimed parliamentary votes for herself or for her sex.

84 For an examination of all the main arguments alleged on either side see Dicey, *Letters to a Friend on Votes for Women.*

and also of unmarried women has greatly increased; and this class has by success in literature, as well as in other fields, acquired year by year greater influence. In the United Kingdom there exists among the actual population an excess of women over men, and this excess is increased by the emigration of Englishmen to our colonies and elsewhere. The low rate of payment received by women as compared with men, for services of any kind in which men and women enter into competition, has excited much notice. The spreading belief, or, as it used to be considered, the delusion, that wages can be raised by legislation, has naturally suggested the inference that want of a parliamentary vote inflicts severe pecuniary loss upon women. The extension of the power of the state and the enormous outgrowth of social legislation results in the daily enactment of laws which affect the very matters in which every woman has a personal interest. In an era of peace and of social reform the electors themselves constantly claim the sympathy and the active co-operation of women on behalf of causes which are treated, at any rate by partisans, as raising grave moral or religious controversy. Hence the agitation in favour of Woman Suffrage often commends itself to ministers of religion and notably to the English clergy, who believe, whether rightly or not, that the political power of women would practically add to the authority in the political world of the Church of England. These circumstances, and others which may be suggested by the memory or the ingenuity of my readers, are enough to explain the prominence and weight acquired for the movement in favour of giving the parliamentary franchise to women.

The Main Lines of Argument

These may be brought under two heads; they are most clearly and briefly exhibited if under each head is stated the argument of the Suffragist and the answer or reasoning in reply of the Anti-Suffragist.

First Argument

Every citizen, or, as the point is generally put, every person who pays taxes under the law of the United Kingdom, is entitled as a matter of right to a vote for a member of Parliament. Hence the obvious conclusion that as every Englishwoman pays taxes under the law of the United Kingdom, every Englishwoman is at any rate *prima facie* entitled to a vote.

Answer

This line of reasoning proves too much. It inevitably leads to the conclusion that any form of popular government ought to be based on the existence of strictly universal suffrage. An extreme suffragette will say that this result is not a *reductio ad absurdum*. But there are thousands of sensible Englishmen and Englishwomen who, while they doubt the advisability of introducing into England even manhood suffrage, refuse to admit the cogency of reasoning which leads to the result that every Englishman and Englishwoman of full age must have a right to vote for a member of Parliament. But the full strength of an anti-suffragist's reply cannot be shown by any man who does not go a little further into the nature of things. A fairminded man prepared to do this will, in the first place, admit that many democratic formulas, *e.g.* the dictum that "liability to taxation involves the right to representation," do verbally cover a woman's claim to a parliamentary vote. His true answer is that many so-called democratic principles, as also many so-called conservative principles, are in reality not principles at all but war-cries, or shibboleths which may contain a good deal of temporary or relative truth but are mixed up with a vast amount of error. The idea, he will ultimately say, that the possession of a vote is a personal right is a delusion. It is in truth the obligation to discharge a public duty, and whether this miscalled right should be conferred upon or withheld from Englishwomen can be decided only by determining whether their possession of the parliamentary vote will conduce to the welfare of England.

Second Argument

The difference of sex presents no apparent or necessary reason for denying to Englishwomen the same political rights as are conferred upon Englishmen. It is found by experience, as suffragists will add, that some women have in many ways even greater capacity for the exercise of government than have some men. This argument may best be put in its full strength if it be placed, as it often is, in the form of a question: Was it reasonable that Florence Nightingale should not have possessed the right to vote for a member of Parliament when even in her day her footman or her coachman, if he had happened to be a ten-pound householder, or a forty-shilling freeholder, might have exercised a right denied to a lady who, as appears from her biography, possessed many statesmanlike qualities, who did in fact in some lines of action exert more political power than most M.P.s, and who always exercised power disinterestedly, and generally exercised it with admitted benefit to the country? There is not the remotest doubt that the argument involved in this inquiry (in whatever form it is stated) seems to many women, to a great number of parliamentary electors, and also to a considerable number of M.P.s, to afford an unanswerable and conclusive reason in favour of giving parliamentary votes to women.

Answer

The claim of parliamentary votes for women as now put forward in England is in reality a claim for the absolute political equality of the two sexes. Whether its advocates are conscious of the fact or not, it is a demand on behalf of women for seats in Parliament and in the Cabinet. It means that Englishwomen should share the jury box and should sit on the judicial bench. It treats as insignificant for most purposes that difference of sex which, after all, disguise the matter as you will, is one of the most fundamental and far-reaching differences which can distinguish one body of human beings from another. It is idle to repeat again and again reasoning which, for the last thirty years and more, has been pressed upon the attention of every English reader and elector. One thing is certain: the real strength (and it is great) of the whole conservative argument against the demand of votes for women lies in the fact that this line of reasoning, on the face thereof, conforms to the nature of things. The anti-suffragists can re-echo the words of Burke whilst adapting them to a controversy unknown to him and practically unknown to his age:

> The principles that guide us, in public and in private, as they are not of our devising, but moulded into the nature and the essence of things, will endure with the sun and moon—long, very long after whig and tory, Stuart and Brunswick [suffragist, suffragette, and anti-suffragist], and all such misera-

ble bubbles and playthings of the hour, are vanished from existence and from memory.[85]

Proportional Representation[86]

The case in favour of the introduction of proportional representation into England rests on the truth of three propositions.

First Proposition

The House of Commons often fails to represent with precision or accuracy the state of opinion *e.g.* as to woman suffrage, existing among the electorate of England. In other words, the House of Commons often fails to be, as it is sometimes expressed, "the mirror of the national mind," or to exactly reflect the will of the electors.

Second Proposition

It is quite possible by some system of proportional representation to frame a House of Commons which would reflect much more than at present the opinion of the nation, or, in other words, of the electorate.

Third Proposition

It is pre-eminently desirable that every opinion *bonâ fide* existing among the electors should be represented in the House of Commons in as nearly as possible the same proportion in which it exists among the electors, or, to use popular language, among the nation.

Now of these three propositions the substantial truth of the first and second must, in my judgment, be admitted. No one can doubt the possibility, and even the high probability, that, for example, the cause of woman suffrage may, at the present moment, obtain more than half the votes of the House of Commons while it would not obtain as many as half the votes of the electorate. Nor again is it at all inconceivable that at some other period the cause of woman suffrage

---

85 Burke, *Correspondence*, i. pp. 332, 333.

86 See Humphreys, *Proportional Representation*; J. Fischer Williams, *Proportional Representation and British Politics*; Lowell, *Public Opinion and Popular Government*, pp. 122–124.

should, while receiving the support of half the electorate, fail to obtain the votes of half the House of Commons. No one, in the second place, can, I think, with reason dispute that, among the numerous plans for proportional representation thrust upon the attention of the public, some one, and probably several, would tend to make the House of Commons a more complete mirror of what is called the mind of the nation than the House is at present; and this concession, it may with advantage be noted, does not involve the belief that under any system of popular government whatever, a representative body can be created which at every moment will absolutely and with complete accuracy reflect the opinions held by various classes of the people of England. Now my belief in the substantial truth of the first and the second of our three propositions makes it needless for me, at any rate for the purpose of this Introduction, to consider the reservations with which their absolute accuracy ought to be assumed. For the sake of argument, at any rate, I treat them as true. My essential objection to the system of proportional representation consists in my grave doubt as to the truth of the third of the above three propositions, namely, that it is desirable that any opinion existing among any large body of electors should be represented in the House of Commons as nearly as possible in the same proportion in which it exists among such electors.

Before, however, any attempt is made to state the specific objections which in my judgment lie against the introduction of proportional representation into the parliamentary constitution of England, it is essential to discriminate between two different ideas which are confused together under the one demand for proportional representation. The one of these ideas is the desirability that every opinion entertained by a substantial body of Englishmen should obtain utterance in the House of Commons, or, to use a vulgar but effective piece of political slang, "be voiced by" some member or members of that House. Thus it has been laid down by the leader of the Liberal party that

it was infinitely to the advantage of the House of Commons, if it was to be a real reflection and mirror of the national mind, that there should be no strain of opinion honestly entertained by any substantial body of the King's subjects which should not find there representation and speech.[87]

To this doctrine any person who has been influenced by the teaching of Locke, Bentham, and Mill will find it easy to assent, for it is well known that in any country, and especially in any country where popular government exists, the thoughts, even the bad or the foolish thoughts, of the people should be known to the national legislature. An extreme example will best show my meaning. If among the people of any land the hatred of the Jews or of Judaism should exist, it would certainly be desirable that this odious prejudice should find some exponent or advocate in the Parliament of such country, for the knowledge of popular errors or delusions may well be essential to the carrying out of just government or wise administration. Ignorance is never in truth the source of wisdom or of justice. The other idea or meaning attached by Proportionalists to proportional representation is that every influential opinion should not only find utterance in the House of Commons, but, further, and above all, be represented in the House of Commons by the same proportionate number of votes which it obtains from the voters at an election. Thus the eminent man who advocated the desirability of every opinion obtaining a hearing in the House of Commons, used on another occasion the following words: "It is an essential and integral feature of our policy that we shall go forward with the task of making the House of Commons not only the mouthpiece but the mirror of the national mind."[88] Now the doctrine of proportional representation thus interpreted is a dogma to which a fair-minded man may well refuse his assent. It is by no means obviously true; it is open to the following (among other) objections that admit of clear statement.

Objections to the Third Proposition

First Objection   The more complicated any system of popular election is made, the more power is thrown into the hands of election

---

87 See Mr. Asquith's speech at St. Andrews, Feb. 19, 1906, cited by J. Fischer Williams, *Proportional Representation*, p. 17.

88 Mr. Asquith at Burnley, Dec. 5, 1910, cited by J. Fischer Williams, *Proportional Representation*, p. 17.

agents or wire-pullers. This of itself increases the power and lowers the character of the party machine; but the greatest political danger with which England is now threatened is the inordinate influence of party mechanism. This objection was long ago insisted upon by Bagehot.[89] It explains, if it does not wholly justify, John Bright's denunciation of fancy franchises.

Second Objection   The House of Commons is no mere debating society. It is an assembly entrusted with great though indirect executive authority; it is, or ought to be, concerned with the appointment and the criticism of the Cabinet. Grant, for the sake of argument, that every influential opinion should in the House of Commons gain a hearing. This result would be obtained if two men, or only one man, were to be found in the House who could ensure a hearing whenever he spoke in favour of some peculiar opinion. The argument for woman suffrage was never stated with more force in Parliament than when John Mill represented Westminster. The reasons in its favour would not, as far as argument went, have commanded more attention if a hundred members had been present who shared Mill's opinions but were not endowed with his logical power and his lucidity of expression. But where a body of men such as constitute the House of Commons are at all concerned with government, unity of action is of more consequence than variety of opinion. The idea, indeed, of representation may be, and often is, carried much too far. A Cabinet which represented all shades of opinion would be a Ministry which could not act at all. No one really supposes that a Government could in ordinary circumstances be formed in which two opposite parties balanced one another. Nor can it often be desirable that an opinion held by, say, a third of a ministerial party should necessarily be represented by a third of the Cabinet. It may well be doubted whether even on commissions appointed partly, at any rate, for the purpose of inquiry, it is at all desirable that distinctly opposite views should obtain recognition. The Commission which laid down the leading lines of Poor Law Reform in 1834 rendered an immense service to England. Would there have been any real advantage in plac-

---

89 Bagehot, *English Constitution*, pp. 148–159.

ing on that Commission men who condemned any change in the existing poor law?

Third Objection   Proportional representation, just because it aims at the representation of opinions rather than of persons, tends to promote the existence in the House of Commons of numerous party groups and also fosters the admitted evil of log-rolling. The working of English parliamentary government has owed half of its success to the existence of two leading and opposed parties, and of two such parties only. Using somewhat antiquated but still intelligible terms, let me call them by the name of Tories and Whigs.[90] These two parties have, if one may speak in very broad terms, tended, the one to uphold the rule of the well-born, the well-to-do, and therefore, on the whole, of the more educated members of the community; the other has promoted the power of numbers, and has therefore aimed at increasing the political authority of the comparatively poor, that is, of the comparatively ignorant. Each tendency has obviously some good and some bad effects. If, for a moment, one may adopt modern expressions while divesting them of any implied blame or praise, one may say that Conservatism and Liberalism each play their part in promoting the welfare of any country where popular government exists. Now, that the existence of two leading parties, and of two such parties only, in England has favoured the development of English constitutionalism is past denial. It is also certain that during the nineteenth century there has been a notable tendency in English public life to produce in the House of Commons separate groups or parties which stood more or less apart from Tories and Whigs, and were all but wholly devoted to the attainment of some one definite change or reform. The Repealers, as led by O'Connell, and still more the Free Traders, as led by Cobden[91] are early examples of such

---

90 I choose these old expressions which have been in use, at any rate from 1689 till the present day, because they make it easier to keep somewhat apart from the burning controversies of 1914.

91 Cobden would have supported any Premier, whether a Tory or a Whig, who undertook to repeal the Corn Laws. O'Connell would have supported any Premier who had pledged himself to repeal the Act of Union with Ireland; but O'Connell's position was peculiar. He took an active interest in English politics, he was a Benthamite Liberal, and during a part of his career acted in alliance with the Whigs.

groups. These groups avowedly held the success of the cause for which they fought of greater consequence than the maintenance in office either of Tories or of Whigs. Even in 1845 they had perplexed the working of our constitution; they had gone far to limit the operation of the very valuable rule that a party, which persuades Parliament to adopt the party's policy, should be prepared to take office and carry that policy into effect. The Free Traders, in fact, give the best, if not the earliest, example of an English group organised to enforce the adoption by the English parliament of an opinion, doctrine, or theory to which that group was devoted. Now an observer of the course of events during the last sixty years will at once note the increasing number of such groups in the House of Commons. To-day we have Ministerialists and Unionists (corresponding roughly with the old Whigs and Tories), we have also Irish Nationalists and the Labour Party. These parties have each separate organisations. But one can easily observe the existence of smaller bodies each devoted to its own movement or cause, such, for example, as the temperance reformers, as the advocates of woman suffrage, or as the members who hold that the question of the day is the disestablishment of the Church. This state of things already invalidates our constitutional customs. Nor is it easy to doubt that any fair system of proportional representation must increase the number of groups existing in Parliament, for the very object of Proportionalists is to ensure that every opinion which exists among an appreciable number of British electors shall have an amount of votes in Parliament proportionate to the number of votes it obtains among the electors. If, for example, a tenth of the electors should be anti-vaccinators, the anti-vaccinators ought, under a perfect scheme of representation, to command sixty-seven votes in the House of Commons. Sixty-seven anti-vaccinators who might accidentally obtain seats in the House of Commons, *e.g.* as Conservatives or Liberals, would, be it noted, constitute a very different body from sixty-seven members sent to the House of Commons to represent the cause of anti-vaccination. The difference is this: In the first case each anti-vaccinator would often perceive that there were matters of more pressing importance than anti-vaccination; but the sixty-seven men elected under a system of proportional representation to obtain the total repeal of the vaccination laws would, one may almost say must, make that repeal the one dominant object of their parliamentary action. That the multiplication of groups might weaken the whole system of our parliamentary government is a probable conjecture. That proportional representation might tend to extend the vicious system of log-rolling is all but demonstrable. Let me suppose the sixty-seven anti-vaccinators to be already in existence; let me suppose, as would probably be the case, that they are elected because of their firm faith in anti-vaccination, and that, both from their position and from their creed, they feel that to destroy the vaccination laws is the supreme object at which every good man should aim. They will soon find that their sixty-seven votes, though of high importance, are not enough to save the country. The course which these patriots must follow is obvious. They are comparatively indifferent about Home Rule, about Disestablishment, about the objects of the Labour Party. Let them promise their support to each of the groups advocating each of these objects in return for the help in repealing legislation which originates, say our anti-vaccinators, in the delusions of Jenner. A political miracle will have been performed. A majority in favour of anti-vaccination will have been obtained; the voice of fanatics will have defeated the common sense of the nation. Let me, as an illustration of my contention, recall to public attention a forgotten fact. Some forty years ago the Claimant, now barely remembered as Arthur Orton, was a popular hero. His condemnation to imprisonment for fourteen or fifteen years excited much indignation. He obtained one representative, and one representative only, of his grievances in the House of Commons. Under a properly organised system of proportional representation, combined with our present household suffrage, he might well have obtained twenty. Does any one doubt that these twenty votes would have weighed with the Whips of any party in power? Is it at all certain that the Claimant might not, thus supported, have obtained a mitigation of his punishment, if not a re-trial of his case? This is an extreme illustration of popular folly. For this very reason it is a good test of a logical theory. I do not contend that proportional representation cannot be defended by weighty considerations; my contention is that it is open to some grave objections which have not received an adequate answer.[92]

Federalism[93]

In 1884 the peculiarities and the merits of federal government had not attracted the attention of the English public. Here and there a statesman whose mind was turned towards the relation of England and her colonies had perceived that some of the self-governing colonies might with advantage adopt federal constitutions. In 1867 Parliament had readily assented to the creation of the Canadian Dominion and thereby transformed the colonies possessed by England on the continent of America into a federal state. In truth it may be said that the success of the Northern States of the American Commonwealth in the War of Secession had, for the first time, impressed upon Englishmen the belief that a democratic and a federal state might come with success through a civil war, carried on against states which asserted their right to secede from the Republic of which they were a part. Still in 1884 hardly a statesman whose name carried weight with Englishmen advocated the formation of a federal system as a remedy for the defects, whatever they were, of the English constitution, or as the means for uniting the widely scattered countries which make up the British Empire. Walter Bagehot was in his day, as he still is, the most eminent of modern English constitutionalists. He compared the constitution of England with the constitution of the United States. But the result of such comparison was, in almost every case, to illustrate some hitherto unnoted merit of the English constitution which was not to be found in the constitution of the great American Repub-

---

92 Proportional representation was in Mill's day known as minority representation. The change of name is not without significance. In 1870 the demand for minority representation was put forward mainly as the means for obtaining a hearing for intelligent minorities whose whisper might easily be drowned by the shouts of an unintelligent majority. In 1914 minority representation is recommended mainly as the means of ensuring that the true voice of the nation shall be heard. It was once considered a check upon democracy; it is now supported as the best method for giving effect to the true will of the democracy.

93 Compare especially as to federal government, Chap. III. p. 73, *post.*

lic. Sir Henry Maine was in his time the most brilliant of the writers who had incidentally turned their thoughts towards constitutional problems. Maine's *Popular Government,* published in 1885, expressed his admiration for the rigidity or the conservatism of American federalism. But he never hinted at the conviction, which he probably never entertained, that either the United Kingdom or the British Empire would gain by transformation into a federal state. Thirty years ago the nature of federalism had received in England very inadequate investigation.[94] In this, as in other matters, 1914 strangely contrasts with 1884. The notion is now current that federalism contains the solution of every constitutional problem which perplexes British statesmanship. Why not, we are told, draw closer the bonds which maintain peace and goodwill between the United Kingdom and all her colonies, by constructing a new and grand Imperial federation governed by a truly Imperial Parliament, which shall represent every state, including England, which is subject to the government of the King? Why not, we are asked, establish a permanent reconciliation between England and Ireland by the conversion of the United Kingdom into a federalised kingdom whereof England, Scotland, Ireland, and Wales, and, for aught I know, the Channel Islands and the Isle of Man, shall form separate states? This new constitutional idea of the inherent excellence of federalism is a new faith or delusion which deserves examination. My purpose, therefore, is to consider two different matters—namely, first, the general characteristics of federalism; secondly, the bearing of these characteristics on the proposal popularly known as Imperial federalism, for including England[95] and the five self-governing colonies in a federal constitution, and also the proposal (popularly known as Home Rule all round) for federalising the United Kingdom.

---

94 In Chap. III., *post,* federalism was analysed (1885) as illustrating, by way of contrast, that sovereignty of the English Parliament which makes England one of the best examples of a unitary state.

95 In treating of Imperial federalism, as often in other parts of this book, I purposely and frequently, in accordance with popular language, use "England" as equivalent to the United Kingdom.

Leading Characteristics of Federal Government[96]

Federalism is a natural constitution for a body of states which desire union and do not desire unity. Take as countries which exhibit this state of feeling the United States, the English federated colonies, the Swiss Confederation, and the German Empire, and contrast with this special condition of opinion the deliberate rejection by all Italian patriots of federalism, which in the case of Italy presented many apparent advantages, and the failure of union between Sweden and Norway to produce any desire for unity or even for a continued political connection, though these Scandinavian lands differ little from each other in race, in religion, in language, or in their common interest to maintain their independence against neighbouring and powerful countries.

The physical contiguity, further, of countries which are to form a confederated state is certainly a favourable, and possibly a necessary, condition for the success of federal government.

The success of federal government is greatly favoured by, if it does not absolutely require, approximate equality in the wealth, in the population, and in the historical position of the different countries which make up a confederation. The reason for this is pretty obvious. The idea which lies at the bottom of federalism is that each of the separate states should have approximately equal political rights and should thereby be able to maintain the "limited independence" (if the term may be used) meant to be secured by the terms of federal union. Hence the provision contained in the constitution of the United States under which two Senators, and no more, are given to each state, though one be as populous, as large, and as wealthy as is New York, and another be as small in area and contain as few citizens as Rhode Island. Bagehot, indeed, points out that the equal power in the Senate of a small state and of a large state is from some points of view an evil. It is, however, an arrangement obviously congenial to

---

96 See especially Chap. III. p. 73, *post.* It is worth observing that the substance of this chapter was published before the production by Gladstone of his first Home Rule Bill for Ireland.

federal sentiment. If one state of a federation greatly exceed in its
numbers and in its resources the power of each of the other states,
and still more if such "dominant partner," to use a current expression, greatly exceed the whole of the other Confederated States in
population and in wealth, the confederacy will be threatened with
two dangers. The dominant partner may exercise an authority almost
inconsistent with federal equality. But, on the other hand, the other
states, if they should possess under the constitution rights equal to
the rights or the political power left to the dominant partner, may
easily combine to increase unduly the burdens, in the way of taxation
or otherwise, imposed upon the one most powerful state.

Federalism, when successful, has generally been a stage towards
unitary government. In other words, federalism tends to pass into
nationalism. This has certainly been the result of the two most successful of federal experiments. The United States, at any rate as they
now exist, have been well described as a nation concealed under the
form of a federation. The same expression might with considerable
truth be applied to Switzerland. Never was there a country in which
it seemed more difficult to produce national unity. The Swiss cantons
are divided by difference of race, by difference of language, by
difference of religion. These distinctions till nearly the middle of the
nineteenth century produced a kind of disunion among the Swiss
people which in 1914 seems almost incredible. They forbade the existence of a common coinage; they allowed any one canton to protect
the financial interest of its citizens against competition by the inhabitants of every other canton. In 1847 the Sonderbund threatened to
destroy the very idea of Swiss unity, Swiss nationality, and Swiss
independence. Patriots had indeed for generations perceived that the
federal union of Switzerland afforded the one possible guarantee for
the continued existence of their country. But attempt after attempt to
secure the unity of Switzerland had ended in failure. The victory of
the Swiss federalists in the Sonderbund war gave new life to Switzerland: this was the one indubitable success directly due to the
movements of 1847–48. It is indeed happy that the victory of the
federal armies took place before the fall of the French Monarchy, and
that the Revolution of February, combined with other movements

which distracted Europe, left the Swiss free to manage their own affairs in their own way. Swiss patriotism and moderation met with their reward. Switzerland became master of her own fate. Each step in the subsequent progress of the new federal state has been a step along the path leading from confederate union to national unity.

A federal constitution is, as compared with a unitary constitution, a weak form of government. Few were the thinkers who in 1884 would have denied the truth of this proposition. In 1914 language is constantly used which implies that a federal government is in itself superior to a unitary constitution such as that of France or of England. Yet the comparative weakness of federalism is no accident. A true federal government is based on the division of powers. It means the constant effort of statesmanship to balance one state of the confederacy against another. No one can rate more highly than myself the success with which a complicated system is worked by the members of the Swiss Council or, to use expressions familiar to Englishmen, by the Swiss Cabinet. Yet everywhere throughout Swiss arrangements you may observe the desire to keep up a sort of balance of advantages between different states. The members of the Council are seven in number; each member must, of necessity, belong to a different canton. The federal Parliament meets at Bern; the federal Court sits at Lausanne in the canton of Vaud; the federal university is allotted to a third canton, namely Zurich. Now rules or practices of this kind must inevitably restrict the power of bringing into a Swiss Cabinet all the best political talent to be found in Switzerland. Such a system applied to an English or to a French Cabinet would be found almost unworkable. Federalism again would mean, in any country where English ideas prevail, the predominance of legalism or, in other words, a general willingness to yield to the authority of the law courts. Nothing is more remarkable, and in the eyes of any impartial critic more praiseworthy, than the reverence paid on the whole by American opinion to the Supreme Court of the United States. Nor must one forget that the respect paid to the opinion of their own judges, even when deciding questions on which political feeling runs high, is, on the whole, characteristic of the citizens of each particular state. The Supreme Court, *e.g.*, of Massachusetts may be called upon to determine in effect whether a law passed by the legislature of Massachusetts is, or is not, constitutional; and the decision of the Court will certainly meet with obedience. Now, what it is necessary to insist upon is that this legalism which fosters and supports the rule of law is not equally displayed in every country. No French court has ever definitely pronounced a law passed by the French legislature invalid, nor, it is said, has any Belgian court ever pronounced invalid a law passed by the Belgian Parliament. Whether English electors are now strongly disposed to confide to the decision of judges questions which excite strong political feeling is doubtful. Yet—and this is no insignificant matter—under every federal system there must almost of necessity exist some body of persons who can decide whether the terms of the federal compact have been observed. But if this power be placed in the hands of the Executive, the law will, it may be feared, be made subservient to the will of any political party which is for the moment supreme. If it be placed in the hands of judges, who profess and probably desire to practise judicial impartiality, it may be very difficult to ensure general respect for any decision which contradicts the interests and the principles of a dominant party. Federalism, lastly, creates divided allegiance. This is the most serious and the most inevitable of the weaknesses attaching to a form of government under which loyalty to a citizen's native state may conflict with his loyalty to the whole federated nation. Englishmen, Scotsmen, and Irishmen have always, as soldiers, been true to the common flag. The whole history of the Sonderbund in Switzerland and of Secession in the United States bears witness to the agonised perplexity of the noblest among soldiers when called upon to choose between loyalty to their country and loyalty to their canton or state. One example of this difficulty is amply sufficient for my purpose. General Scott and General Lee alike had been trained as officers of the American Army; each was a Virginian; each of them was determined from the out-break of the Civil War to follow the dictates of his own conscience; each was placed in a position as painful as could be occupied by a soldier of bravery and honour; each was a victim of that double allegiance which is all but inherent in federalism. General Scott followed the impulse of loyalty to the Union. General Lee felt that as a matter of duty he must obey the sentiment of loyalty to Virginia.

In any estimate of the strength or the weakness of federal government it is absolutely necessary not to confound, though the confusion is a very common one, federalism with nationalism. A truly federal government is the denial of national independence to every state of the federation. No single state of the American Commonwealth is a separate nation; no state, it may be added, *e.g.* the State of New York, has anything like as much of local independence as is possessed by New Zealand or by any other of the five Dominions.[97] There is of course a sense, and a very real sense, in which national tradition and national feeling may be cultivated in a state which forms part of a confederacy. The French inhabitants of Quebec are Frenchmen to the core. But their loyalty to the British Empire is certain. One indisputable source of their Imperial loyalty is that the break-up of the Empire might, as things now stand, result to Canada in union with the United States. But Frenchmen would with more difficulty maintain their French character if Quebec became a state of the Union and ceased to be a province of the Dominion. In truth national character in one sense of that term has less necessary connection than Englishmen generally suppose with political arrangements. It would be simple folly to assert that Sir Walter Scott did not share the sentiment of Scottish nationalism; yet the influence of Scott's genius throughout Europe was favoured by, and in a sense was the fruit of, the union with England. But the aspiration and the effort towards actual national independence is at least as inconsistent with the conditions of a federal as with the conditions of a unitary government. Any one will see that this is so who considers how patent would have been the folly of the attempt to establish a confederacy which should have left Italy a state of the Austrian Empire. Nor does historical experience countenance the idea that federalism, which may certainly be a step towards closer national unity, can be used as a method for gradually bringing political unity to an end.

---

97 As to meaning of "Dominions" see p. xlii, note 21, *ante.*

The Characteristics of Federal Government in Relation to Imperial Federalism

Many Englishmen of to-day advocate the building up of some grand federal constitution which would include the United Kingdom (or, to use popular language, England) and at any rate the five Dominions. This splendid vision of the advantages to be obtained by increased unity of action between England and her self-governing colonies is suggested by obvious and important facts. The wisdom of every step which may increase the reciprocal goodwill, strong as it now is, of England and her Dominions is proved by the success of each Imperial Conference. It is perfectly plain already, and will become every day plainer both to Englishmen and to the inhabitants of the British Empire outside England, that the existence of the Empire ought to secure both England and her colonies against even the possibility of attack by any foreign power. It to-day in reality secures the maintenance of internal peace and order in every country inhabited by British subjects. It is further most desirable, it may probably become in no long time an absolute necessity, that every country throughout the Empire should contribute in due measure to the cost of Imperial defence. To this it should be added that the material advantages accruing to millions of British subjects from the Imperial power of England may more and more tend to produce that growth of loyalty and goodwill towards the Empire which in 1914 is a characteristic and splendid feature both of England and of her colonies. Any man may feel pride in an Imperial patriotism grounded on the legitimate belief that the Empire built up by England furthers the prosperity and the happiness of the whole body of British subjects.[98]

---

98 "But this Empire of ours is distinguished from [other Empires] by special and dominating characteristics. From the external point of view it is made up of countries which are not geographically conterminous or even contiguous, which present every variety of climate, soil, people, and religion, and, even in those communities which have attained to complete self-government, and which are represented in this room to-day, does not draw its unifying and cohesive force solely from identity of race or of language. Yet you have here a political organisation which, by its mere existence, rules out the possibility of war between populations numbering something like a third of the human race. There is, as there must be among communities so differently situated and circumstanced, a vast variety of constitutional methods, and of social and political institutions and ideals. But to speak for a moment for that part of the Empire which is represented here to-day, what is it that we have in common, which amidst every diversity of external and material conditions, makes us and

But, when every admission which the most ardent of Imperialists can ask for, is made of the benefits conferred in every quarter of the world upon the inhabitants of different countries, by the existence of England's Imperial power, it is quite possible for a calm observer to doubt whether the so-called federalisation of the British Empire is an object which ought to be aimed at by the statesmen either of England or of the Dominions. The objections to the creed of federalism, in so far as it means the building up of a federal constitution for the Empire, or rather for England and her Dominions, may be summed up in the statement that this belief in a new-fangled federalism is at bottom a delusion, and a delusion perilous not only to England but to the whole British Empire. But this general statement may be best justified by the working out of two criticisms.

First: The attempt to form a federal constitution for the Empire is at this moment full of peril to England, to the Dominions, and, it may well be, to the maintenance of the British Empire. The task imposed upon British and upon colonial statesmanship is one of infinite difficulty. As we all know, the creation of the United States was for the thirteen independent colonies a matter of absolute necessity. But the highest statesmanship of the ablest leaders whom a country ever possessed was hardly sufficient for the transformation of thirteen different states into one confederated nation. Even among countries differing little in race, religion, and history, it was found all but impossible to reconcile the existence of state rights with the creation of a strong central and national power. If any one considers the infinite diversity of the

---

keeps us one? There are two things in the self-governing British Empire which are unique in the history of great political aggregations. The first is the reign of Law: wherever the King's writ runs, it is the symbol and messenger not of an arbitrary authority, but of rights shared by every citizen, and capable of being asserted and made effective by the tribunals of the land. The second is the combination of local autonomy—absolute, unfettered, complete—with loyalty to a common head, co-operation, spontaneous and unforced, for common interests and purposes, and, I may add, a common trusteeship, whether it be in India or in the Crown Colonies, or in the Protectorates, or within our own borders, of the interests and fortunes of fellow-subjects who have not yet attained, or perhaps in some cases may never attain, to the full stature of self-government."—See speech of the Right Hon. H. H. Asquith (President of the Conference), Minutes of Proceedings of the Imperial Conference, 1911 [Cd. 5745], p. 22.

countries which make up the British Empire, if he reflects that they
are occupied by different races whose customs and whose civilisation
are the product of absolutely different histories, that the different
countries of the Empire are in no case contiguous, and in many
instances are separated from England and from each other by seas
extending over thousands of miles, he will rather wonder at the
boldness of the dreams entertained by the votaries of federal Imperialism, than believe that the hopes of federalising the Empire are
likely to meet with fulfilment. I shall be reminded, however, and with
truth, that Imperial federalism, as planned by even its most sanguine
advocates, means something very different from the attempt to frame
a constitution of which the United Kingdom, the Dominions, the
Crown colonies, and British India shall constitute different states.
Our Imperialists really aim, and the fact must be constantly borne in
mind, at federalising the relation not between England and the rest
of the Empire, but between England and the five self-governing
Dominions. But then this admission, while it does away with some
of the difficulties besetting the policy which is miscalled *Imperial*
federalism, raises a whole body of difficult and all but unanswerable
questions. Take a few of the inquiries to which sanguine reformers,
who talk with easy confidence of federalism being the solution of all
the most pressing constitutional problems, must find a reply. What is
to be the relation between the new federated state (consisting of
England and the five Dominions) and British India? Will the millions
who inhabit India readily obey a new and strange sovereign, or will
the states of the new confederacy agree that the rest of the Empire
shall be ruled by the Parliament and Government of England alone?
Is the whole expense of Imperial defence to be borne by the federated
states, or will the new federation of its own authority impose taxes
upon India and the Crown colonies for the advantage of the federated state? Is it certain, after all, that the mutual goodwill entertained
between England and the Dominions really points towards federalism? No doubt England and the states represented at the Imperial
Conferences entertain a genuine and ardent wish that the British
Empire should be strong and be able, as against foreigners, and even
in resistance to secession, to use all the resources of the whole Empire

for its defence and maintenance. But then each one of the Dominions desires rather the increase than the lessening of its own independence. Is there the remotest sign that, for example, New Zealand, though thoroughly loyal to the Empire, would tolerate interference by any Imperial Parliament or Congress with the internal affairs of New Zealand which even faintly resembled the authority exerted by Congress in New York, or the authority exerted by the Parliament of the Canadian Dominion in Quebec? But if the Dominions would not tolerate the interference with their own affairs by any Parliament, whatever its title, sitting at Westminster, is there the remotest reason to suppose that the existing Imperial Parliament will consent to become a Parliament of the Empire in which England, or rather the United Kingdom, and each of the five Dominions shall be fairly represented? But here we come to a further inquiry, to which our new federalists hardly seem to have given a thought: What are they going to do with the old Imperial Parliament which has, throughout the whole history of England, inherited the traditions and often exerted the reality of sovereign power? Under our new federation is the Imperial Parliament to become a Federal Congress wherein every state is to have due representation? Is this Federal Congress to be for Englishmen the English Parliament, or is there to be in addition to or instead of the ancient Parliament of England a new local English Parliament controlling the affairs of England alone? This question itself is one of unbounded difficulty. It embraces two or three inquiries the answers whereto may trouble the thoughts of theorists, and these replies, if they are ever discovered, may give rise throughout England and the British Empire to infinite discord. Is it not one example of the perplexities involved in any plan of Imperial federalism, and of the intellectual levity with which they are met, that our Federalists never have given a clear and, so to speak, intelligible idea of what is to be under a federal government the real position not of the United Kingdom but of that small country limited in size, but still of immense power, which is specifically known by the august name of England? The traditional feuds of Ireland and the ecclesiastical grievances of Wales, the demand of some further recognition of that Scottish nationality, for which no sensible Englishman shows or is tempted to show the least disrespect, all deserve and receive exaggerated attention. But England and English interests, just because Englishmen have identified the greatness of England with the prosperity of the United Kingdom and the greatness and good government of the Empire, are for the moment overlooked. I venture to assure all my readers that this forgetfulness of England—and by England I here mean the country known, and famous, as England before the legal creation either of Great Britain or of the United Kingdom—is a fashion opposed both to common sense and to common justice, and, like all opposition to the nature of things, will ultimately come to nothing.[99] The questions I have mentioned are numerous and full of complexity. The present time, we must add, is intensely unfavourable to the creation of a new federalised and Imperial constitution. The Parliament and the Government of the United Kingdom may be chargeable with grave errors: they have fallen into many blunders. But they have never forgotten—they will never, one trusts, forget—that they hold

> a common trusteeship, whether it be in India or in the Crown Colonies, or in the Protectorates, or within our own borders, of the interests and fortunes of fellow-subjects who have not yet attained, or perhaps in some cases may never attain, to the full stature of self-government.[100]

Is it credible that, for instance, the peoples of India will see with indifference this trusteeship pass from the hands of an Imperial Parliament (which has more or less learned to think imperially, and in England has maintained the equal political rights of all British subjects) into the hands of a new-made Imperial Congress which will

---

99 Sir Joseph Ward is an eminent colonial statesman; he is also an ardent Imperialist of the colonial type. In his plan for an Imperial Council, or in other words for an Imperial Parliament representing the United Kingdom, or rather the countries which now make it up, and also the Dominions, he calmly assumes that Englishmen will without difficulty allow the United Kingdom to be broken up into four countries ruled by four local Parliaments. He supposes, that is to say, as a matter of course, that Englishmen will agree to a radical change in the government of England which no sane English Premier would have thought of pressing upon the Parliaments of the self-governing colonies which now constitute the Dominion of Canada or which now constitute the Commonwealth of Australia. See Minutes of Proceedings of the Imperial Conference, 1911 [Cd. 5745], pp. 59–61.

100 See Mr. Asquith's address, cited pp. xcviii–xcix, note 98, *ante.*

consist in part of representatives of Dominions which, it may be of necessity, cannot give effect to this enlarged conception of British citizenship?[101]

Second: The unity of the Empire does not require the formation of a federal or of any other brand-new constitution. I yield to no man in my passion for the greatness, the strength, the glory, and the moral unity of the British Empire.[102] I am one of the thousands of Englishmen who approved, and still approve, of the war in South Africa because it forbade secession. But I am a student of the British constitution; my unhesitating conviction is that the constitution of the Empire ought to develop, as it is actually developing, in the same way in which grew up the constitution of England.[103] The relation between England and the Dominions, and, as far as possible, between England and the colonies which are not as yet self-governing countries, need not be developed by arduous feats of legislation. It should grow under the influence of reasonable understandings and of fair customs. There are, as I have intimated,[104] two objects on which every Imperialist should fix his eyes. The one is the contribution by every country within the Empire towards the cost of defending the Empire. The second object is the constant consultation between England and the Dominions. The English taxpayer will not, and ought not to, continue for ever paying the whole cost of Imperial defence. The Dominions cannot for an indefinite period bear the risks of Imperial wars without having a voice in determining if such wars should begin, and when and on what terms they should be brought to an end. Imperial statesmanship is rapidly advancing in the right direction. The system of Imperial Conferences[105] and other modes of inter-communication

---

101 See p. liv, and note 43, *ante.*

102 See *A Fool's Paradise,* p. 24.

103 This conviction is strengthened by the facts now daily passing before our eyes (Sept. 1914).

104 See pp. xcviii, xcix, *ante;* and see *A Fool's Paradise,* p. 25.

105 Consider the gradual, the most hopeful, and the most successful development of these conferences from 1887 to the last conference in 1911. A sort of conference was held in 1887, and the conferences of 1897 and 1902 were held in connection with some other celebration.

between England and the Dominions will, we may hope, result in regulating both the contribution which the Dominions ought to make towards the defence of the Empire, and the best method for collecting colonial opinion on the policy of any war which may assume an Imperial character. My full belief is that an Imperial constitution based on goodwill and fairness may within a few years come into real existence, before most Englishmen have realised that the essential foundations of Imperial unity have already been firmly laid. The ground of my assurance is that the constitution of the Empire may, like the constitution of England, be found to rest far less on parliamentary statutes than on the growth of gradual and often unnoted customs.

Characteristics of Federal Government in Relation to Home Rule All Round

Advocates of the so-called "federal solution" apparently believe that the United Kingdom as a whole will gain by exchanging our present unitary constitution for some unspecified form of federal government. To an Englishman who still holds, as was universally held by every English statesman till at the very earliest 1880, that the union between England and Scotland was the wisest and most fortunate among the achievements of British statesmanship, there is great difficulty in understanding the new belief that the federalisation of the United Kingdom will confer benefit upon any of the inhabitants of Great Britain. [106] A candid critic may be able to account for the existence of a political creed which he does not affect to share.

The first regular conference for no other purpose than consultation was held in 1907, in which the Imperial Conference received by resolution a definite constitution. The conference of 1911 was held under the scheme thus agreed upon in 1907.

106 The omission of reference to the policy of Home Rule for Ireland as embodied in the Government of Ireland Act, 1914, is intentional. The true character and effect of that Act cannot become apparent until some years have passed. The Act itself stands in a position never before occupied by any statute of immense and far-reaching importance. It may not come into operation for an indefinite period. Its very authors contemplate its amendment before it shall begin to operate. The Act is at the moment detested by the Protestants of Ulster, and a binding though ambiguous pledge has been given that the Act will not be forced upon Ulster against her will. The people of Great Britain will insist on this pledge being held sacred. To a constitutionalist the Act at present affords better ground for wonder than for criticism. If any reader should be curious to know my views on Home Rule he will find them in a general form in *England's Case against Home Rule,* published in 1887; and as applied to the last Home Rule Bill, in *A Fool's Paradise,* published in 1913.

The faith in Home Rule all round has been stimulated, if not mainly created, by the controversy, lasting for thirty years and more, over the policy of Home Rule for Ireland. British Home Rulers have always been anxious to conceal from themselves that the creation of a separate Irish Parliament, and a separate Irish Cabinet depending for its existence on such Parliament, is a real repeal of the Act of Union between Great Britain and Ireland. This refusal to look an obvious fact in the face is facilitated by the use of that most ambiguous phrase, "Home Rule all round." Federalism has, no doubt, during the last thirty, or one may say fifty, years acquired a good deal of new prestige. The prosperity of the United States, the military authority of the German Empire, may by federalists be put down to the credit of federal government, though in matter of fact no two constitutions can, either in their details or in their spirit, bear less real resemblance than the democratic and, on the whole, unmilitary constitution of the United States and the autocratic Imperial and, above all, military government of Germany. Federal government has also turned out to be the form of government suitable for some of the British Dominions. It has been an undoubted success in the Canadian Dominion. It has not been long tried but has not been a failure in the Australian Commonwealth. It may become, Englishmen are inclined to think it is, the best form of government for the states included in the Union of South Africa. Little reflection, however, is required in order to see that none of these federations resemble the constitution of England either in their historical development or in their actual circumstances. Then, too, it is thought that whereas English statesmen find it difficult to regulate the relation between Great Britain and Ireland, the task will become easier if the same statesmen undertake to transform, by some hocus-pocus of political legerdemain, the whole United Kingdom into a federal government consisting of at least four different states. It is supposed, lastly, though the grounds for the supposition are not very evident, that the federalisation of the United Kingdom is necessary for, or conducive to, the development of Imperial federalism.

Federalism, in short, has at present the vague, and therefore the strong and imaginative, charm which has been possessed at one time throughout Europe by the parliamentary constitutionalism of England and at another by the revolutionary republicanism of France. It may be well, therefore, to state with some precision why, to one who has studied the characteristics of federal government, it must seem in the highest degree improbable that Home Rule all round, or the federal solution, will be of any benefit whatever to any part of the United Kingdom.

1. There is no trace whatever of the existence of the federal spirit throughout the United Kingdom. In England, which is after all by far the most important part of the kingdom, the idea of federalism has hitherto been totally unknown. Politicians may have talked of it when it happened to suit their party interest, but to the mass of the people the idea of federation has always been, and I venture to assert at this moment is, unknown and all but incomprehensible. Scotsmen sometimes complain that Great Britain is often called England. They sometimes talk as though they were in some mysterious manner precluded from a fair share in the benefits accruing from the unity of Great Britain. To any one who investigates the actual course of British politics, and still more of British social life since the beginning of the nineteenth century, these complaints appear to be utterly groundless. The prejudices which, say, in the time of Dr. Johnson, kept Scotsmen and Englishmen apart, have in reality vanished. To take one example of disappearing differences, we may note that while many leading Englishmen fill in Parliament Scottish seats many Scotsmen fill English seats. What is true is that the course of events, and the way in which the steam-engine and the telegraph bring the world everywhere closer together, are unfavourable to that prominence in any country which at one time was attainable by particular localities, or by small bodies of persons living somewhat apart from the general course of national life. This change has, like all other alterations, its weak side. It is quite possible honestly to regret the time when Edinburgh possessed the most intellectual society to be found in Great Britain or Ireland. It is also possible honestly to wish that Lichfield and Norwich might still have, as they had at the beginning of the nineteenth century, a little and not unfamous literary coterie of their own. There is a sense in which the growth of large states is injurious to the individual life of smaller communities. The Roman Republic

and the Roman Empire did not produce thinkers or writers who did as much for the progress of mankind as was done by the philosophers, the historians, and the poets of Greece, and the fruits of Greek genius were mainly due to the intellectual achievements of Athens during not much more than a century. Ireland is, as regards most of its inhabitants, discontented with the Union. But it is idle to pretend that Ireland has ever desired federalism in the sense in which it was desired by the colonies which originally formed the United States, or by the inhabitants of what are now the provinces of the Canadian Dominion. O'Connell for a very short time exhibited a tendency to substitute federalism for repeal. He discovered his mistake and reverted to repeal, which with his more revolutionary followers meant nationalism. No one who reads the last and the strangest of the biographies of Parnell can doubt that "Ireland a Nation" was the cry which met his own instinctive feeling no less than the wishes of his followers, except in so far as their desires pointed towards a revolutionary change in the tenure of land rather than towards the claim for national independence.

2. There is good reason to fear that the federalisation of the United Kingdom, stimulating as it would the disruptive force of local nationalism, might well arouse a feeling of divided allegiance. This topic is one on which I have no wish to dwell, but it cannot be forgotten by any sensible observer who reflects upon the history of secession in the United States, or of the Sonderbund in Switzerland, or who refuses to forget the preeminently uneasy connection between the different parts of the Austrian Empire and the deliberate determination of Norway to sever at all costs the union with Sweden. Nor is it possible to see how the federalisation of the United Kingdom should facilitate the growth of Imperial federalism.

3. Federalism, as the dissolution of the United Kingdom, is absolutely foreign to the historical and, so to speak, instinctive policy of English constitutionalists. Each successive generation from the reign of Edward I. onwards has laboured to produce that complete political unity which is represented by the absolute sovereignty of the Parliament now sitting at Westminster. Let it be remembered that no constitutional arrangements or fictions could get rid of the fact that Eng-

land would, after as before the establishment of Home Rule all round, continue, in virtue of her resources and her population, the predominant partner throughout the United Kingdom, and the partner on whom sovereignty had been conferred, not by the language of any statute or other document, but by the nature of things. It would be hard indeed to prevent the English Parliament sitting at Westminster from not only claiming but exercising sovereign authority; and to all these difficulties must be added one ominous and significant reflection. To every foreign country, whether it were numbered among our allies or among our rivals, the federalisation of Great Britain would be treated as a proof of the declining power alike of England and of the British Empire.[107]

The Referendum[108]

The word Referendum is a foreign expression derived from Switzerland. Thirty years ago it was almost unknown to Englishmen, even though they were interested in political theories. Twenty years ago it was quite unknown to British electors. The word has now obtained popular currency but is often misunderstood. It may be well, therefore, to define, or rather describe, the meaning of the "referendum" as used in this Introduction and as applied to England. The referendum is used by me as meaning the principle that Bills, even

---

107 Any great change in the form of the constitution of England, *e.g.* the substitution of an English republic for a limited monarchy, might deeply affect the loyalty of all the British colonies. Can any one be certain that New Zealand or Canada would, at the bidding of the Parliament of the United Kingdom, transer their loyalty from George V. to a President chosen by the electorate of the United Kingdom, and this even though the revolution were carried out with every legal formality including the assent of the King himself, and even though the King were elected the first President of the new Commonwealth? Is it certain that a federated union of England, Ireland, Scotland, and Wales would command in our colonies the respect paid to the present United Kingdom? These questions may well seem strange: they are not unimportant. The King is what the Imperial Parliament has never been, the typical representative of Imperial unity throughout every part of the Empire.

108 Lowell, *Public Opinion and Popular Government,* part iii. chaps. xi–xv., especially chaps. xii. and xiii. (best thing on the subject); Lowell, *Government of England,* i. p. 411; "The Referendum and its Critics," by A. V. Dicey, *Quarterly Review,* No. 423, April 1910; *The Crisis of Liberalism,* by J. A. Hobson; Low, *The Governance of England,* Intro. p. xvii; "Ought the Referendum to be introduced into England?" by A. V. Dicey, *Contemporary Review,* 1890, and *National Review,* 1894.

when passed both by the House of Commons and by the House of Lords,[109] should not become Acts of Parliament until they have been submitted to the vote of the electors and have received the sanction or approval of the majority of the electors voting on the matter. The referendum is sometimes described, and for general purposes well described, as "the people's veto." This name is a good one; it reminds us that the main use of the referendum is to prevent the passing of any important Act which does not command the sanction of the electors. The expression "veto" reminds us also that those who advocate the introduction of the referendum into England in fact demand that the electors, who are now admittedly the political sovereign of England, should be allowed to play the part in legislation which was really played, and with popular approval, by *e.g.* Queen Elizabeth at a time when the King or Queen of England was not indeed the absolute sovereign of the country, but was certainly the most important part of the sovereign power, namely Parliament.[110] In this Introduction the referendum, or the people's veto, is considered simply with reference to Bills passed by the Houses of Parliament but which have not received the royal assent. The subject is dealt with by no means exhaustively, but with a view in the first place to bring out the causes of the demand in England for the referendum; and in the next place to consider carefully and examine in turn first by far the strongest argument against, and secondly the strongest argument in favour of introducing the referendum into the constitution of England.

---

109 And *a fortiori* when passed under the Parliament Act, without the consent of the House of Lords.

110 The referendum, it should be noted, can be applied to legislation for different purposes and in different ways. It may, for instance, be applied only to a Bill affecting fundamental changes in the constitution, *e.g.* to a Bill affecting the existence of the monarchy, or to any Bill which would in popular language be called a Reform Bill, and to such Bill after it has been passed by the two Houses. In this case the object of the referendum would be to ensure that no Act of transcendent importance shall be passed without the undoubted assent of the electors. The referendum may again be applied, as it is applied in the Commonwealth of Australia, for preventing "deadlocks," as they are called, arising from the fact of one House of Parliament having carried repeatedly, and the other having repeatedly rejected, a given Bill.

The Causes

During forty years faith in parliamentary government has suffered an extraordinary decline or, as some would say, a temporary eclipse.[111] This change is visible in every civilised country. Depreciation of, or contempt for, representative legislatures clearly exists under the parliamentary and republican government of France, under the federal and republican constitution of the Swiss Confederacy, or of the United States, under the essential militarism and the superficial parliamentarism of the German Empire, and even under the monarchical and historical constitutionalism of the British Empire. This condition, whether temporary or permanent, of public opinion greatly puzzles the now small body of surviving constitutionalists old enough to remember the sentiment of the mid-Victorian era, with its prevalent belief that to imitate the forms, or at any rate to adopt the spirit of the English constitution, was the best method whereby to confer upon the people of any civilised country the combined blessings of order and of progress. To explain in any substantial degree the alteration in popular opinion it would be necessary to produce a treatise probably longer and certainly of more profound thought than the book for which I am writing a new Introduction. Yet one or two facts may be noted which, though they do not solve the problem before us, do to some slight extent suggest the line in which its solution must be sought for. Parliamentary government may under favourable circumstances go a great way towards securing such blessings as the prevalence of personal liberty and the free expression of opinion. But neither parliamentary government nor any form of constitution, either which has been invented or may be discovered, will ever of itself remove all or half the sufferings of human beings. Utopias lead to disappointment just because they are utopias. The very extension of constitutional government has itself led to the frustration of high hopes; for constitutions have by force of imitation been set up in states unsuited to popular government. What is even more important, parliamentary government has by its continued existence betrayed two defects hardly suspected by the Liberals or

---

111 Compare *Law and Opinion* (2nd ed.), pp. 440–443.

reformers of Europe, or at any rate of England, between 1832 and 1880. We now know for certain that while popular government may be under wise leadership a good machine for simply destroying existing evils, it may turn out a very poor instrument for the construction of new institutions or the realisation of new ideals. We know further that party government, which to many among the wisest of modern constitutionalists appears to be the essence of England's far-famed constitution, inevitably gives rise to partisanship, and at last produces a machine which may well lead to political corruption and may, when this evil is escaped, lead to the strange but acknowledged result that a not unfairly elected legislature may misrepresent the permanent will of the electors. This fact has made much impression on the political opinion both of England and of the United States. The above considerations taken as a whole afford some explanation of a demand for that referendum which, though it originates in Switzerland, flourishes in reality, though not in name, in almost every state of the American Commonwealth.

The Main Argument Against the Referendum

To almost all Englishmen the chief objection to the referendum is so obvious, and seems to many fair-minded men so conclusive, that it ought to be put forward in its full strength and to be carefully examined before the reader is called upon to consider the possible advantages of a great change in our constitution. This objection may be thus stated:

In England the introduction of the referendum means, it is urged, the transfer of political power from knowledge to ignorance. Let us put this point in a concrete form. The 670 members of the House of Commons together with the 600 and odd members of the House of Lords[112] contain a far greater proportion of educated men endowed with marked intellectual power and trained in the exercise of some high political virtues than would generally be found among, say, 1270 electors collected merely by chance from an electorate of more than 8,000,000. The truth of this allegation can hardly be disputed; the

---

112 Strictly, 638 members. See *Whitaker's Almanack*, 1914, p. 124.

inference is drawn therefrom that to substitute the authority of the electorate for the authority of the House of Commons and the House of Lords is to transfer the government of the country from the rule of intelligence to the rule of ignorance. This line of argument can be put in various shapes. It is, in whatever form it appears, the reasoning on which the most capable censors of the referendum rely. Oddly enough (though the matter admits of explanation) this line of reasoning is adopted at once by a thoughtful conservative, such as Maine, and by revolutionists who wish to force upon England, through the use of authoritative legislation, the ideals of socialism. Maine saw in the referendum a bar to all reasonable reforms. He impresses upon his readers that democracy is not in itself a progressive form of government, and expresses this view in words which deserve quotation and attention:

> The delusion that democracy when it has once had all things put under its feet, is a progressive form of government, lies deep in the convictions of a particular political school; but there can be no delusion grosser. . . . All that has made England famous, and all that has made England wealthy, has been the work of minorities, sometimes very small ones. It seems to me quite certain that, if for four centuries there had been a very widely extended franchise and a very large electoral body in this country, there would have been no reformation of religion, no change of dynasty, no toleration of Dissent, not even an accurate Calendar. The threshing-machine, the power-loom, the spinning-jenny, and possibly the steam-engine, would have been prohibited. Even in our day, vaccination is in the utmost danger, and we may say generally that the gradual establishment of the masses in power is of the blackest omen for all legislation founded on scientific opinion, which requires tension of mind to understand it, and self-denial to submit to it.[113]

And he thence practically infers that democracy as it now exists in England would, combined with the referendum, be probably a death-blow to all reasonable reform.[114] To Maine, in short, the referendum is the last step in the development of democracy, and his censure of the referendum is part of a powerful attack by an intellec-

---

113 Maine, *Popular Government,* pp. 97–98.

114 See *ibid.* pp. 96–97.

tual conservative on democratic government which he distrusted and abhorred. Now revolutionists who probably think themselves democrats have of recent years attacked the referendum on grounds which might have been suggested by Maine's pages. The referendum, we are told by socialistic writers, will work steadily to the disadvantage of the Liberal Party.[115] Would not, we are asked, the anti-reforming press exhaust itself in malignant falsehoods calculated to deceive the people? Such suggestions and others of the same quality may be summed up in an argument which from a socialistic point of view has considerable force. The people, it is said, are too stupid to be entrusted with the referendum; the questions on which the electors are nominally called upon to decide must never be put before them with such clearness that they may understand the true issues submitted to their arbitrament. The party machine, think our new democrats, may be made the instrument for foisting upon the people of England changes which revolutionary radicals or enthusiasts know to be reforms, but which the majority of the electorate, if they understood what was being done, might condemn as revolution or confiscation. The attacks of conservatives and the attacks of socialistic democrats to a certain extent balance one another, but they contain a common element of truth. The referendum is a mere veto. It may indeed often stand in the way of salutary reforms, but it may on the other hand delay or forbid innovations condemned by the weight both of the uneducated and of the educated opinion of England. Thus it is, to say the least, highly probable that, if the demand of votes for women were submitted to the present electorate by means of a referendum, a negative answer would be returned, and an answer of such decision as to check for years the progress or success of the movement in favour of woman suffrage. It must, in short, be admitted that a veto on legislation, whether placed in the hands of the King, or in the hands of the House of Lords, or of the House of Commons, or of the 8,000,000 electors, would necessarily work sometimes well and sometimes ill. It might, for example, in England forbid the enforcement or extension of the vaccination laws; it might forbid the grant of parlia-

---

115 See *Against the Referendum* and *Quarterly Review*, April 1910, No. 423, pp. 551, 552.

mentary votes to Englishwomen; it might have forbidden the passing of the Government of Ireland Act, 1914; it might certainly have forbidden the putting of any tax whatever on the importation of corn into the United Kingdom. Now observe that if you take any person, whether an Englishman or Englishwoman, he or she will probably hold that in some one or more of these instances the referendum would have worked ill, and that in some one or more of these instances it would have worked well. All, therefore, that can be conclusively inferred from the argument against the referendum is that the people's veto, like any other veto, may sometimes be ill, and sometimes be well employed. Still it certainly would be urged by a fair-minded opponent of the referendum that there exists a presumption that the Houses of Parliament acting together will exhibit something more of legislative intelligence than would the mass of the electorate when returning their answer to a question put to them by the referendum. But a reasonable supporter of the referendum, while admitting that such a presumption may exist, will however maintain that it is of very slight weight. The Parliament Act gives unlimited authority to a parliamentary or rather House of Commons majority. The wisdom or experience of the House of Lords is in matters of permanent legislation thereby deprived of all influence. A House of Commons majority acts more and more exclusively under the influence of party interests. It is more than possible that the referendum might, if introduced into England, increase the authority of voters not deeply pledged to the dogmas of any party. The referendum, as I have dealt with it, cannot, be it always borne in mind, enforce any law to which at any rate the House of Commons has not consented. It has the merits as also the weaknesses of a veto. Its strongest recommendation is that it may keep in check the inordinate power now bestowed on the party machine.

The Main Argument in Favour of the Referendum

The referendum is an institution which, if introduced into England, would be *strong* enough to curb the absolutism of a party possessed of a parliamentary majority. The referendum is also an institution which in England promises some *considerable diminution* in the most patent defects of party government. Consider first the *strength* of the referendum. It lies in the fact that the people's veto is at once a democratic institution, and, owing to its merely negative character, may be a strictly conservative institution. It is democratic, for it is in reality, as also on the face thereof, an appeal to the people. It is conservative since it ensures the maintenance of any law or institution which the majority of the electors effectively wish to preserve. Nor can any one who studies the present condition of English society seriously believe that, under any system whatever, an institution deliberately condemned by the voice of the people can for a long time be kept in existence. The referendum is, in short, merely the clear recognition in its negative form of that sovereignty of the nation of which under a system of popular government every leading statesman admits the existence. But the mere consonance of a given arrangement with some received doctrine, such as "the sovereignty of the people," must with a thoughtful man carry little weight, except in so far as this harmony with prevalent ideas promises permanence to some suggested reform or beneficial institution. Let us then consider next the *tendency* of the referendum to *lessen the evils* of the party system. An elected legislature may well misrepresent the will of the nation. This is proved by the constant experience of Switzerland and of each of the States which make up the American Commonwealth. This danger of misrepresenting the will of the nation may exist even in the case of an honest and a fairly-elected legislative body. This misrepresentation is likely or even certain to arise where, as in England, a general election comes more and more to resemble the election of a given man or a given party to hold office for five years. Partisanship must, under such a system, have more weight than patriotism. The issues further to be determined by the electors will year by year become, in the absence of the referendum, more complicated and confused. But in the world of politics confusion naturally begets intrigue, sometimes coming near to fraud. Trust in elected legislative bodies is, as already noted, dying out under every form of popular government. The party machine is regarded with suspicion, and often with detestation, by public-spirited citizens of the United States. Coalitions, log-rolling, and parliamentary intrigue are in England diminishing the moral and political faith in the House of Commons. Some means must, many Englishmen believe, be found for the diminution of evils which are under a large electorate the natural, if not the necessary, outcome of our party system. The obvious corrective is to confer upon the people a veto which may restrict the unbounded power of a parliamentary majority. No doubt the referendum must be used with vigilance and with sagacity. Perpetual watchfulness on the part of all honest citizens is the unavoidable price to be paid for the maintenance of sound popular government. The referendum futher will promote or tend to promote among the electors a kind of intellectual honesty which, as our constitution now works, is being rapidly destroyed. For the referendum will make it possible to detach the question, whether a particular law, *e.g.* a law introducing some system of so-called tariff reform, shall be passed, from the totally different question, whether Mr. A or Mr. B shall be elected for five years Prime Minister of England. Under the referendum an elector may begin to find it possible to vote for or against a given law in accordance with his real view as to its merits or demerits, without being harassed through the knowledge that if he votes against a law which his conscience and his judgment condemns, he will also be voting that A, whom he deems the fittest man in England to be Prime Minister, shall cease to hold office, and that B, whom the elector happens to distrust, shall at once become Prime Minister. And no doubt the referendum, if ever established in England, may have the effect, which it already has in Switzerland, of making it possible that a minister or a Cabinet, supported on the whole by the electorate, shall retain office honestly and openly, though some proposal made by the Prime Minister and his colleagues and assented to by both Houses of Parliament is, through the referendum, condemned by the electorate. These possible results are undoubtedly repulsive to men who see nothing to censure in our party system. But, as I have throughout insisted, the great recommendation of the referendum is that it tends to correct, or at lowest greatly to diminish, the worst and the most patent evils of party government.

No effort has been made by me to exhaust the arguments against or in favour of the referendum. My aim in this Introduction has been to place before my readers the strongest argument against and also the strongest argument in favour of the introduction of the referendum into the constitution of England. It is certain that no man, who is really satisfied with the working of our party system, will ever look with favour on an institution which aims at correcting the vices of party government. It is probable, if not certain, that any one, who realises the extent to which parliamentary government itself is losing credit from its too close connection with the increasing power of the party machine, will hold with myself that the referendum judiciously used may, at any rate in the case of England, by checking the omnipotence of partisanship, revive faith in that parliamentary government which has been the glory of English constitutional history.

CONCLUSIONS

1. The sovereignty of Parliament is still the fundamental doctrine of English constitutionalists. But the authority of the House of Lords has been gravely diminished, whilst the authority of the House of Commons, or rather of the majority thereof during any one Parliament, has been immensely increased. Now this increased portion of sovereignty can be effectively exercised only by the Cabinet which holds in its hands the guidance of the party machine. And of the party which the parliamentary majority supports, the Premier has become at once the legal head and, if he is a man of ability, the real leader.[116] This gradual development of the power of the Cabinet and of the Premier is a change in the working of the English constitution. It is due to at least two interconnected causes. The one is the advance towards democracy resulting from the establishment, 1867 to 1884, of Household Suffrage; the other is the increasing rigidity of the party system. The result of a state of things which is not yet fully recognised inside or outside Parliament is that the Cabinet, under a leader who has fully studied and mastered the arts of modern parliamentary warfare, can defy, on matters of the highest importance, the possible or certain will of the nation. This growth of the authority obtained by

---

116 Lowell, *Government of England*, chaps. xxiv–xxvii., and especially i. pp. 441–447; *Public Opinion and Popular Government*, part ii. pp. 57–110.

the men who can control the party machine is the more formidable if we adopt the view propounded by the ablest of the critics of the Government of England, and hold with Lowell that party government has been for generations not the accident or the corruption but, so to speak, the very foundation of our constitutional system.[117] The best way to measure the extent of a hardly recognised alteration in the working of parliamentary government in England is to note the way in which a system nominally unchanged worked in the days of Palmerston, *i.e.* from 1855 to 1865, that is rather less than sixty years ago. He became Premier in 1855. He was in 1857 the most popular of Prime Ministers. After a contest with a coalition of all his opponents, a dissolution of Parliament gave to the old parliamentary hand a large and decisive majority. For once he lost his head. He became for the minute unpopular in the House of Commons. A cry in which there was little of real substance was raised against him amongst the electors. In 1858 he resigned office; in 1859 another dissolution restored to office the favourite of the people. He remained Premier with the support of the vast majority of the electors till his death in 1865. These transactions were natural enough in the Palmerstonian era; they could hardly recur in 1914. Palmerston, as also Gladstone, did not hold power in virtue of the machine. The Parliament Act is the last and greatest triumph of party government.

2. The increasing influence of the party system has in England, and still more throughout the British Empire, singularly coincided with the growth of the moral influence exercisable by the Crown. From the accession of Victoria to the present day the moral force at the disposal of the Crown has increased. The plain truth is that the King of England has at the present day two sources of moral authority of which writers on the constitution hardly take enough account in regard to the future. The King, whoever he be, is the only man throughout the British Empire who stands outside, if not above, the party system. The King is, in lands outside the United Kingdom, the acknowledged, and indeed the sole, representative and centre of the Empire.[118]

---

117 See note on preceding page.

118 See p. lxviii, *ante.*

3. The last quarter of the nineteenth and, still more clearly, the first fourteen years of the twentieth century are, as already pointed out, marked by declining faith in that rule of law which in 1884 was one of the two leading principles of constitutional government as understood in England.

4. The various ideas for the improvement of the constitution which now occupy the minds of reformers or innovators are intended, at any rate, to provide against the unpopularity of legislation, but for the most part are hardly framed with the object of promoting the wisdom of legislation. No doubt some of these schemes may indirectly increase the chance that injudicious legislation may receive a check. Proportional representation may sometimes secure a hearing in the House of Commons for opinions which, though containing a good deal of truth, command little or comparatively little popularity. The referendum, it is hoped, may diminish the admitted and increasing evil of our party system. Still, as I have insisted, the main object aimed at by the advocates of political change is for the most part to ensure that legislation shall be in conformity with popular opinion.[119]

The conclusions I have enumerated are certainly calculated to excite anxiety in the minds of sensible and patriotic Englishmen. Every citizen of public spirit is forced to put to himself this question: What will be the outcome of the democratic constitutionalism now established and flourishing in England? He is bound to remember that pessimism is as likely to mislead a contemporary critic as optimism. He will find the nearest approach to the answer which his inquiry requires in a sermon or prophecy delivered in 1872 by a constitutionalist who even then perceived possibilities and perils to which forty-two years ago our leading statesmen were for the most part blind. Listen to the words of Walter Bagehot:

> In the meantime, our statemen have the greatest opportunities they have had for many years, and likewise the greatest duty. They have to guide the new voters in the exercise of the franchise; to guide them quietly, and without saying what they are doing, but still to guide them. The leading statesmen in a free country have great momentary power. They settle the conver-

---

119 See pp. lxxvii–lxxx, *ante*.

sation of mankind. It is they who, by a great speech or two, determine what shall be said and what shall be written for long after. They, in conjunction with their counsellors, settle the programme of their party—the "platform," as the Americans call it, on which they and those associated with them are to take their stand for the political campaign. It is by that programme, by a comparison of the programmes of different statesmen, that the world forms its judgment. The common ordinary mind is quite unfit to fix for itself what political question it shall attend to; it is as much as it can do to judge decently of the questions which drift down to it, and are brought before it; it almost never settles its topics; it can only decide upon the issues of these topics. And in settling what these questions shall be, statesmen have now especially a great responsibility if they raise questions which will excite the lower orders of mankind; if they raise questions on which those orders are likely to be wrong; if they raise questions on which the interest of those orders is not identical with, or is antagonistic to, the whole interest of the State, they will have done the greatest harm they can do. The future of this country depends on the happy working of a delicate experiment, and they will have done all they could to vitiate that experiment. Just when it is desirable that ignorant men, new to politics, should have good issues, and only good issues, put before them, these statesmen will have suggested bad issues. They will have suggested topics which will bind the poor as a class together; topics which will excite them against the rich; topics the discussion of which in the only form in which that discussion reaches their ear will be to make them think that some new law can make them comfortable—that it is the present law which makes them uncomfortable—that Government has at its disposal an inexhaustible fund out of which it can give to those who now want without also creating elsewhere other and greater wants. If the first work of the poor voters is to try to create a "poor man's paradise," as poor men are apt to fancy that Paradise, and as they are apt to think they can create it, the great political trial now beginning will simply fail. The wide gift of the elective franchise will be a great calamity to the whole nation, and to those who gain it as great a calamity as to any.[120]

This is the language of a man of genius, who being dead yet speaketh. Whether the warning which his words certainly contain was unnecessary, or whether his implied prophecy of evil has not already been partially fulfilled or may not at some not distant date obtain more complete fulfilment, are inquiries which must be answered by the candour and the thoughtfulness of my readers. The complete reply must be left to the well-informed and more or less

---

120 Bagehot, *English Constitution* (2nd ed.). pp. xvii–xix.

impartial historian, who in 1950 or in 2000 shall sum up the final outcome of democratic government in England. Still it may be allowable to an author writing in 1914, though more than half blinded, as must be every critic of the age in which he lives, by the ignorance and the partialities of his own day, to remember that the present has its teaching no less than the past or the future. National danger is the test of national greatness. War has its lessons which may be more impressive than the lessons, valuable as they always are, of peace. The whole of a kingdom, or rather of an Empire, united for once in spirit, has entered with enthusiasm upon an arduous conflict with a nation possessed of the largest and the most highly trained army which the modern world can produce. This is in itself a matter of grave significance. England and the whole British Empire with her have taken up the sword and thereby have risked the loss of wealth, of prosperity, and even of political existence. And England, with the fervent consent of the people of every land subject to the rule of our King, has thus exchanged the prosperity of peace for the dangers and labours of war, not for the sake of acquiring new territory or of gaining additional military glory, for of these things she has enough and more than enough already, but for the sake of enforcing the plainest rules of international justice and the plainest dictates of common humanity. This is a matter of good omen for the happy development of popular government and for the progress, slow though it be, of mankind along the path of true fortitude and of real righteousness. These facts may rekindle among the youth of England as of France the sense that to be young is very heaven; these facts may console old men whom political disillusion and disappointment which they deem undeserved may have tempted towards despair, and enable them to rejoice with calmness and gravity that they have lived long enough to see the day when the solemn call to the performance of a grave national duty has united every man and every class of our common country in the determination to defy the strength, the delusions, and the arrogance of a militarised nation, and at all costs to secure for the civilised world the triumph of freedom, of humanity, and of justice.

OUTLINE OF SUBJECT

THE TRUE NATURE OF
CONSTITUTIONAL LAW

Optimistic view of English constitution.

*B*urke writes in 1791:

> Great critics have taught us one essential rule. . . . It is this, that if ever we
> should find ourselves disposed not to admire those writers or artists, Livy
> and Virgil for instance, Raphael or Michael Angelo, whom all the learned
> had admired, not to follow our own fancies, but to study them until we
> know how and what we ought to admire; and if we cannot arrive at this
> combination of admiration with knowledge, rather to believe that we are
> dull, than that the rest of the world has been imposed on. It is as good a rule,
> at least, with regard to this admired constitution (of England). We ought to
> understand it according to our measure; and to venerate where we are not
> able presently to comprehend. [1]

Hallam writes in 1818:

> No unbiased observer who derives pleasure from the welfare of his species,
> can fail to consider the long and uninterruptedly increasing prosperity of
> England as the most beautiful phænomenon in the history of mankind.
> Climates more propitious may impart more largely the mere enjoyments of
> existence; but in no other region have the benefits that political institutions
> can confer been diffused over so extended a population; nor have any people
> so well reconciled the discordant elements of wealth, order, and liberty.
> These advantages are surely not owing to the soil of this island, nor to
> the latitude in which it is placed; but to the spirit of its laws, from which,
> through various means, the characteristic independence and industrious-
> ness of our nation have been derived. The constitution, therefore, of Eng-

---

1 Burke, *Works,* iii, (1872 ed.), p. 114.

land must be to inquisitive men of all countries, far more to ourselves, an object of superior interest; distinguished, especially, as it is from all free governments of powerful nations, which history has recorded, by its manifesting, after the lapse of several centuries, not merely no symptom of irretrievable decay, but a more expansive energy.[2]

These two quotations from authors of equal though of utterly different celebrity, recall with singular fidelity the spirit with which our grandfathers and our fathers looked upon the institutions of their country. The constitution was to them, in the quaint language of George the Third, "the most perfect of human formations";[3] it was to them not a mere polity to be compared with the government of any other state, but so to speak a sacred mystery of statesmanship; it "had (as we have all heard from our youth up) not been made but had grown"; it was the fruit not of abstract theory but of that instinct which (it is supposed) has enabled Englishmen, and especially uncivilised Englishmen, to build up sound and lasting institutions, much as bees construct a honeycomb, without undergoing the degradation of understanding the principles on which they raise a fabric more subtlely wrought than any work of conscious art. The constitution was marked by more than one transcendent quality which in the eyes of our fathers raised it far above the imitations, counterfeits, or parodies, which have been set up during the last hundred years throughout the civilised world; no precise date could be named as the day of its birth; no definite body of persons could claim to be its creators, no one could point to the document which contained its clauses; it was in short a thing by itself, which Englishmen and foreigners alike should "venerate, where they are not able presently to comprehend."

Modern view of constitution.

The present generation must of necessity look on the constitution in a spirit different from the sentiment either of 1791 or of 1818. We cannot share the religious enthusiasm of Burke, raised, as it was, to

---

2 Hallam, *Middle Ages* (12th ed.), ii. p. 267. Nothing gives a more vivid idea of English sentiment with regard to the constitution towards the end of the eighteenth century than the satirical picture of national pride to be found in Goldsmith's *Citizen of the World,* Letter IV.

3 See Stanhope, *Life of Pitt,* i. App. p. 10.

the temper of fanatical adoration by just hatred of those "doctors of the modern school," who, when he wrote, were renewing the rule of barbarism in the form of the reign of terror; we cannot exactly echo the fervent self-complacency of Hallam, natural as it was to an Englishman who saw the institutions of England standing and flourishing, at a time when the attempts of foreign reformers to combine freedom with order had ended in ruin. At the present day students of the constitution wish neither to criticise, nor to venerate, but to understand; and a professor whose duty it is to lecture on constitutional law, must feel that he is called upon to perform the part neither of a critic nor of an apologist, nor of an eulogist, but simply of an expounder; his duty is neither to attack nor to defend the constitution, but simply to explain its laws. He must also feel that, however attractive be the mysteries of the constitution, he has good reason to envy professors who belong to countries such as France, Belgium, or the United States, endowed with constitutions of which the terms are to be found in printed documents, known to all citizens and accessible to every man who is able to read. Whatever may be the advantages of a so-called "unwritten" constitution, its existence imposes special difficulties on teachers bound to expound its provisions. Any one will see that this is so who compares for a moment the position of writers, such as Kent or Story, who commented on the Constitution of America, with the situation of any person who undertakes to give instruction in the constitutional law of England.

Special difficulty of commenting on English constitution. When these distinguished jurists delivered, in the form of lectures, commentaries upon the Constitution of the United States, they knew precisely what was the subject of their teaching and what was the proper mode of dealing with it. The theme of their teaching was a definite assignable part of the law of their country; it was recorded in a given document to which all the world had access, namely, "the Constitution of the United States established and ordained by the People of the United States." The articles of this constitution fall indeed far short of perfect logical arrangement, and lack absolute lucidity of expression; but they contain, in a clear and intelligible form, the fundamental law of the Union. This law (be it noted) is made and can only be altered or repealed in a way different from the method by which other enactments are made or altered; it stands forth, therefore, as a separate subject for study; it deals with the legislature, the executive, and the judiciary, and, by its provisions for its own amendment, indirectly defines the body in which resides the legislative sovereignty of the United States. Story and Kent therefore knew with precision the nature and limits of the department of law on which they intended to comment; they knew also what was the method required for the treatment of their topic. Their task as commentators on the constitution was in kind exactly similar to the task of commenting on any other branch of American jurisprudence. The American lawyer has to ascertain the meaning of the Articles of the Constitution in the same way in which he tries to elicit the meaning of any other enactment. He must be guided by the rules of grammar, by his knowledge of the common law, by the light (occasionally) thrown on American legislation by American history, and by the conclusions to be deduced from a careful study of judicial decisions. The task, in short, which lay before the great American commentators was the explanation of a definite legal document in accordance with the received cannons of legal interpretation. Their work, difficult as it might prove, was work of the kind to which lawyers are accustomed, and could be achieved by the use of ordinary legal methods. Story and Kent indeed were men of extraordinary capacity; so, however, were our own Blackstone, and at least one of Blackstone's editors. If, as is undoubtedly the case, the American jurists have produced commentaries on the constitution of the United States utterly unlike, and, one must in truth add, vastly superior to, any commentaries on the constitutional law of England, their success is partly due to the possession of advantages denied to the English commentator or lecturer. His position is entirely different from that of his American rivals. He may search the statute-book from beginning to end, but he will find no enactment which purports to contain the articles of the constitution; he will not possess any test by which to discriminate laws which are constitutional or fundamental from ordinary enactments; he will discover that the very term "constitutional law," which is not (unless my memory deceives me) ever employed by Blackstone, is of comparatively modern origin; and in short, that before commenting on the law of the constitution he must make up his mind what is the nature and the extent of English constitutional law.[4]

Commentator seeks help from constitutional lawyers, constitutional historians and constitutional theorists.

His natural, his inevitable resource is to recur to writers of authority on the law, the history, or the practice of the constitution. He will find (it must be admitted) no lack of distinguished guides; he may avail himself of the works of lawyers such as Blackstone, of the investigations of historians such as Hallam or Freeman, and of the speculations of philosophical theorists such as Bagehot or Hearn. From each class he may learn much, but for reasons which I am about to lay before you for consideration, he is liable to be led by each class of authors somewhat astray in his attempt to ascertain the field of his labours and the mode of working it; he will find, unless he can obtain some clue to guide his steps, that the whole province of so-called "constitutional law" is a sort of maze in which the wanderer is perplexed by unreality, by antiquarianism, and by conventionalism.

I. Lawyer's view of constitution. Its unreality. Blackstone.

Let us turn first to the lawyers, and as in duty bound to Blackstone.

Of constitutional law as such there is not a word to be found in his *Commentaries.* The matters which appear to belong to it are dealt with by him in the main under the head Rights of Persons. The Book which is thus entitled treats (*inter alia*) of the Parliament, of the King and his title, of master and servant, of husband and wife, of parent and child. The arrangement is curious and certainly does not bring into view the true scope or character of constitutional law. This, however, is a trifle. The Book contains much real learning about our system of government. Its true defect is the hopeless confusion both of language and of thought, introduced into the whole subject of constitutional law by Blackstone's habit—common to all the lawyers of his time—of applying old and inapplicable terms to new institu-

---

4 See this point brought out with great clearness by Monsieur Boutmy, *Études de Droit Constitutionnel* (2nd ed.), p. 8, English translation, p. 8. Monsieur Boutmy well points out that the sources of English constitutional law may be considered fourfold, namely—(1) Treaties or Quasi-Treaties, *i.e.* the Acts of Union; (2) The Common Law; (3) Solemn Agreements (pacts), *e.g.* the Bill of Rights; (4) Statutes. This mode of division is not exactly that which would be naturally adopted by an English writer, but it calls attention to distinctions often overlooked between the different sources of English constitutional law.

tions, and especially of ascribing in words to a modern and constitutional King the whole, and perhaps more than the whole, of the
powers actually possessed and exercised by William the Conqueror.
Blackstone writes:

> We are next to consider those branches of the royal prerogative, which
> invest thus our sovereign lord, thus all-perfect and immortal in his kingly
> capacity, with a number of authorities and powers; in the exertion whereof
> consists the executive part of the government. This is wisely placed in a
> single hand by the British constitution, for the sake of unanimity, strength,
> and dispatch. Were it placed in many hands, it would be subject to many
> wills: many wills, if disunited and drawing different ways, create weakness
> in a government; and to unite those several wills, and reduce them to one,
> is a work of more time and delay than the exigencies of state will afford.
> The King of England is, therefore, not only the chief, but properly the sole,
> magistrate of the nation; all others acting by commission from, and in due
> subordination to him; in like manner as, upon the great revolution of the
> Roman state, all the powers of the ancient magistracy of the commonwealth
> were concentrated in the new Emperor: so that, as Gravina expresses it, *in
> ejus unius persona veteris reipublicae vis atque majestas per cumulatas magistratuum
> potestates exprimebatur.*[5]

The language to this passage is impressive; it stands curtailed but
in substance unaltered in Stephen's *Commentaries*. It has but one fault;
the statements it contains are the direct opposite of the truth. The
executive of England is in fact placed in the hands of a committee
called the Cabinet. If there be any one person in whose single hand
the power of the State is placed, that one person is not the King but
the chairman of the committee, known as the Prime Minister. Nor
can it be urged that Blackstone's description of the royal authority
was a true account of the powers of the King at the time when
Blackstone wrote. George the Third enjoyed far more real authority
than has fallen to the share of any of his descendants. But it would be
absurd to maintain that the language I have cited painted his true
position. The terms used by the commentator were, when he used
them, unreal, and known[6] to be so. They have become only a little
more unreal during the century and more which has since elapsed.

---

5 Blackstone, *Commentaries*, i. p. 250.

6 The following passage from Paley's *Moral Philosophy,* published in 1785, is full of instruction. "In the British, and possibly in all other constitutions, there exists a wide difference

The King is considered in domestic affairs . . . as the fountain of justice, and general conservator of the peace of the kingdom. . . . He therefore has alone the right of erecting courts of judicature: for, though the constitution of the kingdom hath entrusted him with the whole executive power of the laws, it is impossible, as well as improper, that he should personally carry into execution this great and extensive trust: it is consequently necessary, that courts should be erected to assist him in executing this power; and equally necessary, that if erected, they should be erected by his authority. And hence it is, that all jurisdictions of courts are either mediately or immediately derived from the Crown, their proceedings run generally in the King's name, they pass under his seal, and are executed by his officers.[7]

Here we are in the midst of unrealities or fictions. Neither the King nor the Executive has anything to do with erecting courts of justice. We should rightly conclude that the whole Cabinet had gone mad if to-morrow's Gazette contained an order in council not authorised by statute erecting a new Court of Appeal. It is worth while here to note what is the true injury to the study of law produced by the tendency of Blackstone, and other less famous constitutionalists, to adhere to unreal expressions. The evil is not merely or mainly that these expressions exaggerate the power of the Crown. For such conventional exaggeration a reader could make allowance, as easily as we do for ceremonious terms of respect or of social courtesy. The harm wrought is, that unreal language obscures or conceals the true extent

---

between the actual state of the government and the theory. The one results from the other; but still they are different. When we contemplate the *theory* of the British government, we see the King invested with the most absolute personal impunity; with a power of rejecting laws, which have been resolved upon by both Houses of Parliament; of conferring by his charter, upon any set or succession of men he pleases, the privilege of sending representatives into one House of Parliament, as by his immediate appointment he can place whom he will in the other. What is this, a foreigner might ask, but a more circuitous despotism? Yet, when we turn our attention from the legal existence to the actual exercise of royal authority in England, we see these formidable prerogatives dwindled into mere ceremonies; and in their stead, a sure and commanding influence, of which the constitution, it seems, is totally ignorant, growing out of that enormous patronage, which the increased extent and opulence of the Empire has placed in the disposal of the executive magistrate."—Paley, *Moral Philosophy,* Book vi. cap. vii. The whole chapter whence this passage is taken repays study. Paley sees far more clearly into the true nature of the then existing constitution than did Blackstone. It is further noticeable that in 1785 the power to create Parliamentary boroughs was still looked upon as in theory an existing prerogative of the Crown. The power of the Crown was still large, and rested in fact upon the possession of enormous patronage.

7 Blackstone, *Commentaries,* i. p. 267.

of the powers, both of the King and of the Government. No one, indeed, but a child, fancies that the King sits crowned on his throne at Westminster, and in his own person administers justice to his subjects. But the idea entertained by many educated men that an English King or Queen reigns without taking any part in the government of the country, is not less far from the truth than the notion that Edward VII. ever exercises judicial powers in what are called his Courts. The oddity of the thing is that to most Englishmen the extent of the authority actually exercised by the Crown—and the same remark applies (in a great measure) to the authority exercised by the Prime Minister, and other high officials—is a matter of conjecture. We have all learnt from Blackstone, and writers of the same class, to make such constant use of expressions which we know not to be strictly true to fact, that we cannot say for certain what is the exact relation between the facts of constitutional government and the more or less artificial phraseology under which they are concealed. Thus to say that the King appoints the Ministry is untrue; it is also, of course, untrue to say that he creates courts of justice; but these two untrue statements each bear a very different relation to actual facts. Moreover, of the powers ascribed to the Crown, some are in reality exercised by the Government, whilst others do not in truth belong either to the King or to the Ministry. The general result is that the true position of the Crown as also the true powers of the Government are concealed under the fictitious ascription to the sovereign of political omnipotence, and the reader of, say, the first Book of Blackstone, can hardly discern the facts of law with which it is filled under the unrealities of the language in which these facts find expression.

II. Historian's view of constitution. Its antiquarianism.

Let us turn from the formalism of lawyers to the truthfulness of our constitutional historians.

Here a student or professor troubled about the nature of constitutional law finds himself surrounded by a crowd of eminent instructors. He may avail himself of the impartiality of Hallam: he may dive into the exhaustless erudition of the Bishop of Oxford: he will discover infinite parliamentary experience in the pages of Sir Thomas May, and vigorous common sense, combined with polemical research, in Mr. Freeman's *Growth of the English Constitution*. Let us take this book as an excellent type of historical constitutionalism. The

Growth of the English Constitution is known to every one. Of its recognised merits, of its clearness, of its accuracy, of its force, it were useless and impertinent to say much to students who know, or ought to know, every line of the book from beginning to end. One point, however, deserves especial notice. Mr. Freeman's highest merit is his unrivalled faculty for bringing every matter under discussion to a clear issue. He challenges his readers to assent or deny. If you deny you must show good cause for your denial, and hence may learn fully as much from rational disagreement with our author as from unhesitating assent to his views. Take, then, the *Growth of the English Constitution* as a first-rate specimen of the mode in which an historian looks at the constitution. What is it that a lawyer, whose object is to acquire the knowledge of law, will learn from its pages? A few citations from the ample and excellent head notes to the first two chapters of the work answer the inquiry.

They run thus:

> The Landesgemeinden of Uri and Appenzell; their bearing on English Constitutional History; political elements common to the whole Teutonic race; monarchic, aristocratic, and democratic elements to be found from the beginning; the three classes of men, the noble, the common freeman, and the slave; universal prevalence of slavery; the Teutonic institutions common to the whole Aryan family; witness of Homer; description of the German Assemblies by Tacitus; continuity of English institutions; English nationality assumed; Teutonic institutions brought into Britain by the English conquerors; effects of the settlement on the conquerors; probable increase of slavery; Earls and Churls; growth of the kingly power; nature of kingship; special sanctity of the King; immemorial distinction between Kings and Ealdormen. . . . Gradual growth of the English constitution; new laws seldom called for; importance of precedent; return to early principles in modern legislation; shrinking up of the ancient national Assemblies; constitution of the Witenagemót; the Witenagemót continued in the House of Lords; Gemóts after the Norman Conquest; the King's right of summons; Life Peerages; origin of the House of Commons; comparison of English and French national Assemblies; of English and French history generally; course of events influenced by particular men; Simon of Montfort . . . Edward the First; the constitution finally completed under him; nature of later changes; difference between English and continental legislatures.

All this is interesting, erudite, full of historical importance, and thoroughly in its place in a book concerned solely with the "growth" of the constitution; but in regard to English law and the law of the constitution, the *Landesgemeinden* of Uri, the witness of Homer, the ealdormen, the constitution of the Witenagemót, and a lot more of fascinating matter are mere antiquarianism. Let no one suppose that to say this is to deny the relation between history and law. It were far better, as things now stand, to be charged with heresy, than to fall under the suspicion of lacking historical-mindedness, or of questioning the universal validity of the historical method. What one may assert without incurring the risk of such crushing imputations is, that the kind of constitutional history which consists in researches into the antiquities of English institutions, has no direct bearing on the rules of constitutional law in the sense in which these rules can become the subject of legal comment. Let us eagerly learn all that is known, and still more eagerly all that is not known, about the Witenagemót. But let us remember that antiquarianism is not law, and that the function of a trained lawyer is not to know what the law of England was yesterday, still less what it was centuries ago, or what it ought to be to-morrow, but to know and be able to state what are the principles of law which actually and at the present day exist in England. For this purpose it boots nothing to know the nature of the Landesgemeinden of Uri, or to understand, if it be understandable, the constitution of the Witenagemót. All this is for a lawyer's purposes simple antiquarianism. It throws as much light on the constitution of the United States as upon the constitution of England; that is, it throws from a legal point of view no light upon either the one or the other.

Contrast between legal and historical view of constitution.

The name of the United States serves well to remind us of the true relation between constitutional historians and legal constitutionalists. They are each concerned with the constitution, but from a different aspect. An historian is primarily occupied with ascertaining the steps by which a constitution has grown to be what it is. He is deeply, sometimes excessively, concerned with the question of "origins." He is but indirectly concerned in ascertaining what are the rules of the constitution in the year 1908. To a lawyer, on the other hand, the primary object of study is the law as it now stands; he is only secondarily occupied with ascertaining how it came into existence. This is absolutely clear if we compare the position of an American historian with the position of an American jurist. The historian of the American Union would not commence his researches at the year 1789; he would have a good deal to say about Colonial history and about the institutions of England; he might, for aught I know, find himself impelled to go back to the Witenagemót; he would, one may suspect, pause in his researches considerably short of Uri. A lawyer lecturing on the constitution of the United States would, on the other hand, necessarily start from the constitution itself. But he would soon see that the articles of the constitution required a knowledge of the Articles of Confederation; that the opinions of Washington, of Hamilton, and generally of the "Fathers," as one sometimes hears them called in America, threw light on the meaning of various constitutional articles; and further, that the meaning of the constitution could not be adequately understood by any one who did not take into account the situation of the colonies before the separation from England and the rules of common law, as well as the general conceptions of law and justice inherited by English colonists from their English forefathers. As it is with the American lawyer compared with the American historian, so it is with the English lawyer as compared with the English historian. Hence, even where lawyers are concerned, as they frequently must be, with the development of our institutions, arises a further difference between the historical and the legal view of the constitution. Historians in their devotion to the earliest phases of ascertainable history are infected with a love which, in the eyes of a lawyer, appears inordinate, for the germs of our institutions, and seem to care little about their later developments. Mr. Freeman gives but one-third of his book to anything as modern as the days of the Stuarts. The period of now more than two centuries which has elapsed since what used to be called the "Glorious Revolution," filled as those two centuries are with change and with growth, seems hardly to have attracted the attention of a writer whom lack, not of knowledge, but of will has alone prevented from sketching out the annals of our modern constitution. A lawyer must look at the matter differently. It is from the later annals of England he derives most help in the study of existing law. What we might have obtained from Dr. Stubbs had he not surrendered to the Episcopate gifts which we hoped were dedicated to the University alone, is now left to conjecture. But, things being as they are, the historian who most nearly meets the wants of lawyers is Mr. Gardiner. The struggles of the seventeenth century, the conflict between James and Coke, Bacon's theory of the prerogative, Charles's effort to substitute the personal will of Charles Stuart for the legal will of the King of England, are all matters which touch not remotely upon the problems of actual law. A knowledge of these things guards us, at any rate, from the illusion, for illusion it must be termed, that modern constitutional freedom has been established by an astounding method of retrogressive progress; that every step towards civilisation has been a step backwards towards the simple wisdom of our uncultured ancestors. The assumption which underlies this view, namely, that there existed among our Saxon forefathers a more or less perfect polity, conceals the truth both of law and of history. To ask how a mass of legal subtleties

> would have looked . . . in the eyes of a man who had borne his part in the elections of Eadward and of Harold, and who had raised his voice and clashed his arms in the great Assembly which restored Godwine to his lands,[8]

is to put an inquiry which involves an untenable assumption; it is like asking what a Cherokee Indian would have thought of the claim of George the Third to separate taxation from representation. In each case the question implies that the simplicity of a savage enables him to solve with fairness a problem of which he cannot understand the terms. Civilisation may rise above, but barbarism sinks below the level of legal fictions, and our respectable Saxon ancestors were, as compared, not with ourselves only, but with men so like ourselves as Coke and Hale, respectable barbarians. The supposition, moreover, that the cunning of lawyers has by the invention of legal fictions corrupted the fair simplicity of our original constitution, underrates the statesmanship of lawyers as much as it overrates the merits of early society. The fictions of the Courts have in the hands of lawyers

---

8 See Freeman, *Growth of the English Constitution* (1st ed.), p. 125.

such as Coke served the cause both of justice and of freedom, and served it when it could have been defended by no other weapons. For there are social conditions under which legal fictions or subtleties afford the sole means of establishing that rule of equal and settled law which is the true basis of English civilisation. Nothing can be more pedantic, nothing more artificial, nothing more unhistorical, than the reasoning by which Coke induced or compelled James to forego the attempt to withdraw cases from the Courts for his Majesty's personal determination.[9] But no achievement of sound argument, or stroke of enlightened statesmanship, ever established a rule more essential to the very existence of the constitution than the principle enforced by the obstinacy and the fallacies of the great Chief-Justice. Oddly enough, the notion of an ideal constitution corrupted by the technicalities of lawyers is at bottom a delusion of the legal imagination. The idea of retrogressive progress is merely one form of the appeal to precedent. This appeal has made its appearance at every crisis in the history of England, and indeed no one has stated so forcibly as my friend Mr. Freeman himself the peculiarity of all English efforts to extend the liberties of the country, namely, that these attempts at innovation have always assumed the form of an appeal to pre-existing rights. But the appeal to precedent is in the law courts merely a useful fiction by which judicial decision conceals its transformation into judicial legislation; and a fiction is none the less a fiction because it has emerged from the Courts into the field of politics or of history. Here, then, the astuteness of lawyers has imposed upon the simplicity of historians. Formalism and antiquarianism have, so to speak, joined hands; they have united to mislead students in search for the law of the constitution.

Let us turn now to the political theorists.

III. View of political theorists. Its defect that it deals solely with conventions of constitution.
No better types of such thinkers can be taken than Bagehot and Professor Hearn. No author of modern times (it may be confidently asserted) has done so much to elucidate the intricate workings of English government as Bagehot. His *English Constitution* is so full of brightness, originality, and wit, that few students notice how full it is

---

9 See 12 *Rep.* 64; Hearn, *Government of England* (2nd ed.), chap. iii.

also of knowledge, of wisdom, and of insight. The slight touches, for example, by which Bagehot paints the reality of Cabinet government, are so amusing as to make a reader forget that Bagehot was the first author who explained in accordance with actual fact the true nature of the Cabinet and its real relation to the Crown and to Parliament. He is, in short, one of those rare teachers who have explained intricate matters with such complete clearness, as to make the public forget that what is now so clear ever needed explanation. Professor Hearn may perhaps be counted an anticipator of Bagehot. In any case he too has approached English institutions from a new point of view, and has looked at them in a fresh light; he would be universally recognised among us as one of the most distinguished and ingenious exponents of the mysteries of the English constitution, had it not been for the fact that he made his fame as a professor, not in any of the seats of learning in the United Kingdom, but in the University of Melbourne. From both these writers we expect to learn, and do learn much, but, as in the case of Mr. Freeman, though we learn much from our teacher which is of value, we do not learn precisely what as lawyers we are in search of. The truth is that both Bagehot and Professor Hearn deal and mean to deal mainly with political understandings or conventions and not with rules of law. What is the precise moral influence which might be exerted by a wise constitutional monarch; what are the circumstances under which a Minister is entitled to dissolve Parliament; whether the simultaneous creation of a large number of Peers for a special purpose is constitutionally justifiable; what is the principle on which a Cabinet may allow of open questions—these and the like are the kind of inquiries raised and solved by writers whom, as being occupied with the conventional understandings of the constitution, we may term conventionalists. These inquires are, many of them, great and weighty; but they are not inquiries which will ever be debated in the law courts. If the Premier should advise the creation of five hundred Peers, the Chancery Division would not, we may be sure, grant an injunction to restrain their creation. If he should on a vote of censure decline to resign office, the King's Bench Division would certainly not issue a *quo warranto* calling upon him to show cause why he continues to be

Prime Minister. As a lawyer, I find these matters too high for me. Their practical solution must be left to the profound wisdom of Members of Parliament; their speculative solution belongs to the province of political theorists.

And conventional view does not explain how conventions enforced.

One suggestion a mere legist may be allowed to make, namely, that the authors who insist upon and explain the conventional character of the understandings which make up a great part of the constitution, leave unexplained the one matter which needs explanation. They give no satisfactory answer to the inquiry how it happens that the understandings of politics are sometimes at least obeyed as rigorously as the commands of law.[10] To refer to public opinion and to considerations of expediency is to offer but a very inadequate solution of a really curious problem. Public opinion approves and public expediency requires the observance of contracts, yet contracts are not always observed, and would (presumably) be broken more often than they are did not the law punish their breach, or compel their performance. Meanwhile it is certain that understandings are not laws, and that no system of conventionalism will explain the whole nature of constitutional law, if indeed "constitutional law" be in strictness law at all.

Is constitutional law really "law" at all?

For at this point a doubt occurs to one's mind which must more than once have haunted students of the constitution. Is it possible that so-called "constitutional law" is in reality a cross between history and custom which does not properly deserve the name of law at all, and certainly does not belong to the province of a professor called upon to learn or to teach nothing but the true indubitable law of England? Can it be that a dark saying of Tocqueville's, "the English constitution has no real existence" (*elle n'existe point*[11]), contains the truth of the whole matter? In this case lawyers would gladly surrender a domain to which they can establish no valid title. The one half of it should, as belonging to history, go over to our historical professors. The other half should, as belonging to conventions which illustrate the growth of law, be transferred either to my friend the Corpus

---

10 See further on this point, Part III. *post.*

11 Tocqueville, *Œuvres Complètes,* i. 166, 167.

Professor of Jurisprudence, because it is his vocation to deal with the oddities or the outlying portions of legal science, or to my friend the Chichele Professor of International Law, because he being a teacher of law which is not law, and being accustomed to expound those rules of public ethics which are miscalled international law, will find himself at home in expounding political ethics which, on the hypothesis under consideration, are miscalled constitutional law.

Before, however, admitting the truth of the supposition that "constitutional law" is in no sense law at all, it will be well to examine a little further into the precise meaning which we attach to the term constitutional law, and then consider how far it is a fit subject for legal exposition.

It consists of two different kinds of rules.

Constitutional law, as the term is used in England, appears to include all rules which directly or indirectly affect the distribution or the exercise of the sovereign power in the state.[12] Hence it includes (among other things) all rules which define the members of the sovereign power, all rules which regulate the relation of such members to each other, or which determine the mode in which the sovereign power, or the members thereof, exercise their authority. Its rules prescribe the order of succession to the throne, regulate the prerogatives of the chief magistrate, determine the form of the legislature and its mode of election. These rules also deal with Ministers, with their responsibility, with their spheres of action, define the territory over which the sovereignty of the state extends and settle who are to be deemed subjects or citizens. Observe the use of the word "rules," not "laws." This employment of terms is intentional. Its object is to call attention to the fact that the rules which make up constitutional law, as the term is used in England, include two sets of principles or maxims of a totally distinct character.

(i.) Rules which are true laws—law of the constitution.

The one set of rules are in the strictest sense "laws," since they are rules which (whether written or unwritten, whether enacted by stat-

---

12 Compare Holland, *Jurisprudence* (10th ed.), pp. 138, 139, and 359–363. "By the constitution of a country is meant so much of its law as relates to the designation and form of the legislature; the rights and functions of the several parts of the legislative body; the construction, office, and jurisdiction of courts of justice. The constitution is one principal division, section, or title of the code of public laws, distinguished from the rest only by the superior importance of the subject of which it treats."—Paley, *Moral Philosophy*, Book vi. chap. vii.

ute or derived from the mass of custom, tradition, or judge-made maxims known as the Common Law) are enforced by the Courts; these rules constitute "constitutional law" in the proper sense of that term, and may for the sake of distinction be called collectively "the law of the constitution."

(ii.) Rules which are not laws —conventions of the constitution.

The other set of rules consist of conventions, understandings, habits, or practices which, though they may regulate the conduct of the several members of the sovereign power, of the Ministry, or of other officials, are not in reality laws at all since they are not enforced by the Courts. This portion of constitutional law may, for the sake of distinction, be termed the "conventions of the constitution," or constitutional morality.

To put the same thing in a somewhat different shape, "constitutional law," as the expression is used in England, both by the public and by authoritative writers, consists of two elements. The one element, here called the "law of the constitution," is a body of undoubted law; the other element, here called the "conventions of the constitution," consists of maxims or practices which, though they regulate the ordinary conduct of the Crown, of Ministers, and of other persons under the constitution, are not in strictness laws at all. The contrast between the law of the constitution and the conventions of the constitution may be most easily seen from examples.

Examples of rules belonging to law of constitution.

To the law of the constitution belong the following rules:

"The King can do no wrong." This maxim, as now interpreted by the Courts, means, in the first place, that by no proceeding known to the law can the King be made personally responsible for any act done by him; if (to give an absurd example) the King were himself to shoot the Premier through the head, no court in England could take cognisance of the act. The maxim means, in the second place, that no one can plead the orders of the Crown or indeed of any superior officer in defence of any act not otherwise justifiable by law; this principle in both its applications is (be it noted) a law and a law of the constitution, but it is not a written law. "There is no power in the Crown to dispense with the obligation to obey a law;" this negation or abolition of the dispensing power now depends upon the Bill of Rights; it is a law of the Constitution and a written law. "Some person is legally responsible for every act done by the Crown." This responsibility of

Ministers appears in foreign countries as a formal part of the constitution; in England it results from the combined action of several legal principles, namely, first, the maxim that the King can do no wrong; secondly, the refusal of the Courts to recognise any act as done by the Crown, which is not done in a particular form, a form in general involving the affixing of a particular seal by a Minister, or the counter-signature or something equivalent to the counter-signature of a Minister; thirdly, the principle that the Minister who affixes a particular seal, or countersigns his signature, is responsible for the act which he, so to speak, endorses;[13] this again is part of the constitution and a law, but it is not a written law. So again the right to personal liberty, the right of public meeting, and many other rights, are part of the law of the constitution, though most of these rights are consequences of the more general law or principle that no man can be punished except for direct breaches of law (*i.e.* crimes) proved in the way provided by law (*i.e.* before the Courts of the realm).

To the conventions of the constitution belong the following maxims:

Examples of rules which belong to conventions of the constitution.

"The King must assent to, or (as it is inaccurately expressed) cannot 'veto'[14] any bill passed by the two Houses of Parliament"; "the House of Lords does not originate any money bill"; "when the House of Lords acts as a Court of Appeal, no peer who is not a law lord takes part in the decisions of the House"; "Ministers resign office when they have ceased to command the confidence of the House of Commons"; "a bill must be read a certain number of times before passing through the House of Commons." These maxims are distinguished from each other by many differences;[15] under a new or written con-

---

13 Compare Hearn, *Government of England* (2nd ed.), chap. iv.

14 As to the meaning of "veto," see Hearn, *Government of England* (2nd ed.), pp. 51, 60, 61, 63, 548, and the article on the word Veto in the last edition of the *Encyclopædia Britannica*, by Professor Orelli.

15 Some of these maxims are never violated, and are universally admitted to be inviolable. Others, on the other hand, have nothing but a slight amount of custom in their favour, and are of disputable validity. The main distinction between different classes of conventional rules may, it is conceived, be thus stated: Some of these rules could not be violated without bringing to a stop the course of orderly and pacific government; others might be violated without any other consequence than that of exposing the Minister or other person by whom they were broken to blame or unpopularity.

stitution some of them probably would and some of them would not take the form of actual laws. Under the English constitution they have one point in common: they are none of them "laws" in the true sense of that word, for if any or all of them were broken, no court would take notice of their violation.

It is to be regretted that these maxims must be called "conventional," for the word suggests a notion of insignificance or unreality. This, however, is the last idea which any teacher would wish to convey to his hearers. Of constitutional conventions or practices some are as important as any laws, though some may be trivial, as may also be the case with a genuine law. My object, however, is to contrast, not shams with realities, but the legal element with the conventional element of so-called "constitutional law."

Distinction between laws and conventions not the same as difference between written and unwritten law.

This distinction differs essentially, it should be noted, from the distinction between "written law" (or statute law) and "unwritten law" (or common law). There are laws of the constitution, as, for example, the Bill of Rights, the Act of Settlement, and Habeas Corpus Acts, which are "written law," found in the statute-books—in other words, are statutory enactments. There are other most important laws of the constitution (several of which have already been mentioned) which are "unwritten" laws, that is, not statutory enactments. Some further of the laws of the constitution, such, for example, as the law regulating the descent of the Crown, which were at one time unwritten or common law, have now become written or

---

This difference will at bottom be found to depend upon the degree of directness with which the violation of a given constitutional maxim brings the wrongdoer into conflict with the law of the land. Thus a Ministry under whose advice Parliament were not summoned to meet for more than a year would, owing to the lapse of the Mutiny Act, etc., become through their agents engaged in a conflict with the Courts. The violation of a convention of the constitution would in this case lead to revolutionary or reactionary violence. The rule, on the other hand, that a Bill must be read a given number of times before it is passed is, though a well-established constitutional principle, a convention which might be disregarded without bringing the Government into conflict with the ordinary law. A Ministry who induced the House of Commons to pass an Act, *e.g.* suspending the Habeas Corpus Act, after one reading, or who induced the House to alter their rules as to the number of times a Bill should be read, would in no way be exposed to a contest with the ordinary tribunals. Ministers who, after Supplies were voted and the Mutiny Act passed, should prorogue the House and keep office for months after the Government had ceased to retain the confidence of the Commons, might or might not incur grave unpopularity, but would not necessarily commit a breach of law. See further Part III. *post.*

statute law. The conventions of the constitution, on the other hand, cannot be recorded in the statute-book, though they may be formally reduced to writing. Thus the whole of our parliamentary procedure is nothing but a mass of conventional law; it is, however, recorded in written or printed rules. The distinction, in short, between written and unwritten law does not in any sense square with the distinction between the law of the constitution (constitutional law properly so called) and the conventions of the constitution. This latter is the distinction on which we should fix our whole attention, for it is of vital importance, and elucidates the whole subject of constitutional law. It is further a difference which may exist in countries which have a written or statutory constitution.[16] In the United States the legal powers of the President, the Senate, the mode of electing the President, and the like, are, as far as the law is concerned, regulated wholly by the law of the constitution. But side by side with the law have grown up certain stringent conventional rules, which, though they would not be noticed by any court, have in practice nearly the force of law. No President has ever been re-elected more than once: the popular approval of this conventional limit (of which the constitution knows nothing) on a President's re-eligibility proved a fatal bar to General Grant's third candidature. Constitutional understandings have entirely changed the position of the Presidential electors. They were by the founders of the constitution intended to be what their name denotes, the persons who chose or selected the President; the chief officer, in short, of the Republic was, according to the law, to be appointed under a system of double election. This intention has failed; the "electors" have become a mere means of voting for a

---

16 The conventional element in the constitution of the United States is far larger than most Englishmen suppose. See on this subject Wilson, *Congressional Government,* and Bryce (3rd ed.), *American Commonwealth,* chaps. xxxiv. and xxxv. It may be asserted without much exaggeration that the conventional element in the constitution of the United States is now as large as in the English constitution. Under the American system, however, the line between "conventional rules" and "laws" is drawn with a precision hardly possible in England.

Under the constitution of the existing French Republic, constitutional conventions or understandings exert a considerable amount of influence. They considerably limit, for instance, the actual exercise of the large powers conferred by the letter of the constitution on the President. See Chardon, *L'Administration de la France—Les Fonctionnaires,* pp. 79–105.

particular candidate; they are no more than so many ballots cast for the Republican or for the Democratic nominee. The understanding that an elector is not really to elect, has now become so firmly established, that for him to exercise his legal power of choice is considered a breach of political honour too gross to be committed by the most unscrupulous of politicians. Public difficulties, not to say dangers, might have been averted if, in the contest between Mr. Hayes and Mr. Tilden, a few Republican electors had felt themselves at liberty to vote for the Democratic candidate. Not a single man among them changed his side. The power of an elector to elect is as completely abolished by constitutional understandings in America as is the royal right of dissent from bills passed by both Houses by the same force in England. Under a written, therefore, as under an unwritten constitution, we find in full existence the distinction between the law and the conventions of the constitution.

Constitutional law as subject of legal study means solely law of constitution.

Upon this difference I have insisted at possibly needless length, because it lies at the very root of the matter under discussion. Once grasp the ambiguity latent in the expression "constitutional law," and everything connected with the subject falls so completely into its right place that a lawyer, called upon to teach or to study constitutional law as a branch of the law of England, can hardly fail to see clearly the character and scope of his subject.

With conventions or understandings he has no direct concern. They vary from generation to generation, almost from year to year. Whether a Ministry defeated at the polling booths ought to retire on the day when the result of the election is known, or may more properly retain office until after a defeat in Parliament, is or may be a question of practical importance. The opinions on this point which prevail today differ (it is said) from the opinions or understandings which prevailed thirty years back, and are possibly different from the opinions or understanding which may prevail ten years hence. Weighty precedents and high authority are cited on either side of this knotty question; the dicta or practice of Russell and Peel may be balanced off against the dicta or practice of Beaconsfield and Gladstone. The subject, however, is not one of law but of politics, and need trouble no lawyer or the class of any professor of law. If he is concerned with it at all, he is so only in so far as he may be called upon to show what is the connection (if any there be) between the conventions of the constitution and the law of the constitution.

This the true constitutional law is his only real concern. His proper function is to show what are the legal rules (*i.e.* rules recognised by the Courts) which are to be found in the several parts of the constitution. Of such rules or laws he will easily discover more than enough. The rules determining the legal position of the Crown, the legal rights of the Crown's Ministers, the constitution of the House of Lords, the constitution of the House of Commons, the laws which govern the established Church, the laws which determine the position of the non-established Churches, the laws which regulate the army,— these and a hundred other laws form part of the law of the constitution, and are as truly part of the law of the land as the articles of the Constitution of the United States form part of the law of the Union.

Law of constitution can be expounded like any other branch of English law.

The duty, in short, of an English professor of law is to state what are the laws which form part of the constitution, to arrange them in their order, to explain their meaning, and to exhibit where possible their logical connection. He ought to expound the unwritten or partly unwritten constitution of England, in the same manner in which Story and Kent have expounded the written law of the American constitution. The task has its special perplexities, but the difficulties which beset the topic are the same in kind, though not in degree, as those which are to be found in every branch of the law of England. You are called upon to deal partly with statute law, partly with judge-made law; you are forced to rely on Parliamentary enactments and also on judicial decisions, on authoritative dicta, and in many cases on mere inferences drawn from judicial doctrines; it is often difficult to discriminate between prevalent custom and acknowledged right. This is true of the endeavour to expound the law of the constitution; all this is true also in a measure of any attempt to explain our law of contract, our law of torts, or our law of real property.

Moreover, teachers of constitutional law enjoy at this moment one invaluable advantage. Their topic has, of recent years,[17] become of

---

17 This treatise was originally published in 1885. Since that date legal decisions and public discussion have thrown light upon several matters of constitutional law, such, for example, as the limits to the right of public meeting and the nature of martial law.

immediate interest and of pressing importance. These years have brought into the foreground new constitutional questions, and have afforded in many instances the answers thereto. The series of actions connected with the name of Mr. Bradlaugh[18] has done as much to clear away the obscurity which envelops many parts of our public law as was done in the eighteenth century by the series of actions connected with the name of John Wilkes. The law of maintenance has been rediscovered; the law of blasphemy has received new elucidation. Everybody now knows the character of a penal action. It is now possible to define with precision the relation between the House of Commons and the Courts of the land; the legal character and solemnity of an oath has been made patent to all the world, or at any rate to all those persons who choose to read the *Law Reports.* Meanwhile circumstances with which Mr. Bradlaugh had no connection have forced upon public attention all the various problems connected with the right of public meeting. Is such a right known to the law? What are the limits within which it may be exercised? What is the true definition of an "unlawful assembly"? How far may citizens lawfully assembled assert their right of meeting by the use of force? What are the limits within which the English constitution recognises the right of self-defence? These are questions some of which have been raised and all of which may any day be raised before the Courts. They are inquiries which touch the very root of our public law. To find the true reply to them is a matter of importance to every citizen. While these inquiries require an answer the study of the law of the constitution must remain a matter of pressing interest. The fact, however, that the provisions of this law are often embodied in cases which have gained notoriety and excite keen feelings of political partisanship may foster a serious misconception. Unintelligent students may infer that the law of the constitution is to be gathered only from famous judgments which embalm the results of grand constitutional or political conflicts. This is not so. Scores of unnoticed cases, such as the *Parlement Belge,*[19] or *Thomas* v. *The Queen,*[20] touch upon or decide principles of constitu-

---

18 Written 1885. See for Bradlaugh's political career, *Dict. Nat. Biog.,* Supplement, vol. i. p. 248.

19 4 P. D. 129; 5 P. D. 197. Compare *Walker* v. *Baird* [1892], A. C. 491, 497.

20 L. R., 10 Q. B. 31.

tional law. Indeed every action against a constable or collector of revenue enforces the greatest of all such principles, namely, that obedience to administrative orders is no defence to an action or prosecution for acts done in excess of legal authority. The true law of the constitution is in short to be gathered from the sources whence we collect the law of England in respect to any other topic, and forms as interesting and as distinct, though not as well explored, a field for legal study or legal exposition as any which can be found. The subject is one which has not yet been fully mapped out. Teachers and pupils alike therefore suffer from the inconvenience as they enjoy the interest of exploring a province of law which has not yet been entirely reduced to order.[21]

This inconvenience has one great compensation. We are compelled to search for the guidance of first principles, and as we look for a clue through the mazes of a perplexed topic, three such guiding principles gradually become apparent. They are, *first,* the legislative sovereignty of Parliament;[22] *secondly,* the universal rule or supremacy throughout the constitution of ordinary law;[23] and *thirdly* (though here we tread on more doubtful and speculative ground), the dependence in the last resort of the conventions upon the law of the constitution.[24] To examine, to elucidate, to test these three principles, forms, at any rate (whatever be the result of the investigation), a suitable introduction to the study of the law of the constitution.

---

21 Since these words were written, Sir William Anson's admirable *Law and Custom of the Constitution* has gone far to provide a complete scheme of English constitutional law.

22 See Part I. *post.*

23 See Part II. *post.*

24 See Part III. *post.*

PART I
THE SOVEREIGNTY OF PARLIAMENT

Chapter I

THE NATURE OF PARLIAMENTARY SOVEREIGNTY

The sovereignty of Parliament is (from a legal point of view) the dominant characteristic of our political institutions.

Aim of chapter.

My aim in this chapter is, in the first place, to explain the nature of Parliamentary sovereignty and to show that its existence is a legal fact, fully recognised by the law of England; in the next place, to prove that none of the alleged legal limitations on the sovereignty of Parliament have any existence; and, lastly, to state and meet certain speculative difficulties which hinder the ready admission of the doctrine that Parliament is, under the British constitution, an absolutely sovereign legislature.

NATURE OF PARLIAMENTARY SOVEREIGNTY

Nature of Parliamentary Sovereignty.

Parliament means, in the mouth of a lawyer (though the word has often a different sense in ordinary conversation), the King, the House of Lords, and the House of Commons; these three bodies acting together may be aptly described as the "King in Parliament," and constitute Parliament.[1]

The principle of Parliamentary sovereignty means neither more nor less than this, namely, that Parliament thus defined has, under the English constitution, the right to make or unmake any law whatever; and, further, that no person or body is recognised by the law of

---

1 Conf. Blackstone, *Commentaries*, i. p. 153.

England as having a right to override or set aside the legislation of Parliament.

A law may, for our present purpose, be defined as "any rule which will be enforced by the Courts." The principle then of Parliamentary sovereignty may, looked at from its positive side, be thus described: Any Act of Parliament, or any part of an Act of Parliament, which makes a new law, or repeals or modifies an existing law, will be obeyed by the Courts. The same principle, looked at from its negative side, may be thus stated: There is no person or body of persons who can, under the English constitution, make rules which override or derogate from an Act of Parliament, or which (to express the same thing in other words) will be enforced by the Courts in contravention of an Act of Parliament. Some apparent exceptions to this rule no doubt suggest themselves. But these apparent exceptions, as where, for example, the Judges of the High Court of Justice make rules of court repealing Parliamentary enactments, are resolvable into cases in which Parliament either directly or indirectly sanctions subordinate legislation. This is not the place for entering into any details as to the nature of judicial legislation;[2] the matter is mentioned here only in order to remove an obvious difficulty which might present itself to some students. It will be necessary in the course of these lectures to say a good deal more about Parliamentary sovereignty, but for the present the above rough description of its nature may suffice. The important thing is to make clear that the doctrine of Parliamentary sovereignty is, both on its positive and on its negative side, fully recognised by the law of England.

Unlimited Legislative Authority of Parliament

Unlimited legislative authority of Parliament.

The classical passage on this subject is the following extract from Blackstone's *Commentaries:* —

Sir Edward Coke,[3] says:

> The power and jurisdiction of Parliament is so transcendent and absolute, that it cannot be confined, either for causes or persons, within any bounds.

---

2 The reader who wishes for fuller information on the nature of judge-made law will find what he wants in Dicey's *Law and Public Opinion in England,* App. Note iv. p. 481, and in Sir Frederick Pollock's *Essays in Jurisprudence and Ethics,* p. 237.

3 *Fourth Institute,* p. 36.

And of this high court, he adds, it may be truly said, *"Si antiquitatem spectes, est vetustissima; si dignitatem, est honoratissima; si jurisdictionem, est capacissima."* It hath sovereign and uncontrollable authority in the making, confirming, enlarging, restraining, abrogating, repealing, reviving, and expounding of laws, concerning matters of all possible denominations, ecclesiastical or temporal, civil, military, maritime, or criminal: this being the place where that absolute despotic power, which must in all governments reside somewhere, is entrusted by the constitution of these kingdoms. All mischiefs and grievances, operations and remedies, that transcend the ordinary course of the laws, are within the reach of this extraordinary tribunal. It can regulate or new-model the succession to the Crown; as was done in the reign of Henry VIII. and William III. It can alter the established religion of the land; as was done in a variety of instances, in the reigns of king Henry VIII. and his three children. It can change and create afresh even the constitution of the kingdom and of parliaments themselves; as was done by the act of union, and the several statutes for triennial and septennial elections. It can, in short, do everything that is not naturally impossible; and therefore some have not scrupled to call its power, by a figure rather too bold, the omnipotence of Parliament. True it is, that what the Parliament doth, no authority upon earth can undo. So that it is a matter most essential to the liberties of this kingdom, that such members be delegated to this important trust, as are most eminent for their probity, their fortitude, and their knowledge; for it was a known apophthegm of the great lord treasurer Burleigh, "that England could never be ruined but by a Parliament": and, as Sir Matthew Hale observes, this being the highest and greatest court over which none other can have jurisdiction in the kingdom, if by any means a misgovernment should any way fall upon it, the subjects of this kingdom are left without all manner of remedy. To the same purpose the president Montesquieu, though I trust too hastily, presages; that as Rome, Sparta, and Carthage have lost their liberty and perished, so the constitution of England will in time lose its liberty, will perish: it will perish whenever the legislative power shall become more corrupt than the executive.[4]

De Lolme has summed up the matter in a grotesque expression which has become almost proverbial. "It is a fundamental principle with English lawyers, that Parliament can do everything but make a woman a man, and a man a woman."

Historical examples of Parliamentary sovereignty. This supreme legislative authority of Parliament is shown historically in a large number of instances.

---

4 Blackstone, *Commentaries*, i. pp. 160, 161. Compare as to sovereignty of Parliament, *De Republica Anglorum; A Discourse on the Commonwealth of England,* by Sir Thomas Smith, edited by L. Alston, Book ii, chap. i. p. 148. The book was originally published in 1583.

Act of
Settle-
ment.

The descent of the Crown was varied and finally fixed under the Act of Settlement, 12 & 13 William III., c. 2; the King occupies the throne under a Parliamentary title; his claim to reign depends upon and is the result of a statute. This is a proposition which, at the present day, no one is inclined either to maintain or to dispute; but a glance at the statute-book shows that not much more than two hundred years ago Parliament had to insist strenuously upon the principle of its own lawful supremacy. The first section of 6 Anne, c. 7, enacts (*inter alia*),

> That if any person or persons shall maliciously, advisedly, and directly by writing or printing maintain and affirm that our sovereign lady the Queen that now is, is not the lawful and rightful Queen of these realms, or that the pretended Prince of Wales, who now styles himself King of Great Britain, or King of England, by the name of James the Third, or King of Scotland, by the name of James the Eighth, hath any right or title to the Crown of these realms, or that any other person or persons hath or have any right or title to the same, otherwise than according to an Act of Parliament made in England in the first year of the reign of their late Majesties King William and Queen Mary, of ever blessed and glorious memory, intituled, An Act declaring the rights and liberties of the subject, and settling the succession of the Crown; and one other Act made in England in the twelfth year of the reign of his said late Majesty King William the Third, intituled, An Act for the further limitation of the Crown, and better securing the rights and liberties of the subject; and the Acts lately made in England and Scotland mutually for the union of the two kingdoms; or that the Kings or Queens of this realm, with and by the authority of Parliament, are not able to make laws and statutes of sufficient force and validity to limit and bind the Crown, and the descent, limitation, inheritance, and government thereof; every such person or persons shall be guilty of high treason, and being thereof lawfully convicted, shall be adjudged traitors, and shall suffer pains of death, and all losses and forfeitures as in cases of high treason.[5]

Acts of
Union.

The Acts of Union (to one of which Blackstone calls attention) afford a remarkable example of the exertion of Parliamentary authority. But there is no single statute which is more significant either as to the theory or as to the practical working of the constitution than the Septennial Act.[6] The circumstances of its enactment and the nature of the Act itself merit therefore special attention.

---

5 6 Anne, c. 41 (otherwise 6 Anne, c. 7), sec. 1. This enactment is still in force.

6 1 George I. st. 2, c. 38.

In 1716 the duration of Parliament was under an Act of 1694 limited to three years, and a general election could not be deferred beyond 1717. The King and the Ministry were convinced (and with reason) that an appeal to the electors, many of whom were Jacobites, might be perilous not only to the Ministry but to the tranquillity of the state. The Parliament then sitting, therefore, was induced by the Ministry to pass the Septennial Act by which the legal duration of parliament was extended from three to seven years, and the powers of the then existing House of Commons were in effect prolonged for four years beyond the time for which the House was elected. This was a much stronger proceeding than passing say an Act which enabled future Parliaments to continue in existence without the necessity for a general election during seven instead of during three years. The statute was justified by considerations of statesmanship and expediency. This justification of the Septennial Act must seem to every sensible man so ample that it is with some surprise that one reads in writers so fair and judicious as Hallam or Lord Stanhope attempts to minimise the importance of this supreme display of legislative authority. Hallam writes:

> Nothing can be more extravagant than what is sometimes confidently pretended by the ignorant, that the legislature exceeded its rights by this enactment; or, if that cannot legally be advanced, that it at least violated the trust of the people, and broke in upon the ancient constitution.

This remark he bases on the ground that

> the law for triennial Parliaments was of little more than twenty years' continuance. It was an experiment, which, as was argued, had proved unsuccessful; it was subject, like every other law, to be repealed entirely, or to be modified at discretion.[7]

Lord Stanhope says:

> We may . . . cast aside the foolish idea that the Parliament overstepped its legitimate authority in prolonging its existence; an idea which was indeed urged by party-spirit at the time, and which may still sometimes pass current

---

7 Hallam, *Constitutional History of England*, iii. (1872 ed.), p. 236.

in harangues to heated multitudes, but which has been treated with utter contempt by the best constitutional writers.[8]

These remarks miss the real point of the attack on the Septennial Act, and also conceal the constitutional importance of the statute. The thirty-one peers who protested against the Bill because (among other grounds)

> it is agreed, that the House of Commons must be chosen by the people, and when so chosen, they are truly the representatives of the people, which they cannot be so properly said to be, when continued for a longer time than that for which they were chosen; for after that time they are chosen by the Parliament, and not the people, who are thereby deprived of the only remedy which they have against those, who either do not understand, or through corruption, do wilfully betray the trust reposed in them; which remedy is, to choose better men in their places,[9]

hit exactly the theoretical objection to it. The peculiarity of the Act was not that it changed the legal duration of Parliament or repealed the Triennial Act; the mere passing of a Septennial Act in 1716 was not and would never have been thought to be anything more startling or open to graver censure than the passing of a Triennial Act in 1694. What was startling was that an existing Parliament of its own authority prolonged its own legal existence. Nor can the argument used by Priestley,[10] and in effect by the protesting Peers

> that Septennial Parliaments were at first a direct usurpation of the rights of the people; for by the same authority that one Parliament prolonged their own power to seven years, they might have continued it to twice seven, or like the Parliament of 1641 have made it perpetual

be treated as a blunder grounded simply on the "ignorant assumption" that the Septennial Act prolonged the original duration of Parliament.[11] The contention of Priestley and others was in substance that members elected to serve for three years were constitutionally so

---

8 Lord Mahon, *History of England*, i. p. 302.

9 Thorold Rogers, *Protests of the Lords,* i. p. 218.

10 See *Priestley on Government* (1771), p. 20.

11 Hallam, *Constitutional History*, iii. (1872 ed.), p. 236 (n.).

far at least the delegates or agents of their constituents that they could not, without an inroad on the constitution, extend their own authority beyond the period for which it was conferred upon them by their principals, *i.e.* the electors. There are countries, and notably the United States, where an Act like the Septennial Act would be held legally invalid; no modern English Parliament would for the sake of keeping a government or party in office venture to pass say a Decennial Act and thus prolong its own duration; the contention therefore that Walpole and his followers in passing the Septennial Act violated the understandings of the constitution has on the face of it nothing absurd. Parliament made a legal though unprecedented use of its powers. To under-rate this exertion of authority is to deprive the Septennial Act of its true constitutional importance. That Act proves to demonstration that in a legal point of view Parliament is neither the agent of the electors nor in any sense a trustee for its constituents. It is legally the sovereign legislative power in the state, and the Septennial Act is at once the result and the standing proof of such Parliamentary sovereignty.

Interference of Parliament with private rights.

Hitherto we have looked at Parliament as legally omnipotent in regard to public rights. Let us now consider the position of Parliament in regard to those private rights which are in civilised states justly held specially secure or sacred. Coke (it should be noted) particularly chooses interference with private rights as specimens of Parliamentary authority.

> Yet some examples are desired. Daughters and heirs apparent of a man or woman, may by Act of Parliament inherit during the life of the ancestor.
> It may adjudge an infant, or minor, of full age.
> To attaint a man of treason after his death.
> To naturalise a mere alien, and make him a subject born. It may bastard a child that by law is legitimate, viz. begotten by an adulterer, the husband being within the four seas.
> To legitimate one that is illegitimate, and born before marriage absolutely. And to legitimate *secundum quid,* but not *simpliciter.* [12]

Coke is judicious in his choice of instances. Interference with public rights is at bottom a less striking exhibition of absolute power than

---

12 Coke, *Fourth Institute,* p. 36.

is the interference with the far more important rights of individuals; a ruler who might think nothing of overthrowing the constitution of his country, would in all probability hesitate a long time before he touched the property or interfered with the contracts of private persons. Parliament, however, habitually interferes, for the public advantage, with private rights. Indeed such interference has now (greatly to the benefit of the community) become so much a matter of course as hardly to excite remark, and few persons reflect what a sign this interference is of the supremacy of Parliament. The statute-book teems with Acts under which Parliament gives privileges or rights to particular persons or imposes particular duties or liabilities upon other persons. This is of course the case with every railway Act, but no one will realise the full action, generally the very beneficial action of Parliamentary sovereignty, who does not look through a volume or two of what are called *Local and Private Acts*. These Acts are just as much Acts of Parliament as any Statute of the Realm. They deal with every kind of topic, as with railways, harbours, docks, the settlement of private estates, and the like. To these you should add Acts such as those which declare valid marriages which, owing to some mistake of form or otherwise, have not been properly celebrated, and Acts, common enough at one time but now rarely passed, for the divorce of married persons.

One further class of statutes deserve in this connection more notice than they have received—these are Acts of Indemnity.

Acts of Indemnity. An Act of Indemnity is a statute, the object of which is to make legal transactions which when they took place were illegal, or to free individuals to whom the statute applies from liability for having broken the law; enactments of this kind were annually passed with almost unbroken regularity for more than a century (1727–1828) to free Dissenters from penalties, for having accepted municipal offices without duly qualifying themselves by taking the sacrament according to the rites of the Church of England. To the subject of Acts of Indemnity, however, we shall return in a later chapter.[13] The point to be now noted is that such enactments being as it were the legalisation

---

13 See Chap. V. *post*.

of illegality are the highest exertion and crowning proof of sovereign power.

So far of the sovereignty of Parliament from its positive side: let us now look at the same doctrine from its negative aspect.

The Absence of Any Competing Legislative Power

No other competing legislative authority.

The King, each House of Parliament, the Constituencies, and the Law Courts, either have at one time claimed, or might appear to claim, independent legislative power. It will be found, however, on examination that the claim can in none of these cases be made good.

The King.

The King   Legislative authority originally resided in the King in Council, [14] and even after the commencement of Parliamentary legislation there existed side by side with it a system of royal legislation under the form of Ordinances, [15] and (at a later period) of Proclamations.

Statute of Proclamations.

These had much the force of law, and in the year 1539 the Act 31 Henry VIII., c. 8, formally empowered the Crown to legislate by means of proclamations. This statute is so short and so noteworthy that it may well be quoted *in extenso*.

> The King for the time being, with the advice of his Council, or the more part of them, may set forth proclamations under such penalties and pains as to him and them shall seem necessary, which shall be observed as though they were made by Act of Parliament; but this shall not be prejudicial to any person's inheritance, offices, liberties, goods, chattels, or life; and whosoever shall willingly offend any article contained in the said proclamations, shall pay such forfeitures, or be so long imprisoned, as shall be expressed in the said proclamations; and if any offending will depart the realm, to the intent he will not answer his said offence, he shall be adjudged a traitor. [16]

This enactment marks the highest point of legal authority ever reached by the Crown, and, probably because of its inconsistency with the whole tenor of English law, was repealed in the reign of Edward the Sixth. It is curious to notice how revolutionary would

---

14 See Stubbs, *Constitutional History*, i. pp. 126–128, and ii. pp. 245–247.

15 Stubbs, *ibid.* ii. chap. xv.

16 31 Henry VIII., c. 8.

have been the results of the statute had it remained in force. It must have been followed by two consequences. An English king would have become nearly as despotic as a French monarch. The statute would further have established a distinction between "laws" properly so called as being made by the legislature and "ordinances" having the force of law, though not in strictness laws as being rather decrees of the executive power than Acts of the legislature. This distinction exists in one form or another in most continental states, and is not without great practical utility. In foreign countries the legislature generally confines itself to laying down general principles of legislation, and leaves them with great advantage to the public to be supplemented by decrees or regulations which are the work of the executive. The cumbersomeness and prolixity of English statute law is due in no small measure to futile endeavours of Parliament to work out the details of large legislative changes. This evil has become so apparent that in modern times Acts of Parliament constantly contain provisions empowering the Privy Council, the judges, or some other body, to make rules under the Act for the determination of details which cannot be settled by Parliament. But this is only an awkward mitigation[17] of an acknowledged evil, and the substance no less than the form of the law would, it is probable, be a good deal improved if the executive government of England could, like that of France, by means of decrees, ordinances, or proclamations having the force of law, work out the detailed application of the general principles embodied in the Acts of the legislature.[18] In this, as in some other instances, restrictions wisely placed by our forefathers on the growth

---

17 A critic has objected to the words "awkward mitigation of an acknowledged evil" on the ground that they condemn in England a system which as it exists abroad is referred to as being not without great practical utility. The expression objected to is, however, justifiable. Under the English system elaborate and detailed statutes are passed, and the power to make rules under the statute, *e.g.* by order in council or otherwise, is introduced only in cases where it is obvious that to embody the rules in the statute is either highly inexpedient or practically impossible. Under the foreign, and especially the French system, the form of laws, or in other words, of statutes, is permanently affected by the knowledge of legislators and draftsmen that any law will be supplemented by decrees. English statutes attempt, and with very little success, to provide for the detailed execution of the laws enacted therein. Foreign laws are, what every law ought to be, statements of general principles.

18 See Duguit, *Manuel de Droit Public Français—Droit Constitutionnel*, ss. 140, 141.

of royal power, are at the present day the cause of unnecessary restraints on the action of the executive government. For the repeal of 31 Henry VIII., c. 8, rendered governmental legislation, with all its defects and merits, impossible, and left to proclamations only such weight as they might possess at common law. The exact extent of this authority was indeed for some time doubtful. In 1610, however, a solemn opinion or protest of the judges[19] established the modern doctrine that royal proclamations have in no sense the force of law; they serve to call the attention of the public to the law, but they cannot of themselves impose upon any man any legal obligation or duty not imposed by common law or by Act of Parliament. In 1766 Lord Chatham attempted to prohibit by force of proclamation the exportation of wheat, and the Act of Indemnity (7 George III., c. 7), passed in consequence of this attempt, may be considered the final legislative disposal of any claim on the part of the Crown to make law by force of proclamation.

The main instances[20] where, in modern times, proclamations or orders in council are of any effect are cases either where, at common law, a proclamation is the regular mode, not of legislation, but of

---

19 See Coke, 12 *Rep.* p. 74; and Gardiner, *History of England*, ii. pp. 104, 105.

20 In rare instances, which are survivals from the time when the King of England was the true "sovereign" in the technical sense of that term, the Crown exercises legislative functions in virtue of the prerogative. Thus the Crown can legislate, by proclamations or orders in council, for a newly conquered country (*Campbell* v. *Hall*, Cowp. 204), and has claimed the right, though the validity thereof is doubtful, to legislate for the Channel Islands by orders in council. *In the Matter of the States of Jersey*, 9 Moore P. C., n. s. 184, 262. See Stephen, *Commentaries* (8th ed.), i. pp. 100–102. "The Channel Islands indeed claim to have conquered England, and are the sole fragments of the dukedom of Normandy which still continue attached to the British Crown. For this reason, in these islands alone of all British possessions does any doubt arise as to whether an Act of the imperial Parliament is of its own force binding law. In practice, when an Act is intended to apply to them, a section is inserted authorising the King in Council to issue an Order for the application of the Act to these islands, and requiring the registration of that Order in the islands, and the Order in Council is made by the King and registered by the States accordingly." Sir H. Jenkyns, *British Rule and Jurisdiction beyond the Seas*, p. 37. But whatever doubt may arise in the Channel Islands, every English lawyer knows that any English court will hold that an Act of Parliament clearly intended to apply to the Channel Islands is in force there *proprio vigore*, whether registered by the States or not.

As to the legislative power of the Crown in Colonies which are not self-governing, see further *British Rule and Jurisdiction beyond the Seas*, p. 95.

announcing the executive will of the King, as when Parliament is summoned by proclamation, or else where orders in council have authority given to them by Act of Parliament.

Houses of Parliament.

Resolutions of Either House of Parliament   The House of Commons, at any rate, has from time to time appeared to claim for resolutions of the House, something like legal authority. That this pretension cannot be supported is certain, but there exists some difficulty in defining with precision the exact effect which the Courts concede to a resolution of either House.

Two points are, however, well established.

Resolutions of either House.

First, the resolution of neither House is a law.

This is the substantial result of the case of *Stockdale* v. *Hansard.*[21] The gist of the decision in that case is that a libellous document did not cease to be a libel because it was published by the order of the House of Commons, or because the House subsequently resolved that the power of publishing the report which contained it, was an essential incident to the constitutional functions of Parliament.

Secondly, each House of Parliament has complete control over its own proceedings, and also has the right to protect itself by committing for contempt any person who commits any injury against, or offers any affront to the House, and no Court of law will inquire into the mode in which either House exercises the powers which it by law possesses.[22]

The practical difficulty lies in the reconciliation of the first with the second of these propositions, and is best met by following out the analogy suggested by Mr. Justice Stephen, between a resolution of the House of Commons, and the decision of a Court from which there is no appeal.

> I do not say that the resolution of the House is the judgment of a Court not subject to our revision; but it has much in common with such a judgment. The House of Commons is not a Court of Justice; but the effect of its privilege to regulate its own internal concerns, practically invests it with a judicial

---

21 9 A. & E. 1.

22 See *Stockdale* v. *Hansard,* 9 A. & E. 1; *Case of Sheriff of Middlesex,* 11 A. & E. 273; *Burdett* v. *Abbot,* 14 East, 1, 111, 131; *Bradlaugh* v. *Gossett,* 12 Q. B. D. 272.

character when it has to apply to particular cases the provisions of Acts of Parliament. We must presume that it discharges this function properly, and with due regard to the laws, in the making of which it has so great a share. If its determination is not in accordance with law, this resembles the case of an error by a judge whose decision is not subject to appeal. There is nothing startling in the recognition of the fact that such an error is possible. If, for instance, a jury in a criminal case give a perverse verdict, the law has provided no remedy. The maxim that there is no wrong without a remedy, does not mean, as it is sometimes supposed, that there is a legal remedy for every moral or political wrong. If this were its meaning, it would be manifestly untrue. There is no legal remedy for the breach of a solemn promise not under seal, and made without consideration; nor for many kinds of verbal slander, though each may involve utter ruin; nor for oppressive legislation, though it may reduce men practically to slavery; nor for the worst damage to person and property inflicted by the most unjust and cruel war. The maxim means only that legal wrong and legal remedy are correlative terms; and it would be more intelligibly and correctly stated, if it were reversed, so as to stand, "Where there is no legal remedy, there is no legal wrong."[23]

Law as to effect of resolutions of either House.

The law therefore stands thus. Either House of Parliament has the fullest power over its own proceedings, and can, like a Court, commit for contempt any person who, in the judgment of the House, is guilty of insult or affront to the House. The *Case of the Sheriff of Middlesex*[24] carries this right to the very farthest point. The Sheriff was imprisoned for contempt under a warrant issued by the Speaker. Every one knew that the alleged contempt was nothing else than obedience by the Sheriff to the judgment of the Court of Queen's Bench in the case of *Stockdale* v. *Hansard*, and that the Sheriff was imprisoned by the House because under such judgment he took the goods of the defendant Hansard in execution. Yet when the Sheriff was brought by *Habeas Corpus* before the Queen's Bench the Judges held that they could not inquire what were the contempts for which the Sheriff was committed by the House. The Courts, in other words, do not claim any right to protect their own officials from being imprisoned by the House of Commons for alleged contempt of the House, even though the so-called contempt is nothing else than an act of obedience to the Courts. A declaration or resolution of either House, on the other

---

23 *Bradlaugh* v. *Gossett*, 12 Q. B. D. 271, 285.

24 11 A. & E. 273.

hand, is not in any sense a law. Suppose that *X* were by order of the House of Commons to assault *A* out of the House, irrespective of any act done in the House, and not under a warrant committing *A* for contempt; or suppose that *X* were to commit some offence by which he incurred a fine under some Act of Parliament, and that such fine were recoverable by *A* as a common informer. No resolution of the House of Commons ordering or approving of *X's* act could be pleaded by *X* as a legal defence to proceedings, either civil or criminal, against him.[25] If proof of this were wanted it would be afforded by the Act 3 & 4 Vict. c. 9. The object of this Act, passed in consequence of the controversy connected with the case of *Stockdale* v. *Hansard,* is to give summary protection to persons employed in the publication of Parliamentary papers, which are, it should be noted, papers published by the order of one or other of the Houses of Parliament. The necessity for such an Act is the clearest proof that an order of the House is not of itself a legal defence for the publication of matters which would otherwise be libellous. The House of Commons

> by invoking the authority of the whole Legislature to give validity to the plea they had vainly set up in the action [of *Stockdale* v. *Hansard*], and by not appealing against the judgment of the Court of Queen's Bench, had, in effect, admitted the correctness of that judgment and affirmed the great principle on which it was founded, viz. that no single branch of the Legislature can, by an assertion of its alleged privileges, alter, suspend, or supersede any known law of the land, or bar the resort of any Englishman to any remedy, or his exercise and enjoyment of any right, by that law established.[26]

---

25 Conf. *Attorney -General* v. *Bradlaugh,* 14 Q. B. D. (C. A.), 667.

26 Arnould, *Memoir of Lord Denman,* ii. p. 70. Nothing is harder to define than the extent of the indefinite powers or rights possessed by either House of Parliament under the head of privilege or law and custom of Parliament. The powers exercised by the Houses, and especially in practice by the House of Commons, make a near approach to an authority above that of the ordinary law of the land. Parliamentary privilege has from the nature of things never been the subject of precise legal definition. One or two points are worth notice as being clearly established.

1. Either House of Parliament may commit for contempt, and the Courts will not go behind the committal and inquire into the facts constituting the alleged contempt. Hence either House may commit to prison for contempt any person whom the House think guilty of contempt.

The Vote of the Parliamentary Electors   Expressions are constantly used in the course of political discussions which imply that the body of persons entitled to choose members of Parliament possess under the English constitution some kind of legislative authority. Such language is, as we shall see, not without a real meaning;[27] it points to the important consideration that the wishes of the constituencies influence the action of Parliament. But any expressions which attribute to Parliamentary electors a legal part in the process of law-making are quite inconsistent with the view taken by the law of the position of an elector. The sole legal right of electors under the English constitution is to elect members of Parliament. Electors have no legal means of initiating, of sanctioning, or of repealing the legislation of Parliament. No Court will consider for a moment the argument that a law is invalid as being opposed to the opinion of the electorate; their opinion can be legally expressed through Parliament, and through Parliament alone. This is not a necessary incident of representative government. In Switzerland no change can be introduced in the constitution[28] which has not been submitted for approval or disapproval to all male citizens who have attained their majority; and even an ordinary law which does not involve a change in the constitution may, after it has been passed by the Federal Assembly, be submitted

---

2. The House of Lords have power to commit an offender to prison for a specified term, even beyond the duration of the session (May, *Parliamentary Practice* (11th ed.), pp. 91, 92). But the House of Commons do not commit for a definite period, and prisoners committed by the House are, if not sooner discharged, released from their confinement on a prorogation. If they were held longer in custody they would be discharged by the Courts upon a writ of Habeas Corpus (May, *Parliamentary Practice,* chap. iii.).

3. A libel upon either House of Parliament or upon a member thereof, in his character of a member, has been often treated as a contempt. (*Ibid.*)

4. The Houses and all the members thereof have all the privileges as to freedom of speech, etc., necessary for the performance of their duties. (See generally May's *Parliamentary Practice,* chap. iii.) Compare as to Parliamentary privilege *Shaftesbury's Case,* 6 St. Tr. 1269; *Flower's Case,* 8 T. R. 314; *Ashby* v. *White,* 1 Sm. L. Cas. (9th ed.), 268; *Wilkes's Case,* 19 St. Tr. 1153; *Burdett* v. *Colman,* 14 East, 163; *Rex* v. *Creevy,* 1 M. & S. 273; *Clarke* v. *Bradlaugh,* 7 Q. B. D. 38, 8. App. Cas. 354; *The Attorney-General* v. *Bradlaugh,* 14 Q. B. D. 667.

27 See pp. 27–30, *post.*

28 *Constitution Fédérale de la Confédération Swisse,* Arts. 118–121; see Adams, *The Swiss Confederation,* chap. vi.

on the demand of a certain number of citizens to a popular vote, and is annulled if a vote is not obtained in its favour.[29]

The Courts.

The Law Courts   A large proportion of English law is in reality made by the judges, and whoever wishes to understand the nature and the extent of judicial legislation in England, should read Pollock's admirable essay on the *Science of Case Law*.[30] The topic is too wide a one to be considered at any length in these lectures. All that we need note is that the adhesion by our judges to precedent, that is, their habit of deciding one case in accordance with the principle, or supposed principle, which governed a former case, leads inevitably to the gradual formation by the Courts of fixed rules for decision, which are in effect laws. This judicial legislation might appear, at first sight, inconsistent with the supremacy of Parliament. But this is not so. English judges do not claim or exercise any power to repeal a Statute, whilst Acts of Parliament may override and constantly do override the law of the judges. Judicial legislation is, in short, subordinate legislation, carried on with the assent and subject to the supervision of Parliament.

ALLEGED LEGAL LIMITATIONS ON THE LEGISLATIVE SOVEREIGNTY OF PARLIAMENT

Alleged limitations.

All that can be urged as to the speculative difficulties of placing any limits whatever on sovereignty has been admirably stated by Austin and by Professor Holland.[31] With these difficulties we have, at this moment, no concern. Nor is it necessary to examine whether it be or be not true, that there must necessarily be found in every state some person, or combination of persons, which, according to the constitution, whatever be its form, can legally change every law, and there-

---

29 *Constitution Fédérale de la Confédération Swisse,* Art. 89.

30 Pollock, *Essays in Jurisprudence and Ethics,* p. 237, and see Dicey, *Law and Opinion in England* (2nd ed.), pp. 361, 483.

31 See Austin, *Jurisprudence,* i. (4th ed.), pp. 270–274, and Holland, *Jurisprudence* (10th ed.), pp. 47–52 and 359–363. The nature of sovereignty is also stated with brevity and clearness in Lewis, *Use and Abuse of Political Terms,* pp. 37–53. Compare, for a different view, Bryce, *Studies in History and Jurisprudence,* ii., Essay ix., Obedience; and Essay x., The Nature of Sovereignty.

fore constitutes the legally supreme power in the state. Our whole business is now to carry a step further the proof that, under the English constitution, Parliament does constitute such a supreme legislative authority or sovereign power as, according to Austin and other jurists, must exist in every civilised state, and for that purpose to examine into the validity of the various suggestions, which have from time to time been made, as to the possible limitations on Parliamentary authority, and to show that none of them are countenanced by English law.

The suggested limitations are three in number.[32]

Moral law.
First, Acts of Parliament, it has been asserted, are invalid if they are opposed to the principles of morality or to the doctrines of international law. Parliament, it is in effect asserted, cannot make a law opposed to the dictates of private or public morality. Thus Blackstone lays down in so many words that the

> law of nature being coeval with mankind, and dictated by God himself, is of course superior in obligation to any other. It is binding over all the globe, in all countries, and at all times: no human laws are of any validity if contrary to this; and such of them as are valid derive all their force and all their authority, mediately or immediately, from this original;[33]

and expressions are sometimes used by modern judges which imply that the Courts might refuse to enforce statutes going beyond the proper limits (internationally speaking) of Parliamentary authority.[34] But to words such as those of Blackstone, and to the *obiter dicta* of the Bench, we must give a very qualified interpretation. There is no legal basis for the theory that judges, as exponents of morality, may overrule Acts of Parliament. Language which might seem to imply this

---

32 Another limitation has been suggested more or less distinctly by judges such as Coke (12 *Rep.* 76; and Hearn, *Government of England* (2nd ed.), pp. 48, 49); an Act of Parliament cannot (it has been intimated) overrule the principles of the common law. This doctrine once had a real meaning (see Maine, *Early History of Institutions*, pp. 381, 382), but it has never received systematic judicial sanction and is now obsolete. See Colonial Laws Validity Act, 1865, 28 & 29 Vict. c. 63.

33 Blackstone, *Commentaries*, i. p. 40; and see Hearn, *Government of England* (2nd ed.), pp. 48, 49.

34 See *Ex parte Blain,* 12 Ch. D. (C. A.), 522, 531, judgment of Cotton, L. J.

amounts in reality to nothing more than the assertion that the judges, when attempting to ascertain what is the meaning to be affixed to an Act of Parliament, will presume that Parliament did not intend to violate[35] the ordinary rules of morality, or the principles of international law, and will therefore, whenever possible, give such an interpretation to a statutory enactment as may be consistent with the doctrines both of private and of international morality. A modern judge would never listen to a barrister who argued that an Act of Parliament was invalid because it was immoral, or because it went beyond the limits of Parliamentary authority. The plain truth is that our tribunals uniformly act on the principle that a law alleged to be a bad law is *ex hypothesi* a law, and therefore entitled to obedience by the Courts.

Prerogative.   *Secondly,* doctrines have at times[36] been maintained which went very near to denying the right of Parliament to touch the Prerogative.

In the time of the Stuarts[37] the doctrine was maintained, not only by the King, but by lawyers and statesmen who, like Bacon, favoured the increase of royal authority, that the Crown possessed under the name of the "prerogative" a reserve, so to speak, of wide and indefinite rights and powers, and that this prerogative or residue of sovereign power was superior to the ordinary law of the land. This doctrine combined with the deduction from it that the Crown could suspend the operation of statutes, or at any rate grant dispensation from obedience to them, certainly suggested the notion that the high powers of the prerogative were to a certain extent beyond the reach of Parliamentary enactment. We need not, however, now enter into the political controversies of another age. All that need be noticed is that though certain powers—as, for example, the right of making treaties—are now left by law in the hands of the Crown, and are exercised in fact by the executive government, no modern lawyer would maintain that these powers or any other branch of royal au-

---

35 See *Colquhoun* v. *Brooks,* 21 Q. B. D. (C. A.), 52; and compare the language of Lord Esher, pp. 57, 58, with the judgment of Fry, L. J., *ibid.* pp. 61. 62.

36 See Stubbs, *Constitutional History,* ii. pp. 239, 486, 513–515.

37 Gardiner, *History,* iii. pp. 1–5; compare, as to Bacon's view of the prerogative, *Francis Bacon,* by Edwin A. Abbott, pp. 140, 260, 279.

thority could not be regulated or abolished by Act of Parliament, or, what is the same thing, that the judges might legally treat as invalid a statute, say, regulating the mode in which treaties are to be made, or making the assent or the Houses of Parliament necessary to the validity of a treaty.[38]

Thirdly, language has occasionally been used in Acts of Parliament which implies that one Parliament can make laws which cannot be touched by any subsequent Parliament, and that therefore the legislative authority of an existing Parliament may be limited by the enactments of its predecessors.[39]

That Parliaments have more than once intended and endeavoured to pass Acts which should tie the hands of their successors is certain, but the endeavour has always ended in failure. Of statutes intended to arrest the possible course of future legislation, the most noteworthy are the Acts which embody the treaties of Union with Scotland[40] and Ireland.[41] The legislators who passed these Acts assuredly intended to give to certain portions of them more than the ordinary effect of statutes. Yet the history of legislation in respect of these very

---

38 Compare the parliamentary practice in accordance with which the consent or recommendation of the Crown is required to the introduction of bills touching the prerogative or the interests of the Crown.

39 This doctrine was known to be erroneous by Bacon. "The principal law that was made this Parliament was a law of a strange nature, rather just than legal, and more magnanimous than provident. This law did ordain, That no person that did assist in arms or otherwise the King for the time being, should after be impeached therefor, or attainted either by the course of law or by Act of Parliament; for if any such act of attainder did hap to be made, it should be void and of none effect. . . . But the force and obligation of this law was in itself illusory, as to the latter part of it; (by a precedent Act of Parliament to bind or frustrate a future). For a supreme and absolute power cannot conclude itself, neither can that which is in nature revocable be made fixed; no more than if a man should appoint or declare by his will that if he made any later will it should be void. And for the case of the Act of Parliament, there is a notable precedent of it in King Henry the Eighth's time, who doubting he might die in the minority of his son, provided an Act to pass, That no statute made during the minority of a king should bind him or his successors, except it were confirmed by the king under his great seal at his full age. But the first Act that passed in King Edward the Sixth's time was an Act of repeal of that former Act; at which time nevertheless the King was minor. But things that do not bind may satisfy for the time." *Works of Francis Bacon*, vi., by Spedding, Ellis, and Heath (1861), pp. 159, 160.

40 The Union with Scotland Act, 1706, 6 Anne, c. 11.

41 The Union with Ireland Act, 1800, 39 & 40 Geo. III., c. 67.

Acts affords the strongest proof of the futility inherent in every attempt of one sovereign legislature to restrain the action of another equally sovereign body. Thus the Act of Union with Scotland enacts in effect that every professor of a Scotch University shall acknowledge and profess and subscribe the Confession of Faith as his profession of faith, and in substance enacts that this provision shall be a fundamental and essential condition of the treaty of union in all time coming.[42] But this very provision has been in its main part repealed by the Universities (Scotland) Act, 1853,[43] which relieves most professors in the Scotch universities from the necessity of subscribing the Confession of Faith. Nor is this by any means the only inroad made upon the terms of the Act of Union; from one point of view at any rate the Act 10 Anne, c. 12,[44] restoring the exercise of lay patronage, was a direct infringement upon the Treaty of Union. The intended unchangeableness, and the real liability of these Acts or treaties to be changed by Parliament, comes out even more strikingly in the history of the Act of Union with Ireland. The fifth Article of that Act runs as follows:

> That it be the fifth article of Union, that the Churches of England and Ireland as now by law established, be united into one Protestant episcopal Church, to be called the United Church of England and Ireland; and that the doctrine, worship, discipline, and government of the said United Church shall be and shall remain in full force for ever, as the same are now by law established for the Church of England; and that the continuance and preservation of the said United Church , as the established Church of England and Ireland, shall be deemed and be taken to be an essential and fundamental part of the Union.

That the statesmen who drew and passed this Article meant to bind the action of future Parliaments is apparent from its language. That the attempt has failed of success is apparent to every one who knows the contents of the Irish Church Act, 1869.

Act limiting right of Parliament to tax colonies.

One Act, indeed, of the British Parliament might, looked at in the light of history, claim a peculiar sanctity. It is certainly an enactment

---

42 See 6 Anne, c. 11, art. 25.

43 16 & 17 Vict. c. 89, s. 1.

44 Compare Innes, *Law of Creeds in Scotland,* pp. 118–121.

of which the terms, we may safely predict, will never be repealed and the spirit will never be violated. This Act is the Taxation of Colonies Act, 1778.[45] It provides that Parliament

> will not impose any duty, tax, or assessment whatever, payable in any of his Majesty's colonies, provinces, and plantations in North America or the West Indies; except only such duties as it may be expedient to impose for the regulation of commerce; the net produce of such duties to be always paid and applied to and for the use of the colony, province, or plantation, in which the same shall be respectively levied, in such manner as other duties collected by the authority of the respective general courts, or general assemblies, of such colonies, provinces, or plantations, are ordinarily paid and applied.[46]

This language becomes the more impressive when contrasted with the American Colonies Act, 1776,[47] which, being passed in that year to repeal the Acts imposing the Stamp Duties, carefully avoids any surrender of Parliament's right to tax the colonies. There is no need to dwell on the course of events of which these two Acts are a statutory record. The point calling for attention is that though policy and prudence condemn the repeal of the Taxation of Colonies Act, 1778, or the enactment of any law inconsistent with its spirit, there is under our constitution no legal difficulty in the way of repealing or overriding this Act. If Parliament were tomorrow to impose a tax, say on New Zealand or on the Canadian Dominion, the statute imposing it would be a legally valid enactment. As stated in short by a very judicious writer—

> It is certain that a Parliament cannot so bind its successors by the terms of any statute, as to limit the discretion of a future Parliament, and thereby disable the Legislature from entire freedom of action at any future time when it might be needful to invoke the interposition of Parliament to legislate for the public welfare.[48]

---

45 18 Geo. III., c. 12.

46 18 Geo. III., c. 12, s. 1.

47 6 Geo. III., c. 12.

48 Todd, *Parliamentary Government in the British Colonies*, p. 192. It is a matter of curious, though not uninstructive, speculation to consider why it is that Parliament, though on several occasions passing Acts which were intended to be immutable, has never in reality succeeded in restricting its own legislative authority.

This question may be considered either logically or historically.

Parliamentary sovereignty is therefore an undoubted legal fact.

It is complete both on its positive and on its negative side. Parliament can legally legislate on any topic whatever which, in the judgment of Parliament, is a fit subject for legislation. There is no power which, under the English constitution, can come into rivalry with the legislative sovereignty of Parliament.

The logical reason why Parliament has failed in its endeavours to enact unchangeable enactments is that a sovereign power cannot, while retaining its sovereign character, restrict its own powers by any particular enactment. An Act, whatever its terms, passed by Parliament might be repealed in a subsequent, or indeed in the same, session, and there would be nothing to make the authority of the repealing Parliament less than the authority of the Parliament by which the statute, intended to be immutable, was enacted. "Limited Sovereignty," in short, is in the case of a Parliamentary as of every other sovereign, a contradiction in terms. Its frequent and convenient use arises from its in reality signifying, and being by any one who uses words with any accuracy understood to signify, that some person, *e.g.* a king, who was at one time a real sovereign or despot, and who is in name treated as an actual sovereign, has become only a part of the power which is legally supreme or sovereign in a particular state. This, it may be added, is the true position of the king in most constitutional monarchies.

Let the reader, however, note that the impossibility of placing a limit of the exercise of sovereignty does not in any way prohibit either logically, or in matter of fact, the abdication of sovereignty. This is worth observation, because a strange dogma is sometimes put forward that a sovereign power, such as the Parliament of the United Kingdom, can never by its own act divest itself of sovereignty. This position is, however, clearly untenable. An autocrat, such as the Russian Czar, can undoubtedly abdicate; but sovereignty or the possession of supreme power in a state, whether it be in the hands of a Czar or of a Parliament, is always one and the same quality. If the Czar can abdicate, so can a Parliament. To argue or imply that because sovereignty is not limitable (which is true) it cannot be surrendered (which is palpably untrue) involves the confusion of two distinct ideas. It is like arguing that because no man can, while he lives, give up, do what he will, his freedom of volition, so no man can commit suicide. A sovereign power can divest itself of authority in two ways, and (it is submitted) in two ways only. It may simply put an end to its own existence. Parliament could extinguish itself by legally dissoving itself and leaving no means whereby a subsequent Parliament could be legally summoned. (See Bryce, *American Commonwealth*, i, (3rd ed.), p. 242, note 1.) A step nearly approaching to this was taken by the Barebones Parliament when, in 1653, it resigned its power into the hands of Cromwell. A sovereign again may transfer sovereign authority to another person or body of persons. The Parliament of England went very near doing this when, in 1539, the Crown was empowered to legislate by proclamation; and though the fact is often overlooked, the Parliaments both of England and of Scotland did, at the time of the Union, each transfer sovereign power to a new sovereign body, namely, the Parliament of Great Britain. This Parliament, however, just because it acquired the full authority of the two legislatures by which it was constituted, became in its turn a legally supreme or sovereign legislature, authorised therefore, though contrary perhaps to the intention of its creators, to modify or

No one of the limitations alleged to be imposed by law on the absolute authority of Parliament has any real existence, or receives any countenance, either from the statute-book or from the practice of the Courts.

This doctrine of the legislative supremacy of Parliament is the very keystone of the law of the constitution. But it is, we must admit, a dogma which does not always find ready acceptance, and it is well worth while to note and examine the difficulties which impede the admission of its truth.

---

abrogate the Act of Union by which it was constituted. If indeed the Act of Union had left alive the Parliaments of England and of Scotland, though for one purpose only, namely, to modify when necessary the Act of Union, and had conferred upon the Parliament of Great Britain authority to pass any law whatever which did not infringe upon or repeal the Act of Union, then the Act of Union would have been a fundamental law unchangeable legally by the British Parliament: but in this case the Parliament of Great Britain would have been, not a sovereign, but a subordinate, legislature, and the ultimate sovereign body, in the technical sense of that term, would have been the two Parliaments of England and of Scotland respectively. The statesmen of these two countries saw fit to constitute a new sovereign Parliament, and every attempt to tie the hands of such a body necessarily breaks down, on the logical and practical impossibility of combining absolute legislative authority with restrictions on that authority which, if valid, would make it cease to be absolute.

The historical reason why Parliament has never succeeded in passing immutable laws, or in other words, has always retained its character of a supreme legislature, lies deep in the history of the English people and in the peculiar development of the English constitution. England has, at any rate since the Norman Conquest, been always governed by an absolute legislator. This lawgiver was originally the Crown, and the peculiarity of the process by which the English constitution has been developed lies in the fact that the legislative authority of the Crown has never been curtailed, but has been transferred from the Crown acting alone (or rather in Council) to the Crown acting first together with, and then in subordination to, the Houses of Parliament. Hence Parliament, or in technical terms the King in Parliament, has become—it would perhaps be better to say has always remained—a supreme legislature. It is well worth notice that on the one occasion when English reformers broke from the regular course of English historical development, they framed a written constitution, anticipating in many respects the constitutionalism of the United States, and placed the constitution beyond the control of the ordinary legislature. It is quite clear that, under the Instrument of Government of 1653, Cromwell intended certain fundamentals to be beyond the reach of Parliament. It may be worth observing that the constitution of 1653 placed the Executive beyond the control of the legislature. The Protector under it occupied a position which may well be compared either with that of the American President or of the German Emperor. See Harrison, *Cromwell*, pp. 194–203. For a view of sovereignty which, though differing to a certain extent from the view put forward in this work, is full of interest and instruction, my readers are referred to Professor Sidgwick's *Elements of Politics*, ch. xxxi. "Sovereignty and Order."

DIFFICULTIES AS TO THE DOCTRINE
OF PARLIAMENTARY SOVEREIGNTY

Difficulties as to Parliamentary sovereignty.

The reasons why many persons find it hard to accept the doctrine of Parliamentary sovereignty are twofold.

Difficulty from Austin's theory.

The dogma sounds like a mere application to the British constitution of Austin's theory of sovereignty, and yet intelligent students of Austin must have noticed that Austin's own conclusion as to the persons invested with sovereign power under the British constitution does not agree with the view put forward, on the authority of English lawyers, in these lectures. For while lawyers maintain that sovereignty resides in "Parliament," *i.e.* in the body constituted by the King, the House of Lords, and the House of Commons, Austin holds[49] that the sovereign power is vested in the King, the House of Lords, and the Commons or the electors.

Difficulty from actual limitation on power of Parliament.

Every one, again, knows as a matter of common sense that, whatever lawyers may say, the sovereign power of Parliament is not unlimited, and that King, Lords, and Commons united do not possess anything like that "restricted omnipotence"—if the term may be excused—which is the utmost authority ascribable to any human institution. There are many enactments, and these laws not in themselves obviously unwise or tyrannical, which Parliament never would and (to speak plainly) never could pass. If the doctrine of Parliamentary sovereignty involves the attribution of unrestricted power to Parliament, the dogma is no better than a legal fiction, and certainly is not worth the stress here laid upon it.

Both these difficulties are real and reasonable difficulties. They are, it will be found, to a certain extent connected together, and well repay careful consideration.

Criticism on Austin's theory.

As to Austin's theory of sovereignty in relation to the British constitution, sovereignty, like many of Austin's conceptions, is a generalisation drawn in the main from English law, just as the ideas

---

49 See Austin, *Jurisprudence*, i. (4th ed.), pp. 251–255. Compare Austin's language as to the sovereign body under the constitution of the United States. (Austin, *Jurisprudence,* i. (4th ed.), p. 268.)

of the economists of Austin's generation are (to a great extent) generalisations suggested by the circumstances of English commerce. In
England we are accustomed to the existence of a supreme legislative
body, *i.e.* a body which can make or unmake every law; and which,
therefore, cannot be bound by any law. This is, from a legal point of
view, the true conception of a sovereign, and the ease with which the
theory of absolute sovereignty has been accepted by English jurists is
due to the peculiar history of English constitutional law. So far, therefore, from its being true that the sovereignty of Parliament is a deduction from abstract theories of jurisprudence, a critic would come
nearer the truth who asserted that Austin's theory of sovereignty is
suggested by the position of the English Parliament, just as Austin's
analysis of the term "law" is at Bottom an analysis of a typical law,
namely, an English criminal statute.

It should, however, be carefully noted that the term "sovereignty,"
as long as it is accurately employed in the sense in which Austin
sometimes[50] uses it, is a merely legal conception, and means simply
the power of law-making unrestricted by any legal limit. If the term
"sovereignty" be thus used, the sovereign power under the English
constitution is clearly "Parliament." But the word "sovereignty" is
sometimes employed in a political rather than in a strictly legal sense.
That body is "politically" sovereign or supreme in a state the will of
which is ultimately obeyed by the citizens of the state. In this sense of
the word the electors of Great Britain may be said to be, together with
the Crown and the Lords, or perhaps, in strict accuracy, independently of the King and the Peers, the body in which sovereign power
is vested. For, as things now stand, the will of the electorate, and
certainly of the electorate in combination with the Lords and the
Crown, is sure ultimately to prevail on all subjects to be determined
by the British government. The matter indeed may be carried a little
further, and we may assert that the arrangements of the constitution
are now such as to ensure that the will of the electors shall by regular
and constitutional means always in the end assert itself as the pre-

---

50 Compare Austin, *Jurisprudence*, i. (4th ed.), p. 268.

dominant influence in the country. But this is a political, not a legal
fact. The electors can in the long run[51] always enforce their will. But
the Courts will take no notice of the will of the electors. The judges
know nothing about any will of the people except in so far as that will
is expressed by an Act of Parliament, and would never suffer the
validity of a statute to be questioned on the ground of its having been
passed or being kept alive in opposition to the wishes of the electors.
The political sense of the word "sovereignty" is, it is true, fully as
important as the legal sense or more so. But the two significations,
though intimately connected together, are essentially different, and
in some part of his work Austin has apparently confused the one
sense with the other. He writes:

> Adopting the language of some of the writers who have treated of the
> British constitution, I commonly suppose that the present parliament, or the
> parliament for the time being, is possessed of the sovereignty: or I commonly
> suppose that the King and the Lords, with the members of the Commons'
> house, form a tripartite body which is sovereign or supreme. But, speaking
> accurately, the members of the Commons' house are merely trustees for
> the body by which they are elected and appointed: and, consequently, the
> sovereignty always resides in the King and the Peers, with the electoral body

---

51 The working of a constitution is greatly affected by the rate at which the will of the
political sovereign can make itself felt. In this matter we may compare the constitutions of
the United States, of the Swiss Confederacy, and of the United Kingdom respectively. In
each case the people of the country, or to speak more accurately the electorate, are politically sovereign. The action of the people of the United States in changing the Federal
Constitution is impeded by many difficulties, and is practically slow; the Federal Constitution has, except after the civil war, not been materially changed during the century which
has elapsed since its formation. The Articles of the Swiss Confederation admit of more easy
change than the Articles of the United States Constitution, and since 1848 have undergone
considerable modification. But though in one point of view the present constitution, revised
in 1874, may be considered a new constitution, it does not differ fundamentally from that of
1848. As things now stand, the people of England can change any part of the law of the
constitution with extreme rapidity. Theoretically there is no check on the action of Parliament whatever, and it may be conjectured that in practice any change however fundamental would be at once carried through, which was approved of by one House of Commons,
and, after a dissolution of Parliament, was supported by the newly elected House. The
paradoxical and inaccurate assertion, therefore, that England is more democratically governed than either the United States or Switzerland, contains a certain element of truth; the
immediate wishes of a decided majority of the electorate of the United Kingdom can be
more rapidly carried into legal effect than can the immediate wishes of a majority among
the people either of America or of Switzerland.

of the Commons. That a trust is imposed by the party delegating, and that the party representing engages to discharge the trust, seems to be imported by the correlative expressions *delegation* and *representation*. It were absurd to suppose that the delegating empowers the representative party to defeat or abandon any of the purposes for which the latter is appointed: to suppose, for example, that the Commons empower their representatives in parliament to relinquish their share in the sovereignty to the King and the Lords.[52]

Austin owns that the doctrine here laid down by him is inconsistent with the language used by writers who have treated of the British constitution. It is further absolutely inconsistent with the validity of the Septennial Act. Nothing is more certain than that no English judge ever conceded, or, under the present constitution, can concede, that Parliament is in any legal sense a "trustee"[53] for the electors. Of such a feigned "trust" the Courts know nothing. The plain truth is that as a matter of law Parliament is the sovereign power in the state, and that the "supposition" treated by Austin as inaccurate is the correct statement of a legal fact which forms the basis of our whole legislative and judicial system. It is, however, equally true that in a political sense the electors are the most important part of, we may even say are actually, the sovereign power, since their will is under the present constitution sure to obtain ultimate obedience. The language therefore of Austin is as correct in regard to "political" sovereignty as it is erroneous in regard to what we may term "legal" sovereignty. The electors are a part of and the predominant part of the politically sovereign power. But the legally sovereign power is assuredly, as maintained by all the best writers on the constitution, nothing but Parliament.

It may be conjectured that the error of which (from a lawyer's point of view) Austin has been guilty arises from his feeling, as every person must feel who is not the slave to mere words, that Parliament is (as already pointed out[54]) nothing like an omnipotent body, but that its powers are practically limited in more ways than one. And

---

52 Austin, *Jurisprudence*, i. (4th ed.), p. 253.

53 This Austin concedes, but the admission is fatal to the contention that Parliament is not in strictness a sovereign. (See Austin *Jurisprudence*, i. (4th ed.), pp. 252, 253.)

54 See p. 26, *ante*.

this limitation Austin expresses, not very happily, by saying that the members of the House of Commons are subject to a trust imposed upon them by the electors. This, however, leads us to our second difficulty, namely, the coexistence of parliamentary sovereignty with the fact of actual limitations on the power of Parliment.

Existence of actual limitations to power not inconsistent with sovereignty. As to the actual limitations on the sovereign power of Parliament, the actual exercise of authority by any sovereign whatever, and notably by Parliament, is bounded or controlled by two limitations. Of these the one is an external, the other is an internal limitation.

External limit. The external limit to the real power of a sovereign consists in the possibility or certainty that his subjects, or a large number of them, will disobey or resist his laws.

This limitation exists even under the most despotic monarchies. A Roman Emperor, or a French King during the middle of the eighteenth century, was (as is the Russian Czar at the present day) in strictness a "sovereign" in the legal sense of that term. He had absolute legislative authority. Any law made by him was binding, and there was no power in the empire or kingdom which could annul such law. It may also be true,—though here we are passing from the legal to the political sense of sovereignty,—that the will of an absolute monarch is in general obeyed by the bulk of his subjects. But it would be an error to suppose that the most absolute ruler who ever existed could in reality make or change every law at his pleasure. That this must be so results from considerations which were long ago pointed out by Hume. Force, he teaches, is in one sense always on the side of the governed, and government therefore in a sense always depends upon opinion. He writes:

> Nothing appears more surprising to those, who consider human affairs with a philosophical eye, than the easiness with which the many are governed by the few; and the implicit submission, with which men resign their own sentiments and passions to those of their rulers. When we inquire by what means this wonder is effected, we shall find, that, as force is always on the side of the governed, the governors have nothing to support them but opinion. It is, therefore, on opinion only that government is founded; and this maxim extends to the most despotic and most military governments, as well as to the most free and most popular. The Soldan of Egypt, or the Emperor of Rome, might drive his harmless subjects, like brute beasts,

against their sentiments and inclination: But he must, at least, have led his *mamalukes* or *prætorian bands*, like men, by their opinion.[55]

Illus-
trations of
external
limit on
exercise of
sovereign
power.

The authority, that is to say, even of a despot, depends upon the readiness of his subjects or of some portion of his subjects to obey his behests; and this readiness to obey must always be in reality limited. This is shown by the most notorious facts of history. None of the early Cæsars could at their pleasure have subverted the worship or fundamental institutions of the Roman world, and when Constantine carried through a religious revolution his success was due to the sympathy of a large part of his subjects. The Sultan could not abolish Mahommedanism. Louis the Fourteenth at the height of his power could revoke the Edict of Nantes, but he would have found it impossible to establish the supremacy of Protestantism, and for the same reason which prevented James the Second from establishing the supremacy of Roman Catholicism. The one king was in the strict sense despotic; the other was as powerful as any English monarch. But the might of each was limited by the certainty of popular disobedience or opposition. The unwillingness of subjects to obey may have reference not only to great changes, but even to small matters. The French National Assembly of 1871 was emphatically the sovereign power in France. The majority of its members were (it is said) prepared for a monarchical restoration, but they were not prepared to restore the white flag: the army which would have acquiesced in the return of the Bourbons, would not (it was anticipated) tolerate the sight of an anti-revolutionary symbol: "the *chassepots* would go off of themselves." Here we see the precise limit to the exercise of legal sovereignty; and what is true of the power of a despot or of the authority of a constituent assembly is specially true of the sovereignty of Parliament; it is limited on every side by the possibility of popular resistance. Parliament might legally establish an Episcopal Church in Scotland; Parliament might legally tax the Colonies; Parliament might without any breach of law change the succession to the throne or abolish the monarchy; but every one knows that in the present state of the world the British Parliament will do none of these things. In

---

55 Hume, *Essays,* i. (1875 ed.), pp. 109, 110.

each case widespread resistance would result from legislation which, though legally valid, is in fact beyond the stretch of Parliamentary power. Nay, more than this, there are things which Parliament has done in other times, and done successfully, which a modern Parliament would not venture to repeat. Parliament would not at the present day prolong by law the duration of an existing House of Commons. Parliament would not without great hesitation deprive of their votes large classes of Parliamentary electors; and, speaking generally, Parliament would not embark on a course of reactionary legislation; persons who honestly blame Catholic Emancipation and lament the disestablishment of the Irish Church do not dream that Parliament could repeal the statutes of 1829 or of 1869. These examples from among a score are enough to show the extent to which the theoretically boundless sovereignty of Parliament is curtailed by the external limit to its exercise.

Internal limit. Illustrations.   The internal limit to the exercise of sovereignty arises from the nature of the sovereign power itself. Even a despot exercises his powers in accordance with his character, which is itself moulded by the circumstances under which he lives, including under that head the moral feelings of the time and the society to which he belongs. The Sultan could not if he would change the religion of the Mahommedan world, but if he could do so it is in the very highest degree improbable that the head of Mahommedanism should wish to overthrow the religion of Mahomet; the internal check on the exercise of the Sultan's power is at least as strong as the external limitation. People sometimes ask the idle question why the Pope does not introduce this or that reform? The true answer is that a revolutionist is not the kind of man who becomes a Pope, and that the man who becomes a Pope has no wish to be a revolutionist. Louis the Fourteenth could not in all probability have established Protestantism as the national religion of France; but to imagine Louis the Fourteenth as wishing to carry out a Protestant reformation is nothing short of imagining him to have been a being quite unlike the *Grand Monarque*. Here again the internal check works together with the external check, and the influence of the internal limitation is as great in the case of a Parliamentary sovereign as of any other; perhaps it is greater. Parlia-

ment could not prudently tax the Colonies; but it is hardly conceivable that a modern Parliament, with the history of the eighteenth
century before its eyes, should wish to tax the Colonies. The combined influence both of the external and of the internal limitation on
legislative sovereignty is admirably stated in Leslie Stephen's *Science
of Ethics,* whose chapter on "Law and Custom" contains one of the
best statements to be met with of the limits placed by the nature of
things on the theoretical omnipotence of sovereign legislatures.

> Lawyers are apt to speak as though the legislature were omnipotent, as
> they do not require to go beyond its decisions. It is, of course, omnipotent in
> the sense that it can make whatever laws it pleases, inasmuch as a law means
> any rule which has been made by the legislature. But from the scientific
> point of view, the power of the legislature is of course strictly limited. It is
> limited, so to speak, both from within and from without; from within, be-
> cause the legislature is the product of a certain social condition, and deter-
> mined by whatever determines the society; and from without, because
> the power of imposing laws is dependent upon the instinct of subordina-
> tion, which is itself limited. If a legislature decided that all blue-eyed babies
> should be murdered, the preservation of blue-eyed babies would be illegal;
> but legislators must go mad before they could pass such a law, and subjects
> be idiotic before they could submit to it.[56]

Limits
may not
coincide.

Though sovereign power is bounded by an external and an internal
limit, neither boundary is very definitely marked, nor need the two
precisely coincide. A sovereign may wish to do many things which
he either cannot do at all or can do only at great risk of serious
resistance, and it is on many accounts worth observation that the
exact point at which the external limitation begins to operate, that is,
the point at which subjects will offer serious or insuperable resistance
to the commands of a ruler whom they generally obey, is never fixed
with precision. It would be rash of the Imperial Parliament to abolish
the Scotch law Courts, and assimilate the law of Scotland to that of
England. But no one can feel sure at what point Scotch resistance to
such a change would become serious. Before the War of Secession
the sovereign power of the United States could not have abolished
slavery without provoking a civil war; after the War of Secession

---

56 Leslie Stephen, *Science of Ethics*, p. 143.

the sovereign power abolished slavery and conferred the electoral franchise upon the Blacks without exciting actual resistance.

In reference to the relation between the external and the internal limit to sovereignty, representative government presents a noteworthy peculiarity. It is this. The aim and effect of such government is to produce a coincidence, or at any rate diminish the divergence, between the external and the internal limitations on the exercise of sovereign power. Frederick the Great may have wished to introduce, and may in fact have introduced, changes or reforms opposed to the wishes of his subjects. Louis Napoleon certainly began a policy of free trade which would not be tolerated by an assembly which truly represented French opinion. In these instances neither monarch reached the external limit to his sovereign power, but it might very well have happened that he might have reached it, and have thereby provoked serious resistance on the part of his subjects. There might, in short, have arisen a divergence between the internal and the external check. The existence of such a divergence, or (in other words) of a difference between the permanent wishes of the sovereign, or rather of the King who then constituted a predominant part of the sovereign power, and the permanent wishes of the nation, is traceable in England throughout the whole period beginning with the accession of James the First and ending with the Revolution of 1688. The remedy for this divergence was found in a transference of power from the Crown to the Houses of Parliament; and in placing on the throne rulers who from their position were induced to make their wishes coincide with the will of the nation expressed through the House of Commons; the difference between the will of the sovereign and the will of the nation was terminated by the foundation of a system of real representative government. Where a Parliament truly represents the people, the divergence between the external and the internal limit to the exercise of sovereign power can hardly arise, or if it arises, must soon disappear. Speaking roughly, the permanent wishes of the representative portion of Parliament can hardly in the long run differ from the wishes of the English people, or at any rate of the electors; that which the majority of the House of Commons command, the majority of the English people usually desire. To prevent the divergence between the wishes of the sovereign and the wishes of subjects is in short the

Representative government produces coincidence between external and internal limit.

effect, and the only certain effect, of bonâ fide representative government. For our present purpose there is no need to determine whether this result be good or bad. An enlightened sovereign has more than once carried out reforms in advance of the wishes of his subjects. This is true both of sovereign kings and, though more rarely, of sovereign Parliaments. But the sovereign who has done this, whether King or Parliament, does not in reality represent his subjects.[57] All that it is here necessary to insist upon is that the essential property of representative government is to produce coincidence between the wishes of the sovereign and the wishes of the subjects; to make, in short, the two limitations on the exercise of sovereignty absolutely coincident. This, which is true in its measure of all real representative government, applies with special truth to the English House of Commons.

Burke writes:

> The House of Commons was supposed originally to be *no part of the standing government of this country*. It was considered as a *control,* issuing *immediately* from the people, and speedily to be resolved into the mass from whence it arose. In this respect it was in the higher part of government what juries are in the lower. The capacity of a magistrate being transitory, and that of a citizen permanent, the latter capacity it was hoped would of course preponderate in all discussions, not only between the people and the standing authority of the Crown, but between the people and the fleeting authority of the House of Commons itself. It was hoped that, being of a middle nature between subject and government, they would feel with a more tender and a nearer interest everything that concerned the people, than the other remoter and more permanent parts of legislature.
>
> Whatever alterations time and the necessary accommodation of business may have introduced, this character can never be sustained, unless the House of Commons shall be made to bear some stamp of the actual disposition of the people at large. It would (among public misfortunes) be an evil more natural and tolerable, that the House of Commons should be infected with every epidemical phrensy of the people, as this would indicate some consanguinity, some sympathy of nature with their constituents, than that they should in all cases be wholly untouched by the opinions and feelings of the people out of doors. By this want of sympathy they would cease to be a House of Commons.[58]

---

57 Compare *Law and Opinion in England,* pp. 4, 5.

58 Burke, *Works,* ii. (1808 ed.), pp. 287, 288. See further in reference to Parliamentary sovereignty, App. Note III., Distinction between a Parliamentary Executive and a Non-Parliamentary Executive.

Chapter II

PARLIAMENT AND NON-SOVEREIGN LAW-MAKING BODIES

Aim of chapter.

*I*n my last chapter I dwelt upon the nature of Parliamentary sovereignty; my object in this chapter is to illustrate the characteristics of such sovereignty by comparing the essential features of a sovereign Parliament like that of England with the traits which mark non-sovereign law-making bodies.

CHARACTERISTICS OF SOVEREIGN PARLIAMENT

Parliamentary sovereignty.

The characteristics of Parliamentary sovereignty may be deduced from the term itself. But these traits are apt to escape the attention of Englishmen, who have been so accustomed to live under the rule of a supreme legislature, that they almost, without knowing it, assume that all legislative bodies are supreme, and hardly therefore keep clear before their minds the properties of a supreme as contrasted with a non-sovereign law-making body. In this matter foreign observers are, as is natural, clearer-sighted than Englishmen. De Lolme, Gneist, and Tocqueville seize at once upon the sovereignty of Parliament as a salient feature of the English constitution, and recognise the far-reaching effects of this marked peculiarity in our institutions.

Tocqueville writes:

> In England, the Parliament has an acknowledged right to modify the constitution; as, therefore, the constitution may undergo perpetual changes,

it does not in reality exist; the Parliament is at once a legislative and a constituent assembly.[1]

His expressions are wanting in accuracy, and might provoke some criticism, but the description of the English Parliament as at once "a legislative and a constituent assembly" supplies a convenient formula for summing up the fact that Parliament can change any law whatever. Being a "legislative" assembly it can make ordinary laws, being a "constituent" assembly it can make laws which shift the basis of the constitution. The results which ensue from this fact may be brought under three heads.

First, there is no law which Parliament cannot change, or (to put the same thing somewhat differently), fundamental or so-called constitutional laws are under our constitution changed by the same body and in the same manner as other laws, namely, by Parliament acting in its ordinary legislative character.

A Bill for reforming the House of Commons, a Bill for abolishing the House of Lords, a Bill to give London a municipality, a Bill to make valid marriages celebrated by a pretended clergyman, who is found after their celebration not to be in orders, are each equally within the competence of Parliament, they each may be passed in substantially the same manner, they none of them when passed will be, legally speaking, a whit more sacred or immutable than the others, for they each will be neither more nor less than an Act of Parliament, which can be repealed as it has been passed by Parliament, and cannot be annulled by any other power.

Secondly, there is under the English constitution no marked or clear distinction between laws which are not fundamental or constitutional and laws which are fundamental or constitutional. The very language therefore, expressing the difference between a "legislative" assembly which can change ordinary laws and a "constituent" assembly which can change not only ordinary but also constitutional and fundamental laws, has to be borrowed from the political phraseology of foreign countries.

No law Parliament cannot change.

No distinction between constitutional and ordinary laws.

---

1 Tocqueville, i. (translation), p. 96, *Œuvres Complètes*, i. pp. 166, 167.

Relation
between
Parliamen-
tary sover-
eignty and
an unwrit-
ten consti-
tution.

This absence of any distinction between constitutional and ordinary laws has a close connection with the non-existence in England of
any written or enacted constitutional statute or charter. Tocqueville
indeed, in common with other writers, apparently holds the unwritten character of the British constitution to be of its essence:
"L'Angleterre n'ayant point de constitution écrite, qui peut dire
qu'on change sa constitution?"[2] But here Tocqueville falls into an
error, characteristic both of his nation and of the weaker side of his
own rare genius. He has treated the form of the constitution as the
cause of its substantial qualities, and has inverted the relation of
cause and effect. The constitution, he seems to have thought, was
changeable because it was not reduced to a written or statutory form.
It is far nearer the truth to assert that the constitution has never been
reduced to a written or statutory form because each and every part of
it is changeable at the will of Parliament. When a country is governed
under a constitution which is intended either to be unchangeable or
at any rate to be changeable only with special difficulty, the constitution, which is nothing else than the laws which are intended to have
a character of permanence or immutability, is necessarily expressed in
writing, or, to use English phraseology, is enacted as a statute.
Where, on the other hand, every law can be legally changed with
equal ease or with equal difficulty, there arises no absolute need for
reducing the constitution to a written form, or even for looking upon
a definite set of laws as specially making up the constitution. One
main reason then why constitutional laws have not in England been
recognised under that name, and in many cases have not been reduced to the form of a statutory enactment, is that one law, whatever
its importance, can be passed and changed by exactly the same
method as every other law. But it is a mistake to think that the whole
law of the English constitution might not be reduced to writing and
be enacted in the form of a constitutional code. The Belgian constitution indeed comes very near to a written reproduction of the English
constitution, and the constitution of England might easily be
turned into an Act of Parliament without suffering any material

---

2 Tocqueville, *Œuvres Complètes*, i. p. 312.

transformation of character, provided only that the English Parliament retained—what the Belgian Parliament, by the way, does not possess—the unrestricted power of repealing or amending the constitutional code.

No person entitled to pronounce Act of Parliament void.

Thirdly, there does not exist in any part of the British Empire any person or body of persons, executive, legislative or judicial, which can pronounce void any enactment passed by the British Parliament on the ground of such enactment being opposed to the constitution, or on any ground whatever, except, of course, its being repealed by Parliament.

These then are the three traits of Parliamentary sovereignty as it exists in England: first, the power of the legislature to alter any law, fundamental or otherwise, as freely and in the same manner as other laws; secondly, the absence of any legal distinction between constitutional and other laws; thirdly, the non-existence of any judicial or other authority having the right to nullify an Act of Parliament, or to treat it as void or unconstitutional.

Flexibility of the constitution.

These traits are all exemplifications of the quality which my friend Mr. Bryce has happily denominated the "flexibility"[3] of the British constitution. Every part of it can be expanded, curtailed, amended, or abolished, with equal ease. It is the most flexible polity in existence, and is therefore utterly different in character from the "rigid" constitutions (to use another expression of Mr. Bryce's) the whole or some part of which can be changed only by some extra-ordinary method of legislation.

CHARACTERISTICS OF
NON-SOVEREIGN LAW-MAKING BODIES

Characteristics of non-sovereign law-making bodies.

From the attributes of a sovereign legislature it is possible to infer negatively what are the characteristics all (or some) of which are the marks of a non-sovereign law-making body, and which therefore may be called the marks or notes of legislative subordination.

---

3 See Bryce, *Studies in History and Jurisprudence,* i. Essay III., Flexible and Rigid Constitutions.

These signs by which you may recognise the subordination of a law-making body are, first, the existence of laws affecting its constitution which such body must obey and cannot change; hence, secondly, the formation of a marked distinction between ordinary laws and fundamental laws; and lastly, the existence of some person or persons, judicial or otherwise, having authority to pronounce upon the validity or constitutionality of laws passed by such law-making body.

Wherever any of these marks of subordination exist with regard to a given law-making body, they prove that it is not a sovereign legislature.

Meaning of term "law-making body." Observe the use of the words "law-making body."

This term is here employed as an expression which may include under one head[4] both municipal bodies, such as railway companies,

---

4 This inclusion has been made the subject of criticism.

The objections taken to it are apparently threefold.

First, there is, it is said, a certain absurdity in bringing into one class things so different in importance and in dignity as, for example, the Belgian Parliament and an English School-board. This objection rests on a misconception. It would be ridiculous to overlook the profound differences between a powerful legislature and a petty corporation. But there is nothing ridiculous in calling attention to the points which they have in common. The sole matter for consideration is whether the alleged similarity be real. No doubt when features of likeness between things which differ from one another both in appearance and in dignity are pointed out, the immediate result is to produce a sense of amusement, but the apparent absurdity is no proof that the likeness is unreal or undeserving of notice. A man differs from a rat. But this does not make it the less true or the less worth noting that they are both vertebrate animals.

Secondly, the powers of an English corporation, it is urged, can in general only be exercised reasonably, and any exercise of them is invalid which is not reasonable, and this is not true of the laws made, *e.g.,* by the Parliament of a British colony.

The objection admits of more than one reply. It is not universally true that the bye-laws made by a corporation are invalid unless they are reasonable. But let it be assumed for the sake of argument that this restriction is always, as it certainly is often, imposed on the making of bye-laws. This concession does not involve the consequence that bye-laws do not partake of the nature of laws. All that follows from it is a conclusion which nobody questions, namely, that the powers of a non-sovereign law-making body may be restricted in very different degrees.

Thirdly, the bye-laws of a corporation are, it is urged, not laws, because they affect only certain persons, *e.g.* in the case of a railway company the passengers on the railway, and do not, like the laws of a colonial legislature, affect all persons coming under the jurisdiction of the legislature; or to put the same objection in another shape, the bye-laws of a railway company apply, it is urged, only to persons using the railway, in addition to the general law school-boards, town councils, and the like, which possess a limited power of making laws, but are not ordinarily called legislatures, and bodies such as the Parliaments of the British Colonies, of Belgium, or of France, which are ordinarily called "legislatures," but are not in reality sovereign bodies.

The reason for grouping together under one name such very different kinds of "law-making" bodies is, that by far the best way of clearing up our ideas as to the nature of assemblies which, to use the foreign formula,[5] are "legislative" without being "constituent," and which therefore are not sovereign legislatures, is to analyse the characteristics of societies, such as English railway companies, which possess a certain legislative authority, though the authority is clearly delegated and subject to the obvious control of a superior legislature.

It will conduce to clearness of thought if we divide non-sovereign law-making bodies into the two great classes of obviously subordinate bodies such as corporations, the Council of India, etc., and such legislatures of independent countries as are legislative without being constituent, *i.e.* are non-sovereign legislative bodies.

The consideration of the position of the non-sovereign legislatures which exist under the complicated form of constitution known as a federal government is best reserved for a separate chapter.[6]

---

of the land by which such persons are also bound, whereas the laws, *e.g.,* of the New Zealand Parliament constitute the general law of the colony.

The objection is plausible, but does not really show that the similarity insisted upon between the position of a corporation and, *e.g.,* a colonial legislature is unreal. In either case the laws made, whether by the corporation or by the legislature, apply only to a limited class of persons, and are liable to be overridden by the laws of a superior legislature. Even in the case of a colony so nearly independent as New Zealand, the inhabitants are bound first by the statutes of the Imperial Parliament, and in addition thereto by the Acts of the New Zealand Parliament. The very rules which are bye-laws when made by a corporation would admittedly be laws if made directly by Parliament. Their character cannot be changed by the fact that they are made by the permission of Parliament through a subordinate legislative body. The Council of a borough, which for the present purpose is a better example of my meaning than a railway company, passes in accordance with the powers conferred upon it by Parliament a bye-law prohibiting processions with music on Sunday. The same prohibition if contained in an Act of Parliament would be admittedly a law. It is none the less a law because made by a body which is permitted by Parliament to legislate.

5 See p. 37, *ante.*

6 See Chap. III., *post.*

Subordinate Law-making Bodies

Subordinate bodies.

Corporations.

Corporations   An English railway company is as good an example as can be found of a subordinate law-making body. Such a company is in the strictest sense a law-making society, for it can under the powers of its Act make laws (called bye-laws) for the regulation (*inter alia*) of travelling upon the railway,[7] and can impose a penalty for the breach of such laws, which can be enforced by proceedings in the Courts. The rules therefore or bye-laws made by a company within the powers of its Act are "laws" in the strictest sense of the term, as any person will discover to his own cost who, when he travels by rail from Oxford to Paddington, deliberately violates a bye-law duly made by the Great Western Railway Company.

But though an English railway company is clearly a law-making body, it is clearly a non-sovereign law-making body. Its legislative power bears all the marks of subordination.

First, the company is bound to obey laws and (amongst others) the Act of Parliament creating the company, which it cannot change. This is obvious, and need not be insisted upon.

Secondly, there is the most marked distinction between the Act constituting the company, not a line of which can be changed by the company, and the bye-laws which, within the powers of its Act, the company can both make and change. Here we have on a very small scale the exact difference between constitutional laws which cannot, and ordinary laws which can, be changed by a subordinate legislature, *i.e.* by the company. The company, if we may apply to it the terms of constitutional law, is not a constituent, but is within certain limits a legislative assembly; and these limits are fixed by the constitution of the company.

Thirdly, the Courts have the right to pronounce, and indeed are bound to pronounce, on the validity of the company's bye-laws; that is, upon the validity, or to use political terms, on the constitutionality of the laws made by the company as a law-making body. Note par-

---

7 See especially the Companies Clauses Consolidation Act, 1845 (8 & 9 Vict. c. 20), secs. 103, 108–111. This Act is always embodied in the special Act constituting the company. Its enactments therefore form part of the constitution of a railway company.

ticularly that it is not the function of any Court or judge to declare void or directly annul a bye-law made by a railway company. The function of the Court is simply, upon any particular case coming before it which depends upon a bye-law made by a railway company, to decide for the purposes of that particular case whether the bye-law is or is not within the powers conferred by Act of Parliament upon the company; that is to say, whether the bye-law is or is not valid, and to give judgment in the particular case according to the Court's view of the validity of the bye-law. It is worth while to examine with some care the mode in which English judges deal with the inquiry whether a particular bye-law is or is not within the powers given to the company by Act of Parliament, for to understand this point goes a good way towards understanding the exact way in which English or American Courts determine the constitutionality of Acts passed by a non-sovereign legislature.

The London and North-Western Railway Company made a bye-law by which

> any person travelling without the special permission of some duly autho-rised servant of the company in a carriage or by a train of a superior class to that for which his ticket was issued is hereby subject to a penalty not exceed-ing forty shillings, and shall, in addition, be liable to pay his fare according to the class of carriage in which he is travelling from the station where the train originally started, unless he shows that he had no intention to defraud.

X, with the intention of defrauding the company, travelled in a first-class carriage instead of a second-class carriage for which his ticket was issued, and having been charged under the bye-law was con-victed in the penalty of ten shillings, and costs. On appeal by X, the Court determined that the bye-law was illegal and void as being repugnant to 8 Vict. c. 20, s. 103, or in effect to the terms of the Act incorporating the company,[8] and that therefore X could not be con-victed of the offence charged against him.

A bye-law of the South-Eastern Railway Company required that a passenger should deliver up his ticket to a servant of the company when required to do so, and that any person travelling without a

---

[8] *Dyson* v. *L. & N.-W. Ry. Co.,* 7 Q. B. D. 32.

ticket or failing or refusing to deliver up his ticket should be required to pay the fare from the station whence the train originally started to the end of his journey. X had a railway ticket enabling him to travel on the South-Eastern Railway. Having to change trains and pass out of the company's station he was asked to show his ticket, and refused to do so, but without any fraudulent intention. He was summoned for a breach of the bye-law, and convicted in the amount of the fare from the station whence the train started. The Queen's Bench Division held the conviction wrong on the ground that the bye-law was for several reasons invalid, as not being authorised by the Act under which it purported to be made.[9]

Now in these instances, and in other cases where the Courts pronounce upon the validity of a bye-law made by a body (*e.g.* a railway company or a school-board) having powers to make bye-laws enforceable by penalties, it is natural to say that the Courts pronounce the bye-laws valid or invalid. But this is not strictly the case. What the judges determine is not that a particular bye-law is invalid, for it is not the function of the Courts to repeal or annul the bye-laws made by railway companies, but that in a proceeding to recover a penalty from X for the breach of a bye-law judgment must be given on the basis of the particular bye-law being beyond the powers of the company, and therefore invalid. It may indeed be thought that the distinction between annulling a bye-law and determining a case upon the assumption of such bye-law being void is a distinction without a difference. But this is not so. The distinction is not without importance even when dealing with the question whether X, who is alleged to have broken a bye-law made by a railway company, is liable to pay a fine; it is of first-rate importance when the question before the Courts is one involving considerations of constitutional law, as for example when the Privy Council is called upon, as constantly happens, to determine cases which involve the validity or constitutionality of laws made by the Dominion Parliament or by one of the provincial Parliaments of Canada. The significance, however, of the

---

9 *Saunders* v. *S.-E. Ry. Co.*, 5 Q. B. D. 456. Compare *Bentham* v. *Hoyle*, 3 Q. B. D. 289, and *L. E. & S. C. Ry. Co.* v. *Watson*, 3 C. P. D. 429; 4 C. P. D. (C. A.), 118.

distinction will become more apparent as we proceed with our subject; the matter of consequence now is to notice the nature of the distinction, and to realise that when a Court in deciding a given case considers whether a bye-law is, or is not, valid, the Court does a different thing from affirming or annulling the bye-law itself.

Council of
British
India.

Legislative Council of British India[10]   Laws are made for British India by a Legislative Council having very wide powers of legislation. This Council, or, as it is technically expressed, the "Governor-General in Council," can pass laws as important as any Acts passed by the British Parliament. But the authority of the Council in the way of law-making is as completely subordinate to, and as much dependent upon, Acts of Parliament as is the power of the London and North-Western Railway Company to make bye-laws.

The legislative powers of the Governor-General and his Council arise from definite Parliamentary enactments.[11] These Acts constitute what may be termed as regards the Legislative Council the constitution of India. Now observe, that under these Acts the Indian Council is in the strictest sense a non-sovereign legislative body, and this independently of the fact that the laws or regulations made by the Governor-General in Council can be annulled or disallowed by the Crown; and note that the position of the Council exhibits all the marks or notes of legislative subordination.

First, the Council is bound by a large number of rules which cannot be changed by the Indian legislative body itself, and which can be changed by the superior power of the Imperial Parliament.

Secondly, the Acts themselves from which the Council derives its authority cannot be changed by the Council, and hence in regard to the Indian legislative body form a set of constitutional or fundamental laws, which, since they cannot be changed by the Council, stand in marked contrast with the laws or regulations which the Council is

---

10 See Ilbert, *Government of India*, pp. 199–216, Digest of Statutory Enactments, ss. 60–69.

11 The Government of India Act, 1833 (3 & 4 Will. IV. c. 85), ss. 45–48, 51, 52; The Indian Councils Act, 1861 (24 & 25 Vict. c. 67), ss. 16–25; The Government of India Act, 1865 (28 & 29 Vict. c. 17).

The Indian Council is in some instances under Acts of Parliament, *e.g.* 24 & 25 Vict. c. 67; 28 & 29 Vict. c. 17; 32 & 33 Vict. c. 98, empowered to legislate for persons outside India.

empowered to make. These fundamental rules contain, it must be added, a number of specific restrictions on the subjects with regard to which the Council may legislate. Thus the Governor-General in Council has no power of making laws which may affect the authority of Parliament, or any part of the unwritten laws or constitution of the United Kingdom, whereon may depend in any degree the allegiance of any person to the Crown of the United Kingdom, or the sovereignty or dominion of the Crown over any part of India.[12]

Thirdly, the Courts in India (or in any other part of the British Empire) may, when the occasion arises, pronounce upon the validity or constitutionality of laws made by the Indian Council.

The Courts treat Acts passed by the Indian Council precisely in the same way in which the King's Bench Division treats the bye-laws of a railway company. No judge in India or elsewhere ever issues a decree which declares invalid, annuls, or makes void a law or regulation made by the Governor-General in Council. But when any particular case comes before the Courts, whether civil or criminal, in which the rights or liabilities of any party are affected by the legislation of the Indian Council, the Court may have to consider and determine with a view to the particular case whether such legislation was or was not within the legal powers of the Council, which is of course the same thing as adjudicating as regards the particular case in hand upon the validity or constitutionality of the legislation in question. Thus suppose that X is prosecuted for the breach of a law or regulation passed by the Council, and suppose the fact to be established past a doubt that X has broken this law. The Court before which the proceedings take place, which must obviously in the ordinary course of things be an Indian Court, may be called upon to consider whether the regulation which X has broken is within the powers given to the Indian Council by the Acts of Parliament making up the Indian constitution. If the law is within such powers, or, in other words, is constitutional, the Court will by giving judgment against X give full effect to the law, just as effect is given to the bye-law of a railway company by the tribunal before whom an offender is sued pronouncing judgment

---

12 See 24 & 25 Vict. c. 67. s. 22.

against him for the penalty. If, on the other hand, the Indian Court deem that the regulation is *ultra vires* or unconstitutional, they will refuse to give effect to it, and treat it as void by giving judgment for the defendant on the basis of the regulation being invalid or having no legal existence. On this point the *Empress* v. *Burah*[13] is most instructive. The details of the case are immaterial; the noticeable thing is that the High Court held a particular legislative enactment of the Governor-General in Council to be in excess of the authority given to him by the Imperial Parliament and therefore invalid, and on this ground entertained an appeal from two prisoners which, if the enactment had been valid, the Court would admittedly have been incompetent to entertain. The Privy Council, it is true, held on appeal[14] that the particular enactment was within the legal powers of the Council and therefore valid, but the duty of the High Court of Calcutta to consider whether the legislation of the Governor-General was or was not constitutional, was not questioned by the Privy Council. To look at the same thing from another point of view, the Courts in India treat the legislation of the Governor-General in Council in a way utterly different from that in which any English Court can treat the Acts of the Imperial Parliament. An Indian tribunal may be called upon to say that an Act passed by the Governor-General need not be obeyed because it is unconstitutional or void. No British Court can give judgment, or ever does give judgment, that an Act of Parliament need not be obeyed because it is unconstitutional. Here, in short, we have the essential difference between subordinate and sovereign legislative power.[15]

English colonies.

English Colonies with Representative and Responsible Governments   Many English colonies, and notably the Dominion of New Zealand (to which country our attention had best for the sake of clearness be specially directed), possess representative assemblies which occupy a somewhat peculiar position.

---

13 3 Ind. L. R. (Calcutta Series), p. 63.

14 *Reg.* v. *Burah*, 3 App. Cas. 889.

15 See especially *Empress* v. *Burah and Book Singh*, 3 Ind. L. R. (Calcutta Series, 1878), 63, 86–89, for the judgment of Markby J.

Powers
exercised
by colonial
Parliaments.

The Parliament of the Dominion of New Zealand exercises through-out that country[16] many of the ordinary powers of a sovereign assembly such as the Parliament of the United Kingdom. It makes and repeals laws, it puts Ministries in power and dismisses them from office, it controls the general policy of the New Zealand Government, and generally makes its will felt in the transaction of affairs after the manner of the Parliament at Westminister. An ordinary observer would, if he looked merely at the everyday proceedings of the New Zealand legislature, find no reason to pronounce it a whit less powerful within its sphere than the Parliament of the United Kingdom. No doubt the assent of the Governor is needed in order to turn colonial Bills into laws: and further investigation would show our inquirer that for the validity of any colonial Act there is required, in addition to the assent of the Governor, the sanction, either express or implied, of the Crown. But these assents are constantly given almost as a matter of course, and may be compared (though not with absolute correctness) to the Crown's so-called "veto" or right of refusing assent to Bills which have passed through the Houses of Parliament.

Limit to
powers.

Yet for all this, when the matter is further looked into, the Dominion Parliament (together with other colonial legislatures) will be found to be a non-sovereign legislative body, and bears decisive marks of legislative subordination. The action of the Dominion Parliament is restrained by laws which it cannot change, and are changeable only by the Imperial Parliament; and further, New Zealand Acts, even when assented to by the Crown, are liable to be treated by the Courts in New Zealand and elsewhere throughout the British dominions as void or unconstitutional, on the ground of their coming

---

16 No colonial legislature has as such any authority beyond the territorial limits of the colony. This forms a considerable restriction on the powers of a colonial Parliament, and a great part of the imperial legislation for the colonies arises from the Act of a colonial legislature having, unless given extended operation by some imperial statute, no effect beyond the limits of the colony.

In various instances, however, imperial Acts have given extended power of legislation to colonial legislatures. Sometimes the imperial Act authorises a colonial legislature to make laws on a specified subject with extra-territorial operation [*e.g.* the Merchant Shipping Act, 1894, ss. 478, 735, 736]. Sometimes an Act of the colonial legislature is given the force of law throughout British dominions. (Compare Jenkyns, *British Rule and Jurisdiction beyond the Seas*, p. 70.)

into conflict with laws of the Imperial Parliament, which the colonial legislature has no authority to touch.[17]

That this is so becomes apparent the moment we realise the exact relation between colonial and Imperial laws. The matter is worth some little examination, both for its own sake and for the sake of the light it throws on the sovereignty of Parliament.

The charter of colonial legislative independence is the Colonial Laws Validity Act, 1865.[18]

Colonial Laws Validity Act, 1865.

This statute seems (oddly enough) to have passed through Parliament without discussion; but it permanently defines and extends the authority of colonial legislatures, and its main provisions are of such importance as to deserve verbal citation:

> Sec. 2. Any colonial law which is or shall be in any respect repugnant to the provisions of any Act of Parliament extending to the colony to which such law may relate, or repugnant to any order or regulation made under authority of such Act of Parliament, or having in the colony the force and effect of such Act, shall be read subject to such Act, order, or regulation, and shall, to the extent of such repugnancy, but not otherwise, be and remain absolutely void and inoperative.
>
> 3. No colonial law shall be or be deemed to have been void or inoperative on the ground of repugnancy to the law of England, unless the same shall be repugnant to the provisions of some such Act of Parliament, order, or regulation as aforesaid.
>
> 4. No colonial law, passed with the concurrence of or assented to by the Governor of any colony, or to be hereafter so passed or assented to, shall be or be deemed to have been void or inoperative, by reason only of any instructions with reference to such law or the subject thereof which may have been given to such Governor by or on behalf of Her Majesty, by any

---

17 As also upon the ground of their being in strictness *ultra vires*, *i.e.* beyond the powers conferred upon the Dominion legislature. This is the ground why a colonial Act is in general void, in so far as it is intended to operate beyond the territory of the colony. ''In 1879, the Supreme Court of New Zealand held that the Foreign Offenders Apprehension Act, 1863, of that colony, which authorises the deportation of persons charged with indictable misdemeanours in other colonies, was beyond the competence of the New Zealand legislature, for it involved detention on the high seas, which the legislature could not authorise, as it could legislate only for peace, order, and good government within the limits of the colony.'' Jenkyns, *British Rule and Jurisdiction beyond the Seas*, p. 70, citing *In re Gleich*. Ollivier Bell and Fitzgerald's N. Z. Rep., S. C. p. 39.

18 28 & 29 Vict. c. 63. See on this enactment, Jenkyns, *British Rule and Jurisdiction beyond the Seas*, pp. 71, 72.

instrument other than the letters-patent or instrument authorising such Governor to concur in passing or to assent to laws for the peace, order, and good government of such colony, even though such instructions may be referred to in such letters-patent or last-mentioned instrument.

5. Every colonial legislature shall have, and be deemed at all times to have had, full power within its jurisdiction to establish courts of judicature, and to abolish and reconstitute the same, and to alter the constitution thereof, and to make provision for the administration of justice therein; and every representative legislature shall, in respect to the colony under its jurisdiction, have, and be deemed at all times to have had, full power to make laws respecting the constitution, powers, and procedure of such legislature; provided that such laws shall have been passed in such manner and form as may from time to time be required by any Act of Parliament, letters-patent, order in council, or colonial law for the time being in force in the said colony.

The importance, it is true, of the Colonial Laws Validity Act, 1865, may well be either exaggerated or quite possibly underrated. The statute is in one sense less important than it at first sight appears, because the principles laid down therein were, before its passing, more or less assumed, though with some hesitation, to be good law and to govern the validity of colonial legislation. From another point of view the Act is of the highest importance, because it determines, and gives legislative authority to, principles which had never before been accurately defined, and were liable to be treated as open to doubt.[19] In any case the terms of the enactment make it now possible to state with precision the limits which bound the legislative authority of a colonial Parliament.

The Dominion Parliament may make laws opposed to the English common law, and such laws (on receiving the required assents) are perfectly valid.

Thus a New Zealand Act which changed the common law rules as to the descent of property, which gave the Governor authority to forbid public meetings, or which abolished trial by jury, might be inexpedient or unjust, but would be a perfectly valid law, and would

---

19 Up to 1865 the prevalent opinion in England seems to have been that any law seriously opposed to the principles of English law was repugnant to the law of England, and colonial laws were from time to time disallowed solely on the ground of such supposed repugnancy and invalidity.

be recognised as such by every tribunal throughout the British Empire.[20]

The Dominion Parliament, on the other hand, cannot make any laws inconsistent with any Act of Parliament, or with any part of an Act of Parliament, intended by the Imperial Parliament to apply to New Zealand.

Suppose, for example, that the Imperial Parliament were to pass an Act providing a special mode of trial in New Zealand for particular classes of offences committed there, no enactment of the colonial Parliament, which provided that such offences should be tried otherwise than as directed by the imperial statute, would be of any legal effect. So again, no New Zealand Act would be valid that legalised the slave trade in the face of the Slave Trade Act, 1824, 5 George IV. c. 113, which prohibits slave trading throughout the British dominions; nor would Acts passed by the Dominion Parliament be valid which repealed, or invalidated, several provisions of the Merchant Shipping Act 1894 meant to apply to the colonies, or which deprived a discharge under the English Bankruptcy Act of the effect which, in virtue of the imperial statute, it has as a release from debts contracted in any part whatever of the British dominions. No colonial legislature, in short, can override imperial legislation which is intended to apply to the colonies. Whether the intention be expressed in so many words, or be apparent only from the general scope and nature of the enactment, is immaterial. Once establish that an imperial law is intended to apply to a given colony, and the consequence follows that any colonial enactment which contravenes that law is invalid and unconstitutional.[21]

Acts of colonial legislature may be pronounced void by Courts.

Hence the Courts in the Dominion of New Zealand, as also in the rest of the British Empire, may be called upon to adjudicate upon the validity or constitutionality of any Act of the Dominion Parliament.

---

20 Assuming, of course, that such Acts are not inconsistent with any imperial statute applying to the colony. (Compare *Robinson* v. *Reynolds*, Macassey's N. Z. Rep. p. 562.)

21 See Tarring, *Law Relating to the Colonies* (2nd ed.), pp. 232–247, for a list of imperial statutes which relate to the colonies in general, and which therefore no colonial legislation can, except under powers given by some Act of the Imperial Parliament, contravene.

For if a New Zealand law really contradicts the provisions of an Act of Parliament extending to New Zealand, no Court throughout the British dominions could legally, it is clear, give effect to the enactment of the Dominion Parliament. This is an inevitable result of the legislative sovereignty exercised by the Imperial Parliament. In the supposed case the Dominion Parliament commands the judges to act in a particular manner, and the Imperial Parliament commands them to act in another manner. Of these two commands the order of the Imperial Parliament is the one which must be obeyed. This is the very meaning of Parliamentary sovereignty. Whenever, therefore, it is alleged that any enactment of the Dominion Parliament is repugnant to the provisions of any Act of the Imperial Parliament extending to the colony, the tribunal before which the objection is raised must pronounce upon the validity or constitutionality of the colonial law.[22]

Colonial Parliament may be a "constituent" as well as legislative body.

The constitution of New Zealand is created by and depends upon the New Zealand Constitution Act, 1852, 15 & 16 Vict. c. 72, and the Acts amending the same. One might therefore expect that the Parliament of the Dominion of New Zealand, which may conveniently be called the New Zealand Parliament, would exhibit that "mark of subordination" which consists in the inability of a legislative body to change fundamental or constitutional laws, or (what is the same thing) in the clearly drawn distinction between ordinary laws which the legislature can change and laws of the constitution which it cannot change, at any rate when acting in its ordinary legislative character. But this anticipation is hardly borne out by an examination into the Acts creating the constitution of New Zealand. A comparison of the Colonial Laws Validity Act, 1865, s. 5, with the New Zealand Constitution Act, as subsequently amended, shows that the New Zealand Parliament can change the articles of the constitution. This power, derived from imperial statutes, is of course in no way inconsistent with the legal sovereignty of the Imperial Parliament.[23] One

---

22 See *Powell* v. *Apollo Candle Co.*, 10 App. Cas. 282; *Hodge* v. *The Queen*, 9 App. Cas. 117.

23 The constitutions of some self-governing colonies, *e.g.* Victoria, certainly show that a Victorian law altering the constitution must in some instances be passed in a manner different from the mode in which other laws are passed. This is a faint recognition of the difference between fundamental and other laws. Compare 18 & 19 Vict. c. 55, Sched. I. s. 60;

may fairly therefore assert that the New Zealand Parliament, in common with many other colonial legislative assemblies, is, though a "subordinate," at once a legislative and a constituent assembly. It is a "subordinate" assembly[24] because its powers are limited by the legislation of the Imperial Parliament; it is a constituent assembly since it can change the articles of the constitution of New Zealand. The authority of the New Zealand Parliament to change the articles of the constitution of New Zealand is from several points of view worth notice.

Reason of this.

We have here a decisive proof that there is no necessary connection between the written character and the immutability of a constitution. The New Zealand constitution is to be found in a written document; it is a statutory enactment. Yet the articles of this constitutional statute can be changed by the Parliament which it creates, and changed in the same manner as any other law. This may seem an obvious matter enough, but writers of eminence so often use language which implies or suggests that the character of a law is changed by its being expressed in the form of a statute as to make it worth while noting that a statutory constitution need not be in any sense an immutable

but there appears to have been considerable laxity in regard to observing these constitutional provisions. See Jenks, *Government of Victoria*, pp. 247–249.

24 It is usually the case that a self-governing colony, such as New Zealand, has the power in one form or another to change the colonial constitution. The extent, however, of this power, and the mode in which it can be exercised, depends upon the terms of the Act of Parliament, or of the charter creating or amending the colonial constitution, and differs in different cases. Thus the Parliament of New Zealand can change almost all, though not quite all, of the articles of the constitution, and can change them in the same manner in which it can change an ordinary colonial law. The Parliament of the Canadian Dominion cannot change the constitution of the Dominion. The Parliament of the Australian Commonwealth, on the other hand, occupies a peculiar position. It can by virtue of the terms of the constitution itself alter, by way of ordinary legislation, certain of the articles of the constitution (see, *e.g.*, Constitution of Commonwealth, ss. 65, 67), whilst it cannot, by way of ordinary legislation, change other articles of the constitution. All the articles, however, of the constitution which cannot be changed by ordinary Parliamentary legislation can— subject, of course, to the sanction of the Crown—be altered or abrogated by the Houses of the Parliament, and a vote of the people of the Commonwealth, as provided by the Constitution of the Commonwealth, s. 128. The point to be specially noted is, that the Imperial Parliament, as a rule, enables a self-governing colony to change the colonial constitution. The exception in the case of Canada is more apparent than real; the Imperial Parliament would no doubt give effect to any change clearly desired by the inhabitants of the Canadian Dominion.

constitution. The readiness again with which the English Parliament has conceded constituent powers to colonial legislatures shows how little hold is exercised over Englishmen by that distinction between fundamental and non-fundamental laws which runs through almost all the constitutions not only of the Continent but also of America. The explanation appears to be that in England we have long been accustomed to consider Parliament as capable of changing one kind of law with as much ease as another. Hence when English statesmen gave Parliamentary government to the colonies, they almost as a matter of course bestowed upon colonial legislatures authority to deal with every law, whether constitutional or not, which affected the colony, subject of course to the proviso, rather implied than expressed, that this power should not be used in a way inconsistent with the supremacy of the British Parliament. The colonial legislatures, in short, are within their own sphere copies of the Imperial Parliament. They are within their own sphere sovereign bodies; but their freedom of action is controlled by their subordination to the Parliament of the United Kingdom.

How conflicts between imperial and colonial legislation are avoided.

The question may naturally be asked how the large amount of colonial liberty conceded to countries like New Zealand has been legally reconciled with Imperial sovereignty?

The inquiry lies a little outside our subject, but is not really foreign to it, and well deserves an answer. Nor is the reply hard to find if we keep in mind the true nature of the difficulty which needs explanation.

The problem is not to determine what are the means by which the English Government keeps the colonies in subjection, or maintains the political sovereignty of the United Kingdom. This is a matter of politics with which this book has no concern.

The question to be answered is how (assuming the law to be obeyed throughout the whole of the British Empire) colonial legislative freedom is made compatible with the legislative sovereignty of Parliament? How are the Imperial Parliament and the colonial legislatures prevented from encroaching on each other's spheres?

No one will think this inquiry needless who remarks that in confederations, such as the United States, or the Canadian Dominion, the Courts are constantly occupied in determining the boundaries which divide the legislative authority of the Central Government from that of the State Legislatures.

The assertion may sound paradoxical, but is nevertheless strictly true, that the acknowledged legal supremacy of Parliament is one main cause of the wide power of legislation allowed to colonial assemblies.

The constitutions of the colonies depend directly or indirectly upon imperial statutes. No lawyer questions that Parliament could legally abolish any colonial constitution, or that Parliament can at any moment legislate for the colonies and repeal or override any colonial law whatever. Parliament moreover does from time to time pass Acts affecting the colonies, and the colonial,[25] no less than the English, Courts completely admit the principle that a statute of the Imperial Parliament binds any part of the British dominions to which the statute is meant to apply. But when once this is admitted, it becomes obvious that there is little necessity for defining or limiting the sphere of colonial legislation. If an Act of the New Zealand Parliament contravenes an imperial statute, it is for legal purposes void; and if an Act of the New Zealand Parliament, though not infringing upon any statute, is so opposed to the interests of the Empire that it ought not to be passed, the British Parliament may render the Act of no effect by means of an imperial statute.

This course, however, is rarely, if ever, necessary; for Parliament exerts authority over colonial legislation by in effect regulating the use of the Crown's "veto" in regard to colonial Acts. This is a matter which itself needs a little explanation.

The Crown's right to refuse assent to bills which have passed through the Houses of Parliament is practically obsolete.[26] The power

---

25 See Todd, *Parliamentary Government*, pp. 168–192.

26 This statement has been questioned—see Hearn (2nd ed.), p. 63—but is, it is submitted, correct. The so-called "veto" has never been employed as regards any public bill since the accession of the House of Hanover. When George the Third wished to stop the passing of Fox's India Bill, he abstained from using the Crown's right to dissent from proposed legislation, but availed himself of his influence in the House of Lords to procure the rejection of the measure. No stronger proof could be given that the right of veto was more than a century ago already obsolete. But the statement that a power is practically obsolete

of the Crown to negative or veto the bills of colonial legislatures stands on a different footing. It is virtually, though not in name, the right of the Imperial Parliament to limit colonial legislative independence, and is frequently exercised.

This check on colonial legislation is exerted in two different manners.[27]

---

does not involve the assertion that it could under no conceivable circumstances be revived. On the whole subject of the veto, and the different senses in which the expression is used, the reader should consult an excellent article by Professor Orelli of Zurich, to be found under the word "Veto" in *Encyclopædia Britannica* (9th ed.), xxiv. p. 208.

The history of the Royal Veto curiously illustrates the advantage which sometimes arises from keeping alive in theory prerogatives which may seem to be practically obsolete. The Crown's legislative "veto" has certainly long been unused in England, but it has turned out a convenient method of regulating the relation between the United Kingdom and the Colonies. If the right of the King to refuse his assent to a bill which had passed the two Houses of Parliament had been abolished by statute, it would have been difficult, if not impossible, for the King to veto, or disallow, Acts passed by the Parliament of a self-governing colony, *e.g.* New Zealand. It would, in other words, have been hard to create a parliamentary veto of colonial legislation. Yet the existence of such a veto, which ought to be, and is, sparingly used, helps to hold together the federation known as the British Empire.

27 The mode in which the power to veto colonial legislation is exercised may be best understood from the following extract from the Rules and Regulations printed some years ago by the Colonial Office:

RULES AND REGULATIONS
CHAPTER III
§1. *Legislative Councils and Assemblies*

48. In every colony the Governor has authority either to give or to withhold his assent to laws passed by the other branches or members of the Legislature, and until that assent is given no such law is valid or binding.

49. Laws are in some cases passed with suspending clauses; that is, although assented to by the Governor they do not come into operation or take effect in the colony until they shall have been specially confirmed by Her Majesty, and in other cases Parliament has for the same purpose empowered the Governor to reserve laws for the Crown's assent, instead of himself assenting or refusing his assent to them.

50. Every law which has received the Governor's assent (unless it contains a suspending clause) comes into operation immediately, or at the time specified in the law itself. But the Crown retains power to disallow the law; and if such power be exercised . . . the law ceases to have operation from the date at which such disallowance is published in the colony.

51. In colonies having representative assemblies the disallowance of any law, or the Crown's assent to a reserved bill, is signified by order in council. The confirmation of an Act passed with a suspending clause, is not signified by order in council unless this mode of confirmation is required by the terms of the suspending clause itself, or by some special provision in the constitution of the colony.

How right of "veto" exercised.

The Governor of a colony, say New Zealand, may directly refuse his assent to a bill passed by both Houses of the New Zealand Parliament. In this case the bill is finally lost, just as would be a bill which had been rejected by the colonial council, or as would be a bill passed

---

52. In Crown colonies the allowance or disallowance of any law is generally signified by despatch.

53. In some cases a period is limited, after the expiration of which local enactments, though not actually disallowed, cease to have the authority of law in the colony, unless before the lapse of that time Her Majesty's confirmation of them shall have been signified there; but the general rule is otherwise.

54. In colonies possessing representative assemblies, laws purport to be made by the Queen or by the Governor on Her Majesty's behalf or sometimes by the Governor alone, omitting any express reference to Her Majesty, with the advice and consent of the council and assembly. They are almost invariably designated as Acts. In colonies not having such assemblies, laws are designated as ordinances, and purport to be made by the Governor, with the advice and consent of the Legislative Council (or in British Guiana of the Court of Policy).

The "veto," it will be perceived, may be exercised by one of two essentially different methods: first, by the refusal of the Governor's assent; secondly, by the exercise of the royal power to disallow laws even when assented to by the Governor. As further, the Governor may reserve bills for the royal consideration, and as colonial laws are sometimes passed containing a clause which suspends their operation until the signification of the royal assent, the check on colonial legislation may be exercised in four different forms—

(1) The refusal of the Governor's assent to a bill.
(2) Reservation of a bill for the consideration of the Crown, and the subsequent lapse of the bill owing to the royal assent being refused, or not being given within the statutory time.
(3) The insertion in a bill of a clause preventing it from coming into operation until the signification of the royal assent thereto, and the want of such royal assent.
(4) The disallowance by the Crown of a law passed by the Colonial Parliament with the assent of the Governor.

The reader should note, however, the essential difference between the three first modes and the fourth mode of checking colonial legislation. Under the three first a proposal law passed by the colonial legislature never comes into operation in the colony. Under the fourth a colonial law which has come into operation in the colony is annulled or disallowed by the Crown from the date of such disallowance. In the case of more than one colony, such disallowance must, under the Constitution Act or letters-patent, be signified within two years. See the British North American Act, 1867, sec. 56. Compare the Australian Constitutions Act, 1842 (5 & 6 Vict. c. 76), secs. 32, 33; the Australian Constitutions Act, 1850, 13 & 14 Vict. c. 59; and the Victoria Constitution Act, 1855 (18 & 19 Vict. c. 55), sec. 3.

Under the Australian Commonwealth Act the King may disallow an Act assented to by the Governor-General within one year after the Governor-General's assent. (Commonwealth of Australia Constitution Act, sec. 59.)

by the English Houses of Parliament if the Crown were to exert the obsolete prerogative of refusing the royal assent. The Governor, again, may, without refusing his assent, reserve the bill for the consideration of the Crown. In such case the bill does not come into force until it has received the royal assent, which is in effect the assent of the English Ministry, and therefore indirectly of the Imperial Parliament.

The Governor, on the other hand, may, as representing the Crown, give his assent to a New Zealand bill. The bill thereupon comes into force throughout New Zealand. But such a bill, though for a time a valid Act, is not finally made law even in New Zealand, since the Crown may, after the Governor's assent has been given, disallow the colonial Act. The case is thus put by Mr. Todd:

> Although a governor as representing the Crown is empowered to give the royal assent to bills, this act is not final and conclusive; the Crown itself having, in point of fact, a second veto. All statutes assented to by the governor of a colony go into force immediately, unless they contain a clause suspending their operation until the issue of a proclamation of approval by the queen in council, or some other specific provision to the contrary; but the governor is required to transmit a copy thereof to the secretary of state for the colonies; and the queen in council may, within two years after the receipt of the same, disallow any such Act.''[28]

The result therefore of this state of things is, that colonial legislation is subject to a real veto on the part of the imperial government, and no bill which the English Ministry think ought for the sake of imperial interests to be negatived can, though passed by the New Zealand or other colonial legislature, come finally into force. The home government is certain to negative or disallow any colonial law which, either in letter or in spirit, is repugnant to Parliamentary legislation, and a large number of Acts can be given which on one ground or another have been either not assented to or disallowed by the Crown. In 1868 the Crown refused assent to a Canadian Act reducing the salary of the Governor-General.[29] In 1872 the Crown refused assent to a

---

28 Todd, *Parliamentary Government in the British Colonies*, p. 137.

29 Todd, *Parliamentary Government in the British Colonies*, p. 144.

Canadian Copyright Act because certain parts of it conflicted with imperial legislation. In 1873 a Canadian Act was disallowed as being contrary to the express terms of the British North America Act, 1868; and on similar grounds in 1878 a Canadian Shipping Act was disallowed.[30] So again the Crown has at times in effect passed a veto upon Australian Acts for checking Chinese immigration.[31] And Acts passed by a colonial legislature, allowing divorce on the ground solely of the husband's adultery or (before the passing of the Deceased Wife's Sister's Marriage Act, 1907, 7 Edward VII. c. 47) legalising marriage with a deceased wife's sister or with a deceased husband's brother, have (though not consistently with the general tenor of our colonial policy) been sometimes disallowed by the Crown, that is, in effect by the home government.

The general answer therefore to the inquiry, how colonial liberty of legislation is made legally reconcilable with imperial sovereignty, is that the complete recognition of the supremacy of Parliament obviates the necessity for carefully limiting the authority of colonial legislatures, and that the home government, who in effect represent Parliament, retain by the use of the Crown's veto the power of preventing the occurrence of conflicts between colonial and imperial laws. To this it must be added that imperial treaties legally bind the colonies, and that the "treaty-making power," to use an American expression, resides in the Crown, and is therefore exercised by the home government in accordance with the wishes of the Houses of Parliament, or more strictly of the House of Commons; whilst the authority to make treaties is, except where expressly allowed by Act of Parliament, not possessed by any colonial government.[32]

It should, however, be observed that the legislature of a self-governing colony is free to determine whether or not to pass laws necessary for giving effect to a treaty entered into between the impe-

---

30 *Ibid.*, pp. 147, 150.

31 As regards the Australian colonies such legislation has, I am informed, been heretofore checked in the following manner. Immigration bills have been reserved for the consideration of the Crown, and the assent of the Crown not having been given, have never come into force.

32 See Todd, *Parliamentary Government in the British Colonies*, pp. 192–218.

rial government and a foreign power; and further, that there might in practice be great difficulty in enforcing within the limits of a colony the terms of a treaty, *e.g.* as to the extradition of criminals, to which colonial sentiment was opposed. But this does not affect the principle of law that a colony is bound by treaties made by the imperial government, and does not, unless under some special provision of an Act of Parliament, possess authority to make treaties with any foreign power.

Policy of imperial government not to interfere with action of colonies.

Any one who wishes justly to appreciate the nature and the extent of the control exerted by Great Britain over colonial legislation should keep two points carefully in mind. The tendency, in the first place, of the imperial government is as a matter of policy to interfere less and less with the action of the colonies, whether in the way of law-making[33] or otherwise.[34] Colonial Acts, in the second place, even when finally assented to by the Crown, are, as already pointed out, invalid if repugnant to an Act of Parliament applying to the colony. The imperial policy therefore of non-intervention in the local affairs of British dependencies combines with the supreme legislative authority of the Imperial Parliament to render encroachments by the Parliament of the United Kingdom on the sphere of colonial legislation, or

---

33 Thus the New Zealand Deceased Husband's Brother Act, 1900, No. 72, legalising marriage with a deceased husband's brother, the Immigration Restriction Act, 1901, passed by the Commonwealth Parliament, the Immigrants' Restriction Act, 1907, No. 15, passed by the Transvaal Legislature, have all received the sanction of the Crown. The last enactment illustrates the immensely wide legislative authority which the home government will under some circumstances concede to a colonial Parliament. The Secretary of State for India (Mr. Morley) "regrets that he cannot agree that the Act in question can be regarded as similar to the legislation already sanctioned in other self-governing colonies. . . . Section 2 (4) of the Transvaal Act introduces a principle to which no parallel can be found in previous legislation. This clause . . . will debar from entry into the Transvaal British subjects who would be free to enter into any other colony by proving themselves capable of passing the educational tests laid down for immigrants. It will, for instance, permanently exclude from the Transvaal members of learned professions and graduates of European Universities of Asiatic origin who may in future wish to enter the colony." See Parl. Paper [Cd. 3887], *Correspondence relating to Legislation affecting Asiatics in the Transvaal*, pp. 52, 53, and compare pp. 31, 32. See p. liv, *ante*.

34 Except in the case of political treaties, such as the Hague Conventions, the imperial government does not nowadays bind the colonies by treaties, but secures the insertion in treaties of clauses allowing colonies to adhere to a treaty if they desire to do so.

by colonial Parliaments on the domain of imperial legislation, of comparatively rare occurrence.[35]

Foreign Non-sovereign Legislatures

Non-
sovereign
legislatures
of inde-
pendent
nations.

We perceive without difficulty that the Parliaments of even those colonies, such as the Dominion of Canada, or the Australian Commonwealth, which are most nearly independent states, are not in reality sovereign legislatures. This is easily seen, because the sovereign Parliament of the United Kingdom, which legislates for the whole British Empire, is visible in the background, and because the colonies, however large their practical freedom of action, do not act as independent powers in relation to foreign states; the Parliament of a dependency cannot itself be a sovereign body. It is harder for Englishmen to realise that the legislative assembly of an independent nation may not be a sovereign assembly. Our political habits of thought indeed are so based upon the assumption of Parliamentary omnipotence, that the position of a Parliament which represents an independent nation and yet is not itself a sovereign power is apt to appear to us exceptional or anomalous. Yet whoever examines the constitutions of civilised countries will find that the legislative assemblies of great nations are, or have been, in many cases legislative without being constituent bodies. To determine in any given case whether a foreign legislature be a sovereign power or not we must examine the constitution of the state to which it belongs, and ascertain whether the legislature whose position is in question bears any of the marks of subordination. Such an investigation will in many or in most instances show that an apparently sovereign assembly is in reality a non-sovereign law-making body.

France.

France has within the last hundred and thirty years made trial of at least twelve constitutions.[36]

---

35 The right of appeal to the Privy Council from the decision of the Courts of the colonies is another link strengthening the connection between the colonies and England.

There have been, however, of recent years a good number of conflicts between imperial and colonial legislation as to matters affecting merchant shipping.

36 Demombynes, *Les Constitutions Européennes,* ii. (2nd ed.), pp. 1–5. See Appendix, Note I., Rigidity of French Constitutions.

These various forms of government have, amidst all their differences, possessed in general one common feature. They have most of them been based upon the recognition of an essential distinction between constitutional or "fundamental" laws intended to be either immutable or changeable only with great difficulty, and "ordinary" laws which could be changed by the ordinary legislature in the common course of legislation. Hence under the constitutions which France has from time to time adopted the common Parliament or legislative body has not been a sovereign legislature.

Constitutional monarchy of Louis Philippe.

The constitutional monarchy of Louis Philippe, in outward appearance at least, was modelled on the constitutional monarchy of England. In the Charter not a word could be found which expressly limits the legislative authority possessed by the Crown and the two Chambers, and to an Englishman it would seem certainly arguable that under the Orleans dynasty the Parliament was possessed of sovereignty. This, however, was not the view accepted among French lawyers. Tocqueville writes:

> The immutability of the Constitution of France is a necessary consequence of the laws of that country. . . . As the King, the Peers, and the Deputies all derive their authority from the Constitution, these three powers united cannot alter a law by virtue of which alone they govern. Out of the pale of the Constitution they are nothing; where, then, could they take their stand to effect a change in its provisions? The alternative is clear: either their efforts are powerless against the Charter, which continues to exist in spite of them, in which case they only reign in the name of the Charter; or they succeed in changing the Charter, and then the law by which they existed being annulled, they themselves cease to exist. By destroying the Charter, they destroy themselves. This is much more evident in the laws of 1830 than in those of 1814. In 1814 the royal prerogative took its stand above and beyond the Constitution; but in 1830 it was avowedly created by, and dependent on, the Constitution. A part, therefore, of the French Constitution is immutable, because it is united to the destiny of a family; and the body of the Constitution is equally immutable, because there appear to be no legal means of changing it. These remarks are not applicable to England. That country having no written Constitution, who can assert when its Constitution is changed?[37]

---

37 A. de Tocqueville, *Democracy in America*, ii. (translation), App. pp. 322, 323. *Œuvres Complètes*, i. p. 311.

Tocqueville's reasoning[38] may not carry conviction to an Englishman, but the weakness of his argument is of itself strong evidence of the influence of the hold on French opinion of the doctrine which it is intended to support, namely, that Parliamentary sovereignty was not a recognised part of French constitutionalism. The dogma which is so naturally assented to by Englishmen contradicts that idea of the essential difference between constitutional and other laws which appears to have a firm hold on most foreign statesmen and legislators.

Republic of 1848.

The Republic of 1848 expressly recognised this distinction; no single article of the constitution proclaimed on 4th November 1848 could be changed in the same way as an ordinary law. The legislative assembly sat for three years. In the last year of its existence, and then only, it could by a majority of three-fourths, and not otherwise, convoke a constituent body with authority to modify the constitution. This constituent and sovereign assembly differed in numbers, and otherwise, from the ordinary non-sovereign legislature.

Present Republic.

The National Assembly of the French Republic exerts at least as much direct authority as the English Houses of Parliament. The French Chamber of Deputies exercises at least as much influence on the appointment of Ministers, and controls the action of the government, at least as strictly as does our House of Commons. The President, moreover, does not possess even a theoretical right of veto. For all this, however, the French Parliament is not a sovereign assembly, but is bound by the laws of the constitution in a way in which no law binds our Parliament. The articles of the constitution, or "fundamental laws," stand in a totally different position from the ordinary law of the land. Under article 8 of the constitution, no one of these fundamental enactments can be legally changed otherwise than subject to the following provisions:

> 8. *Les Chambres auront le droit, par délibérations séparées, prises dans chacune à la majorité absolue des voix, soit spontanément, soit sur la demande du Président de la*

---

38 His view is certainly paradoxical. (See Duguit, *Manuel de droit Constitutionnel Français*, s. 149, p. 1090.) As a matter of fact one provision of the Charter, namely, art. 23, regulating the appointment of Peers, was changed by the ordinary process of legislation. See Law of 29th December 1831, Hélie, Les Constitutions de la France, p. 1006.

République, de déclarer qu'il y a lieu de réviser les lois constitutionnelles. Après que chacune des deux Chambres aura pris cette résolution, elles se réuniront en Assemblée nationale pour procéder à la révision. —Les délibérations portant révision des lois constitutionnelles, en tout ou en partie, devront être prises à la majorité absolue des membres composant l'Assemblée nationale. [39]

Supreme legislative power is therefore under the Republic vested not in the ordinary Parliament of two Chambers, but in a "national assembly," or congress, composed of the Chamber of Deputies and the Senate sitting together.

Distinction between flexible and rigid constitutions.

The various constitutions, in short, of France, which are in this respect fair types of continental polities,[40] exhibit, as compared with the expansiveness or "flexibility" of English institutions, that characteristic which may be conveniently described as "rigidity."[41]

---

39 Duguit et Monnier, *Les Constitutions de la France depuis 1789,* pp. 320, 321. A striking example of the difference between English and French constitutionalism is to be found in the division of opinion which exists between French writers of authority on the answer to the inquiry whether the French Chambers, when sitting together, have constitutionally the right to change the constitution. To an Englishman the question seems hardly to admit of discussion, for Art. 8 of the constitutional laws enacts in so many words that these laws may be revised, in the manner therein set forth, by the Chambers when sitting together as a National Assembly. Many French constitutionalists therefore lay down, as would any English lawyer, that the Assembly is a constituent as well as a legislative body, and is endowed with the right to change the constitution (Duguit, *Manuel,* s. 151; Moreau, *Précis élémentaire de droit constitutionnel* (Paris, 1892), p. 149). But some eminent authorities maintain that this view is erroneous, and that in spite of the words of the constitution the ultimate right of constitutional amendment must be exercised directly by the French people, and that therefore any alteration in the constitutional laws by the Assembly lacks, at any rate, moral validity unless it is ratified by the direct vote of the electors. (See, on the one side, Duguit, *Manuel,* s. 151; Bard et Robiquet, *La Constitution française de 1875* (2nd ed.), pp. 374–390, and on the other side, Esmein, *Droit Constitutionnel* (4th ed.), p. 907; Borgeaud, *Etablissement et Rivision des Constitutions,* pp. 303–307.)

40 No constitution better merits study in this as in other respects than the constitution of Belgium. Though formed after the English model, it rejects or omits the principle of Parliamentary sovereignty. The ordinary Parliament cannot change anything in the constitution; it is a legislative, not a constituent body; it can declare that there is reason for changing a particular constitutional provision, and having done so is *ipso facto* dissolved (*après cette déclaration les deux chambres sont dissoutes de plein droit*). The new Parliament thereupon elected has a right to change the constitutional article which has been declared subject to change (*Constitution de La Belgique,* Arts. 131, 71).

41 See Appendix, Note I., Rigidity of French Constitutions.

And here it is worth while, with a view to understanding the constitution of our own country, to make perfectly clear to ourselves the distinction already referred to between a "flexible" and a "rigid" constitution.

Flexible constitutions.

A "flexible" constitution is one under which every law of every description can legally be changed with the same case and in the same manner by one and the same body. The "flexibility" of our constitution consists in the right of the Crown and the two Houses to modify or repeal any law whatever; they can alter the succession to the Crown or repeal the Acts of Union in the same manner in which they can pass an Act enabling a company to make a new railway from Oxford to London. With us, laws therefore are called constitutional, because they refer to subjects supposed to affect the fundamental institutions of the state, and not because they are legally more sacred or difficult to change than other laws. And as a matter of fact, the meaning of the word "constitutional" is in England so vague that the term "a constitutional law or enactment" is rarely applied to any English statute as giving a definite description of its character.

Rigid constitutions.

A "rigid" constitution is one under which certain laws generally known as constitutional or fundamental laws cannot be changed in the same manner as ordinary laws. The "rigidity" of the constitution, say of Belgium or of France, consists in the absence of any right on the part of the Belgian or French Parliament, when acting in its ordinary capacity, to modify or repeal certain definite laws termed constitutional or fundamental. Under a rigid constitution the term "constitutional" as applied to a law has a perfectly definite sense. It means that a particular enactment belongs to the articles of the constitution, and cannot be legally changed with the same ease and in the same manner as ordinary laws. The articles of the constitution will no doubt generally, though by no means invariably, be found to include all the most important and fundamental laws of the state. But it certainly cannot be asserted that where a constitution is rigid all its articles refer to matters of supreme importance. The rule that the French Parliament must meet at Versailles was at one time one of the constitutional laws of the French Republic. Such an enactment, however practically important, would never in virtue of its own character have been termed constitutional; it was constitutional simply because it was included in the articles of the constitution.[42]

The contrast between the flexibility of the English and the rigidity of almost every foreign constitution suggests two interesting inquiries.

Whether rigidity of constitution secures permanence?

First, does the rigidity of a constitution secure its permanence and invest the fundamental institutions of the state with practical immutability?

To this inquiry historical experience gives an indecisive answer.

In some instances the fact that certain laws or institutions of a state have been marked off as placed beyond the sphere of political controversy, has, apparently, prevented that process of gradual innovation which in England has, within not much more than sixty years, transformed our polity. The constitution of Belgium stood for more than half a century without undergoing, in form at least, any material change whatever. The constitution of the United States has lasted for more than a hundred years, but has not undergone anything like the amount of change which has been experienced by the constitution of England since the death of George the Third.[43] But if the inflexibility of constitutional laws has in certain instances checked the gradual and unconscious process of innovation by which the foundations of a commonwealth are undermined, the rigidity of constitutional forms has in other cases provoked revolution. The twelve unchangeable

---

42 The terms "flexible" and "rigid" (originally suggested by my friend Mr. Bryce) are, it should be remarked, used throughout this work without any connotation either of praise or of blame. The flexibility and expansiveness of the English constitution, or the rigidity and immutability of, *e.g.,* the constitution of the United States, may each be qualities which according to the judgment of different critics deserve either admiration or censure. With such judgments this treatise has no concern. My whole aim is to make clear to my readers the exact difference between a flexible and a rigid constitution. It is not my object to pronounce any opinion on the question whether the flexibility or rigidity of a given polity be a merit or a defect.

43 No doubt the constitution of the United States has in reality, though not in form, changed a good deal since the beginning of last century; but the change has been effected far less by formally enacted constitutional amendments than by the growth of customs or institutions which have modified the working without altering the articles of the constitution.

constitutions of France have each lasted on an average for less than ten years, and have frequently perished by violence. Louis Philippe's monarchy was destroyed within seven years of the time when Tocqueville pointed out that no power existed legally capable of altering the articles of the Charter. In one notorious instance at least—and other examples of the same phenomenon might be produced from the annals of revolutionary France—the immutability of the constitution was the ground or excuse for its violent subversion. The best plea for the *Coup d'état* of 1851 was, that while the French people wished for the re-election of the President, the article of the constitution requiring a majority of three-fourths of the legislative assembly in order to alter the law which made the President's re-election impossible, thwarted the will of the sovereign people. Had the Republican Assembly been a sovereign Parliament, Louis Napoleon would have lacked the plea, which seemed to justify, as well as some of the motives which tempted him to commit, the crime of the 2nd of December.

Nor ought the perils in which France was involved by the immutability with which the statesmen of 1848 invested the constitution to be looked upon as exceptional; they arose from a defect which is inherent in every rigid constitution. The endeavour to create laws which cannot be changed is an attempt to hamper the exercise of sovereign power; it therefore tends to bring the letter of the law into conflict with the will of the really supreme power in the state. The majority of French electors were under the constitution the true sovereign of France; but the rule which prevented the legal re-election of the President in effect brought the law of the land into conflict with the will of the majority of the electors, and produced, therefore, as a rigid constitution has a natural tendency to produce, an opposition between the letter of the law and the wishes of the sovereign. If the inflexibility of French constitutions has provoked revolution, the flexibility of English institutions has, once at least, saved them from violent overthrow. To a student, who at this distance of time calmly studies the history of the first Reform Bill, it is apparent, that in 1832 the supreme legislative authority of Parliament enabled the nation to carry through a political revolution under the guise of a legal reform.

The rigidity, in short, of a constitution tends to check gradual innovation; but, just because it impedes change, may, under unfavourable circumstances, occasion or provoke revolution.

Secondly, what are the safeguards which under a rigid constitution can be taken against unconstitutional legislation?

The general answer to our inquiry (which of course can have no application to a country like England, ruled by a sovereign Parliament) is that two methods may be, and have been, adopted by the makers of constitutions, with a view to rendering unconstitutional legislation, either impossible, or inoperative.

Reliance may be placed upon the force of public opinion and upon the ingenious balancing of political powers for restraining the legislature from passing unconstitutional enactments. This system opposes unconstitutional legislation by means of moral sanctions, which resolve themselves into the influence of public sentiment.

Authority, again, may be given to some person or body of persons, and preferably to the Courts, to adjudicate upon the constitutionality of legislative acts, and treat them as void if they are inconsistent with the letter or the spirit of the constitution. This system attempts not so much to prevent unconstitutional legislation as to render it harmless through the intervention of the tribunals, and rests at bottom on the authority of the judges.

This general account of the two methods by which it may be attempted to secure the rigidity of a constitution is hardly intelligible without further illustration. Its meaning may be best understood by a comparison between the different policies in regard to the legislature pursued by two different classes of constitutionalists.

French constitution-makers and their continental followers have, as we have seen, always attached vital importance to the distinction between fundamental and other laws, and therefore have constantly created legislative assemblies which possessed "legislative" without possessing "constituent" powers. French statesmen have therefore been forced to devise means for keeping the ordinary legislature within its appropriate sphere. Their mode of procedure has been marked by a certain uniformity; they have declared on the face of the constitution the exact limits imposed upon the authority of the legis-

(margin note: What are the safeguards against unconstitutional legislation?)

(margin note: Safeguards provided by continental constitutionalists.)

lature; they have laid down as articles of the constitution whole bodies of maxims intended to guide and control the course of legislation; they have provided for the creation, by special methods and under special conditions, of a constituent body which alone should be entitled to revise the constitution. They have, in short, directed their attention to restraining the ordinary legislature from attempting any inroad upon the fundamental laws of the state; but they have in general trusted to public sentiment,[44] or at any rate to political considerations, for inducing the legislature to respect the restraints imposed on its authority, and have usually omitted to provide machinery for annulling unconstitutional enactments, or for rendering them of no effect.

French Revolutionary constitutions.

These traits of French constitutionalism are specially noticeable in the three earliest of French political experiments. The Monarchical constitution of 1791, the Democratic constitution of 1793, the Directorial constitution of 1795 exhibit, under all their diversities, two features in common.[45] They each, on the one hand, confine the power of the legislature within very narrow limits indeed; under the Directory, for instance, the legislative body could not itself change any one of the 377 articles of the constitution, and the provisions for creating a constituent assembly were so framed that not the very least alteration in any of these articles could have been carried out within a period of less than nine years.[46] None of these constitutions, on the other

---

44 "Aucun des pouvoirs institués par la constitution n'a le droit de la changer dans son ensemble ni dans ses parties, sauf les réformes qui pourront y être faites par la voie de la révision, conformément aux dispositions du titre VII. ci-dessus.

"L'Assemblée nationale constituante en remet le dépôt à la fidélité du Corps législatif, du Roi et des juges, à la vigilance des pères de famille, aux épouses et aux méres, à l'affection des jeunes citoyens, au courage de tous les Français."—Constitution de 1791, Tit. vii. Art. 8; Duguit et Monnier, *Les Constitutions de la France depuis 1789*, p. 34.

These are the terms in which the National Assembly entrusts the Constitution of 1791 to the guardianship of the nation. It is just possible, though not likely, that the reference to the judges is intended to contain a hint that the Courts should annul or treat as void unconstitutional laws. Under the Constitution of the Year VIII. the senate had authority to annul unconstitutional laws. But this was rather a veto on what in England we should call Bills than a power to make void laws duly enacted. See Constitution of Year VIII., Tit. ii. Arts. 26, 28, Hélie, *Les Constitutions de la France*, p. 579.

45 See Appendix, Note I, Rigidity of French Constitutions.

46 See Constitution of 1795, Tit. xiii. Art. 338, Hélie, *Les Constitutions de la France*, p. 463.

hand, contain a hint as to the mode in which a law is to be treated which is alleged to violate the constitution. Their framers indeed hardly seem to have recognised the fact that enactments of the legislature might, without being in so many words opposed to the constitution, yet be of dubious constitutionality, and that some means would be needed for determining whether a given law was or was not in opposition to the principles of the constitution.

Existing Republican constitution.

These characteristics of the revolutionary constitutions have been repeated in the works of later French constitutionalists. Under the present French Republic there exist a certain number of laws (not it is true a very large number), which the Parliament cannot change; and what is perhaps of more consequence, the so-called Congress[47] could at any time increase the number of fundamental laws, and thereby greatly decrease the authority of future Parliaments. The constitution, however, contains no article providing against the possibility of an ordinary Parliament carrying through legislation greatly in excess of its constitutional powers. Any one in fact who bears in mind the respect paid in France from the time of the Revolution onwards to the legislation of *de facto* governments and the traditions of the French judicature, will assume with confidence that an enactment passed through the Chambers, promulgated by the President, and published in the *Bulletin des Lois,* will be held valid by every tribunal throughout the Republic.

Are the articles of continental constitutions "laws"?

This curious result therefore ensues. The restrictions placed on the action of the legislature under the French constitution are not in reality laws, since they are not rules which in the last resort will be enforced by the Courts. Their true character is that of maxims of political morality, which derive whatever strength they possess from being formally inscribed in the constitution and from the resulting support of public opinion. What is true of the constitution of France applies with more or less force to other politics which have been formed under the influence of French ideas. The Belgian constitution, for example, restricts the action of the Parliament no less than does

---

47 The term is used by French writers, but does not appear in the *Lois Constitutionnelles,* and one would rather gather that the proper title for a so-called Congress is *L'Assemblée Nationale.*

the Republican constitution of France. But it is at least doubtful whether Belgian constitutionalists have provided any means whatever for invalidating laws which diminish or do away with the rights (*e.g.* the right of freedom of speech) "guaranteed" to Belgian citizens. The jurists of Belgium maintain, in theory at least, that an Act of Parliament opposed to any article of the constitution ought to be treated by the Courts as void. But during the whole period of Belgian independence, no tribunal, it is said, has ever pronounced judgment upon the constitutionality of an Act of Parliament. This shows, it may be said, that the Parliament has respected the constitution, and certainly affords some evidence that, under favourable circumstances, formal declarations of rights may, from their influence on popular feeling, possess greater weight than is generally attributed to them in England; but it also suggests the notion that in Belgium, as in France, the restrictions on Parliamentary authority are supported mainly by moral or political sentiment, and are at bottom rather constitutional understandings than laws.

To an English critic, indeed, the attitude of continental and especially of revolutionary statesmen towards the ordinary legislature bears an air of paradox. They seem to be almost equally afraid of leaving the authority of the ordinary legislature unfettered, and of taking the steps by which the legislature may be prevented from breaking through the bonds imposed upon its power. The explanation of this apparent inconsistency is to be found in two sentiments which have influenced French constitution-makers from the very outbreak of the Revolution—an over-estimate of the effect to be produced by general declarations of rights, and a settled jealousy of any intervention by the judges in the sphere of politics.[48] We shall see, in a later chapter, that the public law of France is still radically influenced by the belief, even now almost universal among Frenchmen, that the law Courts must not be allowed to interfere in any way whatever with matters of state, or indeed with anything affecting the machinery of government.[49]

---

48 A. de Tocqueville, *Œuvres Complètes*, i. pp. 167, 168.

49 See Chap. XII.

Safeguards
provided
by found-
ers of
United
States.

The authors of the American constitution have, for reasons that will appear in my next chapter, been even more anxious than French statesmen to limit the authority of every legislative body throughout the Republic. They have further shared the faith of continental politicians in the value possessed by general declarations of rights. But they have, unlike French constitution-makers, directed their attention, not so much to preventing Congress and other legislatures from making laws in excess of their powers, as to the invention of means by which the effect of unconstitutional laws may be nullified; and this result they have achieved by making it the duty of every judge throughout the Union to treat as void any enactment which violates the constitution, and thus have given to the restrictions contained in the constitution on the legislative authority either of Congress or the State legislatures the character of real laws, that is, of rules enforced by the Courts. This system, which makes the judges the guardians of the constitution, provides the only adequate safeguard which has hitherto been invented against unconstitutional legislation.

Chapter III

PARLIAMENTARY SOVEREIGNTY AND FEDERALISM

My present aim is to illustrate the nature of Parliamentary sovereignty as it exists in England, by a comparison with the system of government known as Federalism as it exists in several parts of the civilised world, and especially in the United States of America.[1]

There are indeed to be found at the present time three other noteworthy examples of federal government—the Swiss Confederation, the Dominion of Canada, and the German Empire.[2] But while from a study of the institutions of each of these states one may draw illustrations which throw light on our subject, it will be best to keep our attention throughout this chapter fixed mainly on the institutions of the great American Republic. And this for two reasons. The Union, in the first place, presents the most completely developed type of federalism. All the features which mark that scheme of government, and above all the control of the legislature by the Courts, are there exhibited in their most salient and perfect form; the Swiss Confederation[3], moreover, and the Dominion of Canada, are more or less

---

1 On the whole subject of American Federalism the reader should consult Mr. Bryce's *American Commonwealth,* and with a view to matters treated of in this chapter should read with special care vol. i. part i.

2 To these we must now (1908) add the Commonwealth of Australia. (See Appendix, Note IX., Australian Federalism), [and see further the South Africa Act, 1909, 9 Ed. VII. c. 9].

3 Swiss federalism deserves an amount of attention which it has only of recent years begun to receive. The essential feature of the Swiss Commonwealth is that it is a genuine and

copied from the American model, whilst the constitution of the German Empire is too full of anomalies, springing both from historical and from temporary causes, to be taken as a fair representative of any known form of government. The Constitution of the United States, in the second place, holds a very peculiar relation towards the institutions of England. In the principle of the distribution of powers which determines its form, the Constitution of the United States is the exact opposite of the English constitution, the very essence of which is, as I hope I have now made clear, the unlimited authority of Parliament. But while the formal differences between the constitution of the American Republic and the constitution of the English monarchy are, looked at from one point of view, immense, the institutions of America are in their spirit little else than a gigantic development of the ideas which lie at the basis of the political and legal institutions of England. The principle, in short, which gives its form to our system of government is (to use a foreign but convenient expression) "unitarianism," or the habitual exercise of supreme legislative authority by one central power, which in the particular case is the British Parliament. The principle which, on the other hand, shapes every part of the American polity, is that distribution of limited, executive, legislative, and judical authority among bodies each co-ordinate with and independent of the other which, we shall in a moment see, is essential to the federal form of government. The contrast therefore between the two polities is seen in its most salient form, and the results of this difference are made all the more visible because in every other respect the institutions of the English people on each side the Atlantic rest upon the same notions of law, of justice, and of the relation between the rights of individuals and the rights of the government, or the state.

We shall best understand the nature of federalism and the points in which a federal constitution stands in contrast with the Parliamentary constitution of England if we note, first, the conditions essential to

---

natural democracy, but a democracy based on Continental, and not on Anglo-Saxon, ideas of freedom and of government.

The constitution of the Commonwealth of Australia contains at least one feature apparently suggested by Swiss federalism. See Appendix, Note IX., Australian Federalism.

the existence of a federal state and the aim with which such a state is formed; secondly, the essential features of a federal union; and lastly, certain characteristics of federalism which result from its very nature, and form points of comparison, or contrast, between a federal polity and a system of Parliamentary sovereignty.

Conditions and aim of federalism.

A federal state requires for its formation two conditions.[4]

Countries capable of union.

There must exist, in the first place, a body of countries such as the Cantons of Switzerland, the Colonies of America, or the Provinces of Canada, so closely connected by locality, by history, by race, or the like, as to be capable of bearing, in the eyes of their inhabitants, an impress of common nationality. It will also be generally found (if we appeal to experience) that lands which now form part of a federal state were at some stage of their existence bound together by close alliance or by subjection to a common sovereign. It were going further than facts warrant to assert that this earlier connection is essential to the formation of a federal state. But it is certain that where federalism flourishes it is in general the slowly-matured fruit of some earlier and looser connection.

Existence of federal sentiment.

A second condition absolutely essential to the founding of a federal system is the existence of a very peculiar state of sentiment among the inhabitants of the countries which it is proposed to unite. They must desire union, and must not desire unity. If there be no desire to unite, there is clearly no basis for federalism; the wild scheme entertained (it is said) under the Commonwealth of forming a union between the English Republic and the United Provinces was one of those dreams which may haunt the imagination of politicians but can

---

4 For United States see Story, *Commentaries on the Constitution of the United States* (4th ed.), and Bryce, *American Commonwealth*.

For Canada see the British North America Act, 1867, 30 Vict., c. 3; Bourinot, *Parliamentary Procedure and Practice in the Dominion of Canada*.

For Switzerland see *Constitution Fédérale de la Confédération Swisse du 29 Mai 1874*; Blumer, *Handbuch des Schweizerischen Bundesstaatsrechtes*; Lowell, *Governments and Parties in Continental Europe*, ii. chaps. xi.–xiii.; Sir F. O. Adams's *Swiss Confederation*; and Appendix, Note VIII., Swiss Federalism.

For the Commonwealth of Australia, the Constitution whereof deserves careful examination, the reader should consult Quick and Garran, *Annotated Constitution of the Australian Commonwealth*; Moore, *The Commonwealth of Australia*; and Bryce, *Studies in History and Jurisprudence*, i. Essay VIII., "The Constitution of the Commonwealth of Australia." See further, Appendix, Note IX., Australian Federalism.

never be transformed into fact. If, on the other hand, there be a desire for unity, the wish will naturally find its satisfaction, not under a federal, but under a unitarian constitution; the experience of England and Scotland in the eighteenth and of the states of Italy in the nineteenth century shows that the sense of common interests, or common national feeling, may be too strong to allow of that combination of union and separation which is the foundation of federalism. The phase of sentiment, in short, which forms a necessary condition for the formation of a federal state is that the people of the proposed state should wish to form for many purposes a single nation, yet should not wish to surrender the individual existence of each man's State or Canton. We may perhaps go a little farther, and say, that a federal government will hardly be formed unless many of the inhabitants of the separate States feel stronger allegiance to their own State than to the federal state represented by the common government. This was certainly the case in America towards the end of the eighteenth century, and in Switzerland at the middle of the nineteenth century. In 1787 a Virginian or a citizen of Massachusetts felt a far stronger attachment to Virginia or to Massachusetts than to the body of the confederated States. In 1848 the citizens of Lucerne felt far keener loyalty to their Canton than to the confederacy, and the same thing, no doubt, held true in a less degree of the men of Berne or of Zurich. The sentiment therefore which creates a federal state is the prevalence throughout the citizens of more or less allied countries of two feelings which are to a certain extent inconsistent—the desire for national unity and the determination to maintain the independence of each man's separate State. The aim of federalism is to give effect as far as possible to both these sentiments.

The aim of federalism.

A federal state is a political contrivance intended to reconcile national unity and power with the maintenance of "state rights." The end aimed at fixes the essential character of federalism. For the method by which Federalism attempts to reconcile the apparently inconsistent claims of national sovereignty and of state sovereignty consists of the formation of a constitution under which the ordinary powers[5] of sovereignty are elaborately divided between the common

---

5 See Appendix, Note II., Division of Powers in Federal States.

or national government and the separate states. The details of this division vary under every different federal constitution, but the general principle on which it should rest is obvious. Whatever concerns the nation as a whole should be placed under the control of the national government. All matters which are not primarily of common interest should remain in the hands of the several States. The preamble to the Constitution of the United States recites that

> We, the people of the United States, in order to form a more perfect union, establish justice, ensure domestic tranquillity, provide for the common defence, promote the general welfare, and secure the blessings of liberty to ourselves and our posterity, do ordain and establish this Constitution for the United States of America.

The tenth amendment enacts that "the powers not delegated to the United States by the Constitution nor prohibited by it to the States are reserved to the States respectively or to the people." These two statements, which are reproduced with slight alteration in the constitution of the Swiss Confederation,[6] point out the aim and lay down the fundamental idea of federalism.

Essential characteristics of federalism. United States.

From the notion that national unity can be reconciled with state independence by a division of powers under a common constitution between the nation on the one hand and the individual States on the other, flow the three leading characteristics of completely developed federalism,—the supremacy of the constitution—the distribution among bodies with limited and co-ordinate authority of the different powers of government—the authority of the Courts to act as interpreters of the constitution.

Supremacy of constitution.

A federal state derives its existence from the constitution, just as a corporation derives its existence from the grant by which it is created. Hence, every power, executive, legislative, or judicial, whether it belong to the nation or to the individual States, is subordinate to and controlled by the constitution. Neither the President of the United States nor the Houses of Congress, nor the Governor of Massachusetts, nor the Legislature or General Court of Massachusetts, can legally exercise a single power which is inconsistent with the articles

---

6 *Constitution Fédérale*, Preamble, and art. 3.

of the Constitution. This doctrine of the supremacy of the constitution is familiar to every American, but in England even trained lawyers find a difficulty in following it out of its legitimate consequences. The difficulty arises from the fact that under the English constitution no principle is recognised which bears any real resemblance to the doctrine (essential to federalism) that the Constitution constitutes the "supreme law of the land."[7] In England we have laws which may be called fundamental[8] or constitutional because they deal with important principles (as, for example, the descent of the Crown or the terms of union with Scotland) lying at the basis of our institutions, but with us there is no such thing as a supreme law, or law which tests the validity of other laws. There are indeed important statutes, such as the Act embodying the Treaty of Union with Scotland, with which it would be political madness to tamper gratuitously; there are utterly unimportant statutes, such, for example, as the Dentists Act, 1878, which may be repealed or modified at the pleasure or caprice of Parliament; but neither the Act of Union with Scotland nor the Dentists Act, 1878, has more claim than the other to be considered a supreme law. Each embodies the will of the sovereign legislative power; each can be legally altered or repealed by Parliament; neither tests the validity of the other. Should the Dentists Act, 1878, unfortunately contravene the terms of the Act of Union, the Act of Union would be *pro tanto* repealed, but no judge would dream of maintaining that the Dentists Act, 1878, was thereby rendered invalid or unconstitutional. The one fundamental dogma of English constitutional law is the absolute legislative sovereignty or despotism of the King in Parliament. But this dogma is incompatible with the existence of a fundamental compact, the provisions of which control every authority existing under the constitution.[9]

Consequences. Written constitution. In the supremacy of the constitution are involved three consequences:

---

7 See Constitution of United States, art. 6, cl. 2.

8 The expression "fundamental laws of England" became current during the controversy as to the payment of ship-money (1635). See Gardiner, *History of England,* viii. pp. 84, 85.

9 Compare especially Kent, *Commentaries,* i. pp. 447–449.

The constitution must almost necessarily be a "written" constitution.

The foundations of a federal state are a complicated contract. This compact contains a variety of terms which have been agreed to, and generally after mature deliberation, by the States which make up the confederacy. To base an arrangement of this kind upon understandings or conventions would be certain to generate misunderstandings and disagreements. The articles of the treaty, or in other words of the consitution, must therefore be reduced to writing. The constitution must be a written document, and, if possible, a written document of which the terms are open to no misapprehension. The founders of the American Union left at least one great question unsettled. This gap in the Constitution gave an opening to the dispute which was the plea, if not the justification, for the War of Secession.[10]

Rigid constitution. The constitution must be what I have termed a "rigid"[11] or "inexpansive" constitution.

The law of the constitution must be either legally immutable, or else capable of being changed only by some authority above and beyond the ordinary legislative bodies, whether federal or state legislatures, existing under the constitution.

In spite of the doctrine enunciated by some jurists that in every country there must be found some person or body legally capable of changing every institution thereof, it is hard to see why it should be held inconceivable[12] that the founders of a polity should have delib-

---

10 No doubt it is conceivable that a federation might grow up by the force of custom, and under agreements between different States which were not reduced into writing, and it appears to be questionable how far the Achæan League was bound together by anything equivalent to a written constitution. It is, however, in the highest degree improbable, even if it be not practically impossible, that in modern times a federal state could be formed without the framing of some document which, whatever the name by which it is called, would be in reality a written constitution, regulating the rights and duties of the federal government and the States composing the Federation.

11 See pp. 39, 64–66, *ante.*

12 Eminent American lawyers, whose opinion is entitled to the highest respect, maintain that under the Constitution there exists no person, or body of persons, possessed of legal sovereignty, in the sense given by Austin to that term, and it is difficult to see that this opinion involves any absurdity. Compare Constitution of United States, art. 5. It would appear further that certain rights reserved under the Constitution of the German Empire to

erately omitted to provide any means for lawfully changing its bases. Such an omission would not be unnatural on the part of the authors of a federal union, since one main object of the States entering into the compact is to prevent further encroachments upon their several state rights; and in the fifth article of the United States Constitution may still be read the record of an attempt to give to some of its provisions temporary immutability. The question, however, whether a federal constitution necessarily involves the existence of some ultimate sovereign power authorised to amend or alter its terms is of merely speculative interest, for under existing federal governments the constitution will be found to provide the means for its own improvement.[13] It is, at any rate, certain that whenever the founders of a federal government hold the maintenance of a federal system to be of primary importance, supreme legislative power cannot be safely vested in any ordinary legislature acting under the constitution.[14] For so to vest legislative sovereignty would be inconsistent with the aim of federalism, namely, the permanent division between the spheres of the national government and of the several States. If Congress could legally change the Constitution, New York and Massachusetts would have no legal guarantee for the amount of independence reserved to them under the Constitution, and would be as subject to the sovereign power of Congress as is Scotland to the sovereignty of Parliament; the Union would cease to be a federal state, and would become a unitarian republic. If, on the other hand, the legislature of

---

particular States cannot under the Constitution be taken away from a State without its assent. (See *Reichsverfassung,* art. 78.) The truth is that a Federal Constitution partakes of the nature of a treaty, and it is quite conceivable that the authors of the Constitution may intend to provide no constitutional means of changing its terms except the assent of all the parties to the treaty.

13 See *e.g.* South Africa Act, 1909, s. 152.

14 Under the Constitution of the German Empire the Imperial legislative body can amend the Constitution. But the character of the Federal Council (*Bundesrath*) gives ample security for the protection of State rights. No change in the Constitution can be effected which is opposed by fourteen votes in the Federal Council. This gives a veto on change to Prussia and to various combinations of some among the other States. The extent to which national sentiment and State patriotism respectively predominate under a federal system may be conjectured from the nature of the authority which has the right to modify the Constitution. See Appendix, Note II., Division of Powers in Federal States.

South Carolina could of its own will amend the Constitution, the authority of the central government would (from a legal point of view) be illusory; the United States would sink from a nation into a collection of independent countries united by the bond of a more or less permanent alliance. Hence the power of amending the Constitution has been placed, so to speak, outside the Constitution, and one may say, with sufficient accuracy for our present purpose, that the legal sovereignty of the United States resides in the States' governments as forming one aggregate body represented by three-fourths of the several States at any time belonging to the Union.[15] Now from the necessity for placing ultimate legislative authority in some body outside the Constitution a remarkable consequence ensues. Under a federal as under a unitarian system there exists a sovereign power, but the sovereign is in a federal state a despot hard to rouse. He is not, like the English Parliament, an ever-wakeful legislator, but a monarch who slumbers and sleeps. The sovereign of the United States has been roused to serious action but once during the course of more than a century. It needed the thunder of the Civil War to break his repose, and it may be doubted whether anything short of impending revolution will ever again arouse him to activity. But a monarch who slumbers for years is like a monarch who does not exist. A federal constitution is capable of change, but for all that a federal constitution is apt to be unchangeable.[16]

---

15 "The Congress, whenever two-thirds of both houses shall deem it necessary, shall propose amendments to this Constitution, or, on the application of the legislatures of two-thirds of the several States, shall call a convention for proposing amendments, which, in either case, shall be valid to all intents and purposes, as part of this Constitution, when ratified by the legislatures of three-fourths of the several States, or by conventions in three-fourths thereof, as the one or the other mode of ratification may be proposed by the Congress; provided that no amendments which may be made prior to the year one thousand eight hundred and eight shall in any manner affect the first and fourth clauses in the ninth section of the first article; and that no State, without its consent, shall be deprived of its equal suffrage in the Senate."—Constitution of United States, art. 5. Compare Austin, i. p. 278, and see Bryce, *American Commonwealth,* i. (3rd ed.), chap. xxxii., on the Amendment of the Constitution.

16 [Note, however, the ease with which the provisions of the Constitution of the U.S., with regard to the election of Senators by the Legislature and the transference of such election to the people of each State, have been carried through by Amendment xvii., passed in 1913.]

Every legislature under federal constitution is a subordinate law-making body.

Every legislative assembly existing under a federal constitution is merely[17] a subordinate law-making body, whose laws are of the nature of bye-laws, valid whilst within the authority conferred upon it by the constitution, but invalid or unconstitutional if they go beyond the limits of such authority.

There is an apparent absurdity[18] in comparing the legislature of the United States to an English railway company or a municipal corporation, but the comparison is just. Congress can, within the limits of its legal powers, pass laws which bind every man throughout the United States. The Great Eastern Railway Company can, in like manner, pass laws which bind every man throughout the British dominions. A law passed by Congress which in in excess of its legal powers, as contravening the Constitution, is invalid; a law passed by the Great Eastern Railway Company in excess of the powers given by Act of Parliament, or, in other words, by the legal constitution of the company, is also invalid; a law passed by Congress is called an "Act" of Congress, and if *ultra vires* is described as "unconstitutional"; a law passed by the Great Eastern Railway Company is called a "bye-law," and if *ultra vires* is called, not "unconstitutional," but "invalid." Differences, however, of words must not conceal from us essential similarity in things. Acts of Congress, or of the Legislative Assembly of New York or of Massachusetts, are at bottom simply "bye-laws," depending for their validity upon their being within the powers given to Congress or to the state legislatures by the Constitution. The bye-laws of the Great Eastern Railway Company, imposing fines upon passengers who travel over their line without a ticket, are laws, but they are laws depending for their validity upon their being within the powers conferred upon the Company by Act of Parliament, *i.e.* by the Company's constitution. Congress and the Great Eastern Railway Company are in truth each of them nothing more than subordinate law-making bodies. Their power differs not in degree, but in kind,

---

17 This is so in the United States, but it need not necessarily be so. The Federal Legislature may be a sovereign power but may be so constituted that the rights of the States under the Constitution are practically protected. This condition of things exists in the German Empire.

18 See p. 40, note 4, *ante.*

from the authority of the sovereign Parliament of the United Kingdom.[19]

Distribution of powers. The distribution of powers is an essential feature of federalism. The object for which a federal state is formed involves a division of authority between the national government and the separate States. The powers given to the nation form in effect so many limitations upon the authority of the separate States, and as it is not intended that the central government should have the opportunity of encroaching upon the rights retained by the States, its sphere of action necessarily becomes the object of rigorous definition. The Constitution, for instance, of the United States delegates special and closely defined powers to the executive, to the legislature, and to the judiciary of the Union, or in effect to the Union itself, whilst it provides that the powers "not delegated to the United States by the Constitution nor prohibited by it to the States are reserved to the States respectively or to the people."[20]

Division of powers carried in fact beyond necessary limit. This is all the amount of division which is essential to a federal constitution. But the principle of definition and limitation of powers harmonises so well with the federal spirit that it is generally carried much farther than is dictated by the mere logic of the constitution. Thus the authority assigned to the United States under the Constitution is not concentrated in any single official or body of officials. The

---

19 See as to bye-laws made by municipal corporations, and the dependence of their validity upon the powers conferred upon the corporation: *Johnson* v. *Mayor of Croydon*, 16 Q. B. D. 708; *Reg.* v. *Powell*, 51 L. T. 92; *Munro* v. *Watson*, 57 L. T. 366. See Bryce, *American Commonwealth*, i. (3rd ed.), pp. 244, 245.

20 Constitution of United States, Amendments, art. 10. See provisions of a similar character in the Swiss Constitution, *Constitution Fédérale*, art. 3. Compare the Constitution of the Canadian Dominion, British North America Act, 1867, secs. 91, 92.

There exists, however, one marked distinction in principle between the Constitution of the United States and the Constitution of the Canadian Dominion. The Constitution of the United States in substance reserves to the separate States all powers not expressly conferred upon the national government. The Canadian Constitution in substance confers upon the Dominion government all powers not assigned exclusively to the Provinces. In this matter the Swiss Constitution follows that of the United States.

The Constitution of the Australian Commonwealth follows in effect the example of the Constitution of the United States. The powers conferred upon the Commonwealth Parliament are, though very large, definite; the powers reserved to the Parliaments of the States are indefinite. See Commonwealth Act, ss. 51, 52, and 107, and Appendix, Note II., Division of Powers in Federal States, and Note IX., Australian Federalism.

President has definite rights, upon which neither Congress nor the judicial department can encroach. Congress has but a limited, indeed a very limited, power of legislation, for it can make laws upon eighteen topics only; yet within its own sphere it is independent both of the President and of the Federal Courts. So, lastly, the judiciary have their own powers. They stand on a level both with the President and with Congress, and their authority (being directly derived from the constitution) cannot, without a distinct violation of law, be trenched upon either by the executive or by the legislature. Where, further, States are federally united, certain principles of policy or of justice must be enforced upon the whole confederated body as well as upon the separate parts thereof, and the very inflexibility of the constitution tempts legislators to place among constitutional articles maxims which (though not in their nature constitutional) have special claims upon respect and observance. Hence spring additional restrictions on the power both of the federation and of the separate states. The United States Constitution prohibits both to Congress[21] and to the separate States[22] the passing of a bill of attainder or an *ex post facto* law, the granting of any title of nobility, or in effect the laying of any tax on articles exported from any State,[23] enjoins that full faith shall be given to the public acts and judicial proceedings of every other State, hinders any State from passing any law impairing the obligation of contracts,[24] and prevents every State from entering into any treaty, alliance, or confederation; thus it provides that the elementary principles of justice, freedom of trade, and the rights of individual property shall be absolutely respected throughout the length and breadth of the Union. It further ensures that the right of the people to keep and bear arms shall not be infringed, while it also provides that no member can be expelled from either House of Congress without the concurrence of two-thirds of the House. Other federal constitutions go far beyond that of the United States in ascribing among

---

21 Constitution of United States, art. 1, sec. 9.

22 *Ibid.*, art. 1, sec. 10.

23 *Ibid.*, art. 1, sec. 9. But conf. art. 1, sec. 10.

24 *Ibid.*, art. 1, sec. 10.

constitutional articles either principles or petty rules which are supposed to have a claim of legal sanctity; the Swiss Constitution is full of "guaranteed" rights.

Nothing, however, would appear to an English critic to afford so striking an example of the connection between federalism and the "limitation of powers" as the way in which the principles of the federal Constitution pervade in America the constitutions of the separate States. In no case does the legislature of any one State possess all the powers of "state sovereignty" left to the States by the Constitution of the Republic, and every state legislature is subordinated to the constitution of the State.[25] The ordinary legislature of New York or Massachusetts can no more change the state constitution than it can alter the Constitution of the United States itself; and, though the topic cannot be worked out here in detail, it may safely be asserted that state government throughout the Union is formed upon the federal model, and (what is noteworthy) that state constitutions have carried much further than the Constitution of the Republic the tendency to clothe with constitutional immutability any rules which strike the people as important. Illinois has embodied, among fundamental laws, regulations as to elevators.[26]

But here, as in other cases, there is great difficulty in distinguishing cause and effect. If a federal form of government has affected, as it probably has, the constitutions of the separate States, it is certain that features originally existing in the State constitutions have been reproduced in the Constitution of the Union; and, as we shall see in a moment, the most characteristic institution of the United States, the Federal Court, appears to have been suggested at least to the founders of the Republic, by the relation which before 1789 already existed between the state tribunals and the state legislatures.[27]

---

25 Contrast with this the indefinite powers left to State Parliaments under the Commonwealth of Australia Constitution Act, ss. 106, 107. The Constitutionalists of Australia who created the Commonwealth have been as much influenced by the traditions of English Parliamentary sovereignty as American legislators have in their dealings with the State Constitutions been influenced by the spirit of federalism.

26 See *Munn* v. *Illinois,* 4 Otto, 113.

27 European critics of American federalism have, as has been well remarked by an eminent French writer, paid in general too little attention to the working and effect of the state

Division of powers distinguishes federal from unitarian system of government.

The tendency of federalism to limit on every side the action of government and to split up the strength of the state among co-ordinate and independent authorities is specially noticeable, because it forms the essential distinction between a federal system such as that of America or Switzerland, and a unitarian system of government such as that which exists in England or Russia. We talk indeed of the English constitution as resting on a balance of powers, and as maintaining a division between the executive, the legislative, and the judicial bodies. These expressions have a real meaning. But they have quite a different significance as applied to England from the sense which they bear as applied to the United States. All the power of the English state is concentrated in the Imperial Parliament, and all departments of government are legally subject to Parliamentary despotism. Our judges are independent, in the sense of holding their office by a permanent tenure, and of being raised above the direct influence of the Crown or the Ministry; but the judicial department does not pretend to stand on a level with Parliament; its functions might be modified at any time by an Act of Parliament; and such a statute would be no violation of the law. The Federal Judiciary, on the other hand, are co-ordinate with the President and with Congress, and cannot without a revolution be deprived of a single right by President or Congress. So, again, the executive and the legislature are with us distinct bodies, but they are not distinct in the sense in which the President is distinct from and independent of the Houses of Congress. The House of Commons interferes with administrative matters, and the Ministry are in truth placed and kept in office by the

---

constitutions, and have overlooked the great importance of the action of the state legislatures. See Boutmy, *Études de Droit Constitutionnel* (2nd ed.), pp. 103–111.

"It has been truly said that nearly every provision of the Federal Constitution that has worked well is one borrowed from or suggested by some State Constitution; nearly every provision that has worked badly is one which the Convention, for want of a precedent, was obliged to devise for itself."—Bryce, *American Commonwealth*, i. (3rd ed.), p. 35. One capital merit of Mr. Bryce's book is that it for the first time reveals, even to those who had already studied American institutions, the extent to which the main features of the Constitution of the United States were suggested to its authors by the characteristics of the State governments.

House. A modern Cabinet would not hold power for a week if censured by a newly elected House of Commons. An American President may retain his post and exercise his very important functions even though his bitterest opponents command majorities both in the Senate and in the House of Representatives. Unitarianism, in short, means the concentration of the strength of the state in the hands of one visible sovereign power, be that power Parliament or Czar. Federalism means the distribution of the force of the state among a number of co-ordinate bodies each originating in and controlled by the constitution.

Authority
of Courts. Whenever there exists, as in Belgium or in France, a more or less rigid constitution, the articles of which cannot be amended by the ordinary legislature, the difficulty has to be met of guarding against legislation inconsistent with the constitution. As Belgian and French statesmen have created no machinery for the attainment of this object, we may conclude that they considered respect for the constitution to be sufficiently secured by moral or political sanctions, and treated the limitations placed on the power of Parliament rather as maxims of policy than as true laws. During a period, at any rate of more than sixty years, no Belgian judge has (it is said) ever pronounced a Parliamentary enactment unconstitutional. No French tribunal, as has been already pointed out, would hold itself at liberty to disregard an enactment, however unconstitutional, passed by the National Assembly, inserted in the *Bulletin des Lois,* and supported by the force of the government; and French statesmen may well have thought, as Tocqueville certainly did think, that in France possible Parliamentary invasions of the constitution were a less evil than the participation of the judges in political conflicts. France, in short, and Belgium being governed under unitarian constitutions, the nonsovereign character of the legislature is in each case an accident, not an essential property of their polity. Under a federal system it is otherwise. The legal supremacy of the constitution is essential to the existence of the state; the glory of the founders of the United States is to have devised or adopted arrangements under which the Constitution became in reality as well as name the supreme law of the land.

This end they attained by adherence to a very obvious principle, and by the invention of appropriate machinery for carrying this principle into effect.

How
authority
of the
Courts is
exerted.

The principle is clearly expressed in the Constitution of the United States (article 6):

> The Constitution and the laws of the United States which shall be made in pursuance thereof . . . shall be the supreme law of the land, and the judges in every State shall be bound thereby, anything in the constitution or laws of any State to the contrary notwithstanding.[28]

The import of these expressions is unmistakable. Chancellor Kent writes:

> Every Act of Congress and every Act of the legislatures of the States, and every part of the constitution of any State, which are repugnant to the Constitution of the United States, are necessarily void. This is a clear and settled principle of [our] constitutional jurisprudence.[29]

The legal duty therefore of every judge, whether he act as a judge of the State of New York or as a judge of the Supreme Court of the United States, is clear. He is bound to treat as void every legislative act, whether proceeding from Congress or from the state legislatures, which is inconsistent with the Constitution of the United States. His duty is as clear as that of an English judge called upon to determine the validity of a bye-law made by the Great Eastern or any other Railway Company. The American judge must in giving judgment obey the terms of the Constitution, just as his English brother must in giving judgment obey every Act of Parliament bearing on the case.

Supremacy
of constitu-
tion se-
cured by
creation of
Supreme
Court.

To have laid down the principle with distinctness is much, but the great problem was how to ensure that the principle should be obeyed; for there existed a danger that judges depending on the federal government should wrest the Constitution in favour of the central power, and that judges created by the States should wrest it in favour of State rights or interests. This problem has been solved by the creation of the Supreme Court and of the Federal Judiciary.

---

28 Constitution of United States, art. 6.

29 Kent, *Commentaries*, i. (12th ed.), p. 314, and conf. *Ibid.*, p. 449.

Of the nature and position of the Supreme Court itself thus much alone need for our present purpose be noted. The Court derives its existence from the Constitution, and stands therefore on an equality with the President and with Congress; the members thereof (in common with every judge of the Federal Judiciary) hold their places during good behaviour, at salaries which cannot be diminished during a judge's tenure of office.[30] The Supreme Court stands at the head of the whole federal judicial department, which, extending by its subordinate Courts throughout the Union, can execute its judgments through its own officers without requiring the aid of state officials. The Supreme Court, though it has a certain amount of original jurisdiction, derives its importance from its appellate character; it is on every matter which concerns the interpretation of the Constitution a supreme and final Court of Appeal from the decision of every Court (whether a Federal Court or a State Court) throughout the Union. It is in fact the final interpreter of the Constitution, and therefore has authority to pronounce finally as a Court of Appeal whether a law passed either by Congress or by the legislature of a State, *e.g.* New York, is or is not constitutional. To understand the position of the Supreme Court we must bear in mind that there exist throughout the Union two classes of Courts in which proceedings can be commenced, namely, the subordinate federal Courts deriving their authority from the Constitution, and the state Courts, *e.g.* of New York or Massachusetts, created by and existing under the state constitutions; and that the jurisdiction of the federal judiciary and the state judiciary is in many cases concurrent, for though the jurisdiction of the federal Courts is mainly confined to cases arising under the Constitution and laws of the United States, it is also frequently dependent upon the character of the parties, and though there are cases with which no state Court can deal, such a Court may often entertain cases which might be brought in a federal Court, and constantly has to consider the effect of the Constitution on the validity either of a law passed by Congress or of state legislation. That the Supreme Court should be a Court of Appeal from the decision of the subordinate

---

30 Constitution of United States, art. 3, secs. 1, 2.

federal tribunals is a matter which excites no surprise. The point to be noted is that it is also a Court of Appeal from decisions of the Supreme Court of any State, *e.g.* New York, which turn upon or interpret the articles of the Constitution or Acts of Congress. The particular cases in which a party aggrieved by the decision of a state Court has a right of appeal to the Supreme Court of the United States are regulated by an Act of Congress of 24th September 1789, the twenty-fifth section of which provides that

> a final judgment or decree, in any suit in the highest court of law or equity of a State, may be brought up on error in point of law, to the Supreme Court of the United States, provided the validity of a treaty, or statute of, or authority exercised under the United States, was drawn in question in the state court, and the decision was against the validity; or provided the validity of any state authority was drawn in question, on the ground of its being repugnant to the Constitution, treaties, or laws of the United States, and the decision was in favour of its validity; or provided the construction of any clause of the Constitution or of a treaty, or statute of, or commission held under the United States, was drawn in question, and the decision was against the title, right, privilege, or exemption, specially claimed under the authority of the Union.[31]

Strip this enactment of its technicalities and it comes to this. A party to a case in the highest Court, say of New York, who bases his claim or defence upon an article in the Constitution or law made under it, stands in this position: If judgment be in his favour there is no further appeal; if judgment goes against him, he has a right of appeal to the Supreme Court of the United States. Any lawyer can see at a glance how well devised is the arrangement to encourage state Courts in the performance of their duty as guardians of the Constitution, and further that the Supreme Court thereby becomes the ultimate arbiter of all matters affecting the Constitution.

Let no one for a moment fancy that the right of every Court, and ultimately of the Supreme Court, to pronounce on the constitutionality of legislation and on the rights possessed by different authorities under the Constitution is one rarely exercised, for it is in fact a right which is constantly exerted without exciting any more surprise on the

---

31 Kent, *Commentaries*, i. (12th ed.), pp. 299, 300.

part of the citizens of the Union than does in England a judgment of the King's Bench Division treating as invalid the bye-law of a railway company. The American tribunals have dealt with matters of supreme consequence; they have determined that Congress has the right to give priority to debts due to the United States,[32] can lawfully incorporate a bank,[33] has a general power to levy or collect taxes without any restraint, but subject to definite principles of uniformity prescribed by the Constitution; the tribunals have settled what is the power of Congress over the militia, who is the person who has a right to command it,[34] and that the power exercised by Congress during the War of Secession of issuing paper money was valid.[35] The Courts again have controlled the power of the separate States fully as vigorously as they have defined the authority of the United States. The judiciary have pronounced unconstitutional every *ex post facto* law, every law taxing even in the slightest degree articles exported from any State, and have again deprived of effect state laws impairing the obligation of contracts. To the judiciary in short are due the maintenance of justice, the existence of internal free trade, and the general respect for the rights of property; whilst a recent decision shows that the Courts are prepared to uphold as consistent with the Constitution any laws which prohibit modes of using private property, which seem to the judges inconsistent with public interest.[36] The power moreover of the Courts which maintains the articles of the Constitution as the law of the land, and thereby keeps each authority within its proper sphere, is exerted with an ease and regularity which has astounded and perplexed continental critics. The explanation is that while the judges of the United States control the action of the Constitution, they nevertheless perform purely judicial functions, since they never decide anything but the cases before them. It is natural to

---

32 Kent, *Commentaries*, i. (12th ed.), pp. 244–248.

33 *Ibid.*, pp. 248–254.

34 *Ibid.*, pp. 262–266.

35 Story, *Commentaries on the Constitution* (4th ed.), ii. secs. 1116, 1117. See *Hepburn* v. *Griswold*, 8 Wallace, 603, Dec. 1869, and *Knox* v. *Lee*, 12 Wallace, 457.

36 *Munn* v. *Illinois*, 4 Otto, Rep. 113. See especially the Judgments of Marshall, C. J., collected in *The Writings of John Marshall upon the Federal Constitution* (1839).

say that the Supreme Court pronounces Acts of Congress invalid, but in fact this is not so. The Court never directly pronounces any opinion whatever upon an Act of Congress. What the Court does do is simply to determine that in a given case *A* is or is not entitled to recover judgment against *X*; but in determining that case the Court may decide that an Act of Congress is not to be taken into account, since it is an Act beyond the constitutional powers of Congress.[37]

The true merit of the founders of the United States.

If any one thinks this is a distinction without a difference he shows some ignorance of politics, and does not understand how much the authority of a Court is increased by confining its action to purely judicial business. But persons who, like Tocqueville, have fully appreciated the wisdom of the statesmen who created the Union, have formed perhaps an exaggerated estimate of their originality. Their true merit was that they applied with extraordinary skill the notions which they had inherited from English law to the novel circumstances of the new republic. To any one imbued with the traditions of English procedure it must have seemed impossible to let a Court decide upon anything but the case before it. To any one who had inhabited a colony governed under a charter the effect of which on the validity of a colonial law was certainly liable to be considered by the Privy Council, there was nothing startling in empowering the judiciary to pronounce in given cases upon the constitutionality of Acts passed by assemblies whose powers were limited by the Constitution, just as the authority of the colonial legislatures was limited by charter or by Act of Parliament. To a French jurist, indeed, filled with the traditions of the French Parliaments, all this might well be incomprehensible, but an English lawyer can easily see that the fathers of the republic treated Acts of Congress as English Courts treat bye-laws, and in forming the Supreme Court may probably have had in mind the functions of the Privy Council. It is still more certain that they had before their eyes cases in which the tribunals of particular States had treated as unconstitutional, and therefore pronounced void, Acts of the state legislature which contravened the state constitution. The earliest case of declaring a law unconstitutional

---

37 See Chap. II. pp. 42–45, *ante.*

dates (it is said) from 1786, and took place in Rhode Island, which was then, and continued till 1842, to be governed under the charter of Charles II. An Act of the legislature was declared unconstitutional by the Courts of North Carolina in 1787[38] and by the Courts of Virginia in 1788,[39] whilst the Constitution of the United States was not adopted till 1789, and *Marbury* v. *Madison,* the first case in which the Supreme Court dealt with the question of constitutionality, was decided in 1803.[40]

But if their notions were conceptions derived from English law, the great statesmen of America gave to old ideas a perfectly new expansion, and for the first time in the history of the world formed a constitution which should in strictness be "the law of the land," and in so doing created modern federalism. For the essential characteristics of federalism—the supremacy of the constitution—the distribution of powers—the authority of the judiciary—reappear, though no doubt with modifications, in every true federal state.

The Canadian Dominion.

Turn for a moment to the Canadian Dominion. The preamble to the British North America Act, 1867, asserts with diplomatic inaccuracy that the Provinces of the present Dominion have expressed their desire to be united into one Dominion "with a constitution similar in principle to that of the United *Kingdom.*" If preambles were intended to express anything like the whole truth, for the word *"Kingdom"* ought to have been substituted *"States"*: since it is clear that the Constitution of the Dominion is in its essential features modelled on that of the Union. This is indeed denied, but in my judgment without adequate grounds, by competent Canadian critics.[41] The differences

---

38 Martin, 421.

39 1 Va. Cas. 198.

40 1 Cranch, 137. For the facts as to the early action of the State Courts in declaring legislative enactments unconstitutional I am indebted, as for much other useful criticism, to that eminent constitutionalist my friend the late Professor Thayer of Harvard University.

41 The difference between the judgment as to the character of the Canadian Constitution formed by myself, and the judgment of competent and friendly Canadian critics, may easily be summarised and explained. If we look at the federal character of the Constituton of the Dominion, we must inevitably regard it as a copy, though by no means a servile copy, of the Constitution of the United States. Now in the present work the Canadian Constitution is regarded exclusively as a federal government. Hence my assertion, which I still hold to be

between the institutions of the United States and of the Dominion are of course both considerable and noteworthy. But no one can study the provisions of the British North America Act, 1867, without seeing that its authors had the American Constitution constantly before their eyes, and that if Canada were an independent country it would be a Confederacy governed under a Constitution very similar to that of the United States. The Constitution is the law of the land; it cannot be changed (except within narrow limits allowed by the British North America Act, 1867) either by the Dominion Parliament[42] or by the Provincial Parliaments;[43] it can be altered only by the sovereign power of the British Parliament.[44] Nor does this arise from the Canadian Dominion being a dependency. New Zealand is, like Canada, a colony, but the New Zealand Parliament can with the assent of the Crown do what the Canadian Parliament cannot do—change the colonial constitution. Throughout the Dominion, therefore, the Constitution is in the strictest sense the immutable law of the land. Under this law again, you have, as you would expect, the distribution of powers among bodies of co-ordinate authority;[45] though undoubtedly the powers bestowed on the Dominion Government and Parliament are greater when compared with the powers reserved to the

---

correct, that the government of the Dominion is modelled on that of the Union. If, on the other hand, we compare the Canadian Executive with the American Executive, we perceive at once that Canadian government is modelled on the system of Parliamentary cabinet government as it exists in England, and does not in any wise imitate the Presidential government of America. This, it has been suggested to me by a friend well acquainted with Canadian institutions, is the point of view from which they are looked upon by my Canadian critics, and is the justification for the description of the Constitution of the Dominion given in the preamble to the British North America Act, 1867. The suggestion is a just and valuable one; in deference to it some of the expressions used in the earlier editions of this book have undergone a slight modification.

42 See, however, British North America Act, 1867 (30 Vict. c. 3), s. 94, which gives the Dominion Parliament a limited power (when acting in conjunction with a Provincial legislature) of changing to a certain extent the provisions of the British North America Act, 1867.

43 The legislatures of each Province have, nevertheless, authority to make laws for "the amendment from time to time, notwithstanding anything [in the British North America Act, 1867] of the Constitution of the Province, except as regards the office of Lieutenant Governor." See British North America Act, 1867, s. 92.

44 See for an example of an amendment of the Dominion Constitution by an Imperial statute, the Parliament of Canada Act, 1875.

45 British North America Act, 1867, secs. 91, 92.

Provinces than are the powers which the Constitution of the United States gives to the federal government. In nothing is this more noticeable than in the authority given to[46] the Dominion Government to disallow Provincial Acts.[47]

This right was possibly given with a view to obviate altogether the necessity for invoking the law Courts as interpreters of the Constitution; the founders of the Confederation appear in fact to have believed that

> the care taken to define the respective powers of the several legislative bodies in the Dominion would prevent any troublesome or dangerous conflict of authority arising between the central and local governments.[48]

The futility, however, of a hope grounded on a misconception of the nature of federalism is proved by the existence of two thick volumes of reports filled with cases on the constitutionality of legislative enactments, and by a long list of decisions as to the respective powers possessed by the Dominion and by the Provincial Parliaments—judgments given by the true Supreme Court of the Dominion, namely, the Judicial Committee of the Privy Council. In Canada, as in the United States, the Courts inevitably become the interpreters of the Constitution.

The Swiss Confederation.

Swiss federalism repeats, though with noteworthy variations, the essential traits of the federal polity as it exists across the Atlantic. The Constitution is the law of the land, and cannot be changed either by the federal or by the cantonal legislative bodies; the Constitution enforces a distribution of powers between the national government and the Cantons, and directly or indirectly defines and limits the power of every authority existing under it. The Common Government has in Switzerland, as in America, three organs—a Federal Legislature, a Federal Executive (*Bundesrath*), and a Federal Court (*Bundesgericht*).

Of the many interesting and instructive peculiarities which give to Swiss federalism an individual character, this is not the occasion to

---

46 *Ibid.*, secs. 56, 90.

47 Bourinot, *Parliamentary Procedure and Practice in the Dominion of Canada,* p. 76.

48 Bourinot, *Parliamentary Procedure and Practice in the Dominion of Canada,* p. 694.

write in detail. It lies, however, within the scope of this chapter to note that the Constitution of the Confederation differs in two most important respects from that of the United States. It does not, in the first place, establish anything like the accurate division between the executive and the judicial departments of government which exists both in America and in Canada; the Executive exercises, under the head of "administrative law," many functions[49] of a judicial character, and thus, for example, till 1893 dealt in effect with questions[50] having reference to the rights of religious bodies. The Federal Assembly is the final arbiter on all questions as to the respective jurisdiction of the Executive and of the Federal Court. The judges of that Court are elected by the Federal Assembly, they are occupied greatly with questions of public law (*Staatsrecht*), and so experienced a statesman as Dr. Dubs laments that the Federal Court should possess jurisdiction in matters of private law.[51] When to this it is added that the judgments of the Federal Court are executed by the government, it at once becomes clear that, according to any English standard, Swiss statesmanship has failed as distinctly as American statesmanship has succeeded in keeping the judicial apart from the executive department of government, and that this failure constitutes a serious flaw in the Swiss Constitution. That Constitution, in the second place, does not in reality place the Federal Court on an absolute level with the Federal Assembly. That tribunal cannot question the constitutionality of laws or decrees passed by the Federal Parliament.[52] From this fact one might suppose that the Federal Assembly is (unlike Congress) a sovereign body, but this is not so. The reason why all Acts of the Assembly must be treated as constitutional by the Federal Tribunal is that the Constitution itself almost precludes the possibility of encroachment upon its articles by the federal legislative body. No

---

49 *Constitution Fédérale*, art. 113, *Loi*; 27 June 1874, art. 59; and Dubs, *Das öffentliche Recht der schweizerischen Eidgenossenschaft*, ii. (2nd ed.), p. 90.

50 The decision thereof belonged till 1893 to the Assembly, guided by the Federal Council; it now belongs to the Federal Court. See Dubs, ii. pp. 92–95; Lowell, *Governments and Parties*, ii. pp. 217, 218.

51 *Constitution Fédérale*, art. 113; and Dubs, ii. (2nd ed.), pp. 92–95.

52 *Constitution Fédérale*, art. 113; and Dubs, ii. (2nd ed.), pp. 92–95.

legal revision can take place without the assent both of a majority of Swiss citizens and of a majority of the Cantons, and an ordinary law duly passed by the Federal Assembly may be legally annulled by a popular veto. The authority of the Swiss Assembly nominally exceeds the authority of Congress, because in reality the Swiss legislative body is weaker than Congress. For while in each case there lies in the background a legislative sovereign capable of controlling the action of the ordinary legislature, the sovereign power is far more easily brought into play in Switzerland than in America. When the sovereign power can easily enforce its will, it may trust to its own action for maintaining its rights; when, as in America, the same power acts but rarely and with difficulty, the Courts naturally become the guardians of the sovereign's will expressed in the articles of the Constitution.

Compari-
son be-
tween sys-
tem of
federalism
and of par-
liamentary
sovereignty.
Our survey from a legal point of view of the characteristics common to all federal governments forcibly suggests conclusions of more than merely legal interest, as to the comparative merits of federal government, and the system of Parliamentary sovereignty.

Weakness
of federal-
ism.
Federal government means weak government.[53]

The distribution of all the powers of the state among co-ordinate authorities necessarily leads to the result that no one authority can wield the same amount of power as under a unitarian constitution as

---

53 This weakness springs from two different causes: first, the division of powers between the central government and the States; secondly, the distribution of powers between the different members (*e.g.* the President and the Senate) of the national government. The first cause of weakness is inherent in the federal system; the second cause of weakness is not (logically at least) inherent in federalism. Under a federal constitution the whole authority of the national government might conceivably be lodged in one person or body, but we may feel almost certain that in practice the fears entertained by the separate States of encroachments by the central government on their State rights will prohibit such a concentration of authority.

The statement that federal government means weak government should be qualified or balanced by the consideration that a federal system sometimes makes it possible for different communities to be united as one state when they otherwise could not be united at all. The bond of federal union may be weak, but it may be the strongest bond which circumstances allow.

The failure and the calamities of the Helvetic Republic are a warning against the attempt to force upon more or less independent states a greater degree of political unity than they will tolerate.

possessed by the sovereign. A scheme again of checks and balances in which the strength of the common government is so to speak pitted against that of the state governments leads, on the face of it, to a certain waste of energy. A federation therefore will always be at a disadvantage in a contest with unitarian states of equal resources. Nor does the experience either of the United States or of the Swiss confederation invalidate this conclusion. The Union is threatened by no powerful neighbours and needs no foreign policy.[54] Circumstances unconnected with constitutional arrangements enable Switzerland to preserve her separate existence, though surrounded by powerful and at times hostile nations. The mutual jealousies moreover incident to federalism do visibly weaken the Swiss Republic. Thus, to take one example only, each member of the Executive must belong to a different canton.[55] But this rule may exclude from the government statesmen of high merit, and therefore diminish the resources of the state. A rule that each member of the Cabinet should be the native of a different county would appear to Englishmen palpably absurd. Yet this absurdity is forced upon Swiss politicians, and affords one among numerous instances in which the efficiency of the public service is sacrificed to the requirements of federal sentiment. Switzerland, moreover, is governed under a form of democratic federalism which tends towards unitarianism. Each revision increases the authority of the nation at the expense of cantonal independence. This is no doubt in part due to the desire to strengthen the nation against foreign attack. It is perhaps also due to another circumstance. Federalism, as it defines, and therefore limits, the powers of each department of the administration, is unfavourable to the interference or to the activity of government. Hence a federal government can hardly render services to the nation by undertaking for the national benefit functions which may be performed by individuals. This may be a merit of the federal system; it is, however, a merit which does not commend itself to modern democrats, and no more curious instance can be found of the inconsistent currents of popular opinion

---

54 The latter part of statement is perhaps less true in 1908 than it was in 1885.

55 *Constitution Fédérale,* art. 96.

which may at the same time pervade a nation or a generation than the coincidence in England of a vague admiration for federalism alongside with a far more decided feeling against the doctrines of so-called *laissez faire.* A system meant to maintain the *status quo* in politics is incompatible with schemes for wide social innovation.

Federalism tends to produce conservatism.

Conservatism of federalism.

This tendency is due to several causes. The constitution of a Federal state must, as we have seen, generally be not only a written but a rigid constitution, that is, a constitution which cannot be changed by any ordinary process of legislation. Now this essential rigidity of federal institutions is almost certain to impress on the minds of citizens the idea that any provision included in the constitution is immutable and, so to speak, sacred. The least observation of American politics shows how deeply the notion that the Constitution is something placed beyond the reach of amendment has impressed popular imagination. The difficulty of altering the Constitution produces conservative sentiment, and national conservatism doubles the difficulty of altering the Constitution. The House of Lords has lasted for centuries; the American Senate has now existed for more than one hundred years, yet to abolish or alter the House of Lords might turn out to be an easier matter than to modify the constitution of the Senate.[56] To this one must add that a federal constitution always lays down general principles which, from being placed in the constitution, gradually come to command a superstitious reverence, and thus are in fact, though not in theory, protected from change or criticism. The principle that legislation ought not to impair obligation of contracts has governed the whole course of American opinion. Of the conservative effect of such a maxim when forming an article of the constitution we may form some measure by the following reflection. If any principle of the like kind had been recognised in England as legally binding on the Courts, the Irish Land Act would have been unconstitutional and void; the Irish Church Act, 1869, would, in great part at least, have been from a legal point of view so much waste paper, and there would have been great difficulty in legislating in the

---

56 See, however, note 16, p. 81, *ante.*

way in which the English Parliament has legislated for the reform of the Universities. One maxim only among those embodied in the Constitution of the United States would, that is to say, have been sufficient if adopted in England to have arrested the most vigorous efforts of recent Parliamentary legislation.

Legal spirit of federalism.

Federalism, lastly, means legalism—the predominance of the judiciary in the constitution—the prevalence of a spirit of legality among the people.

That in a confederation like the United States the Courts become the pivot on which the constitutional arrangements of the country turn is obvious. Sovereignty is lodged in a body which rarely exerts its authority and has (so to speak) only a potential existence; no legislature throughout the land is more than a subordinate law-making body capable in strictness of enacting nothing but bye-laws; the powers of the executive are again limited by the constitution; the interpreters of the constitution are the judges. The Bench therefore can and must determine the limits to the authority both of the government and of the legislature; its decision is without appeal; the consequence follows that the Bench of judges is not only the guardian but also at a given moment the master of the constitution.[57] Nothing

---

57 The expression "master of the constitution" has been criticised on the ground of exaggeration (Sidgwick, *Elements of Politics*, p. 616). The expression, however, though undoubtedly strong, is, it is submitted, justifiable, if properly understood. It is true, as my friend Mr. Sidgwick well pointed out, that the action of the Supreme Court is restrained, first, by the liability of the judges to impeachment for misconduct, and, secondly, by the fear of provoking disorder. And to these restraints a third and more efficient check must be added. The numbers of the Court may be increased by Congress, and its decision in a given case has not even in theory that force as a decisive precedent which is attributable to a decision of the House of Lords; hence if the Supreme Court were to pronounce judgments which ran permanently counter to the opinion of the party which controlled the government of the Union, its action could be altered by adding to the Court lawyers who shared the convictions of the ruling party. (See Davis, *American Constitutions; the Relations of the Three Departments as adjusted by a Century*, pp. 52–54.) It would be idle therefore to maintain, what certainly cannot be asserted with truth, that the Supreme Court is the sovereign of the United States. It is, however, I conceive, true that at any given moment the Court may, on a case coming before it, pronounce a judgment which determines the working of the Constitution. The decision in the *Dred Scott Case* for example, and still more the judicial opinions delivered in deciding the case, had a distinct influence on the interpretation of the Constitution both by slave-owners and by Abolitionists. In terming the Court the "master of the constitution" it was not my intention to suggest the exercise by it of irregular or revolu-

puts in a stronger light the inevitable connection between federalism and the prominent position of the judicial body than the history of modern Switzerland. The statesmen of 1848 desired to give the *Bundesgericht* a far less authoritative position than is possessed by the American Supreme Court. They in effect made the Federal Assembly for most, what it still is for some purposes, a final Court of Appeal. But the necessities of the case were too strong for Swiss statesmanship; the revision of 1874 greatly increased the power of the Federal Tribunal.

Dangers arising from position of judiciary.

From the fact that the judicial Bench supports under federal institutions the whole stress of the constitution, a special danger arises lest the judiciary should be unequal to the burden laid upon them. In no country has greater skill been expended on constituting an august and impressive national tribunal than in the United States. Moreover, as already pointed out, the guardianship of the Constitution is in America confided not only to the Supreme Court but to every judge throughout the land. Still it is manifest that even the Supreme Court can hardly support the duties imposed upon it. No one can doubt that the varying decisions given in the legal-tender cases, or in the line of recent judgments of which *Munn* v. *Illinois* is a specimen, show that the most honest judges are after all only honest men, and when set to determine matters of policy and statesmanship will necessarily be swayed by political feeling and by reasons of state. But the moment that this bias becomes obvious a Court loses its moral authority, and decisions which might be justified on grounds of policy excite natural indignation and suspicion when they are seen not to be fully justified on grounds of law. American critics indeed are to be found

---

tionary powers. No doubt, again, the Supreme Court may be influenced in delivering its judgments by fear of provoking violence. This apprehension is admittedly a limit to the full exercise of its theoretical powers by the most absolute of despots. It was never my intention to assert that the Supreme Court, which is certainly not the sovereign of the United States, was in the exercise of its functions free from restraints which limit the authority of even a sovereign power. It must further be noted, in considering how far the Supreme Court could in fact exert all the authority theoretically vested in it, that it is hardly conceivable that the opinions of the Court as to, say, the constitutional limits to the authority of Congress should not be shared by a large number of American citizens. Whenever in short the Court differed in its view of the Constitution from that adopted by the President or the Congress, the Court, it is probable, could rely on a large amount of popular support.

who allege that the Supreme Court not only is proving but always has proved too weak for the burden it is called upon to bear, and that it has from the first been powerless whenever it came into conflict with a State, or could not count upon the support of the Federal Executive. These allegations undoubtedly hit a weak spot in the constitution of the great tribunal. Its judgments are without force, at any rate as against a State if the President refuses the means of putting them into execution. "John Marshall," said President Jackson, according to a current story,[58] "has delivered his judgment; let him now enforce it, if he can"; and the judgment was never put into force. But the weight of criticisms repeated from the earliest days of the Union may easily be exaggerated.[59] Laymen are apt to mistake the growth of judicial caution for a sign of judicial weakness. Foreign observers, moreover, should notice that in a federation the causes which bring a body such as the Supreme Court into existence, also supply it with a source of ultimate power. The Supreme Court and institutions like it are the protectors of the federal compact, and the validity of that compact is, in the long run, the guarantee for the rights of the separate States. It is the interest of every man who wishes the federal constitution to be observed, that the judgments of the federal tribunals should be respected. It is therefore no bold assumption that, as long as the people of the United States wish to keep up the balanced system of federalism, they will ultimately compel the central government to support the authority of the federal Court. Critics of the Court are almost driven to assert that the American people are indifferent to State Rights. The assertion may or may not be true; it is a matter on which no English critic should speak with confidence. But censures on the working of a federal Court tell very little against such an institution if they establish nothing more than the almost self-evident proposition that a federal tribunal will be ineffective and superfluous when the United States shall have ceased

---

58 See W. G. Sumner, *Andrew Jackson*, American Statesmen Series, p. 182.

59 See Davis, *American Constitutions; the Relations of the Three Departments as adjusted by a Century*. Mr. Davis is distinctly of opinion that the power of the Courts both of the United States and of the separate States has increased steadily since the foundation of the Union. See Davis, *American Constitutions*, pp. 55–57.

to be in reality a federation. A federal Court has no proper place in a unitarian Republic.

Judges, further, must be appointed by some authority which is not judicial, and where decisions of a Court control the action of government there exists an irresistible temptation to appoint magistrates who agree (honestly it may be) with the views of the executive. A strong argument pressed against Mr. Blaine's election was, that he would have the opportunity as President of nominating four judges, and that a politician allied with railway companies was likely to pack the Supreme Court with men certain to wrest the law in favour of mercantile corporations. The accusation may have been baseless; the fact that it should have been made, and that even "Republicans" should declare that the time had come when "Democrats" should no longer be excluded from the Bench of the United States, tells plainly enough of the special evils which must be weighed against the undoubted benefits of making the Courts rather than the legislature the arbiters of the constitution.

That a federal system again can flourish only among communities imbued with a legal spirit and trained to reverence the law is as certain as can be any conclusion of political speculation. Federalism substitutes litigation for legislation, and none but a law-fearing people will be inclined to regard the decision of a suit as equivalent to the enactment of a law. The main reason why the United States has carried out the federal system with unequalled success is that the people of the Union are more thoroughly imbued with legal ideas than any other existing nation. Constitutional questions arising out of either the constitutions of the separate States or the articles of the federal Constitution are of daily occurrence and constantly occupy the Courts. Hence the citizens become a people of constitutionalists, and matters which excite the strongest popular feeling, as, for instance, the right of Chinese to settle in the country, are determined by the judicial Bench, and the decision of the Bench is acquiesced in by the people. This acquiescence or submission is due to the Americans inheriting the legal notions of the common law, *i.e.* of the "most legal system of law" (if the expression may be allowed) in the world. Tocqueville long ago remarked that the Swiss fell far short of the

Americans in reverence for law and justice.[60] The events of the last sixty years suggest that he perhaps underrated Swiss submission to law. But the law to which Switzerland is accustomed recognises wide discretionary power on the part of the executive, and has never fully severed the functions of the judge from those of the government. Hence Swiss federalism fails, just where one would expect it to fail, in maintaining that complete authority of the Courts which is necessary to the perfect federal system. But the Swiss, though they may not equal the Americans in reverence for judicial decisions, are a law-respecting nation. One may well doubt whether there are many states to be found where the mass of the people would leave so much political influence to the Courts. Yet any nation who cannot acquiesce in the finality of possibly mistaken judgments is hardly fit to form part of a federal state.[61]

---

60 See passage cited, pp. 108–109, *post*.

61 See Appendix, Note VIII., Swiss Federalism.

PART II
THE RULE OF LAW

Chapter IV

THE RULE OF LAW: ITS NATURE AND GENERAL APPLICATIONS

Two features have at all times since the Norman Conquest characterised the political institutions of England.

The first of these features is the omnipotence or undisputed supremacy throughout the whole country of the central government. This authority of the state or the nation was during the earlier periods of our history represented by the power of the Crown. The King was the source of law and the maintainer of order. The maxim of the Courts, *"tout fuit in luy et vient de lui al commencement,"*[1] was originally the expression of an actual and undoubted fact. This royal supremacy has now passed into that sovereignty of Parliament which has formed the main subject of the foregoing chapters.[2]

The second of these features, which is closely connected with the first, is the rule or supremacy of law. This peculiarity of our polity is well expressed in the old saw of the Courts, *"La ley est le plus haute inheritance, que le roy ad; car par la ley it même et toutes ses sujets sont rulés, et si la ley ne fuit, nul roi, et nul inheritance sera."*[3]

This supremacy of the law, or the security given under the English constitution to the rights of individuals looked at from various points of view, forms the subject of this part of this treatise.

---

1 Year Books, xxiv. Edward III.; cited Gneist, *Englische Verwaltungsrecht,* i. p. 454.

2 See Part I.

3 Year Books, xix. Henry VI., cited Gneist, *Englische Verwaltungsrecht,* i. p. 455.

Foreign observers of English manners, such for example as Voltaire, De Lolme, Tocqueville, or Gneist, have been far more struck than have Englishmen themselves with the fact that England is a country governed, as is scarcely any other part of Europe, under the rule of law; and admiration or astonishment at the legality of English habits and feeling is nowhere better expressed than in a curious passage from Tocqueville's writings, which compares the Switzerland and the England of 1836 in respect of the spirit which pervades their laws and manners. He writes:

I am not about to compare Switzerland[4] with the United States, but with Great Britain. When you examine the two countries, or even if you only pass through them, you perceive, in my judgment, the most astonishing differences between them. Take it all in all, England seems to be much more republican than the Helvetic Republic. The principal differences are found in the institutions of the two countries, and especially in their customs (*moeurs*).

1. In almost all the Swiss Cantons liberty of the press is a very recent thing.

2. In almost all of them individual liberty is by no means completely guaranteed, and a man may be arrested administratively and detained in prison without much formality.

3. The Courts have not, generally speaking, a perfectly independent position.

4. In all the Cantons trial by jury is unknown.

5. In several Cantons the people were thirty-eight years ago entirely without political rights. Aargau, Thurgau, Tessin, Vaud, and parts of the Cantons of Zurich and Berne were in this condition.

The preceding observations apply even more strongly to customs than to institutions.

i. In many of the Swiss Cantons the majority of the citizens are quite without the taste or desire for *self-government,* and have not acquired the habit of it. In any crisis they interest themselves about their affairs, but you never see in them the thirst for political rights and the craving to take part in public affairs which seem to torment Englishmen throughout their lives.

ii. The Swiss abuse the liberty of the press on account of its being a recent form of liberty, and Swiss newspapers are much more *revolutionary* and much less *practical* than English newspapers.

iii. The Swiss seem still to look upon associations from much the same point of view as the French, that is to say, they consider them as a means

---

4 Many of Tocqueville's remarks are not applicable to the Switzerland of 1902; they refer to a period before the creation in 1848 of the Swiss Federal Constitution.

of revolution, and not as a slow and sure method for obtaining redress of wrongs. The art of associating and of making use of the right of association is but little understood in Switzerland.

iv. The Swiss do not show the love of justice which is such a strong characteristic of the English. Their Courts have no place in the political arrangements of the country, and exert no influence on public opinion. The love of justice, the peaceful and legal introduction of the judge into the domain of politics, are perhaps the most standing characteristics of a free people.

v. Finally, and this really embraces all the rest, the Swiss do not show at bottom that respect for justice, that love of law, that dislike of using force, without which no free nation can exist, which strikes strangers so forcibly in England.

I sum up these impressions in a few words.

Whoever travels in the United States is involuntarily and instinctively so impressed with the fact that the spirit of liberty and the taste for it have pervaded all the habits of the American people, that he cannot conceive of them under any but a Republican government. In the same way it is impossible to think of the English as living under any but a free government. But if violence were to destroy the Republican institutions in most of the Swiss Cantons, it would be by no means certain that after rather a short state of transition the people would not grow accustomed to the loss of liberty. In the United States and in England there seems to be more liberty in the customs than in the laws of the people. In Switzerland there seems to be more liberty in the laws than in the customs of the country.[5]

Bearing of Tocqueville's remarks on meaning of rule of law.

Tocqueville's language has a twofold bearing on our present topic. His words point in the clearest manner to the rule, predominance, or supremacy of law as the distinguishing characteristic of English institutions. They further direct attention to the extreme vagueness of a trait of national character which is as noticeable as it is hard to portray. Tocqueville, we see, is clearly perplexed how to define a feature of English manners of which he at once recognises the existence; he mingles or confuses together the habit of self-government, the love of order, the respect for justice and a legal turn of mind. All these sentiments are intimately allied, but they cannot without confusion be identified with each other. If, however, a critic as acute as Tocqueville found a difficulty in describing one of the most marked peculiarities of English life, we may safely conclude that we ourselves, whenever we talk of Englishmen as loving the government of law, or

---

5 See Tocqueville, *Œuvres Complètes*, viii. pp. 455–457.

of the supremacy of law as being a characteristic of the English constitution, are using words which, though they possess a real significance, are nevertheless to most persons who employ them full of vagueness and ambiguity. If therefore we are ever to appreciate the full import of the idea denoted by the term "rule, supremacy, or predominance of law," we must first determine precisely what we mean by such expressions when we apply them to the British constitution.

Three meanings of rule of law.
When we say that the supremacy or the rule of law is a characteristic of the English constitution, we generally include under one expression at least three distinct though kindred conceptions.

Absence of arbitrary power on part of the government.
We mean, in the first place, that no man is punishable or can be lawfully made to suffer in body or goods except for a distinct breach of law established in the ordinary legal manner before the ordinary Courts of the land. In this sense the rule of law is contrasted with every system of government based on the exercise by persons in authority of wide, arbitrary, or discretionary powers of constraint.

Contrast between England and the Continent at present day.
Modern Englishmen may at first feel some surprise that the "rule of law" (in the sense in which we are now using the term) should be considered as in any way a peculiarity of English institutions, since, at the present day, it may seem to be not so much the property of any one nation as a trait common to every civilised and orderly state. Yet, even if we confine our observation to the existing condition of Europe, we shall soon be convinced that the "rule of law" even in this narrow sense is peculiar to England, or to those countries which, like the United States of America, have inherited English traditions. In almost every continental community the executive exercises far wider discretionary authority in the matter of arrest, of temporary imprisonment, of expulsion from its territory, and the like, than is either legally claimed or in fact exerted by the government in England; and a study of European politics now and again reminds English readers that wherever there is discretion there is room for arbitrariness, and that in a republic no less than under a monarchy discretionary authority on the part of the government must mean insecurity for legal freedom on the part of its subjects.

Contrast between England and Continent during eighteenth century.

If, however, we confined our observation to the Europe of the twentieth century, we might well say that in most European countries the rule of law is now nearly as well established as in England, and that private individuals at any rate who do not meddle in politics have little to fear, as long as they keep the law, either from the Government or from any one else; and we might therefore feel some difficulty in understanding how it ever happened that to foreigners the absence of arbitrary power on the part of the Crown, of the executive, and of every other authority in England, has always seemed a striking feature, we might almost say the essential characteristic, of the English constitution.[6]

Our perplexity is entirely removed by carrying back our minds to the time when the English constitution began to be criticised and admired by foreign thinkers. During the eighteenth century many of the continental governments were far from oppressive, but there was no continental country where men were secure from arbitrary power. The singularity of England was not so much the goodness or the leniency as the legality of the English system of government. When Voltaire came to England—and Voltaire represented the feeling of his age—his predominant sentiment clearly was that he had passed out of the realm of despotism to a land where the laws might be harsh, but where men were ruled by law and not by caprice.[7] He had good reason to know the difference. In 1717 Voltaire was sent to the Bastille for a poem which he had not written, of which he did not know the author, and with the sentiment of which he did not agree. What adds to the oddity, in English eyes, of the whole transaction is

---

6 ''La liberté est le droit de faire tout ce que les lois permettent; et si un citoyen pouvoit faire ce qu'elles défendent, il n'auroit plus de liberté, paree que les autres auroient tout de même ce pouvoir.''—Montesquieu, *De l'Esprit des Lois,* Livre XI. chap. iii.

''Il y a aussi une nation dans le monde qui a pour objet direct de sa constitution la liberté politique.''—*Ibid.* chap. v. The English are this nation.

7 ''Les circonstances qui contraignaient Voltaire à chercher un refuge chez nos voisins devaient lui inspirer une grande sympathie pour des institutions où il n'y avait nulle place à l'arbitraire. 'La raison est libre ici et n'y connaît point de contrainte.' On y respire un air plus généreux, l'on se sent au milieu de citoyens qui n'ont pas tort de porter le front haut, de marcher fièrement, sûrs qu'on n'eût pu toucher à un seul cheveu de leur tête, et n'ayant à redoubter ni lettres de cachet, ni captivité immotivée.''—Desnoiresterres, *Voltaire,* i. p. 365.

that the Regent treated the affair as a sort of joke, and, so to speak, "chaffed" the supposed author of the satire *"I have seen"* on being about to pay a visit to a prison which he "had not seen."[8] In 1725 Voltaire, then the literary hero of his country, was lured off from the table of a Duke, and was thrashed by lackeys in the presence of their noble master; he was unable to obtain either legal or honourable redress, and because he complained of this outrage, paid a second visit to the Bastille. This indeed was the last time in which he was lodged within the walls of a French gaol, but his whole life was a series of contests with arbitrary power, and nothing but his fame, his deftness, his infinite resource, and ultimately his wealth, saved him from penalties far more severe than temporary imprisonment. Moreover, the price at which Voltaire saved his property and his life was after all exile from France. Whoever wants to see how exceptional a phenomenon was that supremacy of law which existed in England during the eighteenth century should read such a book as Morley's *Life of Diderot*. The effort lasting for twenty-two years to get the *Encyclopédie* published was a struggle on the part of all the distinguished literary men in France to obtain utterance for their thoughts. It is hard to say whether the difficulties or the success of the contest bear the strongest witness to the wayward arbitrariness of the French Government.

Royal lawlessness was not peculiar to specially detestable monarchs such as Louis the Fifteenth: it was inherent in the French system of administration. An idea prevails that Louis the Sixteenth at least was not an arbitrary, as he assuredly was not a cruel ruler. But it is an error to suppose that up to 1789 anything like the supremacy of law existed under the French monarchy. The folly, the grievances, and the mystery of the Chevalier D'Eon made as much noise little more than a century ago as the imposture of the Claimant in our own day. The memory of these things is not in itself worth reviving. What does deserve to be kept in remembrance is that in 1778, in the days of Johnson, of Adam Smith, of Gibbon, of Cowper, of Burke, and of Mansfield, during the continuance of the American war and within

---

8 Desnoiresterres, i. pp. 344–364.

eleven years of the assembling of the States General, a brave officer and a distinguished diplomatist could for some offence still unknown, without trial and without conviction, be condemned to undergo a penance and disgrace which could hardly be rivalled by the fanciful caprice of the torments inflicted by Oriental despotism.[9]

Nor let it be imagined that during the latter part of the eighteenth century the government of France was more arbitrary than that of other countries. To entertain such a supposition is to misconceive utterly the condition of the continent. In France, law and public opinion counted for a great deal more than in Spain, in the petty States of Italy, or in the Principalities of Germany. All the evils of despotism which attracted the notice of the world in a great kingdom such as France existed under worse forms in countries where, just because the evil was so much greater, it attracted the less attention. The power of the French monarch was criticised more severely than the lawlessness of a score of petty tyrants, not because the French King ruled more despotically than other crowned heads, but because the French people appeared from the eminence of the nation to have a special claim to freedom, and because the ancient kingdom of France was the typical representative of despotism. This explains the thrill of enthusiasm with which all Europe greeted the fall of the Bastille. When the fortress was taken, there were not ten prisoners within its walls; at that very moment hundreds of debtors languished in English goals. Yet all England hailed the triumph of the French populace with a fervour which to Englishmen of the twentieth century is at first sight hardly comprehensible. Reflection makes clear enough the cause of a feeling which spread through the length and breadth of the civilised world. The Bastille was the outward and visible sign of lawless power. Its fall was felt, and felt truly, to herald in for the rest of Europe that rule of law which already existed in England.[10]

---

9 It is worth notice that even after the meeting of the States General the King was apparently reluctant to give up altogether the powers exercised by *lettres de cachet*. See "Déclaration des intentions du Roi," art. 15, Plouard, *Les Constitutions Françaises*, p. 10.

10 For English sentiment with reference to the servitude of the French, see Goldsmith, *Citizen of the World*, iii. Letter iv.; and see *Ibid.*, Letter xxxvii. p. 143, for a contrast between

Every man subject to ordinary law administered by ordinary tribunals.

We mean in the second place,[11] when we speak of the "rule of law" as a characteristic of our country, not only that with us no man is above the law, but (what is a different thing) that here every man, whatever be his rank or condition, is subject to the ordinary law of the realm and amenable to the jurisdiction of the ordinary tribunals.

In England the idea of legal equality, or of the universal subjection of all classes to one law administered by the ordinary Courts, has been pushed to its utmost limit. With us every official, from the Prime Minister down to a constable or a collector of taxes, is under the same responsibility for every act done without legal justification as any other citizen. The Reports abound with cases in which officials have been brought before the Courts, and made, in their personal capacity, liable to punishment, or to the payment of damages, for acts done in their official character but in excess of their lawful authority. A colonial governor,[12] a secretary of state,[13] a military officer,[14] and all subordinates, though carrying out the commands of their official superiors, are as responsible for any act which the law does not authorise as is any private and unofficial person. Officials, such for example as soldiers[15] or clergymen of the Established Church, are, it is true, in England as elsewhere, subject to laws which do not affect the rest of the nation, and are in some instances amenable to tribunals which have no jurisdiction over their fellow-countrymen; officials, that is to say, are to a certain extent governed under what may be termed official law. But this fact is in no way inconsistent with the

---

the execution of Lord Ferrers and the impunity with which a French nobleman was allowed to commit murder because of his relationship to the Royal family; and for the general state of feeling throughout Europe, Tocqueville, *Œuvres Complètes*, viii. pp. 57–72. The idea of the rule of law in this sense implies, or is at any rate closely connected with, the absence of any dispensing power on the part either of the Crown or its servants. See Bill of Rights, Preamble 1, Stubbs, *Select Charters* (2nd ed.), p. 523. Compare *Miller* v. *Knox*, 6 Scott, 1; *Attorney-General* v. *Kissane*, 32 L.R. Ir. 220.

11 For first meaning see p. 110, *ante*.

12 *Mostyn* v. *Fabregas*, Cowp. 161; *Musgrave* v. *Pulido*, 5 App. Cas. 102; *Governor Wall's Case*, 28 St. Tr. 51.

13 *Entick* v. *Carrington*, 19 St. Tr. 1030.

14 *Phillips* v. *Eyre*, L. R., 4 Q. B. 225.

15 As to the legal position of soldiers, see Chaps. VIII. and IX., *post*.

principle that all men are in England subject to the law of the realm; for though a soldier or a clergyman incurs from his position legal liabilities from which other men are exempt, he does not (speaking generally) escape thereby from the duties of an ordinary citizen.

An Englishman naturally imagines that the rule of law (in the sense in which we are now using the term) is a trait common to all civilised societies. But this supposition is erroneous. Most European nations had indeed, by the end of the eighteenth century, passed through that stage of development (from which England emerged before the end of the sixteenth century) when nobles, priests, and others could defy the law. But it is even now far from universally true that in continental countries all persons are subject to one and the same law, or that the Courts are supreme throughout the state. If we take France as the type of a continental state, we may assert, with substantial accuracy, that officials—under which word should be included all persons employed in the service of the state—are, or have been, in their official capacity, to some extent exempted from the ordinary law of the land, protected from the jurisdiction of the ordinary tribunals, and subject in certain respects only to official law administered by official bodies.[16]

There remains yet a third and a different sense in which the "rule of law" or the predominance of the legal spirit may be described as a special attribute of English institutions. We may say that the constitution is pervaded by the rule of law on the ground that the general principles of the constitution (as for example the right to personal liberty, or the right of public meeting) are with us the result of judicial decisions determining the rights of private persons in particular cases brought before the Courts;[17] whereas under many foreign constitutions the security (such as it is) given to the rights of individuals results, or appears to result, from the general principles of the constitution.

---

16 See Chapter XII. as to the contrast between the rule of law and foreign administrative law.

17 Compare *Calvin's Case*, 7 Coke, Rep. 1; *Campbell* v. *Hall*, Cowp. 204; *Wilkes* v. *Wood*, 19 St. Tr. 1153; *Mostyn* v. *Fabregas*, Cowp. 161. Parliamentary declarations of the law such as the Petition of Right and the Bill of Rights have a certain affinity to judicial decisions.

This is one portion at least of the fact vaguely hinted at in the current but misguiding statement that "the constitution has not been made but has grown." This dictum, if taken literally, is absurd.

> Political institutions (however the proposition may be at times ignored) are the work of men, owe their origin and their whole existence to human will. Men did not wake up on a summer morning and find them sprung up. Neither do they resemble trees, which, once planted, are "aye growing" while men "are sleeping." In every stage of their existence they are made what they are by human voluntary agency.[18]

Yet, though this is so, the dogma that the form of a government is a sort of spontaneous growth so closely bound up with the life of a people that we can hardly treat it as a product of human will and energy, does, though in a loose and inaccurate fashion, bring into view the fact that some politics, and among them the English constitution, have not been created at one stroke, and, far from being the result of legislation, in the ordinary sense of that term, are the fruit of contests carried on in the Courts on behalf of the rights of individuals. Our constitution, in short, is a judge-made constitution, and it bears on its face all the features, good and bad, of judge-made law.

Contrast between the English constitution and Foreign constitutions. Hence flow noteworthy distinctions between the constitution of England and the constitutions of most foreign countries.

There is in the English constitution an absence of those declarations or definitions of rights so dear to foreign constitutionalists. Such principles, moreover, as you can discover in the English constitution are, like all maxims established by judicial legislation, mere generalisations drawn either from the decisions or dicta of judges, or from statutes which, being passed to meet special grievances, bear a close resemblance to judicial decisions, and are in effect judgments pronounced by the High Court of Parliament. To put what is really the same thing in a somewhat different shape, the relation of the rights of individuals to the principles of the constitution is not quite the same in countries like Belgium, where the constitution is the result of a legislative act, as it is in England, where the constitution itself is based upon legal decisions. In Belgium, which may be taken as a type of

---

18 Mill, *Representative Government*, p. 4.

countries possessing a constitution formed by a deliberate act of legislation, you may say with truth that the rights of individuals to personal liberty flow from or are secured by the constitution. In England the right to individual liberty is part of the constitution, because it is secured by the decisions of the Courts, extended or confirmed as they are by the *Habeas Corpus* Acts. If it be allowable to apply the formulas of logic to questions of law, the difference in this matter between the constitution of Belgium and the English constitution may be described by the statement that in Belgium individual rights are deductions drawn from the principles of the constitution, whilst in England the so-called principles of the constitution are inductions or generalisations based upon particular decisions pronounced by the Courts as to the rights of given individuals.

This is of course a merely formal difference. Liberty is as well secured in Belgium as in England, and as long as this is so it matters nothing whether we say that individuals are free from all risk of arbitrary arrest, because liberty of person is guaranteed by the constitution, or that the right to personal freedom, or in other words to protection from arbitrary arrest, forms part of the constitution because it is secured by the ordinary law of the land. But though this merely formal distinction is in itself of no moment, provided always that the rights of individuals are really secure, the question whether the right to personal freedom or the right to freedom of worship is likely to be secure does depend a good deal upon the answer to the inquiry whether the persons who consciously or unconsciously build up the constitution of their country begin with definitions or declarations of rights, or with the contrivance of remedies by which rights may be enforced or secured. Now, most foreign constitution-makers have begun with declarations of rights. For this they have often been in nowise to blame. Their course of action has more often than not been forced upon them by the stress of circumstances, and by the consideration that to lay down general principles of law is the proper and natural function of legislators. But any knowledge of history suffices to show that foreign constitutionalists have, while occupied in defining rights, given insufficient attention to the absolute necessity for the provision of adequate remedies by which the rights they proclaimed might be enforced. The Constitution of 1791 proclaimed liberty of conscience, liberty of the press, the right of public meeting, the responsibility of government officials.[19] But there never was a period in the recorded annals of mankind when each and all of these rights were so insecure, one might almost say so completely non-existent, as at the height of the French Revolution. And an observer may well doubt whether a good number of these liberties or rights are even now so well protected under the French Republic as under the English Monarchy. On the other hand, there runs through the English constitution that inseparable connection between the means of enforcing a right and the right to be enforced which is the strength of judicial legislation. The saw, *ubi jus ibi remedium*, becomes from this point of view something much more important than a mere tautologous proposition. In its bearing upon constitutional law, it means that the Englishmen whose labours gradually framed the complicated set of laws and institutions which we call the Constitution, fixed their minds far more intently on providing remedies for the enforcement of particular rights or (what is merely the same thing looked at from the other side) for averting definite wrongs, than upon any declaration of the Rights of Man or of Englishmen. The *Habeas Corpus* Acts declare no principle and define no rights, but they are for practical purposes worth a hundred constitutional articles guaranteeing individual liberty. Nor let it be supposed that this connection between rights and remedies which depends upon the spirit of law pervading English institutions is inconsistent with the existence of a written constitution, or even with the existence of constitutional declarations of rights. The Constitution of the United States and the constitutions of the separate States are embodied in written or printed documents, and contain declarations of rights.[20] But the statesmen of America

---

19 See Plouard, *Les Constitutions Françaises*, pp. 14–16; Duguit and Monnier, *Les Constitutions de la France* (2nd ed.), pp. 4, 5.

20 The Petition of Right, and the Bill of Rights, as also the American Declarations of Rights, contain, it may be said, proclamations of general principles which resemble the declarations of rights known to foreign constitutionalists, and especially the celebrated Declaration of the Rights of Man (*Declaration des Droits de l'Homme et du Citoyen*) of 1789. But the English and American Declarations on the one hand, and foreign declarations of rights on the other, though bearing an apparent resemblance to each other, are at bottom remarkable

have shown unrivalled skill in providing means for giving legal security to the rights declared by American constitutions. The rule of law is as marked a feature of the United States as of England.

The fact, again, that in many foreign countries the rights of individuals, *e.g.* to personal freedom, depend upon the constitution, whilst in England the law of the constitution is little else than a generalisation of the rights which the Courts secure to individuals, has this important result. The general rights guaranteed by the constitution may be, and in foreign countries constantly are, suspended. They are something extraneous to and independent of the ordinary course of the law. The declaration of the Belgian constitution, that individual liberty is "guaranteed," betrays a way of looking at the rights of individuals very different from the way in which such rights are regarded by English lawyers. We can hardly say that one right is more guaranteed than another. Freedom from arbitrary arrest, the right to express one's opinion on all matters subject to the liability to pay compensation for libellous or to suffer punishment for seditious or blasphemous statements, and the right to enjoy one's own property, seem to Englishmen all to rest upon the same basis, namely, on the law of the land. To say that the "constitution guaranteed" one class of rights more than the other would be to an Englishman an unnatural or a senseless form of speech. In the Belgian constitution the words have a definite meaning. They imply that no law invading personal freedom can be passed without a modification of the constitution made in the special way in which alone the constitution can be legally changed or amended. This, however, is not the point to which our immediate attention should be directed. The matter to be noted is, that where the right to individual freedom is a result de-

---

rather by way of contrast than of similarity. The Petition of Right and the Bill of Rights are not so much "declarations of rights" in the foreign sense of the term, as judicial condemnations of claims or practices on the part of the Crown, which are thereby pronounced illegal. It will be found that every, or nearly every, clause in the two celebrated documents negatives some distinct claim made and put into force on behalf of the prerogative. No doubt the Declarations contained in the American Constitutions have a real similarity to the continental declarations of rights. They are the product of eighteenth-century ideas; they have, however, it is submitted, the distinct purpose of legally controlling the action of the legislature by the Articles of the Constitution.

duced from the principles of the constitution, the idea readily occurs that the right is capable of being suspended or taken away. Where, on the other hand, the right to individual freedom is part of the constitution because it is inherent in the ordinary law of the land, the right is one which can hardly be destroyed without a thorough revolution in the institutions and manners of the nation. The so-called "suspension of the *Habeas Corpus* Act" bears, it is true, a certain similarity to what is called in foreign countries "suspending the constitutional guarantees." But, after all, a statute suspending the *Habeas Corpus* Act falls very far short of what its popular name seems to imply; and though a serious measure enough, is not, in reality, more than a suspension of one particular remedy for the protection of personal freedom. The *Habeas Corpus* Act may be suspended and yet Englishmen may enjoy almost all the rights of citizens. The constitution being based on the rule of law, the suspension of the constitution, as far as such a thing can be conceived possible, would mean with us nothing less than a revolution.

Summary of mean- ings of Rule of Law That "rule of law," then, which forms a fundamental principle of the constitution, has three meanings, or may be regarded from three different points of view.

It means, in the first place, the absolute supremacy or predominance of regular law as opposed to the influence of arbitrary power, and excludes the existence of arbitrariness, of prerogative, or even of wide discretionary authority on the part of the government. Englishmen are ruled by the law, and by the law alone; a man may with us be punished for a breach of law, but he can be punished for nothing else.

It means, again, equality before the law, or the equal subjection of all classes to the ordinary law of the land administered by the ordinary Law Courts; the "rule of law" in this sense excludes the idea of any exemption of officials or others from the duty of obedience to the law which governs other citizens or from the jurisdiction of the ordinary tribunals; there can be with us nothing really corresponding to the "administrative law" (*droit administratif*) or the "administrative tribunals" (*tribunaux administratifs*) of France.[21] The notion which lies

---

21 See Chap. XII.

at the bottom of the "administrative law" known to foreign countries is, that affairs or disputes in which the government or its servants are concerned are beyond the sphere of the civil Courts and must be dealt with by special and more or less official bodies. This idea is utterly unknown to the law of England, and indeed is fundamentally inconsistent with our traditions and customs.

The "rule of law," lastly, may be used as a formula for expressing the fact that with us the law of the constitution, the rules which in foreign countries naturally form part of a constitutional code, are not the source but the consequence of the rights of individuals, as defined and enforced by the Courts; that, in short, the principles of private law have with us been by the action of the Courts and Parliament so extended as to determine the position of the Crown and of its servants; thus the constitution is the result of the ordinary law of the land.

Influence of "Rule of Law" on leading provisions of constitution.

General propositions, however, as to the nature of the rule of law carry us but a very little way. If we want to understand what that principle in all its different aspects and developments really means, we must try to trace its influence throughout some of the main provisions of the constitution. The best mode of doing this is to examine with care the manner in which the law of England deals with the following topics, namely, the right to personal freedom;[22] the right to freedom of discussion;[23] the right of public meeting;[24] the use of martial law;[25] the rights and duties of the army;[26] the collection and expenditure of the public revenue;[27] and the responsibility of Ministers.[28] The true nature further of the rule of law as it exists in England will be illustrated by contrast with the idea of *droit administratif*, or administrative law, which prevails in many continental countries.[29] These topics will each be treated of in their due order. The object, however, of this treatise, as the reader should remember, is not to provide minute and full information, *e.g.* as to the *Habeas Corpus* Acts, or other enactments protecting the liberty of the subject; but simply to show that these leading heads of constitutional law, which have

---

22 Chap. V.

23 Chap. VI.

24 Chap. VII.

25 Chap. VIII.

26 Chap. IX.

27 Chap. X.

28 Chap. XI.

29 Chap. XII.

been enumerated, these "articles," so to speak, of the constitution, are both governed by, and afford illustrations of, the supremacy throughout English institutions of the law of the land.[30] If at some future day the law of the constitution should be codified, each of the topics I have mentioned would be dealt with by the sections of the code. Many of these subjects are actually dealt with in the written constitutions of foreign countries, and notably in the articles of the Belgian constitution, which, as before noticed, makes an admirable summary of the leading maxims of English constitutionalism. It will therefore often be a convenient method of illustrating our topic to take the article of the Belgian, or it may be of some other constitution, which bears on the matter in hand, as for example the right to personal freedom, and to consider how far the principle therein embodied is recognised by the law of England; and if it be so recognised, what are the means by which it is maintained or enforced by our Courts. One reason why the law of the constitution is imperfectly understood is, that we too rarely put it side by side with the constitutional provisions of other countries. Here, as elsewhere, comparison is essential to recognition.

---

30 The rule of equal law is in England now exposed to a new peril. "The Legislature has thought fit," writes Sir F. Pollock, "by the Trade Disputes Act, 1906, to confer extraordinary immunities on combinations both of employers and of workmen, and to some extent on persons acting in their interests. Legal science has evidently nothing to do with this violent empirical operation on the body politic, and we can only look to jurisdictions beyond seas for the further judicial consideration of the problems which our Courts were endeavouring (it is submitted, not without a reasonable measure of success) to work out on principles of legal justice."—Pollock, *Law of Torts* (8th ed.), p. v.

Chapter V

THE RIGHT TO PERSONAL FREEDOM

The seventh article of the Belgian constitution establishes in that country principles which have long prevailed in England. The terms thereof so curiously illustrate by way of contrast some marked features of English constitutional law as to be worth quotation.

> *Art 7. La liberté individuelle est garantie.*
>
> *Nul ne peut être poursuivi que dans les cas prévus par la loi, et dans la forme qu'elle prescrit.*
>
> *Hors le cas de flagrant délit, mul ne peut être arrêté qu'en vertu de l'ordonnance motivée du juge, qui doit être signifiée au moment de l'arrestation, ou au plus tard dans les vingt-quatre heures.* [1]

How secured in England.

The security which an Englishman enjoys for personal freedom does not really depend upon or originate in any general proposition contained in any written document. The nearest approach which our statute-book presents to the statement contained in the seventh article of the Belgian constitution is the celebrated thirty-ninth article[2] of the Magna Charta:

> *Nullus liber homo capiatur, vel imprisonetur, aut dissaisiatur, aut utlagetur, aut exuletur, aut aliquo modo destruatur, nec super eum ibimus, nec super eum mittemus, nisi per legale judicium parium suorum vel per legem terrae,*

---

1 *Constitution de la Belgique,* art. 7.

2 See Stubbs, *Charters* (2nd ed.), p. 301.

which should be read in combination with the declarations of the
Petition of Right. And these enactments (if such they can be called)
are rather records of the existence of a right than statutes which
confer it. The expression again, "guaranteed," is, as I have already
pointed out, extremely significant; it suggests the notion that personal liberty is a special privilege insured to Belgians by some power
above the ordinary law of the land. This is an idea utterly alien to
English modes of thought, since with us freedom of person is not a
special privilege but the outcome of the ordinary law of the land
enforced by the Courts. Here, in short, we may observe the application to a particular case of the general principle that with us individual rights are the basis, not the result, of the law of the constitution.

The proclamation in a constitution or charter of the right to personal freedom, or indeed of any other right, gives of itself but slight
security that the right has more than a nominal existence, and students who wish to know how far the right to freedom of person is in
reality part of the law of the constitution must consider both what is
the meaning of the right and, a matter of even more consequence,
what are the legal methods by which its exercise is secured.

The right to personal liberty as understood in England means in
substance a person's right not to be subjected to imprisonment, arrest, or other physical coercion in any manner that does not admit of
legal justification. That anybody should suffer physical restraint is in
England *prima facie* illegal, and can be justified (speaking in very
general terms) on two grounds only, that is to say, either because the
prisoner or person suffering restraint is accused of some offence and
must be brought before the Courts to stand his trial, or because he
has been duly convicted of some offence and must suffer punishment
for it. Now personal freedom in this sense of the term is secured in
England by the strict maintenance of the principle that no man can be
arrested or imprisoned except in due course of law, *i.e.* (speaking
again in very general terms indeed) under some legal warrant or
authority,[3] and, what is of far more consequence, it is secured by the

---

3 See as to arrests, Stephen, *Commentaries,* iv. (14th ed.), pp. 303–312.

provision of adequate legal means for the enforcement of this principle. These methods are twofold;[4] namely, redress for unlawful arrest
or imprisonment by means of a prosecution or an action, and de-
liverance from unlawful imprisonment by means of the writ of *habeas corpus.* Let us examine the general character of each of these
remedies.

REDRESS FOR ARREST

Proceed-
ings for
wrongful
arrest.

If we use the term redress in a wide sense, we may say that a
person who has suffered a wrong obtains redress either when he gets
the wrongdoer punished or when he obtains compensation for the
damage inflicted upon him by the wrong.

Each of these forms of redress is in England open to every one
whose personal freedom has been in any way unlawfully interfered
with. Suppose, for example, that *X* without legal justification assaults
A, by knocking him down, or deprives *A* of his freedom—as the
technical expression goes, "imprisons" him—whether it be for a
length of time, or only for five minutes; *A* has two courses open to
him. He can have *X* convicted of an assault and thus cause him to be
punished for his crime, or he can bring an action of trespass against *X*
and obtain from *X* such compensation for the damage which *A* has
sustained from *X*'s conduct as a jury think that *A* deserves. Suppose
that in 1725 Voltaire had at the instigation of an English lord been
treated in London as he was treated in Paris. He would not have
needed to depend for redress upon the goodwill of his friends or
upon the favour of the Ministry. He could have pursued one of two
courses. He could by taking the proper steps have caused all his
assailants to be brought to trial as criminals. He could, if he had
preferred it, have brought an action against each and all of them: he
could have sued the nobleman who caused him to be thrashed, the
footmen who thrashed him, the policemen who threw him into gaol,

---

4 Another means by which personal liberty or other rights may be protected is the allowing
a man to protect or assert his rights by force against a wrongdoer without incurring legal
liability for injury done to the aggressor. The limits within which English law permits
so-called "self-defence," or, more accurately, "the assertion of legal rights by the use of a
person's own force," is one of the obscurest among legal questions. See Appendix, Note
IV., Right of Self-Defence.

and the gaoler or lieutenant who kept him there. Notice particularly that the action for trespass, to which Voltaire would have had recourse, can be brought, or, as the technical expression goes, "lies," against every person throughout the realm. It can and has been brought against governors of colonies, against secretaries of state, against officers who have tried by Court-martial persons not subject to military law, against every kind of official high or low. Here then we come across another aspect of the "rule of law." No one of Voltaire's enemies would, if he had been injured in England, have been able to escape from responsibility on the plea of acting in an official character or in obedience to his official superiors.[5] Nor would any one of them have been able to say that the degree of his guilt could in any way whatever be determined by any more or less official Court. Voltaire, to keep to our example, would have been able in England to have brought each and all of his assailants, including the officials who kept him in prison, before an ordinary Court, and therefore before judges and jurymen who were not at all likely to think that official zeal or the orders of official superiors were either a legal or a moral excuse for breaking the law.

Before quitting the subject of the redress afforded by the Courts for the damage caused by illegal interference with any one's personal freedom, we shall do well to notice the strict adherence of the judges in this as in other cases to two maxims or principles which underlie the whole law of the constitution, and the maintenance of which has gone a great way both to ensure the supremacy of the law of the land and ultimately to curb the arbitrariness of the Crown. The first of these maxims or principles is that every wrongdoer is individually responsible for every unlawful or wrongful act in which he takes part, and, what is really the same thing looked at from another point of view, cannot, if the act be unlawful, plead in his defence that he did it under the orders of a master or superior. Voltaire, had he been arrested in England, could have treated each and all of the persons engaged in the outrage as individually responsible for the wrong done to him. Now this doctrine of individual responsibility is the real

---

5 Contrast the French *Code Pénal*, art. 114.

foundation of the legal dogma that the orders of the King himself are no justification for the commission of a wrongful or illegal act. The ordinary rule, therefore, that every wrongdoer is individually liable for the wrong he has committed, is the foundation on which rests the great constitutional doctrine of Ministerial responsibility. The second of these noteworthy maxims is, that the Courts give a remedy for the infringement of a right whether the injury done be great or small. The assaults and imprisonment from which Voltaire suffered were serious wrongs; but it would be an error to fancy, as persons who have no experience in the practice of the Courts are apt to do, the proceedings for trespass or for false imprisonment can be taken only where personal liberty is seriously interfered with. Ninety-nine out of every hundred actions for assault or false imprisonment have reference to injuries which in themselves are trifling. If one ruffian gives another a blow, if a policeman makes an arrest without lawful authority, if a schoolmaster keeps a scholar locked up at school for half an hour after he ought to have let the child go home,[6] if in short X interferes unlawfully to however slight a degree with the personal liberty of A, the offender exposes himself to proceedings in a Court of law, and the sufferer, if he can enlist the sympathies of a jury, may recover heavy damages for the injury which he has or is supposed to have suffered. The law of England protects the right to personal liberty, as also every other legal right, against every kind of infringement, and gives the same kind of redress (I do not mean, of course, inflicts the same degree of punishment or penalty) for the pettiest as for the gravest invasions of personal freedom. This seems to us so much a matter of course as hardly to call for observation, but it may be suspected that few features in our legal system have done more to maintain the authority of the law than the fact that all offences great and small are dealt with on the same principles and by the same Courts. The law of England now knows nothing of exceptional offences punished by extraordinary tribunals.[7]

---

6 *Hunter* v. *Johnson*, 13 Q. B. D. 225.

7 Contrast with this the extraordinary remedies adopted under the old French monarchy for the punishment of powerful criminals. As to which see Fléchier, *Mémoires sur les Grand-Jours tenues à Clermont en* 1665–66.

The right of a person who has been wrongfully imprisoned on regaining his freedom to put his oppressor on trial as a criminal, or by means of an action to obtain pecuniary compensation for the wrong which he has endured, affords a most insufficient security for personal freedom. If *X* keeps *A* in confinement, it profits *A* little to know that if he could recover his freedom, which he cannot, he could punish and fine *X*. What *A* wants is to recover his liberty. Till this is done he cannot hope to punish the foe who has deprived him of it. It would have been little consolation for Voltaire to know that if he could have got out of the Bastille he could recover damages from his enemies. The possibility that he might when he got free have obtained redress for the wrong done him might, so far from being a benefit, have condemned him to lifelong incarceration. Liberty is not secure unless the law, in addition to punishing every kind of interference with a man's lawful freedom, provides adequate security that every one who without legal justification is placed in confinement shall be able to get free. This security is provided by the celebrated writ of *habeas corpus* and the *Habeas Corpus* Acts.

WRIT OF HABEAS CORPUS[8]

Writ of *habeas corpus*.

It is not within the scope of these lectures to give a history of the writ of *habeas corpus* or to provide the details of the legislation with regard to it. For minute information, both about the writ and about the *Habeas Corpus* Acts, you should consult the ordinary legal textbooks. My object is solely to explain generally the mode in which the law of England secures the right to personal freedom. I shall therefore call attention to the following points: first, the nature of the writ; secondly, the effect of the so-called *Habeas Corpus* Acts; thirdly, the precise effect of what is called (not quite accurately) the Suspension of the *Habeas Corpus* Act; and, lastly, the relation of any Act suspending the operation of the *Habeas Corpus* Act to an Act of Indemnity. Each of these matters has a close bearing on the law of the constitution.

---

8 See Stephen, *Commentaries* (14th ed.), iii. pp. 697–707; 16 Car. I. c. 10; 31 Car. II. c. 2; 56 George III. c. 100; Forsyth, *Opinions*, 436–452, 481.

Nature of Writ

Legal documents constantly give the best explanation and illustration of legal principles. We shall do well therefore to examine with care the following copy of a writ of *habeas corpus:*

> *Victoria, by the Grace of God, of the United Kingdom of Great Britain and Ireland Queen, Defender of the Faith,*
>
> *To J. K., Keeper of our Gaol of Jersey, in the Island of Jersey, and to J. C. Viscount of said Island, greeting. We command you that you have the body of C. C. W. detained in our prison under your custody, as it is said, together with the day and cause of his being taken and detained, by whatsoever name he may be called or known, in our Court before us, at Westminster, on the 18th day of January next, to undergo and receive all and singular such matters and things which our said Court shall then and there consider of him in this behalf; and have there then this Writ. Witness* THOMAS *Lord* DENMAN, *at Westminster, the 23rd day of December in the 8th year of our reign.*
>
>

By the Court,
Robinson. [9]

>
> *At the instance of C. C. W.*
>
> *R. M. R.*
>
>

W. A. L., 7 Gray's Inn Square, London,
Attorney for the said C. W.

The character of the document is patent on its face. It is an order issued, in the particular instance, by the Court of Queen's Bench, calling upon a person by whom a prisoner is alleged to be kept in confinement to bring such prisoner—to "have his body," whence the name *habeas corpus*—before the Court to let the Court know on what ground the prisoner is confined, and thus to give the Court the opportunity of dealing with the prisoner as the law may require. The essence of the whole transaction is that the Court can by the writ of *habeas corpus* cause any person who is imprisoned to be actually brought before the Court and obtain knowledge of the reason why he is imprisoned; and then having him before the Court, either then and there set him free or else see that he is dealt with in whatever way the law requires, as, for example, brought speedily to trial.

---

9 *Carus Wilson's Case,* 7 Q. B. 984, 988. In this particular case the writ calls upon the gaoler of the prison to have the body of the prisoner before the Court by a given day. It more ordinarily calls upon him to have the prisoner before the Court "immediately after the receipt of this writ."

The writ can be issued on the application either of the prisoner himself or of any person on his behalf, or (supposing the prisoner cannot act) then on the application of any person who believes him to be unlawfully imprisoned. It is issued by the High Court, or during vacation by any judge thereof; and the Court or a judge should and will always cause it to be issued on being satisfied by affidavit that there is reason to suppose a prisoner to be wrongfully deprived of his liberty. You cannot say with strictness that the writ is issued "as a matter of course," for some ground must be shown for supposing that a case of illegal imprisonment exists. But the writ is granted "as a matter of right,"—that is to say, the Court will always issue it if *prima facie* ground is shown for supposing that the person on whose behalf it is asked for is unlawfully deprived of his liberty. The writ or order of the Court can be addressed to any person whatever, be he an official or a private individual, who has, or is supposed to have, another in his custody. Any disobedience to the writ exposes the offender to summary punishment for contempt of Court,[10] and also in many cases to heavy penalties recoverable by the party aggrieved.[11] To put the matter, therefore, in the most general terms, the case stands thus. The High Court of Justice possesses, as the tribunals which make up the High Court used to possess, the power by means of the writ of *habeas corpus* to cause any person who is alleged to be kept in unlawful confinement to be brought before the Court. The Court can then inquire into the reason why he is confined, and can, should it see fit, set him then and there at liberty. This power moreover is one which the Court always will exercise whenever ground is shown by any applicant whatever for the belief that any man in England is unlawfully deprived of his liberty.

The Habeas Corpus Acts

Habeas Corpus Acts.

The right to the writ of *habeas corpus* existed at common law long before the passing in 1679 of the celebrated *Habeas Corpus* Act,[12] 31

---

10 *Rex* v. *Winton*, 5 T. R. 89, and conf. 56 Geo. III. c. 100, s. 2; see Corner, *Practice of the Crown Side of the Court of Queen's Bench*.

11 31 Car. II. c. 2, s. 4.

12 See also 16 Car. I. c. 10, s. 6.

Car. II. c. 2, and you may wonder how it has happened that this and the subsequent Act, 56 Geo. III. c. 100, are treated, and (for practical purposes) rightly treated, as the basis on which rests an Englishman's security for the enjoyment of his personal freedom. The explanation is, that prior to 1679 the right to the writ was often under various pleas and excuses made of no effect. The aim of the *Habeas Corpus* Acts has been to meet all the devices by which the effect of the writ can be evaded, either on the part of the judges, who ought to issue the same, and if necessary discharge the prisoner, or on the part of the gaoler or other person who has the prisoner in custody. The earlier Act of Charles the Second applies to persons imprisoned on a charge of crime; the later Act of George the Third applies to persons deprived of their liberty otherwise than on a criminal accusation.

Take these two classes of persons separately.

Habeas Corpus Act, 1679, 31 Car. II. c. 2.

A person is imprisoned on a charge of crime. If he is imprisoned without any legal warrant for his imprisonment, he has a right to be set at liberty. If, on the other hand, he is imprisoned under a legal warrant, the object of his detention is to ensure his being brought to trial. His position in this case differs according to the nature of the offence with which he is charged. In the case of the lighter offences known as misdemeanours he has, generally [13] the right to his liberty on giving security with proper sureties that he will in due course surrender himself to custody and appear and take his trial on such indictment as may be found against him in respect of the matter with which he is charged, or (to use technical expressions) he has the right to be admitted to bail. In the case, on the other hand, of the more serious offences, such as felonies or treasons, a person who is once committed to prison is not entitled to be let out on bail. The right of the prisoner is in this case simply the right to a speedy trial. The effect of the writ of *habeas corpus* would be evaded either if the Court did not examine into the validity of the warrant on which the prisoner was detained, and if the warrant were not valid release him, or if the Court, on ascertaining that he was legally imprisoned, did not cause

---

13 See Stephen, *Digest of the Law of Criminal Procedure,* art. 276, note 1, and also art. 136 and p. 89, note 1. Compare the Indictable Offences Act, 1848 (11 & 12 Vict. c. 42), s. 23.

him according to circumstances either to go out on bail or to be speedily brought to trial.

The Act provides against all these possible failures of justice. The law as to persons imprisoned under accusations of crime stands through the combined effect of the rules of the common law and of the statute in substance as follows. The gaoler who has such person in custody is bound when called upon to have the prisoner before the Court with the true cause of his commitment. If the cause is insufficient, the prisoner must of course be discharged; if the cause is sufficient, the prisoner, in case he is charged with a misdemeanour, can in general insist upon being bailed till trial; in case, on the other hand, the charge is one of treason or felony, he can insist upon being tried at the first sessions after his committal, or if he is not then tried, upon being bailed, unless the witnesses for the Crown cannot appear. If he is not tried at the second sessions after his commitment, he can insist upon his release without bail. The net result, therefore, appears to be that while the *Habeas Corpus* Act is in force no person committed to prison on a charge of crime can be kept long in confinement, for he has the legal means of insisting upon either being let out upon bail or else of being brought to a speedy trial.

Habeas Corpus Act, 1816, 56 Geo. III. c. 100.

A person, again, who is detained in confinement but not on a charge of crime needs for his protection the means of readily obtaining a legal decision on the lawfulness of his confinement, and also of getting an immediate release if he has by law a right to his liberty. This is exactly what the writ of *habeas corpus* affords. Whenever any Englishman or foreigner is alleged to be wrongfully deprived of liberty, the Court will issue the writ, have the person aggrieved brought before the Court, and if he has a right to liberty set him free. Thus if a child is forcibly kept apart from his parents,[14] if a man is wrongfully

---

14 See *The Queen* v. Nash, 10 Q. B. D. (C. A.) 454; and compare *Re Agar-Ellis*, 24 Ch. D. (C. A.) 317. For recent instances of effect of *Habeas Corpus* Act see *Barnardo* v. *Ford* [1892], A. C. 326; *Barnardo* v. *McHugh* [1891], A. C. 388; *Reg.* v. *Jackson* [1891], 1 Q. B. (C. A.) 671; *Cox* v. *Hakes*, 15 App. Cas. 506; *Reg.* v. *Barnardo*, 24 Q. B. D. (C. A.) 283; and 23 Q. B. D. (C. A.) 305. Compare as to power of Court of Chancery for protection of children independently of *Habeas Corpus* Acts, *Reg.* v. *Gyngall* [1893], 2 Q. B. (C. A.) 232.

As to appeal to Privy Council, see *Att. Gen. for Hong Kong* v. *Kwok-A-Sing* (1873), L. R. 5 P. C. 179.

kept in confinement as a lunatic, if a nun is alleged to be prevented from leaving her convent,—if, in short, any man, woman, or child is, or is asserted on apparently good grounds to be, deprived of liberty, the Court will always issue a writ of *habeas corpus* to any one who has the aggrieved person in his custody to have such person brought before the Court, and if he is suffering restraint without lawful cause, set him free. Till, however, the year 1816 (56 Geo. III.) the machinery for obtaining the writ was less perfect[15] in the case of persons not accused of crime than in the case of those charged with criminal offences, and the effect of 56 Geo. III. c. 100, was in substance to apply to non-criminal cases the machinery of the great *Habeas Corpus* Act, 31 Car. II. c. 2.

At the present day, therefore, the securities for personal freedom are in England as complete as laws can make them. The right to its enjoyment is absolutely acknowledged. Any invasion of the right entails either imprisonment or fine upon the wrongdoer; and any person, whether charged with crime or not, who is even suspected to be wrongfully imprisoned, has, if there exists a single individual willing to exert himself on the victim's behalf, the certainty of having his case duly investigated, and, if he has been wronged, of recovering his freedom. Let us return for a moment to a former illustration, and suppose that Voltaire has been treated in London as he was treated in Paris. He most certainly would very rapidly have recovered his freedom. The procedure would not, it is true, have been in 1726 quite as easy as it is now under the Act of George the Third. Still, even then it would have been within the power of any one of his friends to put the law in motion. It would have been at least as easy to release Voltaire in 1726 as it was in 1772 to obtain by means of *habeas corpus* the freedom of the slave James Sommersett when actually confined in irons on board a ship lying in the Thames and bound for Jamaica.[16]

---

15 The inconvenience ultimately remedied by the *Habeas Corpus* Act, 1816, was in practice small, for the judges extended to all cases of unlawful imprisonment the spirit of the *Habeas Corpus* Act, 1679, and enforced immediate obedience to the writ of *habeas corpus,* even when issued not under the statue, but under the common law authority of the Courts. Blackstone, *Comm.* iii. p. 138.

16 *Sommersett's Case,* 20 St. Tr. 1.

The whole history of the writ of *habeas corpus* illustrates the predominant attention paid under the English constitution to "remedies," that is, to modes of procedure by which to secure respect for a legal right, and by which to turn a merely nominal into an effective or real right. The *Habeas Corpus* Acts are essentially procedure Acts, and simply aim at improving the legal mechanism by means of which the acknowledged right to personal freedom may be enforced. They are intended, as is generally the case with legislation which proceeds under the influence of lawyers, simply to meet actual and experienced difficulties. Hence the *Habeas Corpus* Act of Charles the Second's reign was an imperfect or very restricted piece of legislative work, and Englishmen waited nearly a century and a half (1679–1816) before the procedure for securing the right to discharge from unlawful confinement was made complete. But this lawyer-like mode of dealing with a fundamental right had with all its defects the one great merit that legislation was directed to the right point. There is no difficulty, and there is often very little gain, in declaring the existence of a right to personal freedom. The true difficulty is to secure its enforcement. The *Habeas Corpus* Acts have achieved this end, and have therefore done for the liberty of Englishmen more than could have been achieved by any declaration of rights. One may even venture to say that these Acts are of really more importance not only than the general proclamations of the Rights of Man which have often been put forward in foreign countries, but even than such very lawyer-like documents as the Petition of Right or the Bill of Rights, though these celebrated enactments show almost equally with the *Habeas Corpus* Act that the law of the English constitution is at bottom judge-made law.[17]

Effect of writ of *habeas corpus* on authority of judges.

Every critic of the constitution has observed the effect of the *Habeas Corpus* Acts in securing the liberty of the subject; what has received less and deserves as much attention is the way in which the right to issue a writ of *habeas corpus*, strengthened as that right is by statute, determines the whole relation of the judicial body towards the execu-

---

17 Compare Imperial Constitution of 1804, ss. 60–63, under which a committee of the Senate was empowered to take steps for putting an end to illegal arrests by the Government. See Plouard, *Les Constitutions Françaises*, p. 161.

tive. The authority to enforce obedience to the writ is nothing less than the power to release from imprisonment any person who in the opinion of the Court is unlawfully deprived of his liberty, and hence in effect to put an end to or to prevent any punishment which the Crown or its servants may attempt to inflict in opposition to the rules of law as interpreted by the judges. The judges therefore are in truth, though not in name, invested with the means of hampering or supervising the whole administrative action of the government, and of at once putting a veto upon any proceeding not authorised by the letter of the law. Nor is this power one which has fallen into disuse by want of exercise. It has often been put forth, and this too in matters of the greatest consequence; the knowledge moreover of its existence governs the conduct of the administration. An example or two will best show the mode in which the "judiciary" (to use a convenient Americanism) can and do by means of the writ of *habeas corpus* keep a hold on the acts of the executive. In 1839 Canadian rebels, found guilty of treason in Canada and condemned to transportion, arrived in official custody at Liverpool on their way to Van Diemen's Land. The friends of the convicts questioned the validity of the sentence under which they were transported; the prisoners were thereupon taken from prison and brought upon a writ of *habeas corpus* before the Court of Exchequer. Their whole position having been considered by the Court, it was ultimately held that the imprisonment was legal. But had the Court taken a different view, the Canadians would at once have been released from confinement.[18] In 1859 an English officer serving in India was duly convicted of manslaughter and sentenced to four years' imprisonment: he was sent to England in military custody to complete there his term of punishment. The order under which he was brought to this country was technically irregular, and the convict having been brought on a writ of *habeas corpus* before the Queen's Bench, was on this purely technical ground set at liberty.[19] So, to take a very notorious instance of judicial authority in matters most nearly concerning the executive, the Courts have again

---

18 *The Case of the Canadian Prisoners*, 5 M & W. 32.

19 *In re Allen*, 30 L. J. (Q. B.), 38.

and again considered, in the case of persons brought before them by the writ of *habeas corpus,* questions as to the legality of impressment, and as to the limits within which the right of impressment may be exercised; and if, on the one hand, the judges have in this particular instance (which by the way is almost a singular one) supported the arbitrary powers of the prerogative, they have also strictly limited the exercise of this power within the bounds prescribed to it by custom or by statute.[20] Moreover, as already pointed out, the authority of the civil tribunals even when not actually put into force regulates the action of the government. In 1854 a body of Russian sailors were found wandering about the streets of Guildford, without any visible means of subsistence; they were identified by a Russian naval officer as deserters from a Russian man-of-war which had put into an English port; they were thereupon, under his instructions and with the assistance of the superintendent of police, conveyed to Portsmouth for the purpose of their being carried back to the Russian ship. Doubts arose as to the legality of the whole proceeding. The law officers were consulted, who thereupon gave it as their opinion that "the delivering-up of the Russian sailors to the Lieutenant and the assistance offered by the police for the purpose of their being conveyed back to the Russian ship were contrary to law."[21] The sailors were presumably released; they no doubt would have been delivered by the Court had a writ of *habeas corpus* been applied for. Here then we see the judges in effect restraining the action of the executive in a matter which in most countries is considered one of administration or of policy lying beyond the range of judicial interference. The strongest examples, however, of interference by the judges with administrative proceedings are to be found in the decisions given under the Extradition Acts. Neither the Crown nor any servant of the Crown has any right to expel a foreign criminal from the country or to sur-

---

20 See *Case of Pressing Mariners,* 18 St. Tr. 1323; Stephen, *Commentaries,* ii. (14th ed.), p. 574; conf. Corner, *Forms of Writs on Crown Side of Court of Queen's Bench,* for form of *habeas corpus* for an impressed seaman.

21 See Forsyth, *Opinions,* p. 468.

render him to his own government for trial.[22] A French forger, robber, or murderer who escapes from France to England cannot, independently of statutory enactments, be sent back to his native land for trial or punishment. The absence of any power on the part of the Crown to surrender foreign criminals to the authorities of their own state has been found so inconvenient, that in recent times Extradition Acts have empowered the Crown to make treaties with foreign states for the mutual extradition of criminals or of persons charged with crime. The exercise of this authority is, however, hampered by restrictions which are imposed by the statute under which alone it exists. It therefore often happens that an offender arrested under the warrant of a Secretary of State and about to be handed over to the authorities of his own country conceives that, on some ground or other, his case does not fall within the precise terms of any Extradition Act. He applies for a writ of *habeas corpus;* he is brought up before the High Court; every technical plea he can raise obtains full consideration,[23] and if on any ground whatever it can be shown that the terms of the Extradition Act have not been complied with, or that they do not justify his arrest and surrender, he is as a matter of course at once set at liberty.[24] It is easy to perceive that the authority of the judges, exercised, as it invariably must be, in support of the strict rules of law, cuts down the discretionary powers of the Crown. It

---

22 See, however, *Rex, v. Lundy,* 2 Ventris, 314; *Rex* v. *Kimberley,* 2 Stra., 848; *East India Company* v. *Campbell,* 1 Ves. Senr., 246; *Mure* v. *Kaye,* 4 Taunt. 34; and Chitty, *Criminal Law* (1826), pp. 14, 16, in support of the opinion that the Crown possessed a common law right of extradition as regards foreign criminals. This opinion may possibly once have been correct. (Compare, however, *Reg.* v. *Bernard,* Annual Register for 1858, p. 328, for opinion of Campbell, C. J., cited *In re Castioni* [1891], 1 Q. B. 149, 153, by Sir C. Russell, *arguendo.*) It has, however, in any case (to use the words of a high authority) "ceased to be law now. If any magistrate were now to arrest a person on this ground, the validity of the commitment would certainly be tested, and, in the absence of special legislative provisions, the prisoner as certainly discharged upon application to one of the superior Courts."—Clarke, *Extradition* (3rd ed.), p. 27. The case of *Musgrove* v. *Chun Teeong Toy* [1891], A. C. 272, which establishes that an alien has not a legal right, enforceable by action, to enter British territory, suggests the possible existence of a common law right on the part of the Crown to expel an alien from British territory.

23 *In re Bellencontre* [1891], 2 Q. B. 122.

24 *In re Coppin,* L. R. 2 Ch. 47; *The Queen* v. *Wilson,* 3 Q. B. D. 42.

often prevents the English government from meeting public danger by measures of precaution which would as a matter of course be taken by the executive of any continental country. Suppose, for example, that a body of foreign anarchists come to England and are thought by the police on strong grounds of suspicion to be engaged in a plot, say for blowing up the Houses of Parliament. Suppose also that the existence of the conspiracy does not admit of absolute proof. An English Minister, if he is not prepared to put the conspirators on their trial, has no means of arresting them, or of expelling them from the country.[25] In case of arrest or imprisonment they would at once be brought before the High Court on a writ of *habeas corpus*, and unless some specific legal ground for their detention could be shown they would be forthwith set at liberty. Of the political or, to use foreign expressions, of the "administrative" reasons which might make the arrest or expulsion of a foreign refugee highly expedient, the judges would hear nothing; that he was arrested by order of the Secretary of State, that his imprisonment was a simple administrative act, that the Prime Minister or the Home Secretary was prepared to make affidavit that the arrest was demanded by the most urgent considerations of public safety, or to assure the Court that the whole matter was one of high policy and concerned national interests, would be no answer whatever to the demand for freedom under a writ of *habeas corpus*. All that any judge could inquire into would be, whether there was any rule of common or of statute law which would authorise interference with a foreigner's personal freedom. If none such could be found, the applicants would assuredly obtain their liberty. The plain truth is that the power possessed by the judges of controlling the administrative conduct of the executive has been, of necessity, so exercised as to prevent the development with us of any system corresponding to the "administrative law" of continental states. It strikes at the root of those theories as to the nature of administrative acts, and as to the "separation of powers," on which, as will be shown in a later chapter,[26] the *droit administratif* of France

---

25 Contrast the dealings of Louis Philippe's Government in 1833 with the *Duchesse de Berry*, for which see Grégoire, *Histoire de France*, i. pp. 356–361.

26 See Chap. XII.

depends, and it deprives the Crown, which now means the Ministry of the day, of all discretionary authority. The actual or possible intervention, in short, of the Courts, exercisable for the most part by means of the writ of *habeas corpus,* confines the action of the government within the strict letter of the law; with us the state can punish, but it can hardly prevent the commission of crimes.

Contests of seventeenth century about position of judges.

We can now see why it was that the political conflicts of the seventeenth century often raged round the position of the judges, and why the battle might turn on a point so technical as the inquiry, what might be a proper return to a writ of *habeas corpus.*[27] Upon the degree of authority and independence to be conceded to the Bench depended the colour and working of our institutions. To supporters, on the one hand, of the prerogative who, like Bacon, were not unfrequently innovators or reformers, judicial independence appeared to mean the weakness of the executive, and the predominance throughout the state of the conservative legalism, which found a representative in Coke. The Parliamentary leaders, on the other hand, saw, more or less distinctly, that the independence of the Bench was the sole security for the maintenance of the common law, which was nothing else than the rule of established customs modified only by Acts of Parliament, and that Coke in battling for the power of the judges was asserting the rights of the nation; they possibly also saw, though this is uncertain, that the maintenance of rigid legality, inconvenient as it might sometimes prove, was the certain road to Parliamentary sovereignty.[28]

Suspension of the Habeas Corpus Act

Suspension of *Habeas Corpus* Act.

During periods of political excitement the power or duty of the Courts to issue a writ of *habeas corpus,* and thereby compel the speedy trial or release of persons charged with crime, has been found an inconvenient or dangerous limitation on the authority of the executive government. Hence has arisen the occasion for statutes which are popularly called *Habeas Corpus* Suspension Acts. I say "popularly

---

27 *Darnel's Case,* 3 St. Tr. 1.

28 See Gardiner, *History of England,* ii. chap. xxii., for an admirable statement of the different views entertained as to the position of the judges.

called," because if you take (as you may) the Act 34 Geo. III. c. 54[29] as a type of such enactments, you will see that it hardly corresponds with its received name. The whole effect of the Act, which does not even mention the *Habeas Corpus* Act, is to make it impossible for any person imprisoned under a warrant signed by a Secretary of State on a charge of high treason, or on suspicion of high treason, to insist upon being either discharged or put on trial. No doubt this is a great diminution in the securities for personal freedom provided by the *Habeas Corpus* Acts; but it falls very far short of anything like a general suspension of the right to the writ of *habeas corpus*; it in no way affects the privileges of any person not imprisoned on a charge of high treason; it does not legalise any arrest, imprisonment, or punishment which was not lawful before the Suspension Act passed; it does not in any wise touch the claim to a writ of *habeas corpus* possessed by every one, man, woman, or child, who is held in confinement other-wise than on a charge of crime. The particular statute 34 Geo. III. c. 54 is, and (I believe) every other *Habeas Corpus* Suspension Act affecting

---

29 Of which s. 1 enacts "that every person or persons that are or shall be in prison within the kingdom of Great Britain at or upon the day on which this Act shall receive his Majesty's royal assent, or after, by warrant of his said Majesty's most honorable Privy Council, signed by six of the said Privy Council, for high treason, suspicion of high treason, or treasonable practices, or by warrant, signed by any of his Majesty's secretaries of state, for such causes as aforesaid, may be detained in safe custody, without bail or mainprize, until the first day of *February* one thousand seven hundred and ninety-five; and that no judge or justice of the peace shall bail or try any such person or persons so committed, without order from his said Majesty's Privy Council, signed by six of the said Privy Council, till the said first day of *February* one thousand seven hundred and ninety-five; and law or statute to the contrary notwithstanding."

The so-called suspension of the *Habeas Corpus* Act under a statute such as 34 Geo. III. c. 54, produces both less and more effect than would the total repeal of the *Habeas Corpus* Acts. The suspension, while it lasts, makes it possible for the government to arrest and keep in prison any persons declared in effect by the government to be guilty or suspected of treasonable practices, and such persons have no means of obtaining either a discharge or a trial. But the suspension does not affect the position of persons not detained in custody under suspicion of treasonable practices. It does not therefore touch the ordinary liberty of ordinary citizens. The repeal of the *Habeas Corpus* Acts, on the other hand, would deprive every man in England of one security against wrongful imprisonment, but since it would leave alive the now unquestionable authority of the judges to issue and compel obedience to a writ of *habeas corpus* at common law, it would not, assuming the Bench to do their duty, increase the power of the government to imprison persons suspected of treasonable practices, nor materially diminish the freedom of any class of Englishmen. Compare Blackstone, *Comm.* iii. p. 138.

England, has been an annual Act, and must, therefore, if it is to continue in force, be renewed year by year. The sole, immediate, and direct result, therefore, of suspending the *Habeas Corpus* Act is this: the Ministry may for the period during which the Suspension Act continues in force constantly defer the trial of persons imprisoned on the charge of treasonable practices. This increase in the power of the executive is no trifle, but it falls far short of the process known in some foreign countries as "suspending the constitutional guarantees," or in France as the "proclamation of a state of siege";[30] it, indeed, extends the arbitrary powers of the government to a far less degree than many so-called Coercion Acts. That this is so may be seen by a mere enumeration of the chief of the extraordinary powers which were conferred by comparatively recent enactments on the Irish executive. Under the Act of 1881 (44 Vict. c. 4) the Irish executive obtained the absolute power of arbitrary and preventive arrest, and could without breach of law detain in prison any person arrested on suspicion for the whole period for which the Act continued in force. It is true that the Lord Lieutenant could arrest only persons suspected of treason or of the commission of some act tending to interfere with the maintenance of law and order. But as the warrant itself to be issued by the Lord Lieutenant was made under the Act conclusive evidence of all matters contained therein, and therefore (*inter alia*) of the truth of the assertion that the arrested person or "suspect" was reasonably suspected, *e.g.* of treasonable practices, and therefore liable to arrest, the result clearly followed that neither the Lord Lieutenant nor any official acting under him could by any possibility be made liable to any legal penalty for any arrest, however groundless or malicious, made in due form within the words of the Act. The Irish government, therefore, could arrest any person whom the Lord Lieutenant thought fit to imprison, provided only that the warrant was in the form and contained the allegations required by the statute. Under the Prevention of Crime (Ireland) Act, 1882—45 & 46 Vict. c. 25—the Irish executive was armed with the following (among other) extraordinary powers. The government could in the case of certain

---

30 See Duguit, *Manuel de Droit Constitutionnel,* pp. 510–513, and article "État de Siège" in Chéruel, *Dictionnaire Historique des Institutions de la France* (6th ed.).

crimes[31] abolish the right to trial by jury,[32] could arrest strangers found out of doors at night under suspicious circumstances,[33] could seize any newspaper which, in the judgment of the Lord Lieutenant, contained matter inciting to treason or violence,[34] and could prohibit any public meeting which the Lord Lieutenant believed to be dangerous to the public peace or safety. Add to this that the Prevention of Crime Act, 1882, re-enacted (incidentally as it were) the Alien Act of 1848, and thus empowered the British Ministry to expel from the United Kingdom any foreigner who had not before the passing of the Act been resident in the country for three years.[35] Not one of these extraordinary powers flows directly from a mere suspension of the *Habeas Corpus* Act; and, in truth, the best proof of the very limited legal effect of such so-called suspension is supplied by the fact that before a *Habeas Corpus* Suspension Act runs out its effect is, almost invariably, supplemented by legislation of a totally different character, namely, an Act of Indemnity.

An Act of Indemnity

Act of
Indemnity.

Reference has already been made to Acts of Indemnity as the supreme instance of Parliamentary sovereignty.[36] They are retrospective statutes which free persons who have broken the law from responsibility for its breach, and thus make lawful acts which when they were committed were unlawful. It is easy enough to see the connection between a *Habeas Corpus* Suspension Act and an Act of Indemnity. The Suspension Act, as already pointed out, does not free any person from civil or criminal liability for a violation of the law. Suppose that a Secretary of State or his subordinates should, during the suspension of the *Habeas Corpus* Act, arrest and imprison a per-

---

31 Viz, (*a*) treason or treason-felony; (*b*) murder or manslaughter; (*c*) attempt to murder; (*d*) aggravated crime of violence against the person; (*e*) arson, whether by law or by statute; attack on dwelling-house.

32 Sect. 1.

33 Sect. 12.

34 Sect. 13.

35 Sect. 15.

36 See pp. 10, 11, *ante*.

fectly innocent man without any cause whatever, except (it may be) the belief that it is conducive to the public safety that the particular person—say, an influential party leader such as Wilkes, Fox, or O'Connell—should be at a particular crisis kept in prison, and thereby deprived of influence. Suppose, again, that an arrest should be made by orders of the Ministry under circumstances which involve the unlawful breaking into a private dwelling-house, the destruction of private property, or the like. In each of these instances, and in many others which might easily be imagined, the Secretary of State who orders the arrest and the officials who carry out his commands have broken the law. They may have acted under the *bona fide* belief that their conduct was justified by the necessity of providing for the maintenance of order. But this will not of itself, whether the *Habeas Corpus* Act be suspended or not, free the persons carrying out the arrests from criminal and civil liability for the wrong they have committed. The suspension, indeed, of the *Habeas Corpus* Act may prevent the person arrested from taking at the moment any proceedings against a Secretary of State or the officers who have acted under his orders. For the sufferer is of course imprisoned on the charge of high treason or suspicion of treason, and therefore will not, while the suspension lasts, be able to get himself discharged from prison. The moment, however, that the Suspension Act expires he can, of course, apply for a writ of *habeas corpus*, and ensure that, either by means of being put on his trial or otherwise, his arbitrary imprisonment shall be brought to an end. In the cases we have supposed the prisoner has been guilty of no legal offence. The offenders are in reality the Secretary of State and his subordinates. The result is that on the expiration of the Suspension Act they are liable to actions or indictments for their illegal conduct, and can derive no defence whatever from the mere fact that, at the time when the unlawful arrest took place, the *Habeas Corpus* Act was, partially at any rate, not in force. It is, however, almost certain that, when the suspension of the *Habeas Corpus* Act makes it possible for the government to keep suspected persons in prison for a length of time without bringing them to trial, a smaller or greater number of unlawful acts will be committed, if not by the members of the Ministry themselves, at any rate by their agents. We may even go farther than this, and say that the unavowed object of a *Habeas Corpus* Suspension Act is to enable the government to do acts which, though politically expedient, may not be strictly legal. The Parliament which destroys one of the main guarantees for individual freedom must hold, whether wisely or not, that a crisis has arisen when the rights of individuals must be postponed to considerations of state. A Suspension Act would, in fact, fail of its main object, unless officials felt assured that, as long as they *bona fide,* and uninfluenced by malice or by corrupt motives, carried out the policy of which the Act was the visible sign, they would be protected from penalties for conduct which, though it might be technically a breach of law, was nothing more than the free exertion for the public good of that discretionary power which the suspension of the *Habeas Corpus* Act was intended to confer upon the executive. This assurance is derived from the expectation that, before the Suspension Act ceases to be in force, Parliament will pass an Act of Indemnity, protecting all persons who have acted, or have intended to act, under the powers given to the government by the statute. This expectation has not been disappointed. An Act suspending the *Habeas Corpus* Act, which has been continued for any length of time, has constantly been followed by an Act of Indemnity. Thus the Act to which reference has already been made, 34 Geo. III. c. 54, was continued in force by successive annual re-enactments for seven years, from 1794 to 1801. In the latter year an Act was passed, 41 Geo. III. c. 66, "indemnifying such persons as since the first day of February, 1793, have acted in the apprehending, imprisoning, or detaining in custody in Great Britain of persons suspected of high treason or treasonable practices." It cannot be disputed that the so-called suspension of the *Habeas Corpus* Act, which every one knows will probably be followed by an Act of Indemnity, is, in reality, a far greater interference with personal freedom than would appear from the very limited effect, in a merely legal point of view, of suspending the right of persons accused of treason to demand a speedy trial. The Suspension Act, coupled with the prospect of an Indemnity Act, does in truth arm the executive with arbitrary powers. Still, there are one or two considerations which limit the practical importance that can fairly be given to an expected Act of Indemnity. The relief to be obtained from it is prospective and uncertain. Any suspicion on the part of the public, that officials had grossly abused their powers, might make it difficult to obtain a Parliamentary indemnity for things done while the *Habeas Corpus* Act was suspended. As regards, again, the protection to be derived from the Act by men who have been guilty of irregular, illegal, oppressive, or cruel conduct, everything depends on the terms of the Act of Indemnity. These may be either narrow or wide. The Indemnity Act, for instance, of 1801, gives a very limited amount of protection to official wrongdoers. It provides, indeed, a defence against actions or prosecutions in respect of anything done, commanded, ordered, directed, or advised to be done in Great Britain for apprehending, imprisoning, or detaining in custody any person charged with high treason or treasonable practices. Any no doubt such a defence would cover any irregularity or merely formal breach of the law, but there certainly could be imagined acts of spite or extortion, done under cover of the Suspension Act, which would expose the offender to actions or prosecutions, and could not be justified under the terms of the Indemnity Act. Reckless cruelty to a political prisoner, or, still more certainly, the arbitrary punishment or the execution of a political prisoner, between 1793 and 1801, would, in spite of the Indemnity Act, have left every man concerned in the crime liable to suffer punishment. Whoever wishes to appreciate the moderate character of an ordinary Act of Indemnity passed by the Imperial Parliament, should compare such an Act as 41 Geo. III. c. 66, with the enactment whereby the Jamaica House of Assembly attempted to cover Governor Eyre from all liability for unlawful deeds done in suppressing rebellion during 1866. An Act of Indemnity, again, though it is the legalisation of illegality, is also, it should be noted, itself a law. It is something in its essential character, therefore, very different from the proclamation of martial law, the establishment of a state of siege, or any other proceeding by which the executive government at its own will suspends the law of the land. It is no doubt an exercise of arbitrary sovereign power; but where the legal sovereign is a Parliamentary assembly, even acts of state assume the form of regular legislation, and this fact of itself maintains in no small degree the real no less than the apparent supremacy of law.

Chapter VI

THE RIGHT TO FREEDOM OF DISCUSSION

The Declaration of the Rights of Man[1] and the French Constitution of 1791 proclaim freedom of discussion and the liberty of the press in terms which are still cited in text-books[2] as embodying maxims of French jurisprudence.

Principles
laid down
in foreign
constitution.

> *La libre communication des pensées et des opinions est un des droits les plus précieux de l'homme; tout citoyen peut donc parler, écrire, imprimer librement, sauf à répondre de l'abus de cette liberté dans les cas déterminés par la loi.''[3]*
>
> *La constitution garantit, comme droit naturel et civil . . . la libreté à tout homme de parler, d'écrire, d'imprimer et publier ses pensées, sans que ses écrits puissent être soumis à aucune censure ou inspection avant leur publication.[4]*

Belgian law, again, treats the liberty of the press as a fundamental article of the constitution.

> *Art. 18. La presse est libre; la censure ne pourra jamais être établie: il ne peut être exigé de cautionnement des écrivains, éditeurs ou imprimeurs.*
>
> *Lorsque l'auteur est connu et domicilié en Belgique, l'éditeur, l'imprimeur ou le distributeur ne peut être poursuivi.[5]*

---

1 Duguit et Monnier, *Les Constitutions de la France,* p. 1.

2 Bourguignon, *Éléments Généraux de Législation Française,* p. 468.

3 *Déclar. des droits,* art. 11, Plouard, p. 16, Duguit et Monnier, p. 2.

4 *Constitution de 1791, Tit.* 1; Plouard, p. 18, Duguit et Monnier, p. 4.

5 *Constitution de la Belgique,* art. 18.

No principle of freedom of discussion recognised by English law.

Both the revolutionists of France and the constitutionalists of Belgium borrowed their ideas about freedom of opinion and the liberty of the press from England, and most persons form such loose notions as to English law that the idea prevails in England itself that the right to the free expression of opinion, and especially that form of it which is known as the "liberty of the press," are fundamental doctrines of the law of England in the same sense in which they were part of the ephemeral constitution of 1791 and still are embodied in the articles of the existing Belgian constitution; and, further, that our Courts recognise the right of every man to say and write what he pleases, especially on social, political, or religious topics, without fear of legal penalties. Yet this notion, justified though it be, to a certain extent, by the habits of modern English life, is essentially false, and conceals from students the real attitude of English law towards what is called "freedom of thought," and is more accurately described as the "right to the free expression of opinion." As every lawyer knows, the phrases "freedom of discussion" or "liberty of the press" are rarely found in any part of the statute-book nor among the maxims of the common law.[6] As terms of art they are indeed quite unknown to our Courts. At no time has there in England been any proclamation of the right to liberty of thought or to freedom of speech. The true state of things cannot be better described than in these words from an excellent treatise on the law of libel:

English law only secures that no one shall be punished except for statements proved to be breach of law.

> Our present law permits any one to say, write, and publish what he pleases; but if he make a bad use of this liberty he must be punished. If he unjustly attack an individual, the person defamed may sue for damages; if, on the other hand, the words be written or printed, or if treason or immorality be thereby inculcated, the offender can be tried for the misdemeanour either by information or indictment.[7]

Any man may, therefore, say or write whatever he likes, subject to the risk of, it may be, severe punishment if he publishes any statement (either by word of mouth, in writing, or in print) which he is not legally entitled to make. Nor is the law of England specially

---

6 It appears, however, in the Preamble to Lord Campbell's Act, 1843, 6 & 7 Vict. c. 96.

7 Odgers, *Libel and Slander*, Introd. (3rd ed.), p. 12.

favourable to free speech or to free writing in the rules which it maintains in theory and often enforces in fact as to the kind of statements which a man has a legal right to make. Above all, it recognises in general no special privilege on behalf of the "press," if by that term we mean, in conformity with ordinary language, periodical literature in general, and particularly the newspapers. In truth there is little in the statute-book which can be called a "press law."[8] The law of the press as it exists here is merely part of the law of libel, and it is well worth while to trace out with some care the restrictions imposed by the law of libel on the "freedom of the press," by which expression I mean a person's right to make any statement he likes in books or newspapers.

Libels on individuals.

There are many statements with regard to individuals which no man is entitled to publish in writing or print; it is a libel (speaking generally) thus to publish any untrue statement about another which is calculated to injure his interests, character, or reputation. Every man who directly or indirectly makes known or, as the technical expression goes, "publishes" such a statement, gives currency to a libel and is liable to an action for damages. The person who makes a defamatory statement and authorises its publication in writing, the person who writes, the publisher who brings out for sale, the printer who prints, the vendor who distributes a libel, are each guilty of publication, and may each severally be sued. The gist of the offence being the making public, not the writing of the libel, the person who having read a libel sends it on to a friend, is a libeller; and it would seem that a man who reads aloud a libel, knowing it to be such, may be sued. This separate liability of each person concerned in a wrongful act is, as already pointed out, a very noticeable characteristic of our law. Honest belief, moreover, and good intentions on the part of

---

8 For exceptions to this, see *e.g.* 8 & 9 Vict. c. 75; 44 & 45 Vict. c. 60, s. 2. It is, however, true, as pointed out by one of my critics (see the *Law of the Press,* by Fisher & Strahan, 2nd ed. p. iii.), that "there is slowly growing up a distinct law of the press." The tendency of recent press legislation is to a certain extent to free the proprietors of newspapers from the full amount of liability which attaches to other persons for the *bona fide* publication of defamatory statements made at public meetings and the like. See especially the Libel Law Amendment Act, 1888 (51 & 52 Vict. c. 64), s. 4. Whether this deviation from the principles of the common law is, or is not, of benefit to the public, is an open question which can be answered only by experience.

a libeller, are no legal defence for his conduct. Nor will it avail him to show that he had good reason for thinking the false statement which he made to be true. Persons often must pay heavy damages for giving currency to statements which were not meant to be falsehoods, and which were reasonably believed to be true. Thus it is libellous to publish of a man who has been convicted of felony but has worked out his sentence that he "is a convicted felon." It is a libel on the part of X if X publishes that B has told him that A's bank has stopped payment, if, though B in fact made the statement to X, and X believed the report to be true, it turns out to be false. Nor, again, are expressions of opinion when injurious to another at all certain not to expose the publisher of them to an action. A "fair" criticism, it is often said, is not libellous; but it would be a grave mistake to suppose that critics, either in the press or elsewhere, have a right to publish whatever criticisms they think true. Every one has a right to publish fair and candid criticism. But "a critic must confine himself to criticism, and not make it the veil for personal censure, nor allow himself to run into reckless and unfair attacks merely from the love of exercising his power of denunciation."[9] A writer in the press and an artist or actor whose performances are criticised are apt to draw the line between "candid criticism" and "personal censure" at very different points. And when on this matter there is a difference of opinion between a critic and his victim, the delicate question what is meant by fairness has to be determined by a jury, and may be so answered as greatly to curtail the free expression of critical judgments. Nor let it be supposed that the mere "truth" of a statement is of itself sufficient to protect the person who publishes it from liability to punishment. For though the fact that an assertion is true is an answer to an action for libel, a person may be criminally punished for publishing statements which, though perfectly true, damage an individual without being of any benefit to the public. To write, for example, and with truth of A that he many years ago committed acts of immorality may very well expose the writer X to criminal proceedings, and X if put on his trial will be bound to prove not only that A was in fact guilty of the faults imputed to him, but also that the public had an interest in the knowl-

---

9 *Whistler* v. *Ruskin*, "The Times," Nov. 27, 1878, per Huddleston, B.

edge of *A*'s misconduct. If *X* cannot show this, he will find that no supposed right of free discussion or respect for liberty of the press will before an English judge save him from being found guilty of a misdemeanour and sent to prison.

We have spoken so far in very general terms of the limits placed by the law of libel on freedom of discussion as regards the character of individuals. Let us now observe for a moment the way in which the law of libel restricts in theory, at least, the right to criticise the conduct of the government.

Every person commits a misdemeanour who publishes (orally or otherwise) any words or any document with a seditious intention. Now a seditious intention means an intention to bring into hatred or contempt, or to excite disaffection against the King or the govern-ment and constitution of the United Kingdom as by law established, or either House of Parliament, or the administration of justice, or to excite British subjects to attempt otherwise than by lawful means the alteration of any matter in Church or State by law established, or to promote feelings of illwill and hostility between different classes. [10] And if the matter published is contained in a written or printed document the publisher is guilty of publishing a seditious libel. The law, it is true, permits the publication of statements meant only to show that the Crown has been misled, or that the government has committed errors, or to point out defects in the government or the constitution with a view to their legal remedy, or with a view to recommend alterations in Church or State by legal means, and, in short, sanctions criticism on public affairs which is *bona fide* intended to recommend the reform of existing institutions by legal methods. But any one will see at once that the legal definition of a seditious libel might easily be so used as to check a great deal of what is ordinarily considered allowable discussion, and would if rigidly enforced be inconsistent with prevailing forms of political agitation.

The case is pretty much the same as regards the free expression of opinion on religious or moral questions. [11] Of late years circumstances

---

10 See Stephen, *Digest of the Criminal the Law* (6th ed.), arts. 96, 97, 98.
11 *Ibid.*, arts. 179–183.

have recalled attention to the forgotten law of blasphemy. But it surprises most persons to learn that, on one view of the law, any one who publishes a denial of the truth of Christianity in general or of the existence of God, whether the terms of such publication are decent or otherwise, commits the misdemeanour of publishing a blasphemous libel, and is liable to imprisonment; that, according to another view of the law, any one is guilty of publishing a blasphemous libel who publishes matter relating to God, Jesus Christ, or the Book of Common Prayer intended to wound the feelings of mankind, or to excite contempt against the Church by law established, or to promote immorality; and that it is at least open to grave doubt how far the publications which thus wound the feelings of mankind are exempt from the character of blasphemy because they are intended in good faith to propagate opinions which the person who publishes them regards as true.[12] Most persons, again, are astonished to find that the denial of the truth of Christianity or of the authority of the Scriptures, by "writing, printing, teaching, or advised speaking" on the part of any person who has been educated in or made profession of Christianity in England, is by statute a criminal offence entailing very severe penalities.[13] When once, however, the principles of the common law and the force of the enactments still contained in the statute-book are really appreciated, no one can maintain that the law of England recognises anything like that natural right to the free communication of thoughts and opinions which was proclaimed in France a little over a hundred years ago to be one of the most valuable Rights of Man. It is quite clear, further, that the effect of English law, whether as regards statements made about individuals, or the expression of opinion about public affairs, or speculative matters, depends wholly upon the answer to the question who are to determine whether a given publication is or is not a libel. The reply (as we all

---

12 See especially Stephen, *Digest of the Criminal Law* (6th ed.), art. 179, and contrast Odgers (3rd ed.), pp. 475–490, where a view of the law is maintained differing from that of Sir J. F. Stephen.

13 See 9 & 10 Will. III. c. 35, as altered by 53 Geo. III. c. 160, and Stephen's *Digest of the Criminal Law*, art. 181. Conf. *Attorney-General* v. *Bradlaugh*, 14 Q. B. D. (C. A.), 667, p. 719, judgment of Lindley, L. J.

know) is, that in substance this matter is referred to the decision of a jury. Whether in any given case a particular individual is to be convicted of libel depends wholly upon their judgment, and they have to determine the questions of truth, fairness, intention, and the like, which affect the legal character of a published statement.[14]

Freedom of discussion is, then, in England little else than the right to write or say anything which a jury, consisting of twelve shopkeepers, think it expedient should be said or written. Such "liberty" may vary at different times and seasons from unrestricted license to very severe restraint, and the experience of English history during the last two centuries shows that under the law of libel the amount of latitude conceded to the expression of opinion has, in fact, differed greatly according to the condition of popular sentiment. Until very recent times the law, moreover, has not recognized any privilege on the part of the press. A statement which is defamatory or blasphemous, if made in a letter or upon a card, has exactly the same character if made in a book or a newspaper. The protection given by the Belgian constitution to the editor, printer, or seller of a newspaper involves a recognition of special rights on the part of persons connected with the press which is quite inconsistent with the general theory of English law. It is hardly an exaggeration to say, from this point of view, that liberty of the press is not recognised in England.

Why the liberty of the press has been thought peculiar to England.

Why then has the liberty of the press been long reputed as a special feature of English institutions?

The answer to this inquiry is, that for about two centuries the relation between the government and the press has in England been marked by all those characteristics which make up what we have termed the "rule" or "supremacy" of law, and that just because of this, and not because of any favour shown by the law of England towards freedom of discussion, the press, and especially the newspaper press, has practically enjoyed with us a freedom which till

---

14 "The truth of the matter is very simple when stripped of all ornaments of speech, and a man of plain common sense may easily understand it. It is neither more nor less than this: that a man may publish anything which twelve of his countrymen think is not blamable, but that he ought to be punished if he publishes that which is blamable [*i.e.* that which twelve of his countrymen think is blamable]. This in plain common sense is the substance of all that has been said on the matter."—*Rex* v. *Cutbill,* 27 St. Tr. 642, 675.

recent years was unknown in continental states. Any one will see that this is so who examines carefully the situation of the press in modern England, and then contrasts it either with the press law of France or with the legal condition of the press in England during the sixteenth and seventeenth centuries.

The posi-
tion of the
press in
modern
England.
No censor-
ship.

The present position of the English press is marked by two features.

First, "the liberty of the press," says Lord Mansfield, "consists in printing without any previous license, subject to the consequences of law."[15] Lord Ellenborough says:

> The law of England is a law of liberty, and consistently with this liberty we have not what is called an *imprimatur;* there is no such preliminary license necessary; but if a man publish a paper, he is exposed to the penal consequences, as he is in every other act, if it be illegal.[16]

These dicta show us at once that the so-called liberty of the press is a mere application of the general principle, that no man is punishable except for a distinct breach of the law.[17] This principle is radically inconsistent with any scheme of license or censorship by which a man is hindered from writing or printing anything which he thinks fit, and is hard to reconcile even with the right on the part of the Courts to restrain the circulation of a libel, until at any rate the publisher has been convicted of publishing it. It is also opposed in spirit to any regulation requiring from the publisher of an intending newspaper a preliminary deposit of a certain sum of money, for the sake either of ensuring that newspapers should be published only by solvent persons, or that if a newspaper should contain libels there shall be a certainty of obtaining damages from the proprietor. No sensible person will argue that to demand a deposit from the owner of a newspaper, or to impose other limitations upon the right of publishing periodicals, is of necessity inexpedient or unjust. All that is here insisted upon is, that such checks and preventive measures are inconsistent with the pervading principle of English law, that

---

15 *Rex* v. *Dean of St. Asaph*, 3 T. R. 431 (note).

16 *Rex* v. *Cobbett*, 29 St. Tr. 49; see Odgers, *Libel and Slander* (3rd ed.), p. 10.

17 See p. 110, *ante*.

men are to be interfered with or punished, not because they may or will break the law, but only when they have committed some definite assignable legal offence. Hence, with one exception,[18] which is a quaint survival from a different system, no such thing is known with us as a license to print, or a censorship either of the press or of political newspapers. Neither the government nor any other authority has the right to seize or destroy the stock of a publisher because it consists of books, pamphlets, or papers which in the opinion of the government contain seditious or libellous matter. Indeed, the Courts themselves will, only under very special circumstances, even for the sake of protecting an individual from injury, prohibit the publication or republication of a libel, or restrain its sale until the matter has gone before a jury, and it has been established by their verdict that the words complained of are libellous.[19] Writers in the press are, in short, like every other person, subject to the law of the realm, and nothing else. Neither the government nor the Courts have (speaking generally) any greater power to prevent or oversee the publication of a newspaper than the writing and sending of a letter. Indeed, the simplest way of setting forth broadly the position of writers in the press is to say that they stand in substantially the same position as letterwriters. A man who scribbles blasphemy on a gate[20] and a man who prints blasphemy in a paper or in a book commit exactly the same offence, and are dealt with in England on the same principles. Hence also writers in and owners of newspapers have, or rather had until very recently, no special privilege protecting them from liability.[21] Look at the matter which way you will, the main feature of liberty of the press as understood in England is that the press (which

---

18 *I.e.* the licensing of plays. See the Theatres Act, 1843, 6 & 7 Vict. c. 68; Stephen, *Commentaries* (14th ed.), iii. p. 227.

19 Compare Odgers, *Libel and Slander* (3rd ed.), chap. xiii., especially pp. 388–399, with the first edition of Mr. Odgers' work, pp. 13–16.

20 *Reg.* v. *Pooley*, cited Stephen, *Digest of the Criminal Law* (6th ed.), p. 125.

21 This statement must be to a certain extent qualified in view of the Libel Act, 1843, 6 & 7 Vict. c. 96, the Newspaper Libel and Registration Act, 1881, 44 & 45 Vict. c. 60, and the Law of Libel Amendment Act, 1888, 51 & 52 Vict. c. 64, which do give some amount of special protection to *bona fide* reports, *e.g.* of public meetings, in newspapers.

means, of course, the writers in it) is subject only to the ordinary law of the land.

Press offences dealt with by ordinary Courts.

Secondly, press offences, in so far as the term can be used with reference to English law, are tried and punished only by the ordinary Courts of the country, that is, by a judge and jury.[22]

Since the Restoration,[23] offences committed through the newspapers, or, in other words, the publication therein of libels whether defamatory, seditious, or blasphemous, have never been tried by any special tribunal. Nothing to Englishmen seems more a matter of course than this. Yet nothing has in reality contributed so much to free the periodical press from any control. If the criterion whether a publication be libellous is the opinion of the jury, and a man may publish anything which twelve of his countrymen think is not blamable, it is impossible that the Crown or the Ministry should exert any stringent control over writings in the press, unless (as indeed may sometimes happen) the majority of ordinary citizens are entirely opposed to attacks on the government. The times when persons in power wish to check the excesses of public writers are times at which a large body of opinion or sentiment is hostile to the executive. But under these circumstances it must, from the nature of things, be at least an even chance that the jury called upon to find a publisher guilty of printing seditious libels may sympathise with the language which the officers of the Crown deem worthy of punishment, and hence may hold censures which are prosecuted as libels to be fair and laudable criticism of official errors. Whether the control indirectly exercised over the expression of opinion by the verdict of twelve commonplace Englishmen is at the present day certain to be as great a protection to the free expression of opinion, even in political matters, as it proved a century ago, when the sentiment of the governing

---

22 The existence, however, of process by criminal information, and the rule that truth was no justification, had the result that during the eighteenth century seditious libel rose almost to the rank of a press offence, to be dealt with, if not by separate tribunals, at any rate by special rules enforced by a special procedure.

23 See as to the state of the press under the Commonwealth, Masson, *Life of Milton*, iii. pp. 265–297. Substantially the possibility of trying press offences by special tribunals was put an end to by the abolition of the Star Chamber in 1641, 16 Car. I. c. 10.

body was different from the prevalent feeling of the class from which jurymen were chosen, is an interesting speculation into which there is no need to enter. What is certain is, that the practical freedom of the English press arose in great measure from the trial with us of "press offences," like every other kind of libel, by a jury.

The liberty of the press, then, is in England simply one result of the universal predominance of the law of the land. The terms "liberty of the press," "press offences," "censorship of the press," and the like, are all but unknown to English lawyers, simply because any offence which can be committed through the press is some form of libel, and is governed in substance by the ordinary law of defamation.

These things seem to us at the present day so natural as hardly to be noticeable; let us, however, glance as I have suggested at the press law of France both before and since the Revolution; and also at the condition of the press in England up to nearly the end of the seventeenth century. Such a survey will prove to us that the treatment in modern England of offences committed through the newspapers affords an example, as singular as it is striking, of the legal spirit which now pervades every part of the English constitution.

Compari-
son with
the press
law of
France.

An Englishman who consults French authorities is struck with amazement at two facts: press law[24] has long constituted and still constitutes to a certain extent a special department of French legislation, and press offences have been, under every form of government which has existed in France, a more or less special class of crimes. The Acts which have been passed in England with regard to the press since the days of Queen Elizabeth do not in number equal one-tenth,

---

24 The press is now governed in France by the *Loi sur la liberte de la presse,* 29–30 Juill. 1881. This law repeals all earlier edicts, decrees, laws, ordinances, etc. on the subject. Immediately before this law was passed there were in force more than thirty enactments regulating the position of the French press, and inflicting penalties on offences which could be committed by writers in the press; and the three hundred and odd closely printed pages of Dalloz, treating of laws on the press, show that the enactments then in vigour under the Republic were as nothing compared to the whole mass of regulations, ordinances, decrees, and laws which, since the earliest days of printing down to the year 1881, have been issued by French rulers with the object of controlling the literary expression of opinion and thought. See Dalloz, *Répertoire,* vol. xxxvi., *"Presse,"* pp. 384–776, and especially Tit. I. chap. i., Tit. II. chap. iv.; Roger et Sorel, *Codes et Loi Usuelles,* "Presse," 637–652; Duguit, *Manuel de Droit Constitutionnel,* pp. 575–582.

or even one-twentieth, of the laws enacted during the same period on the same subject in France. The contrast becomes still more marked if we compare the state of things in the two countries since the beginning of the eighteenth century, and (for the sake of avoiding exaggeration) put the laws passed since that date, and which were till 1881 in force in France, against every Act which, whether repealed or unrepealed, has been passed in England since the year 1700. It will be found that the French press code consisted, till after the establishment of the present Republic, of over thirty enactments, whilst the English Acts about the press passed since the beginning of the last century do not exceed a dozen, and, moreover, have gone very little way towards touching the freedom of writers.

The ground of this difference lies in the opposite views taken in the two countries of the proper relation of the state to literature, or, more strictly, to the expression of opinion in print.

In England the doctrine has since 1700 in substance prevailed that the government has nothing to do with the guidance of opinion, and that the sole duty of the state is to punish libels of all kinds, whether they are expressed in writing or in print. Hence the government has (speaking generally) exercised no special control over literature, and the law of the press, in so far as it can be said to have existed, has been nothing else than a branch or an application of the law of libel.

In France, literature has for centuries been considered as the particular concern of the state. The prevailing doctrine, as may be gathered from the current of French legislation, has been, and still to a certain extent is, that it is the function of the administration not only to punish defamation, slander, or blasphemy, but to guide the course of opinion, or, at any rate, to adopt preventive measures for guarding against the propagation in print of unsound or dangerous doctrines. Hence the huge amount and the special and repressive character of the press laws which have existed in France.

Up to the time of the Revolution the whole literature of the country was avowedly controlled by the state. The right to print or sell books and printed publications of any kind was treated as a special privilege or monopoly of certain libraries; the regulations (*réglements*) of 1723 (some part of which was till quite recently in force)[25] and of 1767 confined the right of sale and printing under the severest penalties of librarians who were duly licensed.[26] The right to publish, again, was submitted to the strictest censorship, exercised partly by the University (an entirely ecclesiastical body), partly by the Parliaments, partly by the Crown. The penalties of death, of the galleys, of the pillory, were from time to time imposed upon the printing or sale of forbidden works. These punishments were often evaded; but they after all retained practical force till the very eve of the Revolution. The most celebrated literary works of France were published abroad. Montesquieu's *Esprit des Lois* appeared at Geneva. Voltaire's *Henriade* was printed in England; the most remarkable of his and of Rousseau's writings were published in London, in Geneva, or in Amsterdam. In 1775 a work entitled *Philosophie de la Nature* was destroyed by the order of the Parliament of Paris, the author was decreed guilty of treason against God and man, and would have been burnt if he could have been arrested. In 1781, eight years before the meeting of the States General, Raynal was pronounced by the Parliament guilty of blasphemy on account of his *Histoire des Indes*.[27] The point, however, to remark is, not so much the severity of the punishments which under the *Ancien Régime* were intended to suppress the expression of heterodox or false beliefs, as the strict maintenance down to 1789 of the right and duty of the state to guide the literature of the country. It should further be noted that down to that date the government made no marked distinction between periodical and other literature. When the *Lettres Philosophiques* could be burnt by the hangman, when the publication of the *Henriade* and the *Encyclopédie* depended on the goodwill of the King, there was no need for establishing special restrictions on newspapers. The daily or weekly press, moreover, hardly existed in France till the opening of the States General.[28]

25 See Dalloz, *Répertoire,* vol. xxxvi., *"Presse,"* Tit. I. chap. i. Compare Roger et Sorel, *Codes et Lois,* "Presse," pp. 637–652.

26 *Ibid.*

27 See Dalloz, *Répertoire,* vol. xxxvi., *"Presse,"* Tit. I. chap. i. Compare Roger et Sorel, *Codes et Lois,* "Presse," pp. 637–652.

28 See Rocquain, *L'Esprit Révolutionnaire avant la Révolution,* for a complete list of *"Livres Condamnés"* from 1715 to 1789. Rocquain's book is fill of information on the arbitrariness of the French Government during the reigns of Louis XV. and Louis XVI.

The Revolution (it may be fancied) put an end to restraints upon the press. The Declaration of the Rights of Man proclaimed the right of every citizen to publish and print his opinions, and the language has been cited[29] in which the Constitution of 1791 guaranteed to every man the natural right of speaking, printing, and publishing his thoughts without having his writings submitted to any censorship or inspection prior to publication. But the Declaration of Rights and this guarantee were practically worthless. They enounced a theory which for many years was utterly opposed to the practice of every French government.

The Convention did not establish a censorship, but under the plea of preventing the circulation of seditious works it passed the law of 29th March 1793, which silenced all free expression of opinion. The Directory imitated the Convention. Under the First Empire the newspaper press became the property of the government, and the sale, printing, and publication of books was wholly submitted to imperial control and censorship.[30]

The years which elapsed from 1789 to 1815 were, it may be suggested, a revolutionary era which provoked or excused exceptional measures of state interference. Any one, however, who wants to see how consonant to the ideas which have permanently governed French law and French habits is the notion that the administration should by some means keep its hand on the national literature of the country, ought to note with care the course of legislation from the Restoration to the present day. The attempt, indeed, to control the publication of books has been by slow degrees given up; but one government after another has, with curious uniformity, proclaimed the freedom and ensured the subjection of the newspaper press. From 1814 to 1830 the censorship was practically established (21st Oct. 1814), was partially abolished, was abolished (1819), was re-established and extended (1820), and was re-abolished (1828).[31] The Revolution of July 1830 was occasioned by an attempt to destroy the liberty of the press. The Charter made the abolition of the censorship part of the constitution, and since that date no system of censorship

---

29 See p. 146, *ante.*

30 Dalloz, *Répertoire*, xxxvi., *"Presse,"* Tit. I. chap. i.

31 See Duguit, *Traité de Droit Constitutionnel*, i. pp. 91, 92.

has been in name re-established. But as regards newspapers, the celebrated decree of 17th February 1852 enacted restrictions more rigid than anything imposed under the name of *la censure* by any government since the fall of Napoleon I. The government took to itself under this law, in addition to other discretionary powers, the right to suppress any newspaper without the necessity of proving the commission of any crime or offence by the owner of the paper or by any writer in its columns.[32] No one, further, could under this decree set up a paper without official authorisation. Nor have different forms of the censorship been the sole restrictions imposed in France on the liberty of the press. The combined operations of enactments passed during the existence of the Republic of 1848, and under the Empire, was (among other things) to make the signature of newspaper articles by their authors compulsory,[33] to require a large deposit from any person who wished to establish a paper,[34] to withdraw all press offences whatever from the cognisance of a jury,[35] to re-establish or reaffirm the provision contained in the *réglement* of 1723 by which no one could carry on the trade of a librarian or printer (*commerce de la librairie*) without a license. It may, in fact, be said with substantial truth that between 1852 and 1870 the newspapers of France were as much controlled by the government as was every kind of literature before 1789, and that the Second Empire exhibited a retrogression towards the despotic principles of the *Ancien Régime*. The Republic,[36]

---

32 Décret, 17 Février, 1852, sec. 32, Roger et Sorel, *Codes et Lois*, p. 648.

33 Roger et Sorel, *Codes et Lois*, p. 646. Lois, 16 Julliet 1850.

34 Roger et Sorel, *Codes et Lois*, p. 646. Lois, 16 Juillet 1850.

35 Lois, 31 Déc. 1851.

36 One thing is perfectly clear and deserves notice. The legislation of the existing Republic was not till 1881, any more than that of the Restoration or the Empire, based on the view of the press which pervades the modern law of England. "Press law" still formed a special department of the law of France. "Press offences" were a particular class of crimes, and there were at least two provisions, and probably several more, to be found in French laws which conflicted with the doctrine of the liberty of the press as understood in England. A law passed under the Republic (6th July 1871. Roger et Sorel, *Codes et Lois*, p. 652) reimposed on the proprietors of newspapers the necessity of making a large deposit, with the proper authorities, as a security for the payment of fines or damages incurred in the course of the management of the paper. A still later law (29th December 1875, s. 5. Roger et Sorel, *Codes et Lois*, p. 652), while it submitted some press offences to the judgment of a jury, subjected

it is true, has abolished the restraints on the liberty of the press which grew up both before and under the Empire. But though for the last twenty-seven years the ruling powers in France have favoured the liberty or license of the press, nothing is more plain than that until quite recently the idea that press offences were a peculiar class of offences to be dealt with in a special way and punished by special courts was accepted by every party in France. This is a matter of extreme theoretical importance. It shows how foreign to French notions is the idea that every breach of law ought to be dealt with by the ordinary law of the land. Even a cursory survey—and no other is possible in these lectures—of French legislation with regard to literature proves, then, that from the time when the press came into existence up to almost the present date the idea has held ground that the state, as represented by the executive, ought to direct or control the expression of opinion, and that this control has been exercised by an official censorship—by restrictions on the right to print or sell books—and by the subjection of press offences to special laws administered by special tribunals. The occasional relaxation of these restrictions is of importance. But their recurring revival is of far more significance than their temporary abolition.[37]

Contrast with position of press in England during seventeenth century.

Let us now turn to the position of the English press during the sixteenth and seventeenth centuries.

The Crown originally held all presses in its own hands, allowed no one to print except under special license, and kept all presses subject to regulations put forward by the Star Chamber in virtue of the royal prerogative: the exclusive privilege of printing was thus given to

---

others to the cognisance of Courts of which a jury formed no part. The law of 29th July 1881 establishes the freedom of the press. Recent French legislation exhibits, no doubt, a violent reaction against all attempts to check the freedom of the press, but in its very effort to secure this freedom betrays the existence of the notion that offences committed through the press require in some sort exceptional treatment.

37 Note the several laws passed since 1881 to repress the abuse of freedom in one form or another by the press, *e.g.* the law of 2nd August 1882, modified and completed by the law of 16th March 1898, for the suppression of violations of moral principles (*outrages aux bonnes mœurs*) by the press, the law of 28th July 1894, to suppress the advocacy of anarchical principles by the press, and the law of 16th March 1893, giving the French government special powers with regard to foreign newspapers, or newspapers published in a foreign language. Conf. Duguit, *Manuel de Droit Constitutionnel*, p. 582.

ninety-seven London stationers and their successors, who, as the Stationers' Company, constituted a guild with power to seize all publications issued by outsiders; the printing-presses ultimately conceded to the Universities existed only by a decree of the Star Chamber.

Side by side with the restrictions on printing—which appear to have more or less broken down—there grew up a system of licensing which constituted a true censorship.[38]

Press offences constituted a special class of crimes cognisable by a special tribunal—the Star Chamber—which sat without a jury and administered severe punishments.[39] The Star Chamber indeed fell in 1641, never to be revived, but the censorship survived the Commonwealth, and was under the Restoration (1662) given a strictly legal foundation by the statute 13 & 14 Car. II. c. 33, which by subsequent enactments was kept in force till 1695.[40]

Original likeness and subsequent unlikeness between press law of England and of France.

There existed, in short, in England during the sixteenth and seventeenth centuries every method of curbing the press which was then practised in France, and which has prevailed there almost up to the present day. In England, as on the Continent, the book trade was a monopoly, the censorship was in full vigour, the offences of authors and printers were treated as special crimes and severely punished by special tribunals. This similarity or identity of the principles with regard to the treatment of literature originally upheld by the government of England and by the government of France is striking. It is rendered still more startling by the contrast between the subsequent history of legislation in the two countries. In France (as we have already seen) the censorship, though frequently abolished, has almost as frequently been restored. In England the system of licensing, which was the censorship under another name, was terminated rather than abolished in 1695. The House of Commons, which refused to continue the Licensing Act, was certainly not imbued with any settled enthusiasm for liberty of thought. The English statesmen

---

38 See for the control exercised over the press down to 1695, Odgers, *Libel and Slander* (3rd ed.), pp. 10–13.

39 Gardiner, *History of England*, vii. pp. 51, 130; *ibid.*, viii. pp. 225, 234.

40 See Macaulay, *History of England*, iv. chaps. xix, xxi.

of 1695 neither avowed nor entertained the belief that the "free communication of thoughts and opinions was one of the most valuable of
the rights of man."[41] They refused to renew the Licensing Act, and
thus established freedom of the press without any knowledge of the
importance of what they were doing. This can be asserted with confidence, for the Commons delivered to the Lords a document which
contains the reasons for their refusing to renew the Act.

> This paper completely vindicates the resolution to which the Commons
> had come. But it proves at the same time that they knew not what they were
> doing, what a revolution they were making, what a power they were calling
> into existence. They pointed out concisely, clearly, forcibly, and sometimes
> with a grave irony which is not unbecoming, the absurdities and iniquities of
> the statute which was about to expire. But all their objections will be found to
> relate to matters of detail. On the great question of principle, on the question
> whether the liberty of unlicensed printing be, on the whole, a blessing or a
> curse to society, not a word is said. The Licensing Act is condemned, not as a
> thing essentially evil, but on account of the petty grievances, the exactions,
> the jobs, the commercial restrictions, the domiciliary visits, which were inci-
> dental to it. It is pronounced mischievous because it enables the Company of
> Stationers to extort money from publishers, because it empowers the agents
> of the government to search houses under the authority of general warrants,
> because it confines the foreign book trade to the port of London; because it
> detains valuable packages of books at the Custom House till the pages are
> mildewed. The Commons complain that the amount of the fee which the
> licenser may demand is not fixed. They complain that it is made penal in an
> officer of the Customs to open a box of books from abroad, except in the
> presence of one of the censors of the press. How, it is very sensibly asked, is
> the officer to know that there are books in the box till he has opened it? Such
> were the arguments which did what Milton's *Areopagitica* had failed to do.[42]

How slight was the hold of the principle of the liberty of the press
on the statesmen who abolished the censorship is proved by their
entertaining, two years later, a bill (which, however, never passed) to
prohibit the unlicensed publication of news.[43] Yet while the solemn
declaration by the National Assembly of 1789 of the right to the free
expression of thought remained a dead letter, or at best a speculative

---

41 See *Declaration of the Rights of Man,* art. 11, p. 146, *ante.*

42 Macaulay, *History of England,* iv. pp. 541, 542.

43 Macaulay, *History of England,* iv. pp. 771, 772.

maxim of French jurisprudence which, though not without influence, was constantly broken in upon by the actual law of France, the refusal of the English Parliament in 1695 to renew the Licensing Act did permanently establish the freedom of the press in England. The fifty years which followed were a period of revolutionary disquiet fairly comparable with the era of the Restoration in France. But the censorship once abolished in England was never revived, and all idea of restrictions on the liberty of the press other than those contained in the law of libel have been so long unknown to Englishmen, that the rare survivals in our law of the notion that literature ought to be controlled by the state appear to most persons inexplicable anomalies, and are tolerated only because they produce so little inconvenience that their existence is forgotten.

Questions suggested by original similarity and final difference between press law of France and of England.

To a student who surveys the history of the liberty of the press in France and in England two questions suggest themselves. How does it happen that down to the end of the seventeenth century the principles upheld by the Crown in each country were in substance the same? What, again, is the explanation of the fact that from the beginning of the eighteenth century the principles governing the law of the press in the two countries have been, as they still continue to be, essentially different? The similarity and the difference each seems at first sight equally perplexing. Yet both one and the other admit of explanation, and the solution of an apparent paradox is worth giving because of its close bearing on the subject of this lecture, namely, the predominance of the spirit of legality which distinguishes the law of the constitution.

Reasons for original similarity.

The ground of the similarity between the press law of England and of France from the beginning of the sixteenth till the beginning of the eighteenth century, is that the governments, if not the people, of each country were during that period influenced by very similar administrative notions and by similar ideas as to the relation between the state and individuals. In England, again, as in every European country, the belief prevailed that a King was responsible for the religious belief of his subjects. This responsibility involves the necessity for regulating the utterance and formation of opinion. But this direction or control cannot be exercised without governmental interference with that liberty of the press which is at bottom the right of every man to print any opinion which he chooses to propagate, subject only to risk of punishment if his expressions contravene some distinct legal maxim. During the sixteenth and seventeenth centuries, in short, the Crown was in England, as in France, extending its administrative powers; the Crown was in England, as in France, entitled, or rather required by public opinion, to treat the control of literature as an affair of state. Similar circumstances produced similar results; in each country the same principles prevailed; in each country the treatment of the press assumed, therefore, a similar character.

Reasons for later dissimilarity. The reason, again, why, for nearly two centuries, the press has been treated in France on principles utterly different from those which have been accepted in England, lies deep in the difference of the spirit which has governed the customs and laws of the two countries.

In France the idea has always flourished that the government, whether Royal, Imperial, or Republican, possesses, as representing the state, rights and powers as against individuals superior to and independent of the ordinary law of the land. This is the real basis of that whole theory of a *droit administratif,*[44] which it is so hard for Englishmen fully to understand. The increase, moreover, in the authority of the central government has at most periods both before and since the Revolution been, or appeared to most Frenchmen to be, the means of removing evils which oppressed the mass of the people. The nation has in general looked upon the authority of the state with the same favour with which Englishmen during the sixteenth century regarded the prerogative of the Crown. The control exercised in different forms by the executive over literature has, therefore, in the main fully harmonised with the other institutions of France. The existence, moreover, of an elaborate administrative system, the action of which has never been subject to the control of the ordinary tribunals, has always placed in the hands of whatever power was supreme in France the means of enforcing official surveillance of literature. Hence the censorship (to speak of no other modes of checking

---

44 See Chap. XII. *post.*

the liberty of the press) has been on the whole in keeping with the
general action of French governments and with the average sentiment of the nation, whilst there has never been wanting appropriate
machinery by which to carry the censorship into effect.

No doubt there were heard throughout the eighteenth century,
and have been heard ever since, vigorous protests against the censorship, as against other forms of administrative arbitrariness; and at the
beginning of the Great Revolution, as at other periods since, efforts
were made in favour of free discussion. Hence flowed the abolition of
the censorship, but this attempt to limit the powers of the government in one particular direction was quite out of harmony with the
general reverence for the authority of the state. As long, moreover, as
the whole scheme of French administration was left in force, the
government, in whatever hands it was placed, always retained the
means of resuming its control over the press, whenever popular
feeling should for a moment favour the repression of free speech.
Hence arose the constantly recurring restoration of the abolished
censorship or of restraints which, though not called by the unpopular
name of *la censure,* were more stringent than has ever been any
Licensing Act. Restrictions, in short, on what Englishmen understand by the liberty of the press have continued to exist in France and
are hardly now abolished, because the exercise of preventive and
discretionary authority on the part of the executive harmonises with
the general spirit of French law, and because the administrative
machinery, which is the creation of that spirit, has always placed (as it
still places) in the hands of the executive the proper means for enforcing discretionary authority.

In England, on the other hand, the attempt made by the Crown
during the sixteenth and seventeenth centuries to form a strong central administration, though it was for a time attended with success,
because it met some of the needs of the age, was at bottom repugnant
to the manners and traditions of the country; and even at a time
when the people wished the Crown to be strong, they hardly liked
the means by which the Crown exerted its strength.

Hundreds of Englishmen who hated toleration and cared little for
freedom of speech, entertained a keen jealousy of arbitrary power,

and a fixed determination to be ruled in accordance with the law of the land.[45] These sentiments abolished the Star Chamber in 1641, and made the re-establishment of the hated Court impossible even for the frantic loyalty of 1660. But the destruction of the Star Chamber meant much more than the abolition of an unpopular tribunal; it meant the rooting up from its foundations of the whole of the administrative system which had been erected by the Tudors and extended by the Stuarts. This overthrow of a form of administration which contradicted the legal habits of Englishmen had no direct connection with any desire for the uncontrolled expression of opinion. The Parliament which would not restore the Star Chamber or the Court of High Commission passed the Licensing Act, and this statute, which in fact establishes the censorship, was, as we have seen, continued in force for some years after the Revolution. The passing, however, of the statute, though not a triumph of toleration, was a triumph of legality. The power of licensing depended henceforward, not on any idea of inherent executive authority, but on the statute law. The right of licensing was left in the hands of the government, but this power was regulated by the words of a statute; and, what was of more consequence, breaches of the Act could be punished only by proceedings in the ordinary Courts. The fall of the Star Chamber deprived the executive of the means for exercising arbitrary power. Hence the refusal of the House of Commons in 1695 to continue the Licensing Act was something very different from the proclamation of freedom of thought contained in the French Declaration of Rights, or from any of the laws which have abolished the censorship in France. To abolish the right of the government to control the press, was, in England, simply to do away with an exceptional authority, which was opposed to the general tendency of the law, and the abolition was final, because the executive had already lost the means by which the control of opinion could be effectively enforced.

To sum the whole matter up, the censorship though constantly abolished has been constantly revived in France, because the exertion of discretionary powers by the government has been and still is in

---

45 See Selden's remarks on the illegality of the decrees of the Star Chamber, cited Gardiner, *History of England*, vii. p. 51.

harmony with French laws and institutions. The abolition of the censorship was final in England, because the exercise of discretionary power by the Crown was inconsistent with our system of administration and with the ideas of English law. The contrast is made the more striking by the paradoxical fact, that the statesmen who tried with little success to establish the liberty of the press in France really intended to proclaim freedom of opinion, whilst the statesmen who would not pass the Licensing Act, and thereby founded the liberty of the press in England, held theories of toleration which fell far short of favouring unrestricted liberty of discussion. This contrast is not only striking in itself, but also affords the strongest illustration that can be found of English conceptions of the rule of law.

Chapter VII

THE RIGHT OF PUBLIC MEETING [1]

Right of public meeting.

The law of Belgium [2] with regard to public meetings is contained in the nineteenth article of the constitution, which is probably intended in the main to reproduce the law of England, and runs as follows:

Rules of Belgian constitution.

> *Art. 19. Les Belges ont le droit de s'assembler paisiblement et sans armes, en se conformant aux lois, qui peuvent régler l'exercice de ce droit, sans néanmoins le soumettre à une autorisation préalable.*
>
> *Cette disposition ne s'applique point aux rassemblements en plein air, qui restent entièrement soumis aux lois de police.* [3]

Principles of English law as to right of public meeting.

The restrictions on the practice of public meeting appear to be more stringent in Belgium than in England, for the police have with us no special authority to control open-air assemblies. Yet just as it cannot with strict accuracy be asserted that English law recognises the liberty of the press, so it can hardly be said that our constitution knows of such a thing as any specific right of public meeting. No better in-

---

1 See generally as to the right of public meeting, Stephen, *Commentaries*, iv. (14th ed.), pp. 174–178, and Kenny, *Outlines of Criminal Law* (3rd ed.), pp. 280–286. See Appendix, Note V., Questions connected with the Right of Public Meeting.

2 See *Law Quarterly Review*, iv. p. 159. See also as to right of public meeting in Italy, *ibid.* p. 78; in France, *ibid.* p. 165; in Switzerland, *ibid.* p. 169; in United States, *ibid.* p. 257. See as to history of law of public meeting in France, Duguit, *Manuel de Droit Constitutionnel*, pp. 554–559.

3 *Constitution de la Belgique*, art. 19.

stance can indeed be found of the way in which in England the constitution is built up upon individual rights than our rules as to public assemblies. The right of assembling is nothing more than a result of the view taken by the Courts as to individual liberty of person and individual liberty of speech. There is no special law allowing *A, B,* and *C* to meet together either in the open air or elsewhere for a lawful purpose, but the right of *A* to go where he pleases so that he does not commit a trespass, and to say what he likes to *B* so that his talk is not libellous or seditious, the right of *B* to do the like, and the existence of the same rights of *C, D, E,* and *F,* and so on *ad infinitum,* lead to the consequence that *A, B, C, D,* and a thousand or ten thousand other persons, may (as a general rule)[4] meet together in any place where otherwise they each have a right to be for a lawful purpose and in a lawful manner. *A* has a right to walk down the High Street or to go on to a common. *B* has the same right. *C, D,* and all their friends have the same right to go there also. In other words, *A, B, C,* and *D,* and ten thousand such, have a right to hold a public meeting; and as *A* may say to *B* that he thinks an Act ought to be passed abolishing the House of Lords, or that the House of Lords are bound to reject any bill modifying the constitution of their House, and as *B* may make the same remark to any of his friends, the result ensues that *A* and ten thousand more may hold a public meeting either to support the government or to encourage the resistance of the Peers. Here then you have in substance that right of public meeting for political and other purposes which is constantly treated in foreign countries as a special privilege, to be exercised only subject to careful restrictions. The assertion, however, that *A, B, C,* and *D,* and a hundred thousand more persons, just because they may each go where they like, and each say what they please, have a right to hold meetings for the discussion of political and other topics, does not of course mean that it is impossible for persons so to exercise the right of meeting as to break the law. The object of a meeting may be to commit a crime by open force, or in some way or other to break the

---

4 It is not intended here to express any opinion on the point whether an agreement on the part of *A, B,* and *C* to meet together may not under exceptional circumstances be a conspiracy.

peace, in which case the meeting itself becomes an unlawful assembly.[5] The mode in which a meeting is held may threaten a breach of the peace on the part of those holding the meeting, and therefore inspire peaceable citizens with reasonable fear; in which case, again, the meeting will be unlawful. In either instance the meeting may lawfully be broken up, and the members of it expose themselves to all the consequences, in the way of arrest, prosecution, and punishment, which attend the doing of unlawful acts, or, in other words, the commission of crimes.

Meeting not unlawful because it will excite unlawful opposition.

A public meeting which, from the conduct of those engaged in it, as, for example, through their marching together in arms, or through their intention to excite a breach of the peace on the part of opponents,[6] fills peaceable citizens with reasonable fear that the peace will be broken, is an unlawful assembly. But a meeting which in not otherwise illegal does not[7] become an unlawful assembly solely because it will excite violent and unlawful opposition, and thus may indirectly lead to a breach of the peace. Suppose, for example, that the members of the Salvation Army propose to hold a meeting at Oxford, suppose that a so-called Skeleton Army announce that they will attack the Salvationists and disperse them by force, suppose, lastly, that thereupon peaceable citizens who do not like the quiet of the town to be disturbed and who dread riots, urge the magistrates to stop the meeting of the Salvationists. This may seem at first sight a reasonable request, but the magistrates cannot, it is submitted,[8] legally take the course suggested to them. That under the present state of the law this must be so is on reflection pretty clear. The right of *A*

---

5 For the meaning of the term "unlawful assembly" see Appendix, Note V., Questions connected with the Right of Public Meeting.

6 Compare *O'Kelly* v. *Harvey*, 14 L. R. Ir. 105, *Humphries* v. *Connor*, 17 Ir. C. L. R. 1, 8, 9, judgment of Fitzgerald, J.

7 This statement must be read subject to the limitations stated, p. 174, *post*.

8 I assume, of course, that the Salvationists meet together, as they certainly do, for a lawful purpose, and meet quite peaceably, and without any intent either themselves to break the peace or to incite others to a breach thereof. The magistrates, however, could require the members of the Skeleton Army, or perhaps even the members of the Salvation Army, to find sureties for good behaviour or to keep the peace. Compare Kenny, *Outlines of Criminal Law* (3rd ed.), pp. 282, 486; *Wise* v. *Dunning* [1902], 1 K. B. 167.

to walk down the High Street is not, as a rule,[9] taken away by the threat of X to knock A down if A takes his proposed walk. It is true that A's going into the High Street may lead to a breach of the peace, but A no more causes the breach of the peace than a man whose pocket is picked causes the theft by wearing a watch. A is the victim, not the author of a breach of the law. Now, if the right of A to walk down the High Street is not affected by the threats of X, the right of A, B, and C to march down the High Street together is not diminished by the proclamation of X, Y, and Z that they will not suffer A, B, and C to take their walk. Nor does it make any difference that A, B, and C call themselves the Salvation Army, or that X, Y, and Z call themselves the Skeleton Army. The plain principle is that A's right to do a lawful act, namely, walk down the High Street, cannot be diminished by X's threat to do an unlawful act, namely, to knock A down. This is the principle established, or rather illustrated, by the case of *Beatty* v. *Gillbanks*.[10] The Salvation Army met together at Weston-super-Mare with the knowledge that they would be opposed by the Skeleton Army. The magistrates had put out a notice intended to forbid the meeting. The Salvationists, however, assembled, were met by the police, and told to obey the notice. X, one of the members, declined to obey and was arrested. He was subsequently, with others, convicted by the magistrates of taking part in an unlawful assembly. It was an undoubted fact that the meeting of the Salvation Army was likely to lead to an attack by the Skeleton Army, and in this sense cause a breach of the peace. The conviction, however, of X by the magistrates was quashed on appeal to the Queen's Bench Division.

Field, J. says:

> What has happened here is that an unlawful organisation [the Skeleton Army] has assumed to itself the right to prevent the appellants and others from lawfully assembling together, and the finding of the justices amounts to this, that a man may be convicted for doing a lawful act if he knows that

---

9 See p. 178, *post*, and compare *Humphries* v. *Connor*, 17 Ir. C. L. R. 1.

10 9 Q. B. D. 308.

his doing it may cause another to do an unlawful act. There is no authority for such a proposition.[11]

The principle here laid down is thus expressed by an Irish judge in a case which has itself received the approval of the English King's Bench Division.[12]

> Much has been said on both sides in the course of the argument about the case of *Beatty* v. *Gillbanks*.[13] I am not sure that I would have taken the same view of the facts of that case as was adopted by the Court that decided it; but I agree with both the law as laid down by the Judges, and their application of it to the facts as they understood them. The principle underlying the decision seems to me to be that an act innocent in itself, done with innocent intent, and reasonably incidental to the performance of a duty, to the carrying on of business, to the enjoyment of legitimate recreation, or generally to the exercise of a legal right, does not become criminal because it may provoke persons to break the peace, or otherwise to conduct themselves in an illegal way.[14]

Nor is it in general an answer to the claim of, *e.g.* the Salvationists, to exercise their right of meeting, that whilst such exercise may excite wrongdoers to break the peace, the easiest way of keeping it is to prevent the meeting, for "if danger arises from the exercise of lawful rights resulting in a breach of the peace, the remedy is the presence of sufficient force to prevent that result, not the legal condemnation of those who exercise those rights."[15]

---

11 *Beatty* v. *Gillbanks*, 9 Q. B. D. 308, at p. 314. *Beaty* v. *Glenister*, W. N. 1884, p. 93; *Reg.* v. *Justices of Londonderry*, 28 L. R. Ir. 440; with which contrast *Wise* v. *Dunning* [1902], 1 K. B. 167, and the Irish cases, *Humphries* v. *Connor*, 17 Ir. C. L. R. 1; *Reg.* v. *M'Naghton*, 14 Cox C. C. 572; *O'Kelly* v. *Harvey*, 14 L. R. Ir. 105.

It is to noted that the King's Bench Division in deciding *Wise* v. *Dunning* did not mean to overrule *Beatty* v. *Gillbanks*, and apparently conceived that they were following *Reg.* v. *Justices of Londonderry*.

See also Appendix, Note V., Questions connected with the Right of Public Meeting.

12 See *Reg.* v. *Justices of Londonderry*, 28 L. R. Ir. 440; *Wise* v. *Dunning* [1902], 1 K. B. 167, 179, judgment of Darling, J.

13 9 Q. B. D. 308.

14 *The Queen* v. *Justices of Londonderry*, 28 L. R. Ir. 440, pp. 461, 462, judgment of Holmes, J.

15 *Reg.* v. *Justices of Londonderry*, 28 L. R. Ir. 440, p. 450, judgment of O'Brien, J.

The principle, then, that a meeting otherwise in every respect lawful and peaceable is not rendered unlawful merely by the possible or probable misconduct of wrongdoers, who to prevent the meeting are determined to break the peace, is, it is submitted,[16] well established, whence it follows that in general an otherwise lawful public meeting cannot be forbidden or broken up by the magistrates simply because the meeting may probably or naturally lead to a breach of the peace on the part of wrongdoers.

To the application of this principle there exist certain limitations or exceptions. They are grounded on the absolute necessity for preserving the King's peace.

FIRST LIMITATION

(1) Where illegality in meeting provokes breach of peace.

If there is anything unlawful in the conduct of the persons convening or addressing a meeting, and the illegality is of a kind which naturally provokes opponents to a breach of the peace, the speakers at and the members of the meeting may be held to cause the breach of the peace, and the meeting itself may thus become an unlawful meeting. If, for example, a Protestant controversialist surrounded by his friends uses in some public place where there is a large Roman Catholic population, abusive language which is in fact slanderous of Roman Catholics, or which he is by a local by-law forbidden to use in the streets, and thereby provokes a mob of Roman Catholics to break the peace, the meeting may become an unlawful assembly. And the same result may ensue where, though there is nothing in the mode in which the meeting is carried on which provokes a breach of the

---

16 *Wise* v. *Dunning* [1902], 1 K. B. 167, or rather some expressions used in the judgments in that case, may undoubtedly be cited as laying down the broader rule, that a public meeting in itself lawful, and carried on, so far as the promoters and the members of it are concerned, perfectly peaceably, may become unlawful solely because the natural consequence of the meeting will be to produce an unlawful act, viz. a breach of the peace on the part of opponents (see pp. 175, 176, judgment of Alverstone, C. J.; p. 178, judgment of Darling, J.; pp. 179, 180, judgment of Channell, J.). It should be noted, however, that *Wise* v. *Dunning* has reference, not to the circumstances under which a meeting becomes an unlawful assembly, but to the different question, what are the circumstances under which a person may be required to find sureties for good behaviour? (see Kenny, *Outlines of Criminal Law*, p. 486).

peace, yet the object of the meeting is in itself not strictly lawful, and may therefore excite opponents to a breach of the peace.[17]

SECOND LIMITATION

(2) Where meeting lawful but peace can only be kept by dispersing it.

Where a public meeting, though the object of the meeting and the conduct of the members thereof are strictly lawful, provokes a breach of the peace, and it is impossible to preserve or restore the peace by any other means than by dispersing the meeting, then magistrates, constables, and other persons in authority may call upon the meeting to disperse, and, if the meeting does not disperse, it becomes an unlawful assembly.[18] Let us suppose, for example, that the Salvation Army hold a meeting at Oxford, that a so-called Skeleton Army come together with a view to preventing the Salvationists from assembling, and that it is in strictness impossible for the peace to be preserved by any other means than by requiring the Salvationists to disperse. Under these circumstances, though the meeting of the Salvation Army is in itself perfectly lawful, and though the wrongdoers are the members of the Skeleton Army, yet the magistrates may, it would seem, if they can in no other way preserve the peace, require the Salvationists to disperse, and if the Salvationists do not do so, the meeting becomes an unlawful assembly; and it is possible that, if the magistrates have no other means of preserving the peace, *i.e.* cannot protect the Salvationists from attack by the Skeleton Army, they may lawfully prevent the Salvationists from holding the meeting.[19] But the only justification for preventing the Salvationists from exercising their legal rights is the *necessity of the case*. If the peace can be preserved, not by breaking up an otherwise lawful meeting, but by arresting the wrongdoers—in this case the Skeleton Army—the

---

17 Compare *Wise* v. *Dunning* [1902], 1 K. B. 167, and *O'Kelly* v. *Harvey*, 14 L. R. Ir. 105.

18 See especially *O'Kelly* v. *Harvey*, 14 L. R. Ir. 105.

19 It is particularly to be noted that in *O'Kelly* v. *Harvey*, 14 L. R. Ir. 105, the case in which is carried furthest the right of magistrates to preserve the peace by dispersing a lawful meeting, *X*, the magistrate against whom an action for assault was brought, believed that there would be a breach of the peace if the meeting broken up continued assembled, and that there was no other way by which the breach of the peace could be avoided but by stopping and dispersing the meeting. *Ibid.* p. 109, judgment of Law, C.

magistrates or constables are bound, it is submitted, to arrest the wrongdoers and to protect the Salvationists in the exercise of their lawful rights.[20]

One point, however, deserves special notice since it is apt to be overlooked.

Limitations on right of public meeting are really limitations on individual freedom.

The limitations or restrictions which arise from the paramount necessity for preserving the King's peace are, whatever their extent, —and as to their exact extent some fair doubt exists,—in reality nothing else than restraints, which, for the sake of preserving the peace, are imposed upon the ordinary freedom of individuals.

Thus if *A,* a religious controversialist, acting alone and unaccompanied by friends and supporters, addresses the public in, say, the streets of Liverpool, and uses language which is defamatory or abusive, or, without being guilty of defamation, uses terms of abuse which he is by a local by-law forbidden to use in the streets, and thereby, as a natural result of his oratory, excites his opponents to a breach of the peace, he may be held liable for the wrongful acts of which his language is the cause though not the legal justification, and this though he does not himself break the peace, nor intend to cause others to violate it. He may, certainly, be called upon to find sureties for his good behaviour, and he may, probably, be prevented by the police from continuing addresses which are exciting a breach of the peace, for

> the cases with respect to apprehended breaches of the peace show that the law does regard the infirmity of human temper to the extent of considering that a breach of the peace, although an illegal act, may be the natural consequence of insulting or abusive language or conduct."[21]

So again it may, where the public peace cannot otherwise be preserved, be lawful to interfere with the legal rights of an individual and to prevent him from pursuing a course which in itself is perfectly legal. Thus *A,* a zealous Protestant lady, walks through a crowd of Roman Catholics wearing a party emblem, namely, an orange lily,

---

20 This is particularly well brought out in *O'Kelly* v. *Harvey,* 14 L. R. Ir. 105.

21 *Wise* v. *Dunning* [1902], 1 K. B. 167, at pp. 179, 180, judgment of Channell, J.

which under the circumstances of the case is certain to excite, and does excite, the anger of the mob. She has no intention of provoking a breach of the peace, she is doing nothing which is in itself unlawful; she exposes herself, however, to insult, and to pressing danger of public attack. A riot has begun; *X*, a constable who has no other means of protecting *A*, or of restoring the peace, requests her to remove the lily. She refuses to do so. He then, without use of any needless force, removes the flower and thereby restores the peace. The conduct of *X* is apparently legal, and *A* has no ground of action for what would otherwise have been an assault. The legal vindication of *X*'s conduct is not that *A* was a wrongdoer, or that the rioters were within their rights, but that the King's peace could not be restored without compelling *A* to remove the lily.[22]

Meeting
not made
unlawful
by official
proclama-
tion of its
illegality.

No public meeting, further, which would not otherwise be illegal, becomes so (unless in virtue of some special Act of Parliament) in consequence of any proclamation or notice by a Secretary of State, by a magistrate, or by any other official. Suppose, for example, that the Salvationists advertise throughout the town that they intend holding a meeting in a field which they have hired near Oxford, that they intend to assemble in St. Giles's and march thence with banners flying and bands playing to their proposed place of worship. Suppose that the Home Secretary thinks that, for one reason or another, it is undesirable that the meeting should take place, and serves formal notice upon every member of the army, or on the officers who are going to conduct the so-called "campaign" at Oxford, that the gath-

---

22 *Humphries* v. *Connor*, 17 Ir. C. L. R. 1. The case is very noticeable; it carries the right of magistrates or constables to interfere with the legal conduct of *A*, for the sake of preventing or terminating a breach of the peace by *X*, to its very furthest extent. The interference, if justifiable at all, can be justified only by necessity, and an eminent Irish judge has doubted whether it was not in this case carried too far. "I do not see where we are to draw the line. If [*X*] is at liberty to take a lily from one person [*A*] because the wearing of it is displeasing to others, who may make it an excuse for a breach of the peace, where are we to stop? It seems to me that we are making, not the law of the land, but the law of the mob supreme, and recognising in constables a power of interference with the rights of the Queen's subjects, which, if carried into effect to the full extent of the principle, might be accompanied by constitutional danger. If it had been alleged that the lady wore the emblem with an intent to provoke a breach of the peace, it would render her a wrongdoer; and she might be chargeable as a person creating a breach of the peace," *Humphries* v. *Connor*, 17 Ir. C. L. R. 1, at pp. 8, 9, per Fitzgerald, J.

ering must not take place. This notice does not alter the character of the meeting, though, if the meeting be illegal, the notice makes any one who reads it aware of the character of the assembly, and thus affects his responsibility for attending it.[23] Assume that the meeting would have been lawful if the notice had not been issued, and it certainly will not become unlawful because a Secretary of State has forbidden it to take place. The proclamation has under these circumstances as little legal effect as would have a proclamation from the Home Office forbidding me or any other person to walk down the High Street. It follows, therefore, that the government has little or no power of preventing meetings which to all appearance are lawful, even though they may in fact turn out when actually convened to be unlawful because of the mode in which they are conducted. This is certainly a singular instance of the way in which adherence to the principle that the proper function of the state is the punishment, not the prevention, of crimes, deprives the executive of discretionary authority.

Meeting may be lawful though its holding contrary to public interest.

A meeting, lastly, may be lawful which, nevertheless, any wise or public-spirited person would hesitate to convene. For *A, B,* and *C* may have a right to hold a meeting, although their doing so will as a matter of fact probably excite opponents to deeds of violence, and possibly produce bloodshed. Suppose a Protestant zealot were to convene a meeting for the purpose of denouncing the evils of the confessional, and were to choose as the scene of the open-air gathering some public place where meetings were usually held in the midst of a large town filled with a population of Roman Catholic poor. The meeting would, it is conceived, be lawful, but no one can doubt that it might provoke violence on the part of opponents. Neither the government, however, nor the magistrates could (it is submitted), as a rule, at any rate, prohibit and prevent the meeting from taking place. They might, it would seem, prevent the meeting if the Protestant controversialist and his friends intended to pursue a course of conduct, *e.g.* to give utterance to libellous abuse, which would be both illegal and might naturally produce a breach of the peace, or if the

---

23 See *Rex* v. *Fursey,* 6 C. & P. 81; 3 St. Tr. (n.s.) 543.

circumstances were such that the peace could not be preserved otherwise than by preventing the meeting.[24] But neither the government nor the magistrates can, it is submitted, solely on the ground that a public meeting may provoke wrongdoers to a breach of the peace, prevent loyal citizens from meeting together peaceably and for a lawful purpose. Of the policy or of the impolicy of denying to the highest authority in the state very wide power to take in their discretion precautionary measures against the evils which may flow from the injudicious exercise of legal rights, it is unnecessary here to say anything. The matter which is worth notice is the way in which the rules as to the right of public meeting illustrate both the legal spirit of our institutions and the process by which the decisions of the courts as to the rights of individuals have in effect made the right of public meeting a part of the law of the constitution.

---

24 See pp. 171–172, *ante,* and compare *O'Kelly* v. *Harvey,* 14 L. R. Ir. 105, with *Reg.* v. *Justices of Londonderry,* 28 L. R. Ir. 440, and *Wise* v. *Dunning* [1902], 1 K. B. 167, with *Beatty* v. *Gillbanks,* 9 Q. B. D. 308. And the magistrates might probably bind over the conveners of the meeting to find sureties for their good behaviour. The law on this point may, it appears, be thus summed up: "Even a person who has not actually committed any offence at all may be required to find sureties for good behaviour, or to keep the peace, if there be reasonable grounds to fear that he may commit some offence, or may incite others to do so, or even that he may act in some manner which would naturally tend to induce other people (against his desire) to commit one."—Kenny, *Outlines of Criminal Law,* p. 486.

Chapter VIII

MARTIAL LAW

No sharp line can be drawn between rules of private law or of criminal law and constitutional law.

The rights already treated of in the foregoing chapter, as for example the right to personal freedom or the right to free expression of opinion, do not, it may be suggested, properly belong to the province of constitutional law at all, but form part either of private law strictly so called, or of the ordinary criminal law. Thus *A*'s right to personal freedom is, it may be said, only the right of *A* not to be assaulted, or imprisoned, by *X*, or (to look at the same thing from another point of view) is nothing else than the right of *A*, if assaulted by *X*, to bring an action against *X*, or to have *X* punished as a criminal for the assault. Now in this suggestion there lies an element of important truth, yet it is also undoubted that the right to personal freedom, the right to free discussion, and the like, appear in the forefront of many written constitutions, and are in fact the chief advantages which citizens hope to gain by the change from a despotic to a constitutional form of government.

The truth is that these rights may be looked upon from two points of view. They may be considered simply parts of private or, it may be, of criminal law; thus the right to personal freedom may, as already pointed out, be looked at as the right of *A* not to have the control of his body interfered with by *X*. But in so far as these rights hold good against the governing body in the state, or in other words, in so far as these rights determine the relation of individual citizens towards the executive, they are part, and a most important part, of the law of the constitution.

Now the noticeable point is that in England the rights of citizens as against each other are (speaking generally) the same as the rights of citizens against any servant of the Crown. This is the significance of the assertion that in this country the law of the constitution is part of the ordinary law of the land. The fact that a Secretary of State cannot at his discretion and for reasons of state arrest, imprison, or punish any man, except, of course, where special powers are conferred upon him by statute, as by an Alien Act or by an Extradition Act, is simply a result of the principle that a Secretary of State is governed in his official as in his private conduct by the ordinary law of the realm. Were the Home Secretary to assault the leader of the Opposition in a fit of anger, or were the Home Secretary to arrest him because he thought his political opponent's freedom dangerous to the state, the Secretary of State would in either case be liable to an action, and all other penalties to which a person exposes himself by committing an assault. The fact that the arrest of an influential politician whose speeches might excite disturbance was a strictly administrative act would afford no defence to the Minister or to the constables who obeyed his orders.

The subjects treated of in this chapter and in the next three chapters clearly belong to the field of constitutional law, and no one would think of objecting to their treatment in a work on the law of the constitution that they are really part of private law. Yet, if the matter be looked at carefully, it will be found that, just as rules which at first sight seem to belong to the domain of private law are in reality the foundation of constitutional principles, so topics which appear to belong manifestly to the law of constitution depend with us at bottom on the principles of private or of criminal law. Thus the position of a soldier is in England governed, as we shall see, by the principle, that though a soldier is subject to special liabilities in his military capacity, he remains while in the ranks, as he was when out of them, subject to all the liabilities of an ordinary citizen. So, from a legal point of view, ministerial responsibility is simply one application of the doctrine which pervades English law,[1] that no one can plead the command of a superior, were it the order of the Crown itself, in defence of conduct otherwise not justified by law.

Turn the matter which way you will, you come back to the all-important consideration on which we have already dwelt, that whereas under many foreign constitutions the rights of individuals flow, or appear to flow, from the articles of the constitution, in England the law of the constitution is the result, not the source of the rights of individuals. It becomes, too, more and more apparent that the means by which the Courts have maintained the law of the constitution have been the strict insistence upon the two principles, first of "equality before the law," which negatives exemption from the liabilities of ordinary citizens or from the jurisdiction of the ordinary Courts, and, secondly, of "personal responsibility of wrongdoers," which excludes the notion that any breach of law on the part of a subordinate can be justified by the orders of his superiors; the legal dogma, as old at least as the time of Edward the Fourth, that, if any man arrest another without lawful warrant, even by the King's command, he shall not be excused, but shall be liable to an action for false imprisonment, is not a special limitation imposed upon the royal prerogative, but the application to acts done under royal orders of that principle of individual responsibility which runs through the whole law of torts.[2]

Martial Law.

"Martial law,"[3] in the proper sense of that term, in which it means the suspension of ordinary law and the temporary government of a country or parts of it by military tribunals, is unknown to the law of England.[4] We have nothing equivalent to what is called in France the

---

1 See Mommsen, *Romische Staatsrecht*, p. 672, for the existence of what seems to have been a similar principle in early Roman law.

2 See Hearn, *Government of England* (2nd ed.), chap. iv.; and compare Gardiner, *History*, x. pp. 144, 145.

3 See Forsyth, *Opinions*, pp. 188–216, 481–563; Stephen, *History of the Criminal Law*, i. pp. 201–216; *Rex* v. *Pinney*, 5 C. & P. 254; 3 St. Tr. (n. s.) 11; *Reg.* v. *Vincent*, 9 C. & P. 91; 3 St. Tr. (n. s.) 1037; *Reg.* v. *Neale*, 9 C. & P. 431.

4 This statement has no reference to the law of any other country than England, even though such country may form part of the British Empire. With regard to England in time of peace the statement is certainly true. As to how far, if at all, it ought to be qualified with

"Declaration of the State of Siege,"[5] under which the authority ordinarily vested in the civil power for the maintenance of order and police passes entirely to the army (*autorité militaire*). This is an unmistakable proof of the permanent supremacy of the law under our constitution.

The assertion, however, that no such thing as martial law exists under our system of government, though perfectly true, will mislead any one who does not attend carefully to the distinction between two utterly different senses in which the term "martial law" is used by English writers.

In what sense martial law recognised by English law. Martial law is sometimes employed as a name for the common law right of the Crown and its servants to repel force by force in the case of invasion, insurrection, riot, or generally of any violent resistance to the law. This right, or power, is essential to the very existence of orderly government, and is most assuredly recognised in the most ample manner by the law of England. It is a power which has in itself no special connection with the existence of an armed force. The Crown has the right to put down breaches of the peace. Every subject, whether a civilian or a soldier, whether what is called a "servant of the government," such for example as a policeman, or a person in no way connected with the administration, not only has the right, but is, as a matter of legal duty,[6] bound to assist in putting down breaches of the peace. No doubt policemen or soldiers are the persons who, as being specially employed in the maintenance of order, are most generally called upon to suppress a riot, but it is clear that all loyal subjects are bound to take their part in the suppression of riots.

It is also clear that a soldier has, as such, no exemption from liability to the law for his conduct in restoring order. Officers, magistrates,

---

regard to a state of war, see Appendix, Note X., Martial Law in England during Time of War or Insurrection.

5 See *Loi sur l'état de siège*, 9 *Aout* 1849, Roger et Sorel, *Codes et Lois*, p. 436; *Loi* 3 *Avril* 1878, art. 1, and generally Duguit, *Manuel de Droit Constitutionnel*, s. 76, pp. 510–513, 926. See p. 186, *post*.

6 Compare *Miller* v. *Knox*, 6 Scott 1. See statement of Commissioners including Bowen, L. J., and R. B. Haldane, Q. C., for Inquiring into the Disturbances at Featherstone in 1893 [C. 7234], and see Appendix, Note VI., Duty of Soldiers called upon to disperse Unlawful Assembly.

soldiers, policemen, ordinary citizens, all occupy in the eye of the law the same position; they are, each and all of them, bound to withstand and put down breaches of the peace, such as riots and other disturbances; they are, each and all of them authorised to employ so much force, even to the taking of life, as may be necessary for that purpose, and they are none of them entitled to use more; they are, each and all of them, liable to be called to account before a jury for the use of excessive, that is, of unnecessary force; they are each, it must be added—for this is often forgotten—liable, in theory at least, to be called to account before the Courts for non-performance of their duty as citizens in putting down riots, though of course the degree and kind of energy which each is reasonably bound to exert in the maintenance of order may depend upon and differ with his position as officer, magistrate, soldier, or ordinary civilian. Whoever doubts these propositions should study the leading case of *Rex* v. *Pinney*,[7] in which was fully considered the duty of the Mayor of Bristol in reference to the Reform Riots of 1831.

So accustomed have people become to fancy that the maintenance of the peace is the duty solely of soldiers or policemen, that many students will probably feel surprise on discovering, from the doctrine laid down in *Rex* v. *Pinney*, how stringent are the obligations of a magistrate in time of tumult, and how unlimited is the amount of force which he is bound to employ in support of the law. A student, further, must be on his guard against being misled, as he well might be, by the language of the Riot Act.[8] That statute provides, in substance, that if twelve rioters continue together for an hour after a magistrate has made a proclamation to them in the terms of the Act (which proclamation is absurdly enough called reading the Riot Act) ordering them to disperse, he may command the troops to fire upon the rioters or charge them sword in hand.[9] This, of course, is not the language, but it is the effect of the enactment. Now the error into which an uninstructed reader is likely to fall, and into which magis-

---

7 5 C. & P. 254; 3 St. Tr. (n. s.) 11.

8 1 Geo. I. stat. 2, c. 5.

9 See Stephen, *History of the Criminal Law,* i. pp. 202–205.

trates and officers have from time to time (and notably during the Gordon riots of 1780) in fact fallen, is to suppose that the effect of the Riot Act is negative as well as positive, and that, therefore, the military cannot be employed without the fulfilment of the conditions imposed by the statute. This notion is now known to be erroneous; the occasion on which force can be employed, and the kind and degree of force which it is lawful to use in order to put down a riot, is determined by nothing else than the necessity of the case.

If, then, by martial law be meant the power of the government or of loyal citizens to maintain public order, at whatever cost of blood or property may be necessary, martial law is assuredly part of the law of England. Even, however, as to this kind of martial law one should always bear in mind that the question whether the force employed was necessary or excessive will, especially where death has ensued, be ultimately determined by a judge and jury,[10] and that the estimate of what constitutes necessary force formed by a judge and jury, sitting in quiet and safety after the suppression of a riot, may differ considerably from the judgment formed by a general or magistrate, who is surrounded by armed rioters, and knows that at any moment a riot may become a formidable rebellion, and the rebellion if unchecked become a successful revolution.

In what sense martial law not recognised by English law. Martial law is, however, more often used as the name for the government of a country or a district by military tribunals, which more or less supersede the jurisdiction of the Courts. The proclamation of martial law in this sense of the term is, as has been already pointed out,[11] nearly equivalent to the state of things which in France and many other foreign countries is known as the declaration of a

---

10 This statement does not contradict anything decided by *Ex parte D. F. Marais* [1902], A. C. 109, nor is it inconsistent with the language used in the judgment of the Privy Council, if that language be strictly construed, as it ought to be, in accordance with the important principles that, first, "a case is only an authority for what it actually decides" (*Quinn* v. *Leathem* [1901], A. C. 506, judgment of Halsbury, L. C.), and, secondly, "every judgment must be read as applicable to the particular facts proved, or assumed to be proved, since the generality of the expressions which may be found there are not intended to be expositions of the whole law, but governed and qualified by the particular facts of the case in which such expressions are to be found" (*ibid.*).

11 See p. 182, *ante.*

"state of siege," and is in effect the temporary and recognised government of a country by military force. The legal aspect of this condition of affairs in states which recognise the existence of this kind of martial law can hardly be better given than by citing some of the provisions of the law which at the present day regulates the state of siege in France:

French
Law as to
state of
siege.

> 7. *Aussitôt l'état de siège déclaré, les pouvoirs dont l'autorité civile était revêtue pour le maintien de l'ordre et de la police passent tout entiers à l'autorité militaire. —L'autorité civile continue neanmoins à exercer ceux de ces pouvoirs dont l'autorité militaire ne l'a pas dessaisie.*
>
> 8. *Lest ribunaux militaires peuvent être saisis de la connaissance des crimes et délits contre la sûreté de la République, contre la constitution, contre l'ordre et la paix publique, quelle que soit la qualité des auteurs principaux et des complices.*
>
> 9. *L'autorité militaire a le droit, —1° De faire des perquisitions, de jour et de nuit, dans le domicile des citoyens; —2° D'éloigner les repris de justice et les individus qui n'ont pas leur domicile dans les lieux, soumis à l'état de siège; —3° D'ordonner la remise des armes et munitions, et de procedér à leur recherche et à leur enlèvement; —4° D'interdire les publications et les réunions qu'elle juge de nature à exciter ou à entretenir le desordre.* [12]

We may reasonably, however, conjecture that the terms of the law give but a faint conception of the real condition of affairs when, in consequence of tumult or insurrection, Paris, or some other part of France, is declared in a state of siege, and, to use a significant expression known to some continental countries, "the constitutional guarantees are suspended." We shall hardly go far wrong if we assume that, during this suspension of ordinary law, any man whatever is liable to arrest, imprisonment, or execution at the will of a military tribunal consisting of a few officers who are excited by the passions natural to civil war. However this may be, it is clear that in France, even under the present Republican government, the suspension of law involved in the proclamation of a state of siege is a thing fully recognised by the constitution, and (strange though the fact may appear) the authority of military Courts during a state of siege is greater under the Republic than it was under the monarchy of Louis Philippe. [13]

---

12 Roger et Sorel, *Codes et Lois*, pp. 436, 437.

13 See *Geoffroy's Case*, 24 *Journal du Palais*, p. 1218, cited by Forsyth, *Opinions*, p. 483. Conf.,

Now, this kind of martial law is in England utterly unknown to the constitution. Soldiers may suppress a riot as they may resist an invasion, they may fight rebels just as they may fight foreign enemies, but they have no right under the law to inflict punishment for riot or rebellion. During the effort to restore peace, rebels may be lawfully killed just as enemies may be lawfully slaughtered in battle, or prisoners may be shot to prevent their escape, but any execution (independently of military law) inflicted by a Court-martial is illegal, and technically murder. Nothing better illustrates the noble energy with which judges have maintained the rule of regular law, even at periods of revolutionary violence, than *Wolfe Tone's Case.* [14] In 1798, Wolfe Tone, an Irish rebel, took part in a French invasion of Ireland. The man-of-war in which he sailed was captured, and Wolfe Tone was brought to trial before a Court-martial in Dublin. He was thereupon sentenced to be hanged. He held, however, no commission as an English officer, his only commission being one from the French Republic. On the morning when his execution was about to take place application was made to the Irish King's Bench for a writ of *habeas corpus*. The ground taken was that Wolfe Tone, not being a military person, was not subject to punishment by a Court-martial, or, in effect, that the officers who tried him were attempting illegally to enforce martial law. The Court of King's Bench at once granted the writ. When it is remembered that Wolfe Tone's substantial guilt was admitted, that the Court was made up of judges who detested the rebels, and that in 1798 Ireland was in the midst of a revolutionary crisis, it will be admitted that no more splendid assertion of the supremacy of the law can be found than the protection of Wolfe Tone by the Irish Bench.

---

however, for statement of limits imposed by French law on action of military authorities during state of siege, Duguit, *Manuel de Droit Constitutionnel*, pp. 512, 513.

14 27 St. Tr. 614.

Chapter IX

THE ARMY[1]

The Army.

The English army may for the purposes of this treatise be treated as consisting of the Standing Army or, in technical language, the Regular Forces[2] and of the Territorial Force,[3] which, like the Militia,[4] is a territorial army for the defence of the United Kingdom.

Each of these forces has been rendered subordinate to the law of the land. My object is not to give even an outline of the enactments affecting the army, but simply to explain the legal principles on which this supremacy of the law throughout the army has been secured.

---

1 See Stephen, *Commentaries*, ii. book iv. chap. viii.; Gneist, *Das Englische Verwaltungsrecht*, ii. 952–966; *Manual of Military Law.*

As to Standing Army, 1 Will. & Mary, c. 5; see the Army Discipline and Regulation Act, 1879, 42 & 43 Vict. c. 33; the Army Act, *i.e.* the Army Act, 1881, 44 & 45 Vict. c. 58, with the amendments made up to 1907.

2 "The expressions 'regular forces' and 'His Majesty's regular forces' mean officers and soldiers who by their commission, terms of enlistment, or otherwise, are liable to render continuously for a term military service to His Majesty in any part of the world, including, subject to the modifications in this Act mentioned, the Royal Marines and His Majesty's Indian forces and the Royal Malta Artillery, and subject to this qualification, that when the reserve forces are subject to military law such forces become during the period of their being so subject part of the regular forces" (Army Act, s. 190 (8)).

3 See the Territorial and Reserve Forces Act, 1907 (7 Edw. VII. c. 9), especially s. 6, s. 1, sub-s. (6), and the Army Act.

4 *The Militia*—the Territorial and Reserve Forces Act, 1907, does not repeal the various Militia Acts. Until these Acts are repealed the statutory power of raising the militia, either regular or local, and of forming thereof regiments and corps will continue to exist. (For the law regulating the militia see 13 Car. II. stat. 1. c. 6; 14 Car. II. c. 3; 15 Car. II. c. 4; the Militia

It will be convenient in considering this matter to reverse the order pursued in the common text-books; these contain a great deal about the militia, the territorial force of its day, and comparatively little about the regular forces, or what we now call the "army." The reason of this is that historically the militia is an older institution than the permanent army, and the existence of a standing army is historically, and according to constitutional theories, an anomaly. Hence the standing army has often been treated by writers of authority as a sort of exceptional or subordinate topic, a kind of excrescence, so to speak, on the national and constitutional force known as the militia.[5] As a matter of fact, of course, the standing army is now the real national force, and the territorial force is a body of secondary importance.

THE STANDING ARMY

Standing Army. Its existence reconciled with Parliamentary government by the annual Mutiny Acts.

A permanent army of paid soldiers, whose main duty is one of absolute obedience to commands, appears at first sight to be an institution inconsistent with that rule of law or submission to the civil authorities, and especially to the judges, which is essential to popular

---

Act, 1802, 42 Geo. III. c. 90; Militia Act, 1882, 45 & 46 Vict. c. 49; and Regulation of the Forces Act, 1881, 44 & 45 Vict. c. 57.) The militia as long as it exists is in theory a local force levied by conscription, but the power of raising it by ballot has been for a considerable time suspended, and the militia has been in fact recruited by voluntary enlistment. Embodiment converts the militia into a regular army, but an army which cannot be called upon to serve abroad. Embodiment can lawfully take place only in case "of imminent national danger or of great emergency," the occasion being first communicated to Parliament if sitting, or if not sitting, proclaimed by Order in Council (Militia Act, 1882, s. 18; 2 Steph. Comm. (14th ed.) p. 469). The maintenance of discipline among the members of the militia when embodied depends on the passing of the Army (Annual) Act, or in popular language, on the continuance of the Mutiny Act (see p. 232, *post*).

The position of the militia, however, is affected by the Territorial and Reserve Forces Act, 1907, in two ways:

(1) All the units of the general (or regular) militia may, and will, it is said, in a short time have either been transferred to the Army Reserve (under s. 34) or have been disbanded.

(2) The personnel of the regular militia will shortly, it is said, cease to exist as such.

The actual position of the militia, however, until the Acts on which its existence depends have been repealed, is worth noting, as it is conceivable that Parliament may think it worth while to keep alive the historical right of the Crown to raise the militia.

5 In the seventeenth century Parliament apparently meant to rely for the defence of England upon this national army raised from the counties and placed under the guidance of country gentlemen. See 14 Car. II. c. 3.

CHAPTER IX   189

or Parliamentary government; and in truth the existence of permanent paid forces has often in most countries and at times in England—notably under the Commonwealth—been found inconsistent with the existence of what, by a lax though intelligible mode of speech, is called a free government.[6] The belief, indeed, of our statesmen down to a time considerably later than the Revolution of 1689 was that a standing army must be fatal to English freedom, yet very soon after the Revolution it became apparent that the existence of a body of paid soldiers was necessary to the safety of the nation. Englishmen, therefore, at the end of the seventeenth and the beginning of the eighteenth centuries, found themselves placed in this dilemma. With a standing army the country could not, they feared, escape from despotism; without a standing army the country could not, they were sure, avert invasion; the maintenance of national liberty appeared to involve the sacrifice of national independence. Yet English statesmanship found almost by accident a practical escape from this theoretical dilemma, and the Mutiny Act, though an enactment passed in a hurry to meet an immediate peril, contains the solution of an apparently insolvable problem.

In this instance, as in others, of success achieved by what is called the practical good sense, the political instinct, or the statesmanlike tact of Englishmen, we ought to be on our guard against two errors.

We ought not, on the one hand, to fancy that English statesmen acted with some profound sagacity or foresight peculiar to themselves, and not to be found among the politicians of other countries. Still less ought we, on the other, to imagine that luck or chance helps Englishmen out of difficulties with which the inhabitants of other countries cannot cope. Political common sense, or political instinct, means little more than habitual training in the conduct of affairs; this

---

6 See, *e.g.* Macaulay, *History*, iii. pp. 42–47. "Throughout the period [of the Civil War and the Interregnum] the military authorities maintained with great strictness their exclusive jurisdiction over offences committed both by officers and soldiers. More than once conflicts took place between the civil magistrates and the commanders of the army over this question."—Firth, *Cromwell's Army*, p. 310, Mr. Firth gives several examples (pp. 310–312) of the assertion or attempted assertion of the authority of the civil power even during a period of military predominance.

practical acquaintance with public business was enjoyed by educated Englishmen a century or two earlier than by educated Frenchmen or Germans; hence the early prevalence in England of sounder principles of government than have till recently prevailed in other lands. The statesmen of the Revolution succeeded in dealing with difficult problems, not because they struck out new and brilliant ideas, or because of luck, but because the notions of law and government which had grown up in England were in many points sound, and because the statesmen of 1689 applied to the difficulties of their time the notions which were habitual to the more thoughtful Englishmen of the day. The position of the army, in fact, was determined by an adherence on the part of the authors of the first Mutiny Act to the fundamental principle of English law, that a soldier may, like a clergyman, incur special obligations in his official character, but is not thereby exempted from the ordinary liabilities of citizenship.

The object and principles of the first Mutiny Act[7] of 1689 are exactly the same as the object and principles of the Army Act,[8] under which the English army is in substance now governed. A comparison of the two statutes shows at a glance what are the means by which the maintenance of military discipline has been reconciled with the maintenance of freedom, or, to use a more accurate expression, with the supremacy of the law of the land.

The preamble to the first Mutiny Act has reappeared with slight alterations in every subsequent Mutiny Act, and recites that

> Whereas no man may be forejudged of life or limb, or subjected to any kind of punishment by martial law, or in any other manner than by the judgment of his peers, and according to the known and established laws of this realm; yet, nevertheless, it [is] requisite for retaining such forces as are, or shall be, raised during this exigence of affairs, in their duty an exact discipline be observed; and that soldiers who shall mutiny or stir up sedition, or shall desert their majesties' service, be brought to a more exemplary and speedy punishment than the usual forms of law will allow.[9]

---

7 1 Will. & Mary, c. 5.

8 Combined with the Army (Annual) Act, passed each year.

9 See Clode, *Military Forces of the Crown,* i. p. 499. Compare 47 Vict. c. 8. The variations in the modern Acts, though slight, are instructive.

This recital states the precise difficulty which perplexed the states-men in 1689. Now let us observe the way in which it has been met.

A soldier, whether an officer or a private, in a standing army, or (to use the wider expression of modern Acts) "a person subject to military law,"[10] stands in a two-fold relation: the one is his relation towards his fellow-citizens outside the army; the other is his relation towards the members of the army, and especially towards his military superiors; any man, in short, subject to military law has duties and rights as a citizen as well as duties and rights as a soldier. His position is each respect is under English law governed by definite principles.

A SOLDIER'S POSITION AS A CITIZEN

Soldier's position as citizen.

The fixed doctrine of English law is that a soldier, though a member of a standing army, is in England subject to all the duties and liabilities of an ordinary citizen. "Nothing in this Act contained" (so runs the first Mutiny Act) "shall extend or be construed to exempt any officer or soldier whatsoever from the ordinary process of law."[11] These words contain the clue to all our legislation with regard to the standing army whilst employed in the United Kingdom. A soldier by his contract of enlistment undertakes many obligations in addition to the duties incumbent upon a civilian. But he does not escape from any of the duties of an ordinary British subject.

The results of this principle are traceable throughout the Mutiny Acts.

---

10 Part V. of the Army Act points out who under English law are "persons subject to military law," that is to say, who are liable to be tried and punished by Court-martial for military, and in some circumstances for civil, offences under the provisions of the Act.

For our present purpose such persons (speaking broadly at any rate) appear to come within three descriptions:—first, persons belonging to the regular forces, or, in popular language, the standing army (see Army Act, ss. 175 (1), 190 (8)); secondly, persons belonging to the territorial force, in certain circumstances, viz. when they are being trained, when acting with any regular forces, when embodied, and when called out for actual military service for purposes of defence (Army Act, ss. 176, 190 (6) (a)); thirdly, persons not belonging to the regular forces or to the auxiliary forces who are either employed by, or followers of, the army on active service beyond the seas (*ibid.* s. 176 (9) (10)). The regular forces include the Royal Marines when on shore and the reserve forces when called out. See Army Act, secs. 175, 176; conf. *Marks* v. *Frogley* [1898], 1 Q. B. (C. A.) 888.

11 Will. & Mary, c. 5, s. 6; see Clode, *Military Forces of the Crown,* i. p. 500.

Criminal liability.

A soldier is subject to the same criminal liability as a civilian.[12] He may when in the British dominions be put on trial before any competent "civil" (*i.e.* non-military) Court for any offence for which he would be triable if he were not subject to military law, and there are certain offences, such as murder, for which he must in general be tried by a civil tribunal.[13] Thus, if a soldier murders a companion or robs a traveller whilst quartered in England or in Van Diemen's Land, his military character will not save him from standing in the dock on the charge of murder or theft.

Civil liability.

A soldier cannot escape from civil liabilities, as, for example, responsibility for debts; the only exemption which he can claim is that he cannot be forced to appear in Court, and could not, when arrest for debt was allowable, be arrested for any debt not exceeding £30.[14]

No one who has entered into the spirit of continental legislation can believe that (say in France or Prussia) the rights of a private individual would thus have been allowed to override the claims of the public service.

In all conflicts of jurisdiction between a military and a civil Court the authority of the civil Court prevails. Thus, if a soldier is acquitted or convicted of an offence by a competent civil Court, he cannot be tried for the same offence by a Court-martial;[15] but an acquittal or conviction by a Court-martial, say for manslaughter or robbery, is no plea to an indictment for the same offence at the Assizes.[16]

Order of superiors no defence to charge of crime.

When a soldier is put on trial on a charge of crime, obedience to superior orders is not of itself a defence.[17]

---

12 Compare Army Act, secs. 41, 144, 162.

13 Compare, however, the Jurisdiction in Homicide Act, 1862, 25 & 26 Vict. c. 65, and Clode, *Military Forces of the Crown*, i. pp. 206, 207.

14 See Army Act, s. 144. Compare Clode, *Military Forces of the Crown*, i. pp. 207, 208, and *Thurston v. Mills,* 16 East, 254.

15 Army Act, s. 162, sub-ss. 1–6.

16 *Ibid.* Contrast the position of the army in relation to the law of the land in France. The fundamental principle of French law is, as it apparently always has been, that every kind of crime or offence committed by a soldier or person subject to military law must be tried by a military tribunal. See *Code de Justice Militaire,* arts. 55, 56, 76, 77, and Le Faure, *Les Lois Militaires,* pp. 167, 173.

17 Stephen, *History of the Criminal Law,* i. pp. 204–206, and compare Clode, *Military Forces of the Crown,* ii. pp. 125–155. The position of a soldier is curiously illustrated by the following

This is a matter which requires explanation.

A soldier is bound to obey any lawful order which he receives from his military superior. But a soldier cannot any more than a civilian avoid responsibility for breach of the law by pleading that he broke the law in *bona fide* obedience to the orders (say) of the commander-in-chief. Hence the position of a soldier is in theory and may be in practice a difficult one. He may, as it has been well said, be liable to be shot by a Court-martial if he disobeys an order, and to be hanged by a judge and jury if he obeys it. His situation and the line of his duty may be seen by considering how soldiers ought to act in the following cases.

During a riot an officer orders his soldiers to fire upon rioters. The command to fire is justified by the fact that no less energetic course of action would be sufficient to put down the disturbance. The soldiers are, under these circumstances, clearly bound from a legal, as well as from a military, point of view to obey the command of their officer. It is a lawful order, and the men who carry it out are performing their duty both as soldiers and as citizens.

An officer orders his soldiers in a time of political excitement then and there to arrest and shoot without trial a popular leader against whom no crime has been proved, but who is suspected of treasonable designs. In such a case there is (it is conceived) no doubt that the

---

case. *X* was a sentinel on board the *Achille* when she was paying off. "The orders to him from the preceding sentinel were, to keep off all boats, unless they had officers with uniforms in them, or unless the officer on deck allowed them to approach; and he received a musket, three blank cartridges, and three balls. The boats pressed; upon which he called repeatedly to them to keep off; but one of them persisted and came close under the ship; and he then fired at a man who was in the boat, and killed him. It was put to the jury to find, whether the sentinel did not fire under the mistaken impression that it was his duty; and they found that he did. But a case being reserved, the judges were unanimous that it was, nevertheless, murder. They thought it, however, a proper case for a pardon; and further, they were of opinion, that if the act had been necessary for the preservation of the ship, as if the deceased had been stirring up a mutiny, the sentinel would have been justified."—Russell, *Crimes and Misdemeanors* (4th ed.), i. p. 823, on the authority of *Rex* v. *Thomas*, East, T., 1816, MS., Bayley, J. The date of the decision is worth noticing; no one can suppose that the judges of 1816 were disposed to underrate the rights of the Crown and its servants. The judgment of the Court rests upon and illustrates the incontrovertible principle of the common law that the fact of a person being a soldier and of his acting strictly under orders, does not of itself exempt him from criminal liability for acts which would be crimes if done by a civilian.

soldiers who obey, no less than the officer who gives the command, are guilty of murder, and liable to be hanged for it when convicted in due course of law. In such an extreme instance as this the duty of soldiers is, even at the risk of disobeying their superior, to obey the law of the land.

An officer orders his men to fire on a crowd who he thinks could not be dispersed without the use of firearms. As a matter of fact the amount of force which he wishes to employ is excessive, and order could be kept by the mere threat that force would be used. The order, therefore, to fire is not in itself a lawful order, that is, the colonel, or other officer, who gives it is not legally justified in giving it, and will himself be held criminally responsible for the death of any person killed by the discharge of firearms. What is, from a legal point of view, the duty of the soldiers? The matter is one which has never been absolutely decided; the following answer, given by Mr. Justice Stephen, is, it may fairly be assumed, as nearly correct a reply as the state of the authorities makes it possible to provide:

> I do not think, however, that the question how far superior orders would justify soldiers or sailors in making an attack upon civilians has ever been brought before the Courts of law in such a manner as to be fully considered and determined. Probably upon such an argument it would be found that the order of a military superior would justify his inferiors in executing any orders for giving which they might fairly suppose their superior officer to have good reasons. Soldiers might reasonably think that their officer had good grounds for ordering them to fire into a disorderly crowd which to them might not appear to be at that moment engaged in acts of dangerous violence, but soldiers could hardly suppose that their officer could have any good grounds for ordering them to fire a volley down a crowded street when no disturbance of any kind was either in progress or apprehended. The doctrine that a soldier is bound under all circumstances whatever to obey his superior officer would be fatal to military discipline itself, for it would justify the private in shooting the colonel by the orders of the captain, or in deserting to the enemy on the field of battle on the order of his immediate superior. I think it is not less monstrous to suppose that superior orders would justify a soldier in the massacre of unoffending civilians in time of peace, or in the exercise of inhuman cruelties, such as the slaughter of women and children, during a rebellion. The only line that presents itself to my mind is that a soldier should be protected by orders for which he might reasonably believe his officer to have good grounds. The inconvenience of being subject to two jurisdictions, the sympathies of which are not unlikely to be opposed to each

other, is an inevitable consequence of the double necessity of preserving on the one hand the supremacy of the law, and on the other the discipline of the army.[18]

The hardship of a soldier's position resulting from this inconvenience is much diminished by the power of the Crown to nullify the effect of an unjust conviction by means of a pardon.[19] While, however, a soldier runs no substantial risk of punishment for obedience to orders which a man of common sense may honestly believe to involve no breach of law, he can under no circumstances escape the chance of his military conduct becoming the subject of inquiry before a civil tribunal, and cannot avoid liability on the ground of obedience to superior orders for any act which a man of ordinary sense must have known to be a crime.[20]

A SOLDIER'S POSITION AS A MEMBER OF THE ARMY

Soldier's position as member of army.

A citizen on entering the army becomes liable to special duties as being "a person subject to military law." Hence acts which if done by a civilian would be either no offence at all or only slight misdemeanours, *e.g.* an insult or a blow offered to an officer, may when done by a soldier become serious crimes and expose the person guilty of them to grave punishment. A soldier's offences, moreover, can be tried and punished by a Court-martial. He therefore in his military character of a soldier occupies a position totally different from that of a civilian; he has not the same freedom, and in addition to his duties as

---

18 Stephen, *History of the Criminal Law of England,* i. pp. 205, 206. Compare language of Willes, J., in *Keighly* v. *Bell,* 4 F. & F. 763. See also opinion of Lord Bowen, cited in Appendix, Note VI., Duty of Soldiers called upon to disperse an Unlawful Assembly.

19 As also by the right of the Attorney-General as representing the Crown to enter a *nolle prosequi.* See Stephen, *History of the Criminal Law,* i. p. 496, and Archbold, *Pleading in Criminal Cases* (22nd ed.), p. 125.

20 *Buron* v. *Denman,* 2 Ex. 167, is sometimes cited as showing that obedience to the orders of the Crown is a legal justification to an officer for committing a breach of law, but the decision in that case does not, in any way, support the doctrine erroneously grounded upon it. What the judgment in *Buron* v. *Denman* shows is, that an act done by an English military or naval officer in a foreign country to a foreigner, in discharge of orders received from the Crown, may be an act of war, but does not constitute any breach of law for which an action can be brought against the officer in an English Court. Compare *Feather* v. *The Queen,* 6 B. & S. 257, 295, *per Curiam.*

a citizen is subject to all the liabilities imposed by military law; but though this is so, it is not to be supposed that, even as regards a soldier's own position as a military man, the rule of the ordinary law is, at any rate in time of peace, excluded from the army.

The general principle on this subject is that the Courts of law have jurisdiction to determine who are the persons subject to military law, and whether a given proceeding, alleged to depend upon military law, is really justified by the rules of law which govern the army.

Hence flow the following (among other) consequences.

The civil Courts determine[21] whether a given person is or is not "a person subject to military law."[22]

Enlistment, which constitutes the contract[23] by which a person becomes subject to military law, is a civil proceeding, and a civil Court may sometimes have to inquire whether a man has been duly enlisted, or whether he is or is not entitled to his discharge.[24]

If a Court-martial exceeds its jurisdiction, or an officer, whether acting as a member of a Court-martial or not, does any act not authorised by law, the action of the Court, or of the officer, is subject to the supervision of the Courts.

The proceedings by which the Courts of law supervise the acts of Courts-martial and of officers may be criminal or civil. Criminal proceedings take the form of an indictment for assault, false imprisonment, manslaughter, or

---

21 See *Wolfe Tone's Case,* 27 St. Tr. 614; *Douglas's Case,* 3 Q. B. 825; *Fry* v. *Ogle,* cited *Manual of Military Law,* chap. vii. s. 41.

22 See Army Act, ss. 175–184.

23 "The enlistment of the soldier is a species of contract between the sovereign and the soldier, and under the ordinary principles of law cannot be altered without the consent of both parties. The result is that the conditions laid down in the Act under which a man was enlisted cannot be varied without his consent."—*Manual of Military Law,* chap. x. s. 18.

24 See Army Act, s. 96, for special provisions as to the delivering to a master of an apprentice who, being under twenty-one, has enlisted as a soldier. Under the present law, at any rate, it can very rarely happen that a Court should be called upon to consider whether a person is improperly detained in military custody as a soldier. See Army Act, s. 100, sub-ss. 2, 3. The Courts used to interfere, when soldiers were impressed, in cases of improper impressment. See Clode, *Military Forces,* ii. pp. 8, 587.

A civil Court may also be called upon to determine whether a person subject to military law has, or has not, a right to resign his commission, *Hearson* v. *Churchill* [1892], 2 Q. B. (C. A.) 144.

even murder. Civil proceedings may either be preventive, *i.e.* to restrain the commission or continuance of an injury; or remedial, *i.e.* to afford a remedy for injury actually suffered. Broadly speaking, the civil jurisdiction of the Courts of law is exercised as against the tribunal of a Court-martial by writs of prohibition or certiorari; and as against individual officers by actions for damages. A writ of *habeas corpus* also may be directed to any officer, governor of a prison, or other, who has in his custody any person alleged to be improperly detained under colour of military law.[25]

Lastly, the whole existence and discipline of the standing army, at any rate in time of peace, depends upon the passing of what is known as an annual Mutiny Act,[26] or in strict correctness of the Army (Annual) Act. If this Act were not in force a soldier would not be bound by military law. Desertion would be at most only a breach of contract, and striking an officer would be no more than an assault.

THE TERRITORIAL FORCE

Territorial Force.

This force in many respects represents the militia and the volunteers. It is, as was in fact the militia in later times, raised by voluntary enlistment. It cannot be compelled to serve outside the United Kingdom. It is from its nature, in this too like the militia, a body hardly capable of being used for the overthrow of Parliamentary government. But even with regard to the territorial force, care has been taken to ensure that it shall be subject to the rule of law. The members of this local army are (speaking in general terms) subject to military law only when in training or when the force is embodied.[27] Embodi-

---

25 *Manual of Military Law,* chap. viii. s. 8. It should, however, be noted that the Courts of law will not, in general at any rate, deal with rights dependent on military status and military regulations.

26 The case stands thus: The discipline of the standing army depends on the Army Act, 1881, 44 & 45 Vict. c. 58, which by s. 2 continues in force only for such time as may be specified in an annual Act, which is passed yearly, and called the Army (Annual) Act. This Act keeps in existence the standing army and continues the Army Act in force. It is therefore, in strictness, upon the passing of the Army (Annual) Act that depends the existence and the discipline of the standing army.

27 But in one case at least, *i.e.* failure to attend on embodiment, a man of the territorial force may be liable to be tried by Court-martial, though not otherwise subject to military law. (Territorial and Reserve Forces Act, 1907, s. 20; see also as to cases of concurrent jurisdiction of a Court-martial and a Court of summary jurisdiction, *ibid.* ss. 24, 25.)

ment indeed converts the territorial force into a territorial army, though an army which cannot be required to serve abroad.

But the embodiment can lawfully take place only in case of imminent national danger or great emergency, or unless the emergency requires it, until Parliament has had an opportunity of presenting an address against the embodiment of the territorial force. The general effect of the enactments on the subject is that, at any rate when there is a Parliament in existence, the embodiment of the territorial force cannot, except under the pressure of urgent necessity, be carried out without the sanction of Parliament.[28] Add to this, that the maintenance of discipline among the members of the territorial force when it is embodied depends on the continuance in force of the Army Act and of the Army (Annual) Act.[29]

---

28 Compare the Territorial and Reserve Forces Act, 1907, s. 7, the Reserve Forces Act, 1882, ss. 12, 13, and the Militia Act, 1882, s. 18, and see note 4, p. 188, *ante.*

29 There exists an instructive analogy between the position of persons subject to military law, and the position of the clergy of the Established Church.

A clergyman of the National Church, like a soldier of the National Army, is subject to duties and to Courts to which other Englishmen are not subject. He is bound by restrictions, as he enjoys privileges peculiar to his class, but the clergy are no more than soldiers exempt from the law of the land. Any deed which would be a crime or a wrong when done by a layman, is a crime or a wrong when done by a clergyman, and is in either case dealt with by the ordinary tribunals.

Moreover, as the Common Law Courts determine the legal limits to the jurisdiction of Courts-martial, so the same Courts in reality determine (subject, of course, to Acts of Parliament) what are the limits to the jurisdiction of ecclesiastical Courts.

The original difficulty, again, of putting the clergy on the same footing as laymen, was at least as great as that of establishing the supremacy of the civil power in all matters regarding the army. Each of these difficulties was met at an earlier date and had been overcome with more completeness in England than in some other countries. We may plausibly conjecture that this triumph of law was due to the acknowledged supremacy of the King in Parliament, which itself was due to the mode in which the King, acting together with the two Houses, manifestly represented the nation, and therefore was able to wield the whole moral authority of the state.

Chapter X

THE REVENUE[1]

Revenue. As in treating of the army my aim was simply to point out what were the principles determining the relation of the armed forces of the country to the law on the land, so in treating of the revenue my aim is not to give even a sketch of the matters connected with the raising, the collection, and the expenditure of the national income, but simply to show that the collection and expenditure of the revenue, and all things appertaining thereto, are governed by strict rules of law. Attention should be fixed upon three points, — the *source* of the public revenue—the *authority* for expending the public revenue—and the *securities* provided by law for the due appropriation of the public revenue, that is, for its being expended in the exact manner which the law directs.

SOURCE OF PUBLIC REVENUE

Source.

It is laid down by Blackstone and other authorities that the revenue consists of the hereditary or "ordinary" revenue of the Crown and of the "extraordinary" revenue depending upon taxes imposed by Parliament. Historically this distinction is of interest. But for our purpose we need hardly trouble ourselves at all with the hereditary revenue of the Crown, arising from Crown lands, droits of admiralty, and the

---

1 Stephen, *Commentaries*, ii. bk. iv. chap. vii.; Hearn, *Government of England* (2nd ed.), c. 13, pp. 351–388; May, *Parliamentary Practice,* chap. xxi.; see Exchequer and Audit Act, 1866, 29 & 30 Vict. c. 39, and 1 & 2 Vict. c. 2, s. 2.

like. It forms an insignificant portion of the national resources, amounting to not much more than £500,000 a year. It does not, moreover, at the present moment belong specially to the Crown, for it was commuted at the beginning of the reign of the present King,[2] as it was at the beginning of the reign of William IV. and of the reign of Queen Victoria, for a fixed "civil list,"[3] or sum payable yearly for the support of the dignity of the Crown. The whole then of the hereditary revenue is now paid into the national exchequer and forms part of the income of the nation. We may, therefore, putting the hereditary revenue out of our minds, direct our whole attention to what is oddly enough called the "extraordinary," but is in reality the ordinary, or Parliamentary, revenue of the nation.

The whole of the national revenue had come to amount in a normal year to somewhere about £144,000,000.[4] It is (if we put out of sight the small hereditary revenue of the Crown) raised wholly by taxes imposed by law. The national revenue, therefore, depends wholly upon law and upon statute-law; it is the creation of Acts of Parliament.

While no one can nowadays fancy that taxes can be raised otherwise than in virtue of an Act of Parliament, there prevails, it may be suspected, with many of us a good deal of confusion of mind as to the exact relation between the raising of the revenue and the sitting of Parliament. People often talk as though, if Parliament did not meet, no taxes would be legally payable, and the assembling of Parliament were therefore secured by the necessity of filling the national exchequer. This idea is encouraged by the study of periods, such as the reign of Charles I., during which the Crown could not legally obtain necessary supplies without the constant intervention of Parliament. But the notion that at the present day no money could legally be levied if Parliament ceased to meet is unfounded. Millions of money would come into the Exchequer even though Parliament did not sit at

---

2 Civil List Act, 1901, 1 Ed. VII. c. 4.

3 See as to civil list, May, *Constitutional Hist.* i. chap. iv.

4 The Chancellor of the Exchequer, in his Budget speech of 18th April 1907 (172 Hansard (4th ser.), col. 1180), gave the total revenue for the year (Exchequer receipts) 1906–7 at £144,814,000. [See as to the burden of taxes and rates in later years, *Law and Opinion* (2nd ed.), pp. lxxxiv.–lxxxvii.]

all. For though all taxation depends upon Act of Parliament, it is far from being the case that all taxation now depends upon annual or temporary Acts.

Taxes are made payable in two different ways, *i.e.* either by permanent or by yearly Acts.

Taxes, the proceeds of which amounted in the year 1906–7 to at least three-fourths of the whole yearly revenue, are imposed by permanent Acts; such taxes are the land tax,[5] the excise,[6] the stamp duties,[7] and by far the greater number of existing taxes. These taxes would continue to be payable even though Parliament should not be convened for years. We should all, to take an example which comes home to every one, be legally compellable to buy the stamps for our letters even though Parliament did not meet again till (say) A.D. 1910.

Other taxes—and notably the income tax—the proceeds of which make up the remainder of the national income, are imposed by yearly Acts.[8] If by any chance Parliament should not be convened for a year, no one would be under any legal obligation to pay income tax.

This distinction between revenue depending upon permanent Acts and revenue depending upon temporary Acts is worth attention, but the main point, of course, to be borne in mind is that all taxes are imposed by statute, and that no one can be forced to pay a single shilling by way of taxation which cannot be shown to the satisfaction of the judges to be due from him under Act of Parliament.

AUTHORITY FOR EXPENDING REVENUE

Authority for expenditure.

At one time revenue once raised by taxation was in truth and in reality a grant or gift by the Houses of Parliament to the Crown. Such grants as were made to Charles the First or James the First were

---

5 38 George III. c. 5.

6 See Stephen, *Commentaries*, ii. pp. 552, 553.

7 Stamp Act, 1891, 54 & 55 Vict. c. 39.

8 The only taxes imposed annually or by yearly Acts are the customs duty on tea, which for the year ending 31st March 1907 amounted to £5,888,288, and the income tax, which for the same year amounted to £31,891,949, giving a total of annual taxation raised by annual grant of £37,780,237.

moneys truly given to the King. He was, as a matter of moral duty, bound, out of the grants made to him, as out of the hereditary revenue, to defray the expenses of government; and the gifts made to the King by Parliament were never intended to be "money to put into his own pocket," as the expression goes. Still it was in truth money of which the King or his Ministers could and did regulate the distribution. One of the singularities which mark the English constitution is the survival of mediæval notions, which more or less identified the Kings's property with the national revenue, after the passing away of the state of society to which such ideas naturally belonged; in the time of George the Third many public expenses, as, for example, the salaries of the judges, were charged upon the civil list, and thus were mixed up with the King's private expenditure. At the present day, however, the whole public revenue is treated, not as the King's property, but as public income; and as to this two matters deserve special observation.

First, the whole revenue of the nation is paid into the Bank of England[9] to the "account of his Majesty's Exchequer,"[10] mainly through the Inland Revenue Office. That office is a mere place for the receipt of taxes; it is a huge money-box into which day by day moneys paid as taxes are dropped, and whence such moneys are taken daily to the Bank. What, I am told, takes place is this. Each day large amounts are received at the Inland Revenue Office; two gentlemen come there each afternoon in a cab from the Bank; they go through the accounts for the day with the proper officials; they do not leave till every item is made perfectly clear; they then take all the money received, and drive off with it and pay it into the Bank of England.

Secondly, not a penny of revenue can be legally expended except under the authority of some Act of Parliament.

---

9 Or into the Bank of Ireland. See Exchequer and Audit Departments Act, 1866 (29 & 30 Vict. c. 39), s. 10.

10 *Ibid.* and *Control and Audit of Public Receipts and Expenditure,* pp. 7, 8. But a system of appropriations in aid has been introduced during the last few years under which certain moneys which before were treated as extra receipts, and paid into the Exchequer, are not paid into the Exchequer, but are applied by the department where they are received in reduction of the money voted by Parliament.

This authority may be given by a permanent Act, as, for example, by the Civil List Act, 1 & 2 Vict. c. 2, or by the National Debt and Local Loans Act, 1887; or it may be given by the Appropriation Act, that is, the annual Act by which Parliament "appropriates" or fixes the sums payable to objects (the chief of which is the support of the army and navy) which are not provided for, as is the payment of the National Debt, by permanent Acts of Parliament.

The whole thing, to express it in general terms, stands thus.

There is paid into the Bank of England in a normal year[11] a national income raised by different taxes amounting to nearly £144,000,000 per annum. This £144,000,000 constitutes the revenue or "consolidated fund."

Every penny of it is, unless the law is broken, paid away in accordance with Act of Parliament. The authority to make payments from it is given in many cases by permanent Acts; thus the whole of the interest on the National Debt is payable out of the Consolidated Fund under the National Debt and Local Loans Act, 1887. The order or authority to make payments out of it is in other cases given by a yearly Act, namely, the Appropriation Act, which determines the mode in which the supplies granted by Parliament (and not otherwise appropriated by permanent Acts) are to be spent. In either case, and this is the point to bear in mind, payments made out of the national revenue are made by and under the authority of the law, namely, under the directions of some special Act of Parliament.

The details of the method according to which supplies are annually voted and appropriated by Parliament are amply treated of in works which deal with Parliamentary practice.[12] The matter which requires our attention is the fact that each item of expenditure (such, for example, as the wages paid to the army and navy) which is not directed and authorised by some permanent Act is ultimately authorised by the Appropriation Act for the year, or by special Acts which for convenience are passed prior to the Appropriation Act and

---

11 See p. 201, *ante* (3).

12 See especially May, *Parliamentary Practice*, chap. xxi.

are enumerated therein. The expenditure, therefore, no less than the raising of taxation, depends wholly and solely upon Parliamentary enactment.

SECURITY FOR THE PROPER APPROPRIATION OF THE REVENUE

Security for proper expenditure. What, it may be asked, is the real security that moneys paid by the taxpayers are expended by the government in accordance with the intention of Parliament?

The answer is that this security is provided by an elaborate scheme of control and audit. Under this system not a penny of public money can be obtained by the government without the authority or sanction of persons (quite independent, be it remarked, of the Cabinet) whose duty it is to see that no money is paid out of the Exchequer except under legal authority. To the same official ultimately comes the knowledge of the way in which money thus paid out is actually expended, and they are bound to report to Parliament upon any expenditure which is or may appear to be not authorised by law.

The centre of this system of Parliamentary control is the Comptroller and Auditor General. [13]

He is a high official, absolutely independent of the Cabinet; he can take no part in politics, for he cannot be either a member of the House of Commons, or a peer of Parliament. He in common with his subordinate—the Assistant Comptroller and Auditor General—is appointed by a patent under the Great Seal, holds his office during good behaviour, and can be removed only on an address from both Houses of Parliament. [14] He is head of the Exchequer and Audit Department. He thus combines in his own person two characters which formerly belonged to different officials. He is controller of the issue of public money; he is auditor of public accounts. He is called upon, therefore, to perform two different functions, which the reader ought, in his own mind, to keep carefully distinct from each other.

---

13 *Control and Audit of Public Receipts and Expenditure,* 1885.

14 The Exchequer and Audit Departments Act, 1886 (29 & 30 Vict. c. 39), sec. 3.

In exercise of his duty of control the Comptroller General is bound, with the aid of the officials under him, to see that the whole of the national revenue, which, it will be remembered, is lodged in the Bank of England to the account of the Exchequer, is paid out under legal authority, that is, under the provisions of some Act of Parliament.

The Comptroller General is enabled to do this because, whenever the Treasury (through which office alone the public moneys are drawn out from the Bank) needs to draw out money for the public service, the Treasury must make a requisition to the Comptroller General authorising the payment from the public moneys at the Bank of the definite sum required.[15]

The payments made by the Treasury are, as already pointed out, made either under some permanent Act, for what are technically called "Consolidated Fund services," as, for example, to meet the interest on the National Debt, or under the yearly Appropriation Act, for what are technically called "supply services," as, for example, to meet the expenses of the army or the navy.

In either case the Comptroller General must, before granting the necessary credit, satisfy himself that he is authorised in doing so by the terms of the Act under which it is demanded. He must also satisfy himself that every legal formality, necessary for obtaining public money from the Bank, has been duly complied with. Unless, and until, he is satisfied he ought not to grant, and will not grant, a credit for the amount required; and until this credit is obtained, the money required cannot be drawn out of the Bank.

The obtaining from the Comptroller General of a grant of credit may appear to many readers a mere formality, and we may suppose that it is in most cases given as a matter of course. It is, however, a formality which gives an opportunity to an official, who has no interest in deviating from the law, for preventing the least irregularity on the part of the government in the drawing out of public money.

The Comptroller's power of putting a check on government expenditure has, oddly enough, been pushed to its extreme length in

---

15 See *Control and Audit of Public Receipts and Expenditure,* 1885, pp. 61–64, and Forms, No. 8 to No. 12.

comparatively modern times. In 1811 England was in the midst of the great war with France; the King was a lunatic, a Regency Bill was not yet passed, and a million pounds were required for the payment of the navy. Lord Grenville, the then Auditor of the Exchequer, whose office corresponded to a certain extent with that of the present Comptroller and Auditor General, refused to draw the necessary order on the Bank, and thus prevented the million, though granted by Parliament, from being drawn out. The ground of his lordship's refusal was that he had received no authority under the Great Seal or the Privy Seal, and the reason why there was no authority under the Privy Seal was that the King was incapable of affixing the Sign Manual, and that the Sign Manual not being affixed, the clerks of the Privy Seal felt, or said they felt, that they could not consistently with their oaths allow the issue of letters of Privy Seal upon which the warrant under the Privy Seal was then prepared. All the world knew the true state of the case. The money was granted by Parliament, and the irregularity in the issue of the warrants was purely technical, yet the law officers—members themselves of the Ministry—advised that Lord Grenville and the clerks of the Privy Seal were in the right. This inconvenient and, as it seems to modern readers, unreasonable display of legal scrupulosity masked, it may be suspected, a good deal of political byplay. If Lord Grenville and his friends had not been anxious that the Ministry should press on the Regency Bill, the officials of the Exchequer would perhaps have seen their way through the technical difficulties which, as it was, appeared insurmountable, and it is impossible not to suspect that Lord Grenville acted rather as a party leader than as Auditor of the Exchequer. But be this as it may, the debates of 1811[16] prove to demonstration that a Comptroller General can, if he chooses, put an immediate check on any irregular dealings with public moneys.

In exercise of his duty as Auditor the Comptroller General audits all the public accounts;[17] he reports annually to Parliament upon the

---

16 Cobbett's *Parl. Debates,* xviii. pp. 678, 734, 787.

17 In auditing the accounts he inquires into the legality of the purposes for which public money has been spent, and in his report to Parliament calls attention to any expenditure of doubtful legality.

accounts of the past year. Accounts of the expenditure under the Appropriation Act are submitted by him at the beginning of every session to the Public Accounts Committee of the House of Commons —a Committee appointed for the examination of the accounts— showing the appropriation of the sums granted by Parliament to meet the public expenditure. This examination is no mere formal or perfunctory supervision; a glance at the reports of the Committee shows that the smallest expenses which bear the least appearance of irregularity, even if amounting only to a pound or two, are gone into and discussed by the Committee. The results of their discussions are published in reports submitted to Parliament.

The general result of this system of control and audit is, that in England we possess accounts of the national expenditure of an accuracy which cannot be rivalled by the public accounts of other countries, and that every penny of the national income is expended under the authority and in accordance with the provisions of some Act of Parliament.[18]

How, a foreign critic might ask, is the authority of the Comptroller General compatible with the orderly transaction of public business; how, in short, does it happen that difficulties like those which arose in 1811 are not of constant recurrence?

---

18 The main features of the system for the control and audit of national expenditure have been authoritatively summarised as follows:

"The gross revenue collected is paid into the Exchequer.

"Issues from the Exchequer can only be made to meet expenditure which has been sanctioned by Parliament, and to an amount not exceeding the sums authorised.

"The issues from the Exchequer and the audit of Accounts are under the control of the Comptroller and Auditor General, who is an independent officer responsible to the House of Commons, and who can only be removed by vote of both Houses of Parliament.

"Such payments only can be charged against the vote of a year as actually came in course of payment within the year.

"The correct appropriation of each item of Receipt and Expenditure is ensured.

"All unexpended balances of the grants of a year are surrendered to the Exchequer, as also are all extra Receipts and the amount of Appropriations-in-Aid received in excess of the sum estimated to be taken in aid of the vote.

"The accounts of each year are finally reviewed by the House of Commons, through the Committee of Public Accounts, and any excess of expenditure over the amount voted by Parliament for any service must receive legislative sanction."—*Control and Audit of Public Receipts and Expenditure,* 1885, pp. 24, 25.

The general answer of course is, that high English officials, and especially officials removed from the sphere of politics, have no wish or temptation to hinder the progress of public business; the Auditor of the Exchequer was in 1811, be it noted, a peer and a statesman. The more technical reply is, that the law provides two means of overcoming the perversity or factiousness of any Comptroller who should without due reason refuse his sanction to the issue of public money. He can be removed from office on an address of the two Houses, and he probably might, it has been suggested, be coerced into the proper fulfilment of his duties by a mandamus[19] from the High Court of Justice. The worth of this suggestion, made by a competent lawyer, has never been, and probably never will be tested. But the possibility that the executive might have to seek the aid of the Courts in order to get hold of moneys granted by Parliament, is itself a curious proof of the extent to which the expenditure of the revenue is governed by law, or, what is the same thing, may become dependent on the decision of the judges upon the meaning of an Act of Parliament.

---

19 See Bowyer, *Commentaries on Constitutional Law*, p. 210; Hearn, *Government of England* (2nd ed.), p. 375.

Chapter XI

THE RESPONSIBILITY OF MINISTERS

Ministerial responsibility means two utterly different things. It means in ordinary parlance the responsiblity of Ministers to Parliament, or, the liability of Ministers to lose their offices if they cannot retain the confidence of the House of Commons.

This is a matter depending on the conventions of the constitution with which law has no direct concern.

It means, when used in its strict sense, the legal responsibility of every Minister for every act of the Crown in which he takes part.

This responsibility, which is a matter of law, rests on the following foundation. There is not to be found in the law of England, as there is found in most foreign constitutions, an explicit statement that the acts of the monarch must always be done through a Minister, and that all orders given by the Crown must, when expressed in writing, as they generally are, be countersigned by a Minister. Practically, however, the rule exists.

In order that an act of the Crown may be recognised as an expression of the Royal will and have any legal effect whatever, it must in general be done with the assent of, or through some Minister or Ministers who will be held responsible for it. For the Royal will can, speaking generally, be expressed only in one of three different ways, viz. (1) by order in Council; (2) by order, commission, or warrant under the sign-manual; (3) by proclamations, writs, patents, letters, or other documents under the Great Seal.

An order in Council is made by the King "by and with the advice of his Privy Council"; and those persons who are present at the meeting of the Council at which the order was made, bear the responsibility for what was there done. The sign-manual warrant, or other document to which the sign-manual is affixed, bears in general the countersignature of one responsible Minister or of more than one; though it is not unfrequently authenticated by some one of the seals for the use of which a Secretary of State is responsible. The Great Seal is affixed to a document on the responsibility of the Chancellor, and there may be other persons also, who, as well as the Chancellor, are made responsible for its being affixed. The result is that at least one Minister and often more must take part in, and therefore be responsible for, any act of the Crown which has any legal effect, *e.g.* the making of a grant, the giving of an order, or the signing of a treaty.[1]

The Minister or servant of the Crown who thus takes part in giving expression to the Royal will is legally responsible for the act in which he is concerned, and he cannot get rid of his liability by pleading that he acted in obedience to royal orders. Now supposing that the act done is illegal, the Minister concerned in it becomes at once liable to criminal or civil proceedings in a Court of Law. In some instances, it is true, the only legal mode in which his offence could be reached may be an impeachment. But an impeachment itself is a regular though unusual mode of legal procedure before a recognised tribunal, namely, the High Court of Parliament. Impeachments indeed may, though one took place as late as 1805, be thought now obsolete, but the cause why this mode of enforcing Ministerial responsibility is almost out of date is partly that Ministers are now rarely in a position where there is even a temptation to commit the sort of crimes for which impeachment is an appropriate remedy, and partly that the result aimed at by impeachment could now in many cases be better obtained by proceedings before an ordinary Court. The point,

---

1 On the whole of this subject the reader should consult Anson, *Law and Custom of the Constitution*, vol. ii., The Crown (3rd ed.), App. to ch. i. pp. 50–59. Anson gives by far the best and fullest account with which I am acquainted of the forms for the expression of the Royal pleasure and of the effect of these forms in enforcing the legal responsibility of Ministers. See also Clode, *Military Forces of the Crown*, ii. pp. 320, 321; *Buron v. Denman*, 2 Ex. 167, 189, and the Great Seal Act, 1884, 47 & 48 Vict. c. 30.

however, which should never be forgotten is this: it is now well-established law that the Crown can act only through Ministers and according to certain prescribed forms which absolutely require the co-operation of some Minister, such as a Secretary of State or the Lord Chancellor, who thereby becomes not only morally but legally responsible for the legality of the act in which he takes part. Hence, indirectly but surely, the action of every servant of the Crown, and therefore in effect of the Crown itself, is brought under the supremacy of the law of the land. Behind Parliamentary responsibility lies legal liability, and the acts of Ministers no less than the acts of subordinate officials are made subject to the rule of law.

Chapter XII

RULE OF LAW COMPARED WITH DROIT ADMINISTRATIF[1]

Intro-
duction.

*I*n many continental countries, and notably in France, there exists a scheme of administrative law[2]—known to Frenchmen as *droit administratif*—which rests on ideas foreign to the fundamental assumptions of our English common law, and especially to what we have termed the rule of law. This opposition is specially apparent in the protection given in foreign countries to servants of the State, or, as we say in England, of the Crown, who, whilst acting in pursuance

---

1 On *droit administratif* see Aucoc, *Conferences sur l'administration et le droit administratif* (3rd ed.); Berthélemy, *Traité Élémentaire de Droit Administratif* (5th ed. 1908); Chardon, *L'Administration de la France, Les Fonctionnaires* (1908); Duguit, *Manuel de Droit Constitutionnel* (1907); Duguit, *Traité de Droit Constitutionnel* (1911); Duguit, *L'État, les gouvernants et les agents* (1903); Esmein, *Éléments de Droit Constitutionnel* (1896); Hauriou, *Précis de Droit Administratif*; Jacquelin, *La Juridiction Administrative* (1891); Jacquelin, *Les Principes Dominants du Contentieux Administratif* (1899); Jéze, *Les Principes Généraux du Droit Administratif* (1904); Laferrière. *Traité de la Juridiction Administrative,* 2 vols. (2nd ed. 1896); Teissier, *La Responsabilité de la Puissance Publique* (1906).

It is not my aim in this chapter to give a general account of *droit administratif*. My object is to treat of *droit administratif* in so far as its fundamental principles conflict with modern English ideas of the rule of law, and especially to show how it always has given, and still does give, special protection or privileges to the servants of the state. I cannot, however, avoid mentioning some other aspects of a noteworthy legal system or omit some notice of the mode in which the administrative law of France, based as it originally was on the prerogatives of the Crown under the *ancien régime,* has of recent years, by the genius of French legists, been more or less "judicialised"—if so I may render the French term *"juridictionnaliser"*—and incorporated with the law of the land.

2 Known in different countries by different names, *e.g.* in Germany as *Verwaltungsrecht.* The administrative law of France comes nearer than does the *Verwaltungsrecht* of Germany

---

of official orders, or in the *bona fide* attempt to discharge official duties, are guilty of acts which in themselves are wrongful or unlawful. The extent of this protection has in France—with which country we are for the most part concerned—varied from time to time. It was once all but complete; it is now far less extensive than it was thirty-six years ago.[3] It forms only one portion of the whole system of *droit administratif,* but it is the part of French law to which in this chapter I wish to direct particularly the attention of students. I must, however, impress upon them that the whole body of *droit administratif* is well worth their study. It has been imitated in most of the countries of continental Europe. It illustrates, by way of contrast, the full meaning of that absolute supremacy of the ordinary law of the land—a foreign critic might say of that intense legalism—which we have found to be a salient feature of English institutions. It also illustrates, by way of analogy rather than of contrast, some phases in the constitutional history of England. For *droit administratif* has, of recent years, been so developed as to meet the requirements of a modern and a democratic society, and thus throws light upon one stage at least in the growth of English constitutional law.[4]

Our subject falls under two main heads. The one head embraces the nature and the historical growth of *droit administratif,* and especially of that part thereof with which we are chiefly concerned. The other head covers a comparison between the English rule of law and the *droit administratif* of France.

(A) *Droit Administratif.*

For the term *droit administratif* English legal phraseology supplies no proper equivalent. The words "administrative law," which are its most natural rendering, are unknown to English judges and counsel, and are in themselves hardly intelligible without further explanation.

(conf. Otto Mayer, *Le Droit Administratif Allemand,* i. (French translation), p. 293 s. 17), to the rule of law as understood by Englishmen. Here, as elsewhere, it is the similarity as much as the dissimilarity between France and England which prompts comparison. The historical glories of French arms conceal the important fact that among the great States of Europe, France and England have the most constantly attempted, though with unequal success, to maintain the supremacy of the civil power against any class which defies the legitimate sovereignty of the nation.

3 Or than it still is throughout the German Empire. See Duguit, *L'État,* p. 624, note 1.

4 See pp. 246–251, *post.*

This absence from our language of any satisfactory equivalent for the expression *droit administratif* is significant; the want of a name arises at bottom from our non-recognition of the thing itself. In England, and in countries which, like the United States, derive their civilisation from English sources, the system of administrative law and the very principles on which it rests are in truth unknown. This absence from the institutions of the American Commonwealth of anything answering to *droit administratif* arrested the observation of Tocqueville from the first moment when he began his investigations into the characteristics of American democracy. In 1831 he writes to an experienced French judge (*magistrat*), Monsieur De Blosseville, to ask both for an explanation of the contrast in this matter between French and American institutions, and also for an authoritative explanation of the general ideas (*notions générales*) governing the *droit administratif* of his country.[5] He grounds his request for information on his own ignorance[6] about this special branch of French jurisprudence, and clearly implies that this want of knowledge is not uncommon among French lawyers.

When we know that a legist of Tocqueville's genius found it necessary to ask for instruction in the "general ideas" of administrative law, we may safely assume that the topic was one which, even in the eyes of a French lawyer, bore an exceptional character, and need not wonder that Englishmen find it difficult to appreciate the nature of rules which are, admittedly, foreign to the spirit and traditions of our

---

5 Tocqueville's language is so remarkable and bears so closely on our topic that it deserves quotation: *"Ce qui m'empêche le plus, je vous avoue, de savoir ce qui se fait sur ces différents points en Amérique, c'est d'ignorer, à peu près complètement, ce qui existe en France. Vous savez que, chez nous, le droit administratif et le droit civil forment comme deux mondes séparés, qui ne vivent point toujours en paix, mais qui ne sont ni assez amis ni assez ennemis pour se bien connaître. J'ai toujours vécu dans l'un et suis fort ignorant de ce qui se passe dans l'autre. En même temps que j'ai senti le besoin d'acquérir les notions générales qui me manquent à cet égard, j'ai pensé que je ne pouvais mieux faire que de m'adresser à vous."* —Tocqueville, *Œuvres Complètes*, vii. pp. 67, 68.

6 This want of knowledge is explainable, if not justifiable. In 1831 Tocqueville was a youth of not more than twenty-six years of age. There were at that date already to be found books on *droit administratif* written to meet the wants of legal practitioners. But the mass of interesting constitutional literature represented by the writings of Laferrière, Hauriou, Duguit, Jéze, or Berthélemy which now elucidates the theory, and traces the history of a particular and most curious branch of French law, had not come into existence.

institutions. It is, however, this very contrast between administrative law as it exists in France, and still more as it existed during by far the greater part of the nineteenth century, and the notions of equality before the law of the land which are firmly established in modern England, that mainly makes it worth while to study, not of course the details, but what Tocqueville calls the *notions générales* of French *droit administratif*. Our aim should be to seize the general nature of administrative law and the principles on which the whole system of *droit administratif* depends, to note the salient characteristics by which this system is marked, and, lastly, to make clear to ourselves how it is that the existence of a scheme of administrative law makes the legal situation of every government official in France different from the legal situation of servants of the State in England, and in fact establishes a condition of things fundamentally inconsistent with what Englishmen regard as the due supremacy of the ordinary law of the land.

(1) Nature of *droit administratif*.

Droit administratif, or "administrative law," has been defined by French authorities in general terms as "the body of rules which regulate the relations of the administration or of the administrative authority towards private citizens";[7] and Aucoc in his work on *droit administratif* describes his topic in this very general language:[8]

> Administrative law determines (1) the constitution and the relations of those organs of society which are charged with the care of those social interests (*intérêts collectifs*) which are the object of public administration, by which term is meant the different representatives of society among which the State is the most important, and (2) the relation of the administrative authorities toward the citizens of the State.

These definitions are wanting in precision, and their vagueness is not without significance. As far, however, as an Englishman may venture to deduce the meaning of *droit administratif* from foreign treatises, it may, for our present purpose, be best described as that

---

7 "On le définit ordinairement l'ensemble des règles qui régissent les rapports de l'administration ou de l'autorité administrative avec les citoyens." — Aucoc, *Droit Administratif*, i. s. 6.

8 "Nous préférerions dire, pour notre part: Le droit administratif détermine: 1° la constitution et les rapports des organes de la société chargés du soin des intérêts collectifs qui font l'objet de l'administration publique, c'est-à-dire des différentes personnifications de la société, dont l'État est la plus importante; 2° les rapports des autorités administratives avec les citoyens." —Ibid.

portion of French law which determines, (i.) the position and liabilities of all State officials, (ii.) the civil rights and liabilities of private individuals in their dealings with officials as representatives of the State, and (iii.) the procedure by which these rights and liabilities are enforced.

An English student will never, it should particularly be noticed, understand this branch of French law unless he keeps his eye firmly fixed upon its historical aspect, and carefully notes the changes, almost amounting to the transformation, which *droit administratif* has undergone between 1800 and 1908, and above all during the last thirty or forty years. The fundamental ideas which underlie this department of French law are, as he will discover, permanent, but they have at various times been developed in different degrees and in different directions. Hence any attempt to compare the administrative law of France with our English rule of law will be deceptive unless we note carefully what are the stages in the law of each country which we bring into comparison. If, for instance, we compare the law of England and the law of France as they stand in 1908, we are likely to fancy (in my judgment erroneously) that, *e.g.* in regard to the position or privileges of the State and its servants when dealing with private citizens, there may be little essential difference between the laws of the two countries. It is only when we examine the administrative law of France at some earlier date, say between 1800 and 1815, or between the accession to the throne of Louis Philippe (1830) and the fall of the Second Empire (1870), that we can rightly appreciate the essential opposition between our existing English rule of law and the fundamental ideas which lie at the basis of administrative law not only in France but in any country where this scheme of State or official law has obtained recognition.

(2) Historical development. The modern administrative law of France has grown up, or at any rate taken its existing form, during the nineteenth century; it is the outcome of more than a hundred years of revolutionary and constitutional conflict.[9] Its development may conveniently be divided into three periods, marked by the names of the Napoleonic Empire and

---

9 For the history of *droit administratif* see especially Laferrière, i. (2nd ed.), bk. i. c. i.–iv. pp. 137–301. The Second Republic (1848–1851) produced little permanent effect on French administrative law. I have included it in the second of our three periods.

the Restoration (1800–1830), the Orleanist Monarchy and the Second Empire (1830–1870), the Third Republic (1870–1908).

FIRST PERIOD: NAPOLEON
AND THE RESTORATION, 1800–1830

Napoleon and the Restoration.

In the opinion of French men true *droit administratif* owes its origin to the consular constitution of the Year VIII. (1800) created by Bonaparte after the *coup d'état* of the 18th of Brumaire. But legists,[10] no less than historians, admit that the ideas on which *droit administratif* rests, may be rightly traced back, as they have been by Tocqueville,[11] to the *ancien régime;* every feature of Bonaparte's governmental fabric recalls some characteristic of the ancient monarchy; his *Conseil d'État* revives the *Conseil du Roi,* his Prefects are copies of the royal Intendants. Yet in this instance public opinion has come to a right conclusion. It was from Bonaparte that modern *droit administratif* received its form. If he was the restorer of the *ancien régime,* he was also the preserver of the Revolution. Whatever he borrowed from the traditions of old France he adapted to the changed conditions of the new France of 1800. At his touch ancient ideas received a new character and a new life. He fused together what was strongest in the despotic traditions of the monarchy with what was strongest in the equally despotic creed of Jacobinism. Nowhere is this fusion more clearly visible than in the methods by which Bonaparte's legislation and policy gave full ex-

---

10 *"Aussi haut que l'on remonte dans notre histoire, depuis que des juridictions régulières ont été instituées, on ne trouve p chargés d'époque où les corps judiciaires chargés d'appliquer les lois civiles et criminelles aient été en même temps appelés à statuer sur les difficultés en matière d'administration publique."*—Laferrière, i. p. 139, and compare *ibid.* p. 640.

11 *"Ce qui apparaît . . . quand on étudie les paperasses administratives, c'est l'intervention continuelle du pouvoir administratif dans la sphère judiciaire. Les légistes administratifs nous disent sans cesse, que le plus grand vice du gouvernement intérieur de l'ancien régime était que les juges administraient. On pourrait se plaindre avec autant de raison de ce que les administrateurs jugeaient. La seule différence est que nous avons corrigé l'ancien régime sur le premier point, et l'avons imité sur le second. J'avais eu jusqu'à présent la simplicité de croire que ce que nous appelons la justice administrative était une création de Napoléon. C'est du pur ancien régime conservé; et le principe que lors même qu'il s'agit de contrat, c'est-à-dire d'un engagement formel et réguilièrement pris entre un particulier et l'État, c'est à l'État à juger la cause, cet axiome, inconnu chez la plupart des nations modernes, était tenu pour aussi sacré par un intendant de l'ancien régime, qu'il pourrait l'être de nos jours par le personnage qui ressemble le plus à celui-là, je veux dire un préfet."*—Tocqueville, *Œuvres Complètes,* vi. pp. 221, 222.

pression to the ideas or conceptions of royal prerogative underlying the administrative practice of the *ancien régime,* and emphasised the jealousy felt in 1800 by every Frenchman of the least interference by the law Courts with the free action of the government. This jealousy itself, though theoretically justified by revolutionary dogma, was inherited by the Revolution from the statecraft of the monarchy.

Droit adminis-tratif—its two leading principles.

Any one who considers with care the nature of the *droit adminis-tratif* of France, or the topics to which it applies, will soon discover that it rests, and always has rested, at bottom on two leading ideas alien to the conceptions of modern Englishmen.

Privileges of the State.

The first of these ideas is that the government, and every servant of the government, possesses, as representative of the nation, a whole body of special rights, privileges, or prerogatives as against private citizens, and that the extent of these rights, privileges, or prerogatives is to be determined on principles different from the considerations which fix the legal rights and duties of one citizen towards another. An individual in his dealings with the State does not, according to French ideas, stand on anything like the same footing as that on which he stands in dealings with his neighbour.[12]

Separation of powers.

The second of these general ideas is the necessity of maintaining the so-called "separation of powers" (*séparation des pouvoirs*), or, in other words, of preventing the government, the legislature, and the Courts from encroaching upon one another's province. The expression, however, separation of powers, as applied by Frenchmen to the relations of the executive and the Courts, with which alone we are here concerned, may easily mislead. It means, in the mouth of a

---

12 *"Un particulier qui n'exécute pas un marché doit à l'entrepreneur une indemnité proportionnée au gain dont il le prive; le Code civil l'établit ainsi. L'administration qui rompt un tel marché ne doit d'indemnité qu'en raison de la perte éprouvée. C'est la règle de la jurisprudence administrative. A moins que le droit ne s'y oppose, elle tient que l'État, c'est-à-dire la collection de tous les citoyens, et le trésor public, c'est-à-dire l'ensemble de tous les contribuables, doivent passer avant le citoyen ou le contribuable isolés, défendant un intérêt individuel."* —Vivien, *Études Administratives,* i. pp. 141–142. This was the language of a French lawyer of high authority writing in 1853. The particular doctrine which it contains is now repudiated by French lawyers. Vivien's teaching, however, even though it be no longer upheld, illustrates the general view taken in France of the relation between the individual and the state. That Vivien's application of this view is now repudiated, illustrates the change which French *droit administratif* and the opinion of Frenchmen has undergone during the last fifty-five years.

French statesman or lawyer, something different from what we mean in England by the "independence of the judges," or the like expressions. As interpreted by French history, by French legislation, and by the decisions of French tribunals, it means neither more nor less than the maintenance of the principle that while the ordinary judges ought to be irremovable and thus independent of the executive, the government and its officials ought (whilst acting officially) to be independent of and to a great extent free from the jurisdiction of the ordinary Courts.[13] It were curious to follow out the historical growth of the whole theory as to the "separation of powers." It rests apparently upon Montesquieu's *Esprit des Lois*, Book XI. c. 6, and is in some sort the offspring of a double misconception; Montesquieu misunderstood on this point the principles and practice of the English constitution, and his doctrine was in turn, if not misunderstood, exaggerated, and misapplied by the French statesmen of the Revolution. Their judgment was biassed, at once by knowledge of the inconveniences and indeed the gross evils which had resulted from the interference of the French "parliaments" in matters of State and by the belief that these Courts would offer opposition, as they had done before, to fundamental and urgently needed reforms. Nor were the leaders of French opinion uninfluenced by the traditional desire, felt as strongly by despotic democrats as by despotic kings, to increase the power of the central government by curbing the authority of the law Courts. The investigation, however, into the varying fate of a dogma which has undergone a different development on each side of the Atlantic would lead us too far from our immediate topic. All that we need note is the extraordinary influence exerted in France, and in all countries which have followed French examples, by this part of Montesquieu's teaching, and the extent to which it still underlies the political and legal institutions of the French Republic.

Charac-
teristics.

To the combination of these two general ideas may be traced four distinguishing characteristics of French administrative law.

(1) Rights
of State
determined
by special
rules.

The first of these characteristics is, as the reader will at once perceive, that the relation of the government and its officials towards

---

13 See Aucoc, *Droit Administratif*, ss. 20, 24.

private citizens must be regulated by a body of rules which are in reality laws, but which may differ considerably from the laws which govern the relation of one private person to another. This distinction between ordinary law and administrative law is one which since 1800 has been fully recognised in France, and forms an essential part of French public law, as it must form a part of the public law of any country where administrative law in the true sense exists.[14]

(2) Law Courts without jurisdiction in matters concerning the State and administrative litigation to be determined by administrative Courts.

The second of these characteristics is that the ordinary judicial tribunals which determine ordinary questions, whether they be civil or criminal, between man and man, must, speaking generally, have no concern whatever with matters at issue between a private person and the State, *i.e.* with questions of administrative law, but that such questions, in so far as they form at all matter of litigation (*contentieux administratif*), must be determined by administrative Courts in some way connected with the government or the administration.

No part of revolutionary policy or sentiment was more heartily accepted by Napoleon than the conviction that the judges must never be allowed to hamper the action of the government. He gave effect to this conviction in two different ways.

In the first place, he constituted, or reconstituted, two classes of Courts. The one class consisted of "judicial" or, as we should say, "common law" Courts. They performed, speaking generally, but two functions. The one function was the decision of disputes in strictness between private persons; this duty was discharged by such Courts as the Courts of First Instance and the Courts of Appeal. The other function was the trial of all criminal cases; this duty was discharged by such Courts as the Correctional Courts (*Tribunaux Correctionnels*) or the Courts of Assize[15] (*Cours d'Assises*). At the head of all these judicial tribunals was placed, and still stands, the Court of Cassation (*Cour de Cassation*), whereof it is the duty to correct the errors in law of the inferior judicial Courts.[16] The other class of so-called Courts were and are the administrative Courts, such as the Courts of the Prefects

---

14 Of course it is possible that rules of administrative law may exist in a country, *e.g.* in Belgium, where these rules are enforced only by the ordinary Courts.

15 The Courts of Assize are the only Courts in France where there is trial by jury.

16 The *Cour de Cassation* is not in strictness a Court of Appeal.

(*Conseil de Préfecture*)[17] and the Council of State. The function of these bodies, in so far as they acted judicially (for they fulfilled many duties that were not judicial), was to determine questions of administrative law. The two kinds of Courts stood opposed to one another. The judicial Courts had, speaking generally,[18] no concern with questions of administrative law, or, in other words, with cases in which the interest of the State or its servants was at issue; to entrust any judicial Court with the decision of any administrative suit would have been deemed in 1800, as indeed it is still deemed by most Frenchmen, a violation of the doctrine of the separation of powers, and would have allowed the interference by mere judges with cases in which the interest of the State or its servants was at issue. The administrative Courts, on the other hand, had, speaking generally, no direct concern with matters which fell within the jurisdiction of the judicial tribunals, but when we come to examine the nature of the Council of State we shall find that this restriction on the authority of a body which in Napoleon's time formed part of the government itself was far less real than the strict limitations imposed on the sphere of action conceded to the common law Courts.

Napoleon, in the second place, displayed towards the ordinary judges the sentiment of contemptuous suspicion embodied in revolutionary legislation. The law of 16–24 August 1790[19] is one among a score of examples which betray the true spirit of the Revolution. The judicial tribunals are thereby forbidden to interfere in any way whatever with any acts of legislation. Judicial functions, it is laid down, must remain separate from administrative functions. The judges must not, under penalty of forfeiture, disturb or in any way interfere

---

17 With the Courts, or Councils, of the Prefects an English student need hardly concern himself.

18 There existed even under Napoleon exceptional instances, and their number has been increased, in which, mainly from motives of immediate convenience, legislation has given to judicial Courts the decision of matters which from their nature should fall within the sphere of the administrative tribunals, just as legislation has exceptionally given to administrative tribunals matters which would naturally fall within the jurisdiction of the judicial Courts. These exceptional instances cannot be brought within any one clear principle, and may for our purpose be dismissed from consideration.

19 Tit. ii. arts. 11–13.

with the operations of administrative bodies, or summon before them administrative officials on account of anything done by reason of their administrative duties. Napoleon had imbibed to the utmost the spirit of these enactments. He held, as even at a much later date did all persons connected with the executive government, that

> the judges are the *enemies* of the servants of the State, and that there is always reason to fear their attempts to compromise the public interests by their malevolent, or at best rash, interference in the usual course of government business.[20]

This fear was during the Empire, at any rate, assuredly groundless. Administrative officials met with no resistance from the Courts. After the Revolution the judges exhibited boundless humility and servile submission, they trembled before the power and obeyed the orders, often insolent enough, of the government.[21] It is difficult, however, to see how in the days of Napoleon the ordinary judges could, whatever their courage or boldness, have interfered with the conduct of the government or its agents. They are even now, as a rule, without jurisdiction in matters which concern the State. They have no right to determine, for instance, the meaning and legal effect in case it be seriously disputed of official documents, as, for example, of a letter addressed by a Minister of State to a subordinate, or by a general to a person under his command. They are even now in certain cases without jurisdiction as to questions arising between a private person and a department of the government. In Napoleon's time[22] they could not, without the consent of the government, have entertained criminal or civil proceedings against an official for a wrong done or a

---

20 *"On a subi l'influence de ce préjugé dominant chez les gouvernants, dans l'administration et même chez la plupart des jurisconsultes, que les agents judiciaires sont les* ennemis nés *des agents administratifs, qu'il y a toujours à craindre leurs tentatives de compromettre la chose publique par leur intervention—malveillante ou tout au moins inconsidérée—dans la marche normale de l'administration."*—Jéze (ed. 1904), p. 139.

21 *"Les agents administratifs, dans leur arbitraire véritablement inouï, ne recontrèrent aucune résistance chez les agents judiciaires. Ceux-ci, après la Révolution, ont montré une humilité sans limite et une soumission servile. C'est en tremblant qu'ils ont toujours obéi aux ordres parfois insolents du Gouvernement."*—Jéze, p. 128.

22 See Constitution of Year VIII., art. 75, p. 227, *post.*

crime committed by such official in respect of private individuals when acting in discharge of his official duties. The incompetence, however, of the judicial Courts did not mean, even under Napoleon, that a person injured by an agent of the government was without a remedy. He might bring his grievance before, and obtain redress from, the administrative tribunals, *i.e.* in substance the Council of State, or proceedings might, where a crime or a wrong was complained of, be, with the permission of the government, taken before the ordinary Courts.

(3) Conflicts of jurisdiction.   The co-existence of judicial Courts and of administrative Courts results of necessity in raising questions of jurisdiction. *A*, for example, in some judicial Court claims damages against *X* for a breach of contract, or it may be for what we should term an assault or false imprisonment. *X*'s defence in substance is that he acted merely as a servant of the State, and that the case raises a point of administrative law determinable only by an administrative tribunal, or, speaking broadly, by the Council of State. The objection, in short, is that the judicial Court has no jurisdiction. How is this dispute to be decided? The natural idea of an Englishman is that the conflict must be determined by the judicial Courts, *i.e.* the ordinary judges, for that the judges of the land are the proper authorities to define the limits of their own jurisdiction. This view, which is so natural to an English lawyer, is radically opposed to the French conception of the separation of powers, since it must, if systematically carried out, enable the Courts to encroach on the province of the administration. It contradicts the principle still recognised as valid by French law that administrative bodies must never be troubled in the exercise of their functions by any act whatever of the judicial power;[23] nor can an Englishman, who recollects the cases on general warrants, deny that our judges have often interfered with the action of the administration. The worth of Montesquieu's doctrine is open to question, but if his theory be sound, it is clear that judicial bodies ought not to be allowed to pronounce a final judgment upon the limits of their own authority.

---

23 See Aucoc, *Droit Administratif,* s. 24.

Under the legislation of Napoleon the right to determine such questions of jurisdiction was in theory reserved to the head of the State, but was in effect given to the Council of State, that is, to the highest of administrative Courts. Its authority in this matter was, as it still is, preserved in two different ways. If a case before an ordinary or judicial Court clearly raised a question of administrative law, the Court was bound to see that the inquiry was referred to the Council of State for decision. Suppose, however, the Court exceeded, or the government thought that it exceeded, its jurisdiction and trenched upon the authority of the administrative Court, a prefect, who, be it remarked, is a mere government official, could raise a conflict, that is to say, could, by taking the proper steps, insist upon the question of jurisdiction being referred for decision to the Council of State. We can hardly exaggerate the extent of the authority thus conferred upon the Council. It has the right to fix the limits of its own power, it could in effect take out of the hands of a judicial Court a case of which the Court was already seised.[24]

(4) Protection of officials.

The fourth and most despotic characteristic of *droit administratif* lies in its tendency to protect[25] from the supervision or control of the ordinary law Courts any servant of the State who is guilty of an act, however illegal, whilst acting in *bona fide* obedience to the orders of his superiors and, as far as intention goes, in the mere discharge of his official duties.

Such an official enjoyed from 1800 till 1872 a triple protection (*garantie des fonctionnaires*).

Act of State.

In the first place, he could not be made responsible before any Court, whether judicial or administrative, for the performance of any act of State (*acte de gouvernement*).

---

24 Up to 1828 it was possible to raise a conflict (*élever un conflit*) in any criminal no less than in any civil case. Nor is it undeserving of notice that, whilst a conflict could be raised in order to prevent a judicial Court from encroaching on the sphere of an administrative Court, there was in Napoleon's time and still is no legal means for raising a conflict with a view to prevent an administrative Court from encroaching on the sphere of a judicial Court.

25 This protection of officials may be displayed in parts of French law (*e.g.* Code Pénal, art. 114) which do not technically belong to *droit administratif,* but it is in reality connected with the whole system of administrative law.

The law of France has always recognised an indefinite class of acts, *i.e.* acts of State, which, as they concern matters of high policy or of public security, or touch upon foreign policy or the execution of treaties, or concern dealings with foreigners, must be left to the uncontrolled discretion of the government, and lie quite outside the jurisdiction of any Court whatever. What may be the exact definition of an act of State is even now, it would appear in France, a moot point on which high authorities are not entirely agreed. It is therefore impossible for any one but a French lawyer to determine what are the precise qualities which turn conduct otherwise illegal into an act of State of which no French Court could take cognisance. Of recent years the tendency of French lawyers has certainly been to narrow down the sense of an ambiguous term which lends itself easily to the justification of tyranny. We may feel sure, however, that during the Napoleonic era and for long afterwards any transaction on the part of the government or its servants was deemed to be an act of State which was carried out *bona fide* with the object of furthering the interest or the security of the country.

Obedience to orders. In the second place, the French Penal Code, Art. 114,[26] protected, as it still protects, an official from the penal consequences of any interference with the personal liberty of fellow citizens when the act complained of is done under the orders of his official superior.[27]

---

26 "Art. 114. *Lorsqu'un fonctionnaire public, un agent ou un préposé du Gouvernement, aura ordonné ou fait quelque acte arbitraire, et attentatoire soit à la liberté individuelle, soit aux droits civiques d'un ou de plusieurs citoyens, soit à la Charte, il sera condamné à la peine de la dégradation civique.*

"*Si néanmoins il justifie qu'il a agi par ordre de ses supérieurs pour des objets du ressort de ceux-ci, sur lesquels il leur était dû obéissance hiérarchique, il sera exempté de la peine, laquelle sera, dans ce cas, appliquée seulement aux supérieurs qui auront donné l'ordre.*" —*Code Pénal*, art. 114; and Garçon, *Code Pénal annoté*, p. 245. With this read Garçon, *Code Pénal*, arts. 34 and 87, compare *Code d'instruction criminelle*, art. 10; Duguit, *Manuel*, pp. 524–527, and generally Duguit, *L'État*. ch. v. s. 10, pp. 615–634.

27 None but a French criminalist can pronounce with anything like certainty on the full effect of Art. 114, but Garçon's comment thereon (*Code Pénal*, pp. 245–255) suggests to an English lawyer that an offender who brings himself within the exemption mentioned in the second clause of the Article, though he may be found guilty of the offence charged, cannot be punished for it under Art. 114, or any other Article of the Penal Code, and that Art. 114 protects a very wide class of public servants. (See Garçon, comment under heads D and E, pp. 249–252, and under G, p. 253, and para. 100, p. 254. Read also Duguit, *Manuel*, ss. 75–77, especially pp. 504, 527; Duguit, *L'État*, pp. 615–634.)

In the third place, under the celebrated Article 75[28] of the Constitution of the Year VIII., *i.e.* of 1800, no official could, without the permission of the Council of State, be prosecuted or otherwise be proceeded against, for any act done in relation to his official duties.

The protection given was ample. Article 75 reads indeed as if it applied only to prosecutions, but was construed by the Courts so as to embrace actions for damages.[29] Under the Napoleonic Constitution no servant of the State, whether a prefect, a mayor, or a policeman, whose conduct, however unlawful, met with the approval of the government, ran any real risk of incurring punishment or of paying damages for any act which purported to be done in discharge of his official duties.

The effect practically produced by the four characteristics of *droit administratif,* and especially the amount of the protection provided for officials acting in obedience to the orders of their superiors, depends in the main on the answer to one question: What at a given time is found to be the constitution and the character of the Council of State? Was it then under Napoleon a law Court administering judicially a particular branch of French law, or was it a department of the executive government? The answer is plain. The Council, as constituted or revived by Bonaparte, was the very centre of his whole governmental fabric. It consisted of the most eminent administrators whom Napoleon could gather round him. The members of the Council were entitled and were bound to give the supreme ruler advice. The Council, or some of the Councillors, took part in affairs of all descriptions. It is hardly an exaggeration to say that, subject to the absolute will of Napoleon, the members of the Council constituted the government. They held office at his pleasure. The Councillors dealt with policy,

---

It is difficult for an Englishman to understand how under the *Code Pénal* a prefect, a policeman, or any other servant of the State, acting *bona fide* under the orders of his proper official superior, can be in danger of punishment for crimes such as assault, unlawful imprisonment, and the like.

28 *"Les agents du Gouvernement, autres que les ministres, ne peuvent être poursuivis pour des faits relatifs à leurs fonctions, qu'en vertu d'une décision du conseil d'état: en ce cas, la poursuite a lieu devant les tribunaux ordinaires."* —Duguit and Monnier, *Les Constitutions de la France* (deuxième ed.), p. 127.

29 See Jacquelin, *Les Principes Dominants du Contentieux Administratif,* p. 127.

with questions of administration, with questions of administrative law. In 1800 it is probable that administrative suits were not very clearly separated from governmental business. The Council, moreover, even when acting judicially, was more of a Ministry than of a Court, and when the Council, acting as a Court, had given its decision, or tendered its advice, it possessed no means for compelling the executive to give effect to its decisions. As a matter of fact, years have sometimes elapsed before the executive of the day has thought fit to put the judgments of the Council into force, and it was not till 1872 that its decisions acquired by law the character of real judgments. It was, moreover, as we have already pointed out, originally the final Conflict-Court. It had a right to determine whether a given case did or did not concern administrative law, and therefore whether it fell within its own jurisdiction or within the jurisdiction of the ordinary Courts. Thus the state of things which existed in France at the beginning of the nineteenth century bore some likeness to what would be the condition of affairs in England if there were no, or little, distinction between the Cabinet as part of the Privy Council and the Judicial Committee of the Privy Council, and if the Cabinet, in its character of a Judicial Committee, determined all questions arising between the government on the one side, and private individuals on the other, and determined them with an admitted reference to considerations of public interest or of political expediency. Nor was any material change produced by the fall of Napoleon. The restored monarchy eagerly grasped the prerogatives created by the Empire. There was even a sort of return to the unrestrained arbitrariness of the Directory. It was not until 1828, that is, within two years of the expulsion of Charles X., that public opinion enforced some restriction on the methods by which the administrative authorities, *i.e.* the government, invaded the sphere of the judicial Courts.

There are two reasons why it is worth while to study with care the *droit administratif* of our first period. The administrative law of to-day has been built up on the foundations laid by Napoleon. The Courts created by him still exist; their jurisdiction is still defined in accordance, in the main, with the lines which he laid down. True it is that machinery invented to support a scheme of rational absolutism has in later times been used by legists and reformers for the promotion of legal liberty. But it is a fact never to be forgotten that the administrative law of France originated in ideas which favour the prerogatives of the government as the proper defence for the interest of the nation.

SECOND PERIOD: THE ORLEANS MONARCHY AND THE SECOND EMPIRE 1830–1870 [30]

Monarchical period.

 This period deserves the special attention of English students. Napoleonic Imperialism was absolutism; the Restoration was reaction; neither admits of satisfactory comparison with any governmental system known to modern England. The forty years, on the other hand, which intervened between the expulsion of Charles X. and the fall of Napoleon III., though marked by three violent changes —the Revolution of 1848, the *coup d'état* of 1851, the overthrow of the Second Empire in 1870—form, as a whole, a time of civil order. During these forty years France was, with the exception of not more than six months, governed under the established law of the land. An age of peaceful progress gives an opening for illuminative comparison between the public law of France and the public law of England. This remark is particularly applicable to the reign of Louis Philippe. He was, in the eyes of Englishmen, above all things, a constitutional king.[31] His Parliamentary ministries, his House of peers, and his House of deputies, the whole framework and the very spirit of his government, seemed to be modelled upon the constitution of England; under his rule the supremacy of the ordinary law of the land, administered by the ordinary law Courts, was, as Englishmen supposed, as securely established in France as in England. They learn with surprise, that during the whole of these forty years few, if any, legislative or Parliamentary reforms[32] touched the essential characteristics of *droit administratif* as established by Napoleon. It re-

---

30 Little account need be taken of the Second Republic, 1848–1851. Its legislative reforms in administrative law did not outlive its brief and troubled duration.

31 His accession to the throne was aided by an obvious, but utterly superficial, analogy between the course of the English Revolution in the seventeenth century and of the great French Revolution in the eighteenth and nineteenth centuries. Louis Philippe, it was supposed, was exactly the man to perform in France the part which William III. had played in England, and close the era of revolution.

32 It was, however, gradually reformed to a great extent by a process of judicial legislation, *i.e.* by the Council of State acting in the spirit of a law Court.

mained, as it still does, a separate body of law, dealt with by administrative Courts. With this law the judicial Courts continued to have, as they still have, no concern. The introduction of Parliamentary government took from the Council of State, during the reign of Louis Philippe, many of its political functions. It remained, however, as it does to-day, the great administrative Court. It preserved what it does not now retain,[33] the right to define the jurisdiction of the judicial Courts. Servants of the State remained in possession of every prerogative or privilege ensured to them by custom or by Napoleonic legislation. *Droit administratif*, in short, retained till 1870 all its essential features. That this was so is apparent from two considerations:—

The Council not an absolutely judicial body. First, the Council of State never, during the period with which we are concerned, became a thoroughly judicial body.

This indeed is a point on which an English critic must speak with some hesitation. He will remember how easily a Frenchman, even though well acquainted with England, might at the present moment misinterpret the working of English institutions, and imagine, for instance, from the relation of the Lord Chancellor to the Ministry, that the Cabinet, of which the Chancellor is always a member, could influence the judgment given in an action entered in the Chancery Division of the High Court, whereas, as every Englishman knows, centuries have passed since the Lord Chancellor, when acting as a judge in Chancery, was in the slightest degree guided by the interest or the wishes of the Cabinet. An English critic will also remember that at the present day the Council of State commands as profound respect as any Court in France, and stand in popular estimation on a level with the Court of Cassation—the highest of judicial tribunals—and further, that the repute of the Council has risen during every year since 1830. Yet, subject to the hesitation which becomes any one who comments on the working of institutions which are not those of his own country, an English lawyer must conclude that between 1830 and 1870 the Council, while acting as an administrative tribunal, though tending every year to become more and more judicialised, was to a considerable extent an official or governmental

---

33 See as to present Conflict-Court, p. 238, *post.*

body, the members of which, when acting in the discharge of quasi-judicial functions, were likely to be swayed by ministerial or official sentiment. This assertion does not imply that the Council, consisting of persons of the highest eminence and character, did not aim at doing or did not constantly do justice. What is meant is that the Council's idea of justice was not likely to be exactly the same as that entertained by judicial or common law Courts.

No diminution in protection of officials.

Secondly, the legal protection of officials suffered no diminution.

No man could be made liable before any Court whatever for carrying out an act of State (*acte de gouvernement*).[34] And under the rule of Louis Philippe, as under the Second Empire, wide was the extension given, both in theory and in practice, to this indefinite and undefined expression.

In 1832 the Duchesse de Berry attempted to raise a civil war in La Vendée. She was arrested. The king dared not let her leave the country. He would not put on trial the niece of his wife. Republicans and Legitimists alike wished her to be brought before a law Court. The one class desired that "Caroline Berry" should be treated as an ordinary criminal, the other hoped to turn the Duchess into a popular heroine. The case was debated in Parliament again and again. Petitions demanded that she should either be set at liberty or brought before a jury. The government refused to take either course. She was detained in prison until private circumstances deprived her both of credit and of popularity. She was then quietly shipped off to Sicily. The conduct of the government, or in fact of the king, was illegal from beginning to end. The Ministry confessed, through the mouth of Monsieur Thiers, that the law had been violated. A vote of the Chamber of Deputies—not be it noted an act of legislation—supplied, it was held, full justification for a breach of the law.[35] This was the kind of authority ascribed in 1832 by the constitutional Ministers of a constitutional monarch to an act of State. This most elastic of

---

34 See p. 225, *ante.*

35 *"M. Thiers, dans la séance du 20 juin, avoua hautement tout ce qu'il y avait eu d'illégal dans l'arrestation, la détention, la mise en liberté de la duchesse; c'était à la Chambre à decider si l'on avait agi dans l'intérêt bien entendu du salut public. La Chambre passa à l'ordre du jour."* — Grégoire, *Histoire de France,* i. p. 364. See also *ibid.* pp. 292–308, 356–364.

pleas was, it would seem, the excuse or the defence for the dealings of Napoleon III. with the property of the Orleans family; nor is it easy to believe that even as late as 1880 some of the proceedings against the unauthorised congregations were not examples of the spirit which places an act of State above the law of the land.

The Penal Code Article 114,[36] protecting from punishment, though not from legal condemnation, an agent of the government who though he committed a crime acted in obedience to the commands of his official superiors, remained, as it still remains, in full force.

The celebrated Article 75 of the Constitution of the Year VIII.,[37] which made it impossible to take legal proceedings for a crime or a wrong against any official without the permission of the Council of State, which surely in this case must have acted in accordance with the government of the day, still stood unrepealed.

Public opinion refused to regard the Council as a judicial tribunal, and condemned the protection extended to official wrongdoers. Hear on this point the language of Alexis de Tocqueville:

> In the Year VIII. of the French Republic a constitution was drawn up in which the following clause was introduced: "Art. 75. All the agents of the government below the rank of ministers can only be prosecuted[38] for offences relating to their several functions by virtue of a decree of the Conseil d'État; in which case the prosecution takes place before the ordinary tribunals." This clause survived the "Constitution de l'An VIII.," and it is still maintained in spite of the just complaints of the nation. I have always found the utmost difficulty in explaining its meaning to Englishmen or Americans. They were at once led to conclude that the Conseil d'État in France was a great tribunal, established in the centre of the kingdom, which exercised a preliminary and somewhat tyrannical jurisdiction in all political causes. But when I told them that the Conseil d'État was not a judicial body, in the common sense of the term, but an administrative council composed of men dependent on the Crown, so that the King, after having ordered one of his servants, called a Prefect, to commit an injustice, has the power of commanding another of his servants, called a Councillor of State, to prevent the former from being punished; when I demonstrated to them that the citizen

---

36 See p. 226, note 26, *ante*.

37 See pp. 226–227, *ante*.

38 This term was extended by legal decisions so as to cover actions for damages. See Jacquelin, *Les Principes Dominants du Contentieux Administratif,* p. 127.

who has been injured by the order of the sovereign is obliged to solicit from the sovereign permission to obtain redress, they refused to credit so flagrant an abuse, and were tempted to accuse me of falsehood or of ignorance. It frequently happened before the Revolution that a Parliament issued a warrant against a public officer who had committed an offence, and sometimes the proceedings were stopped by the authority of the Crown, which enforced compliance with its absolute and despotic will. It is painful to perceive how much lower we are sunk than our forefathers, since we allow things to pass under the colour of justice and the sanction of the law which violence alone could impose upon them.[39]

This classical passage from Tocqueville's *Democracy in America* was published in 1835, when, at the age of 30, he had obtained a fame which his friends compared to that of Montesquieu. His estimate of *droit administratif* assuredly had not changed when towards the end of his life he published *L'Ancien Régime et la Révolution*, by far the most powerful and the most mature of his works. He writes:

We have, it is true, expelled the judicial power from the sphere of government into which the *ancien régime* had most unhappily allowed its introduction, but at the very same time, as any one can see, the authority of the government has gradually been introducing itself into the natural sphere of the Courts, and there we have suffered it to remain as if the confusion of powers was not as dangerous if it came from the side of the government as if it came from the side of the Courts, or even worse. For the intervention of the Courts of Justice into the sphere of government only impedes the management of business, whilst the intervention of government in the administration of justice depraves citizens and turns them at the same time both into revolutionists and slaves.[40]

These are the words of a man of extraordinary genius who well knew French history, who was well acquainted with the France of his day, who had for years sat in Parliament, who at least once had been

---

39 A. de Tocqueville, *Democracy in America*, i. (translation), p. 101; *Œuvres Complètes*, i. pp. 174, 175.

40 *"Nous avons, il est vrai, chassé la justice de la sphère administrative où l'ancien régime l'avait laissée s'introduire fort indûment; mais dans le même temps, comme on le voit, le gouvernement s'introduisait sans cesse dans la sphère naturelle de la justice, et nous l'y avons laissé: comme si la confusion des pouvoirs n'était pas aussi dangereuse de ce côté que de l'autre, et même pire; car l'intervention de la justice dans l'administration ne nuit qu'aux affaires, tandis que l'intervention de l'administration dans la justice déprave les hommes et tend à les rendre tout à la fois révolutionnaires et serviles."*—Tocqueville, *L'Ancien Régime et la Révolution*, septième édition, p. 81.

a member of the Cabinet, and to whom the public life of his own country was as well known as the public life of England to Macaulay. Tocqueville's language may bear marks of an exaggeration, explainable partly by his turn of mind, and partly by the line of thought which made him assiduously study and possibly overrate the closeness of the connection between the weaknesses of modern democracy and the vices of the old monarchy. Be this as it may, he assuredly expressed the educated opinion of his time. A writer who has admirably brought into view the many merits of the Council of State and the methods by which it has in matters of administrative litigation acquired for itself more and more of a judicial character, acutely notes that till the later part of the nineteenth century the language of everyday life, which is the best expression of popular feeling, applied the terms "courts of justice" or "justice" itself only to the judicial or common law Courts.[41] What stronger confirmation can be found of the justice of Tocqueville's judgment for the time at least in which he lived?

Effect of *droit administratif* on position of French officials. We can now understand the way in which from 1830 to 1870 the existence of a *droit administratif* affected the whole legal position of French public servants, and rendered it quite different from that of English officials.

Persons in the employment of the government, who formed, be it observed, a more important part of the community than do the whole body of English civil servants, occupied in France a situation in some respects resembling that of soldiers in England. For the breach of official discipline they were, we may safely assume, readily punishable in one form or another. But if like English soldiers they were subject to official discipline, they enjoyed what even soldiers in England do not possess, a very large amount of protection against proceedings before the judicial Courts for wrongs done to private citizens. The position, for instance, of say a prefect or a policeman, who in the over-zealous discharge of his duties had broken the law by committing an assault or a trespass, was practically unassailable. He might plead that the wrong done was an act of State. If this defence

---

41 Jéze, p. 138, note 1.

would not avail him he might shelter himself behind Article 114 of the Penal Code, and thus escape not indeed an adverse verdict but the possibility of punishment. But after all, if the Ministry approved of his conduct, he had no need for legal defences. He could not, without the assent of the Council of State, be called upon to answer for his conduct before any Court of law. Article 75 was the palladium of official privilege or irresponsibility. Nor let any one think that this arm of defence had grown rusty with time and could not in practice be used. Between 1852 and 1864 there were 264 applications for authorisations under Article 75 to take proceedings against officials. Only 34 were granted, or, in other words, 230 were refused.[42] The manifest injustice of the celebrated Article had been long felt. Even in 1815 Napoleon had promised its modification.

THIRD PERIOD: THE THIRD REPUBLIC, 1870–1908

Within two years from the fall of the Second Empire public opinion insisted upon three drastic reforms in the administrative or official law of France.

Repeal of
Art. 75. On the 19th of September 1870 Article 75 was repealed.

It had survived the Empire, the Restoration, the Orleans Monarchy, the Republic of 1848, and the Second Empire. The one thing which astonishes an English critic even more than the length of time during which the celebrated Article had withstood every assault, is the date, combined with the method of its abolition. It was abolished on the 19th of September 1870, when the German armies were pressing on to Paris. It was abolished by a Government which had come into office through an insurrection, and which had no claim to actual power or to moral authority except the absolute necessity for protecting France against invasion. It is passing strange that a provisional government, occupied with the defence of Paris, should have repealed a fundamental principle of French law. Of the motives which led men placed in temporary authority by the accidents of a revolution to carry through a legal innovation which, in appearance

---

42 See Jacquelin, *Les Principes Dominants du Contentieux Administratif,* p. 364.

It is worth notice that the principle of Article 75 was, at any rate till lately, recognised in more than one State of the German Empire.

at least, alters the whole position of French officials, no foreign observer can form a certain opinion. It is, however, a plausible conjecture, confirmed by subsequent events, that the repeal of Article 75 was lightly enacted and easily tolerated, because, as many lawyers may have suspected, it effected a change more important in appearance than in reality, and did not after all gravely touch the position of French functionaries or the course of French administration.[43]

A circumstance which fills an English lawyer with further amazement is that the repeal of Article 75 became, and still without any direct confirmation by any legislative assembly remains, part of the law of the land. Here we come across an accepted principle of French constitutional law which betrays the immense authority conceded both by the law and by the public opinion of France to any *de facto* and generally accepted government. Such a body, even if like the provisional government of 1848 it is called to office one hardly knows how, by the shouts of a mob consisting of individuals whose names for the most part no one now knows at all, is deemed to possess whilst it continues in power the fullest legislative authority. It is, to use French terms, not only a legislative but a constituent authority. It can issue decrees, known by the technical name of decree laws (*decréts lois*),[44] which, until regularly repealed by some person or body with acknowledged legislative authority, are often as much law of the land as any Act passed with the utmost formality by the present French National Assembly. Contrast with this ready acceptance of gov-

---

43 For some confirmation of this view, see Aucoc, *Droit Administratif*, ss. 419–426; Jacquelin, *Juridiction Administrative*, p. 427; Laferrière, i. bk. iii. ch. vii.

The admission, however, involved in the repeal of Article 75 of the general principle that officials are at any rate *prima facie* liable for illegal acts, in the same way as private persons, marks, it is said by competent authorities, an important change in the public opinion of France, and is one among other signs of a tendency to look with jealousy on the power of the State.

44 See for the legal doctrine and for examples of such decree laws, Duguit, *Manuel*, pp. 1037, 1038; Moreau, *Le Règlement Administratif*, pp. 103, 104. Such decree laws were passed by the provisional government between the 24th of February and the 4th of May 1848; by Louis Napoleon between the *coup d'état* of 2nd December 1851 and 29th March 1852, that is, a ruler who, having by a breach both of the law of the land and of his oaths usurped supreme power, had not as yet received any recognition by a national vote; and lastly, by the Government of National Defence between 4th September 1870 and 12th February 1871, that is, by an executive which might in strictness be called a government of necessity.

ernmental authority the view taken by English Courts and Parliaments of every law passed from 1642 to 1660 which did not receive the Royal assent. Some of them were enacted by Parliaments of a ruler acknowledged both in England and in many foreign countries as the head of the English State; the Protector, moreover, died in peace, and was succeeded without disturbance by his son Richard. Yet not a single law passed between the outbreak of the Rebellion and the Restoration is to be found in the English Statute Book. The scrupulous legalism of English lawyers acknowledged in 1660 no Parliamentary authority but that Long Parliament which, under a law regularly passed and assented to by Charles I., could not be dissolved without its own consent. A student is puzzled whether most to admire or to condemn the sensible but, it may be, too easy acquiescence of Frenchmen in the actual authority of any *de facto* government, or the legalism carried to pedantic absurdity of Englishmen, who in matters of statesmanship placed technical legality above those rules of obvious expediency which are nearly equivalent to principles of justice. This apparent digression is in reality germane to our subject. It exhibits the different light in which, even in periods of revolution, Frenchmen and Englishmen have looked upon the rule of law.

The strange story of Article 75 needs a few words more for its completion. The decree law of 19th September 1870 reads as if it absolutely subjected officials accused of any breach of the law to the jurisdiction of the judicial Courts. This, moreover, was in fact the view taken by both the judicial and the administrative Courts between 1870 and 1872.[45] But judicial decisions can in France, as elsewhere, frustrate the operation of laws which they cannot repeal. After 1870 proceedings against officials, and officials of all ranks, became frequent. This fact is noteworthy. The government wished to protect its own servants. It brought before the newly constituted Conflict-Court[46] a case raising for reconsideration the effect of the decree law of 19th September 1870. The Court held that, though proceedings against officials might be taken without the leave of the

---

45 See in support of this view, Jacquelin, *Les Principes Dominants du Contentieux Administratif*, pp. 127–144.

46 See pp. 239–240, *post*.

Council of State, yet that the dogma of the separation of powers must still be respected, and that it was for the Conflict-Court to determine whether any particular case fell within the jurisdiction of the judicial Courts or of the administrative Courts, that is in effect of the Council of State.[47] The principle of this decision has now obtained general acceptance. Thus a judgment grounded on that doctrine of the separation of powers which embodies traditional jealousy of interference by ordinary judges in affairs of State has, according, at any rate, to one high authority, reduced the effect of the repeal of Article 75 almost to nothing. "To sum the matter up," writes Duguit, "the only difference between the actual system and that which existed under the Constitution of the Year VIII. is that before 1870 the prosecution of State officials was subject to the authorisation of the Council of State, whilst to-day it is subject to the authorisation of the Conflict-Court."[48]

(2) Decisions of Council of State become judgments.

Under the law of 24th May 1872,[49] the decisions of the Council of State concerning cases of administrative law received for the first time the obligatory force of judgments. They had hitherto been in theory, and from some points of view even in practice, as already pointed out,[50] nothing but advice given to the head of the State.

(3) Creation of independent Conflict-Court.

The same law[51] which enhanced the authority of the Council's decisions diminished its jurisdiction. The Council had, since 1800, decided whether a given case, or a point that might arise in a given case, fell within the jurisdiction of the judicial Courts or of the administrative Courts, *i.e.* in substance of the Council itself. This au-

---

47 See *Pelletier's Case,* decided 26th July 1873; and in support of an interpretation of the law which has now received general approval, Laferrière, i. pp. 637–654; Berthélemy, p. 65; Duguit, *Manuel,* s. 67, pp. 463, 464; Jéze, pp. 133–135.

48 "*Finalement la seule différence entre le système actuel et celui de la constitution de l'an VIII., c'est qu'avant 1870 la poursuite contre les fonctionnaires était subordonnée à l'autorisation du Conseil d'État, et qu'aujourd'hui elle est subordonné à l'autorisation du tribunal des conflits.*"—Duguit, *Manuel,* p. 464.

49 Sect. 9.

50 See pp. 227–228, *ante.*

51 Law of 24th May 1872, Tit. iv. art. 25–28.

thority or power was, in 1872, transferred to a separate and newly constituted Conflict-Court.[52]

This Conflict-Court has been carefully constituted so as to represent equally the authority of the Court of Cassation—the highest judicial Court in France—and the authority of the Council of State—the highest administrative Court in France. It consists of nine members:—three members of the Court of Cassation elected by their colleagues; three members of the Council of State, also elected by their colleagues; two other persons elected by the above six judges of the Conflict-Court. All these eight members of the Court hold office for three years. They are re-eligible, and are almost invariably re-elected. The Minister of Justice (*garde des sceaux*) for the time being, who is a member of the Ministry, is *ex officio* President of the Court. He rarely attends. The Court elects from its own members a Vice-President who generally presides.[53] The Conflict-Court comes near to an absolutely judicial body; it commands, according to the best authorities, general confidence. But its connection with the Government of the day through the Minister of Justice (who is not necessarily a lawyer) being its President, and the absence on the part of its members of that permanent tenure of office,[54] which is the best security for perfect judicial independence, are defects, which, in the opinion of the fairest among French jurists, ought to be removed,[55] and which, as long as they exist, detract from the judicial character of the Conflict-Court. An Englishman, indeed, can hardly fail to surmise that the Court must still remain a partly official body which may occasionally be swayed by the policy of a Ministry, and still more often be influenced by official or governmental ideas. Nor is this suspicion diminished by the knowledge that a Minister of Justice has

---

52 Such a separate Conflict-Court had been created under the Second Republic, 1848–1851. It fell to the ground on the fall of the Republic itself in consequence of the *coup d'état* of 1851.

53 See Appendix, Note XI., Constitution of *Tribunal des Conflits;* Berthèlemy (5th ed.), pp. 880, 881; Chardon, p. 412.

54 A member of the Council of State does not hold this position as Councillor for life. He may be removed from the Council by the government. But no Councillor has been removed since 1875.

55 Laferrière, i. p. 24; Chardon, p. 4, note 2; Jéze, pp. 133, 134.

within the year 1908 defended his position as President of the Court on the ground that it ought to contain some one who represents the interests of the government.[56]

These three thorough-going reforms were carried out by legislative action. They obviously met the requirements of the time.[57] They were rapid; they appeared to be sudden. This appearance is delusive. They were in reality the outcome of a slow but continuous revolution in French public opinion and also of the perseverance with which the legists of the Council of State, under the guidance of French jurisprudence and logic, developed out of the arbitrariness of administrative practice a fixed system of true administrative law. To understand this evolution of *droit administratif* during the lapse of more than a century (1800–1908) we must cast a glance over the whole development of this branch of French law and regard it in the light in which it presents itself, not so much to an historian of France as to a lawyer who looks upon the growth of French public law from an historical point of view. We shall then see that the years under consideration fall into three periods or divisions.[58] They are:

The Period of Unnoticed Growth, 1800–18
(Période D'élaboration Secrète)

During these years the Council, by means of judicial precedents, created a body of maxims, in accordance with which the Council in fact acted when deciding administrative disputes.

The Period of Publication, 1818–60
(Période de Divulgation)

During these forty-two years various reforms were carried out, partly by legislation, but, to a far greater extent, by judge-made law.

---

56 See Jéze, *Revue de Droit public,* etc. (1908), vol. xxv. p. 257.

57 They were either tacitly sanctioned (decree law of 19th September 1870) or enacted (law of 24th May 1872) even before the formal establishment of the Republic (1875) by a National Assembly of which the majority were so far from being revolutionists, or even reformers, that they desired the restoration of the monarchy.

58 See Hauriou, pp. 245–268. These periods do not precisely correspond with the three eras marked by political changes in the annals of France under which we have already considered (see pp. 217–218, *ante*) the history of *droit administratif.*

The judicial became more or less separated off from the administrative functions of the Council. Litigious business (*le contentieux administratif*) was in practice assigned to and decided by a special committee (*section*), and, what is of equal consequence, such business was decided by a body which acted after the manner of a Court which was addressed by advocates, heard arguments, and after public debate delivered judicial decisions. These decisions were reported, became the object of much public interest, and were, after a manner with which English lawyers are well acquainted, moulded into a system of law. The judgments, in short, of the Council acquired the force of precedent. The political revolutions of France, which have excited far too much notice, whilst the uninterrupted growth of French institutions has received too little attention, sometimes retarded or threw back, but never arrested the continuous evolution of *droit administratif;* even under the Second Empire this branch of French jurisprudence became less and less arbitrary and developed more and more into a system of fixed and subtle legal rules.

The Period of Organisation, 1860–1908
(Période d'Organisation)

During the last forty-eight years, marked as they have been in France by the change from the Empire to a Republic, by the German invasion, and by civil war, the development of *droit administratif* has exhibited a singular and tranquil regularity. Sudden innovations have been rare and have produced little effect. The reforms introduced by the decree law of 19th September 1870, and by the law of 24th May 1872, are, taken together, considerable; but they in reality give effect to ideas which had since 1800 more or less guided the judicial legislation and practice both of the Council of State and of the Court of Cassation. If the legal history of France since 1800 be looked at as a whole, an Englishman may reasonably conclude that the arbitrary authority of the executive as it existed in the time of Napoleon, and even as it was exercised under the reign of Louis Philippe or of Louis Napoleon, has gradually, as far as the jurisdiction of the administrative Courts is concerned, been immensely curtailed, if not absolutely brought to an end. *Droit administratif,* though administered by bodies which are perhaps not in strictness Courts, and though containing provisions not reconcilable with the modern English conception of the rule of law, comes very near to law, and is utterly different from the capricious prerogatives of despotic power.

(B) Comparison between *droit administratif* and rule of law.

I. Likeness.

1st Point. *Droit administratif* not opposed to English ideas current in sixteenth and seventeenth centuries.

A comparison between the administrative law of France and our English rule of law, if taken from the right point of view, suggests some interesting points of likeness, no less than of unlikeness.

It will be observed that it is "modern" English notions which we have contrasted with the ideas of administrative law prevalent in France and other continental states. The reason why the opposition between the two is drawn in this form deserves notice. At a period which historically is not very remote from us, the ideas as to the position of the Crown which were current, if not predominant in England, bore a very close analogy to the doctrines which have given rise to the *droit administratif* of France.[59] Similar beliefs moreover necessarily produced similar results, and there was a time when it must have seemed possible that what we now call administrative law should become a permanent part of English institutions. For from the accession of the Tudors till the final expulsion of the Stuarts the Crown and its servants maintained and put into practice, with more or less success and with varying degrees of popular approval, views of government essentially similar to the theories which under different forms have been accepted by the French people. The personal failings of the Stuarts and the confusion caused by the combination of a religious with a political movement have tended to mask the true character of the legal and constitutional issues raised by the political contests of the seventeenth century. A lawyer, who regards the matter from an exclusively legal point of view, is tempted to assert that the real subject in dispute between statesmen such as Bacon and Wentworth on the one hand, and Coke or Eliot on the other, was whether a strong administration of the continental type should, or should not, be permanently established in England. Bacon and men like him no doubt underrated the risk that an increase in the power of

---

[59] This is illustrated by the similarity between the views at one time prevailing both in England and on the continent as to the relation between the government and the press. See pp. 161–164, *ante*.

the Crown should lead to the establishment of despotism. But advocates of the prerogative did not (it may be supposed) intend to sacrifice the liberties or invade the ordinary private rights of citizens; they were struck with the evils flowing from the conservative legalism of Coke, and with the necessity for enabling the Crown as head of the nation to cope with the selfishness of powerful individuals and classes. They wished, in short, to give the government the sort of rights conferred on a foreign executive by the principles of administrative law. Hence for each feature of French *droit administratif* one may find some curious analogy either in the claims put forward or in the institutions favoured by the Crown lawyers of the seventeenth century.

The doctrine, propounded under various metaphors by Bacon, that the prerogative was something beyond and above the ordinary law is like the foreign doctrine that in matters of high policy (*acte de gouvernement*) the administration has a discretionary authority which cannot be controlled by any Court. The celebrated dictum that the judges, though they be "lions," yet should be "lions under the throne, being circumspect that they do not check or oppose any points of sovereignty,"[60] is a curious anticipation of the maxim formulated by French revolutionary statesmanship that the judges are under no circumstances to disturb the action of the administration, and would, if logically worked out, have led to the exemption of every administrative act, or, to use English terms, of every act alleged to be done in virtue of the prerogative, from judicial cognisance. The constantly increasing power of the Star Chamber and of the Council gave practical expression to prevalent theories as to the Royal prerogative, and it is hardly fanciful to compare these Courts, which were in reality portions of the executive government, with the *Conseil d'état* and other *Tribunaux administratifs* of France. Nor is a parallel wanting to the celebrated Article 75 of the Constitution of the Year VIII.[61] This parallel is to be found in Bacon's attempt to prevent the judges by means of the writ *De non procedendo Rege inconsulto* from

---

60 Gardiner, *History of England*, iii. p. 2.

61 See p. 227, *ante*.

proceeding with any case in which the interests of the Crown were concerned. Mr. Gardiner observes:

> The working of this writ, if Bacon had obtained his object, would have been, to some extent, analogous to that provision which has been found in so many French constitutions, according to which no agent of the Government can be summoned before a tribunal, for acts done in the exercise of his office, without a preliminary authorisation by the Council of State. The effect of the English writ being confined to cases where the King was himself supposed to be injured, would have been of less universal application, but the principle on which it rested would have been equally bad.[62]

The principle moreover admitted of unlimited extension, and this, we may add, was perceived by Bacon. He writes to the King:

> The writ is a mean provided by the ancient law of England to bring any case that may *concern your Majesty in profit or power from the ordinary Benches, to be tried and judged before the Chancellor of England,* by the ordinary and legal part of this power. And your Majesty knoweth *your Chancellor is ever a principal counsellor and instrument of monarchy, of immediate dependence on the king; and therefore like to be a safe and tender guardian of the regal rights.*[63]

Bacon's innovation would, if successful, have formally established the fundamental dogma of administrative law, that administrative questions must be determined by administrative bodies.

The analogy between the administrative ideas which still prevail on the Continent[64] and the conception of the prerogative which was maintained by the English crown in the seventeenth century has considerable speculative interest. That the administrative ideas supposed by many French writers to have been originated by the statesmanship of the great Revolution or of the first Empire are to a great extent developments of the traditions and habits of the French monarchy is past a doubt, and it is a curious inquiry how far the efforts made by the Tudors or Stuarts to establish a strong govern-

---

62 Gardiner, *History of England,* iii. p. 7, note 2.

63 Abbot, *Francis Bacon,* p. 234.

64 It is worth noting that the system of "administrative law," though more fully judicialised in France than elsewhere, exists in one form or another in most of the Continental States.

ment were influenced by foreign examples. This, however, is a problem for historians. A lawyer may content himself with noting that French history throws light on the causes both of the partial success and of the ultimate failure of the attempt to establish in England a strong administrative system. The endeavour had a partial success, because circumstances, similar to those which made French monarchs ultimately despotic, tended in England during the sixteenth and part of the seventeenth century to augment the authority of the Crown. The attempt ended in failure, partly because of the personal deficiencies of the Stuarts, but chiefly because the whole scheme of administrative law was opposed to those habits of equality before the law which had long been essential characteristics of English institutions.

2nd Point. Droit administratif is case-law.

Droit administratif is in its contents utterly unlike any branch of modern English law, but in the method of its formation it resembles English law far more closely than does the codified civil law of France. For *droit administratif* is, like the greater part of English law, "case-law," or "judge-made law."[65] The precepts thereof are not to be found in any code; they are based upon precedent: French lawyers cling to the belief that *droit administratif* cannot be codified, just as English and American lawyers maintain, for some reason or other which they are never able to make very clear, that English law, and especially the common law, does not admit of codification. The true meaning of a creed which seems to be illogical because its apologists cannot, or will not, give the true grounds for their faith, is that the devotees of *droit administratif* in France, in common with the devotees of the common law in England, know that the system which they each admire is the product of judicial legislation, and dread that codification might limit, as it probably would, the essentially legislative authority of the *tribunaux administratifs* in France, or of the judges in England. The prominence further given throughout every treatise on *droit administratif* to the *contentieux administratif* recalls the importance in English lawbooks given to matters of procedure. The cause is

---

65 See Dicey, *Law and Opinion in England,* Lect. XI. p. 359, and Appendix, Note IV. p. 481. It may be suspected that English lawyers underrate the influence at the present day exerted by precedent (*Jurisprudence*) in French Courts.

in each case the same, namely, that French jurists and English lawyers are each dealing with a system of law based on precedent.

Nor is it irrelevant to remark that the *droit administratif* of France, just because it is case-law based on precedents created or sanctioned by tribunals, has, like the law of England, been profoundly influenced by the writers of text-books and commentaries. There are various branches of English law which have been reduced to a few logical principles by the books of well-known writers. Stephen transformed pleading from a set of rules derived mainly from the experience of practitioners into a coherent logical system. Private international law, as understood in England at the present day, has been developed under the influence first of Story's *Commentaries on the Conflict of Laws*, and next, at a later date, of Mr. Westlake's *Private International Law*. And the authority exercised in every field of English law by these and other eminent writers has in France been exerted, in the field of administrative law, by authors or teachers such as Cormenin, Macarel, Vivien, Laferrière, and Hauriou. This is no accident. Wherever Courts have power to form the law, there writers of text-books will also have influence. Remark too that, from the very nature of judge-made law, Reports have in the sphere of *droit administratif* an importance equal to the importance which they possess in every branch of English law, except in the rare instances in which a portion of our law has undergone codification.

3rd point. Evolution of *droit administratif*.

But in the comparison between French *droit administratif* and the law of England a critic ought not to stop at the points of likeness arising from their each of them being the creation of judicial decisions. There exists a further and very curious analogy between the process of their historical development. The *Conseil d'État* has been converted from an executive into a judicial or quasi-judicial body by the gradual separation of its judicial from its executive functions through the transference of the former to committees (*sections*), which have assumed more and more distinctly the duties of Courts. These "judicial committees" (to use an English expression) at first only advised the *Conseil d'État* or the whole executive body, though it was soon understood that the Council would, as a general rule, follow or ratify the decision of its judicial committees. This recalls to a student of English law the fact that the growth of our whole judicial system may historically be treated as the transference to parts of the King's Council of judicial powers originally exercised by the King in Council; and it is reasonable to suppose that the rather ill-defined relations between the *Conseil d'État* as a whole, and the *Comité du contentieux*,[66] may explain to a student the exertion, during the earlier periods of English history, by the King's Council, of hardly distinguishable judicial and executive powers; it explains also how, by a natural process which may have excited very little observation, the judicial functions of the Council became separated from its executive powers, and how this differentiation of functions gave birth at last to Courts whose connection with the political executive were merely historical. This process, moreover, of differentiation assisted at times, in France no less than in England, by legislation, has of quite recent years changed the *Conseil d'État* into a real tribunal of *droit administratif,* as it created in England the Judicial Committee of the Privy Council for the regular and judicial decision of appeals from the colonies to the Crown in Council. Nor, though the point is a minor one, is it irrelevant to note that, as the so-called judgments of the *Conseil d'État* were, till 1872, not strictly "judgments," but in reality advice on questions of *droit administratif* given by the *Conseil d'État* to the head of the Executive, and advice which he was not absolutely bound to follow, so the "judgments" of the Privy Council, even when acting through its judicial committee, though in reality judgments, are in form merely humble advice tendered by the Privy Council to the Crown. This form, which is now a mere survival, carries us back to an earlier period of English constitutional history, when the interference by the Council, *i.e.* by the executive, with judicial functions, was a real menace to that supremacy of the law which has been the guarantee of English freedom, and this era in the history of England again is curiously illustrated by the annals of *droit administratif* after the restoration of the Bourbons, 1815–30.

At that date the members of the *Conseil d'État,* as we have seen,[67] held, as they still hold, office at the pleasure of the Executive; they were to a great extent a political body; there existed further no Con-

---

66 See Laferrière, i. p. 236.

67 See pp. 227–228, *ante.*

flict-Court; or rather the *Conseil d'État* was itself the Conflict-Court, or the body which determined the reciprocal jurisdiction of the ordinary law Courts and of the administrative Courts, *i.e.* speaking broadly, the extent of the Council's own jurisdiction. The result was that the *Conseil d'État* used its powers to withdraw cases from the decision of the law Courts, and this at a time when government functionaries were fully protected by Article 75 of the Constitution of the Year VIII. from being made responsible before the Courts for official acts done in excess of their legal powers. Nevertheless, the *Conseil d'État*, just because it was to a great extent influenced by legal ideas, resisted, and with success, exertions of arbitrary power inspired by the spirit of Royalist reaction. It upheld the sales of the national domain made between 1789 and 1814; it withstood every attempt to invalidate decisions given by administrative authorities during the period of the Revolution or under the Empire. The King, owing, it may be assumed, to the judicial independence displayed by the *Conseil d'État*, took steps which were intended to transfer the decision of administrative disputes from the Council or its committees, acting as Courts, to Councillors, acting as part of the executive. Ordinances of 1814 and of 1817 empowered the King to withdraw any administrative dispute which was connected with principles of public interest (*toutes les affaires du contentieux de l'administration qui se lieraient à des vues d'intérêt général*) from the jurisdiction of the *Conseil d'État* and bring it before the Council of Ministers or, as it was called, the *Conseil d'en haut*, and the general effect of this power and of other arrangements, which we need not follow out into detail, was that questions of *droit administratif*, in the decision of which the government were interested, were ultimately decided, not even by a quasi-judicial body, but by the King and his Ministers, acting avowedly under the bias of political considerations.[68] In 1828 France insisted upon and obtained from Charles X. changes in procedure which diminished the arbitrary power of the Council.[69] But no one can wonder that Frenchmen feared the increase of arbitrary power, or that French liberals demanded, after the

---

68 See Laferrière, i. pp. 226–234, and Cormenin, *Du Conseil d'État envisagé comme conseil et comme juridiction* (1818).

69 Ordinance of 1st June 1828, Laferrière, i. p. 232.

Revolution of 1830, the abolition of administrative law and of administrative Courts. They felt towards the jurisdiction of the *Counseil d'État* the dread entertained by Englishmen of the sixteenth and seventeenth centuries with regard to the jurisdiction of the Privy Council, whether exercised by the Privy Council itself, by the Star Chamber, or even by the Court of Chancery. In each country there existed an appreciable danger lest the rule of the prerogative should supersede the supremacy of the law.

The comparison is in many ways instructive; it impresses upon us how nearly it came to pass that something very like administrative law at one time grew up in England. It ought, too, to make us perceive that such law, if it be administered in a judicial spirit, has in itself some advantages. It shows us also the inherent danger of its not becoming in strictness law at all, but remaining, from its close connection with the executive, a form of arbitrary power above or even opposed to the regular law of the land. It is certain that in the sixteenth and seventeenth centuries the jurisdiction of the Privy Council and even of the Star Chamber, odious as its name has remained, did confer some benefits on the public. It should always be remembered that the patriots who resisted the tyranny of the Stuarts were fanatics for the common law, and could they have seen their way to do so would have abolished the Court of Chancery no less than the Star Chamber. The Chancellor, after all, was a servant of the Crown holding his office at the pleasure of the King, and certainly capable, under the plea that he was promoting justice or equity, of destroying the certainty no less than the formalism of the common law. The parallel therefore between the position of the English puritans, or whigs, who, during the seventeenth century, opposed the arbitrary authority of the Council, and the position of the French liberals who, under the Restoration (1815–30), resisted the arbitrary authority of the *Conseil d'État* and the extension of *droit administratif,* is a close one. In each case, it may be added, the friends of freedom triumphed.

The result, however, of this triumph was, it will be said, as regards the matter we are considering, markedly different. Parliament destroyed, and destroyed for ever, the arbitrary authority of the Star Chamber and of the Council, and did not suffer any system of ad-

ministrative Courts or of administrative law to be revived or developed in England. The French liberals, on the expulsion of the
Bourbons, neither destroyed the *tribunaux administratifs* nor made a
clean sweep of *droit administratif*.

The difference is remarkable, yet any student who looks beyond
names at things will find that even here an obvious difference conceals a curious element of fundamental resemblance. The Star Chamber was abolished; the arbitrary jurisdiction of the Council dis-
appeared, but the judicial authority of the Chancellor was touched
neither by the Long Parliament nor by any of the Parliaments which
met yearly after the Revolution of 1688. The reasons for this difference
are not hard to discover. The law administered by the Lord Chancellor, or, in other words, Equity, had in it originally an arbitrary or
discretionary element, but it in fact conferred real benefits upon the
nation and was felt to be in many respects superior to the common
law administered by the common-law Judges. Even before 1660 acute
observers might note that Equity was growing into a system of fixed
law. Equity, which originally meant the discretionary, not to say
arbitrary interference of the Chancellor, for the avowed and often real
purpose of securing substantial justice between the parties in a given
case, might, no doubt, have been so developed as to shelter and
extend the despotic prerogative of the Crown. But this was not the
course of development which Equity actually followed; at any rate
from the time of Lord Nottingham (1673) it was obvious that Equity
was developing into a judicial system for the application of principles
which, though different from those of the common law, were not less
fixed. The danger of Equity turning into the servant of despotism had
passed away, and English statesmen, many of them lawyers, were
little likely to destroy a body of law which, if in one sense an anomaly, was productive of beneficial reforms. The treatment of *droit
administratif* in the nineteenth century by Frenchmen bears a marked
resemblance to the treatment of Equity in the seventeenth century by
Englishmen. *Droit administratif* has been the subject of much attack.
More than one publicist of high reputation has advocated its abolition, or has wished to transfer to the ordinary or civil Courts (*tribunaux judiciaires*) the authority exercised by the administrative tri-

bunals, but the assaults upon *droit administratif* have been repulsed, and the division between the spheres of the judicial and the spheres of the administrative tribunals has been maintained. Nor, again, is there much difficulty in seeing why this has happened. *Droit administratif* with all its peculiarities, and administrative tribunals with all their defects, have been suffered to exist because the system as a whole is felt by Frenchmen to be beneficial. Its severest critics concede that it has some great practical merits, and is suited to the spirit of French institutions. Meanwhile *droit administratif* has developed under the influence rather of lawyers than of politicians; it has during the last half-century and more to a great extent divested itself of its arbitrary character, and is passing into a system of more or less fixed law administered by real tribunals; administrative tribunals indeed still lack some of the qualities, such as complete independence of the Government, which Englishmen and many Frenchmen also think ought to belong to all Courts, but these tribunals are certainly very far indeed from being mere departments of the executive government. To any person versed in the judicial history of England, it would therefore appear to be possible, or even probable, that *droit administratif* may ultimately, under the guidance of lawyers, become, through a course of evolution, as completely a branch of the law of France (even if we use the word "law" in its very strictest sense) as Equity has for more than two centuries become an acknowledged branch of the law of England.

4th Point. Rapid growth of case-law.

The annals of *droit administratif* during the nineteenth century elucidate again a point in the earlier history of English law which excites some perplexity in the mind of a student, namely, the rapidity with which the mere existence and working of law Courts may create or extend a system of law. Any reader of the *History of English Law* by Pollock and Maitland may well be surpised at the rapidity with which the law of the King's Court became the general or common law of the land. This legal revolution seems to have been the natural result of the vigorous exertion of judicial functions by a Court of great authority. Nor can we feel certain that the end attained was deliberately aimed at. It may, in the main, have been the almost undesigned effect of two causes: the first is the disposition always exhibited by capable judges to refer the decision of particular cases to general principles, and to be guided by precedent; the second is the tendency of inferior tribunals to follow the lead given by any Court of great power and high dignity. Here, in short, we have one of the thousand illustrations of the principle developed in M. Tarde's *Lois de l'imitation*, that the innate imitativeness of mankind explains the spread, first, throughout one country, and, lastly, throughout the civilised world, of any institution or habit on which success or any other circumstance has conferred prestige. It may still, however, be urged that the creation under judicial influence of a system of law is an achievement which requires for its performance a considerable length of time, and that the influence of the King's Court in England in moulding the whole law of the country worked with incredible rapidity. It is certainly true that from the Norman Conquest to the accession of Edward I. (1066–1272) is a period of not much over two centuries, and that by 1272 the foundations of English law were firmly laid; whilst if we date the organisation of our judicial system from the accession of Henry II. (1154), we might say that a great legal revolution was carried through in not much more than a century. It is at this point that the history of *droit administratif* helps the student of comparative law.

One need not, however, be greatly astonished at rapidity in the development of legal principles and of legal procedure at a period when the moral influence or the imaginative impressiveness of powerful tribunals was much greater than during the later stages of human progress. In any case it is certain—and the fact is a most instructive one—that under the conditions of modern civilisation a whole body of legal rules and maxims, and a whole system of quasi-judicial procedure, have in France grown up within not much more than a century. The expression "grown up" is here deliberately used; the development of *droit administratif* between 1800 and 1908 resembles a natural process. It is as true of this branch of French law as of the English constitution that it "has not been made but has grown."

An intelligent student soon finds that *droit administratif* contains rules as to the status, the privileges, and the duties of government officials. He therefore thinks he can identify it with the laws, regula-

II. Unlikeness. 1st Point. *Droit administratif* not to be identified with any part of law of England.

tions, or customs which in England determine the position of the servants of the Crown, or (leaving the army out of consideration) of the Civil Service. Such "official law" exists, though only to a limited extent, in England no less than in France, and it is of course possible to identify and compare this official law of the one country with the official law of the other. But further investigation shows that official law thus understood, though it may form part of, is a very different thing from *droit administratif*. The law, by whatever name we term it, which regulates the privileges or disabilities of civil servants is the law of a class, just as military law is the law of a class, namely, the army. But *droit administratif* is not the law of a class, but—a very different thing—a body of law which, under given circumstances, may affect the rights of any French citizen, as for example, where an action is brought by *A* against *X* in the ordinary Courts (*tribunaux judiciaires*), and the rights of the parties are found to depend on an administrative act (*acte administratif*), which must be interpreted by an administrative tribunal (*tribunal administratif*). In truth, *droit administratif* is not the law of the Civil Service, but is that part of French public law which affects every Frenchman in relation to the acts of the public administration as the representative of the State. The relation indeed of *droit administratif* to the ordinary law of France may be best compared not with the relation of the law governing a particular class (*e.g.* military law) to the general law of England, but with the relation of Equity to the common law of England. The point of likeness, slight though in other respects it be, is that *droit administratif* in France and Equity in England each constitute a body of law which differs from the ordinary law of the land, and under certain circumstances modifies the ordinary civil rights of every citizen.

When our student finds that *droit administratif* cannot be identified with the law of the Civil Service, he naturally enough imagines that it may be treated as the sum of all the laws which confer special powers and impose special duties upon the administration, or, in other words, which regulate the functions of the Government. Such laws, though they must exist in every country, have till recently been few in England, simply because in England the sphere of the State's activity has, till within the last fifty or sixty years, been extremely limited. But even in England laws imposing special functions upon government officials have always existed, and the number thereof has of late vastly increased; to take one example among a score, the Factory legislation, which has grown up mainly during the latter half of the nineteenth century, has, with regard to the inspection and regulation of manufactories and workshops, given to the Government and its officials wide rights, and imposed upon them wide duties. If, then, *droit administratif* meant nothing more than the sum of all the laws which determine the functions of civil servants, *droit administratif* might be identified in its general character with the governmental law of England. The idea that such an identification is possible is encouraged by the wide definitions of *droit administratif* to be gathered from French works of authority,[70] and by the vagueness with which English writers occasionally use the term "administrative law." But here, again, the attempted identification breaks down. *Droit administratif*, as it exists in France, is not the sum of the powers possessed or of the functions discharged by the administration; it is rather the sum of the principles which govern the relation between French citizens, as individuals, and the administration as the representative of the State. Here we touch upon the fundamental difference between English and French ideas. In England the powers of the Crown and its servants may from time to time be increased as they may also be diminished. But these powers, whatever they are, must be exercised in accordance with the ordinary common law principles which govern the relation of one Englishman to another. A factory inspector, for example, is possessed of peculiar powers conferred upon him by Act of Parliament; but if in virtue of the orders of his superior officials he exceeds the authority given him by law, he becomes at once responsible for the wrong done, and cannot plead in his defence strict obedience of official orders, and, further, for the tort he has committed he becomes amenable to the ordinary Courts. In France, on the other hand, whilst the powers placed in the hands of the administration might be diminished, it is always assumed that the relation of individual citizens to the State is regulated by principles

---

70 See Aucoc, *Droit Administratif*, i. s. 6; Hauriou, *Précis de Droit Administratif*, 3rd ed., p. 242, and 6th ed., pp. 391, 392; Laferrière, i. pp. 1–8.

different from those which govern the relation of one French citizen to another. *Droit administratif,* in short, rests upon ideas absolutely foreign to English law: the one, as I have already explained,[71] is that the relation of individuals to the State is governed by principles essentially different from those rules of private law which govern the rights of private persons towards their neighbours; the other is that questions as to the application of these principles do not lie within the jurisdiction of the ordinary Courts. This essential difference renders the identification of *droit administratif* with any branch of English law an impossibility. Hence inquiries which rightly occupy French jurists, such, for example, as what is the proper definition of the *contentieux administratif;* what is the precise difference between *actes de gestion* and *actes de puissance publique,* and generally, what are the boundaries between the jurisdiction of the ordinary Courts (*tribunaux judiciaires*) and the jurisdiction of the administrative Courts (*tribunaux administratifs*) have under English law no meaning.

2nd Point. Droit administratif not in reality introduced into law of England. Has *droit administratif* been of recent years introduced in any sense into the law of England?

This is an inquiry which has been raised by writers of eminence,[72] and which has caused some perplexity. We may give thereto a decided and negative reply.

The powers of the English Government have, during the last sixty years or so, been largely increased; the State has undertaken many new functions, such, for example, as the regulation of labour under the Factory Acts, and the supervision of public education under the

---

71 See p. 219, *ante.*

72 See Laferrière, i. pp. 97–106. To cite such enactments as the Public Authorities Protection Act 1893, which by the way does little more than generalise provisions, to be found in a lot of Acts extending from 1601 to 1900, as an example of the existence of administrative law in England, seems to me little else than playing with words. The Act assumes that every person may legally do the act which by law he is ordered to do. It also gives a person who acts in pursuance of his legal duty, *e.g.* under an Act of Parliament, special privileges as to the time within which an action must be brought against him for any wrong committed by him in the course of carrying out his duty, but it does not to the least extent provide that an order from a superior official shall protect, *e.g.* a policeman, for any wrong done by him.

There are, indeed, one or two instances in which no legal remedy can be obtained except against the actual wrong-doer for damage inflicted by the conduct of a servant of the Crown. These instances are practically unimportant. See Appendix, Note XII., "Proceedings against the Crown."

Education Acts. Nor is the importance of this extension of the activity of the State lessened by the consideration that its powers are in many cases exercised by local bodies, such, for example, as County Councils. But though the powers conferred on persons or bodies who directly or indirectly represent the State have been greatly increased in many directions, there has been no intentional introduction into the law of England of the essential principles of *droit administratif.* Any official who exceeds the authority given him by the law incurs the common law responsibility for his wrongful act; he is amenable to the authority of the ordinary Courts, and the ordinary Courts have themselves jurisdiction to determine what is the extent of his legal power, and whether the orders under which he has acted were legal and valid. Hence the Courts do in effect limit and interfere with the action of the "administration," using that word in its widest sense. The London School Board, for example, has claimed and exercised the right to tax the ratepayers for the support of a kind of education superior to the elementary teaching generally provided by School Boards; the High Court of Justice has decided that such right does not exist. A year or two ago some officials, acting under the distinct orders of the Lords of the Admiralty, occupied some land alleged to belong to the Crown; the title of the Crown being disputed, a court of law gave judgment against his officials as wrong-doers. In each of these cases nice and disputable points of law were raised, but no English lawyer, whatever his opinion of the judgments given by the Court, has ever doubted that the High Court had jurisdiction to determine what were the rights of the School Board or of the Crown.

Droit administratif, therefore, has obtained no foothold in England, but, as has been pointed out by some foreign critics, recent legislation has occasionally, and for particular purposes, given to officials something like judicial authority. It is possible in such instances, which are rare, to see a slight approximation to *droit administratif,* but the innovations, such as they are, have been suggested merely by considerations of practical convenience, and do not betray the least intention on the part of English statesmen to modify the essential principles of English law. There exists in England no true *droit administratif.*

An English lawyer, however, who has ascertained that no branch of English law corresponds with the administrative law of foreign countries must be on his guard against falling into the error that the *droit administratif* of modern France is not "law" at all, in the sense in which that term is used in England, but is a mere name for maxims which guide the executive in the exercise if not of arbitrary yet of discretionary power. That this notion is erroneous will, I hope, be now clear to all my readers. But for its existence there is some excuse and even a certain amount of justification.

The French Government does in fact exercise, especially as regards foreigners, a wide discretionary authority which is not under the control of any Court whatever. For an act of State the Executive or its servants cannot be made amenable to the jurisdiction of any tribunal, whether judicial or administrative. Writers of high authority have differed[73] indeed profoundly as to the definition of an act of State (*acte de gouvernement*).[74] Where on a question of French law French jurists disagree, an English lawyer can form no opinion; he may be allowed, however, to conjecture that at times of disturbance a French Government can exercise discretionary powers without the dread of interference on the part of the ordinary Courts, and that administrative tribunals, when they can intervene, are likely to favour that interpretation of the term act of State which supports the authority of the Executive. However this may be, the possession by the French Executive of large prerogatives is apt, in the mind of an Englishman, to be confused with the character of the administrative law enforced by Courts composed, in part at any rate, of officials.

The restrictions, again, placed by French law on the jurisdiction of the ordinary Courts (*tribunaux judiciaires*) whereby they are prevented from interfering with the action of the Executive and its servants, seem to an Englishman accustomed to a system under which the Courts of law determine the limits of their own jurisdiction, to be

---

73 See p. 226, *ante.*

74 Compare Laferrière, ii. bk. iv. ch. ii. p. 32, and Hauriou, pp. 282–287, with Jacquelin, pp. 438–447.

much the same thing as the relegating of all matters in which the authority of the State is concerned to the discretion of the Executive. This notion is erroneous, but it has been fostered by a circumstance which may be termed accidental. The nature and the very existence of *droit administratif* has been first revealed to many Englishmen, as certainly to the present writer, through the writings of Alexis de Tocqueville, whose works have exerted, in the England of the nineteenth century, an influence equal to the authority exerted by the works of Montesquieu in the England of the eighteenth century. Now Tocqueville by his own admission knew little or nothing of the actual working of *droit administratif* in his own day.[75] He no doubt in his later years increased his knowledge, but to the end of his life he looked upon *droit administratif,* not as a practising lawyer but as the historian of the *ancien régime,* and even as an historian he studied the subject from a very peculiar point of view, for the aim of *L'Ancien Régime et la Révolution* is to establish the doctrine that the institutions of modern France are in many respects in spirit the same as the institutions of the ancient monarchy; and Tocqueville, moved by the desire to maintain a theory of history which in his time sounded like a paradox, but, owing greatly to his labours, has now become a generally accepted truth, was inclined to exaggerate the similarity between the France of the Revolution, the Empire, or the Republic, and the France of the *ancien régime.* Nowhere is this tendency more obvious than in his treatment of *droit administratif.* He demonstrates that the ideas on which *droit administratif* is based had been accepted by French lawyers and statesmen long before 1789; he notes the arbitrariness of *droit administratif* under the monarchy; he not only insists upon but deplores the connection under the *ancien régime* between the action of the Executive and the administration of justice, and he certainly suggests that the *droit administratif* of the nineteenth century was all but as closely connected with the exercise of arbitrary power as was the *droit administratif* of the seventeenth or the eighteenth century.

---

75 Tocqueville, vii. *Œuvres Complètes,* p. 66.

He did not recognise the change in the character of *droit administratif* which was quietly taking place in his own day. He could not by any possibility anticipate the reforms which have occurred during the lapse of well-nigh half a century since his death. What wonder that English lawyers who first gained their knowlege of French institutions from Tocqueville should fail to take full account of that judicialisation (*juridictionnalisation*) of administrative law which is one of the most surprising and noteworthy phenomena in the legal history of France.

III. Merits and demerits.

It is not uninstructive to compare the merits and defects, on the one hand, of our English rule of law, and, on the other, of French *droit administratif.*

Rule of law—its merits.

Our rigid rule of law has immense and undeniable merits. Individual freedom is thereby more thoroughly protected in England against oppression by the government than in any other European country; the Habeas Corpus Acts[76] protect the liberty no less of foreigners than of British subjects; martial law[77] itself is reduced within the narrowest limits, and subjected to the supervision of the Courts; an extension of judicial power which sets at nought the dogma of the separation of powers, happily combined with judicial independence, has begotten reverence for the bench of judges. They, rather than the government, represent the august dignity of the State, or, in accordance with the terminology of English law, of the Crown. Trial by jury is open to much criticism; a distinguished French thinker may be right in holding that the habit of submitting difficult problems of fact to the decision of twelve men of not more than average education and intelligence will in the near future be considered an absurdity as patent as ordeal by battle. Its success in England is wholly due to, and is the most extraordinary sign of, popular confidence in the judicial bench. A judge is the colleague and the readily accepted guide of the jurors. The House of Commons shows the feeling of the electors, and has handed over to the High

---

76 See pp. 130–131, *ante.*

77 See p. 180, *ante.*

Court of Justice the trial of election petitions. When rare occasions arise, as at Sheffield in 1866, which demand inquiries of an exceptional character which can hardly be effected by the regular procedure of the Courts, it is to selected members of the bench that the nation turns for aid. In the bitter disputes which occur in the conflicts between capital and labour, employers and workmen alike will often submit their differences to the arbitration of men who have been judges of the High Court. Reverence, in short, for the supremacy of the law is seen in its very best aspect when we recognise it as being in England at once the cause and the effect of reverence for our judges.

Defects.   The blessings, however, conferred upon the nation by the rule of law are balanced by undeniable, though less obvious, evils. Courts cannot without considerable danger be turned into instruments of government. It is not the end for which they are created; it is a purpose for which they are ill suited at any period or in any country where history has not produced veneration for the law and for the law Courts.[78] Respect for law, moreover, easily degenerates into legalism which from its very rigidity may work considerable injury to the nation. Thus the refusal to look upon an agent or servant of the State as standing, from a legal point of view, in a different position from the servant of any other employer, or as placed under obligations or entitled to immunities different from those imposed upon or granted to an ordinary citizen, has certainly saved England from the development of the arbitrary prerogatives of the Crown, but it has also in more ways than one been injurious to the public service.

The law, for instance, has assuredly been slow to recognise the fact that violations of duty by public officials may have an importance and deserve a punishment far greater than the same conduct on the part of an agent of an ordinary employer. Some years ago a copyist in a public office betrayed to the newspapers a diplomatic document of the highest importance. Imagination can hardly picture a more flagrant breach of duty, but there then apparently existed no available

---

78 In times of revolutionary passion trial by jury cannot secure respect for justice. The worst iniquities committed by Jeffreys at the Bloody Assize would have been impossible had he not found willing accomplices in the jurors and freeholders of the western counties.

means for punishing the culprit. If it could have been proved that he had taken from the office the paper on which the communication of state was written, he might conceivably have been put on trial for larceny.[79] But a prisoner put on trial for a crime of which he was in fact morally innocent, because the gross moral offence of which he was really guilty was not a crime, might have counted on an acquittal. The Official Secrets Act, 1889,[80] now, it is true, renders the particular offence, which could not be punished in 1878, a misdemeanour, but the Act, after the manner of English legislation, does not establish the general principle that an official breach of trust is a crime. It is therefore more than possible that derelictions of duty on the part of public servants which in some foreign countries would be severely punished may still in England expose the wrong-doer to no legal punishment.

Nor is it at all wholly a benefit to the public that *bona fide* obedience to the orders of superiors is not a defence available to a subordinate who, in the discharge of his functions as a government officer, has invaded the legal rights of the humblest individual, or that officials are, like everybody else, accountable for their conduct to an ordinary Court of law, and to a Court, be it noted, where the verdict is given by a jury.

In this point of view few things are more instructive than an examination of the actions which have been brought against officers of the Board of Trade for detaining ships about to proceed to sea. Under the Merchant Shipping Acts since 1876 the Board have been and are bound to detain any ship which from its unsafe and unseaworthy condition cannot proceed to sea without serious danger to human life.[81] Most persons would suppose that the officials of the Board, as long as they, *bona fide,* and without malice or corrupt motive, endeavoured to carry out the provisions of the statute, would be safe

---

79 See *Annual Register, 1878, Chronicle,* p. 71.

80 Repealed and superseded by the Official Secrets Act, 1911, 1 & 2 Geo. 5, c. 28, described as "An Act to re-enact the Official Secrets Act, 1889, with Amendments." See especially sec. 2.

81 Merchant Shipping Act, 1894 (57 & 58 Vict. c. 60), s. 459.

from an action at the hands of a shipowner. This, however, is not so. The Board and its officers have more than once been sued with success.[82] They have never been accused of either malice or negligence, but the mere fact that the Board act in an administrative capacity is not a protection to the Board, nor is mere obedience to the orders of the Board an answer to an action against its servants. Any deviation, moreover, from the exact terms of the Acts—the omission of the most unmeaning formality—may make every person, high and low, concerned in the detention of the ship, a wrong-doer. The question, on the answer to which the decision in each instance at bottom depends, is whether there was reasonable cause for detaining the vessel, and this inquiry is determined by jurymen who sympathise more keenly with the losses of a shipowner, whose ship may have been unjustly detained, than with the zeal of an inspector anxious to perform his duty and to prevent loss of life. The result has (it is said) been to render the provisions of the Merchant Shipping Acts, with regard to the detention of unseaworthy ships, nugatory. Juries are often biassed against the Government. A technical question is referred for decision, from persons who know something about the subject, and are impartial, to persons who are both ignorant and prejudiced. The government, moreover, which has no concern but the public interest, is placed in the false position of a litigant fighting for his own advantage. These things ought to be noticed, for they explain, if they do not justify, the tenacity with which statesmen, as partial as Tocqueville to English ideas of government, have clung to the conviction that administrative questions ought to be referred to administrative Courts.

Droit admin-istratif— merits.

The merits of administrative law as represented by modern French *droit administratif,* that is, when seen at its very best, escape the attention, and do not receive the due appreciation of English constitutionalists.[83] No jurist can fail to admire the skill with which the Council of State, the authority and the jurisdiction whereof as an administrative Court year by year receives extension, has worked out

---

82 See *Thomson* v. *Farrer,* 9 Q. B. D. (C. A.), 372.

83 One, and not the least of them, is that access to the Council of State as an administrative Court is both easy and inexpensive.

new remedies for various abuses which would appear to be hardly touched by the ordinary law of the land. The Council, for instance, has created and extended the power of almost any individual to attack, and cause to be annulled, any act done by any administrative authority (using the term in a very wide sense) which is in excess of the legal power given to the person or body from whom the act emanates. Thus an order issued by a prefect or a bye-law made by a corporation which is in excess of the legal power of the prefect or of the corporate body may, on the application of a plaintiff who has any interest in the matter whatever, be absolutely set aside or annulled for the benefit not only of the plaintiff, but of all the world, and this even though he has not himself suffered, from the act complained of, any pecuniary loss or damage. The ingenious distinction[84] again, which has been more and more carefully elaborated by the Council of State, between damage resulting from the personal fault (*faute personnelle*), *e.g.* spite, violence, or negligence of an official, *e.g.* a prefect or a mayor, in the carrying out of official orders, and the damage resulting, without any fault on the part of the official, from the carrying out of official orders, illegal or wrongful in themselves (*faute de service*), has of recent years afforded a valuable remedy to persons who have suffered from the misuse of official power, and has also, from one point of view, extended or secured the responsibility of officials—a responsibility enforceable in the ordinary Courts—for wrongful con-

---

84 French law draws an important distinction between an injury caused to a private individual by act of the administration or government which is in excess of its powers (*faute de service*), though duly carried out, or at any rate, carried out without any gross fault on the part of a subordinate functionary, *e.g.* a policeman acting in pursuance of official orders, and injury caused to a private individual by the negligent or malicious manner (*faute personnelle*) in which such subordinate functionary carries out official orders which may be perfectly lawful. In the first case the policeman incurs no liability at all, and the party aggrieved must proceed in some form or other against the State in the administrative Courts (*tribunaux administratifs*). In the second case the policeman is personally liable, and the party aggrieved must proceed against him in the ordinary Courts (*tribunaux judiciaires*) (see Hauriou, pp. 170, 171; Laferrière, i. p. 652), and apparently cannot proceed against the State.

French authorities differ as to what is the precise criterion by which to distinguish a *faute personnelle* from a *faute de service,* and show a tendency to hold that there is no *faute personnelle* on the part, *e.g.* of a policeman, when he has *bona fide* attempted to carry out his official duty. See Duguit, *L'État,* pp. 638–640; [Duguit, *Traité de Droit Constitutionnel,* i. pp. 553–559.]

duct, which is in strictness attributable to their personal action. And in no respect does this judge-made law of the Council appear to more advantage than in cases, mostly I conceive of comparatively recent date, in which individuals have obtained compensation for governmental action, which might possibly be considered of technical legality, but which involves in reality the illegitimate use of power conferred upon the government or some governmental body for one object, but in truth used for some end different from that contemplated by the law. One example explains my meaning. The State in 1872 had, as it still has, a monopoly of matches. To the government was given by law the power of acquiring existing match factories under some form of compulsory purchase. It occurred to some ingenious minister that the fewer factories there were left open for sale, the less would be the purchase-money which the State would need to pay. A prefect, the direct servant of the government, had power to close factories on sanitary grounds. Under the orders of the minister he closed a factory belonging to *A,* nominally on sanitary grounds, but in reality to lessen the number of match factories which the State, in the maintenance of its monopoly, would require to purchase. There was no personal fault on the part of the prefect. No action could with success be maintained against him in the judicial Courts,[85] nor, we may add, in the administrative Courts.[86] *A,* however, attacked the act itself before the Council of State, and got the order of the prefect annulled, and ultimately obtained, through the Council of State, damages from the State of over £2000 for the illegal closing of the factory, and this in addition to the purchase-money received from the State for taking possession of the factory.[87]

Defects.　　No Englishman can wonder that the jurisdiction of the Council of State, as the greatest of administrative Courts, grows apace; the extension of its power removes, as did at one time the growth of Equity in England, real grievances, and meets the need of the ordinary citizen. Yet to an Englishman imbued with an unshakeable faith in

---

85 Dalloz, 1875, i. 495.

86 Dalloz, 1878, iii. 13.

87 Dalloz, 1880, iii. 41.

the importance of maintaining the supremacy of the ordinary law of the land enforced by the ordinary Law Courts, the *droit administratif* of modern France is open to some grave criticism.

The high and increasing authority of the Council of State must detract, he surmises, from the dignity and respect of the judicial Courts. "The more there is of the more, the less there is of the less" is a Spanish proverb of profound wisdom and wide application. There was a time in the history of England when the judicial power of the Chancellor, bound up as it was with the prerogative of the Crown, might have overshadowed the Courts of Law, which have protected the hereditary liberties of England and the personal freedom of Englishmen. It is difficult not to suppose that the extension of the Council's jurisdiction, beneficial as may be its direct effects, may depress the authority of the judicial tribunals. More than one writer, who ought to represent the ideas of educated Frenchmen, makes the suggestion that if the members of the Council of State lack that absolute security of tenure which is universally acknowledged to be the best guarantee of judicial independence, yet irremovable judges, who, though they may defy dismissal, are tormented by the constant longing for advancement,[88] are not more independent of the Government at whose hands they expect promotion than are members of the Council of State who, if legally removable, are by force of custom hardly ever removed from their high position.

Trial by jury, we are told, is a joke, and, as far as the interests of the public are concerned, a very bad joke.[89] Prosecutors and criminals alike prefer the Correctional Courts, where a jury is unknown, to the Courts of Assize, where a judge presides and a jury gives a verdict. The prosecutor knows that in the Correctional Court proved guilt will lead to condemnation. The criminal knows that though in the inferior Court he may lose the chance of acquittal by good-natured or sentimental jurymen, he also avoids the possibility of undergoing severe punishment. Two facts are certain. In 1881 the judges were deprived of the right of charging the jury. Year by year the number of causes

---

88 See Chardon, pp. 326–328.

89 *Ibid.*

tried in the Assize Courts decreases. Add to this that the procedure of the judicial Courts, whether civil or criminal, is antiquated and cumbrous. The procedure in the great administrative Court is modelled on modern ideas, is simple, cheap, and effective. The Court of Cassation still commands respect. The other judicial Courts, one can hardly doubt, have sunk in popular estimation. Their members neither exercise the power nor enjoy the moral authority of the judges of the High Court.

It is difficult, further, for an Englishman to believe that, at any rate where politics are concerned, the administrative Courts can from their very nature give that amount of protection to individual freedom which is secured to every English citizen, and indeed to every foreigner residing in England. However this may be, it is certain that the distinction between ordinary law and administrative law (taken together with the doctrine of the separation of powers, at any rate as hitherto interpreted by French jurists), implies the general belief that the agents of the government need, when acting in *bona fide* discharge of their official duties, protection from the control of the ordinary law Courts. That this is so is proved by more than one fact. The desire to protect servants of the State has dictated the enactment of the *Code Pénal*, Article 114. This desire kept alive for seventy years Article 75 of the Constitution of the Year VIII. It influenced even the men by whom that Article was repealed, for the repeal itself is expressed in words which imply the intention of providing some special protection for the agents of the government. It influenced the decisions which more or less nullified the effect of the law of 19th December 1870, which was at first supposed to make the judicial Courts the sole judges of the liability of civil servants to suffer punishment or make compensation for acts of dubious legality done in the performance of their official duties. Oddly enough, the success with which administrative Courts have extended the right of private persons to obtain damages from the State itself for illegal or injurious acts done by its servants, seems, as an English critic must think, to supply a new form of protection for the agents of the government when acting in obedience to orders. There surely can be little inducement to take proceedings against a subordinate, whose guilt consists merely in carrying out a wrongful or illegal order, given him by his official superior, if the person damaged can obtain compensation from the government, or, in other words, from the State itself.[90] But turn the matter which way you will, the personal immunities of officials who take part, though without other fault of their own, in any breach of the law, though consistent even with the modern *droit administratif* of France, are inconsistent with the ideas which underlie the common law of England. This essential opposition has been admirably expressed by a French jurist of eminence. Hauriou writes:

> Under every legal system, the right to proceed against a servant of the government for wrongs done to individuals in his official capacity exists in some form or other; the right corresponds to the instinctive impulse felt by every victim of a legal wrong to seek compensation from the immediately visible wrong-doer. But on this point the laws of different countries obey utterly different tendencies. There are countries [such, for example, as England or the United States] where every effort is made to shelter the liability of the State behind the personal responsibility of its servant. There are other countries where every effort is made to cover the responsibility of the servant of the State behind the liability of the State itself, to protect him against, and to save him from, the painful consequences of faults committed in the service of the State. The laws of centralised countries, and notably the law of France, are of this type. There you will find what is called the protection of officials (*garantie des fonctionnaries*).[91]

---

90 Consider, too, the extended protection offered to every servant of the State by the doctrine, suggested by at least one good authority, that he cannot be held personally responsible for any wrong (*faute*) committed whilst he is acting in the spirit of his official duty. *"Si, en effet, le fonctionnaire a agi dans l'esprit de sa fonction, c'est-à-dire en poursuivant effectivement le but qu'avait l'État en établissant cette fonction, il ne peut être responsable ni vis-à-vis de l'État, ni vis-à-vis des particuliers, alors même qu'il ait commis une faute."*—Duguit, *L'État*, p. 638.

91 *"Ce principe est admis par toutes les législations, la poursuite du fonctionnaire existe partout, d'autant qu'elle répond à un mouvement instinctif qui est, pour la victime d'un méfait, de s'en prendre à l'autuer immédiatement visible. Mais les législations obéissent à deux tendances bien opposées: il en est qui s'efforçent d'abriter l'État derrière le fonctionnaire, il en est d'autres, au contraire, qui s'efforçent de faire couvrir le fonctionnaire par l'État, de le protéger, de le rassurer contre les conséquences fâcheuses de ses erreurs. Les législations des pays centralisés et notamment celle de la France sont de ce dernier type; il y a ce que l'on appelle une* garantie des fonctionnaires.*"*—Hauriou, *Précis de Droit Administratif*, Troisième édit., pp. 170, 171.

Chapter XIII

RELATION BETWEEN PARLIAMENTARY SOVEREIGNTY AND THE RULE OF LAW

T he sovereignty of Parliament and the supremacy of the law of the land—the two principles which pervade the whole of the English constitution—may appear to stand in opposition to each other, or to be at best only counterbalancing forces. But this appearance is delusive; the sovereignty of Parliament, as contrasted with other forms of sovereign power, favours the supremacy of the law, whilst the predominance of rigid legality throughout our institutions evokes the exercise, and thus increases the authority, of Parliamentary sovereignty.

Parliamentary sovereignty favours rule of law.

The sovereignty of Parliament favours the supremacy of the law of the land.

That this should be so arises in the main from two characteristics or peculiarities which distinguish the English Parliament from other sovereign powers.

The first of these characteristics is that the commands of Parliament (consisting as it does of the Crown, the House of Lords, and the House of Commons) can be uttered only through the combined action of its three constituent parts, and must, therefore, always take the shape of formal and deliberate legislation. The will of Parliament[1] can be expressed only through an Act of Parliament.

---

1 A strong, if not the strongest, argument in favour of the so-called "bi-cameral" system, is to be found in the consideration that the coexistence of two legislative chambers prevents the confusion of resolutions passed by either House with laws, and thus checks the sub-

This is no mere matter of form; it has most important practical effects. It prevents those inroads upon the law of the land which a despotic monarch, such as Louis XIV., Napoleon I., or Napoleon III., might effect by ordinances or decrees, or which the different constituent assemblies of France, and above all the famous Convention, carried out by sudden resolutions. The principle that Parliament speaks only through an Act of Parliament greatly increases the authority of the judges. A Bill which has passed into a statute immediately becomes subject to judicial interpretation, and the English Bench have always refused, in principle at least, to interpret an Act of Parliament otherwise than by reference to the words of the enactment. An English judge will take no notice of the resolutions of either House, of anything which may have passed in debate (a matter of which officially he has no cognisance), or even of the changes which a Bill may have undergone between the moment of its first introduction to Parliament and of its receiving the Royal assent. All this, which seems natural enough to an English lawyer, would greatly surprise many foreign legists, and no doubt often does give a certain narrowness to the judicial construction of statutes. It contributes greatly, however, both (as I have already pointed out) to the authority of the judges and to the fixity of the law.[2]

The second of these characteristics is that the English Parliament as such has never, except at periods of revolution, exercised direct executive power or appointed the officials of the executive government.

No doubt in modern times the House of Commons has in substance obtained the right to designate for appointment the Prime Minister and the other members of the Cabinet. But this right is, historically speaking, of recent acquisition, and is exercised in a very

---

stitution of the arbitrary will of an assembly for the supremacy of the ordinary law of the land. Whoever wishes to appreciate the force of this argument should weigh well the history, not only of the French Convention but also of the English Long Parliament.

2 The principle that the sovereign legislature can express its commands only in the particular form of an Act of Parliament originates of course in historical causes; it is due to the fact that an Act of Parliament was once in reality, what it still is in form, a law "enacted by the King by and with the advice and consent of the Lords and Commons in Parliament assembled."

roundabout manner; its existence does not affect the truth of the assertion that the Houses of Parliament do not directly appoint or dismiss the servants of the State; neither the House of Lords nor the House of Commons, nor both Houses combined, could even now issue a direct order to a military officer, a constable, or a tax-collector; the servants of the State are still in name what they once were in reality—"servants of the Crown"; and, what is worth careful notice, the attitude of Parliament towards government officials was determined originally, and is still regulated, by considerations and feelings belonging to a time when the "servants of the Crown" were dependent upon the King, that is, upon a power which naturally excited the jealousy and vigilance of Parliament.

Hence several results all indirectly tending to support the supremacy of the law. Parliament, though sovereign, unlike a sovereign monarch who is not only a legislator but a ruler, that is, head of the executive government, has never hitherto been able to use the powers of the government as a means of interfering with the regular course of law;[3] and what is even more important, Parliament has looked with disfavour and jealousy on all exemptions of officials from the ordinary liabilities of citizens or from the jurisdiction of the ordinary Courts; Parliamentary sovereignty has been fatal to the growth of "administrative law." The action, lastly, of Parliament has tended as naturally to protect the independence of the judges, as that of other sovereigns to protect the conduct of officials. It is worth notice that Parliamentary care for judicial independence has, in fact, stopped just at that point where on *a priori* grounds it might be expected to end. The judges are not in strictness irremovable; they can be removed from office on an address of the two Houses; they have been made by Parliament independent of every power in the State except the Houses of Parliament.

Tendency to support rule of law often not found in foreign representative assemblies.

The idea may suggest itself to a reader that the characteristics or peculiarities of the English Parliament on which I have just dwelt must now be common to most of the representative assemblies which exist in continental Europe. The French National Assembly, for

3 Contrast with this the way in which, even towards the end of the eighteenth century, French Kings interfered with the action of the Courts.

example, bears a considerable external resemblance to our own Parliament. It is influenced, however, by a different spirit; it is the heir, in more ways than one, of the Bourbon Monarchy and the Napoleonic Empire. It is apparently, though on this point a foreigner must speak with hesitation, inclined to interfere in the details of administration. It does not look with special favour on the independence or authority of the ordinary judges. It shows no disapprobation of the system of *droit administratif* which Frenchmen—very likely with truth—regard as an institution suited to their country, and it certainly leaves in the hands of the government wider executive and even legislative powers than the English Parliament has ever conceded either to the Crown or to its servants. What is true of France is true under a different form of many other continental states, such, for example, as Switzerland or Prussia. The sovereignty of Parliament as developed in England supports the supremacy of the law. But this is certainly not true of all the countries which now enjoy representative or Parliamentary government.

Rule of law favours Parliamentary sovereignty.

The supremacy of the law necessitates the exercise of Parliamentary sovereignty.

The rigidity of the law constantly hampers (and sometimes with great injury to the public) the action of the executive, and from the hard-and-fast rules of strict law, as interpreted by the judges, the government can escape only by obtaining from Parliament the discretionary authority which is denied to the Crown by the law of the land. Note with care the way in which the necessity for discretionary powers brings about the recourse to exceptional legislation. Under the complex conditions of modern life no government can in times of disorder, or of war, keep the peace at home, or perform its duties towards foreign powers, without occasional use of arbitrary authority. During periods, for instance, of social disturbance you need not only to punish conspirators, but also to arrest men who are reasonably suspected of conspiracy; foreign revolutionists are known to be spreading sedition throughout the land; order can hardly be maintained unless the executive can expel aliens. When two foreign nations are at war, or when civil contests divide a friendly country into two hostile camps, it is impossible for England to perform her duties

as a neutral unless the Crown has legal authority to put a summary
check to the attempts of English sympathisers to help one or other of
the belligerents. Foreign nations, again, feel aggrieved if they are
prevented from punishing theft and homicide,—if, in short, their
whole criminal law is weakened because every scoundrel can ensure
impunity for his crimes by an escape to England. But this result must
inevitably ensue if the English executive has no authority to surrender French or German offenders to the government of France or of
Germany. The English executive needs therefore the right to exercise
discretionary powers, but the Courts must prevent, and will prevent
at any rate where personal liberty is concerned, the exercise by the
government of any sort of discretionary power. The Crown cannot,
except under statute, expel from England any alien[4] whatever, even
though he were a murderer who, after slaughtering a whole family at
Boulogne, had on the very day crossed red-handed to Dover. The
executive therefore must ask for, and always obtains, aid from Parliament. An Alien Act enables the Ministry in times of disturbance to
expel any foreigner from the country; a Foreign Enlistment Act makes
it possible for the Ministry to check intervention in foreign contests or
the supply of arms to foreign belligerents. Extradition Acts empower
the government at the same time to prevent England from becoming
a city of refuge for foreign criminals, and to co-operate with foreign
states in that general repression of crime in which the whole civilised
world has an interest. Nor have we yet exhausted the instances in
which the rigidity of the law necessitates the intervention of Parliament. There are times of tumult or invasion when for the sake of
legality itself the rules of law must be broken. The course which the
government must then take is clear. The Ministry must break the law
and trust for protection to an Act of Indemnity. A statute of this kind
is (as already pointed out[5]) the last and supreme exercise of Parliamentary sovereignty. It legalises illegality; it affords the practical
solution of the problem which perplexed the statesmanship of the
sixteenth and seventeenth centuries, how to combine the mainte-

---

4 See, however, p. 137, note 22, *ante.*

5 See pp. 10, 11, 142–145, *ante.*

nance of law and the authority of the Houses of Parliament with the free exercise of that kind of discretionary power or prerogative which, under some shape or other, must at critical junctures be wielded by the executive government of every civilised country.

This solution may be thought by some critics a merely formal one, or at best only a substitution of the despotism of Parliament for the prerogative of the Crown. But this idea is erroneous. The fact that the most arbitrary powers of the English executive must always be exercised under Act of Parliament places the government, even when armed with the widest authority, under the supervision, so to speak, of the Courts. Powers, however extraordinary, which are conferred or sanctioned by statute, are never really unlimited, for they are confined by the words of the Act itself, and, what is more, by the interpretation put upon the statute by the judges. Parliament is supreme legislator, but from the moment Parliament has uttered its will as lawgiver, that will becomes subject to the interpretation put upon it by the judges of the land, and the judges, who are influenced by the feelings of magistrates no less than by the general spirit of the common law, are disposed to construe statutory exceptions to common law principles in a mode which would not commend itself either to a body of officials, or to the Houses of Parliament, if the Houses were called upon to interpret their own enactments. In foreign countries, and especially in France, administrative ideas—notions derived from the traditions of a despotic monarchy—have restricted the authority and to a certain extent influenced the ideas of the judges. In England judicial notions have modified the action and influenced the ideas of the executive government. By every path we come round to the same conclusion, that Parliamentary sovereignty has favoured the rule of law, and that the supremacy of the law of the land both calls forth the exertion of Parliamentary sovereignty, and leads to its being exercised in a spirit of legality.

PART III

THE CONNECTION BETWEEN THE LAW OF THE CONSTITUTION AND THE CONVENTIONS OF THE CONSTITUTION

Chapter XIV

NATURE OF CONVENTIONS OF CONSTITUTION

Questions
remaining
to be
answered.

In an earlier part of this work[1] stress was laid upon the essential distinction between the "law of the constitution," which, consisting (as it does) of rules enforced or recognised by the Courts, makes up a body of "laws" in the proper sense of that term, and the "conventions of the constitution," which consisting (as they do) of customs, practices, maxims, or precepts which are not enforced or recognised by the Courts, make up a body not of laws, but of constitutional or political ethics; and it was further urged that the law, not the morality of the constitution, forms the proper subject of legal study.[2] In accordance with this view, the reader's attention has been hitherto exclusively directed to the meaning and applications of two principles which pervade the law of the constitution, namely, the Sovereignty of Parliament[3] and the Rule of Law.[4]

But a lawyer cannot master even the legal side of the English constitution without paying some attention to the nature of those constitutional understandings which necessarily engross the attention of historians or of statesmen. He ought to ascertain, at any rate, how, if at all, the law of the constitution is connected with the conventions of the constitution; and a lawyer who undertakes this task

---

1 See pp. cxl–cxlvi, *ante.*

2 See pp. cxlv–cxlvi, *ante.*

3 See Part I.

4 See Part II.

will soon find that in so doing he is only following one stage farther the path on which we have already entered, and is on the road to discover the last and most striking instance of that supremacy of the law which gives to the English polity the whole of its peculiar colour.

My aim therefore throughout the remainder of this book is to define, or ascertain, the relation or connection between the legal and the conventional elements in the constitution, and to point out the way in which a just appreciation of this connection throws light upon several subordinate questions or problems of constitutional law.

This end will be attained if an answer is found to each of two questions: What is the nature of the conventions or understandings of the constitution? What is the force or (in the language of jurisprudence) the "sanction" by which is enforced obedience to the conventions of the constitution? These answers will themselves throw light on the subordinate matters to which I have made reference.

Nature of constitutional understandings. The salient characteristics, the outward aspects so to speak, of the understandings which make up the constitutional morality of modern England, can hardly be better described than in the words of Mr. Freeman:

> We now have a whole system of political morality, a whole code of precepts for the guidance of public men, which will not be found in any page of either the statute or the common law, but which are in practice held hardly less sacred than any principle embodied in the Great Charter or in the Petition of Right. In short, by the side of our written Law, there has grown up an unwritten or conventional Constitution. When an Englishman speaks of the conduct of a public man being constitutional or unconstitutional, he means something wholly different from what he means by conduct being legal or illegal. A famous vote of the House of Commons, passed on the motion of a great statesman, once declared that the then Ministers of the Crown did not possess the confidence of the House of Commons, and that their continuance in office was therefore at variance with the spirit of the constitution. The truth of such a position, according to the traditional principles on which public men have acted for some generations, cannot be disputed; but it would be in vain to seek for any trace of such doctrines in any page of our written Law. The proposer of that motion did not mean to charge the existing Ministry with any illegal act, with any act which could be made the subject either of a prosecution in a lower court or of impeachment in the High Court of Parliament itself. He did not mean that they, Ministers of the Crown, appointed during the pleasure of the Crown, committed any

breach of the Law of which the Law could take cognisance, by retaining possession of their offices till such time as the Crown should think good to dismiss them from those offices. What he meant was that the general course of their policy was one which to a majority of the House of Commons did not seem to be wise or beneficial to the nation, and that therefore, according to a conventional code as well understood and as effectual as the written Law itself, they were bound to resign offices of which the House of Commons no longer held them to be worthy.[5]

The one exception which can be taken to this picture of our conventional constitution is the contrast drawn in it between the "written law" and the "unwritten constitution"; the true opposition, as already pointed out, is between laws properly so called, whether written or unwritten, and understandings, or practices, which, though commonly observed, are not laws in any true sense of that word at all. But this inaccuracy is hardly more than verbal, and we may gladly accept Mr. Freeman's words as a starting-point whence to inquire into the nature or common quality of the maxims which make up our body of constitutional morality.

Examples of constitutional understandings.

The following are examples[6] of the precepts to which Mr. Freeman refers, and belong to the code by which public life in England is (or is supposed to be) governed. "A Ministry which is outvoted in the House of Commons is in many cases bound to retire from office." "A Cabinet, when outvoted on any vital question, may appeal once to the country by means of a dissolution." "If an appeal to the electors goes against the Ministry they are bound to retire from office, and have no right to dissolve Parliament a second time." "The Cabinet are responsible to Parliament as a body, for the general conduct of affairs." "They are further responsible to an extent, not however very definitely fixed, for the appointments made by any of their number, or to speak in more accurate language, made by the Crown under the advice of any member of the Cabinet." "The party who for the time being command a majority in the House of Commons, have (in general) a right to have their leaders placed in office." "The most influential of these leaders ought (generally speaking) to be the Premier, or

---

5 Freeman, *Growth of the English Constitution* (1st ed.), pp. 109, 110.

6 See, for further examples, pp. cxlii, cxliii, *ante*.

head of the Cabinet." There are precepts referring to the position and formation of the Cabinet. It is, however, easy to find constitutional maxims dealing with other topics. "Treaties can be made without the necessity for any Act of Parliament; but the Crown, or in reality the Ministry representing the Crown, ought not to make any treaty which will not command the approbation of Parliament." "The foreign policy of the country, the proclamation of war, and the making of peace ought to be left in the hands of the Crown, or in truth of the Crown's servants. But in foreign as in domestic affairs, the wish of the two Houses of Parliament or (when they differ) of the House of Commons ought to be followed." "The action of any Ministry would be highly unconstitutional if it should involve the proclamation of war, or the making of peace, in defiance of the wishes of the House." "If there is a difference of opinion between the House of Lords and the House of Commons, the House of Lords ought, at some point, not definitely fixed, to give way, and should the Peers not yield, and the House of Commons continue to enjoy the confidence of the country, it becomes the duty of the Crown, or of its responsible advisers, to create or to threaten to create enough new Peers to override the opposition of the House of Lords, and thus restore harmony between the two branches of the legislature."[7] "Parliament ought to be summoned for the despatch of business at least once in every year." "If a sudden emergency arise, *e.g.* through the outbreak of an insurrection, or an invasion by a foreign power, the Ministry ought, if they require additional authority, at once to have Parliament convened and obtain any powers which they may need for the protection of the country. Meanwhile Ministers ought to take every step, even at the peril of breaking the law, which is necessary either for restoring order or for repelling attack, and (if the law of the land is violated) must rely for protection on Parliament passing an Act of Indemnity."

Common characteristic of constitutional understandings.

These rules (which I have purposely expressed in a lax and popular manner), and a lot more of the same kind, make up the constitutional morality of the day. They are all constantly acted upon, and, since they cannot be enforced by any Court of law, have no claim to be

---

7 See however Hearn, *Government of England* (2nd ed.), p. 178.

considered laws. They are multifarious, differing, as it might at first sight appear, from each other not only in importance but in general character and scope. They will be found however, on careful examination, to possess one common quality or property; they are all, or at any rate most of them, rules for determining the mode in which the discretionary powers of the Crown (or of the Ministers as servants of the Crown) ought to be exercised; and this characteristic will be found on examination to be the trait common not only to all the rules already enumerated, but to by far the greater part (though not quite to the whole) of the conventions of the constitution. This matter, however, requires for its proper understanding some further explanation.

Constitutional conventions are mainly rules for governing exercise of prerogative.

The discretionary powers of the government mean every kind of action which can legally be taken by the Crown, or by its servants, without the necessity for applying to Parliament for new statutory authority. Thus no statute is required to enable the Crown to dissolve or to convoke Parliament, to make peace or war, to create new Peers, to dismiss a Minister from office or to appoint his successor. The doing of all these things lies legally at any rate within the discretion of the Crown; they belong therefore to the discretionary authority of the government. This authority may no doubt originate in Parliamentary enactments, and, in a limited number of cases, actually does so originate. Thus the Naturalization Act, 1870, gives to a Secretary of State the right under certain circumstances to convert an alien into a naturalized British subject; and the Extradition Act, 1870, enables a Secretary of State (under conditions provided by the Act) to override the ordinary law of the land and hand over a foreigner to his own government for trial. With the exercise, however, of such discretion as is conferred on the Crown or its servants by Parliamentary enactments we need hardly concern ourselves. The mode in which such discretion is to be exercised is, or may be, more or less clearly defined by the Act itself, and is often so closely limited as in reality to become the subject of legal decision, and thus pass from the domain of constitutional morality into that of law properly so called. The discretionary authority of the Crown originates generally, not in Act of Parliament, but in the "prerogative"—a term which has caused more perplexity to students than any other expression referring to the constitution. The "prerogative" appears to be both historically and as a matter of actual fact nothing else than the residue of discretionary or arbitrary authority, which at any given time is legally left in the hands of the Crown. The King was originally in truth what he still is in name, "the sovereign," or, if not strictly the "sovereign" in the sense in which jurists use that word, at any rate by far the most powerful part of the sovereign power. In 1791 the House of Commons compelled the government of the day, a good deal against the will of Ministers, to put on trial Mr. Reeves, the learned author of the *History of English Law,* for the expression of opinions meant to exalt the prerogative of the Crown at the expense of the authority of the House of Commons. Among other statements for the publication of which he was indicted, was a lengthy comparison of the Crown to the trunk, and the other parts of the constitution to the branches and leaves of a great tree. This comparison was made with the object of drawing from it the conclusion that the Crown was the source of all legal power, and that while to destroy the authority of the Crown was to cut down the noble oak under the cover of which Englishmen sought refuge from the storms of Jacobinism, the House of Commons and other institutions were but branches and leaves which might be lopped off without serious damage to the tree.[8] The publication of Mr. Reeves's theories during a period of popular excitement may have been injudicious. But a jury, one is happy to know, found that it was not seditious; for his views undoubtedly rested on a sound basis of historical fact.

The power of the Crown was in truth anterior to that of the House of Commons. From the time of the Norman Conquest down to the Revolution of 1688, the Crown possessed in reality many of the attributes of sovereignty. The prerogative is the name for the remaining portion of the Crown's original authority, and is therefore, as already pointed out, the name for the residue of discretionary power left at any moment in the hands of the Crown, whether such power be in fact exercised by the King himself or by his Ministers. Every act which

---

8 See 26 St. Tr. 530–534.

the executive government can lawfully do without the authority of
the Act of Parliament is done in virtue of this prerogative. If therefore
we omit from view (as we conveniently may do) powers conferred on
the Crown or its servants by Parliamentary enactments, as for example under an Alien Act, we may use the term "prerogative" as equivalent to the discretionary authority of the executive, and then lay
down that the conventions of the constitution are in the main precepts for determining the mode and spirit in which the prerogative is
to be exercised, or (what is really the same thing) for fixing the manner in which any transaction which can legally be done in virtue
of the Royal prerogative (such as the making of war or the declaration
of peace) ought to be carried out. This statement holds good, it
should be noted, of all the discretionary powers exercised by the
executive, otherwise than under statutory authority; it applies to acts
really done by the King himself in accordance with his personal
wishes, to transactions (which are of more frequent occurrence than
modern constitutionalists are disposed to admit) in which both the
King and his Ministers take a real part, and also to that large and
constantly increasing number of proceedings which, though carried
out in the King's name, are in truth wholly the acts of the Ministry.
The conventions of the constitution are in short rules intended to
regulate the exercise of the whole of the remaining discretionary
powers of the Crown, whether these powers are exercised by the
King himself or by the Ministry. That this is so may be seen by the
ease and the technical correctness with which such conventions may
be expressed in the form of regulations in reference to the exercise of
the prerogative. Thus, to say that a Cabinet when outvoted on any
vital question are bound in general to retire from office, is equivalent
to the assertion, that the prerogative of the Crown to dismiss its
servants at the will of the King must be exercised in accordance with
the wish of the Houses of Parliament; the statement that Ministers
ought not to make any treaty which will not command the approbation of the Houses of Parliament, means that the prerogative of the
Crown in regard to the making of treaties—what the Americans call
the "treaty-making power"—ought not to be exercised in opposition
to the will of Parliament. So, again, the rule that Parliament must

meet at least once a year, is in fact the rule that the Crown's legal right or prerogative to call Parliament together at the King's pleasure must be so exercised that Parliament meet once a year.

Some constitutional conventions refer to exercise of Parliamentary privilege.
This analysis of constitutional understandings is open to the one valid criticism, that, though true as far as it goes, it is obviously incomplete; for there are some few constitutional customs or habits which have no reference to the exercise of the royal power. Such, for example, is the understanding—a very vague one at best—that in case of a permanent conflict between the will of the House of Commons and the will of the House of Lords the Peers must at some point give way to the Lower House. Such, again, is, or at any rate was, the practice by which the judicial functions of the House of Lords are discharged solely by the Law Lords, or the understanding under which Divorce Acts were treated as judicial and not as legislative proceedings. Habits such as these are at bottom customs or rules meant to determine the mode in which one or other or both of the Houses of Parliament shall exercise their discretionary powers, or, to use the historical term, their "privileges." The very use of the word "privilege" is almost enough to show us how to embrace all the conventions of the constitution under one general head. Between "prerogative" and "privilege" there exists a close analogy: the one is the historical name for the discretionary authority of the Crown; the other is the historical name for the discretionary authority of each House of Parliament. Understandings then which regulate the exercise of the prerogative determine, or are meant to determine, the way in which one member of the sovereign body, namely the Crown, should exercise its discretionary authority; understandings which regulate the exercise of privilege determine, or are meant to determine, the way in which the other members of the sovereign body should each exercise their discretionary authority. The result follows, that the conventions of the constitution, looked at as a whole, are customs, or understandings, as to the mode in which the several members of the sovereign legislative body, which, as it will be remembered, is the "King in Parliament,"[9] should each exercise their

---

9 See p. 3, *ante.*

discretionary authority, whether it be termed the prerogative of the Crown or the privileges of Parliament. Since, however, by far the most numerous and important of our constitutional understandings refer at bottom to the exercise of the prerogative, it will conduce to brevity and clearness if we treat the conventions of the constitution, as rules or customs determining the mode in which the discretionary power of the executive, or in technical language the prerogative, ought (*i.e.* is expected by the nation) to be employed.

Aim of constitutional understandings. Having ascertained that the conventions of the constitution are (in the main) rules for determining the exercise of the prerogative, we may carry our analysis of their character a step farther. They have all one ultimate object. Their end is to secure that Parliament, or the Cabinet which is indirectly appointed by Parliament, shall in the long run give effect to the will of that power which in modern England is the true political sovereign of the State—the majority of the electors or (to use popular though not quite accurate language) the nation.

At this point comes into view the full importance of the distinction already insisted upon[10] between "legal" sovereignty and "political" sovereignty. Parliament is, from a merely legal point of view, the absolute sovereign of the British Empire, since every Act of Parliament is binding on every Court throughout the British dominions, and no rule, whether of morality or of law, which contravenes an Act of Parliament binds any Court throughout the realm. But if Parliament be in the eye of the law a supreme legislature, the essence of representative government is, that the legislature should represent or give effect to the will of the political sovereign, *i.e.* of the electoral body, or of the nation. That the conduct of the different parts of the legislature should be determined by rules meant to secure harmony between the action of the legislative sovereign and the wishes of the political sovereign, must appear probable from general considerations. If the true ruler or political sovereign of England were, as was once the case, the King, legislation might be carried out in accordance with the King's will by one of two methods. The Crown might itself legislate, by royal proclamations, or decrees; or some other body,

---

10 See pp. 26–29, *ante.*

such as a Council of State or Parliament itself, might be allowed to legislate as long as this body conformed to the will of the Crown. If the first plan were adopted, there would be no room or need for constitutional conventions. If the second plan were adopted, the proceedings of the legislative body must inevitably be governed by some rules meant to make certain that the Acts of the legislature should not contravene the will of the Crown. The electorate is in fact the sovereign of England. It is a body which does not, and from its nature hardly can, itself legislate, and which, owing chiefly to historical causes, has left in existence a theoretically supreme legislature. The result of this state of things would naturally be that the conduct of the legislature, which (*ex hypothesi*) cannot be governed by laws, should be regulated by understandings of which the object is to secure the conformity of Parliament to the will of the nation. And this is what has actually occurred. The conventions of the constitution now consist of customs which (whatever their historical origin) are at the present day maintained for the sake of ensuring the supremacy of the House of Commons, and ultimately, through the elective House of Commons, of the nation. Our modern code of constitutional morality secures, though in a roundabout way, what is called abroad the "sovereignty of the people."

That this is so becomes apparent if we examine into the effect of one or two among the leading articles of this code. The rule that the powers of the Crown must be exercised through Ministers who are members of one or other House of Parliament and who "command the confidence of the House of Commons," really means, that the elective portion of the legislature in effect, though by an indirect process, appoints the executive government; and, further, that the Crown, or the Ministry, must ultimately carry out, or at any rate not contravene, the wishes of the House of Commons. But as the process of representation is nothing else than a mode by which the will of the representative body or House of Commons is made to coincide with the will of the nation, it follows that a rule which gives the appointment and control of the government mainly to the House of Commons is at bottom a rule which gives the election and ultimate control of the executive to the nation. The same thing holds good of the understanding, or habit, in accordance with which the House of Lords are expected in every serious political controversy to give way at some point or other to the will of the House of Commons as expressing the deliberate resolve of the nation, or of that further custom which, though of comparatively recent growth, forms an essential article of modern constitutional ethics, by which, in case the Peers should finally refuse to acquiesce in the decision of the Lower House, the Crown is expected to nullify the resistance of the Lords by the creation of new Peerages.[11] How, it may be said, is the "point" to be fixed at which, in case of a conflict between the two Houses, the Lords must give way, or the Crown ought to use its prerogative in the creation of new Peers? The question is worth raising, because the answer throws great light upon the nature and aim of the articles which make up our conventional code. This reply is, that the point at which the Lords must yield or the Crown intervene is properly determined by anything which conclusively shows that the House of Commons represents on the matter in dispute the deliberate decision of the nation. The truth of this reply will hardly be questioned, but to admit that the deliberate decision of the electorate is decisive, is in fact to concede that the understandings as to the action of the House of Lords and of the Crown are, what we have found them to be, rules meant to ensure the ultimate supremacy of the true political sovereign, or, in other words, of the electoral body.[12]

Rules as to dissolution of Parliament. By far the most striking example of the real sense attaching to a whole mass of constitutional conventions is found in a particular instance, which appears at first sight to present a marked exception to the general principles of constitutional morality. A Ministry placed in a minority by a vote of the Commons have, in accordance with received doctrines, a right to demand a dissolution of Parliament. On the other hand, there are certainly combinations of circumstances under which the Crown has a right to dismiss a Ministry who command a Parliamentary majority, and to dissolve the Parliament by which the Ministry are supported. The prerogative, in short, of dis-

---

11 Mr. Hearn denies, as it seems to me on inadequate grounds, the existence of this rule or understanding. See Hearn, *Government of England* (2nd ed.), p. 178.

12 Compare Bagehot, *English Constitution*, pp. 25–27.

solution may constitutionally be so employed as to override the will of the representative body, or, as it is popularly called, "The People's House of Parliament." This looks at first sight like saying that in certain cases the prerogative can be so used as to set at nought the will of the nation. But in reality it is far otherwise. The discretionary power of the Crown occasionally may be, and according to constitutional precedents sometimes ought to be, used to strip an existing House of Commons of its authority. But the reason why the House can in accordance with the constitution be deprived of power and of existence is that an occasion has arisen on which there is fair reason to suppose that the opinion of the House is not the opinion of the electors. A dissolution is in its essence an appeal from the legal to the political sovereign. A dissolution is allowable, or necessary, whenever the wishes of the legislature are, or may fairly be presumed to be, different from the wishes of the nation.

The dissolutions of 1784 and 1834.

This is the doctrine established by the celebrated contests of 1784 and of 1834. In each instance the King dismissed a Ministry which commanded the confidence of the House of Commons. In each case there was an appeal to the country by means of a dissolution. In 1784 the appeal resulted in a decisive verdict in favour of Pitt and his colleagues, who had been brought into office by the King against the will of the House of Commons. In 1834 the appeal led to a verdict equally decisive against Peel and Wellington, who also had been called to office by the Crown against the wishes of the House. The essential point to notice is that these contests each in effect admit the principle that it is the verdict of the political sovereign which ultimately determines the right or (what in politics is much the same thing) the power of a Cabinet to retain office, namely, the nation.

Much discussion, oratorical and literary, has been expended on the question whether the dissolution of 1784 or the dissolution of 1834 was constitutional.[13] To a certain extent the dispute is verbal, and depends upon the meaning of the word "constitutional." If we mean by it "legal," no human being can dispute that George the Third and his son could without any breach of law dissolve Parliament. If we

---

13 See Appendix, Note VII., The Meaning of an Unconstitutional Law.

mean "usual," no one can deny that each monarch took a very un-usual step in dismissing a Ministry which commanded a majority in the House of Commons. If by "constitutional" we mean "in conform-ity with the fundamental principles of the constitution," we must without hesitation pronounce the conduct of George the Third con-stitutional, *i.e.* in conformity with the principles of the constitution as they are now understood. He believed that the nation did not ap-prove of the policy pursued by the House of Commons. He was right in this belief. No modern constitutionalist will dispute that the au-thority of the House of Commons is derived from its representing the will of the nation, and that the chief object of a dissolution is to ascertain that the will of Parliament coincides with the will of the nation. George the Third then made use of the prerogative of dissolu-tion for the very purpose for which it exists. His conduct, therefore, on the modern theory of the constitution, was, as far as the dissolu-tion went, in the strictest sense constitutional. But it is doubtful whether in 1784 the King's conduct was not in reality an innovation, though a salutary one, on the then prevailing doctrine. Any one who studies the questions connected with the name of John Wilkes, or the disputes between England and the American colonies, will see that George the Third and the great majority of George the Third's states-men maintained up to 1784 a view of Parliamentary sovereignty which made Parliament in the strictest sense the sovereign power. To this theory Fox clung, both in his youth as a Tory and in his later life as a Whig. The greatness of Chatham and of his son lay in their perceiving that behind the Crown, behind the Revolution Families, behind Parliament itself, lay what Chatham calls the "great public," and what we should call the nation, and that on the will of the nation depended the authority of Parliament. In 1784 George the Third was led by the exigencies of the moment to adopt the attitude of Chatham and Pitt. He appealed (oddly enough) from the sovereignty of Par-liament, of which he had always been the ardent champion, to that sovereignty of the people which he never ceased to hold in abhor-rence. Whether this appeal be termed constitutional or revolutionary is now of little moment; it affirmed decisively the fundamental prin-ciple of our existing constitution that not Parliament but the nation is, politically speaking, the supreme power in the State. On this very ground the so-called "penal" dissolution was consistently enough denounced by Burke, who at all periods of his career was opposed to democratic innovation, and far less consistently by Fox, who blended in his political creed doctrines of absolute Parliamentary sovereignty with the essentially inconsistent dogma of the sovereignty of the people.

Of William the Fourth's action it is hard to speak with decision. The dissolution of 1834 was, from a constitutional point of view, a mistake; it was justified (if at all) by the King's belief that the House of Commons did not represent the will of the nation. The belief itself turned out erroneous, but the large minority obtained by Peel, and the rapid decline in the influence of the Whigs, proved that, though the King had formed a wrong estimate of public sentiment, he was not without reasonable ground for believing that Parliament had ceased to represent the opinion of the nation. Now if it be constitutionally right for the Crown to appeal from Parliament to the electors when the House of Commons has in reality ceased to represent its constituents, there is great difficulty in maintaining that a dissolution is unconstitutional simply because the electors do, when appealed to, support the opinions of their representatives. Admit that the electors are the political sovereign of the State, and the result appears naturally to follow, that an appeal to them by means of a dissolution is constitutional, whenever there is valid and reasonable ground for supposing that their Parliamentary representatives have ceased to represent their wishes. The constitutionality therefore of the dissolution in 1834 turns at bottom upon the still disputable question of fact, whether the King and his advisers had reasonable ground for supposing that the reformed House of Commons had lost the confidence of the nation. Whatever may be the answer given by historians to this inquiry, the precedents of 1784 and 1834 are decisive; they determine the principle on which the prerogative of dissolution ought to be exercised, and show that in modern times the rules as to the dissolution of Parliament are, like other conventions of the constitution, intended to secure the ultimate supremacy of the electorate as the true political sovereign of the State; that, in short, the validity of constitutional maxims is subordinate and subservient to the fundamental principle of popular sovereignty.

Relation of right of dissolution to Parliamentary sovereignty. The necessity for dissolutions stands in close connection with the existence of Parliamentary sovereignty. Where, as in the United States, no legislative assembly is a sovereign power, the right of dissolution may be dispensed with; the constitution provides security that no change of vital importance can be effected without an appeal to the people; and the change in the character of a legislative body by the re-election of the whole or of part thereof at stated periods makes it certain that in the long run the sentiment of the legislature will harmonise with the feeling of the public. Where Parliament is supreme, some further security for such harmony is necessary, and this security is given by the right of dissolution, which enables the Crown or the Ministry to appeal from the legislature to the nation. The security indeed is not absolutely complete. Crown, Cabinet, and Parliament may conceivably favour constitutional innovations which do not approve themselves to the electors. The Septennial Act could hardly have been passed in England, the Act of Union with Ireland would not, it is often asserted, have been passed by the Irish Parliament, if, in either instance, a legal revolution had been necessarily preceded by an appeal to the electorate. Here, as elsewhere, the constitutionalism of America proves of a more rigid type than the constitutionalism of England. Still, under the conditions of modern political life, the understandings which exist with us as to the right of dissolution afford nearly, if not quite, as much security for sympathy between the action of the legislature and the will of the people, as do the limitations placed on legislative power by the constitutions of American States. In this instance, as in others, the principles explicitly stated in the various constitutions of the States, and in the Federal Constitution itself, are impliedly involved in the working of English political institutions. The right of dissolution is the right of appeal to the people, and thus underlies all those constitutional conventions which, in one way or another, are intended to produce harmony between the legal and the political sovereign power.

Chapter XV

THE SANCTION BY WHICH THE CONVENTIONS OF THE CONSTITUTION ARE ENFORCED

What is the sanction by which obedience to the conventions of the constitution is at bottom enforced?

This is by far the most perplexing of the speculative questions suggested by a study of constitutional law. Let us bear in mind the dictum of Paley, that it is often far harder to make men see the existence of a difficulty, than to make them, when once the difficulty is perceived, understand its explanation, and in the first place try to make clear to ourselves what is the precise nature of a puzzle of which most students dimly recognise the existence.

Constitutional understandings are admittedly not laws; they are not (that is to say) rules which will be enforced by the Courts. If a Premier were to retain office after a vote of censure passed by the House of Commons, if he were (as did Lord Palmerston under like circumstances) to dissolve, or strictly speaking to get the Crown to dissolve, Parliament, but, unlike Lord Palmerston, were to be again censured by the newly elected House of Commons, and then, after all this had taken place, were still to remain at the head of the government,—no one could deny that such a Prime Minister had acted unconstitutionally. Yet no Court of law would take notice of his conduct. Suppose, again, that on the passing by both Houses of an important bill, the King should refuse his assent to the measure, or (in popular language) put his "veto" on it. Here there would be a gross violation of usage, but the matter could not by any proceeding known to English law be brought before the judges. Take another instance. Suppose that Parliament were for more than a year not summoned for the despatch of business. This would be a course of proceeding of the most unconstitutional character. Yet there is no Court in the land before which one could go with the complaint that Parliament had not been assembled.[1] Still the conventional rules of the constitution, though not laws, are, as it is constantly asserted, nearly if not quite as binding as laws. They are, or appear to be, respected quite as much as most statutory enactments, and more than many. The puzzle is to see what is the force which habitually compels obedience to rules which have not behind them the coercive power of the Courts.

Partial answer, that constitutional understandings often disobeyed.

The difficulty of the problem before us cannot indeed be got rid of, but may be shifted and a good deal lessened, by observing that the invariableness of the obedience to constitutional understandings is itself more or less fictitious. The special articles of the conventional code are in fact often disobeyed. A Minister sometimes refuses to retire when, as his opponents allege, he ought constitutionally to resign office; not many years have passed since the Opposition of the day argued, if not convincingly yet with a good deal of plausibility, that the Ministry had violated a rule embodied in the Bill of Rights; in 1784 the House of Commons maintained, not only by argument but by repeated votes, that Pitt had deliberately defied more than one constitutional precept, and the Whigs of 1834 brought a like charge against Wellington and Peel. Nor is it doubtful that any one who searches through the pages of Hansard will find other instances in which constitutional maxims of long standing and high repute have been set at nought. The uncertain character of the deference paid to the conventions of the constitution is concealed under the current phraseology, which treats the successful violation of a constitutional rule as a proof that the maxim was not in reality part of the constitution. If a habit or precept which can be set at nought is thereby shown

---

1 See 4 Edward III. c. 14; 16 Car. II. c. 1; and 1 Will. & Mary, Sess. 2, c. 2. Compare these with the repealed 16 Car. I. c. 1, which would have made the assembling of Parliament a matter of law.

not to be a portion of constitutional morality, it naturally follows that no true constitutional rule is ever disobeyed.

But princi-
ple of con-
formity to
will of the
nation al-
ways
obeyed.

Yet, though the obedience supposed to be rendered to the separate understandings or maxims of public life is to a certain extent fictitious, the assertion that they have nearly the force of law is not without meaning. Some few of the conventions of the constitution are rigorously obeyed. Parliament, for example, is summoned year by year with as much regularity as though its annual meeting were provided for by a law of nature; and (what is of more consequence) though particular understandings are of uncertain obligation, neither the Crown nor any servant of the Crown ever refuses obedience to the grand principle which, as we have seen, underlies all the conventional precepts of the constitution, namely, that government must be carried on in accordance with the will of the House of Commons, and ultimately with the will of the nation as expressed through that House. This principle is not a law; it is not to be found in the statute-book, nor is it a maxim of the common law; it will not be enforced by any ordinary judicial body. Why then has the principle itself, as also have certain conventions or understandings which are closely connected with it, the force of law? This, when the matter is reduced to its simplest form, is the puzzle with which we have to deal. It sorely needs a solution. Many writers, however, of authority, chiefly because they do not approach the constitution from its legal side, hardly recognise the full force of the difficulty which requires to be disposed of. They either pass it by, or else apparently acquiesce in one of two answers, each of which contains an element of truth, but neither of which fully removes the perplexities of any inquirer who is determined not to be put off with mere words.

A reply more often suggested than formulated in so many words, is that obedience to the conventions of the constitution is ultimately enforced by the fear of impeachment.

If this view were tenable, these conventions, it should be remarked, would not be "understandings" at all, but "laws" in the truest sense of that term, and their sole peculiarity would lie in their being laws the breach of which could be punished only by one extraordinary tribunal, namely, the High Court of Parliament.

But though it may well be conceded—and the fact is one of great importance—that the habit of obedience to the constitution was originally generated and confirmed by impeachments, yet there are insuperable difficulties to entertaining the belief that the dread of the Tower and the block exerts any appreciable influence over the conduct of modern statesmen. No impeachment for violations of the constitution (since for the present purpose we may leave out of account such proceedings as those taken against Lord Macclesfield, Warren Hastings, and Lord Melville) has occurred for more than a century and a half. The process, which is supposed to ensure the retirement from office of a modern Prime Minister, when placed in a hopeless minority, is, and has long been, obsolete. The arm by which attacks on freedom were once repelled has grown rusty by disuse; it is laid aside among the antiquities of the constitution, nor will it ever, we may anticipate, be drawn again from its scabbard. For, in truth, impeachment, as a means for enforcing the observance of constitutional morality, always laboured under one grave defect. The possibility of its use suggested, if it did not stimulate, one most important violation of political usage; a Minister who dreaded impeachment would, since Parliament was the only Court before which he could be impeached, naturally advise the Crown not to convene Parliament. There is something like a contradiction in terms in saying that a Minister is compelled to advise the meeting of Parliament by the dread of impeachment if Parliament should assemble. If the fear of Parliamentary punishment were the only difficulty in the way of violating the constitution, we may be sure that a bold party leader would, at the present day, as has been done in former centuries, sometimes suggest that Parliament should not meet.

Power of public opinion.   A second and current answer to the question under consideration is, that obedience to the conventional precepts of the constitution is ensured by the force of public opinion.

Now that this assertion is in one sense true, stands past dispute. The nation expects that Parliament shall be convened annually; the nation expects that a Minister who cannot retain the confidence of the House of Commons, shall give up his place, and no Premier even dreams of disappointing these expectations. The assertion, therefore, that public opinion gives validity to the received precepts for the conduct of public life is true. Its defect is that, if taken without further explanation, it amounts to little else than a re-statement of the very problem which it is meant to solve. For the question to be answered is, at bottom, Why is it that public opinion is, apparently at least, a sufficient sanction to compel obedience to the conventions of the constitution? and it is no answer to this inquiry to say that these conventions are enforced by public opinion. Let it also be noted that many rules of conduct which are fully supported by the opinion of the public are violated every day of the year. Public opinion enjoins the performance of promises and condemns the commission of crimes, but the settled conviction of the nation that promises ought to be kept does not hinder merchants from going into the *Gazette,* nor does the universal execration of the villain who sheds man's blood prevent the commission of murders. That public opinion does to a certain extent check extravagance and criminality is of course true, but the operation of opinion is in this case assisted by the law, or in the last resort by the physical power at the disposal of the state. The limited effect of public opinion when aided by the police hardly explains the immense effect of opinion in enforcing rules which may be violated without any risk of the offender being brought before the Courts. To contend that the understandings of the constitution derive their coercive power solely from the approval of the public, is very like maintaining the kindred doctrine that the conventions of international law are kept alive solely by moral force. Every one, except a few dreamers, perceives that the respect paid to international morality is due in great measure, not to moral force, but to the physical force in the shape of armies and navies, by which the commands of general opinion are in many cases supported; and it is difficult not to suspect that, in England at least, the conventions of the constitution are supported and enforced by something beyond or in addition to the public approval.

True answer,— Obedience to conventions enforced by power of law.

What then is this "something"? My answer is, that it is nothing else than the force of the law. The dread of impeachment may have established, and public opinion certainly adds influence to, the prevailing dogmas of political ethics. But the sanction which constrains the boldest political adventurer to obey the fundamental principles of the constitution and the conventions in which these principles are expressed, is in fact that the breach of these principles and of these conventions will almost immediately bring the offender into conflict with the Courts and the law of the land.

This is the true answer to the inquiry which I have raised, but it is an answer which undoubtedly requires both explanation and defence.

Explana-
tion.
The meaning of the statement that the received precepts of the constitution are supported by the law of the land, and the grounds on which that statement is based, can be most easily made apparent by considering what would be the legal results which would inevitably ensue from the violation of some indisputable constitutional maxim.

Yearly
meeting of
Parliament.
No rule is better established than that Parliament must assemble at least once a year. This maxim, as before pointed out, is certainly not derived from the common law, and is not based upon any statutory enactment. Now suppose that Parliament were prorogued once and again for more than a year, so that for two years no Parliament sat at Westminster. Here we have a distinct breach of a constitutional practice or understanding, but we have no violation of law. What, however, would be the consequences which would ensue? They would be, speaking generally, that any Ministry who at the present day sanctioned or tolerated this violation of the constitution, and every person connected with the government, would immediately come into conflict with the law of the land.

A moment's reflection shows that this would be so. The Army (Annual) Act would in the first place expire. Hence the Army Act, on which the discipline of the army depends, would cease to be in force.[2] But thereupon all means of controlling the army without a breach of law would cease to exist. Either the army must be discharged, in which case the means of maintaining law and order would come to an end, or the army must be kept up and discipline must be maintained without legal authority for its maintenance. If

---

2 In popular, though inaccurate language, "the Mutiny Act would expire." See note 26, p. 198, *ante.*

this alternative were adopted, every person, from the Commander-in-Chief downwards, who took part in the control of the army, and indeed every soldier who carried out the commands of his superiors, would find that not a day passed without his committing or sanctioning acts which would render him liable to stand as a criminal in the dock. Then, again, though most of the taxes would still come into the Exchequer, large portions of the revenue would cease to be legally due and could not be legally collected, whilst every official, who acted as collector, would expose himself to actions or prosecutions. The part, moreover, of the revenue which came in, could not be legally applied to the purposes of the government. If the Ministry laid hold of the revenue they would find it difficult to avoid breaches of definite laws which would compel them to appear before the Courts. Suppose however that the Cabinet were willing to defy the law. Their criminal daring would not suffice for its purpose; they could not get hold of the revenue without the connivance or aid of a large number of persons, some of them indeed officials, but some of them, such as the Comptroller General, the Governors of the Bank of England, and the like, unconnected with the administration. None of these officials, it should be noted, could receive from the government or the Crown any protection against legal liability; and any person, *e.g.* the Commander-in-Chief, or the colonel of a regiment, who employed force to carry out the policy of the government would be exposed to resistance supported by the Courts. For the law (it should always be borne in mind) operates in two different ways. It inflicts penalties and punishment upon law-breakers, and (what is of equal consequence) it enables law-respecting citizens to refuse obedience to illegal commands. It legalises passive resistance. The efficacy of such legal opposition is immensely increased by the non-existence in England of anything resembling the *droit administratif* of France,[3] or of that wide discretionary authority which is possessed by every continental government. The result is, that an administration which attempted to dispense with the annual meeting of Parliament could not ensure the obedience even of its own officials, and, unless prepared distinctly to

---

3 See chap. xii., *ante.*

violate the undoubted law of the land, would find itself not only opposed but helpless.

The rule, therefore, that Parliament must meet once a year, though in strictness a constitutional convention which is not a law and will not be enforced by the Courts, turns out nevertheless to be an understanding which cannot be neglected without involving hundreds of persons, many of whom are by no means specially amenable to government influence, in distinct acts of illegality cognisable by the tribunals of the country. This convention therefore of the constitution is in reality based upon, and secured by, the law of the land.

This no doubt is a particularly plain case. I have examined it fully, both because it is a particularly plain instance, and because the full understanding of it affords the clue which guides us to the principle on which really rests such coercive force as is possessed by the conventions of the constitution.

Resignation of Ministry which has lost confidence of the House of Commons.

To see that this is so let us consider for a moment the effect of disobedience by the government to one of the most purely conventional among the maxims of constitutional morality,—the rule, that is to say, that a Ministry ought to retire on a vote that they no longer possess the confidence of the House of Commons. Suppose that a Ministry, after the passing of such a vote, were to act at the present day as Pitt acted in 1783, and hold office in the face of the censure passed by the House. There would clearly be a *primâ facie* breach of constitutional ethics. What must ensue is clear. If the Ministry wished to keep within the constitution they would announce their intention of appealing to the constituencies, and the House would probably assist in hurrying on a dissolution. All breach of law would be avoided, but the reason of this would be that the conduct of the Cabinet would not be a breach of constitutional morality; for the true rule of the constitution admittedly is, not that a Ministry cannot keep office when censured by the House of Commons, but that under such circumstances a Ministry ought not to remain in office unless they can by an appeal to the country obtain the election of a House which will support the government. Suppose then that, under the circumstances I have imagined, the Ministry either would not recommend a dissolution of Parliament, or, having dissolved Parliament and being again censured by the newly elected House of Commons, would not resign office. It would, under this state of things, be as clear as day that the understandings of the constitution had been violated. It is however equally clear that the House would have in their own hands the means of ultimately forcing the Ministry either to respect the constitution or to violate the law. Sooner or later the moment would come for passing the Army (Annual) Act or the Appropriation Act, and the House by refusing to pass either of these enactments would involve the Ministry in all the inextricable embarrassments which (as I have already pointed out) immediately follow upon the omission to convene Parliament for more than a year. The breach, therefore, of a purely conventional rule, of a maxim utterly unknown and indeed opposed to the theory of English law, ultimately entails upon those who break it direct conflict with the undoubted law of the land. We have then a right to assert that the force which in the last resort compels obedience to constitutional morality is nothing else than the power of the law itself. The conventions of the constitution are not laws, but, in so far as they really possess binding force, derive their sanction from the fact that whoever breaks them must finally break the law and incur the penalties of a law-breaker.

Objections.   It is worth while to consider one or two objections which may be urged with more or less plausibility against the doctrine that the obligatory force of constitutional morality is derived from the law itself.

Law may be over-powered by force.   The government, it is sometimes suggested, may by the use of actual force carry through a *coup d'état* and defy the law of the land.

This suggestion is true, but is quite irrelevant. No constitution can be absolutely safe from revolution or from a *coup d'état;* but to show that the laws may be defied by violence does not touch or invalidate the statement that the understandings of the constitution are based upon the law. They have certainly no more force than the law itself. A Minister who, like the French President in 1851, could override the law could of course overthrow the constitution. The theory pro-pounded aims only at proving that when constitutional understand-ings have nearly the force of law they derive their power from the fact that they cannot be broken without a breach of law. No one is concerned to show, what indeed never can be shown, that the law can never be defied, or the constitution never be overthrown.

It should further be observed that the admitted sovereignty of Parliament tends to prevent violent attacks on the constitution. Revolutionists or conspirators generally believe themselves to be supported by the majority of the nation, and, when they succeed, this belief is in general well founded. But in modern England, a party, however violent, who count on the sympathy of the people, can accomplish by obtaining a Parliamentary majority all that could be gained by the success of a revolution. When a spirit of reaction or of innovation prevails throughout the country, a reactionary or revolutionary policy is enforced by Parliament without any party needing to make use of violence. The oppressive legislation of the Restoration in the seventeenth century, and the anti-revolutionary legislation of the Tories from the outbreak of the Revolution till the end of George the Third's reign, saved the constitution from attack. A change of spirit averted a change of form; the flexibility of the constitution proved its strength.

Parliament has never refused to pass Mutiny Act.

If the maintenance of political morality, it may with some plausibility be asked, really depends on the right of Parliament to refuse to pass laws such as the Army (Annual) Act, which are necessary for the maintenance of order, and indeed for the very existence of society, how does it happen that no English Parliament has ever employed this extreme method of enforcing obedience to the constitution?

The true answer to the objection thus raised appears to be that the observance of the main and the most essential of all constitutional rules, the rule, that is to say, requiring the annual meeting of Parliament, is ensured, without any necessity for Parliamentary action, by the temporary character of the Mutiny Act, and that the power of Parliament to compel obedience to its wishes by refusing to pass the Act is so complete that the mere existence of the power has made its use unnecessary. In matter of fact, no Ministry has since the Revolution of 1689 ever defied the House of Commons, unless the Cabinet could confide in the support of the country, or, in other words, could count on the election of a House which would support the policy of the government. To this we must add, that in the rare instances in which a Minister has defied the House, the refusal to pass the Mutiny Act has been threatened or contemplated. Pitt's victory over the Coalition is constantly cited as a proof that Parliament cannot refuse to grant supplies or to pass an Act necessary for the discipline of the army. Yet any one who studies with care the great "Case of the Coalition" will see that it does not support the dogma for which it is quoted. Fox and his friends did threaten and did intend to press to the very utmost all the legal powers of the House of Commons. They failed to carry out their intention solely because they at last perceived that the majority of the House did not represent the will of the country. What the "leading case" shows is, that the Cabinet, when supported by the Crown, and therefore possessing the power of dissolution, can defy the will of a House of Commons if the House is not supported by the electors. Here we come round to the fundamental dogma of modern constitutionalism; the legal sovereignty of Parliament is subordinate to the political sovereignty of the nation. This the conclusion in reality established by the events of 1784. Pitt overrode the customs, because he adhered to the principles, of the constitution. He broke through the received constitutional understandings without damage to his power or reputation; he might in all probability have in case of necessity broken the law itself with impunity. For had the Coalition pressed their legal rights to an extreme length, the new Parliament of 1784 would in all likelihood have passed an Act of Indemnity for illegalities necessitated, or excused, by the attempt of an unpopular faction to drive from power a Minister supported by the Crown, by the Peers, and by the nation. However this may be, the celebrated conflict between Pitt and Fox lends no countenance to the idea that a House of Commons supported by the country would not enforce the morality of the constitution by placing before any Minister who defied its precepts the alternative of resignation or revolution.[4]

---

4 It is further not the case that the idea of refusing supplies is unknown to modern statesmen. In 1868 such refusal was threatened in order to force an early dissolution of Parliament; in 1886 the dissolution took place before the supplies were fully granted, and the supplies granted were granted for only a limited period.

Subordinate inquiries.

A clear perception of the true relation between the conventions of the constitution and the law of the land supplies an answer to more than one subordinate question which has perplexed students and commentators.

Why has impeachment gone out of use?

How is it that the ancient methods of enforcing Parliamentary authority, such as impeachment, the formal refusal of supplies, and the like, have fallen into disuse?

The answer is, that they are disused because ultimate obedience to the underlying principle of all modern constitutionalism, which is nothing else than the principle of obedience to the will of the nation as expressed through Parliament, is so closely bound up with the law of the land that it can hardly be violated without a breach of the ordinary law. Hence the extraordinary remedies, which were once necessary for enforcing the deliberate will of the nation, having become unnecessary, have fallen into desuetude. If they are not altogether abolished, the cause lies partly in the conservatism of the English people, and partly in the valid consideration that crimes may still be occasionally committed for which the ordinary law of the land hardly affords due punishment, and which therefore may well be dealt with by the High Court of Parliament.

Why are constitutional understandings variable?

Why is it that the understandings of the constitution have about them a singular element of vagueness and variability?

Why is it, to take definite instances of this uncertainty and changeableness, that no one can define with absolute precision the circumstances under which a Prime Minister ought to retire from office? Why is it that no one can fix the exact point at which resistance of the House of Lords to the will of the House of Commons becomes unconstitutional? and how does it happen that the Peers could at one time arrest legislation in a way which now would be generally held to involve a distinct breach of constitutional morality? What is the reason why no one can describe with precision the limits to the influence on the conduct of public affairs which may rightly be exerted by the reigning monarch? and how does it happen that George the Third and even George the Fourth each made his personal will or caprice tell on the policy of the nation in a very different way and degree from that in which Queen Victoria ever attempted to exercise personal influence over matters of State?

The answer in general terms to these and the like inquiries is, that the one essential principle of the constitution is obedience by all persons to the deliberately expressed will of the House of Commons in the first instance, and ultimately to the will of the nation as expressed through Parliament. The conventional code of political morality is, as already pointed out, merely a body of maxims meant to secure respect for this principle. Of these maxims some indeed—such, for example, as the rule that Parliament must be convoked at least once a year—are so closely connected with the respect due to Parliamentary or national authority, that they will never be neglected by any one who is not prepared to play the part of a revolutionist; such rules have received the undoubted stamp of national approval, and their observance is secured by the fact that whoever breaks or aids in breaking them will almost immediately find himself involved in a breach of law. Other constitutional maxims stand in a very different position. Their maintenance up to a certain point tends to secure the supremacy of Parliament, but they are themselves vague, and no one can say to what extent the will of Parliament or the nation requires their rigid observance; they therefore obtain only a varying and indefinite amount of obedience.

Withdrawal of confidence by House of Commons.

Thus the rule that a Ministry who have lost the confidence of the House of Commons should retire from office is plain enough, and any permanent neglect of the spirit of this rule would be absolutely inconsistent with Parliamentary government, and would finally involve the Minister who broke the rule in acts of undoubted illegality. But when you come to inquire what are the signs by which you are to know that the House has withdrawn its confidence from a Ministry,—whether, for example, the defeat of an important Ministerial measure or the smallness of a Ministerial majority is a certain proof that a Ministry ought to retire,—you ask a question which admits of no absolute reply.[5] All that can be said is, that a

---

5 See Hearn, *Government of England*, chap. ix., for an attempt to determine the circumstances under which a Ministry ought or ought not to keep office. See debate in House of Commons of 24th July 1905, for consideration of, and reference to, precedents with regard

Cabinet ought not to continue in power (subject, of course, to the one exception on which I have before dwelt)[6] after the expression by the House of Commons of a wish for the Cabinet's retirement. Of course, therefore, a Minister or a Ministry must resign if the House passes a vote of want of confidence. There are, however, a hundred signs of Parliamentary disapproval which, according to circumstances, either may or may not be a sufficient notice that a Minister ought to give up office. The essential thing is that the Ministry should obey the House as representing the nation. But the question whether the House of Commons has or has not indirectly intimated its will that a Cabinet should give up office is not a matter as to which any definite principle can be laid down. The difficulty which now exists, in settling the point at which a Premier and his colleagues are bound to hold that they have lost the confidence of the House, is exactly analogous to the difficulty which often perplexed statesmen of the last century, of determining the point at which a Minister was bound to hold he had lost the then essential confidence of the King. The ridiculous efforts of the Duke of Newcastle to remain at the head of the Treasury, in spite of the broadest hints from Lord Bute that the time had come for resignation, are exactly analogous to the undignified persistency with which later Cabinets have occasionally clung to office in the face of intimations that the House desired a change of government. As long as a master does not directly dismiss a servant, the question whether the employer's conduct betrays a wish that the servant should give notice must be an inquiry giving rise to doubt and discussion. And if there be sometimes a difficulty in determining what is the will of Parliament, it must often of necessity be still more difficult to determine what is the will of the nation, or, in other words, of the majority of the electors.

When House of Lords should give way to Commons.

The general rule that the House of Lords must in matters of legislation ultimately give way to the House of Commons is one of the best-established maxims of modern constitutional ethics. But if any inquirer asks how the point at which the Peers are to give way is to be

---

to the duty of a Ministry to retire from office when they have lost the confidence of the House of Commons.—*Parl. Deb.* 4th ser. vol. 150, col. 50.

6 See pp. 287–291, *ante.*

determined, no answer which even approximates to the truth can be given, except the very vague reply that the Upper House must give way whenever it is clearly proved that the will of the House of Commons represents the deliberate will of the nation. The nature of the proof differs under different circumstances.

When once the true state of the case is perceived, it is easy to understand a matter which, on any cut-and-dried theory of the constitution, can only with difficulty be explained, namely, the relation occupied by modern Cabinets towards the House of Lords. It is certain that for more than half a century Ministries have constantly existed which did not command the confidence of the Upper House, and that such Ministries have, without meeting much opposition on the part of the Peers, in the main carried out a policy of which the Peers did not approve. It is also certain that while the Peers have been forced to pass many bills which they disliked, they have often exercised large though very varying control over the course of legislation. Between 1834 and 1840 the Upper House, under the guidance of Lord Lyndhurst, repeatedly and with success opposed Ministerial measures which had passed the House of Commons. For many years Jews were kept out of Parliament simply because the Lords were not prepared to admit them. If you search for the real cause of this state of things, you will find that it was nothing else than the fact, constantly concealed under the misleading rhetoric of party warfare, that on the matters in question the electors were not prepared to support the Cabinet in taking the steps necessary to compel the submission of the House of Lords. On any matter upon which the electors are firmly resolved, a Premier, who is in effect the representative of the House of Commons, has the means of coercion, namely, by the creation of Peers. In a country indeed like England, things are rarely carried to this extreme length. The knowledge that a power can be exercised constantly prevents its being actually put in force. This is so even in private life; most men pay their debts without being driven into Court, but it were absurd to suppose that the possible compulsion of the Courts and the sheriff has not a good deal to do with regularity in the payment of debts. The acquiescence of the Peers in measures which the Peers do not approve arises at bottom from the fact that the nation, under the present constitution, possesses the power of enforcing, through very cumbersome machinery, the submission of the Peers to the conventional rule that the wishes of the House of Lords must finally give way to the decisions of the House of Commons. But the rule itself is vague, and the degree of obedience which it obtains is varying, because the will of the nation is often not clearly expressed, and further, in this as in other matters, is itself liable to variation. If the smoothness with which the constitutional arrangements of modern England work should, as it often does, conceal from us the force by which the machinery of the constitution is kept working, we may with advantage consult the experience of English colonies. No better example can be given of the methods by which a Representative Chamber attempts in the last resort to compel the obedience of an Upper House than is afforded by the varying phases of the conflict which raged in Victoria during 1878 and 1879 between the two Houses of the Legislature. There the Lower House attempted to enforce upon the Council the passing of measures which the Upper House did not approve, by, in effect, inserting the substance of a rejected bill in the Appropriation Bill. The Council in turn threw out the Appropriation Bill. The Ministry thereupon dismissed officials, magistrates, county court judges, and others, whom they had no longer the means to pay, and attempted to obtain payments out of the Treasury on the strength of resolutions passed solely by the Lower House. At this point, however, the Ministry came into conflict with an Act of Parliament, that is, with the law of the land. The contest continued under different forms until a change in public opinion finally led to the election of a Lower House which could act with the Council. With the result of the contest we are not concerned. Three points, however, should be noticed. The conflict was ultimately terminated in accordance with the expressed will of the electors; each party during its course put in force constitutional powers hardly ever in practice exerted in England; as the Council was elective, the Ministry did not possess any means of producing harmony between the two Houses by increasing the number of the Upper House. It is certain that if the Governor could have nominated members of the Council, the Upper House would have yielded to the will of the Lower, in the same way in which the Peers always in the last resort bow to the will of the House of Commons.

Why is the personal influence of the Crown uncertain? How is it, again, that all the understandings which are supposed to regulate the personal relation of the Crown to the actual work of government are marked by the utmost vagueness and uncertainty?

The matter is, to a certain extent at any rate, explained by the same train of thought as that which we have followed out in regard to the relation between the House of Lords and the Ministry. The revelations of political memoirs and the observation of modern public life make quite clear two points, both of which are curiously concealed under the mass of antiquated formulas which hide from view the real working of our institutions. The first is, that while every act of State is done in the name of the Crown, the real executive government of England is the Cabinet. The second is, that though the Crown has no real concern in a vast number of the transactions which take place under the Royal name, no one of the King's predecessors, nor, it may be presumed, the King himself, has ever acted upon or affected to act upon the maxim originated by Thiers, that "the King reigns but does not govern." George the Third took a leading part in the work of administration; his two sons, each in different degrees and in different ways, made their personal will and predilections tell on the government of the country. No one really supposes that there is not a sphere, though a vaguely defined sphere, in which the personal will of the King has under the constitution very considerable influence. The strangeness of this state of things is, or rather would be to any one who had not been accustomed from his youth to the mystery and formalism of English constitutionalism, that the rules or customs which regulate the personal action of the Crown are utterly vague and undefined. The reason of this will, however, be obvious to any one who has followed these chapters. The personal influence of the Crown exists, not because acts of State are done formally in the Crown's name, but because neither the legal sovereign power, namely Parliament, nor the political sovereign, namely the nation, wishes that the reigning monarch should be without personal weight in the government of the country. The customs or understandings which regulate or control the exercise of the King's personal influence are vague and indefinite, both because statesmen feel that the matter is one hardly to be dealt with by precise rules, and because no human being knows how far and to what extent the nation wishes that the voice of the reigning monarch should command attention. All that can be asserted with certainty is, that on this matter the practice of the Crown and the wishes of the nation have from time to time varied. George the Third made no use of the so-called veto which had been used by William the Third; but he more than once insisted upon his will being obeyed in matters of the highest importance. None of his successors have after the manner of George the Third made their personal will decisive as to general measures of policy. In small things as much as in great one can discern a tendency to transfer to the Cabinet powers once actually exercised by the King. The scene between Jeanie Deans and Queen Caroline is a true picture of a scene which might have taken place under George the Second; George the Third's firmness secured the execution of Dr. Dodd. At the present day the right of pardon belongs in fact to the Home Secretary. A modern Jeanie Deans would be referred to the Home Office; the question whether a popular preacher should pay the penalty of his crimes would now, with no great advantage to the country, be answered, not by the King, but by the Cabinet.

The effect of surviving prerogatives of Crown. What, again, is the real effect produced by the survival of prerogative powers?

Here we must distinguish two different things, namely, the way in which the existence of the prerogative affects the personal influence of the King, and the way in which it affects the power of the executive government.

The fact that all important acts of State are done in the name of the King and in most cases with the cognisance of the King, and that many of these acts, such, for example, as the appointment of judges or the creation of bishops, or the conduct of negotiations with foreign powers and the like, are exempt from the direct control or supervision of Parliament, gives the reigning monarch an opportunity for exercising great influence on the conduct of affairs; and Bagehot has marked out, with his usual subtlety, the mode in which the mere necessity under which Ministers are placed of consulting with and giving information to the King secures a wide sphere for the exercise of legitimate influence by a constitutional ruler.

But though it were a great error to underrate the extent to which the formal authority of the Crown confers real power upon the King, the far more important matter is to notice the way in which the survival of the prerogative affects the position of the Cabinet. It leaves in the hands of the Premier and his colleagues, large powers which can be exercised, and constantly are exercised, free from Parliamentary control. This is especially the case in all foreign affairs. Parliament may censure a Ministry for misconduct in regard to the foreign policy of the country. But a treaty made by the Crown, or in fact by the Cabinet, is valid without the authority or sanction of Parliament; and it is even open to question whether the treaty-making power of the executive might not in some cases override the law of the land.[7] However this may be, it is not Parliament, but the Ministry, who direct the diplomacy of the nation, and virtually decide all questions of peace or war. The founders of the American Union showed their full appreciation of the latitude left to the executive government under the English constitution by one of the most remarkable of their innovations upon it. They lodged the treaty-making power in the hands, not of the President, but of the President and the Senate; and further gave to the Senate a right of veto on Presidential appointments to office. These arrangements supply a valuable illustration of the way in which restrictions on the prerogative become restrictions on the discretionary authority of the executive. Were the House of Lords to have conferred upon it by statute the rights of the Senate, the change in our institutions would be described with technical correctness as the limitation of the prerogative of the Crown as regards the making of treaties and of official appointments. But the true effect

---

7 See the *Parlement Belge,* 4 P. D. 129; 5 P. D. (C. A.) 197. "Whether the power [of the Crown to compel its subjects to obey the provisions of a treaty] does exist in the case of treaties of peace, and whether if so it exists equally in the case of treaties akin to a treaty of peace, or whether in both or either of these cases interference with private rights can be authorised otherwise than by the legislature, are grave questions upon which their Lordships do not find it necessary to express an opinion."—*Walker* v. *Baird* [1892], A. C. 491, 497, judgment of P. C.

of the constitutional innovation would be to place a legal check on the
discretionary powers of the Cabinet.

The survival of the prerogative, conferring as it does wide discretionary authority upon the Cabinet, involves a consequence which
constantly escapes attention. It immensely increases the authority of
the House of Commons, and ultimately of the constituencies by
which that House is returned. Ministers must in the exercise of all
discretionary powers inevitably obey the predominant authority in
the State. When the King was the chief member of the sovereign
body, Ministers were in fact no less than in name the King's servants.
At periods of our history when the Peers were the most influential
body in the country, the conduct of the Ministry represented with
more or less fidelity the wishes of the Peerage. Now that the House of
Commons has become by far the most important part of the sovereign body, the Ministry in all matters of discretion carry out, or
tend to carry out, the will of the House. When however the Cabinet
cannot act except by means of legislation, other considerations come
into play. A law requires the sanction of the House of Lords. No
government can increase its statutory authority without obtaining the
sanction of the Upper Chamber. Thus an Act of Parliament when
passed represents, not the absolute wishes of the House of Commons, but these wishes as modified by the influence of the House of
Lords. The Peers no doubt will in the long run conform to the wishes
of the electorate. But the Peers may think that the electors will disapprove of, or at any rate be indifferent to, a bill which meets with the
approval of the House of Commons. Hence while every action of the
Cabinet which is done in virtue of the prerogative is in fact though
not in name under the direct control of the representative chamber,
all powers which can be exercised only in virtue of a statute are more
or less controlled in their creation by the will of the House of Lords;
they are further controlled in their exercise by the interference of the
Courts. One example, taken from the history of recent years, illustrates the practical effect of this difference.[8] In 1872 the Ministry of the

---

8 On this subject there are remarks worth noting in Stephen's *Life of Fawcett*, pp. 271, 272.

day carried a bill through the House of Commons abolishing the system of purchase in the army. The bill was rejected by the Lords: the Cabinet then discovered that purchase could be abolished by Royal warrant, *i.e.* by something very like the exercise of the prerogative.[9] The system was then and there abolished. The change, it will probably be conceded, met with the approval, not only of the Commons, but of the electors. But it will equally be conceded that had the alteration required statutory authority the system of purchase might have continued in force up to the present day. The existence of the prerogative enabled the Ministry in this particular instance to give immediate effect to the wishes of the electors, and this is the result which, under the circumstances of modern politics, the survival of the prerogative will in every instance produce. The prerogatives of the Crown have become the privileges of the people, and any one who wants to see how widely these privileges may conceivably be stretched as the House of Commons becomes more and more the direct representative of the true sovereign, should weigh well the words in which Bagehot describes the powers which can still legally be exercised by the Crown without consulting Parliament; and should remember that these powers can now be exercised by a Cabinet who are really servants, not of the Crown, but of a representative chamber which in its turn obeys the behests of the electors.

> I said in this book that it would very much surprise people if they were only told how many things the Queen could do without consulting Parliament, and it certainly has so proved, for when the Queen abolished purchase in the army by an act of prerogative (after the Lords had rejected the bill for doing so), there was a great and general astonishment.
>
> But this is nothing to what the Queen can by law do without consulting Parliament. Not to mention other things, she could disband the army (by law she cannot engage more than a certain number of men, but she is not obliged to engage any men); she could dismiss all the officers, from the General commanding-in-chief downwards; she could dismiss all the sailors too; she could sell off all our ships-of-war and all our naval stores; she could make a peace by the sacrifice of Cornwall, and begin a war for the conquest of

---

9 Purchase was not abolished by the prerogative in the ordinary legal sense of the term. A statute prohibited the sale of offices except in so far as might be authorised in the case of the army by Royal warrant. When therefore the warrant authorising the sale was cancelled the statute took effect.

Brittany. She could make every citizen in the United Kingdom, male or female, a peer; she could make every parish in the United Kingdom a "university"; she could dismiss most of the civil servants; she could pardon all offenders. In a word, the Queen could by prerogative upset all the action of civil government within the government, could disgrace the nation by a bad war or peace, and could, by disbanding our forces, whether land or sea, leave us defenceless against foreign nations.[10]

If government by Parliament is ever transformed into government by the House of Commons, the transformation will, it may be conjectured, be effected by use of the prerogatives of the Crown.

Conclusion.

Let us cast back a glance for a moment at the results which we have obtained by surveying the English constitution from its legal side.

The constitution when thus looked at ceases to appear a "sort of maze"; it is seen to consist of two different parts; the one part is made up of understandings, customs, or conventions which, not being enforced by the Courts, are in no true sense of the word laws; the other part is made up of rules which are enforced by the Courts, and which, whether embodied in statutes or not, are laws in the strictest sense of the term, and make up the true law of the constitution.

This law of the constitution is, we have further found, in spite of all appearances to the contrary, the true foundation on which the English polity rests, and it gives in truth even to the conventional element of constitutional law such force as it really possesses.[11]

The law of the constitution, again, is in all its branches the result of two guiding principles, which have been gradually worked out by the more or less conscious efforts of generations of English statesmen and lawyers.

The first of these principles is the sovereignty of Parliament, which means in effect the gradual transfer of power from the Crown to a body which has come more and more to represent the nation.[12] This

---

10 Bagehot, *English Constitution*, Introd. pp. xxxv. and xxxvi.

11 See pp. 292–302, *ante*.

12 A few words may be in place as to the method by which this transfer was accomplished. The leaders of the English people in their contests with Royal power never attempted, except in periods of revolutionary violence, to destroy or dissipate the authority of the Crown as head of the State. Their policy, continued through centuries, was to leave the

curious process, by which the personal authority of the King has been turned into the sovereignty of the King in Parliament, has had two effects: it has put an end to the arbitrary powers of the monarch; it has preserved intact and undiminished the supreme authority of the State.

The second of these principles is what I have called the "rule of law," or the supremacy throughout all our institutions of the ordinary law of the land. This rule of law, which means at bottom the right of the Courts to punish any illegal act by whomsoever committed, is of the very essence of English institutions. If the sovereignty of Parliament gives the form, the supremacy of the law of the land determines the substance of our constitution. The English constitution in short, which appears when looked at from one point of view to be a mere collection of practices or customs, turns out, when examined in its legal aspect, to be more truly than any other polity in the world, except the Constitution of the United States,[13] based on the law of the land.

When we see what are the principles which truly underlie the English polity, we also perceive how rarely they have been followed

---

power of the King untouched, but to bind down the action of the Crown to recognised modes of procedure which, if observed, would secure first the supremacy of the law, and ultimately the sovereignty of the nation. The King was acknowledged to be supreme judge, but it was early established that he could act judicially only in and through his Courts; the King was recognised as the only legislator, but he could enact no valid law except as King in Parliament; the King held in his hands all the prerogatives of the executive government, but, as was after long struggles determined, he could legally exercise these prerogatives only through Ministers who were members of his Council, and incurred responsibility for his acts. Thus the personal will of the King was gradually identified with and transformed into the lawful and legally expressed will of the Crown. This transformation was based upon the constant use of fictions. It bears on its face that it was the invention of lawyers. If proof of this were wanted, we should find it in the fact that the "Parliaments" of France towards the end of the eighteenth century tried to use against the fully-developed despotism of the French monarchy, fictions recalling the arts by which, at a far earlier period, English constitutionalists had nominally checked the encroachments, while really diminishing the sphere, of the royal prerogative. Legal statesmanship bears everywhere the same character. See Rocquain, *L'Esprit Révolutionnaire avant la Revolution.*

13 It is well worth notice that the Constitution of the United States, as it actually exists, rests to a very considerable extent on judge-made law. Chief-Justice Marshall, as the "Expounder of the Constitution," may almost be reckoned among the builders if not the founders of the American polity. See for a collection of his judgments on constitutional questions, *The Writings of John Marshall, late Chief-Justice of the United States, on the Federal Constitution.*

by foreign statesmen who more or less intended to copy the constitution of England. The sovereignty of Parliament is an idea fundamentally inconsistent with the notions which govern the inflexible or rigid constitutions existing in by far the most important of the countries which have adopted any scheme of representative government. The "rule of law" is a conception which in the United States indeed has received a development beyond that which it has reached in England; but it is an idea not so much unknown to as deliberately rejected by the constitution-makers of France, and of other continental countries which have followed French guidance. For the supremacy of the law of the land means in the last resort the right of the judges to control the executive government, whilst the *séparation des pouvoirs* means, as construed by Frenchmen, the right of the government to control the judges. The authority of the Courts of Law as understood in England can therefore hardly coexist with the system of *droit administratif* as it prevails in France. We may perhaps even go so far as to say that English legalism is hardly consistent with the existence of an official body which bears any true resemblance to what foreigners call "the administration." To say this is not to assert that foreign forms of government are necessarily inferior to the English constitution, or unsuited for a civilised and free people. All that necessarily results from the analysis of our institutions, and a comparison of them with the institutions of foreign countries, is, that the English constitution is still marked, far more deeply than is generally supposed, by peculiar features, and that these peculiar characteristics may be summed up in the combination of Parliamentary Sovereignty with the Rule of Law.

APPENDIX

Note I

RIGIDITY OF FRENCH CONSTITUTIONS

*T*welve constitutions[1] have been framed by French constitution-makers since the meeting of the States General in 1789.

A survey of the provisions (if any) contained in these constitutions for the revision thereof leads to some interesting results.

First, with but two exceptions, every French constitution has been marked by the characteristic of "rigidity." Frenchmen of all political schools have therefore agreed in the assumption, that the political foundations of the State must be placed beyond the reach of the ordinary legislature, and ought to be changed, if at all, only with considerable difficulty, and generally after such delay as may give the nation time for maturely reflecting over any proposed innovation.

In this respect the Monarchical Constitution of 1791 is noteworthy. That Constitution formed a legislature consisting of one Assembly,

---

1 Viz. (1) The Monarchical Constitution of 1792; (2) the Republican Constitution of 1793; (3) the Republican Constitution of 1795 (Directory), 5 Fruct. An. III.; (4) the Consular Constitution of the Year VIII. (1799); (5) the Imperial Constitution, 1804; (6) the Constitution proclaimed by the Senate and Provisional Government, 1814; (7) the Constitutional Charter, 1814 (Restoration); (8) the Additional Act (*Acte Additionnel*), 1815, remodelling the Imperial Constitution; (9) the Constitutional Charter of 1830 (Louis Philippe);(10) the Republic of 1848; (11) the Second Imperial Constitution, 1852; (12) the present Republic, 1870–75. See generally Hélie, *Les Constitutions de la France;* and Duguit et Monnier, *Les Constitutions de la France* (Deuxième ed.).

It is possible either to lengthen or to shorten the list of French Constitutions according to the view which the person forming the list takes of the extent of the change in the arrangements of a state necessary to form a new constitution.

but did not give this Assembly or Parliament any authority to revise the Constitution. The only body endowed with such authority was an Assembly of Revision (*Assemblée de Révision*), and the utmost pains were taken to hamper the convening and to limit the action of the Assembly of Revision. The provisions enacted with this object were in substance as follows:—An ordinary Legislative Assembly was elected for two years. No change in the Constitution could take place until three successive Legislative Assemblies should have expressed their wish for a change in some article of the Constitution. On a resolution in favour of such reform having been carried in three successive legislatures or Parliaments, the ensuing Legislative Assembly was to be increased by the addition of 249 members, and this increased Legislature was to constitute an Assembly of Revision.

This Assembly of Revision was tied down, as far as the end could be achieved by the words of the Constitution, to debate on those matters only which were submitted to the consideration of the Assembly by the resolution of the three preceding legislatures. The authority, therefore, of the Assembly was restricted to a partial revision of the Constitution. The moment this revision was finished the 249 additional members were to withdraw, and the Assembly of Revision was thereupon to sink back into the position of an ordinary legislature. If the Constitution of 1791 had continued in existence, no change in its articles could, under any circumstances, have been effected in less than six years. But this drag upon hasty legislation was not, in the eyes of the authors of the Constitution, a sufficient guarantee against inconsiderate innovations.[2] They specially provided that the two consecutive legislative bodies which were to meet after the proclamation of the Constitution, should have no authority even to propose the reform of any article contained therein. The intended consequence was that for at least ten years (1791–1801) the bases of the French government should remain unchanged and unchangeable.[3]

---

2 A resolution was proposed, though not carried, that the articles of the Constitution should be unchangeable for a period of thirty years. Hélie, *Les Constitutions de la France*, p. 302.

3 See Constitution of 1791, Tit. vii.

The Republicans of 1793 agreed with the Constitutionalists of 1791 in placing the foundations of the State outside the limits of ordinary legislation, but adopted in different method of revision. Constitutional changes were under the Constitution of 1793 made dependent, not on the action of the ordinary legislature, but on the will of the people. Upon the demand of a tenth of the primary assemblies in more than half of the Departments of the Republic, the legislature was bound to convoke all the primary assemblies, and submit to them the question of convening a national convention for the revision of the Constitution. The vote of these Assemblies thereupon decided for or against the meeting of a convention, and therefore whether a revision should take place.

Assuming that they decided in favour of a revision, a convention, elected in the same manner as the ordinary legislature, was to be forthwith convened, and to occupy itself as regards the Constitution with those subjects only which should have caused (*ont motivé*) the convention to be assembled. On the expressed wish, in short, of the majority of the citizens, a legislature was to be convoked with a limited authority to reform certain articles of the Constitution.[4]

The Republican and Directorial Constitution again, of 1795, rested, like its predecessors, on the assumption that it was of primary importance to make constitutional changes difficult, and also recognised the danger of again creating a despotic sovereign assembly like the famous, and hated, Convention.

The devices by which it was sought to guard against both sudden innovations, and the tyranny of a constituent assembly, can be understood only by one who remembers that, under the Directorial Constitution, the legislature consisted of two bodies, namely, the Council of Ancients, and the Council of Five Hundred. A proposal for any change in the Constitution was necessarily to proceed from the Council of Ancients, and to be ratified by the Council of Five Hundred. After such a proposal had been duly made and ratified thrice in nine years, at periods distant from each other by at least three years, an Assembly of Revision was to be convoked. This As-

---

4 Constitution du 5 Fructidor, An. III., articles 336–350, Hélie, pp. 436, 463, 464.

sembly constituted what the Americans now term a "constitutional convention." It was a body elected *ad hoc,* whose meeting did not in any way suspend the authority of the ordinary legislature, or of the Executive. The authority of the Assembly of Revision was further confined to the revision of those articles submitted to its consideration by the legislature. It could in no case sit for more than three months, and had no other duty than to prepare a plan of reform (*projet de reforme*) for the consideration of the primary Assemblies of the Republic. When once this duty had been performed, the Assembly of Revision was *ipso facto* dissolved. The Constitution not only carefully provided that the Assembly of Revision should take no part in the government, or in ordinary legislation, but also enacted that until the changes proposed by the Assembly should have been accepted by the people the existing Constitution should remain in force.

The Consular and Imperial Constitutions, all with more or less directness, made changes in the Constitution depend, first, upon a *senatus consultum* or resolution of the Senate; and, next, on the ratification of the change by a popular vote or plebiscite.[5] This may be considered the normal Napoleonic system of constitutional reform. It makes all changes dependent on the will of a body, if effect, appointed by the Executive, and makes them subject to the sanction of a popular vote taken in such a manner that the electors can at best only either reject or, as in fact they always have done, affirm the proposals submitted to them by the Executive. No opportunity is given for debate or for amendments of the proposed innovations. We may assume that even under the form of Parliamentary Imperialism sketched out in the Additional Act of 23rd April 1815, the revision of the Constitution was intended to depend on the will of the Senate and the ratification of the people. The Additional Act is, however, in one respect very remarkable. It absolutely prohibits any proposal which should have for its object the Restoration of the Bourbons, the re-establishment of feudal rights, of tithes, or of an established Church (*culte privilégié et dominant*), or which should in any way re-

---

5 See Hélie, *Les Constitutions de la France,* pp. 696–698.

voke the sale of the national domains, or, in other words, French landowners. This attempt to place certain principles beyond the influence, not only of ordinary legislation but of constitutional change, recalls to the student of English history the Cromwellian Constitution of 1653, and the determination of the Protector that certain principles should be regarded as "fundamentals" not to be touched by Parliament, nor, as far as would appear, by any other body in the State.

The Republic of 1848 brought again into prominence the distinction between laws changeable by the legislature in its ordinary legislative capacity, and articles of the Constitution changeable only with special difficulty, and by an assembly specially elected for the purpose of revision. The process of change was elaborate. The ordinary legislative body was elected for three years. This body could not itself modify any constitutional article. It could however, in its third year, resolve that a total or partial revision of the Constitution was desirable; such a resolution was invalid unless voted thrice at three sittings, each divided from the other by at least the period of a month, unless 500 members voted, and unless the resolution were affirmed by three-fourths of the votes given.

On the resolution in favour of a constitutional change being duly carried, there was to be elected an assembly of revision. This assembly, elected for three months only, and consisting of a larger number than the ordinary legislature, was bound to occupy itself with the revision for which it was convoked, but might, if necessary, pass ordinary laws. It was therefore intended to be a constituent body superseding the ordinary legislature.[6]

The second Empire revived, in substance, the legislative system of the first, and constitutional changes again became dependent upon a resolution of the Senate, and ratification by a popular vote.[7]

The existing Republic is, in many respects, unlike any preceding polity created by French statesmanship. The articles of the Constitution are to be found, not in one document, but in several constitu-

---

6 See Constitution, 1848, art. 111.

7 *Ibid.* 1852, arts. 31, 32; Hélie, p. 1170.

tional laws enacted by the National Assembly which met in 1871.
These laws however cannot be changed by the ordinary legislature
—the Senate and the Chamber of Deputies—acting in its ordinary
legislative character. The two Chambers, in order to effect a change
in the constitutional manner, must, in the first place, each separately
resolve that a revision of the Constitution is desirable. When each
have passed this resolution, the two Chambers meet together, and
when thus assembled and voting together as a National Assembly, or
Congress, have power to change any part, as they have in fact
changed some parts, of the constitutional laws.[8]

I have omitted to notice the constitutional Charter of 1814, granted
by Louis XVIII., and the Charter of 1830, accepted by Louis Philippe.
The omission is intentional. Neither of these documents contains any
special enactments for its amendment. An Englishman would infer
that the articles of the Charter could be abrogated or amended by the
process of ordinary legislation. The inference may be correct. The
constitutionalists of 1814 and 1830 meant to found a constitutional
monarchy of the English type, and therefore may have meant the
Crown and the two Houses to be a sovereign Parliament. The inference however, as already pointed out,[9] is by no means certain. Louis
XVIII. may have meant that the articles of a constitution granted as a
charter by the Crown, should be modifiable only at the will of the
grantor. Louis Philippe may certainly have wished that the foundations of his system of government should be legally immutable.
However this may have been, one thing is clear, namely, that French
constitutionalists have, as a rule, held firmly to the view that the
foundations of the Constitution ought not to be subject to sudden
changes at the will of the ordinary legislature.

Secondly, French statesmen have never fully recognised the inconveniences and the perils which may arise from the excessive rigidity
of a constitution. They have hardly perceived that the power of
a minority to place a veto for a period of many years on a reform
desired by the nation provides an excuse or a reason for revolution.

---

8 See Constitutional Law, 1855, art. 8.

9 See pp. 62–63, *ante.*

The authors of the existing Republic have, in this respect, learnt something from experience. They have indeed preserved the distinction between the Constitution and ordinary laws, but they have included but a small number of rules among constitutional articles, and have so facilitated the process of revision as to make the existing chambers all but a sovereign Parliament. Whether this is on the whole a gain or not, is a point on which it were most unwise to pronounce an opinion. All that is here insisted upon is that the present generation of Frenchmen have perceived that a constitution may be too rigid for use or for safety.[10]

Thirdly, an English critic smiles at the labour wasted in France on the attempt to make immutable Constitutions which, on the average, have lasted about ten years apiece. The edifice, he reflects, erected by the genius of the first great National Assembly, could not, had it stood, have been legally altered till 1801—that is, till the date when, after three constitutions had broken down, Bonaparte was erecting a despotic Empire. The Directorial Republic of 1795 could not, if it had lasted, have been modified in the smallest particular till 1804, at which date the Empire was already in full vigour.

But the irony of fate does not convict its victims of folly, and, if we look at the state of the world as it stood when France began her experiments in constitution-making, there was nothing ridiculous in the idea that the fundamental laws of a country ought to be changed but slowly, or in the anticipation that the institutions of France would not require frequent alteration. The framework of the English Constitution had, if we except the Union between England and Scotland, stood, as far as foreigners could observe, unaltered for a century, and if the English Parliament was theoretically able to modify any institution whatever, the Parliaments of George III. were at least as little likely to change any law which could be considered constitutional as a modern Parliament to abolish the Crown. In fact it was not till nearly forty years after the meeting of the States General (1829) that

---

10 See as to the circumstances which explain the character of the existing Constitution of France, Lowell, *Governments and Parties in Continental Europe*, i. pp. 7–14, and note that the present constitution has already lasted longer than any constitution which has existed in France since 1789.

any serious modification was made in the form of the government of England. No one in France or in England could a century ago foresee the condition of pacific revolution to which modern Englishmen had become so accustomed as hardly to feel its strangeness. The newly-founded Constitution of the United States showed every sign of stability, and has lasted more than a century without undergoing any material change of form. It was reasonable enough therefore for the men of 1789 to consider that a well-built constitution might stand for a long time without the need of repair.

Fourthly, the errors committed by French constitutionalists have been, if we may judge by the event, in the main, twofold. Frenchmen have always been blind to the fact that a constitution may be undermined by the passing of laws which, without nominally changing its provisions, violate its principles. They have therefore failed to provide any adequate means, such as those adopted by the founders of the United States, for rendering unconstitutional legislation inoperative. They have in the next place, generally, though not invariably, underrated the dangers of convoking a constituent assembly, which, as its meeting suspends the authority of the established legislature and Executive, is likely to become a revolutionary convention.

Fifthly, the Directorial Constitution of 1795 is, from a theoretical point of view, the most interesting among the French experiments in the art of constitution-making. Its authors knew by experience the risks to which revolutionary movements are exposed, and showed much ingenuity in their devices for minimising the perils involved in revisions of the Constitution. In entrusting the task of revision to an assembly elected *ad hoc,* which met for no other purpose, and which had no authority to interfere with or suspend the action of the established legislative bodies or of the Executive, they formed a true constitutional convention in the American sense of that term,[11] and, if we may judge by transatlantic experience, adopted by far the wisest method hitherto invented for introducing changes into a written and rigid constitution. The establishment, again, of the principle that all

---

11 See the word *"Convention"* in the American *Encyclopædia of American Science;* and Bryce, *American Commonwealth,* i. (3rd ed.), App. on Constitutional Conventions, p. 667.

amendments voted by the Assembly of Revision must be referred to a popular vote, and could not come into force until accepted by the people, was an anticipation of the Referendum which has now taken firm root in Switzerland, and may, under one shape or another, become in the future a recognised part of all democratic politics. It is worth while to direct the reader's attention to the ingenuity displayed by the constitution-makers of 1795, both because their resourcefulness stands in marked contrast with the want of inventiveness which marks the work of most French constitutionalists, and because the incapacity of the Directorial Government, in the work of administration, has diverted attention from the skill displayed by the founders of the Directorate in some parts of their constitutional creation.

Note II

DIVISION OF POWERS IN FEDERAL STATES

A student who wishes to understand the principles which, under a given system of federalism, determine the division of authority between the nation or the central government on the one hand, and the States on the other, should examine the following points:—*first,* whether it is the National Government or the States to which belong only "definite" powers, *i.e.* only the powers definitely assigned to it under the Constitution; *secondly,* whether the enactments of the Federal legislature can be by any tribunal or other authority nullified or treated as void; *thirdly,* to what extent the Federal government can control the legislation of the separate States; and *fourthly,* what is the nature of the body (if such there be) having authority to amend the Constitution.

It is interesting to compare on these points the provisions of five different federal systems.

THE UNITED STATES

1. The powers conferred by the Constitution on the United States are strictly "definite" or defined; the powers left to the separate States

are "indefinite" or undefined. "The powers not delegated to the United States by the Constitution, nor prohibited by it to the States, are reserved to the States respectively, or to the people."[12] The consequence is that the United States (that is, the National Government) can claim no power not conferred upon the United States either directly or impliedly by the Constitution. Every State in the Union can claim to exercise any power belonging to an independent nation which has not been directly or indirectly taken away from the States by the Constitution.

2. Federal legislation is as much subject to the Constitution as the legislation of the States. An enactment, whether of Congress or of a State legislature, which is opposed to the Constitution, is void, and will be treated as such by the Courts.

3. The Federal government has no power to annul or disallow State legislation. The State Constitutions do not owe their existence to the Federal government, nor do they require its sanction. The Constitution of the United States, however, guarantees to every State a Republican Government, and the Federal government has, it is submitted, the right to put down, or rather is under the duty of putting down, any State Constitution which is not "Republican," whatever be the proper definition of that term.

4. Changes in the Constitution require for their enactment the sanction of three-fourths of the States, and it would appear that constitutionally no State can be deprived of its equal suffrage in the Senate without its consent.[13]

THE SWISS CONFEDERATION

1. The authority of the national government or Federal power is definite, the authority of each of the Cantons is indefinite.[14]

2. Federal legislation must be treated as valid by the Courts. But a law passed by the Federal Assembly must, on demand of either 30,000

---

12 Constitution of United States, Amendment 10.

13 Constitution of United States, art. 5.

14 See Constitution Fédérale, art. 3.

citizens or of eight Cantons, be referred to a popular vote for approval or rejection. It would appear that the Federal Court can treat as invalid Cantonal laws which violate the Constitution.

3. The Federal authorities have no power of disallowing or annulling a Cantonal law. But the Cantonal Constitutions, and amendments thereto, need the guarantee of the Confederacy. This guarantee will not be given to articles in a Cantonal Constitution which are repugnant to the Federal Constitution, and amendments to a Cantonal Constitution do not, I am informed, come into force until they receive the Federal Guarantee.

4. The Federal Constitution can be revised only by a combined majority of the Swiss people, and of the Swiss Cantons. No amendment of the Constitution can be constitutionally effected which is not approved of by a majority of the Cantons.

THE CANADIAN DOMINION

1. The authority of the Dominion, or Federal, government is indefinite or undefined; the authority of the States or Provinces is definite or defined, and indeed defined within narrow limits.[15]

From a federal point of view this is the fundamental difference between the Constitution of the Dominion on the one hand, and the Constitution of the United States or of Switzerland on the other.

The Dominion Parliament can legislate on all matters not exclusively assigned to the Provincial legislatures. The Provincial or State Legislatures can legislate only on certain matters exclusively assigned to them. Congress, on the other hand, or the Swiss Federal Assembly, can legislate only on certain definite matters assigned to it by the Constitution; the States or Cantons retain all powers exercised by legislation or otherwise not specially taken away from them by the Constitution.

2. The legislation of the Federal, or Dominion, Parliament is as much subject to the Constitution (*i.e.* the British North America Act, 1867) as the legislation of the Provinces. Any Act passed, either by the

---

15 See British North America Act, 1867, ss. 91, 92.

Dominion Parliament or by a Provincial Legislature, which is inconsistent with the Constitution is void, and will be treated as void by the Courts.

3. The Dominion Government has authority to disallow the Act passed by a Provincial legislature. This disallowance may be exercised even in respect of Provincial Acts which are constitutional, *i.e.* within the powers assigned to the Provincial legislatures under the Constitution.[16]

4. The Constitution of the Dominion depends on an Imperial statute; it can, therefore, except as provided by the statute itself, be changed only by an Act of the Imperial Parliament. The Parliament of the Dominion cannot, as such, change any part of the Canadian Constitution. It may however, to a limited extent, by its action when combined with that of a Provincial legislature, modify the Constitution for the purpose of producing uniformity of laws in the Provinces of the Dominion.[17]

But a Provincial legislature can under the British North America Act, 1867, s. 92, sub-s. 1, amend the Constitution of the Province. The law, however, amending the Provincial Constitution is, in common with other Provincial legislation, subject to disallowance by the Dominion government.

THE COMMONWEALTH OF AUSTRALIA

1. The authority of the Federal government is definite; the authority of each of the States, vested in the Parliament thereof, is indefinite.[18]

2. Federal legislation (*i.e.* the legislation of the Commonwealth Parliament) is as much subject to the constitution as the legislation of the State Parliaments. An enactment whether of the Commonwealth Parliament or of a State legislature which is opposed to the Constitu-

---

16 See British North America Act, 1867, s. 90; and Bourinot, *Parliamentary Practice and Procedure,* pp. 76–81.

17 British North America Act, 1867, s. 94.

18 Commonwealth Constitution Act, ss. 51, 52, 106, 107.

tion of the Commonwealth, is void and will be treated as such by the Courts.

3. The Federal or Commonwealth government has no power to annul or disallow either directly or indirectly the legislation of a State Parliament.

4. Amendments of the Commonwealth Constitution may be effected by a bill passed by the Commonwealth Parliament, or under some circumstances by one only of the Houses of the Commonwealth Parliament, and approved of by a majority of the voting electors of the Commonwealth, and also by a majority of the States thereof.[19]

Note however that (i) many provisions of the Constitution may under the Constitution be changed by an ordinary Act of the Commonwealth Parliament.[20]

(ii) The Commonwealth Constitution being an Act of the Imperial Parliament may be altered or abolished by an Act of the Imperial Parliament.

THE GERMAN EMPIRE

1. The authority under the Constitution of the Imperial (Federal) power is apparently finite or defined, whilst the authority of the States making up the Federation is indefinite or undefined.

This statement, however, must be understood subject to two limitations: *first,* the powers assigned to the Imperial government are very large; *secondly,* the Imperial legislature can change the Constitution.[21]

2. Imperial legislation at any rate, if carried through in a proper form, cannot apparently be "unconstitutional,"[22] but it would appear

---

19 Constitution, s. 128.

20 See *e.g.* Constitution, ss. 7, 10.

21 See Reichsverfassung, arts. 2. and 78.

22 See on the moot question whether the Reichsgericht and the Courts generally can treat a statute passed by the Diet (Reichstag) as unconstitutional, Lowell, *Governments and Parties in Continental Europe,* i. pp. 282–284.

that State legislation is void, if it conflicts with the Constitution, or with Imperial legislation.[23]

3. Whether the Imperial government has any power of annulling a State law on the ground of unconstitutionality is not very clear, but as far as a foreigner can judge, no such power exists under the Imperial Constitution. The internal constitutional conflicts which may arise within any State may, under certain circumstances, be ultimately determined by Imperial authority.[24]

4. The Constitution may be changed by the Imperial (Federal) legislature in the way of ordinary legislation. But no law amending the Constitution can be carried, if opposed by fourteen votes in the Federal Council (Bundesrath). This gives in effect a "veto" on constitutional changes to Prussia and to several combinations of other States.

Certain rights, moreover, are reserved to several States which cannot be changed under the Constitution, except with the assent of the State possessing the right.[25]

---

23 Reichsverfassung, art. 2; and Labaud, *Staatsrecht des Deutschen Reiches*, s. 10.

24 Reichsverfassung, art. 76.

25 *The South African Union.* — The constitution of the South African Union, it has been well said, "is frankly not in any real sense federal." The Act under which it is framed "does not restrict in any substantial manner the Parliament's power to alter the provisions of the Constitution. It is especially laid down in s. 152 that Parliament may by law repeal or alter any of the provisions of the Act, provided that no provision thereof for the operation of which a definite period of time is fixed shall be repealed or altered before the expiration of such period, and also provided that no repeal or alteration of the provisions of the section itself, or of ss. 33 and 34 relative to the numbers of the members of the Legislative Assembly, prior to the expiration of ten years, or until the total number of members of the Assembly has reached 150, whichever occurs later, or of the provisions of s. 35 relative to the qualifications of electors to the House of Assembly, or of s. 137 as to the use of languages, shall be valid, unless the Bill containing the alterations is passed at a joint sitting of the Houses, and at its third reading by not less than two-thirds of the total number of members of both Houses. The section is well worded, as it obviates the possible evasion of its spirit by the alteration of the section itself." Keith, *South African Union*, Reprinted from the Journal of the Society of Comparative Legislation, pp. 50, 51. See also Brand, *The Union of South Africa*, especially chap. xi.

Note III

DISTINCTION BETWEEN A PARLIAMENTARY EXECUTIVE AND A NON-PARLIAMENTARY EXECUTIVE

Representative government, of one kind or another, exists at this moment in most European countries, as well as in all countries which come within the influence of European ideas; there are few civilised states in which legislative power is not exercised by a wholly, or partially, elective body of a more or less popular or representative character. Representative government, however, does not mean everywhere one and the same thing. It exhibits or tends to exhibit two different forms, or types, which are discriminated from each other by the difference of the relation between the executive and the legislature. Under the one form of representative government the legislature, or, it may be, the elective portion thereof, appoints and dismisses the executive which under these circumstances is, in general, chosen from among the members of the legislative body. Such an executive may appropriately be termed a "parliamentary executive." Under the other form of representative government the executive, whether it be an Emperor and his Ministers, or a President and his Cabinet, is not appointed by the legislature. Such an executive may appropriately be termed a "non-parliamentary executive." As to this distinction between the two forms of representative government, which, though noticed of recent times by authors of eminence, has hardly been given sufficient prominence in treatises on the theory or the practice of the English constitution, two or three points are worth attention.

First, the distinction affords a new principle for the classification of constitutions, and brings into light new points both of affinity and difference. Thus if the character of polities be tested by the nature of their executives, the constitutions of England, of Belgium, of Italy, and of the existing French Republic, all, it will be found, belong substantially to one and the same class; for under each of these constitutions there exists a parliamentary executive. The constitutions, on the other hand, of the United States and of the German Empire, as also the constitution of France in the time of the Second Republic, all belong to another and different class, since under each of these constitutions there is to be found a non-parliamentary executive. This method of grouping different forms of representative government is certainly not without its advantages. It is instructive to perceive that the Republican democracy of America and the Imperial government of Germany have at least one important feature in common, which distinguishes them no less from the constitutional monarchy of England than from the democratic Republic of France.

Secondly, the practical power of a legislative body, or parliament, greatly depends upon its ability to appoint and dismiss the executive; the possession of this power is the source of at least half the authority which, at the present day, has accrued to the English House of Commons. The assertion, indeed, would be substantially true that parliamentary government, in the full sense of that term, does not exist, unless, and until, the members of the executive body hold office at the pleasure of parliament, and that, when their tenure of office does depend on the pleasure of parliament, parliamentary government has reached its full development and been transformed into government by parliament. But, though this is so, it is equally true that the distinction between a constitution with a parliamentary executive and a constitution with a non-parliamentary executive does not square with the distinction insisted upon in the body of this work, between a constitution in which there exists a sovereign parliament and a constitution in which there exists a non-sovereign parliament. The English Parliament, it is true, is a sovereign body, and the real English executive—the Cabinet—is in fact, though not in name, a parliamentary executive. But the combination of parliamentary sovereignty with a parliamentary executive is not essential but accidental. The English Parliament has been a sovereign power for centuries, but down at any rate to the Revolution of 1689 the government of England was in the hands of a non-parliamentary executive. So again it is at least maintainable that in Germany the Federal Council (Bundesrath) and the Federal Diet (Reichstag) constitute together a sovereign legislature.[26] But no one with recent events before his eyes can assert that the German Empire is governed by a parliamentary executive. In this matter, as in many others, instruction may be gained from a study of the history of parliamentary government in Ireland. In modern times both the critics and the admirers of the constitution popularly identified with the name of Grattan, which existed from 1782 to 1800, feel that there is something strange and perplexing in the position of the Irish Parliament. The peculiarity of the case, which it is far easier for us to perceive than it was for Grattan and his contemporaries, lies mainly in the fact that, while the Irish Parliament was from 1782 an admittedly sovereign legislature, and whilst it was probably intended by all parties that the Irish Houses of Parliament should, in their legislation for Ireland, be as little checked by the royal veto as were the English Houses of Parliament, yet the Irish executive was as regards the Irish Parliament in no sense a parliamentary executive, for it was in reality appointed and dismissed by the English Ministry. It would be idle to suppose that mere defects in constitutional mechanism would in themselves have caused, or that the most ingenious of constitutional devices would of themselves have averted, the failure of Grattan's attempt to secure the parliamentary independence of Ireland. But a critic of constitutions may, without absurdity, assert that in 1782 the combination of a sovereign parliament with a non-parliamentary executive made it all but certain that Grattan's constitution must either be greatly modified or come to an end. For our present purpose, however, all that need be noted is that this combination, which to modern critics seems a strange one, did in fact exist during the whole period of Irish parliamentary independence. And as the existence of a sovereign parliament does not necessitate the existence of a parliamentary executive, so a parliamentary executive constantly coexists with a non-sovereign parliament. This is exemplified by the constitution of Belgium as of every English colony endowed with representative institutions and responsible government.

---

26 See the Imperial Constitution, Arts 2 and 78.

The difference again between a parliamentary and a non-parliamentary executive, though it covers, does not correspond with a distinction, strongly insisted on by Bagehot, between Cabinet Government and Presidential Government.[27] Cabinet Government, as that term is used by him and by most writers, is one form, and by far the most usual form, of a parliamentary executive, and the Presidential Government of America which Bagehot had in his mind, is one form, though certainly not the only form, of a non-parliamentary executive. But it would be easy to imagine a parliamentary executive which was not a Cabinet, and something of the sort, it may be suggested, actually existed in France during the period when Monsieur Thiers and Marshal MacMahon were each successively elected chief of the executive power by the French National Assembly, [28] and there certainly may exist a non-parliamentary executive which cannot be identified with Presidential government. Such for example is at the present moment the executive of the German Empire. The Emperor is its real head; he is not a President; neither he, nor the Ministers he appoints, are appointed or dismissible by the body which we may designate as the Federal Parliament.

Thirdly, the English constitution as we now know it presents here, as elsewhere, more than one paradox. The Cabinet is, in reality and in fact, a parliamentary executive, for it is in truth chosen, though by a very indirect process, and may be dismissed by the House of Commons, and its members are invariably selected from among the members of one or other House of Parliament. But, in appearance and in name, the Cabinet is now what it originally was, a non-parliamentary executive; every Minister is the servant of the Crown, and is in form appointed and dismissible, not by the House of Commons, not by the Houses of Parliament, but by the King.

It is a matter of curious speculation, whether the English Cabinet may not at this moment be undergoing a gradual and, as yet, scarcely noticed change of character, under which it may be transformed from a parliamentary into a non-parliamentary executive. The possibility of

27 See Bagehot, *English Constitution* (ed. 1878), pp. 16 and following.
28 See Hélie, *Les Constitutions de la France*, pp. 1360, 1397.

such a change is suggested by the increasing authority of the electorate. Even as it is, a general election may be in effect, though not in name, a popular election of a particular statesman to the Premiership. It is at any rate conceivable that the time may come when, though all the forms of the English constitution remain unchanged, an English Prime Minister will be as truly elected to office by a popular vote as is an American President. It should never be forgotten that the American President is theoretically elected by electors who never exercise any personal choice whatever, and is in fact chosen by citizens who have according to the letter of the constitution no more right to elect a President than an English elector has to elect a Prime Minister.

Fourthly, each kind of executive possesses certain obvious merits and certain obvious defects.

A parliamentary executive, which for the sake of simplicity we may identify with a Cabinet, can hardly come into conflict with the legislature, or, at any rate, with that part of it by which the Cabinet is appointed and kept in power. Cabinet government has saved England from those conflicts between the executive and the legislative power which in the United States have impeded the proper conduct of public affairs, and in France, as in some other countries, have given rise to violence and revolution. A parliamentary Cabinet must from the necessity of the case be intensely sensitive and amenable to the fluctuations of parliamentary opinion, and be anxious, in matters of administration no less than in matters of legislation, to meet the wishes, and even the fancies, of the body to which the Ministry owes its existence. The "flexibility," if not exactly of the constitution yet of our whole English system of government, depends, in practice, quite as much upon the nature of the Cabinet as upon the legal sovereignty of the English Parliament. But Cabinet government is inevitably marked by a defect which is nothing more than the wrong side, so to speak, of its merits. A parliamentary executive must by the law of its nature follow, or tend to follow, the lead of Parliament. Hence under a system of Cabinet government the administration of affairs is apt, in all its details, to reflect not only the permanent will, but also the temporary wishes, or transient passions and fancies, of a parliamentary majority, or of the electors from whose good will the majority derives its authority. A parliamentary executive, in short, is likely to become the creature of the parliament by which it is created, and to share, though in a modified form, the weaknesses which are inherent in the rule of an elective assembly.

The merits and defects of a non-parliamentary executive are the exact opposite of the merits and defects of a parliamentary executive. Each form of administration is strong where the other is weak, and weak where the other is strong. The strong point of a non-parliamentary executive is its comparative independence. Wherever representative government exists, the head of the administation, be he an Emperor or a President, of course prefers to be on good terms with and to have the support of the legislative body. But the German Emperor need not pay anything like absolute deference to the wishes of the Diet; an American President can, if he chooses, run counter to the opinion of Congress. Either Emperor or President, if he be a man of strong will and decided opinions, can in many respects give effect as head of the executive to his own views of sound policy, even though he may, for the moment, offend not only the legislature but also the electors. Nor can it be denied that the head of a non-parliamentary executive may, in virtue of his independence, occasionally confer great benefits on the nation. Many Germans would now admit that the King of Prussia and Prince Bismarck did, just because the Prussian executive was in fact, whatever the theory of the constitution, a non-parliamentary executive, pursue a policy which, though steadily opposed by the Prussian House of Representatives, laid the foundation of German power. There was at least one occasion, and probably more existed, on which President Lincoln rendered an untold service to the United States by acting, in defiance of the sentiment of the moment, on his own conviction as to the course required by sound policy. But an executive which does not depend for its existence on parliamentary support, clearly may, and sometimes will, come into conflict with parliament. The short history of the second French Republic is, from the election of Louis Napoleon to the Presidency down to the *Coup d'État* of the 2nd of December, little else than the story of the contest between the French executive and the French legislature. This struggle, it may be said, arose from the peculiar position of Louis Napoleon as being at once the President of the Republic and the representative of the Napoleonic dynasty. But the contest between Andrew Johnson and Congress, to give no other examples, proves that a conflict between a non-parliamentary executive and the legislature may arise where there is no question of claim to a throne, and among a people far more given to respect the law of the land than are the French.

Fifthly, the founders of constitutions have more than once attempted to create a governing body which should combine the characteristics, and exhibit, as it was hoped, the merits without the defects both of a parliamentary and of a non-parliamentary executive. The means used for the attainment of this end have almost of necessity been the formation under one shape or another of an administration which, while created, should not be dismissible, by the legislature. These attempts to construct a semi-parliamentary executive repay careful study, but have not been crowned, in general, with success.

The Directory which from 1795 to 1799 formed the government of the French Republic was, under a very complicated system of choice, elected by the two councils which constituted the legislature or parliament of the Republic. The Directors could not be dismissed by the Councils. Every year one Director at least was to retire from office. "The foresight," it has been well said,

> of [the Directorial] Constitution was infinite: it prevented popular violence, the encroachments of power, and provided for all the perils which the different crises of the Revolution had displayed. If any Constitution could have become firmly established at that period [1795], it was the directorial constitution.[29]

It lasted for four years. Within two years the majority of the Directory and the Councils were at open war. Victory was determined in favour of the Directors by a *coup d'état,* followed by the transportation of their opponents in the legislature.

It may be said, and with truth, that the Directorial Constitution never had a fair trial, and that at a time when the forces of reaction

---

29 Mignet, *French Revolution* (English Translation) p. 303.

and of revolution were contending for supremacy with alternating success and failure, nothing but the authority of a successful general could have given order, and no power whatever could have given constitutional liberty, to France. In 1875 France was again engaged in the construction of a Republican Constitution. The endeavour was again made to create an executive power which should neither be hostile to, nor yet absolutely dependent upon, the legislature. The outcome of these efforts was the system of Presidential government, which nominally still exists in France. The President of the Republic is elected by the National Assembly, that is, by the Chamber of Deputies and the Senate (or, as we should say in England, by the two Houses of Parliament) sitting together. He holds office for a fixed period of seven years, and is re-eligible; he possesses, nominally at least, considerable powers; he appoints the Ministry or Cabinet, in whose deliberations he, sometimes at least, takes part, and, with the concurrence of the Senate, can dissolve the Chamber of Deputies. The Third French Republic, as we all know, has now lasted for thirty-eight years, and the present Presidential Constitution has been in existence for thirty-three years. There is no reason, one may hope, why the Republic should not endure for an indefinite period; but the interesting endeavour to form a semi-parliamentary executive may already be pronounced a failure. Of the threatened conflict between Marshal MacMahon and the Assembly, closed by his resignation, we need say nothing; it may in fairness be considered the last effort of reactionists to prevent the foundation of a Republican Commonwealth. The breakdown of the particular experiment with which we are concerned is due to the events which have taken place after MacMahon's retirement from office. The government of France has gradually become a strictly parliamentary executive. Neither President Grévy nor President Carnot attempted to be the real head of the administration. President Faure and President Loubet followed in their steps. Each of these Presidents filled, or tried to fill, the part, not of a President, in the American sense of the word, but of a constitutional King. Nor is this all. As long as the President's tenure of office was in practice independent of the will of the Assembly, the expectation was reasonable that, whenever a statesman of vigour and reputation was called to the Presidency, the office might acquire a new character, and the President become, as were in a sense both Thiers and MacMahon, the real head of the Republic. But the circumstances of President Grévy's fall, as also of President Casimir Périer's retirement from office, show that the President, like his ministers, holds his office in the last resort by the favour of the Assembly. It may be, and no doubt is, a more difficult matter for the National Assembly to dismiss a President than to change a Ministry. Still the President is in reality dismissible by the legislature. Meanwhile the real executive is the Ministry, and a French Cabinet is, to judge from all appearances, more completely subject than is an English Cabinet to the control of an elective chamber. The plain truth is that the semi-parliamentary executive which the founders of the Republic meant to constitute has turned out a parliamentary executive of a very extreme type.

The statesmen who in 1848 built up the fabric of the Swiss Confederation have, it would seem, succeeded in an achievement which has twice at least baffled the ingenuity of French statesmanship. The Federal Council[30] of Switzerland is a Cabinet or Ministry elected, but not dismissible, by each Federal Assembly. For the purpose of the election the National Council and the Council of States sit together. The national Council continues in existence for three years. The Swiss Ministry being elected for three years by each Federal Assembly holds office from the time of its election until the first meeting of the next Federal Assembly. The working of this system is noteworthy. The Swiss Government is elective, but as it is chosen by each Assembly Switzerland thus escapes the turmoil of a presidential election, and each new Assembly begins its existence in harmony with the executive. The Council, it is true, cannot be dismissed by the legislature, and the legislature cannot be dissolved by the Council. But conflicts between the Government and the Assembly are unknown. Switzerland is the most democratic country in Europe, and democracies are supposed, not without reason, to be fickle; yet the Swiss executive power possesses a permanence and stability which

---

30 As to the character of the Swiss Federal Council, see Lowell, *Governments and Parties in Continental Europe,* ii. pp. 191–208.

does not characterise any parliamentary Cabinet. An English Ministry, to judge by modern experience, cannot often retain power for more than the duration of one parliament; the Cabinets of Louis Philippe lasted on an average for about three years; under the Republic the lifetime of a French administration is measured by months. The members of the Swiss Ministry, if we may use the term, are elected only for three years; they are however re-eligible, and re-election is not the exception but the rule. The men who make up the administration are rarely changed. You may, it is said, find among them statesmen who have sat in the Council for fifteen or sixteen years consecutively. This permanent tenure of office does not, it would seem, depend upon the possession by particular leaders of extraordinary personal popularity, or of immense political influence; it arises from the fact that under the Swiss system there is no more reason why the Assembly should not re-elect a trusted administrator, than why in England a joint-stock company should not from time to time reappoint a chairman in whom they have confidence. The Swiss Council, indeed, is—as far as a stranger dare form an opinion on a matter of which none but Swiss citizens are competent judges—not a Ministry or a Cabinet in the English sense of the term. It may be described as a Board of Directors appointed to manage the concerns of the Confederation in accordance with the articles of the Constitution and in general deference to the wishes of the Federal Assembly. The business of politics is managed by men of business who transact national affairs, but are not statesmen who, like a Cabinet, are at once the servants and the leaders of a parliamentary majority. This system, one is told by observers who know Switzerland, may well come to an end. The reformers, or innovators, who desire a change in the mode of appointing the Council, wish to place the election thereof in the hands of the citizens. Such a revolution, should it ever be carried out, would, be it noted, create not a parliamentary but a non-parliamentary executive.[31]

---

31 See Adams, *Swiss Confederation*, ch. iv.

Note IV

THE RIGHT OF SELF-DEFENCE

How far has an individual a right to defend his person, liberty, or property, against unlawful violence by force, or (if we use the word "self-defence" in a wider sense than that usually assigned to it) what are the principles which, under English law, govern the right of self-defence?[32]

The answer to this inquiry is confessedly obscure and indefinite, and does not admit of being given with dogmatic certainty; nor need this uncertainty excite surprise, for the rule which fixes the limit to the right of self-help must, from the nature of things, be a compromise between the necessity, on the one hand, of allowing every citizen to maintain his rights against wrongdoers, and the necessity, on the other hand, of suppressing private warfare. Discourage self-help, and loyal subjects become the slaves of ruffians. Over-stimulate self-assertion, and for the arbitrament of the Courts you substitute the decision of the sword or the revolver.

Let it further be remarked that the right of natural self-defence, even when it is recognised by the law, "does not imply a right of attacking, for instead of attacking one another for injuries past or impending, men need only have recourse to the proper tribunals of justice."[33]

A notion is current,[34] for which some justification may be found in the loose dicta of lawyers, or the vague language of legal text-books, that a man may lawfully use any amount of force which is necessary,

---

32 Report of Criminal Code Commission, 1879, pp. 43–46 [C. 2345], Notes A and B; Stephen, *Criminal Digest* (6th ed.), art. 221; 1 East, P. C. 271–294; Foster, *Discourse II.* ss. 2, 3, pp. 270, 271.

33 Stephen, *Commentaries* (8th ed.), iv. pp. 53, 54.

34 This doctrine is attributed by the Commissioners, who in 1879 reported on the Criminal Code Bill, to Lord St. Leonards. As a matter of criticism it is however open to doubt whether Lord St. Leonards held precisely the dogma ascribed to him. See Criminal Code Bill Commission, Report [C. 2345], p. 44, Note B.

and not more than necessary, for the protection of his legal rights. This notion, however popular, is erroneous. If pushed to its fair consequences, it would at times justify the shooting of trespassers, and would make it legal for a schoolboy, say of nine years old, to stab a hulking bully of eighteen who attempted to pull the child's ears. Some seventy years ago or more a worthy Captain Moir carried this doctrine out in practice to its extreme logical results. His grounds were infested by trespassers. He gave notice that he should fire at any wrongdoer who persisted in the offence. He executed his threat, and, after fair warning, shot a trespasser in the arm. The wounded lad was carefully nursed at the captain's expense. He unexpectedly died of the wound. The captain was put on his trial for murder; he was convicted by the jury, sentenced by the judge, and, on the following Monday, hanged by the hangman. He was, it would seem, a well-meaning man, imbued with too rigid an idea of authority. He perished from ignorance of law. His fate is a warning to theorists who incline to the legal heresy that every right may lawfully be defended by the force necessary for its assertion.

The maintainable theories as to the legitimate use of force necessary for the protection or assertion of a man's rights, or in other words the possible answers to our inquiry, are, it will be found, two, and two only.

FIRST THEORY

In defence of a man's liberty, person, or property, he may lawfully use any amount of force which is both "necessary"—*i.e.* not more than enough to attain its object—and "reasonable" or "proportionate" —*i.e.* which does not inflict upon the wrongdoer mischief out of proportion to the injury or mischief which the force used is intended to prevent; and no man may use in defending his rights an amount of force which is either unnecessary or unreasonable.

This doctrine of the "legitimacy of necessary and reasonable force" is adopted by the Criminal Code Bill Commissioners. It had better be given in their own words:

We take [they write] one great principle of the common law to be, that though it sanctions the defence of a man's person, liberty, and property against illegal violence, and permits the use of force to prevent crimes, to preserve the public peace, and to bring offenders to justice, yet all this is subject to the restriction that the force used is necessary; that is, that the mischief sought to be prevented could not be prevented by less violent means; and that the mischief done by, or which might reasonably be anticipated from the force used is not disproportioned to the injury or mischief which it is intended to prevent. This last principle will explain and justify many of our suggestions. It does not seem to have been universally admitted; and we have therefore thought it advisable to give our reasons for thinking that it not only ought to be recognised as the law in future, but that it is the law at present.[35]

The use of the word "necessary" is, it should be noted, somewhat peculiar, since it includes the idea both of necessity and of reasonableness. When this is taken into account, the Commissioners' view is, it is submitted, as already stated, that a man may lawfully use in defence of his rights such an amount of force as is needful for their protection and as does not inflict, or run the risk of inflicting, damage out of all proportion to the injury to be averted, or (if we look at the same thing from the other side) to the value of the right to be protected. This doctrine is eminently rational. It comes to us recommended by the high authority of four most distinguished judges. It certainly represents the principle towards which the law of England tends to approximate. But there is at least some ground for the suggestion that a second and simpler view more accurately represents the result of our authorities.

SECOND THEORY

A man, in repelling an unlawful attack upon his person or liberty, is justified in using against his assailant so much force, even amounting to the infliction of death, as is necessary for repelling the attack—*i.e.* as is needed for self-defence; but the infliction upon a wrongdoer of grievous bodily harm, or death, is justified, speaking

---

35 C. C. B. Commission, Report, p. 11.

generally, only by the necessities of self-defence—*i.e.* the defence of life, limb, or permanent liberty.[36]

This theory may be designated as the doctrine of "the legitimacy of force necessary for self-defence." Its essence is that the right to inflict grievous bodily harm or death upon a wrongdoer originates in, and is limited by, the right of every loyal subject to use the means necessary for averting serious danger to life or limb, and serious interference with his personal liberty.

The doctrine of the "legitimacy of necessary and reasonable force" and the doctrine of the "legitimacy of force necessary for self-de-fence" conduct in the main, and in most instances, to the same practical results.

On either theory *A,* when assaulted by *X,* and placed in peril of his life, may, if he cannot otherwise repel or avoid the assault, strike *X* dead. On the one view, the force used by *A* is both necessary and reasonable; on the other view, the force used by *A* is employed strictly in self-defence. According to either doctrine *A* is not justified in shooting at *X* because *X* is wilfully trespassing on *A*'s land. For the damage inflicted by *A* upon *X*—namely, the risk to *X* of losing his life—is unreasonable, that is, out of all proportion to the injury done to *A* by the trespass, and *A* in firing at a trespasser is clearly using force, not for the purpose of self-defence, but for the purpose of defending his property. Both theories, again, are consistent with the elaborate and admitted rules which limit a person's right to wound or slay another even in defence of life or limb.[37] The gist of these rules is

---

36 See Stephen, *Commentaries* (14th ed.), i. p. 79; iii. p. 267; iv. pp. 42–46. "In the case of justifiable self-defence the injured party may repel force with force in defence of his person, habitation, or property, against one who manifestly intendeth and endeavoureth with violence or surprise to commit a known felony upon either. In these cases he is not obliged to retreat, but may pursue his adversary 'till he findeth himself out of danger, and if in a conflict between them he happeneth to kill, such killing is justifiable.

"Where a known felony is attempted upon the person, be it to rob or murder, here the party assaulted may repel force with force, and even his servant then attendant on him, or any other person present, may interpose for preventing mischief; and if death ensueth, the party so interposing will be justified. In this case nature and social duty co-operate."
—Foster, *Discourse II*. chap. iii. pp. 273, 274.

37 See Stephen, *Criminal Digest* (6th ed.), art. 221, but compare *Commentaries* (8th ed.), iv. pp. 54–56; and 1 Hale, P. C. 479. The authorities are not precisely in agreement as to the

that no man must slay or severly injure another until he has done
everything he possibly can to avoid the use of extreme force. *A* is
struck by a ruffian, *X*; *A* has a revolver in his pocket. He must not
then and there fire upon *X*, but, to avoid crime, must first retreat as
far as he can. *X* pursues; *A* is driven up against a wall. Then, and not
till then, *A*, if he has no other means of repelling attack, may justifi-
ably fire at *X*. Grant that, as has been suggested, the minute provisos
as to the circumstances under which a man assaulted by a ruffian
may turn upon his assailant, belong to a past state of society, and are
more or less obsolete, the principle on which they rest is, nevertheless, clear and most important. It is, that a person attacked, even by a
wrongdoer, may not in self-defence use force which is not "necessary," and that violence is not necessary when the person attacked
can avoid the need for it by retreat; or, in other words, by the temporary surrender of his legal right to stand in a particular place—*e.g.* in a
particular part of a public square, where he has a lawful right to
stand.[38] Both theories, in short, have reference to the use of "necessary" force, and neither countenances the use of any force which is
more than is necessary for its purpose. *A* is assaulted by *X*, he can on
neither theory justify the slaying or wounding of *X*, if *A* can provide
for his own safety simply by locking a door on *X*. Both theories
equally well explain how it is that as the intensity of an unlawful
assault increases, so the amount of force legitimately to be used in
self-defence increases also, and how defence of the lawful possession
of property, and especially of a man's house, may easily turn into the
lawful defence of a man's person. "A justification of a battery in

---

right of *A* to wound *X* before he has retreated as far as he can. But the general principle
seems pretty clear. The rule as to the necessity for retreat by the person attacked must be
always taken in combination with the acknowledged right and duty of every man to stop
the commission of a felony, and with the fact that defence of a man's house seems to be
looked upon by the law as nearly equivalent to the defence of his person. "If a thief assaults
a true man, either abroad or in his house, to rob or kill him, the true man is not bound to
give back, but may kill the assailant, and it is not felony."—1 Hale, P. C. 481. See as to
defence of house, 1 East, P. C. 287.

38 Stephen, *Commentaries* (14th ed.), iv. pp. 42–46; compare 1 Hale, P. C. 481, 482, Stephen,
Criminal Digest, art. 222; Foster, *Discourse II.* cap. iii. It should be noted that the rule
enjoining that a man shall retreat from an assailant before he uses force, applies, it would
appear, only to the use of such force as may inflict grievous bodily harm or death.

defence of possession, though it arose in defence of possession, yet in the end it is the defence of the person."[39] This sentence contains the gist of the whole matter, but must be read in the light of the caution insisted upon by Blackstone, that the right of self-protection cannot be used as a justification for attack.[40]

Whether the two doctrines may not under conceivable circumstances lead to different results, is an inquiry of great interest, but in the cases which generally come before the Courts, of no great importance. What usually requires determination is how far a man may lawfully use all the force necessary to repel an assault, and for this purpose it matters little whether the test of legitimate force be its "reasonableness" or its "self-defensive character." If, however, it be necessary to choose between the two theories, the safest course for an English lawyer is to assume that the use of force which inflicts or may inflict grievous bodily harm or death—of what, in short, may be called "extreme" force—is justifiable only for the purpose of strict self-defence.

This view of the right of self-defence, it may be objected, restricts too narrowly a citizen's power to protect himself against wrong.

The weight of this objection is diminished by two reflections.

For the advancement of public justice, in the first place, every man is legally justified in using, and indeed is often bound to use, force, which may under some circumstances amount to the infliction of death.

Hence a loyal citizen may lawfully interfere to put an end to a breach of the peace, which takes place in his presence, and use such force as is reasonably necessary for the purpose.[41] Hence, too, any private person who is present when any felony is committed, is bound by law to arrest the felon, on pain of fine and imprisonment if he negligently permit him to escape.[42]

---

39 Rolle's Ab. Trespass, g. 8.

40 Blacks. *Comm.* iv. pp. 183, 184.

41 See *Timothy* v. *Simpson,* 1 C. M. & R. 757.

42 Stephen, *Commentaries* (14th ed.), iv. p. 309; Hawkins, P. C. book ii. cap. 12.

Where a felony is committed and the felon flyeth from justice, or a dangerous wound is given, it is the duty of every man to use his best endeavours
for preventing an escape. And if in the pursuit the party flying is killed,
where he cannot otherwise be overtaken, this will be deemed justifiable homicide.
For the pursuit was not barely warrantable; it is what the law requireth, and
will punish the *wilful* neglect of.[43]

No doubt the use of such extreme force is justifiable only in the case
of felony, or for the hindrance of crimes of violence. But

such homicide as is committed for the *prevention of any forcible and atrocious
crime,* is justifiable . . . by the law of England . . . as it stands at the present
day. If any person attempts the robbery or murder of another, or attempts to
break open a house *in the night-time,* and shall be killed in such attempt,
either by the party assaulted, or the owner of the house, or the servant
attendant upon either, or by any other person, and interposing to prevent
mischief, the slayer shall be acquitted and discharged. This reaches not to
any crime unaccompanied with force—as, for example, the picking of pock-
ets; nor to the breaking open of a house *in the day-time,* unless such entry
carries with it an attempt of robbery, arson, murder, or the like.[44]

Acts therefore which would not be justifiable in protection of a person's own property, may often be justified as the necessary means,
either of stopping the commission of a crime, or of arresting a felon.
Burglars rob *A*'s house, they are escaping over his garden wall, carrying off *A*'s jewels with them. *A* is in no peril of his life, but he
pursues the gang, calls upon them to surrender, and *having no other
means of preventing their escape,* knocks down one of them, *X,* who dies
of the blow; *A,* it would seem, if Foster's authority may be trusted,
not only is innocent of guilt, but has also discharged a public duty.[45]

---

43 Foster, *Discourse II.* of Homicide, pp. 271, 272, and compare pp. 273, 274.

"The intentional infliction of death is not a crime when it is done by any person . . . in
order to arrest a traitor, felon, or pirate, or keep in lawful custody a traitor, felon, or pirate,
who has escaped, or is about to escape from such custody, although such traitor, felon, or
pirate, offers no violence to any person."—Stephen, *Digest* (6th ed.), art. 222.

44 Stephen, *Commentaries* (8th ed.), iv. pp. 49, 50, and compare 14th ed. p. 40.

45 A story told of the eminent man and very learned judge, Mr. Justice Willes, and related
by an ear-witness, is to the following effect:—Mr. Justice Willes was asked: "If I look into
my drawing-room, and see a burglar packing up the clock, and he cannot see me, what
ought I to do?" Willes replied, as nearly as may be: "My advice to you, which I give as a

Let it be added that where *A* may lawfully inflict grievous bodily harm upon *X*—*e.g.* in arresting him—*X* acts unlawfully in resisting *A*, and is responsible for the injury caused to *A* by *X*'s resistance.[46]

Every man, in the second place, acts lawfully as long as he merely exercises his legal rights, and he may use such moderate force as in effect is employed simply in the exercise of such rights.

A is walking along a public path on his way home, *X* tries to stop him; *A* pushes *X* aside, *X* has a fall and is hurt. *A* has done no wrong; he has stood merely on the defensive and repelled an attempt to interfere with his right to go along a public way. *X* thereupon draws a sword and attacks *A* again. It is clear that if *A* can in no other way protect himself—*e.g.* by running away from *X*, or by knocking *X* down—he may use any amount of force necessary for his self-defence. He may stun *X*, or fire at *X*.

Here, however, comes into view the question of real difficulty. How far is *A* bound to give up the exercise of his rights, in this particular instance the right to walk along a particular path, rather than risk the maiming or the killing of *X*?

Suppose, for example, that *A* knows perfectly well that *X* claims, though without any legal ground, a right to close the particular foot-path, and also knows that, if *A* turns down another road which will also bring him home, though at the cost of a slightly longer walk, he will avoid all danger of an assault by *X*, or of being driven, in so-called self-defence, to inflict grievous bodily harm upon *X*.

Of course the case for *A*'s right to use any force necessary for his purpose may be put in this way. *A* has a right to push *X* aside. As *X*'s violence grows greater, *A* has a right to repel it. He may thus turn a scuffle over a right of way into a struggle for the defence of *A*'s life, and so justify the infliction even of death upon *X*. But this manner of

---

man, as a lawyer, and as an English judge, is as follows: In the supposed circumstance this is what you have a right to do, and I am by no means sure that it is not your duty to do it. Take a double-barrelled gun, carefully load both barrels, and then, without attracting the burglar's attention, aim steadily at his heart and shoot him dead." See *Saturday Review*, Nov. 11, 1893, p. 534.

46 Foster, *Discourse II*. p. 272.

looking at the matter is unsound. Before *A* is justified in, say, firing at *X* or stabbing *X*, he must show distinctly that he comes within one at least of the two principles which justify the use of extreme force against an assailant. But if he can avoid *X*'s violence by going a few yards out of his way, he cannot justify his conduct under either of these principles. The firing at *X* is not "reasonable," for the damage inflicted by *A* upon *X* in wounding him is out of all proportion to the mischief to *A* which it is intended to prevent—namely, his being forced to go a few yards out of his way on his road home. The firing at *X*, again, is not done in strict self-defence, for *A* could have avoided all danger by turning into another path. *A* uses force, not for the defence of his life, but for the vindication of his right to walk along a particular pathway. That this is the true view of *A*'s position is pretty clearly shown by the old rules enjoining a person assaulted to retreat as far as he can before he grievously wounds his assailant.

Reg. v. *Hewlett,* a case tried as late as 1858, contains judicial doctrine pointing in the same direction. *A* was struck by *X*, *A* thereupon drew a knife and stabbed *X.* The judge laid down that "unless the prisoner [*A*] apprehended robbery or some similar offence, or danger to life, or serious bodily danger (not simply being knocked down), he would not be justified in using the knife in self-defence."[47] The essence of this dictum is, that the force used by *A* was not justifiable, because, though it did ward off danger to *A*—namely, the peril of being knocked down—it was not necessary for the defence of *A*'s life or limb, or property. The case is a particularly strong one, because *X* was not a person asserting a supposed right, but a simple wrongdoer.

Let the last case be a little varied. Let *X* be not a ruffian but a policeman, who, acting under the orders of the Commissioner of Police, tries to prevent *A* from entering the Park at the Marble Arch. Let it further be supposed that the Commissioner has taken an erroneous view of his authority, and that therefore the attempt to hinder *A* from going into Hyde Park at the particular entrance does not

---

47 Foster & Finlason, 91, per Crowder J.

admit of legal justification. *X*, under these circumstances, is therefore legally in the wrong, and *A* may, it would seem,[48] push by *X*. But is there any reason for saying that if *A* cannot simply push *X* aside he can lawfully use the force necessary—*e.g.* by stabbing *X*—to effect an entrance? There clearly is none. The stabbing of *X* is neither a reasonable nor a self-defensive employment of force.

A dispute, in short, as to legal rights must be settled by legal tribunals, "for the King and his Courts are the *vindices injuriarum,* and will give to the party wronged all the satisfaction he deserves";[49] no one is allowed to vindicate the strength of his disputed rights by the force of his arm. Legal controversies are not to be settled by blows. A bishop who in the last century attempted, by means of riot and assault, to make good his claim to remove a deputy registrar, was admonished from the Bench that his view of the law was erroneous, and was saved from the condemnation of the jury only by the rhetoric and the fallacies of Erskine.[50]

From whatever point therefore the matter be approached, we come round to the same conclusion. The only undoubted justification for the use of extreme force in the assertion of a man's rights is, subject to the exceptions or limitations already mentioned, to be found in, as it is limited by, the necessities of strict self-defence.

Note V

QUESTIONS CONNECTED WITH THE RIGHT OF PUBLIC MEETING

Four important questions connected with the right of public meeting require consideration.

These inquiries are: *first,* whether there exist any general right of meeting in public places? *secondly,* what is the meaning of the term

---

48 It is of course assumed in this imaginary case that Acts of Parliament are not in force empowering the Commissioner of Police to regulate the use of the right to enter into the Park. It is not my intention to discuss the effect of the Metropolitan Police Acts, or to intimate any opinion as to the powers of the Commissioner of Police.

49 Stephen, *Commentaries* (14th ed.), iv. p. 44.

50 *The Bishop of Bangor's Case,* 26 St. Tr. 463.

"an unlawful assembly"? *thirdly,* what are the rights of the Crown or its servants in dealing with an unlawful assembly? and *fourthly,* what are the rights possessed by the members of a lawful assembly when the meeting is interfered with or dispersed by force?

For the proper understanding of the matters under discussion, it is necessary to grasp firmly the truth and the bearing of two indisputable but often neglected observations.

The first is that English law does not recognise any special right of public meeting either for a political or for any other purpose.[51]

The right of assembling is nothing more than the result of the view taken by our Courts of individual liberty of person and individual liberty of speech.

Interference therefore with a lawful meeting is not an invasion of a public right, but an attack upon the individual rights of *A* or *B*, and must generally resolve itself into a number of assaults upon definite persons, members of the meeting. A wrongdoer who disperses a crowd is not indicted or sued for breaking up a meeting, but is liable (if at all) to a prosecution or an action for assaulting *A,* a definite member of the crowd.[52] Hence further the answer to the question how far persons present at a lawful meeting may resist any attempt to disperse the assembly, depends at bottom on a determination of the methods prescribed by law to a given citizen *A,* for punishing or repelling an assault.

The second of these preliminary observations is that the most serious of the obscurities which beset the law of public meetings arise from the difficulty of determining how far a citizen is legally justified in using force for the protection of his person, liberty, or property, or, if we may use the word "self-defence" in its widest sense, from uncertainty as to the true principles which govern the right of self-defence.[53]

The close connection of these introductory remarks with the questions to be considered will become apparent as we proceed.

---

51 See chap. vii., *ante.*

52 See *Redford* v. *Birley,* 1 St. Tr. (n. s.) 1017.

53 See Note IV., *ante.*

DOES THERE EXIST ANY GENERAL RIGHT OF MEETING IN PUBLIC PLACES?

The answer is easy. No such right is known to the law of England.

Englishmen, it is true, meet together for political as well as for other purposes, in parks, on commons, and in other open spaces accessible to all the world. It is also true that in England meetings held in the open air are not subject, as they are in other countries—for instance, Belgium—to special restrictions. A crowd gathered together in a public place, whether they assemble for amusement or discussion, to see an acrobat perform his somersaults or to hear a statesman explain his tergiversations, stand in the same position as a meeting held for the same purpose in a hall or a drawing-room. An assembly convened, in short, for a lawful object, assembled in a place which the meeting has a right to occupy, and acting in a peaceable manner which inspires no sensible person with fear, is a lawful assembly, whether it be held in Exeter Hall, in the Grounds of Hatfield or Blenheim, or in the London parks. With such a meeting no man has a right to interfere, and for attending it no man incurs legal penalites.

But the law which does not prohibit open-air meetings does not, speaking generally, provide that there shall be spaces where the public can meet in the open air, either for political discussion or for amusement. There may of course be, and indeed there are, special localities which by statute, by custom or otherwise, are so dedicated to the use of the public as to be available for the purpose of public meetings. But speaking in general terms, the Courts do not recognise certain spaces as set aside for that end. In this respect, again, a crowd of a thousand people stand in the same position as an individual person. If *A* wants to deliver a lecture, to make a speech, or to exhibit a show, he must obtain some room or field which he can legally use for his purpose. He must not invade the rights of private property —*i.e.* commit a trespass. He must not interfere with the convenience of the public—*i.e.* create a nuisance.

The notion that there is such a thing as a right of meeting in public places arises from more than one confusion or erroneous assumption. The right of public meeting—that is, the right of all men to come together in a place where they may lawfully assemble for any lawful purpose, and especially for political discussion—is confounded with the totally different and falsely alleged right of every man to use for the purpose of holding a meeting any place which in any sense is open to the public. The two rights, did they both exist, are essentially different, and in many countries are regulated by totally different rules. It is assumed again that squares, streets, or roads, which every man may lawfully use, are necessarily available for the holding of a meeting. The assumption is false. A crowd blocking up a highway will probably be a nuisance in the legal, no less than in the popular, sense of the term, for they interfere with the ordinary citizen's right to use the locality in the way permitted to him by law. Highways, indeed, are dedicated to the public use, but they must be used for passing and going along them,[54] and the legal mode of use negatives the claim of politicians to use a highway as a forum, just as it excludes the claim of actors to turn it into an open-air theatre. The crowd who collect, and the persons who cause a crowd, for whatever purpose, to collect in a street, create a nuisance.[55] The claim on the part of persons so minded to assemble in any numbers and for so long a time as they please, to remain assembled "to the detriment of others having equal rights, is in its nature irreconcilable with the right of free passage, and there is, so far as we have been able to ascertain, no authority whatever in favour of it."[56] The general public cannot make out a right to hold meetings even on a common.[57] The ground of popular delusions as to the right of public meeting in open places is at bottom the prevalent notion that the law favours meetings held for the sake of political discussion or agitation, combined with the tacit assumption that when the law allows a right it provides the means for its exercise. No ideas can be more unfounded. English law no more favours or provides for the holding of political meetings than for the giving of public concerts. A man has a right to hear an orator

---

54 *Dovaston* v. *Payne,* 2 Hy. Bl. 527.

55 *Rex* v. *Carlile,* 6 C. & P. 628, 636; the *Tramways Case, The Times,* 7th September 1888.

56 *Ex parte Lewis,* 21 Q. B. D. 191, 197; *per Curiam.*

57 *Bailey* v. *Williamson,* L. R. 8 Q. B. 118; *De Morgan* v. *Metropolitan Board of Works,* 5 Q. B. D. 155.

as he has a right to hear a band, or to eat a bun. But each right must be exercised subject to the laws against trespass, against the creation of nuisances, against theft.

The want of a so-called forum may, it will be said, prevent ten thousand worthy citizens from making a lawful demonstration of their political wishes. The remark is true, but, from a lawyer's point of view, irrelevant. Every man has a right to see a Punch show, but if Punch is exhibiting in a theatre for money, no man can see him who cannot provide the necessary shilling. Every man has a right to hear a band, but if there be no place where a band can perform without causing a nuisance, then thousands of excellent citizens must forgo their right to hear music. Every man has a right to worship God after his own fashion, but if all the landowners of a parish refuse ground for the building of a Wesleyan chapel, parishioners must forgo attendance at a Methodist place of worship.

WHAT IS THE MEANING OF THE TERM "AN UNLAWFUL ASSEMBLY"?

The expression "unlawful assembly" does not signify any meeting of which the purpose is unlawful. If, for example, five cheats meet in one room to concoct a fraud, to indite a libel, or to forge a bank-note, or to work out a scheme of perjury, they assemble for an unlawful purpose, but they can hardly be said to constitute an "unlawful assembly." These words are, in English law, a term of art. This term has a more or less limited and definite signification, and has from time to time been defined by different authorities[58] with varying degrees of precision. The definitions vary, for the most part, rather in words than in substance. Such differences as exist have, however, a twofold importance. They show, in the first place, that the circumstances which may render a meeting an unlawful assembly have not been

---

58 See Hawkins, P. C. book i. cap. 65, ss. 9, 11; Blackstone, iv. p. 146; Stephen, *Commentaries* (14th ed.), iv. p. 174; Stephen, *Criminal Digest*, art. 75; Criminal Code Bill Commission, Draft Code, sec. 84, p. 80; *Rex* v. *Pinney*, 5 C. & P. 254; *Rex* v. *Hunt*, 1 St. Tr. (n. s.) 171; *Redford* v. *Birley, ibid.* 1071; *Rex* v. *Morris, ibid,* 521; *Reg.* v. *Vincent*, 3 St. Tr. (n. s.) 1037, 1082; *Beatty* v. *Gillbanks*, 9 Q. B. D. 308; *Reg.* v. *M'Naughton* (Irish), 14 Cox, C. C. 576; *O'Kelly* v. *Harvey* (Irish), 15 Cox, C. C. 435.

absolutely determined, and that some important questions with regard to the necessary characteristics of such an assembly are open to discussion. They show, in the second place, that the rules defining the right of public meeting are the result of judicial legislation, and that the law which has been created may be further developed by the judges, and hence that any lawyer bent on determining the character of a given meeting must consider carefully the tendency, as well as the words, of reported judgments.

The general and prominent characteristic of an unlawful assembly (however defined) is, to any one who candidly studies the authorities, clear enough. It is a meeting of persons who either intend to commit or do commit, or who lead others to entertain a reasonable fear that the meeting will commit, a breach of the peace. This actual or threatened breach of the peace is, so to speak, the essential characteristic or "property" connoted by the term "unlawful assembly." A careful examination, however, of received descriptions or definitions and of the authoritative statements contained in Sir James Stephen's *Digest* and in the Draft Code drawn by the Criminal Code Commissioners, enables an inquirer to frame a more or less accurate definition of an "unlawful assembly."

It may (it is submitted) be defined as any meeting of three or more persons who

1. Assemble to commit, or, when assembled do commit, a breach of the peace; or
2. Assemble with intent to commit a crime by open force; or
3. Assemble for any common purpose, whether lawful or unlawful, in such a manner as to give firm and courageous persons in the neighbourhood of the assembly reasonable cause to fear a breach of the peace, in consequence of the assembly; or
4. Assemble with intent to incite disaffection among the Crown's subjects, to bring the Constitution and Government of the realm, as by law established, into contempt, and generally to carry out, or prepare for carrying out, a public conspiracy.[59]

---

59 *O'Kelly* v. *Harvey* (Irish), 15 Cox, C. C. 435. The portion of this definition contained in brackets must perhaps be considered as, in England, of doubtful authority (see, however, *Reg.* v. *Ernest Jones*, 6 St. Tr. (n. s.) 783, 816, 817, summing up of Wilde, C. J., and *Reg.* v.

The following points require notice:

1. A meeting is an unlawful assembly which either disturbs the peace, or inspires reasonable persons in its neighbourhood with a fear that it will cause a breach of the peace.

Hence the state of public feeling under which a meeting is convened, the class and the number of the persons who come together, the mode in which they meet (whether, for instance, they do or do not carry arms), the place of their meeting (whether, for instance, they assemble on an open common or in the midst of a populous city), and various other circumstances, must all be taken into account in determining whether a given meeting is an unlawful assembly or not.

2. A meeting need not be the less an unlawful assembly because it meets for a legal object.

A crowd collected to petition for the release of a prisoner or to see an acrobatic performance, though meeting for a lawful object, may easily be, or turn into, an unlawful assembly. The lawfulness of the aim with which a hundred thousand people assemble may affect the reasonableness of fearing that a breach of the peace will ensue. But the lawfulness of their object does not of itself make the meeting lawful.

3. A meeting for an unlawful purpose is not, as already pointed out, necessarily an unlawful assembly.

The test of the character of the assembly is whether the meeting does or does not contemplate the use of unlawful force, or does or does not inspire others with reasonable fear that unlawful force will be used—*i.e.* that the King's peace will be broken.

4. There is some authority for the suggestion that a meeting for the purpose of spreading sedition, of exciting class against class, or of bringing the constitution of the country into contempt, is *ipso facto* an unlawful assembly,[60] and that a meeting to promote an unlawful

---

Fussell, ibid. 723, 764, summing up of Wilde, C. J.), but would, it is conceived, certainly hold good if the circumstances of the time were such that the seditious proceedings at the meeting would be likely to endanger the public peace.

60 See *Redford* v. *Birley*, 1 St. Tr. (n. s.) 1071; *Rex* v. *Hunt, ibid.* 171; *Rex* v. *Morris, ibid.* 521; *Reg.* v. *M'Naughton* (Irish), 14 Cox. C. C. 572; *O'Kelly* v. *Harvey* (Irish), 15 Cox, C. C. 435; *Reg.* v. *Burns,* 16 Cox, C. C. 355; *Reg.* v. *Ernest Jones,* 6 St. Tr. (n. s.) 783; *Reg.* v. *Fussell, ibid.* 723.

conspiracy of a public character, even though it does not directly menace a breach of the peace, is also an unlawful assembly.

This is a matter on which it is prudent to speak with reserve and hesitation, and to maintain a suspended judgment until the point suggested has come fairly before the English Courts. The true rule (possibly) may be, that a meeting assembled for the promotion of a purpose which is not only criminal, but also if carried out will promote a breach of the peace, is itself an unlawful assembly.

5. Two questions certainly remain open for decision.

Is a meeting an unlawful assembly because, though the meeting itself is peaceable enough, it excites reasonable dread of future disturbance to the peace of the realm; as where political leaders address a meeting in terms which it is reasonably supposed may, after the meeting has broken up, excite insurrection?

The answer to this inquiry is doubtful.[61]

Need again the breach of the peace, or fear thereof, which gives a meeting the character of illegality, be a breach caused by the members of the meeting?

To this inquiry an answer has already been given in the body of this treatise.[62]

The reply is, in general terms, that, on the one hand, a meeting which, as regards its object and the conduct of the members of it, is perfectly lawful, does not become an unlawful assembly from the mere fact that possibly or probably it may cause wrongdoers who dislike the meeting to break the peace,[63] but, on the other hand, a

---

61 See *Rex* v. *Hunt,* 1 St. Tr. (n. s.) 171; *Rex* v. *Dewhurst, ibid.* 530, 599. "Upon the subject of terror, there may be cases in which, from the general appearance of the meeting, there could be no fear of immediate mischief produced before that assembly should disperse; and I am rather disposed to think that the probability or likelihood of immediate terror before the meeting should disperse is necessary in order to fix the charge upon that second count to which I have drawn your attention. But if the evidence satisfies you there was a present fear produced of future rising, which future rising would be a terror and alarm to the neighbourhood, I should then desire that you would present that as your finding in the shape of what I should then take it to be, a special verdict": per Bailey, J. See also *Reg.* v. *Ernest Jones,* 6 St. Tr. (n. s.) 783; *Reg.* v. *Fussell, ibid.* 723.

62 See chap. vii., *ante.*

63 *Beatty* v. *Gillbanks,* 9 Q. B. D. 308; *Reg.* v. *Justices of Londonderry,* 28 L. R. Ir. 440, pp. 461, 462, judgment of Holmes, J.

meeting which, though perhaps not in strictness an unlawful assembly, does from some illegality in its object, or in the conduct of its members, cause a breach of the peace by persons opposed to the meeting, may thereby become an unlawful assembly,[64] and a meeting which, though in every way perfectly lawful, if it in fact causes a breach of the peace on the part of wrongdoers who dislike the meeting may, if *the peace can be restored by no other means,* be required by the magistrates or other persons in authority to break up, and on the members of the meeting refusing to disperse, becomes an unlawful assembly.[65]

WHAT ARE THE RIGHTS OF THE CROWN OR ITS SERVANTS IN DEALING WITH AN UNLAWFUL ASSEMBLY?

1. Every person who takes part in an unlawful assembly is guilty of a misdemeanour, and the Crown may therefore prosecute every such person for his offence.

Whether a given man *A,* who is present at a particular meeting, does thereby incur the guilt of "taking part" in an unlawful assembly, is in each case a question of fact.

A, though present, may not be a member of the meeting; he may be there accidentally; he may know nothing of its character; the crowd may originally have assembled for a lawful purpose; the circumstances, *e.g.* the production of arms, or the outbreak of a riot, which render the meeting unlawful, may have taken place after it began, and in these transactions *A* may have taken no part. Hence the importance of an official notice, *e.g.* by a Secretary of State, or by a magistrate, that a meeting is convened for a criminal object. A citizen after reading the notice or proclamation, goes to the meeting at his peril. If it turns out in fact an unlawful assembly, he cannot plead ignorance of its character as a defence against the charge of taking part in the meeting.[66]

---

64 *Wise* v. *Dunning* [1902], 1 K. B. 167.

65 On this point see especially *Humphries* v. *Connor,* 17 Ir. C. L. R. 1.

66 *Rex* v. *Fursey,* 6 C. & P. 81; 3 St. Tr. (n. s.) 543.

2. Magistrates, policemen, and all loyal citizens not only are entitled, but indeed are bound to disperse an unlawful assembly, and, if necessary, to do so by the use of force; and it is a gross error to suppose that they are bound to wait until a riot has occurred, or until the Riot Act has been read.[67] The prevalence of this delusion was the cause, during the Gordon Riots, of London being for days in the hands of the mob. The mode of dispersing a crowd when unlawfully assembled, and the extent of force which it is reasonable to use, differ according to the circumstances of each case.

3. If any assembly becomes a riot—*i.e.* has begun to act in a tumultuous manner to the disturbance of the peace—a magistrate on being informed that twelve or more persons are unlawfully, riotously, and tumultuously assembled together to the disturbance of the public peace, is bound to make the short statutable proclamation which is popularly known as "reading the Riot Act."[68]

The consequences are as follows: first, that any twelve rioters who do not disperse within an hour thereafter, are guilty of felony; and, secondly, that the magistrate and those acting with him may, after such hour, arrest the rioters and disperse the meeting by the employment of any amount of force necessary for the purpose, and are protected from liability for hurt inflicted or death caused in dispersing the meeting. The magistrates are, in short, empowered by the Riot Act to read the proclamation before referred to, and thereupon, after waiting for an hour, to order troops and constables to fire upon the rioters, or charge them sword in hand.[69] It is particularly to be noticed that the powers given to magistrates for dealing with riots under the Riot Act in no way lessen the common law right of a magistrate, and indeed of every citizen, to put an end to a breach of the peace, and hence to disperse an unlawful assembly.[70]

---

67 *Reg.* v. *Neale,* 9 C. & P. 431; *Burdet* v. *Abbot,* 4 Taunt. 401, 449. See pp. 285, 286, *ante.*

68 1 Geo. I. stat. 2, cap. 5, s. 2.

69 See Stephen, *Hist. Crim. Law,* i. 203; Criminal Code Bill Commission, Draft Code, ss. 88, 99.

70 *Rex* v. *Fursey,* 6 C. & P. 81; 3 St. Tr. (n. s.) 543.

WHAT ARE THE RIGHTS POSSESSED BY THE MEMBERS OF A LAWFUL ASSEMBLY WHEN THE MEETING IS INTERFERED WITH OR DISPERSED BY FORCE?

The Salvation Army assemble in a place where they have a right to meet, say an open piece of land placed at their disposal by the owner, and for a lawful purpose, namely, to hear a sermon. Certain persons who think the meeting either objectionable or illegal attempt to break it up, or do break it up, by force. What, under these circumstances, are the rights of the Salvationists who have come to listen to a preacher? This in a concrete form is the problem for consideration. [71]

An attempt, whether successful or not, to disperse a lawful assembly involves assaults of more or less violence upon the persons *A, B,* and *C* who have met together. The wrong thus done by the assailants is, as already pointed out, a wrong done, not to the meeting—a body which has legally no collective rights—but to *A, B,* or *C,* an individual pushed, hustled, struck, or otherwise assaulted.

Our problem is, then, in substance—What are the rights of *A,* the member of a meeting, when unlawfully assaulted? And this inquiry, in its turn, embraces two different questions, which, for clearness sake, ought to be carefully kept apart from each other.

First, what are the remedies of *A* for the wrong done to him by the assault?

The answer is easy. *A* has the right to take civil, or (subject to one reservation) criminal proceedings against any person, be he an officer, a soldier, a commissioner of police, a magistrate, a policeman, or a private ruffian, who is responsible for the assault upon *A.* If, moreover, *A* be killed, the person or persons by whom his death has been caused may be indicted, according to circumstances, for manslaughter or murder.

---

71 For the sake of convenience, I have taken a meeting of the Salvation Army as a typical instance of a lawful public meeting. It should, however, be constantly remembered that the rights of the Salvationists are neither more nor less than those of any other crowd lawfully collected together—*e.g.* to hear a band of music.

This statement as to *A*'s rights or (what is, however, the same thing from another point of view) as to the liabilities of *A*'s assailants, is made subject to one reservation. There exists considerable doubt as to the degree and kind of liability of soldiers (or possibly of policemen) who, under the orders of a superior, do some act (*e.g.* arrest *A* or fire at *A*) which is not on the face of it unlawful, but which turns out to be unlawful because of some circumstance of which the subordinate was not in a position to judge, as, for example, because the meeting was not technically an unlawful assembly, or because the officer giving the order had in some way exceeded his authority.

> I hope [says Willes, J.] I may never have to determine that difficult question, how far the orders of a superior officer are a justification. Were I compelled to determine that question, I should probably hold that the orders are an absolute justification in time of actual war—at all events, as regards enemies or foreigners—and, I should think, even with regard to English-born subjects of the Crown, unless the orders were such as could not legally be given. I believe that the better opinion is, that an officer or soldier, acting under the orders of his superior—not being necessarily or manifestly illegal—would be justified by his orders.[72]

A critic were rash who questioned the suggestion of a jurist whose dicta are more weighty than most considered judgments. The words, moreover, of Mr. Justice Willes enounce a principle which is in itself pre-eminently reasonable. If its validity be not admitted, results follow as absurd as they are unjust: every soldier is called upon to determine on the spur of the moment legal subtleties which, after a lengthy consultation, might still perplex experienced lawyers, and the private ordered by his commanding officer to take part in the suppression of a riot runs the risk, if he disobeys, of being shot by order of a court-martial, and, if he obeys, of being hanged under the sentence of a judge. Let it further be carefully noted that the doctrine of Mr. Justice Willes, which is approved of by the Criminal Code Commissioners,[73] applies, it would seem, to criminal liability only.

---

72 *Keighly* v. *Bell*, 4 F. & F. 763, 790, per Willes, J. See also Note VI. p. 512, *post*, Duty of Soldiers called upon to disperse an Unlawful Assembly.

73 See C. C. B. Commission, Draft Code, ss. 49–53.

The soldier or policeman who, without full legal justification, assaults or arrests *A* incurs (it is submitted), even though acting under orders, full civil liability.

Secondly, how far is *A* entitled to maintain by force against all assailants his right to take part in a lawful public meeting, or, in other words, his right to stand in a place where he lawfully may stand —*e.g.* ground opened to *A* by the owner, for a purpose which is in itself lawful—*e.g.* the hearing of an address from a captain of the Salvation Army?

In order to obtain a correct answer to this inquiry we should bear in mind the principles which regulate the right of self-defence,[74] and should further consider what may be the different circumstances under which an attempt may be made without legal warrant to disperse a meeting of the Salvation Army. The attack upon the meeting, or in other words upon *A*, may be made either by mere wrongdoers, or by persons who believe, however mistakenly, that they are acting in exercise of a legal right or in discharge of a legal duty. Let each of these cases be examined separately.

Let us suppose, in the first place, that the Salvationists, and *A* among them, are attacked by the so-called Skeleton Army or other roughs, and let it further be supposed that the object of the assault is simply to break up the meeting, and that therefore, if *A* and others disperse, they are in no peril of damage to life or limb.

A and his friends may legally, it would seem, stand their ground, and use such moderate force as amounts to simple assertion of the right to remain where they are. *A* and his companions may further give individual members of the Skeleton Army in charge for a breach of the peace. It may, however, happen that the roughs are in large numbers, and press upon the Salvationists so that they cannot keep their ground without the use of firearms or other weapons. The use of such force is in one sense necessary, for the Salvationists cannot hold their meeting without employing it. Is the use of such force legal? The strongest way of putting the case in favour of *A* and his friends is that, in firing upon their opponents, they are using force to

---

74 See Note IV. p. 341, *ante.*

put down a breach of the peace. On the whole, however, there can, it is submitted, be no doubt that the use of firearms or other deadly weapons, to maintain their right of meeting, is under the circumstances not legally justifiable. The principle on which extreme acts of self-defence against a lawless assailant cannot be justified until the person assaulted has retreated as far as he can, is applicable to *A, B, C,* etc., just as it would be to *A* singly. Each of the Salvationists is defending, under the supposed circumstances, not his life, but his right to stand on a given plot of ground.

Next, suppose that the attempt to disperse the Salvationists is made, not by the Skeleton Army, but by the police, who act under the order of magistrates who hold *bonâ fide,* though mistakenly,[75] that a notice from the Home Secretary forbidding the Army to meet, makes its meeting an unlawful assembly.

Under these circumstances, the police are clearly in the wrong. A policeman who assaults *A, B,* or *C,* does an act not admitting of legal justification. Nor is it easy to maintain that the mere fact of the police acting as servants of the Crown in supposed discharge of their duty makes it of itself incumbent upon *A* to leave the meeting.

The position, however, of the police differs in two important respects from that of mere wrongdoers. Policeman *X,* when he tells *A* to move on, and compels him to do so, does not put *A* in peril of life or limb, for *A* knows for certain that, if he leaves the meeting, he will not be further molested, or that if he allows himself to be peaceably arrested, he has nothing to dread but temporary imprisonment and appearance before a magistrate who will deal with his rights in accordance with law. Policeman *X,* further, asserts *bonâ fide* a supposed legal right to make *A* withdraw from a place where *X* believes *A* has no right to stand; there is a dispute between *A* and *X* as to a matter of law. This being the state of affairs, it is at any rate fairly arguable that *A, B,* and *C* have a right to stand simply on the defensive,[76] and

---

75 See *Beatty* v. *Gillbanks*, 9 Q. B. D. 308.

76 The legality, however, of even this amount of resistance to the police is doubtful. "Any man who advises a public assembly when the police come there to disperse them, to stand their ground shoulder by shoulder, if that means to resist the police, although it might not mean to resist by striking them; yet if it meant to resist the police and not to disperse, that

remain where they are as long as they can do so without inflicting grievous bodily harm upon X and other policemen. Suppose, however, as is likely to be the fact, that, under the pressure of a large body of constables, the Salvationists cannot maintain their meeting without making use of arms—*e.g.*, using bludgeons, swords, pistols, or the like. They have clearly no right to make use of this kind of force. A and his friends are not in peril of their lives, and to kill a policeman in order to secure A the right of standing in a particular place is to inflict a mischief out of all proportion to the importance of the mischief to A which he wishes to avert.[77] A, therefore, if he stabs or stuns X, can on no theory plead the right of self-defence. A and X further are, as already pointed out, at variance on a question of legal rights. This is a matter to be determined not by arms, but by an action at law.

Let it further be noted that the supposed case is the most unfavourable for the police which can be imagined. They may well, though engaged in hindering what turns out to be a lawful meeting, stand in a much better situation than that of assailants. The police may, under orders, have fully occupied and filled up the ground which the Salvationists intend to use. When the Salvationists begin arriving, they find there is no place where they can meet. Nothing but the use of force, and indeed of extreme force, can drive the police away. This force the Salvation Army cannot use; if they did, they would be using violence not on any show of self-defence, but to obtain possession of a particular piece of land. Their only proper course is the vindication of their rights by proceedings in Court.

---

was illegal advice. If the police had interfered with them, they were not at liberty to resist in any such circumstances; they ought to have dispersed by law, and have sought their remedy against any unjust interference afterwards. . . . This is a body of police acting under the responsibility of the law, acting under the orders of those who would be responsible for the orders which they gave, charged with the public peace, and who would have authority to disperse when they received those orders, leaving those who should give them a deep responsibility if they should improperly interfere with the exercise of any such public duties. . . . Gentlemen, the peaceable citizens are not in the performance of their duty if they stand shoulder to shoulder, and when the police come and order the assembly to disperse, they do not disperse, but insist on remaining, they are not in the peaceable execution of any right or duty, but the contrary, and from that moment they become an illegal assembly."—*Reg.* v. *Ernest Jones,* 6 St. Tr. (n. s.) 783, 811, summing up of Wilde, C. J.

77 *Rex* v. *Fursey,* 6 C. & P. 81; 3 St. Tr. (n. s.) 543.

Of the older cases, which deal with the question how far it is justifiable to resist by violence an arrest made by an officer of justice without due authority, it is difficult to make much use for the elucidation of the question under consideration,[78] for in these cases the matter discussed seems often to have been not whether *A*'s resistance was justifiable, but whether it amounted to murder or only to manslaughter. There are, however, one or two more or less recent decisions which have a real bearing on the right of the members of a public meeting to resist by force attempts to disperse it. And these cases are, on the whole, when properly understood, not inconsistent with the inferences already drawn from general principles. The doctrine laid down in *Reg.* v. *Hewlett*,[79] that *A* ought not to inflict grievous bodily harm even upon *X* a wrongdoer unless in the strictest self-defence, is of the highest importance. *Rex* v. *Fursey*,[80] a decision of 1833, has direct reference to the right of meeting. At a public meeting held that year in London, *A* carried an American flag which was snatched from him by *X*, a policeman, whereupon *A* stabbed *X*. He was subsequently indicted under 9 Geo. I. c. 31, s. 12, and it appears to have been laid down by the judge that though, if the meeting was a legal one, *X* had no right to snatch away *A*'s flag, still that even on the supposition that the meeting was a lawful assembly, *A*, if *X* had died of his wound, would have been guilty either of manslaughter, or very possibly of murder. Quite in keeping with *Rex* v. *Fursey* is the recent case of *Reg.* v. *Harrison*.[81] Some of the expressions attributed, in a very compressed newspaper report, to the learned judge who tried the case, may be open to criticism, but the principle involved in the defendant's conviction, namely, that a ruffian cannot assert his alleged right to walk down a particular street by stunning or braining a policeman, or a good citizen who is helping the policeman, is good law no less than good sense.[82]

---

78 See, *e.g., Dixon's Case,* 1 East, P. C. 313; *Borthwick's Case, ibid.; Wither's Case,* 1 East, P. C. 233, 309; *Tooley's Case,* 2 Lord Raymond, 1296.

79 1 F. & F. 91.

80 3 St. Tr. (n. s.) 543, and compare Criminal Code Commission Report, pp. 43, 44.

81 *The Times,* 19th December 1887.

82 "Well, if any heads are broken before [after?] men are ordered [by the police] to disperse

Nor does the claim to assert legal rights by recourse to pistols or bludgeons receive countenance from two decisions occasionally adduced in its support.

The one is *Beatty* v. *Gillbanks*.[83] This case merely shows that a lawful meeting is not rendered an unlawful assembly simply because ruffians try to break it up, and, in short, that the breach of the peace which renders a meeting unlawful must, in general,[84] be a breach caused by the members of the meeting, and not by wrongdoers who wish to prevent its being held.[85]

The second is *M'Clenaghan* v. *Waters*.[86] The case may certainly be so explained as to lay down the doctrine that the police when engaged under orders in dispersing a lawful meeting are not engaged in the "execution of their duty," and that therefore the members of the meeting may persist in holding it in spite of the opposition of the police. Whether this doctrine be absolutely sound is open to debate. It does not necessarily, however, mean more than that a man may exercise a right, even though he has to use a moderate amount of force, against a person who attempts to hinder the exercise of the right. But *M'Clenaghan* v. *Waters* certainly does not decide that the member of a lawful assembly may exercise whatever amount of force is necessary to prevent its being dispersed, and falls far short of justifying the proceedings of a Salvationist who brains a policeman rather than surrender the so-called right of public meeting. It is, however, doubtful whether *M'Clenaghan* v. *Waters* really supports even the doctrine that moderate resistance to the police is justifiable in order to prevent the dispersing of a lawful assembly. The case

---

and refuse to disperse, those who break their heads will find their own heads in a very bad situation if they are brought into a court of law to answer for it. No jury would hesitate to convict, and no court would hesitate to punish."—*Reg.* v. *Ernest Jones*, 6 St. Tr. (n. s.) 783, 811, 812, summing up of Wilde. C. J.

83 9 Q. B. D. 308.

84 See p. 356, *ante.*

85 As already pointed out, the principle maintained in *Beatty* v. *Gillbanks* is itself open to some criticism.

86 *The Times*, 18th July 1882.

purports to follow *Beatty* v. *Gillbanks,* and therefore the Court cannot be taken as intentionally going beyond the principle laid down in that case. The question for the opinion of the Court, moreover, in *M'Clanaghan* v. *Waters* was, "whether upon the facts stated the police at the time of their being assaulted by the appellants (Salvationists) were legally justified in interfering to prevent the procession from taking place"; or, in other words, whether the meeting of the Salvationists was a lawful assembly? To this question, in the face of *Beatty* v. *Gillbanks,* but one reply was possible. This answer the Court gave: they determined "that in taking part in a procession the appellants were doing only an act strictly lawful, and the fact that that act was believed likely to cause others to commit such as were unlawful, was no justification for interfering with them." Whether the Court determined anything more is at least open to doubt, and if they did determine, as alleged, that the amount of the resistance offered to the police was lawful, this determination is, to say the least, not inconsistent with the stern punishment of acts like that committed by the prisoner Harrison.

No one, however, can dispute that the line between the forcible exercise of a right in the face of opposition, and an unjustifiable assault on those who oppose its exercise, is a fine one, and that many nice problems concerning the degree of resistance which the members of a lawful meeting may offer to persons who wish to break it up are at present unsolved. The next patriot or ruffian who kills or maims a policeman rather than compromise the right of public meeting will try what, from a speculative point of view, may be considered a valuable legal experiment which promises results most interesting to jurists. The experiment will, however, almost certainly be tried at the cost, according to the vigour of his proceedings, of either his freedom or his life.[87]

---

87 The whole summing up of Wilde, C. J., in *Reg.* v. *Ernest Jones,* 6 St. Tr. (n. s.) 783, 807–816, merits particular attention. His language is extremely strong and if it be taken as a perfectly correct exposition of the law, negatives the right to resist by force policemen who with the *bonâ fide* intention to discharge their duty, disperse an assembly which may ultimately turn out not to have been an unlawful assembly.

Note VI

DUTY OF SOLDIERS CALLED UPON
TO DISPERSE AN UNLAWFUL ASSEMBLY

On 7th September 1893 Captain Barker and a small number of soldiers were placed in the Ackton Colliery, in order to defend it from the attack of a mob. A body of rioters armed with sticks and cudgels entered the colliery yard, and with threats demanded the withdrawal of the soldiers. The mob gradually increased, and broke the windows of the building in which the troops were stationed and threw stones at them. Attempts were made to burn the building, and timber was actually set on fire. The soldiers retreated, but were at last surrounded by a mob of 2000 persons. The crowd was called upon to disperse, and the Riot Act read. More stones were hurled at the troops, and it was necessary to protect the colliery. At last, before an hour from the reading of the Riot Act, and on the crowd refusing to disperse, Captin Barker gave orders to fire. The mob dispersed, but one or two bystanders were killed who were not taking an active part in the riot. Commissioners, including Lord Justice Bowen, afterwards Lord Bowen, were appointed to report on the conduct of the troops. The following passage from the report is an almost judicial statement of the law as to the duty of soldiers when called upon to disperse a mob:

> We pass next to the consideration of the all-important question whether the conduct of the troops in firing on the crowd was justifiable; and it becomes essential, for the sake of clearness, to state succinctly what the law is which bears upon the subject. By the law of this country every one is bound to aid in the suppression of riotous assemblages. The degree of force, however, which may lawfully be used in their suppression depends on the nature of each riot, for the force used must always be moderated and proportioned to the circumstances of the case and to the end to be attained.
>
> The taking of life can only be justified by the necessity for protecting persons or property against various forms of violent crime, or by the necessity of dispersing a riotous crowd which is dangerous unless dispersed, or in the case of persons whose conduct has become felonious through disobedience to the provisions of the Riot Act, and who resist the attempt to disperse or apprehend them. The riotous crowd at the Ackton Hall Colliery was one

whose danger consisted in its manifest design violently to set fire and do serious damage to the colliery property, and in pursuit of that object to assault those upon the colliery premises. It was a crowd accordingly which threatened serious outrage, amounting to felony, to property and persons, and it became the duty of all peaceable subjects to assist in preventing this. The necessary prevention of such outrage on person and property justifies the guardians of the peace in the employment against a riotous crowd of even deadly weapons.

Officers and soldiers are under no special privileges and subject to no special responsibilities as regards this principle of the law. A soldier for the purpose of establishing civil order is only a citizen armed in a particular manner. He cannot because he is a soldier excuse himself if without necessity he takes human life. The duty of magistrates and peace officers to summon or to abstain from summoning the assistance of the military depends in like manner on the necessities of the case. A soldier can only act by using his arms. The weapons he carries are deadly. They cannot be employed at all without danger to life and limb, and in these days of improved rifles and perfected ammunition, without some risk of injuring distant and possibly innocent bystanders. To call for assistance against rioters from those who can only interpose under such grave conditions ought, of course, to be the last expedient of the civil authorities. But when the call for help is made, and a necessity for assistance from the military has arisen, to refuse such assistance is in law a misdemeanour.

The whole action of the military when once called in ought, from first to last, to be based on the principle of doing, and doing without fear, that which is absolutely necessary to prevent serious crime, and of exercising all care and skill with regard to what is done. No set of rules exists which governs every instance or defines beforehand every contingency that may arise. One salutary practice is that a magistrate should accompany the troops. The presence of a magistrate on such occasions, although not a legal obligation, is a matter of the highest importance. The military come, it may be, from a distance. They know nothing, probably, of the locality, or of the special circumstances. They find themselves introduced suddenly on a field of action, and they need the counsel of the local justice, who is presumably familiar with the details of the case. But, although the magistrate's presence is of the highest value and moment, his absence does not alter the duty of the soldier, nor ought it to paralyse his conduct, but only to render him doubly careful as to the proper steps to be taken. No officer is justified by English law in standing by and allowing felonious outrage to be committed merely because of a magistrate's absence.

The question whether, on any occasion, the moment has come for firing upon a mob of rioters, depends, as we have said, on the necessities of the case. Such firing, to be lawful, must, in the case of a riot like the present, be necessary to stop or prevent such serious and violent crime as we have alluded to; and it must be conducted without recklessness or negligence.

When the need is clear, the soldier's duty is to fire with all reasonable caution, so as to produce no further injury than what is absolutely wanted for the purpose of protecting person and property. An order from the magistrate who is present is required by military regulations, and wisdom and discretion are entirely in favour of the observance of such a practice. But the order of the magistrate has at law no legal effect. Its presence does not justify the firing if the magistrate is wrong. Its absence does not excuse the officer for declining to fire when the necessity exists.

With the above doctrines of English law the Riot Act does not interfere. Its effect is only to make the failure of a crowd to disperse for a whole hour after the proclamation has been read a felony; and on this ground to afford a statutory justification for dispersing a felonious assemblage, even at the risk of taking life. In the case of the Ackton Hall Colliery, an hour had not elapsed after what is popularly called the reading of the Riot Act, before the military fired. No justification for their firing can therefore be rested on the provisions of the Riot Act itself, the further consideration of which may indeed be here dismissed from the case. But the fact that an hour had not expired since its reading did not incapacitate the troops from acting when outrage had to be prevented. All their common law duty as citizens and soldiers remained in full force. The justification of Captain Barker and his men must stand or fall entirely by the common law. Was what they did necessary, and no more than was necessary, to put a stop to or prevent felonious crime? In doing it, did they exercise all ordinary skill and caution, so as to do no more harm than could be reasonably avoided?

If these two conditions are made out, the fact that innocent people have suffered does not involve the troops in legal responsibility. A guilty ring-leader who under such conditions is shot dead, dies by justifiable homicide. An innocent person killed under such conditions, where no negligence has occurred, dies by an accidental death. The legal reason is not that the innocent person has to thank himself for what has happened, for it is conceivable (though not often likely) that he may have been unconscious of any danger and innocent of all imprudence. The reason is that the soldier who fired has done nothing except what was his strict legal duty.

In measuring with the aid of subsequent evidence the exact necessities of the case as they existed at the time at Ackton Hall Colliery, we have formed a clear view that the troops were in a position of great embarrassment. The withdrawal of half their original force to Nostell Colliery had reduced them to so small a number as to render it difficult for them to defend the colliery premises effectively at nighttime. The crowd for some hours had been familiarised with their presence, and had grown defiant. All efforts at conciliation had failed. Darkness had meanwhile supervened, and it was difficult for Captain Barker to estimate the exact number of his assailants, or to what extent he was being surrounded and outflanked. Six or seven appeals had been made by the magistrate to the crowd. The Riot Act had been read without result. A charge had been made without avail. Much valuable colliery property was already blazing, and the troops were with difficulty keeping at bay a mob armed with sticks and bludgeons, which was refusing to disperse, pressing where it could into the colliery premises, stoning the fire-engine on its arrival, and keeping up volleys of missiles. To prevent the colliery from being overrun and themselves surrounded, it was essential for them to remain as close as possible to the Green Lane entrance. Otherwise, the rioters would, under cover of the darkness, have been able to enter in force. To withdraw from their position was, as we have already intimated, to abandon the colliery offices in the rear to arson and violence. To hold the position was not possible, except at the risk of the men being seriously hurt and their force crippled. Assaulted by missiles on all sides, we think that, in the events which had happened, Captain Barker and his troops had no alternative left but to fire, and it seems to us that Mr. Hartley was bound to require them to do so.

It cannot be expected that this view should be adopted by many of the crowd in Green Lane who were taking no active part in the riotous proceedings. Such persons had not, at the time, the means of judging of the danger in which the troops and the colliery stood. But no sympathy felt by us for the injured bystanders, no sense which we entertain of regret that, owing to the smallness of the military force at Featherstone and the prolonged absence of a magistrate, matters had drifted to such a pass, can blind us to the fact that, as things stood at the supreme moment when the soldiers fired, their action was necessary. We feel it right to express our sense of the steadiness and discipline of the soldiers in the circumstances. We can find no ground for any suggestion that the firing, if it was in fact necessary, was conducted with other than reasonable skill and care. The darkness rendered it impossible to take more precaution than had been already employed to discriminate between the lawless and the peaceable, and it is to be observed that even the first shots fired produced little or no effect upon the crowd in inducing them to withdraw. If our conclusions on these points be, as we believe them to be, correct, it follows that the action of the troops was justified in law.[88]

Note VII

THE MEANING OF AN "UNCONSTITUTIONAL" LAW

The expression "unconstitutional" has, as applied to a law, at least three different meanings varying according to the nature of the constitution with reference to which it is used:

---

88 Report of the committee appointed to inquire into the circumstances connected with the disturbances at Featherstone on the 7th of September 1893 [C. — 7234].

1. The expression, as applied to an English Act of Parliament, means simply that the Act in question, as, for instance, the Irish Church Act, 1869, is, in the opinion of the speaker, opposed to the spirit of the English constitution; it cannot mean that the Act is either a breach of law or is void.

2. The expression, as applied to a law passed by the French Parliament, means that the law, *e.g.* extending the length of the President's tenure of office, is opposed to the articles of the constitution. The expression does not necessarily mean that the law in question is void, for it is by no means certain that any French Court will refuse to enforce a law because it is unconstitutional. The word would probably, though not of necessity, be, when employed by a Frenchman, a term of censure.

3. The expression, as applied to an Act of Congress, means simply that the Act is one beyond the power of Congress, and is therefore void. The word does not in this case necessarily import any censure whatever. An American might, without any inconsistency, say that an Act of Congress was a good law, that is, a law calculated in his opinion to benefit the country, but that unfortunately it was "unconstitutional," that is to say, *ultra vires* and void.

Note VIII

SWISS FEDERALISM[89]

The Swiss Federal Constitution may appear to a superficial observer to be a copy in miniature of the Constitution of the United States; and there is no doubt that the Swiss statesmen of 1848 did in one or two points, and notably in the formation of the Council of States or Senate, intentionally follow American precedents. But for all this, Swiss Federalism is the natural outgrowth of Swiss history, and bears a peculiar character of its own that well repays careful study.

Three ideas underlie the institutions of modern Switzerland.

---

89 See Lowell, *Governments and Parties in Continental Europe,* ii., *Switzerland,* pp. 180—336; Orelli, *Das Staatsrecht der Schweizerischen Eidgenossenschaft;* Marquardsen's *Handbuch des Oeffentlichen Rechts,* iv. i. 2.

The first is the uncontested and direct sovereignty of the nation.

In Switzerland the will of the people, when expressed in the mode provided by the Constitution, is admittedly supreme. This supremacy is not disputed by any political party or by any section of the community. No one dreams of changing the democratic basis of the national institutions. There does not exist in Switzerland any faction which, like the reactionists in France, meditates the overthrow of the Republic. There does not exist any section of the community which, like the Bohemians in Austria, or like the French in Alsace, is, or may be supposed to be, disloyal to the central government. But in Switzerland not only the supremacy but the direct authority of the nation is, practically as well as theoretically, acknowledged. The old idea of the opposition between the government and the people has vanished. All parts of the government, including in that term not only the Executive but also the Legislative bodies, are the recognised agents of the nation, and the people intervene directly in all important acts of legislation. In Switzerland, in short, the nation is sovereign in the sense in which a powerful king or queen was sovereign in the time when monarchy was a predominant power in European countries, and we shall best understand the attitude of the Swiss nation towards its representatives, whether in the Executive or in Parliament, by considering that the Swiss people occupies a position not unlike that held, for example, by Elizabeth of England. However great the Queen's authority, she was not a tyrant, but she really in the last resort governed the country, and her ministers were her servants and carried out her policy. The Queen did not directly legislate, but by her veto and by other means she controlled all important legislation. Such is, speaking roughly, the position of the Swiss people. The Federal Executive and the Federal Parliament pursue the lines of policy approved by the people. Under the name of the Referendum there is exercised a popular veto on laws passed by the Legislature, and of recent years, under the name of the Initiative, an attempt has been made at more or less direct legislation by the people. Whatever be the merits of Swiss institutions, the idea which governs them is obvious. The nation is monarch, the Executive and the members of the Legislature are the people's agents or ministers.

The second idea to which Swiss institutions give expression is that politics are a matter of business. The system of Swiss government is business-like. The affairs of the nation are transacted by men of capacity, who give effect to the will of the nation.

The last and most original Swiss conception is one which it is not easy for foreigners bred up under other constitutional systems to grasp. It is that the existence of political parties does not necessitate the adoption of party government.

These are the principles or conceptions embodied in Swiss institutions; they are closely inter-connected, they pervade and to a great extent explain the operation of the different parts of the Swiss Constitution. Many of its features are of course common to all the federal governments, but its special characteristics are due to the predominance of the three ideas to which the reader's attention has been directed. That this is so will be seen if we examine the different parts of the Swiss Constitution.

THE FEDERAL COUNCIL

This body, which we should in England call the Ministry, consists of seven persons elected at their first meeting by the two Chambers which make up the Swiss Federal Assembly or Congress, and for this purpose sit together. The Councillors hold office for three years, and being elected after the first meeting of the Assembly, which itself is elected for three years, keep their places till the next Federal Assembly meets, when a new election takes place. The Councillors need not be, but in fact are, elected from among the members of the Federal Assembly, and though they lose their seats on election, yet, as they can take part in the debates of each House, may for practical purposes be considered members of the Assembly or Parliament. The powers confided to the Council are wide. The Council is the Executive of the Confederacy and possesses the authority naturally belonging to the national government. It discharges also, strange as this may appear to Englishmen or Americans, many judicial functions. To the Council are in many cases referred questions of "administrative law," and also certain classes of what Englishmen or Americans consider strictly legal questions. Thus the Council in effect determined some years ago what were the rights as to meeting in public of the Salvation Army, and whether and to what extent Cantonal legislation could prohibit or regulate their meetings. The Council again gives the required sanction to the Constitutions or to alterations in the Constitutions of the Cantons, and determines whether clauses in such Constitutions are, or are not, inconsistent with the articles of the Federal Constitution. The Council is in fact the centre of the whole Swiss Federal system; it is called upon to keep up good relations between the Cantons and the Federal or National government, and generally to provide for the preservation of order, and ultimately for the maintenance of the law throughout the whole country. All foreign affairs fall under the Council's supervision, and the conduct of foreign relations must, under the circumstances of Switzerland, always form a most important and difficult part of the duties of the government.

Though the Councillors are elected they are not dismissible by the Assembly, and in so far the Council may be considered an independent body; but from another point of view the Council has no independence. It is expected to carry out, and does carry out, the policy of the Assembly, and ultimately the policy of the nation, just as a good man of business is expected to carry out the orders of his employer. Many matters which are practically determined by the Council might constitutionally be decided by the Assembly itself, which, however, as a rule leaves the transaction of affairs in the hands of the Council. But the Council makes reports to the Assembly, and were the Assembly to express a distinct resolution on any subject, effect would be given to it. Nor is it expected that either the Council or individual Councillors should go out of office because proposals or laws presented by them to the Assembly are rejected, or because a law passed, with the approval of the Council, by the Chambers, is vetoed on being referred to the people. The Council, further, though as the members thereof, being elected by the Federal Assembly, must in general agree with the sentiments of that body, does not represent a Parliamentary majority as does an English or a French Ministry. The Councillors, though elected for a term of three years, are re-eligible, and as a rule are re-elected. The consequence is that a man may hold office for sixteen years or more, and that the character of the Council changes but slowly; and there have, it is said, been cases in which the majority of the Parliament belonged to one party and the majority of the Council to another, and this want of harmony in general political views between the Parliament and the Government did not lead to inconvenience. In truth the Council is not a Cabinet but a Board for the management of business, of which Board the so-called President of the Confederation, who is annually elected from among the members of the Council, is merely the chairman. It may fairly be compared to a Board of Directors chosen by the members of a large joint-stock company. In one sense the Board has no independent power. The majority of the shareholders, did they choose to do so, could always control its action or reverse its policy. In another sense, as we all know, a Board is almost free from control. As long as things are well, or even tolerably, managed, the shareholders have neither the wish nor practically the power to interfere. They know that the directors possess knowledge and experience which the shareholders lack, and that to interfere with the Board's management would imperil the welfare of the association. So it is with the Federal Council. Its dependence is the source of its strength. It does not come into conflict with the Assembly; it therefore is a permanent body, which carries on, and carries on with marked success, the administration of public affairs. It is a body of men of business who transact the business of the State.

It is worth while to dwell at some length on the constitution and character of the Swiss Council or Board, because it gives us a kind of Executive differing both from the Cabinet government of England or France, and from the Presidential government of America. The Council does not, like an English Cabinet, represent, at any rate directly and immediately, a predominant political party. It is not liable to be at any moment dismissed from office. Its members keep their seats for a period longer than the time during which either an English Ministry or an American President can hope to retain office. But the Council, though differing greatly from a Cabinet, is a Parliamentary or semi-Parliamentary Executive.[90] It has not, like an

---

90 See Note III. p. 331, *ante.*

American President, an independent authority of its own which, being derived from popular election, may transcend, and even be opposed to, the authority of the Legislature. The constitutional history of Switzerland since 1848 has exhibited none of those conflicts between the Executive and the legislative body which have occurred more than once in the United States. The position of the Council may, if we seek for an historical parallel, be compared with that of the Council of State under the Cromwellian Instrument of Government, and indeed occupies very nearly the position which the Council of State would have held had the Instrument of Government been, in accordance with the wishes of the Parliamentary Opposition, so modified as to allow of the frequent re-election by Parliament of the members of the Council.[91] If we desire a modern parallel we may perhaps find it in the English Civil Service. The members of the Council are, like the permanent heads of the English Government offices, officials who have a permanent tenure of office, who are in strictness the servants of the State, and who are expected to carry out, and do carry out, measures which they may not have framed, and the policies of which they may not approve. This comparison is the more instructive, because in the absence of the elaborate Civil Service the members of the Council do in effect discharge rather the duties of permanent civil servants than of ministers.

THE FEDERAL ASSEMBLY

This Parliament is certainly modelled to a certain extent on the American Congress. For several purposes, however, the two chambers of which it consists sit together. As already pointed out, when thus combined they elect the Federal Council or Ministry. The Assembly, moreover, is, unlike any representative assembly to which the English people are accustomed, on certain administrative matters a final Court of Appeal from the Council. The main function, however, of the Assembly is to receive reports from the Council and to legislate. It sits but for a short period each year, and confines itself pretty closely to the transaction of business. Laws passed by it may,

---

91 See the "Constitutional Bill of the First Parliament of the Protectorate," cap, 39; Gardiner, *Constitutional Documents of the Puritan Revolution*, pp. 366, 367.

when referred to the people, be vetoed. Its members are pretty constantly re-elected, and it is apparently one of the most orderly and business-like of Parliaments.

The Assembly consists of two chambers or houses.

The Council of States, or, as we may more conveniently call it, the Senate, represents the Cantons, each of which as a rule sends two members to it.

The National Council, like the American House of Representatives, directly represents the citizens. It varies in numbers with the growth of the population, and each Canton is represented in proportion to its population.

In one important respect the Federal Assembly differs from the American Congress. In the United States the Senate has hitherto been the more influential of the two Houses. In Switzerland the Council of States was expected by the founders of the Constitution to wield the sort of authority which belongs to the American Senate. This expectation has been disappointed. The Council of States has played quite a secondary part in the working of the Constitution, and possesses much less power than the National Council. The reasons given for this are various. The members of the Council are paid by the Cantons which they represent. The time for which they hold office is regulated by each Canton, and has generally been short. The Council has no special functions such as has the American Senate, and the general result has been that leading statesmen have sought for seats not in the Council of State, but in the National Council. One cause of the failure on the part of the Council of States to fulfil the expectations of its creators seems to have escaped Swiss attention. The position and functions of the Federal Council or Ministry, its permanence and its relation to the Federal Parliament, make it impossible for the chamber which represents the Cantons to fill the place which is occupied in America by the House which represents the States. The inferior position of the Swiss Council of States deserves notice. It is one of the parts of the Constitution which was suggested by the experience of a foreign country, and for this very reason has, it may be suspected, not fitted in with the native institutions of Switzerland.

THE FEDERAL TRIBUNAL[92]

This Court was constituted by statesmen who knew the weight
and authority which belongs to the Supreme Court of the United
States; but the Federal Tribunal was from the beginning, and is still, a
very different body from, and a much less powerful body than, the
American Supreme Court. It is composed of fourteen judges, and as
many substitutes elected for six years by the Federal Assembly,
which also designates the President and the Vice-President of the
Court for two years at a time. It possesses criminal jurisdiction in
cases of high treason, and in regard to what we may term high crimes
and misdemeanours, though its powers as a criminal Court are rarely
put into operation. It has jurisdiction as regards suits between the
Confederation and the Cantons, and between the Cantons themselves, and generally in all suits in which the Confederation or a
Canton is a party. It also determines all matters of public law, and has
by degrees, in consequence of federal legislation, been made virtually
a general Court of Appeal from the Cantonal tribunals in all cases
arising under federal laws where the amount in dispute exceeds 3000
francs. Add to this that the Court entertains complaints of the violation of the constitutional rights of citizens, and this whether the right
alleged to be violated is guaranteed by a Federal or by a Cantonal
constitution. The primary object for which the Court was constituted
was the giving decisions, or rather the making of judicial declarations
where points of public law are in dispute; and its civil jurisdiction has,
under the stress of circumstances, been increased beyond the limits
within which the founders of the Swiss Constitution intended it to be
restrained. But the Federal Tribunal, though possessed of a wide and
somewhat indefinite jurisdiction, wields nothing like the power possessed by the Supreme Court of the United States. It has no jurisdiction whatever in controversies with reference to "administrative
law"; these are reserved for the Federal Council, and ultimately for
the Federal Assembly,[93] and the term "administrative controversies"
has been given a very extensive signification, so that the Court has

---

92 Lowell, ii. p. 214; Orelli, pp. 38–44.

93 See Swiss Constitution, Art. 85, s. 12, and Art. 113.

been excluded "from the consideration of a long list of subjects, such as the right to carry on a trade, commercial treaties, consumption taxes, game laws, certificates of professional capacity, factory acts, bank-notes, weights and measures, primary public schools, sanitary police, and the validity of cantonal elections,"[94] which would *primâ facie* seem to fall within its competence. The Tribunal, moreover, though it can treat cantonal laws as unconstitutional, and therefore invalid, is bound by the Constitution to treat all federal legislation as valid.[95]

The judges of the Federal Tribunal are appointed by the Federal Assembly, and for short terms. The Tribunal stands alone, instead of being at the head of a national judicial system. It has further no officials of its own for the enforcement of its judgments. They are executed primarily by the cantonal authorities, and ultimately, if the cantonal authorities fail in their duty, by the Federal Council.[96] The control, moreover, exerted by the Federal Tribunal over the acts of Federal officials is incomplete. Any citizen may sue an official, but, as already pointed out, administrative controversies are excluded from the Court's jurisdiction, and in case there is a conflict of jurisdiction between the Federal Council and the Federal Tribunal, it is decided not by the Court but by the Federal Assembly, which one would expect to support the authority of the Council. The Federal Tribunal, at any rate, cannot as regards such disputes fix the limits of its own competence.[97] Under these circumstances it is not surprising that the Tribunal exercises less authority than the Supreme Court of the United States. What may excite some surprise is that, from the very nature of federalism the jurisdiction of the Federal Tribunal has, in spite of all disadvantages under which the Court suffers, year by year increased. Thus until 1893 questions relating to religious liberty, and the rights of different sects, were reserved for the decision of the Federal Assembly. Since that date they have been transferred to the

---

94 Lowell, p. 218.

95 See Swiss Constitution, Art. 113; Brinton Coxe, *Judicial Power and Unconstitutional Legislation*, p. 86.

96 See Adams, *Swiss Confederation*, pp. 74, 75.

97 See Lowell, p. 220.

jurisdiction of the Federal Tribunal. This very transfer, and the whole relation of the Tribunal, the Council, and the Assembly respectively, to questions which would in England or the United States be necessarily decided by a law court, serve to remind the reader of the imperfect recognition in Switzerland of the "rule of law," as it is understood in England, and of the separation of powers as that doctrine is understood in many continental countries.[98]

THE REFERENDUM[99]

If in the constitution of the Federal Tribunal and of the Council of States we can trace the influence of American examples, the referendum, as it exists in Switzerland, is an institution of native growth, which has received there a far more complete and extensive development than in any other country. If we omit all details, and deal with the referendum as it in fact exists under the Swiss Federal Constitution, we may describe it as an arrangement by which no alteration or amendment in the Constitution, and no federal law which any large number of Swiss citizens think of importance, comes finally into force until it has been submitted to the vote of the citizens, and has been sanctioned by a majority of the citizens who actually vote. It may be added that a change in the Constitution thus referred to the people for sanction cannot come into force unless it is approved of both by a majority of the citizens who vote, and by a majority of the Cantons. It must further be noted that the referendum in different forms exists in all but one of the Swiss Cantons, and may therefore now be considered an essential feature of Swiss constitutionalism. The referendum is therefore in effect a nation's veto. It gives to the citizens of Switzerland exactly that power of arresting legislation which is still in theory and was in the time, for example, of Elizabeth actually possessed by an English monarch. A bill could not finally become a law until it had obtained the consent of the Crown. In

---

98 Lowell, pp. 218, 219.

99 See Lowell, ii. chap. xii.; Adams, *Swiss Confederation,* chap. vi. The referendum, though not under that name, exists for many purposes in the different States of the American Union. There is no trace of it, or of any institution corresponding to it, in the Constitution of the United States. Compare Oberholtzer, *Referendum in America.*

popular language, the Crown, in case the monarch dissented, might
be said to veto the bill. A more accurate way of describing the
Crown's action is to say that the King threw out or rejected the bill
just as did the House of Lords or the House of Commons when either
body refused to pass a bill. This is in substance the position occupied
by the citizens of Switzerland when a law passed by the Federal
Assembly is submitted to them for their approbation or rejection. If
they give their assent it becomes the law of the land; if they refuse
their assent it is vetoed, or, speaking more accurately, the proposed
law is not allowed to pass, *i.e.* to become in reality a law.

The referendum has a purely negative effect. It is in many of the
Cantonal Constitutions, and in the Federal Constitution to a certain
extent, supplemented by what is called the Initiative—that is, a de-
vice by which a certain number of citizens can propose a law and
require a popular vote upon it in spite of the refusal of the legislature
to adopt their views.[100] The Initiative has, under the Federal Constitution at any rate, received as yet but little trial. Whether it can be
under any circumstances a successful mode of legislation may be
doubted. All that need here be noted is that while the introduction of
the Initiative is neither in theory nor in fact a necessary consequence
of the maintenance of the referendum, both institutions are examples
of the way in which in Switzerland the citizens take a direct part in
legislation.

The referendum, taken in combination with the other provisions of
the Constitution, and with the general character of Swiss federalism,
tends, it is conceived, to produce two effects.

It alters, in the first place, the position both of the Legislature and
of the Executive. The Assembly and the Federal Council become
obviously the agents of the Swiss people. This state of things, while it
decreases the power, may also increase the freedom of Swiss statesmen. A member of the Council, or the Council itself, proposes a law
which is passed by the Legislature. It is, we will suppose, as has often
happened, referred to the people for approval and then rejected. The
Council and the Assembly bow without any discredit to the popular

---

100 Lowell, p. 280.

decision. There is no reason why the members either of the Council or of the Legislature should resign their seats; it has frequently happened that the electors, whilst disapproving of certain laws submitted for their acceptance by the Federal Assembly, have re-elected the very men whose legislation they have refused to accept. Individual politicians, on the other hand, who advocate particular measures just because the failure to pass these measures into law does not involve resignation or expulsion from office, can openly express their political views even if these views differ from the opinions of the people. The referendum, in the second place, discourages the growth of party government. The electors do not feel it necessary that the Council, or even the Assembly, should strictly represent one party. Where the citizens themselves can veto legislation which they disapprove, it matters comparatively little that some of their representatives should entertain political opinions which do not at the moment commend themselves to the majority of the electorate. The habit, moreover, acquired of taking part in legislation must probably accustom Swiss citizens to consider any proposed law more or less on its merits. They are at any rate less prone than are the voters of most countries to support a party programme which possibly does not as to every one of its provisions command the assent of any one voter. It may, of course, on the other hand, be maintained that it is the incomplete development of party government in Switzerland which favours the adoption of the referendum. However this may be, there can be little doubt that the existence of the most peculiar of Swiss institutions has a close connection with the condition of Swiss parties.

Swiss Federalism has been, as we have already pointed out, considerably influenced by American Federalism, and it is almost impossible for an intelligent student not to compare the most successful federal and democratic government of the New World with the most successful federal and democratic government of Europe, for the history and the institutions of America and of Switzerland exhibit just that kind of likeness and unlikeness which excites comparison.

The United States and Switzerland are both by nature federations; neither country could, it is pretty clear, prosper under any but a federal constitution; both countries are, at the present day at any rate, by nature democracies. In each country the States or Cantons have existed before the federation. In each country state patriotism was originally a far stronger sentiment than the feeling of national unity. In America and in Switzerland national unity has been the growth of necessity. It is also probable that the sentiment of national unity, now that it has been once evoked, will in the long run triumph over the feeling of State rights or State sovereignty. In a very rough manner, moreover, there is a certain likeness between what may be called the federal history of both countries. In America and in Switzerland there existed for a long time causes which prevented and threatened finally to arrest the progress towards national unity. Slavery played in the United States a part which resembled at any rate the part played in Swiss history by religious divisions. In America and in Switzerland a less progressive, but united and warlike, minority of States held for a long time in check the influence of the richer, the more civilised, and the less united States. Constant disputes as to the area of slavery bore at any rate an analogy to the disputes about the common territories which at one time divided the Catholic and Protestant Cantons. Secession was anticipated by the Sonderbund, and the triumph of Grant was not more complete than the triumph of Dufour. Nor is it at all certain that the military genius of the American was greater than the military genius of the Swiss general. The War of Secession and the War of the Sonderbund had this further quality in common. They each absolutely concluded the controversies out of which they had arisen; they each so ended that victors and vanquished alike soon became the loyal citizens of the same Republic. Each country, lastly, may attribute its prosperity, with plausibility at least, to its institutions, and these institutions bear in their general features a marked similarity.

The unlikeness, however, between American and Swiss Federalism is at least as remarkable as the likeness. America is the largest as Switzerland is the smallest of Confederations; more than one American State exceeds in size and population the whole of the Swiss Confederacy. The American Union is from every point of view a modern state; the heroic age of Switzerland, as far as military glory is concerned, had closed before a single European had set foot in

America, and the independence of Switzerland was acknowledged by Europe more than a century before the United States began their political existence. American institutions are the direct outgrowth of English ideas, and in the main of the English ideas which prevailed in England during the democratic movement of the seventeenth century; American society was never under the influence of feudalism. The democracy of Switzerland is imbued in many respects with continental ideas of government, and till the time of the great French Revolution, Swiss society was filled with inequalities originating in feudal ideas. The United States is made up of States which have always been used to representative institutions; the Cantons of Switzerland have been mainly accustomed to non-representative, aristocratic or democratic government. Under these circumstances, it is naturally to be expected that even institutions which possess a certain formal similarity should display an essentially different character in countries which differ so widely as the United States and Switzerland.

These differences may be thus roughly summed up: American Federalism is strong where Swiss Federalism is weak; where American Federalism is weak, Swiss Federalism is strong.

The Senate and the Judiciary of the United States have rightly excited more admiration than any other part of the American Constitution. They have each been, to a certain extent, imitated by the founders of the existing Swiss Republic. But in neither instance has the imitation been a complete success. The Council of States has not the authority of the Senate; the Federal Tribunal, though its power appears to be on the increase, cannot stand comparison with the Supreme Court. The judicial arrangements of Switzerland would appear, at any rate to a foreign critic, to be the least satisfactory of Swiss institutions, and the exercise by the Federal Council and the Federal Assembly of judicial powers is not in unison with the best modern ideas as to the due administration of justice.

The features in American institutions which receive very qualified approval, if not actual censure even from favourable critics, are the mode in which the President is appointed, the relation of the Executive Government to the Houses of Congress, the disastrous development of party organisation, and the waste or corruption which are the consequence of the predominance of party managers or wirepullers.

The Federal Council, on the other hand, forms as good an Executive as is possessed by any country in the world. It would appear to a foreign observer (though on such a matter foreign critics are singularly liable to delusion) to combine in a rare degree the advantages of a Parliamentary and of a non-Parliamentary government. It acts in uniform harmony with the elected representatives of the people, but though appointed by the legislature, it enjoys a permanent tenure of office unknown to Parliamentary Cabinets or to elected Presidents. Though parties, again, exist, and party spirit occasionally runs high in Switzerland, party government is not found there to be a necessity. The evils, at any rate, attributed to government by party are either greatly diminished or entirely averted. The Caucus and the "Machine" are all but unknown. The country is freed from the unwholesome excitement of a Presidential election, or even of a general election, which, as in England, determines which party shall have possession of the government. There is no notion of spoils, and no one apparently even hints at corruption.

Note IX

AUSTRALIAN FEDERALISM [101]

The aim of Australian statesmen has been to combine in the Constitution of the Commonwealth ideas borrowed from the federal and republican constitutionalism of the United States, or, to a certain extent, of Switzerland, with ideas derived from the unitarian [102] and monarchical constitutionalism of England. They have also created for the Commonwealth itself, and retained for each of the several States thereof, the relation which has for years existed between England and the self-governing colonies of Australia.

---

[101] The Commonwealth of Australia Constitution Act, 63 & 64 Vict. c. 12. Quick and Garran, *The Annotated Constitution of the Australian Commonwealth*. Moore, *The Commonwealth of Australia*. Bryce, i. *Studies in History and Jurisprudence*, Essay VIII.

[102] See pp. 73–74, *ante.*

Hence the Commonwealth exhibits four main characteristics: *first,* a Federal form of Government; *secondly,* a Parliamentary Executive; *thirdly,* an effective Method for amending the Constitution; *fourthly,* the maintenance of the Relation which exists between the United Kingdom and a self-governing colony.

FEDERAL GOVERNMENT

The Commonwealth is in the strictest sense a federal government. It owes its birth to the desire for national unity which pervades the whole of Australia, combined[103] with the determination on the part of the several colonies to retain as States of the Commonwealth as large a measure of independence as may be found compatible with the recognition of Australian nationality. The creation of a true federal government has been achieved mainly by following, without however copying in any servile spirit, the fundamental principles of American federalism. As in the United States so in the Australian Commonwealth the Constitution is (subject of course to the sovereign power of the Imperial Parliament) the supreme law of the land;[104] the Constitution itself in the Australian Commonwealth, as in the United States, fixes and limits the spheres of the federal or national government and of the States respectively, and moreover defines these spheres in accordance with the principle that, while the powers of the national or federal government, including in the term government both the Executive and the Parliament of the Commonwealth, are, though wide, definite and limited, the powers of the separate States are indefinite, so that any power not assigned by the Constitution to the federal government remains vested in each of the several States, or, more accurately, in the Parliament of each State.[105] In this point Australian statesmen have followed the example, not of Canada, but of the United States and of Switzerland. The methods again for keeping the government of the Commonwealth on the one side, and the States on the other, within their proper spheres have

---

103 See pp. 75–76, *ante.*

104 Constitution ss. 51, 108.

105 *Ibid.* ss. 106, 107.

been suggested in the main by American experience. The Parliament of the Commonwealth is so constituted as to guarantee within reasonable limits the maintenance of State rights. For whilst the House of Representatives represents numbers, the Senate represents the States of the Commonwealth, and each of the Original States is entitled, irrespective of its size and population, to an equal number of senators.[106] The Constitution, further, is so framed as to secure respect for the Senate; the longer term for which the Senators are elected and the scheme of retirement by rotation, which will, in general, protect the Senate from a dissolution, are intended to make the Senate a more permanent, and therefore a more experienced, body than the House of Representatives, which can under no circumstances exist for more than three years, and may very well be dissolved before that period has elapsed; then too the senators will, as the Constitution now stands, represent the whole of the State for which they sit.[107] The States, again, retain a large amount of legislative independence. Neither the Executive nor the Parliament of the Commonwealth can either directly or indirectly veto the legislation, *e.g.*, of the Victorian Parliament. Lastly, the law Courts, and especially the Federal Supreme Court, are, as in the United States, the guardians of the Constitution, for the Courts are called upon, in any case which comes before them for decision, to pass judgment, should the point be raised, upon the constitutionality, or, in other words, upon the validity under the Constitution of any Act passed either by the Parliament of that Commonwealth or by the Parliament of, *e.g.*, Victoria. That this duty is laid upon the Courts is not indeed expressly stated in the Constitution of the Commonwealth, any more than in the Constitution of the United States; but no English lawyer can doubt that the Courts, and ultimately the Federal Supreme Court, are intended to be the interpreters, and in this sense the protectors of the Constitution. They are, be it noted, in no way

---

106 *Ibid*. s. 7. Such experience however as can be supplied by the events of eight years shows, it is said, that the Senate is absolutely hostile to the maintenance of State rights, and far more so than the House of Representatives.

107 *Ibid*. s. 7.

bound, as is the Swiss Federal tribunal, to assume the constitutionality of laws passed by the federal legislature.

The founders, then, of the Commonwealth have, guided in the main by the example of the United States, created a true federal government; but they have, we shall find, as far as is compatible with the existence of federalism, imported into the Constitution ideas borrowed, or rather inherited, from England. This is specially visible in

THE PARLIAMENTARY EXECUTIVE

The Executive of the Commonwealth is a parliamentary Cabinet, such as has long existed in England, and as exists in all the self-governing British colonies. The authors indeed of the Australian Constitution have, true to English precedent, never made use of the word cabinet; they have not even in so many words enacted that the executive shall be a body of ministers responsible to the federal Parliament; but no one who has the least acquaintance with the history of the English constitution, or of the working of the constitutions which have been conferred upon the self-governing colonies of Australia, can doubt that the federal executive is intended to be, as it in fact is, a parliamentary ministry, which, though nominally appointed by the Governor-General, will owe its power to the support of a parliamentary majority, and will therefore, speaking broadly, consist in general of the leaders of the most powerful parliamentary party of the day. This cabinet possesses the most peculiar among the attributes of an English ministry, namely, the power, in many cases at any rate, to dissolve Parliament, and thus appeal from the body by whom the ministry was created to the people, or in other words to the electors, of the Commonwealth. We should here also observe that the powers of the Australian executive exceed in one respect the authority of an English ministry; an English cabinet may often dissolve the House of Commons, but can never dissolve the House of Lords. But an Australian cabinet can under certain circumstances cause, indirectly at any rate, the dissolution of the Senate. In studying indeed the Constitution of the Commonwealth great attention should be paid to this

existence of the right or power to dissolve Parliament; it is not possessed by the President of the United States or by the Executive
Council of the Swiss Confederation, and it is granted under the constitution of the existing French Republic only in a very limited degree
to the French President; nor is there anything to make it certain that
the President, even if being sure of the assent of the Senate he has the
power to dissolve the Chamber of Deputies, will exert his authority at
the request of the ministry. [108] The point to be specially noted is that
the Federalists of Australia have almost as a matter of course placed
the executive power in the hands of a parliamentary cabinet; they
have neither adopted the American plan of an elected President,
whereby the administration of affairs is placed in the hands of a
non-parliamentary executive, or the Swiss scheme of creating a
semi-parliamentary executive, which, while elected by the federal
Parliament, cannot be dismissed by it. It is true that it might have
been found difficult to adjust the relations between a non-parliamentary or a semi-parliamentary executive and the English cabinet or the Imperial Parliament. But the difficulty is not one which
need necessarily be insuperable. The true reason, it may be conjectured, why Australia has decisively adhered to the system of cabinet
government is that a Parliamentary cabinet is the only form of executive to which the statesmen either of Australia or of England are
accustomed. In one point, indeed, the executive of Australia may
appear to bear an even more parliamentary character than does an
English cabinet, for whilst, in theory at least, a statesman might be
the member of an English ministry, though he were not a member of
either House of Parliament, no Australian minister can hold office,
i.e. in effect be a member of the cabinet for more than three months,
unless he becomes a Senator, or a member of the House of Representatives. [109] But here Australian statesmanship has followed the conventions rather than the law of the English constitution, for in practice an English cabinet always consists of men who are members or
will become members either of the House of Lords or of the House of

---

108 Esmein, *Droit Constitutionnel*, pp. 555–563.

109 Constitution, s. 64.

Commons. Indeed it is worth remark that in several instances where the Australian Constitution deviates from that of England, the deviation is caused by the desire to follow the spirit of modern English constitutionalism. Thus the elaborate and ingenious plan for avoiding in case of disagreement between the two Houses a parliamentary deadlock[110] is simply an attempt to ensure by law that deference for the voice of the electorate which in England constitutional conventions enforce in the long run upon both Houses of the Imperial Parliament.

AMENDMENT OF THE CONSTITUTION

A federal constitution must of necessity be a "rigid" constitution; but the constitutions of each of the Australian self-governing colonies, *e.g.* of Victoria, have been in substance "flexible" constitutions of which the colonial Parliament could change the articles as easily, or nearly as easily, as any other law. Now the people of Australia have, we may safely assume, no desire to forego the advantages of a flexible constitution or to adopt a federal polity which should lend itself as little to amendment as does the Constitution of the United States, or should, like the Constitution of the Canadian Dominion, be amendable only by the action of the Imperial Parliament. Hence Australian Federalists were forced to solve the problem of giving to the Constitution of the Commonwealth as much rigidity as is required by the nature of a federal government, and at the same time such flexibility as should secure to the people of Australia the free exercise of legislative authority, even as regards articles of the Constitution.

Their solution of this problem is ingenious.

The Constitution of the Commonwealth is, looked at as a whole, a rigid constitution, since it cannot be fundamentally altered by the ordinary method of parliamentary legislation.

But this rigidity of the constitution is tempered in three different ways.

First, the Parliament of the Commonwealth is endowed with very wide legislative authority; thus it can legislate on many topics which

---

110 Constitution, s. 57.

lie beyond the competence of the Congress of the United States, and on some topics which lie beyond the competence of the Parliament of the Canadian Dominion;[111] and it is here worth notice that the extension of the powers of the Commonwealth Parliament is facilitated by the fact that on many topics the federal legislature and the State Parliaments have concurrent legislative authority, though of course where a law of the Commonwealth conflicts with the law of a State, the federal law, if within the competence of the Commonwealth Parliament, prevails.[112]

Secondly, a large number of the articles of the constitution remain in force only "until Parliament otherwise provides"; they can therefore be changed like any other law by an Act of Parliament passed in the ordinary manner; in other words, the constitution is as to many of its provisions flexible.[113]

Thirdly, the constitution provides the means for its own alteration[114] and embodies the principle, though not the name, of the Swiss institution known as the referendum. The process of constitutional amendment is broadly and normally as follows: A law changing the constitution must be passed by an absolute majority of each House of Parliament; it must then be submitted to the electors of the Commonwealth for their approval; if in a majority of the States a majority of the electors voting approve the law and also a majority of all the electors voting approve the law, it must be submitted to the Governor-General for the King's assent, and on receiving the due assent becomes, like any other bill, an Act of Parliament. The principle of the whole proceeding is that the constitution can be changed by a vote of the federal Parliament, ratified by the approval both of the majority of the States and of the majority of the Commonwealth electorate.

It should, however, be noted that under certain circumstances a law for changing the constitution which has been passed by an ab-

---

111 Compare Commonwealth Constitution, ss. 51, 52, with Constitution of U. S., art. 1, ss. 1 and 8, and British North America Act, 1867 (30 & 31 Vict. c. 3), ss. 91, 92.

112 See Constitution, s. 109.

113 *Ibid.* s. 51, sub. s. xxxvi. compared *e.g.* with ss. 3, 29, 31, etc.

114 *Ibid.* s. 128.

solute majority of one House of Parliament only, and either is rejected by the other House or not passed by an absolute majority thereof, must be submitted to the electors for their approval, and if approved in the manner already stated, becomes, on the assent of the Crown being duly given, an Act of Parliament.

Add to this that there are a few changes, *e.g.* an alteration diminishing the proportionate representation in any State in either House of Parliament, which cannot be carried through unless the majority of the electors voting in that State approve of the change.[115]

What may be the working of new institutions no one will venture confidently to predict; but a critic of constitutions may entertain the hope that Australian statesmanship has accomplished the feat of framing a polity which shall have the merits both of a rigid and of a flexible constitution, which cannot hastily be changed, but yet admits of easy amendment, whenever alteration or reform is demanded by the deliberate voice of the nation.

MAINTENANCE OF THE RELATION WITH THE UNITED KINGDOM

The founders of the Commonwealth have admittedly been influenced at once by a growing sense of Australian nationality, and by enduring, or even increasing loyalty to the mother-country. The one sentiment has been satisfied by the union of the Australian colonies under a federal government which secures to the people of Australia as complete power of self-government as is compatible with the position of a colony that desires to form part of the British Empire. The other sentiment has been satisfied by placing the Commonwealth itself as regards the mother-country in the position of a self-governing colony, and also by leaving the relation between each State of the Commonwealth and the United Kingdom as little disturbed as is compatible with the creation of the Australian Commonwealth. Each point is worth notice.

The Commonwealth of Australia itself is, as regards the Crown and the Imperial Parliament, nothing but a large self-governing colony.

---

115 Constitution, s. 28.

Thus the Governor-General is appointed by the Crown, *i.e.* by the English ministry, and fills substantially the same position as, before the formation of the Commonwealth, was occupied by the Governor, *e.g.*, of Victoria. A bill passed by the Parliament of the Commonwealth, whether it be an ordinary law or a law which, because it affects the constitution, has been submitted to the electors for their approval, requires in order that it may become an Act the assent of the Crown,[116] and the Crown can negative or veto bills passed by the Parliament of the Commonwealth just as it could, and still can, veto bills passed by the Parliament, *e.g.*, of Victoria. The Imperial Parliament, again, has the admitted right, though it is a right which, except at the wish of the Australian people, would most rarely be exercised, to legislate for Australia, or even to modify the constitution of the Australian Commonwealth. An appeal further lies on most subjects from the decisions of the federal Supreme Court to the English Privy Council, and even the limitations placed on such appeals when certain questions as to the Commonwealth constitution are raised are themselves subject to some qualifications.[117] The broad result therefore is that as regards the Commonwealth the connection with the United Kingdom is retained, and the sovereignty of the Imperial Parliament is untouched.

The position of any State of the Commonwealth in regard to the United Kingdom remains pretty much what it was when the State, *e.g.* Victoria, was still merely a self-governing colony. The Governor of Victoria is now, as then, appointed by the Crown, *i.e.* by the English ministry. A bill passed by the Victorian Parliament still, in order that it may become an Act, requires the assent of the Crown. The Government of the Commonwealth possesses no power of putting a veto on bills passed by the Victorian Parliament. The right of appeal from a Court of Victoria to the English Privy Council stands, in most matters at any rate, substantially where it did before the passing of the Australian Commonwealth Act, except indeed that there is an alternative right of appeal to the High Court of Australia, for "the

---

116 Constitution, ss. 1, 58, 59, and 128.

117 See Constitution, ss. 71, 73, 74.

Constitution grants a new right of appeal from the State Courts to the High Court, but does not take away the existing right of appeal from the State Courts to the Privy Council, which therefore remains unimpaired."[118]

The peculiarities of Australian federalism receive illustration from a comparison between the constitution of the Canadian Dominion[119] and the constitution of the Australian Commonwealth.

The Dominion is from one point of view more, and from another point of view less, directly subject to the control of the Imperial Parliament than is the Commonwealth. The Dominion is more completely subject than the Commonwealth, because the greater part of the Canadian constitution[120] can be amended only by an Act of the Imperial Parliament, whilst the Australian constitution can be amended by the people of the Commonwealth; this distinction, it is well to add, sounds more important than it is in reality, since we may feel morally certain that the Imperial Parliament would introduce any amendment into the constitution of the Dominion which was deliberately desired by the majority at once of the people and of the

---

118 Quick and Garran, *Annotated Constitution*, p. 738. Thus an appeal lies from the Supreme Court of each of the States to the Privy Council from any decision of their Courts; as of right in circumstances defined in the several instruments constituting the Courts; by special leave from the Privy Council in all cases without exception. This rule applies to the exercise of any jurisdiction, whether State or federal, vested in the State Courts, but the State Courts have not full federal jurisdiction. From their power are excepted all cases involving the relation *inter se* of the States, and the States and the Commonwealth.

Appeals lie also from the State Courts to the High Court of Australia in matters both of State and federal jurisdiction on terms defined in the Judicature Act, 1903, of the Commonwealth Parliament. The appellant has of course the choice of appeal. There is nothing to prevent an appeal from such Courts to decide whether any particular case falls under sec. 74 of the constitution or not. Nor is there any mode of preventing contradictory decisions on matters other than questions arising as to the limits *inter se* of the constitutional powers of the Commonwealth and those of any State or States, or to the limits *inter se* of the constitutional powers of any two or more States which cannot reach the Privy Council. The High Court further is not bound to accept the rulings of the Privy Council as superior to its own except in those cases where an actual appeal is successfully brought not from the Superior Court of a State, but from the High Court to the Privy Council.

119 See Munro, *Constitution of Canada*.

120 But certain important though limited powers are under the constitution itself, *i.e.* the British North America Act, 1867, given to the Dominion Parliament and to the Provincial legislatures, enabling them from time to time to amend their constitutions (Munro, *Constitution of Canada*, p. 229). See *e.g.* B. N. A. Act, 1867, ss. 35, 41, 45, 78, 83, 84.

provinces of the Dominion. The Dominion of Canada, on the other hand, is less subject to the Imperial Parliament than is the Commonwealth, because the Provinces of the Dominion are in a sense less directly connected with the Imperial Government and Parliament than are the States of the Commonwealth.

Here however we come across the most important distinction between Canadian federalism and Australian federalism, namely, the difference of the relation of the federal power to the States, or, as in the case of Canada they are called, the Provinces, of the federation. The Dominion possesses all the residuary powers which are not under the Constitution conferred exclusively upon the Provinces; the Commonwealth possesses only those powers which are conferred upon it by the Constitution, whilst all the residuary powers not conferred upon the Commonwealth belong to the States.

The government of the Dominion, again, can exercise very considerable control over the legislation of the Provincial legislatures and over the administration of the Provinces; the government of the Dominion can in all cases put a veto upon laws passed by the Provincial Parliaments; the government of the Dominion appoints the judges of the State Courts; the government of the Dominion, lastly, can appoint and dismiss the Lieutenant-Governor of any Province, who therefore is neither an Imperial official nor a Provincial official, but a Dominion official.

Note X

MARTIAL LAW IN ENGLAND DURING TIME OF WAR OR INSURRECTION [121]

The question for our consideration is, on what principle, and within what limits, does armed resistance to the authority of the Crown, either on the part of an invading army, or on the part of

---

121 See Law Quarterly Review, xviii., Holdsworth, *Martial Law Historically Considered*, pp. 117–132; Richards, *Martial Law, ibid.* pp. 133–142; Pollock, *What is Martial Law? ibid.* pp. 152–158; Dodd, *The Case of Marais, ibid*, pp. 143–151. *The Case of Ship Money*, 3 St. Tr. 826; *Wall's Case*, 28 St. Tr. 51; *Ex parte D. F. Marais* [1902], A. C. 109; Forsyth, *Cases and Opinions*, ch. vi. p. 188; Clode, *Military Forces of the Crown*, ii. ch. xviii.

rebels or rioters, afford a legal justification for acts done in England by the Crown, its servants, or loyal citizens, which, but for the existence of war or insurrection, would be breaches of law?

In considering this question two preliminary observations must be borne in mind.

The first is that this note does not treat of several topics which are often brought within the vague term, martial law. It does not refer to Military Law, *i.e.* the rules contained in the Army Act and the Articles of War for the government of the Army and of all persons included within the term "persons subject to military law"; it has no reference to the laws that govern the action of an English General and his soldiers when carrying on war in a foreign country, or in their treatment of foreign invaders of England; it has no reference to transactions taking place out of England, or to the law of any other country than England. It does not refer, *e.g.*, to the law of Scotland or of Jersey.

The second observation is that, in regard to the subject of this note, we must constantly bear in mind the broad and fundamental principle of English law that a British subject must be presumed to possess at all times in England his ordinary common-law rights, and especially his right to personal freedom, unless it can be conclusively shown, as it often may, that he is under given circumstances deprived of them, either by Act of Parliament or by some well-established principle of law. This presumption in favour of legality is an essential part of that rule of law[122] which is the leading feature of English institutions. Hence, if any one contends that the existence of a war in England deprives Englishmen of any of their common-law rights, *e.g.* by establishing a state of martial law, or by exempting military officers from the jurisdiction of the civil Courts, the burden of proof falls distinctly upon the person putting forward this contention.

Ex parte Milligan (Am.), 4 Wall. 2, and Thayer, *Cases on Constitutional Law,* ii. p. 2376. This, and the other American cases on martial law, though not authorities in an English Court, contain an exposition of the common law in regard to martial law which deserves the most careful attention.

See also Note IV., Right of Self-Defence; Note V., Right of Public Meeting; Note VI., Soldiers and Unlawful Meeting, *ante.*

122 See chap. iv., *ante.*

Our topic may be considered under three heads; first, the nature of martial law; secondly, the inferences which may be drawn from the nature of martial law; thirdly, certain doctrines with regard to martial law which are inconsistent with the view propounded in this note.

NATURE OF MARTIAL LAW

"Martial law," in the sense in which the expression is here used, means the power, right, or duty of the Crown and its servants, or, in other words, of the Government, to maintain public order, or, in technical language, the King's peace, at whatever cost of blood or property may be in strictness necessary for that purpose. Hence martial law comes into existence in times of invasion or insurrection when, where, and in so far as the King's peace cannot be maintained by ordinary means, and owes its existence to urgent and paramount necessity. [123] This power to maintain the peace by the exertion of any amount of force strictly necessary for the purpose is sometimes described as the prerogative of the Crown, but it may more correctly be considered, not only as a power necessarily possessed by the Crown, but also as the power, right, or duty possessed by, or incumbent upon, every loyal citizen of preserving or restoring the King's peace in the case, whether of invasion or of rebellion or generally of armed opposition to the law, by the use of any amount of force whatever necessary to preserve or restore the peace. This power or right arises from the very nature of things. No man, whatever his opinions as to the limits of the prerogative, can question the duty of loyal subjects to aid, subject to the command of the Crown, in resistance, by all necessary means, to an invading army. [124] Nor can it be denied that acts, otherwise tortious, are lawful when necessary for the resistance of invaders. [125]

---

123 See Kent, *Comm.* i. p. 341, and opinion of Sir John Campbell and Sir R. M. Rolfe, Forsyth, *Opinions on Constitutional Law*, pp. 198, 199.

124 See especially the *Case of Ship Money,* 3 St. Tr. 860, 905, 974, 975, 1011–1013, 1134, 1149, 1162, and 1214.

125 See 1 Dyer, 36*b*.

When enemies come against the realm to the sea coast, it is lawful to come upon my land adjoining to the same coast, to make trenches or bulwarks for the defence of the realm, for every subject hath benefit by it. And, therefore, by the common law, every man may come upon my land for the defence of the realm, as appears 8 Ed. IV. 23. And in such case or such extremity they may dig for gravel for the making of bulwarks: for this is for the public, and every one hath benefit by it. . . . And in this case the rule is true, *Princeps et respublica ex justa causa possunt rem meam auferre.* [126]

So to the same effect counsel for the defence in the Case of Ship Money.

My Lords, in these times of war I shall admit not only His Majesty, but likewise every man that hath power in his hands, may take the goods of any within the realm, pull down their houses, or burn their corn, to cut off victuals from the enemy, and do all other things that conduce to the safety of the kingdom, without respect had to any man's property. [127]

And though these authorities refer, as is worth noticing, to interferences with rights of property and not to interferences with personal freedom, between which there exist considerable differences, it will not (it is submitted) be disputed that, in case of invasion, a general and his soldiers acting under the authority of the Crown may lawfully do acts which would otherwise be an interference with the personal liberty, or even, under conceivable circumstances, which may cause the death of British subjects, if these acts are a necessary part of military operations. The point to be borne in mind is that the power to exercise martial law, which is not ill-described by an expression known to the American Courts, viz. the "war power," as it originates in, so it is limited by, the necessity of the case. [128]

On this matter note the opinion of Sir J. Campbell and Sir R. M. Rolfe that "martial law is merely a cessation from necessity of all

---

126 12 Rep. 12.

127 *Case of Ship Money,* 3 St. Tr. 826, 906. Compare especially the language of Holborne in the same case at p. 975, and language of Buller, J., in *British Cast Plate Manufacturers* v. *Meredith,* 4 T. R. at p. 797.

128 See especially opinion of Henley and Yorke, Forsyth, pp. 188, 189; opinion of Hargrave, *ibid.* pp. 189, 190; opinion of Sir John Campbell and Sir R. M. Rolfe, *ibid.* pp. 198, 199.

municipal law, and what necessity requires it justifies";[129] and this description of the circumstances which justify martial law also implies the limits within which it is justifiable; these have been stated with truth, if not with the precise accuracy of legal argument, by Sir James Mackintosh.

> The only principle on which the law of England tolerates what is called Martial Law is necessity; its introduction can be justified only by necessity; its continuance requires precisely the same justification of necessity; and if it survives the necessity on which alone it rests for a single minute, it becomes instantly a mere exercise of lawless violence. When foreign invasion or Civil War renders it impossible for Courts of Law to sit, or to enforce the execution of their judgments, it becomes necessary to find some rude substitute for them, and to employ for that purpose the Military, which is the only remaining Force in the community. While the laws are silenced by the noise of arms, the rulers of the Armed Force must punish, as equitably as they can, those crimes which threaten their own safety and that of society; but no longer.[130]

The existence of martial law thus understood, taken in combination with the rules of the common law as to the duty of loyal subjects, gives very wide authority in England to all persons, and of course above all to a general engaged in repelling an invasion. He holds the armed forces completely under his control; they are governed by military law;[131] so too are all citizens who, though not in strictness soldiers, are persons subject to military law; and in this connection it must be remembered that the King and his servants have a right to call for the help of every loyal subject in resisting an invasion,[132] whence it follows that the number of persons subject to military law may be greatly, indeed almost indefinitely, increased. A general again is clearly entitled to use or occupy any land which he requires for the purpose of military operations and may, if he see fit, erect fortifications thereon, and generally he has the right to use land or any other property which is required for the conduct of the war. It is

---

129 Forsyth, p. 201.

130 Cited Clode, *Military Forces of the Crown*, ii. p. 486.

131 See chaps. viii. and ix., *ante*.

132 See *Case of Ship Money*, 3 St. Tr. 826, 975.

again his right, and indeed his duty, when the necessity arises, to inflict instant punishment upon, and even, if need be, put to death, persons aiding and abetting the enemy or refusing such aid to the English army as can fairly be required of them. It is indeed difficult to picture to one's self any legitimate warlike operation or measure which, while war is raging in England, a general cannot carry out without any breach of the law whatever. Let it too be noted that what is true of a general holds good of every loyal subject according to his situation and the authority which he derives from it, *e.g.* of a subordinate officer, of a magistrate, or even of a private citizen who is helping to resist an invader. Real obvious necessity in this case not only compels but justifies conduct which would otherwise be wrongful or criminal. To this add the consideration, which has been strongly insisted upon by several able writers, that the conditions of modern warfare, such as the existence of the telegraph, whereby acts done, *e.g.*, in London may affect military operations, *e.g.*, in Northumberland, greatly extend the area of necessity, and may, conceivably at least, make it legally allowable, when war or armed insurrection exists in the north of England, to interfere summarily and without waiting for legal process with the freedom of persons residing in London or Bristol. However this may be, it is clear that the existence of the necessity which justifies the use of so-called martial law must depend on the circumstances of each case.

The fact that necessity is the sole justification for martial law or, in other words, for a temporary suspension of the ordinary rights of English citizens during a period of war or insurrection, does however place a very real limit of the lawful exercise of force by the Crown or by its servants. The presence of a foreign army or the outbreak of an insurrection in the north of England, may conceivably so affect the state of the whole country as to justify measures of extra-legal force in every part of England, but neither war nor insurrection in one part of the country *primâ facie* suspends the action of the law in other parts thereof. The fact that the Pretender's army had advanced with unbroken success to Derby did not deprive the citizens of London of the ordinary rights of British subjects. No one has ever suggested that it would have justified the summary execution at Tyburn of an Englishman there found guilty of treason by a court-martial. It is not easy to believe that, without a breach of the law of England, an Englishman imprisoned in London on a charge of high treason could have been taken to a part of the country where in 1745 war was raging, in order that he might there be tried and executed under the authority of a court-martial.[133] Nor does the consideration that the summary execution of rebels, whose crimes could be punished by the ordinary course of law, may check the spread of treason, show that their execution is necessary or legal. We need not, moreover, confine our observation to cases of punishment. It is easy to imagine circumstances under which the arrest and imprisonment on suspicion of persons who are not guilty, or cannot be proved guilty of crime, may be salutary and expedient, but such arrest or imprisonment cannot be legally justified unless it be a matter of necessity.[134] If it be urged, that the respect due in England to the ordinary law of the land places restrictions which may be inconvenient or even noxious on the exercise of the authority of the Crown and its servants, the truth of the observation may be admitted. The reply to it is twofold: first, that the maintenance of the legal rights of citizens is itself a matter of the highest expediency; secondly, that whenever at a period of national danger a breach of law is demanded, if not by absolute necessity, yet by considerations of political expediency, the lawbreaker, whether he be a general, or any other servant of the Crown, who acts *bonâ fide* and solely with a view to the public interest, may confidently count on the protection of an Act of Indemnity.

Nor is it irrelevant at this point to note the striking analogy between the right of an individual to exercise force, even to the extent of causing death, in self-defence, and the right of a general or other loyal citizen to exercise any force whatever necessary for the defence of the realm. In either case the right arises from necessity. An indi-

---

133 If the language in the Charge of Blackburn, J., *Reg.* v. *Eyre,* p. 84, be cited in support of the possible legality of such a transaction, it must be remembered that Blackburn's hypothetical apology for Governor Eyre was based on certain statutes passed by the legislature of Jamaica, and that the whole tendency of the Charge of Cockburn, C. J., in *Reg.* v. *Nelson,* is to show that the execution of Gordon was illegal.

134 See specially language of Holborne, *Case of Ship Money,* 3 St. Tr. p. 975.

vidual may use any amount of force necessary to avert death or grievous bodily harm at the hands of a wrongdoer,[135] but, if he kills a ruffian, he must to justify his conduct show the necessity for the force employed in self-protection. So a general, who under martial law imprisons or kills British subjects in England, must, if he is to escape punishment, justify his conduct by proving its necessity. The analogy between the two cases is not absolutely complete, but it is suggestive and full of instruction.

Observe, further, that the principle which determines the limits of martial law is the principle which also determines the rights and duties of magistrates, of constables, and of loyal citizens generally when called upon to disperse or prevent unlawful assemblies or to suppress a riot. No doubt the degree and the area of the authority exercised by a general when resisting an invading army is far greater than the degree and the area of the authority exercised by a mayor, a magistrate, or a constable when called upon to restore the peace of a town disturbed by riot, but the authority though differing in degree has the same object and has the same source. It is exercised for the maintenance of the King's peace; it is justified by necessity. So true is this, that, when you need to fix the limits of martial law, you are compelled to study the case of *Rex* v. *Pinney*,[136] which refers not to the power and authority of a general in command of soldiers, but to the duty of the Mayor of Bristol to suppress a riot.

In every case in which the legal right or duty arises to maintain the King's peace by the use of force, there will be found to exist two common features. The legal right, *e.g.* of a general or of a mayor, to override the ordinary law of the land is, in the first place, always correlative to his legal duty to do so. Such legal right or duty, in the second place, always lasts so long, and so long only, as the circumstances exist which necessitate the use of force. Martial law exists only during time of war; the right of a mayor to use force in putting an end to a riot ceases when order is restored, just as it only begins when a breach of the peace is threatened or has actually taken place.

---

135 See App., Note IV., The Right of Self-Defence, p. 341, *ante.*

136 3 St. Tr. (n. s.) 11, with which compare Blackburn's Charge in *R.* v. *Eyre,* pp. 58, 59.

The justification and the source of the exercise in England of extraordinary or, as it may be termed, extra-legal power, is always the necessity for the preservation or restoration of the King's peace.

CONCLUSIONS

From the nature of martial law[137] follow four conclusions:—

First, martial law cannot exist in time of peace.

This is on all hands admitted.[138]

What, then, is the test for determining whether a state of peace exists at a given time, in a given part of England, say London?

The answer is that no unfailing test is to be found; the existence of a state of peace is a question of fact to be determined in any case before the Courts in the same way as any other such question.[139]

According, indeed, to a number of old and respectable authorities, a state of war cannot exist, or, in other words, a state of peace always does exist when and where the ordinary Courts are open. But this rule cannot, it would seem, be laid down as anything like an absolute principle of law, for the fact that for some purposes some tribunals have been permitted to pursue their ordinary course in a district in which martial law has been proclaimed, is not conclusive proof that war is not there raging.[140] Yet the old maxim, though not to be accepted as a rigid rule, suggests, it is submitted, a sound principle. At a time and place where the ordinary civil Courts are open, and fully and freely exercise their ordinary jurisdiction, there exists, presumably, a state of peace, and where there is peace there cannot be martial law.

> If, in foreign invasion or civil war, the Courts are actually closed, and it is impossible to administer criminal justice according to law, then, on the theatre of active military operations, where war really prevails, there is a necessity to furnish a substitute for the civil authority, thus overthrown, to preserve the safety of the army and society; and as no power is left but the

---

137 Cockburn's Charge, *Reg. v. Nelson*, p. 85.

138 Compare *Ex parte D. F. Marais* [1902], A. C. 109; *Ex parte Milligan*, 4 Wall. 2 (Am.).

139 Whether the Courts may not take judicial notice of the existence of a state of war?

140 *Ex parte D. F. Marais* [1902], A. C. 109.

military, it is allowed to govern by martial rule until the laws can have their free course. As necessity creates the rule, so it limits its duration; for, if this government is continued after the Courts are reinstated, it is a gross usurpation of power. Martial rule can never exist where the Courts are open, and in the proper and unobstructed exercise of their jurisdiction. It is also confined to the locality of actual war.[141]

Secondly, the existence of martial law does not in any way depend upon the proclamation of martial law.

The proclamation of martial law does not, unless under some statutory provision, add to the power or right inherent in the Government to use force for the repression of disorder, or for resistance to invasion. It does not confer upon the Government any power which the Government would not have possessed without it. The object and the effect of the proclamation can only be to give notice, to the inhabitants of the place with regard to which martial law is proclaimed, of the course which the Government is obliged to adopt for the purpose of defending the country, or of restoring tranquillity.[142]

Thirdly, the Courts have, at any rate in time of peace, jurisdiction in respect of acts which have been done by military authorities and others during a state of war.[143]

"The justification of any particular act done in a state of war is ultimately examinable in the ordinary Courts, and the prior question, whether there was a state of war at a given time and place, is a question of fact."[144]

The truth of this statement of the law is almost self-evident. *A* sues *X* in the High Court for assault and for false imprisonment; *X* justifies the alleged assault on the ground that *X* was at the time of the act complained of the colonel of a regiment, and that the alleged assault was the arrest and imprisonment of *A* by *X* under the orders, say, of the Commander-in-Chief, during a time of war and after the proclamation of martial law. The defence may or may not be good, but it is

---

141 *Ex parte Milligan*, 4 Wall. 2; Thayer, *Cases on Constitutional Law,* part iv. p. 2390.

142 See opinion of Campbell and Rolfe, Forsyth, p. 198.

143 See Cockburn's Charge, *Reg.* v. *Nelson;* Blackburn's Charge, *Reg.* v. *Eyre; Ex parte Milligan,* 4 Wall, 2; and compare *Wall's Case,* 28 St. Tr. 51. *Wright* v. *Fitzgerald,* 27 St. Tr. 759.

144 Sir F. Pollock, *What is Martial Law?* L. Q. R. xviii. pp. 156, 157.

certain that the Courts have, at any rate after the restoration of peace, jurisdiction to inquire into the facts of the case, and that one of the necessary inquiries is whether a state of war did exist at the time when *A* was arrested, though it is quite possible that the existence of a state of war may be a fact of which the Courts take judicial notice. Expressions, indeed, have been used in a recent case[145] which, if taken alone, might seem to assert that the ordinary Courts have no jurisdiction in respect of acts which have been done by military authorities in time of war. But the very width of the language used by the Privy Council in *Ex parte D. F. Marais* warns us that it must be limited to the circumstances of the particular case. It does not necessarily assert more, and as regards transactions taking place in England, cannot be taken to mean more than that the Courts will not, as indeed they in strictness cannot, interfere with actual military operations, or, whilst war is actually raging, entertain proceedings against military men and others for acts done under so-called martial law. The judgment of the Privy Council, in short, whatever the application of its principles to England, asserts nothing as to the jurisdiction of the Courts when peace is restored in respect of acts done during time of war, and eminent lawyers have held that even in time of war the exercise of jurisdiction by the ordinary Courts is rather rendered impossible than superseded.

> The question, how far martial law, when in force, supersedes the ordinary tribunals, can never . . . arise. Martial law is stated by Lord Hale to be in truth no law, but something rather indulged than allowed as a law, and it can only be tolerated because, by reason of open rebellion, the enforcing of any other law has become impossible. It cannot be said in strictness to *supersede* the ordinary tribunals, inasmuch as it only exists by reason of those tribunals having been already practically superseded.[146]

Fourthly, the protection of military men and others against actions or persecutions in respect of unlawful acts done during a time of war, bonâ fide, and in the service of the country, is an Act of Indemnity.[147]

---

145 *Ex parte D. F. Marais* [1902,] A. C. 109, 114, 115, judgment of Privy Council.

146 Joint opinion of Sir J. Campbell and Sir R. M. Rolfe, cited Forsyth, p. 199.

147 See pp. 10, 142, *ante*.

An Act of Indemnity is a statute the object of which is to make legal transactions which, when they took place, were illegal, or to free individuals to whom the statute applies from liability for having broken the law. Statutes of this description have been invariably, or almost invariably, passed after the determination of a period of civil war or disturbance, *e.g.* after the Rebellions of 1715 and of 1745,[148] and their very object has been to protect officials and others who, in the interest of the country, have in a time of danger pursued an illegal course of conduct, *e.g.* have imprisoned citizens whom they had no legal authority to imprison. For our present purpose it is absolutely essential to appreciate the true character of an Act of Indemnity. Such a statute has no application to conduct which, however severe, is strictly lawful. A magistrate who, under proper circumstances, causes an unlawful assembly to be dispersed by force, or an officer who, under proper circumstances, orders his troops to fire on a mob and thereby, in dispersing the mob, wounds or kills some of the crowd, neither of them require to be indemnified. They are sufficiently protected by the common-law justification that in discharge of their duty they used the force, and no more than the force necessary to maintain the King's peace. A general, an officer, a magistrate, or a constable, on the other hand, who, whether in time of war or in time of peace, does without distinct legal justification, any act which injures the property or interferes with the liberty of an Englishman, incurs the penalties to which every man is liable who commits a breach of the law. The law-breaker's motives may be in the highest degree patriotic, his conduct may be politically sagacious, and may confer great benefit on the public, but all this will not, in the absence of legal justification, save him from liability to an action, or, it may be, to a prosecution; he needs for his protection an Act of Indemnity. On this point note the words of a judge of the highest reputation, who was by no means inclined to minimise the authority of the Crown and its servants.

> Where the inquiry is, whether an officer is guilty of misdemeanour from an excess beyond his duty, the principle is very much the same, or rather it is

---

148 See Clode, *Military Forces of the Crown,* ii. pp. 164, 165; 1 Geo. I. St. 2, c. 39, and 19 Geo. II. c. 20.

the complement of that laid down in the case of *Rex* v. *Pinney*. If the officer does some act altogether beyond the power conferred upon him by law, so that it could never under any state of circumstances have been his duty to do it, he is responsible according to the quality of that act; and even if the doing of that illegal act was the salvation of the country, that, though it might be a good ground for the Legislature afterwards passing an Act of Indemnity, would be no bar in law to a criminal prosecution; that is, if he has done something clearly beyond his power. But if the act which he has done is one which, in a proper state of circumstances, the officer was authorised to do, so that in an extreme case, on the principle laid down in *R.* v. *Pinney*, he might be criminally punished for failure of duty for not doing it, then the case becomes very different. [149]

This passage from Blackburn's charge suggests further the proper answer to an objection which is sometimes raised against the view of martial law maintained in this treatise.

How, it is urged, can it be reasonable that a man should be liable to punishment, and therefore need an indemnity for having done an act (*e.g.* having by the use of force dispersed the mob) which it was his duty to do, and for the omission to do which he might have incurred severe punishment?

The answer is, that the supposed difficulty or dilemma cannot in reality arise. The apparent or alleged unreasonableness of the law is created by the ambiguity of the word duty, and by confusing a man's "legal duty" with his "moral duty." Now, for the non-performance of a man's legal duty, he may, of course, be punished, but for the performance of a legal duty he needs no Act of Indemnity. For the performance, on the other hand, of any moral duty, which is not a legal duty, a man may undoubtedly, if he thereby infringes upon the rights of his fellow-citizens, expose himself to punishment of one kind or another, and may therefore need an Act of Indemnity to protect him from the consequences of having done what is legally wrong, though, under the peculiar circumstances of the case, morally right. But then, for the non-performance of a merely moral duty, he will not incur the risk of punishment. If the Mayor of Bristol omits, by the use of the necessary force, to put down a riot, this omission undoubtedly exposes him to punishment, since he neglects to per-

---

149 Blackburn's Charge, *Reg.* v. *Eyre*, p. 58.

form a legal duty; but if he does perform his duty, and by the use of a proper amount of force puts down the riot, he incurs no legal liability to punishment, and needs no Act of Indemnity for his protection. If, on the other hand, at a period of threatened invasion or rebellion, a magistrate, without any legal authority, arrests and imprisons on suspicion a number of persons whom he holds to be disloyal, he may be performing a moral duty, and, if his view of the state of things turns out right, may have rendered a great service to the country; but he assuredly needs an Act of Indemnity to protect him from actions for false imprisonment. But, and this is the point to note, if our magistrate be a man of more prudence than energy, and omits to arrest men whom *ex hypothesi* he has no legal right to arrest, his conduct may incur the blame of patriots, but cannot bring him before the Courts. A man, in short, may be punished for having omitted to do an act which it is his legal duty to perform, but needs no Act of Indemnity for having done his legal duty. A man, on the other hand, who does a legal wrong, whilst performing a moral which is not a legal duty does require an Act of Indemnity for his protection, but then a man will never incur punishment for the simple omission to perform a merely moral duty.

OTHER DOCTRINES WITH REGARD TO MARTIAL LAW

In opposition to the view of martial law upheld in this treatise, which may conveniently be termed the "doctrine of immediate necessity," three other doctrines are, or have been maintained. Of these the first bases the use of martial law on the royal prerogative; the second on the immunity of soldiers from liability to proceedings in the civil Courts as contrasted with the military Courts for any act *bonâ fide* done in the carrying out of military operations; and the third (which extends very widely the meaning of the term necessity) on political necessity or expediency.

The Doctrine of the Prerogative

It is sometimes alleged, or implied, that the Crown may, by virtue of the prerogative, in time of war proclaim martial law, and suspend or override the ordinary law of the land, and this view is supposed to derive support from the consideration that the Petition of Right does not condemn martial law in time of war.

The fatal objection to this doctrine, in so far as it means anything more than the admitted right of the Crown and its servants to use any amount of force necessary for the maintenance of the peace or for repelling invasion, is that it utterly lacks legal authority, whilst to the inference suggested from the language of the Petition of Right no better reply can be given than that supplied by the words of Blackburn, namely, "It would be an exceedingly wrong presumption to say that the Petition of Right, by not condemning martial law in time of war, sanctioned it," though, as he cautiously adds, "it did not in terms condemn it."[150]

The Doctrine of Immunity[151]

This doctrine, it is conceived, may be thus stated. An officer in command of an army must of necessity, in carrying out military operations against an invader, override ordinary rights whether of property or of personal liberty. Decisive authorities may be produced[152] in support of the proposition that he may lawfully violate rights of property, *e.g.* can, without incurring any legal liability, do acts which amount to trespass. But all legal rights stand on the same level; and if an officer can lawfully occupy an Englishman's land, or destroy his property, he can also lawfully, whilst *bonâ fide* carrying on war against a public enemy, imprison Englishmen, inflict punishment upon them, or even deprive them of life, and, in short, interfere with any of the rights of Englishmen in so far as is required for the carrying out of military operations. The soundness of this view is, it is urged, confirmed by the admitted inability of a civil Court to judge of the due discharge of military duties, and by the consideration that no

---

150 Blackburn's Charge, *R.* v. *Eyre*, p. 73, with which should be read pp. 69–73, which suggest the reasons why the authors of the Petition of Right may have omitted all reference to martial law in time of war.

151 See for a very able statement of the theory here criticised, H. Erle Richards' *Martial Law*, L. Q. R. xviii. p. 133.

152 See pp. 399, 400, *ante.*

Court would, or in fact could, during a period of warfare interfere with a general's mode of conducting the war, or with any act done by him or by soldiers acting under his orders, whence, as it is alleged, it follows that acts *bonâ fide* done in the course of military operations fall outside the jurisdiction of the ordinary Courts, not only during war time, but also after the restoration of peace.[153] To put this doctrine of immunity in what appears to me to be its most plausible form, the outbreak of war is to be regarded as a suspension of the ordinary law of the land, as regards, at any rate, officers in command of troops and engaged in resisting invaders. On this view a general would occupy, during the conduct of war, a position analogous to that of a judge when engaged in the discharge of his judicial functions, and no action or other proceeding in the Courts of Common Law would lie against an officer for acts *bonâ fide* done as a part of a military operation, just as no action lies against a judge for acts done in discharge of his official duties.

This doctrine of immunity is, however, open, it is submitted, to the very strongest objections. Most of the undoubted facts on which it rests, *e.g.* the right of a general when resisting an invasion to use freely the land or other property of Englishmen, are merely applications of the principle that a loyal citizen may do any act necessary for the maintenance of the King's peace, and especially for the defeat of an invading army. But for the broad inferences based on this fact and similar facts there appears to exist no sufficient ground.

In support of the doctrine of immunity there can be produced no direct authority, whilst it appears to be absolutely inconsistent, not only with the charge of Cockburn, C.J., in *Rex* v. *Nelson*, but also with the principles or assumptions which are laid down or made in the charge of Blackburn, J., in *Rex* v. *Eyre*. The doctrine, further, is really inconsistent with the constant passing of Acts of Indemnity with a view to covering deeds done in the course of civil war or of rebellion. Nor is it easy to follow the line of reasoning by which it is assumed that if the Courts have no power to interfere with the acts of a general or his soldiers whilst war is raging, the Courts have no jurisdiction to

---

153 See L. Q. R. xviii. p. 140.

entertain during peace proceedings in respect of acts done by a general and his soldiers during a time of war. Here, at any rate, we apparently come into contradiction with some of the best known facts of legal history. The Courts, not only of England, but also of the United States, have never entertained the least doubt of their jurisdiction to inquire into the character of any act done during war time which was *primâ facie* a breach of law.

The Doctrine of Political Necessity or Expediency[154]

The existence of war or invasion justifies—it is maintained by eminent lawyers, whose opinion is entitled to the highest respect—the use of what is called martial law to this extent, namely, that, *e.g.* during an invasion, a general, a mayor, a magistrate, or indeed any loyal citizen, is legally justified in doing any act, even though *primâ facie* a tort or a crime, as to which he can prove to the satisfaction of a jury that he did it for the public service in good faith, and for reasonable and probable cause. This doctrine, which for the sake of convenience I term the doctrine of political expediency, manifestly justifies from a legal point of view many acts not dictated by immediate necessity. The scope thereof may be best understood from an example which I give in the words of its ablest and very learned advocate, Sir Frederick Pollock:

> An enemy's army has landed in force in the north, and is marching on York. The peace is kept in London and Bristol, and the Courts are not closed. It is known that evil-disposed persons have agreed to land at several ports for the purpose of joining the enemy, and giving him valuable aid and information. Bristol is one of the suspected ports. What shall the Lord Mayor of Bristol do? I submit that it is his plain moral duty as a good citizen (putting aside for a moment the question of strict law) to prevent suspected persons from landing, or to arrest and detain them if found on shore; to assume control of the railway traffic, and forbid undesirable passengers to proceed northward, and to exercise a strict censorship and inquisitorial power over letters and telegrams. All these things are in themselves trespasses (except, probably, forbidding an alien to land); some of them may perhaps be justifiable under the statutory powers of the Postmaster-General, but summary restraint by way of prevention must be justified by a common law power

---

154 See Pollock, *What is Martial Law?* L.Q.R. xviii. p. 162.

arising from necessity, if at all. Observe that I say nothing for the present about trial or punishment. The popular (and sometimes official) notion that martial law necessarily means trial by court-martial has caused much confusion. Summary punishment may or may not be necessary. In that respect the Mayor's authority would be like that of the master of a ship.

Now, if the Lord Mayor of Bristol fails to do these things, he will surely find himself in as much trouble as his predecessor [Mr. Pinney] in the time of the Bristol riots. And I do not think he will improve his defence by pleading that the peace was still kept in Bristol, and the Courts were open, and therefore he thought he had no power to do anything beyond the ordinary process of law. Nor yet will he mend matters if he says that he was waiting for an Order in Council which was never issued, or never came to his knowledge. At best it will be a topic of slight mitigation.[155]

The objections to a view which at bottom differs essentially from what I have termed "the doctrine of immediate necessity" are these: The theory under consideration rests on little legal authority, except the case of *Rex* v. *Pinney*;[156] but that case, when its circumstances are examined, does not justify the inferences apparently grounded upon it. The charge against Mr. Pinney was in substance that, being the magistrate specially responsible for the maintenance of order in the town of Bristol, he neglected to take the proper steps to prevent the outbreak of a riot, and after the King's peace had been openly violated by rioters, the prison broken open, and the Bishop's Palace and other houses burned down, he did not take adequate steps to arrest offenders or to restore order. It is impossible to imagine a case under which there could exist a more urgent and stringent necessity for the use of force in the restoration of order. If the charges brought by the Crown could have been made out, Mr. Pinney would have been guilty of as patent a neglect of duty as could have been committed by any public official placed in a position of high authority. That he acted feebly can hardly be doubted; yet, in spite of this, he was, with the apparent approval of the Judge, held innocent of any crime. The point, however, specially to be noted is that, in Pinney's Case, no question whatever was raised as to the possible justification for acts which were *primâ facie* tortious, but were done by a magistrate on

---

155 Pollock, *What is Martial Law?* L. Q. R. xviii. pp. 155, 156.
156 3 St. Tr. (n. s.) 11.

reasonable grounds of public expediency, though lying quite outside the scope of his ordinary authority. How, in short, the case of Mr. Pinney, which at most establishes only that a magistrate who fails to make due efforts to maintain the peace is guilty of a crime, can be supposed to justify the action of the imaginary Mayor of Bristol, who because an invasion is taking place feels it to be his right or his duty to override, in a town where peace prevails, all the ordinary rules of the common law, many lawyers will find it difficult to explain. Still harder will they find it to point out why a mayor, under the circumstances so graphically described by Sir Frederick Pollock, should fear that his failure to show despotic energy should expose him to the legal charges brought against Mr. Pinney. But if Pinney's case does not go far enough to sustain the doctrine of political expediency, I know of no other case which can be produced in its support.

This doctrine, however, is open to the further objection, of which its able advocate recognises the force, that it is inconsistent with the existence of Acts of Indemnity. Sir Frederick Pollock writes:

> It may be objected that, if the view now propounded is correct, Acts of Indemnity are superfluous. But this is not so. An Act of Indemnity is a measure of prudence and grace. Its office is not to justify unlawful acts *ex post facto*, but to quiet doubts, to provide compensation for innocent persons in respect of damage inevitably caused by justifiable acts which would not have supported a legal claim. [157]

The attempt to meet this objection is ingenious, but the endeavour rests on a very inadequate description of an Act of Indemnity. Such a statute may no doubt be in part a measure of prudence and grace, but it is usually far more than this. The Indemnity Acts, whatever their formal language, which for a century or so protected Nonconformists from penalties incurred year by year through the deliberate breach of the Test and Corporation Acts, the Acts of Indemnity passed after the Rebellions of 1715 and of 1745, the Act of Indemnity passed by the Irish Parliament after the Rebellion of 1798 which was not wide

---

157 Pollock, *What is Martial Law?* L. Q. R. xviii. p. 157.

enough to protect Mr. T. Judkin Fitzgerald[158] from actions for acts of cruelty done by him in the suppression of the Rebellion, the further Act finally passed which apparently was wide enough to place him beyond the reach of punishment, and the Act of the legislature of Jamaica which was successfully pleaded by the defendant in *Phillips* v. *Eyre,* were, it is submitted, all of them enactments intended to protect men from the consequences of a breach of the law. An Act of Indemnity in short is, as is insisted upon throughout this treatise, the legalisation of illegality, and is constantly intended to protect from legal penalties men who, though they have acted in the supposed, or even real discharge of a political duty, have broken the law of the land. This is a point on which it is necessary to insist strongly, for the determination of the question at issue between the supporters of the "doctrine of immediate necessity" and the advocates of the "doctrine of political necessity," turns upon the answer to the inquiry, What is the true nature of an Act of Indemnity? If such an Act is essentially the legalisation of illegality, the doctrine of political necessity or expediency falls, it is submitted, to the ground.

Two circumstances give an apparent but merely apparent impressiveness to the doctrine of political expediency. The first is the paradox involved in the contention that action on behalf of the State which is morally right may be legally wrong, and, therefore, be the proper object of an Act of Indemnity. This paradox however is, as already pointed out, apparent only, and after all amounts merely to the assertion that a man's ordinary duty is to keep within the limits of the law, and that, if he is at any moment compelled, on grounds of public interest, to transgress these limits, he must obtain the condonation of the sovereign power, *i.e.* the King in Parliament. The second is the current idea that, at a great crisis, you cannot have too much energy. But this notion is a popular delusion. The fussy activity of a hundred mayors playing the part of public-spirited despots would increase tenfold the miseries and the dangers imposed upon the country by an invasion.

---

158 *Wright* v. *Fitzgerald,* 27 St. Tr. 759; Lecky, *History of England in Eighteenth Century,* viii. pp. 22–27.

Note XI

CONSTITUTION OF THE
TRIBUNAL DES CONFLITS [159]

The Conflict Court consists of the following persons:

I. A President, the Minister of Justice (*Garde des sceaux*). [160] He rarely attends, though he may attend, preside, and vote.

II. Eight elected judges, namely:—

a. Three judges of the Court of Cassation (*Conseillers à la Cour de Cassation*) elected for three years by their colleagues, *i.e.* by the judges of the Court of Cassation.

b. Three members of the Council of State (*Conseillers d'état en service ordinaire*) [161] elected for three years by their colleagues (*i.e.* by the *Conseillers d'état en service ordinaire*).

c. Two other persons elected by the foregoing six judges of the Conflict Court, enumerated under heads *a* and *b*.

These two other persons ought in strictness to be elected neither from the judges of the Court of Cassation nor from the members of the Council of State, but they are in general elected one from the Court of Cassation, the other from the Council of State.

These eight persons, who are re-eligible and usually re-elected, or, if we include the Minister of Justice, these nine persons, constitute the judges of the Conflict Court.

Then there are two substitutes (*suppleants*) elected by the judges coming under the heads *a* and *b* who act only when one of the judges of the Conflict Court cannot act.

There are further two so-called Commissioners of the Government (*Commissaires du Gouvernement*) [162] appointed for a year by the Presi-

---

159 See Berthélemy, *Traité Élémentaire de Droit Administratif* (5th ed.), pp. 880, 881; Chardon, *L'Administration de la France*, p. 411.

160 A Vice-President, who generally presides, is elected by and from the eight elected judges of the Conflict Court.

161 *Conseillers d'état en service ordinaire* are permanent members of the Council of State. They are contrasted with *Conseillers en service extraordinaire*, who are temporary members of the Council, for the discharge of some special duty. See Berthélemy, p. 126.

162 The name may be misleading. These commissioners are, it is said, absolutely free from

dent of the Republic; the one for a year from the Masters of Requests (*Maîtres des requêtes*), who belong to the Council of State, the other from the class of public prosecutors, belonging to the Court of Cassation (*avocats généraux à la Cour de Cassation*).

Note XII

PROCEEDINGS AGAINST THE CROWN

Technically it is impossible under English law to bring an action against the Crown, and this impossibility is often said to be based on the principle that the Crown can do no wrong. Hence well-informed foreign critics, and perhaps some Englishmen also, often think that there is in reality no remedy against the Crown, or in other words, against the Government, for injuries done to individuals by either,

1. The breach of a contract made with the Crown, or with a Government department, or

2. A wrong committed by the Crown, or rather by its servants.

This idea is however in substance erroneous.

AS TO BREACH OF CONTRACT

For the breach of a contract made with a Government department on behalf of the Crown a Petition of Right will in general lie, which though in form a petition, and requiring the sanction of the Attorney-General (which is never refused), is in reality an action.

Many Government departments, further, such for instance as the Commissioners of Works, who have the general charge of public buildings, are corporate bodies, and can be sued as such.

Contracts made with Government departments or their representatives are made on the express or implied terms of payment out of monies to be provided by Parliament, but the risk of Parliament not providing the money is not one which any contractor takes into consideration.

---

pressure by the Government. They are representatives of the law, they are not strictly judges, the opinions which they express often disagree with the opinion of the representative of the Government, viz. the prefect, who has raised the conflict, *i.e.* has brought before the Court the question whether a judicial court has exceeded its jurisdiction by dealing with a question of administrative law.

AS TO WRONGS

Neither an action nor a Petition of Right lies against the Crown for a wrong committed by its servants.

The remedy open to a person injured by a servant of the Crown in the course of his service is an action against the person who has actually done or taken part in doing the wrongful act which has caused damage. But, speaking generally, no injustice results from this, for the Crown, *i.e.* the Government, usually pays damages awarded against a servant of the State for a wrong done in the course of his service. Actions, for instance, have been constantly brought against officers of the Royal Navy for damage done by collisions with other ships caused by the negligence of such officers. The damage recovered against the officer is almost invariably paid by the Admiralty.

It would be an amendment of the law to enact that a Petition of Right should lie against the Crown for torts committed by the servants of the Crown in the course of their service. But the technical immunity of the Crown in respect of such torts is not a subject of public complaint, and in practice works little, if any, injustice.

It should be further remembered that much business which in foreign countries is carried on by persons who are servants of the State is in England transacted by corporate bodies, *e.g.* railway companies, municipal corporations, and the like, which are legally fully responsible for the contracts made on their behalf or wrongs committed by their officials or servants in the course of their service.[163]

Note XIII

PARLIAMENT ACT, 1911
[1 & 2 Geo. 5. Ch. 13.]

An Act to make provision with respect to the powers of the House of Lords in relation to those of the House of Commons, and to limit the duration of Parliament.

[18th August, 1911.]

---

163 See Lowell, *The Government of England*, ii. pp. 490–494.

Whereas it is expedient that provision should be made for regulating the relations between the two Houses of Parliament:

And whereas it is intended to substitute for the House of Lords as it at present exists a Second Chamber constituted on a popular instead of hereditary basis, but such substitution cannot be immediately brought into operation:

And whereas provision will require hereafter to be made by Parliament in a measure effecting such substitution for limiting and defining the powers of the new Second Chamber, but it is expedient to make such provision as in this Act appears for restricting the existing powers of the House of Lords:

Be it therefore enacted by the King's most Excellent Majesty, by and with the advice and consent of the Lords Spiritual and Temporal, and Commons, in this present Parliament assembled, and by the authority of the same, as follows:—

1.—(1) If a Money Bill, having been passed by the House of Commons, and sent up to the House of Lords at least one month before the end of the session, is not passed by the House of Lords without amendment within one month after it is so sent up to that House, the Bill shall, unless the House of Commons direct to the contrary, be presented to His Majesty and become an Act of Parliament on the Royal Assent being signified, notwithstanding that the House of Lords have not consented to the Bill.

(2) A Money Bill means a Public Bill which in the opinion of the Speaker of the House of Commons contains only provisions dealing with all or any of the following subjects, namely, the imposition, repeal, remission, alteration, or regulation of taxation; the imposition for the payment of debt or other financial purposes of charges on the Consolidated Fund, or on money provided by Parliament, or the variation or repeal of any such charges; supply; the appropriation, receipt, custody, issue or audit of accounts of public money; the raising or guarantee of any loan or the repayment thereof; or subordinate matters incidental to those subjects or any of them. In this subsection the expressions "taxation," "public money," and "loan" respectively do not include any taxation, money, or loan raised by local authorities or bodies for local purposes.

(3) There shall be endorsed on every Money Bill when it is sent up to the House of Lords and when it is presented to His Majesty for assent the certificate of the Speaker of the House of Commons signed by him that it is a Money Bill. Before giving his certificate, the Speaker shall consult, if practicable, two members to be appointed from the Chairmen's Panel at the beginning of each Session by the Committee of Selection.

2.—(1) If any Public Bill (other than a Money Bill or a Bill containing any provision to extend the maximum duration of Parliament beyond five years) is passed by the House of Commons in three successive sessions (whether of the same Parliament or not), and, having sent up to the House of Lords at least one month before the end of the session, is rejected by the House of Lords in each of those sessions, that Bill shall, on its rejection for the third time by the House of Lords, unless the House of Commons direct to the contrary, be presented to His Majesty and become an Act of Parliament on the Royal Assent being signified thereto, notwithstanding that the House of Lords have not consented to the Bill: Provided that this provision shall not take effect unless two years have elapsed between the date of the second reading in the first of those sessions of the Bill in the House of Commons and the date on which it passes the House of Commons in the third of those sessions.

(2) When a Bill is presented to His Majesty for assent in pursuance of the provisions of this section, there shall be endorsed on the Bill the certificate of the Speaker of the House of Commons signed by him that the provisions of this section have been duly complied with.

(3) A Bill shall be deemed to be rejected by the House of Lords if it is not passed by the House of Lords either without amendment or with such amendments only as may be agreed to by both Houses.

(4) A Bill shall be deemed to be the same Bill as a former Bill sent up to the House of Lords in the preceding session if, when it is sent up to the House of Lords, it is identical with the former Bill or contains only such alterations as are certified by the Speaker of the House of Commons to be necessary owing to the time which has elapsed since the date of the former Bill, or to represent any amendments which have been made by the House of Lords in the former

Bill in the preceding session, and any amendments which are certified by the Speaker to have been made by the House of Lords in the third session and agreed to by the House of Commons shall be inserted in the Bill as presented for Royal Assent in pursuance of this section:

Provided that the House of Commons may, if they think fit, on the passage of such a Bill through the House in the second or third session, suggest any further amendments without inserting the amendments in the Bill, and any such suggested amendments shall be considered by the House of Lords, and, if agreed to by that House, shall be treated as amendments made by the House of Lords and agreed to by the House of Commons; but the exercise of this power by the House of Commons shall not affect the operation of this section in the event of the Bill being rejected by the House of Lords.

3. Any certificate of the Speaker of the House of Commons given under this Act shall be conclusive for all purposes, and shall not be questioned in any court of law.

4.—(1) In every Bill presented to His Majesty under the preceding provisions of this Act, the words of enactment shall be as follows, that is to say:—

> "Be it enacted by the King's most Excellent Majesty, by and with the advice and consent of the Commons in this present Parliament assembled, in accordance with the provisions of the Parliament Act, 1911, and by authority of the same, as follows."

(2) Any alteration of a Bill necessary to give effect to this section shall not be deemed to be an amendment of the Bill.

5. In this Act the expression "Public Bill" does not include any Bill for confirming a Provisional Order.

6. Nothing in this Act shall diminish or qualify the existing rights and privileges of the House of Commons.

7. Five years shall be substituted for seven years as the time fixed for the maximum duration of Parliament under the Septennial Act, 1715.

8. This Act may be cited as the Parliament Act, 1911.

INDEX

The Palatino typeface used in this volume is the work of Hermann Zapf, the noted European type designer and master calligrapher. Palatino is basically an "old style" letterform, yet strongly endowed with the Zapf distinction of exquisiteness. With concern not solely for the individual letter but also for the working visual relationship in a page of text, Zapf's edged pen has given this type a brisk, natural motion.

Book Design by JMH Corporation, Indianapolis, Indiana
Typography by Typoservice Corporation, Indianapolis, Indiana
Printed and bound by Halliday Lithograph, Inc., West Hanover, Massachusetts